Neptune Public Libra:
25 Neptune Blvd.
P.O. Box 1125
Neptune NJ 07753-11

D0929044

THE ESSENTIAL
GAELIC–ENGLISH DICTIONARY

The Essential Gaelic–English Dictionary

A Dictionary for Students and Learners of Scottish Gaelic

Compiled by
ANGUS WATSON

Birlinn

First published in Great Britain in 2001
by Birlinn Limited
Canongate Venture
5 New Street
Edinburgh EH8 8BH

www.birlinn.co.uk

Copyright © Angus Watson, 2001

The moral right of the author has been asserted.

All rights reserved. No part of this publication may be reproduced, stored in a retrieval system, or transmitted, in any form or by any means, electronic, mechanical, photocopying, recording or otherwise, without the prior permission of the publisher.

British Library Cataloguing-in-Publication Data
A catalogue record for this book is available from the British Library

ISBN 1 874744 92 0

Thug Comhairle nan Leabhraichean tabhartas barantais
dhan fhoillsichear airson obair deasachaidh air an lcabhar seo,
agus chuidich a' Chomhairle le cosgaisean an leabhair

Layout and design by Waverley Typesetters, Galashiels
Printed and bound by Creative Print and Design, Wales

Contents

✍

Neptune Public Libra
25 Neptune Blvd.
P.O. Box 1125
Neptune, NJ 07753-112:

do Sheònaid

Foreword

✧

Dictionary makers often point out that their work is a compromise –
between completeness on the one hand and space and expense on the
other. Even the monumental Dwelly dictionary of Gaelic is not com-
prehensive, and there are stories of copies of Dwelly in Highland homes,
their pages speckled with words added by the family from their own
Gaelic.

Another common defence mechanism among dictionary makers
is for them to acknowledge that their choice of words and expressions
will not please everyone. They are usually right!

In the present volume the aim has been to present as rich a cross-
section of the Gaelic language as possible in the space available, giving
due weight both to the new contexts of our times and to the riches
of the past, as well as to both colloquial and more formal language.
The registers, styles and contexts represented in the dictionary include:
vulgar, familiar, colloquial, formal and traditional words and expressions; examples drawn from modern poetry, modern and traditional
song (an area that attracts many learners to the language), proverbs
and sayings and, occasionally, placenames; the more common
vocabulary of administration, politics and government, journalism and
information technology also figures here.

As a learner of Gaelic myself, I have had the learner in mind
throughout – though I naturally hope the fluent learner, and perhaps
even the native speaker, will find value and interest here also. A priority
has been to include in the entries as many examples as space would
allow, showing words and expressions in actual use. There are many
cases where merely giving a translation equivalent of the headword
would not be adequate. A further aim has been to include the kind of
explanatory information that I would have found useful myself (and
still do!), as a learner of the language.

Novel features of the dictionary include the cross-references given
in many entries. These refer the reader to related words and expressions
(NB, not necessarily exact synonyms) with the aim of increasing the

learner's vocabulary or reminding the more advanced user of alternative words that might be appropriate in a particular context. This gives to the dictionary a little of the nature of a thesaurus, for those who might find that useful, as well as doing a little of the work of an English–Gaelic dictionary by leading the reader to more than one possible Gaelic equivalent for a given word or concept in English. It is hoped that the cross-references might also encourage the learner to learn by browsing. In general, I have tried to make the dictionary into a learning and reference tool a little more flexible than existing Gaelic–English volumes.

Another feature not, I think, found in any other Gaelic dictionary is the giving of a limited number of Scots equivalents for headwords. This is done for two main reasons. Firstly, a Scots equivalent can help to make a particular nuance clearer. For example, 'a wifie', or 'an old wifie' for **cailleach**, or 'give a row to' for the verb **càin**, can give a Scot a clearer idea of some shades of meaning of these words than the English equivalents on their own. Secondly, the presentation of the two languages in the same context might help in a very small way to build bridges between them, encouraging us to think of them as side by side rather than in opposition. As someone with a strong interest in both Gaelic and Scots, I'm saddened and exasperated to see the exchanges that break out from time to time in the press along the lines of 'My language is older than yours, so there!' or 'Why should your language get more money from the government than mine?' It would surely be more productive to concentrate on what should unite us rather than the mostly illusory or irrelevant things that appear to divide us.

Many regret the decline of the pithy, idiomatic Gaelic of the past, and find the Gaelic used today in administration, journalism and broadcasting, for example, pale and fushionless in comparison. But a dictionary has to embrace a language as it is. I make no apology for giving samples of these barer registers of Gaelic, and for going so far as to include examples of calques (expressions closely based on an English model such as **àrdaich ìomhaigh na Gàidhlig** – raise/promote the image of Gaelic), and one or two other expressions or constructions that may well be questionable from the point of view of approved grammar and usage, but which form a part of the language as it is used today.

Language inevitably evolves in step with a society, its technologies, attitudes and preoccupations, and Gaelic has been no exception. And in an age where even a world language such as French has been seriously penetrated by Anglicisms – in spite of a centuries-old official policy of keeping the language 'pure' – it is not surprising if Gaelic too has been radically affected in many of its registers.

At the same time, a good deal of traditional Gaelic survives in the modern language, especially in the form of set expressions, idioms, proverbs and sayings. Users of the language who so wish, therefore, can cultivate a style and a vocabulary that include a goodly leavening of traditional language, enriching their Gaelic without running the risk of sounding too old-fashioned or pretentious. A good selection of such material is included in this dictionary, though it should be noted that the kind of items that are *specifically* marked '(*trad*)' would not always fit comfortably into ordinary conversation. They are given as the kinds of words and expressions that might be useful in a fairly specialised context, or to give information that the more advanced learner might find of interest. For example **is math seachad e** – it's good that it's over – has the traditional feel to it, but would be appropriate and expressive in an everyday context, on completion of some task or other. On the other hand, for example, the traditional dative **ann an Albainn** – in Scotland – or the phrase **fhuair e bàs le nàimhdean** – he died at the hand of enemies – would seem archaic. It goes without saying, though, that many of the items marked '(*trad*)' will be met with in reading Gaelic from earlier decades or centuries, which is another excellent reason for their inclusion here.

It is my view that the learner of a language should, especially in the earlier stages, err on the side of conservatism and not immediately take up the latest changes in colloquial usage. There is the obvious risk of sounding foolish by trying to be trendy when your grasp of the language may not yet be secure! Or at times native speakers may feel you are trying to be *too* clever.

In the entries, for the sake of consistency, I have made one or two conservative choices in presentation. In particular, I have regularly used the genitive case of the noun after a present participle, as in **a' cosnadh airgid** – earning money. I have done this because the genitive is 'grammatically' correct. In fact, though, many speakers have ceased to observe this 'rule', and the construction with the radical form of the noun – **a' cosnadh airgead** – would be acceptable in most contexts except, say, an examination, or a formal talk or speech.

The Layout of the Entries

❧

Within the entries all Gaelic material is in bold type. Italics are used for all text in English that is not translation of the Gaelic material, i.e. abbreviations, instructions such as *see* and *Cf*, and all notes, comments, explanatory material and grammatical information. A generous number of translation equivalents are given for the headwords, without straying too far into the more rarefied areas of English such as Latinate vocabulary. Where appropriate the different senses or usages a headword may have are sub-divided into numbered sections, separated by semi-colons.

The Gaelic spelling used throughout corresponds to up-to-date norms. Exceptions to this occur when an older spelling still occasionally used by some is given for completeness, e.g. '**no** (*older sp* **neo**) *conj* or'. In a good number of instances two acceptable spellings are given. Usually this happens where both spellings correspond to modern spelling conventions and both versions are established in present usage. In other instances a recent loan word, for example, may not yet have settled down into one accepted spelling, so variants are given. Sometimes alternative spellings are indicated by means of brackets as in '**san (fh)radharc** in sight/view'. This of course means that this form of the word can be found as either **fhradharc** or **radharc**. The same example shows how oblique strokes (/) are used in the English translations to save space when giving alternatives. Clearly, in this case the abbreviation shows that 'in sight' and 'in view' would be equally appropriate.

NOUNS

When the headword is a noun the forms normally given are the nominative singular (also called the radical), the genitive singular and the nominative plural, unmarked for case, and in that order. To avoid confusion, in entries where the noun departs from this basic pattern in some way, the forms other than the radical are marked for case, as in '**lasgan,** *gen & pl* **lasgain,** *nm* an outburst', where the genitive singular and the nominative plural are the same, or '**làthair,** *gen* **làthaire,** *nf* presence', where no plural exists, or '**là** *&* **latha,** *gen* **là** *&* **latha,** *pl* **làithean, lathachan** *&* **lathaichean** *nm* a day', where there are variant or alternative forms, or '**leannanachd** *nf invar* courtship', where the noun has only the one form. Nouns are marked for masculine or feminine gender. Some nouns are marked as having both genders, a situation that typically came about when neuter nouns in the older language took on different genders in different dialects as the neuter went out of use.

It is easy to use a noun in a wrong aspect and so I have tried to indicate, for instance, whether a noun is best used in a concrete or abstract sense, collectively, and so on. An entry such as '**amharas,** *gen & pl* **amharais** *nm* suspicion, a suspicion, doubt, a doubt' shows that **amharas** can mean 'suspicion' and 'doubt' the abstract concepts, as well as a particular doubt or suspicion one might have at a particular time. This may be thought to take up a lot of space, but is felt to be worthwhile for the sake of clarity.

VERBS

In the case of verbs, it should be explained that in Gaelic the basic form that is given in grammar books etc. corresponds to the second person singular imperative, rather than to the infinitive which is the form usually given for English verbs. Thus in this dictionary the verbs **gabh, can, siubhal,** for example, are given the equivalents 'take', 'say', 'travel' rather than 'to take', 'to say', 'to travel'.

The verbal forms given in the entries are the imperative form, followed by the present participle, as in '**faighnich** *vi, pres part* **a' faighneachd**, ask', or '**fàillig** *vti, pres part* **a' fàilligeadh**, fail'.

It is important to know whether a verb can be used transitively or intransitively, that is, whether it can be used with or without a direct object, and this is conveyed by the abbreviations *vi, vt* and *vti* given immediately after the imperative of the verb. Taking **faighnich** as an example (see previous paragraph), '*vi*' shows that it cannot be followed by a direct object. To say 'ask a question' we would have to use a different Gaelic verb (**cuir,** with the noun **ceist**), and to say 'ask Morag' we would have to use an *indirect* object in Gaelic (**faighnich de Mhòrag**). The verb **fàillig,** though (see previous paragraph), can be used without a direct object (intransitively) as in **dh'fhàillig mi** 'I failed', or with a direct object (transitively) as in **dh'fhàillig e deuchainn** 'he failed an exam', and this is shown by the label '*vti*'. The label '*vt*' means that the verb concerned is used with a direct object (transitively) and is not normally likely to be used intransitively.

CROSS-REFERENCES

In many entries the reader is referred by the instruction '*Cf*' to other headwords given in the dictionary, as in '**tastan, tastain, tastanan** *nm* (*former currency*) a shilling, *Cf* **sgillinn 2**'. Here, obviously, it is section 2 of the entry under **sgillinn** that is being compared to this sense of **tastan.** The respective entries show that both Gaelic words relate to the idea 'shilling' but in different ways, and that in fact **sgillinn** no longer means 'shilling' but 'penny'. The overall aim, then, is to draw the reader's attention to other items covered in the dictionary that relate to the headword being consulted. As the above example shows, it should not be assumed that the items being compared are exact, or necessarily even close, synonyms. They may in fact even be opposites, in which case this is made clear in the entry, as in section 2 of **smior** 'the best part of something, the best example of something', which ends '*Cf* **brod** *n* **2**, *& opposite* **diù**'.

In most cases the cross-references relate to the basic senses of the headword given at the beginning of the entry, or section of the entry, concerned. Taking the entry '**a cheana** *adv* already, **mar a thuirt mi a cheana** as I've already said, *Cf* **tràth** *adj* **3**', this means that under the adjective **tràth**, in section 3 of that entry, will be found a word or expression (in this case **mu thràth**, a close synonym), which relates to the basic sense given for **a cheana** (in this case 'already').

In a number of entries the cross-reference is in brackets, indicating that it relates only to the part of the entry immediately preceding it. Thus in the entry '**allaidh** *adj* wild (*ie not domesticated*), *usu in set compounds, eg* **madadh-allaidh** *m* a wolf (*Cf* **faol**), **damhan-allaidh** *m* a spider, *Cf* **fiadhaich 1**', the cross-reference '(*Cf* **faol**)' relates only to the immediately preceding item '**madadh-allaidh** a wolf' (**faol** is in fact a synonym), whereas '*Cf* **fiadhaich 1**' relates to the basic sense 'wild'.

Occasionally a cross-reference is applicable to all the sections of an entry. Take the example '**acainn** *&* **acfhainn**, *gen* **ac(fh)ainne**, *pl* **ac(fh)ainnean** *nf coll* **1** apparatus, equipment, tools, **ball-acainn** *m* a (*single*) tool; **2** a set of tools; **3** (*horse*) harness; **4** (*boat*) rigging; *Cf* **uidheam**'. In this case the word **uidheam** has a sense corresponding to each of the four sections of **acainn** and so the reader is referred for comparison to the entire entry for **uidheam**. This is indicated by the fact that '*Cf* **uidheam**' comes at the very end of the entry for **acainn**, and is separated from it by a semi-colon.

Finally, a rough and ready guide to the relative frequency of words is sometimes given in the cross-references, as in '**iarmad, iarmaid, iarmadan** *nm* a remnant, a residue, *Cf more usu* **fuidheall 1**', or '**ifrinn, ifrinn, ifrinnean** *nf* hell, a hell, *Cf less usu* **iutharn(a)**'. Not all Gaelic speakers will necessarily agree with all such indications of relative frequency, but they are based on my own experience of spoken and written Gaelic.

Note: The cross-references are mainly intended to help the intermediate and more advanced learner, and beginners in Gaelic should perhaps ignore them until they have acquired a certain degree of confidence in the language. The cross-references are not, of course, exhaustive. Through them I have tried to give a good amount of useful and stimulating information, but was anxious not to clutter the text unduly.

TABLES OF GRAMMATICAL INFORMATION

At the end of the dictionary will be found a table of the forms of the Gaelic article followed by tables giving the forms of irregular verbs that are most likely to be encountered in mainstream Gaelic. Much other grammatical information is given within individual entries. In particular, the forms of the prepositional pronouns are given in full, and readers should consult the entry for the preposition concerned.

Acknowledgements

I wish to thank my wife for financing the writing of this dictionary and for putting up with me while I was working on it. I would also like to thank Ailean Boyd for his meticulous reading of the text and his many suggestions and corrections. Any shortcomings that remain are mine entirely.

By kind permission of Donald John Macleod, Chair of the Secondary Review Group for Gaelic, the dictionary includes a relatively small number of items from *Faclan Ura Gàidhlig*, produced by the Highland Council. This publication lists a large number of Gaelic equivalents for technical and specialised terms, and for other vocabulary not hitherto readily expressed in Gaelic, and is a useful reference work for those areas.

List of Abbreviations

დი

abbrev	abbreviation
abstr	abstract
adj	adjective, adjectival
admin	administration
adv	adverb, adverbial
agric	agriculture
alt	alternative
anat	anatomy
approx	approximate, approximately
art	article
Bibl	Bible, Biblical
biol	biology
Cf	compare
coll	collective
comp	comparative
con	concrete
conj	conjunction
cons	consonant
corres	correspondence, corresponding
dat	dative case
def	defective
derog	derogatory
dimin	diminutive
ed	education, educational
elec	electric, electrical
emph	emphasis, emphatic
Eng	English
esp	especially
excl(s)	exclamation(s)
expr(s)	expression(s), expressing
f	feminine
fam	familiar

fig	*figurative, figuratively*
fin	*financial*
freq	*frequent, frequently*
fut	*future*
gen	*genitive case*
gram	*grammar, grammatical*
hist	*history, historical*
incl	*including*
inter	*interrogative*
invar	*invariable*
irreg	*irregular*
IT	*information technology, computing*
lang	*language*
lit	*literally*
Lit	*literature, literary*
m	*masculine*
med	*medical*
misc	*miscellaneous*
n	*noun*
neg	*negative*
nf	*noun, feminine*
nm	*noun, masculine*
nmf	*noun, masculine & feminine*
nom	*nominative case*
num(s)	*numeral(s), numerical*
obs	*obsolete*
occas	*occasionally*
pej	*pejorative*
pers pron	*personal pronoun*
philo	*philosophy*
phys	*physical, physically*
pl	*plural*
poet	*poetry, poetic(al)*
pol	*politics, political*
poss	*possessive*
prep pron	*prepositional pronoun*
pres part	*present participle*
pron	*pronoun*
prov	*proverb*
psych	*psychology, psychological*
pt	*part*
rel	*relative*
relig	*religion, religious*
Sc	*Scots (language)*

sing	*singular*
sp	*spelling*
topog	*topography*
trad	*traditional, traditionally*
typog	*typography*
usu	*usual, usually*
v	*verb*
vi	*verb, intransitive*
vt	*verb, transitive*
vti	*verb, transitive & intransitive*
voc	*vocative case*
vulg	*vulgar*

A

a *a particle introducing the numerals* 1 *to* 10 *in counting, or when not followed by a noun*, **a h-aon, a dhà, a trì** one, two, three, **cia mheud a th' agad? a seachd** how many have you got? seven, *in combination with higher numerals* **a h-aon deug** eleven, **a dhà dheug** twelve, **fichead 's a deich** thirty, **ceithir fichead 's a naoi deug** ninety-nine

a *sign of the voc*, **a Chatrìona!** Catherine!, *in corres* **A Charaid** Dear Sir, **A Phàdraig, a charaid** Dear Patrick

a *poss adj* his, her, its, **chunnaic e a mhac 's a mhàthair** he saw his son and his mother, **chunnaic i a mac 's a màthair** she saw her son and her mother, *Note: before a verbal noun the poss adj can express the object of the verb or the subject of a passive construction*, **chan urrainn dhomh a dhèanamh** I can't do it (*lit* I am not capable of its doing), **gus am faicinn** in order to see them (*lit* to their seeing), **bha an leabhar ga fhoillseachadh** the book was being published (*lit* was at its publishing)

a (*in neg* **nach**) *rel pron* who, whom, that, which, **am balach a rinn sin** the boy who did that, **an deoch a dh'òl mi** the drink that I drank, **am film nach fhaca mi** the film I didn't see; *Note: Cf rel pron* **a** *&* *conj* **gu**, *eg* **nach math a rinn thu e!** didn't you do it well! (*lit*) isn't it well that you did it! *&* **nach math gun do rinn thu e?** isn't it a good thing that you did it?

a *combines with a following verbal noun (lenited where possible) to form an infinitive*, **tha mi a' dol a shnàmh** I am going to swim, **cha bu chòir dhut do bhràthair a bhualadh** you ought not to hit your brother

a¹ *prep* (*for* **de**) of, (*causes aspiration/lenition*) **a dhà no a thrì a bhliadhnaichean** two or three years, **uair a thìde** an hour (*lit* an hour of time), *Cf* **de** 1

a² *prep* (*for* **do**) to, (*causes aspiration/lenition*) **thèid i a Ghlaschu** she'll go to Glasgow, (*poem*) **is duilich leam do dhol air ais a dh'Eirinn** (Meg Bateman) hard/sad for me is your going back to Ireland, *Cf* **do** *prep* 2

a' *art, see* **an** *art*

a' *sign of the pres part, see* **ag**

à (*before the art*, **às**) *prep, Note: the pers prons* **mi, thu, e** *&c combine with* **à** *to form the prep prons* **asam(sa), asad(sa), às(-san), aiste(se), asainn(e), asaibh(se), asta(san)** from/out of me, you &c; 1 from, out of, **còmhlan-ciùil à Alba/às an Fhraing** a band from Scotland/

from France, **cò às a tha thu?** where are you from? **cò às a thàinig sin?** where did that come from? **biadh à Tesco's/às a' bhùth** food from Tesco's/from the shop, **bha/chaidh am bus à sealladh** the bus was/went out of sight, **bha mi às mo rian/às mo chiall** I was out of my mind, **cuir às an solas** put out/switch off the light, **a-mach à seo!** (get) out of here! **leig mi sgreuch asam** I let out a shriek; **2** *other uses & idioms* **a' bruidhinn à(s) beul a chèile** speaking with one voice/as one, **tha an fhuil a' tighinn às mo chorraig** my finger's bleeding, **bheir mi an ceann às an amhaich aige!** I'll wring his neck! **chaidh e às mo chuimhne** I forgot it/him, **bha i a' tarraing às** she was teasing him, **tha sinn uabhasach pròiseil asad** we're terribly proud of you, **thug iad na buinn asta** they took to their heels/got the hell out of it, **às aonais sgillinn ruaidh** without a brass farthing, without a penny (to his &c name), **dè a nì sinn às d' aonais?** what will we do without you? **chuir na saighdearan às dha** the soldiers finished him off/did away with him, **cha robh dol às aca a-nis** there was no way out/escape for them now, **dìnnear (&c) ann no às** dinner (&c) or no dinner, **saor-làithean ann no às, tha mi a' dol don oifis!** holidays or no holidays, I'm going to the office!, **fhuair e às leis** he got away with it

ab & **aba**, *gen* **aba**, *pl* **abachan** *nm* an abbot

abachadh, *gen* **abachaidh** *nm* (*fruits &c*) ripening, **àm abachadh nan ubhal** apple ripening time

abaich *adj* **1** (*person*) mature; **2** (*fruit &c*) ripe

abaich *vti*, *pres part* **ag abachadh**, ripen, mature

abaichead, *gen* **abaicheid** *nm* maturity, ripeness, **bha an t-ubhal a' dol an abaichead** the apple was getting riper and riper

abaid, **abaide**, **abaidean** *nf* an abbey

abair *vt irreg* (*see tables p 403*), *pres part* **ag ràdh**, **1** say, **thuirt iad riumsa e** they said it to me, **chan eil mi ag ràdh gu bheil thu ceàrr** I'm not saying you're wrong, *Cf* **can 1**; **2** *in exclamations*, **abair duine gòrach!** what a stupid man! **abair gun robh i sgìth!** how tired she was! **abair bùrach!** what a mess!, talk about a mess!, **abair e!** it sure is!, you bet!

abairt, **abairte**, **abairtean** *nf* **1** a phrase, an expression; **2** (*gram*) a phrase

àbhacas & **àbhachdas**, *gen* **àbhac(hd)ais** *nm* **1** mirth; **2** ridicule, **bha e na bhall àbhachdais** he was a laughing stock, *Cf* **fanaid 1**, **magadh 2**

àbhachd *nf invar* humour

àbhachdach *adj* amusing, humorous, *Cf more usu* **èibhinn**

abhag, **abhaig**, **abhagan** *nf* a terrier

abhainn, aibhne, aibhnichean *nf* a river, a large burn

àbhaist, àbhaiste, àbhaistean *nf* **1** a habit, a custom, *Cf* **cleachdadh 2, gnàth 1**; **2** *usu in exprs* **mar as àbhaist** (*in past* **mar a b' àbhaist**) as usual, & **b' àbhaist dhomh (a bhith a' seinn &c)** I used (to sing &c), *Cf* **cleachd 3**

àbhaisteach *adj* usual, normal, habitual, **anns an àite àbhaisteach aig an àm àbhaisteach** in the usual place at the usual time, *Cf less usu* **gnàthach**

a-bhàn *adv* down, (*song*) **shruth mo dheòir a-bhàn** my tears ran down, *also in expr* **suidh** *v* **a-bhàn** sit down, (*song*) **suidhidh sinn a-bhàn gu socair** we will sit down at our ease, *Cf* **sìos**

a bharrachd air *prep see* **barrachd 4**

a bhòn-dè *adv* the day before yesterday

a bhòn-raoir *adv* the night before last

a bhòn-uiridh *adv* the year before last

a-bhos *adv* here, over here (*with or without implied movement*), hither, **tha e a-bhos airson banais** he is over for a wedding, **thall 's a-bhos** here and there, hither and thither, **seall/thig an taobh a-bhos** look/come over this way, look/come over to this side, *Cf* **a-nall, thall 1**

ablach, ablaich, ablaichean *nm* **1** a mangled carcase, carrion; **2** *usu as term of abuse or contempt*, a wretch, a wreck, **ablach bochd** poor creature, poor wretch, *Cf more sympathetic* **truaghan**; **3** (*fam*) a brat

abradh, abraibh, abrainn, abram, abramaid *pts of irreg v* **abair** *see tables p 403*

abstol, abstoil, abstolan *nm* an apostle, (*Bible*) **Gnìomharan nan Abstol** The Acts of the Apostles

aca(san) *prep pron see* **aig**

acadamh, acadaimh, acadamhan *nmf* an academy, **Acadamh Rìoghail na h-Alba** the Royal Scottish Academy

acaid, acaide, acaidean *nf* a stabbing pain, a stitch

acainn & **acfhainn**, *gen* **ac(fh)ainne**, *pl* **ac(fh)ainnean** *nf coll* **1** apparatus, equipment, tools, **ball-acainn** *m* a (*single*) tool; **2** a set of tools; **3** (*horse*) harness; **4** (*boat*) rigging; *Cf* **uidheam**

acainneach & **acfhainneach** *adj* equipped, tooled up, *Cf* **uidheamaichte 1**; **2** energetic

acair(e), *gen* **acaire** & **acrach**, *pl* **acraichean** *nmf* **1** an anchor; **2** an acre

acarsaid, acarsaide, acarsaidean *nf* an anchorage, a harbour, a mooring, *Cf* **cala, port**[2]

ach *conj* **1** but, **bha dùil againn ris, ach cha tàinig e** we were expecting him, but he didn't come; **2** except, **chan eil duine comasach air ach Dàibhidh** no-one is capable of it except David, *Cf* **a-mhàin**; **3** (*with a verb in the neg*) only, **chan eil agam ach a trì** I only have three; **4** (*occas*) in case, **sheall e oirre ach am b'e fealla-dhà a bha i ris** he looked at her in case/to see if she was joking

achadh, achaidh, achaidhean *nm* (*agric*) a field

a-chaoidh *adv* **1** always, for ever, **bidh gaol agam ort a-chaoidh** I will love you for ever; **2** (*with a verb in the neg*) never, **cha till mi a-chaoidh do thìr nam beann àrda** I will never return to the land of the high bens; *Note: only used in the future tense – when referring to the past use* **a-riamh**; *Cf* **bràth 2 & 3, a-riamh, sìorraidh 2**

achd, achd, achdannan *nf* (*pol, law*) an act, **achd pàrlamaid** an Act of Parliament, **Achd an Aonaidh** the Act of Union (*of the Scots and English parliaments in 1707*)

a cheana *adv* already, **mar a thuirt mi a cheana** as I've already said, *Cf* **tràth** *adj* **3**

a chionn 1 *prep* because of, **a chionn sin** because of that, *Cf* **brìgh 5, sgàth 3; 2 a chionn is gu** *conj* because, **chaill mi an trèana a chionn 's gu robh m' uaireadair briste** I missed the train because my watch was broken

achlais, achlaise, achlaisean *nf* **1** an armpit, (*Sc*) an oxter, **bha neasgaid oirre na h-achlais** she had a boil in her armpit; **2** arm, **bha màileid aice fo a h-achlais** she had a bag under her arm/oxter, **bha iad a' coiseachd romhpa, air achlaisean a chèile** they were walking along with their arms around each other, **thig nam achlais!** come to my arms! (*Cf* **com 1**)

achlasan, *gen & pl* **achlasain** *nm* an armful, *Cf* **ultach 1**

achmhasan, *gen & pl* **achmhasain** *nm* reproof, reproach, adverse criticism, a reprimand, a rebuke

a-chum *prep* (*trad*) **1** for, for the purpose of, **a-chum sin** for that purpose, **a-chum stad a chur air an trioblaid** (in order) to stop the trouble, *Cf more usu* **airson 5, gus** *conj*; **2** *also* **a-chum is gu** *conj* so that, in order that, *Cf more usu* **gus** *conj*

acrach *adj* hungry, *Cf* **acrasach**

acrachadh, *gen* **acrachaidh** *nm* (*the act of*) anchoring, mooring

acraich *vt*, *pres part* **ag acrachadh**, (*boat*) anchor, moor

acras, *gen* **acrais** *nm* hunger, *usu with the art*, **tha/thàinig an t-acras orm** I am/I grew hungry

acrasach *adj* hungry, *cf* **acrach**

actair, actair, actairean *nm* an actor, *Cf* **cleasaiche 1**

ad, aide, adan *nf* a hat

adag, adaig, adagan *nf* a haddock

àdha, àdha, àinean *nm* (*anat*) a liver, *Cf* **grùthan**

a dh'aindeoin *prep see* **aindeòin 2**

a dh'aithghearr *adv see* **aithghearr 3**

adhaltraiche, adhaltraiche, adhaltraichean *nm* an adulterer, **ban-adhaltraiche** *f* an adulteress

adhaltranach *adj* adulterous

adhaltranas, *gen* **adhaltranais** *nm* adultery

adhar, *gen* **adhair** *nm* sky, air, **shuas san adhar** up in the sky/air, *Cf* **speur 1**

adharc, adhairc, adharcan *nf* horn, a horn (*of animal*), **bò air leth-adhairc** a one-horned cow, **spàin adhairc** a horn spoon

adharcach *adj* horned, horny, like horn

adharcan-luachrach, *gen & pl* **adharcain-luachrach** *nm* a lapwing, a peewit, a green plover, (*Sc*) a peesie, *Cf* **curracag**

adhart, *gen* **adhairt** *nm* **1** progress, *Cf more usu* **adhartas, piseach; 2** *usu in expr* **air adhart** *adv* forwards, on, onwards, **tha iad a' tighinn air adhart gu math** they're coming on well, **tha i a' faighinn air adhart** she's getting on, she's making progress, **ceum air adhart** a step forward (*lit & fig*), *Cf less usu* **aghaidh 4**

adhartach *adj* progressive, forward-looking

adhartas, *gen* **adhartais** *nm* progress, **chan eil sinn a' dèanamh adhartais** we're not making (any) progress, *Cf* **piseach 1**

adhbhar, *gen* **adhbhair,** *pl* **adhbharan** *nm* **1** a reason, a cause, **cha robh adhbhar aca greasad dhachaigh** they had no reason to hurry home, **adhbhar mo bhròin** the cause of my sadness, **adhbhar gàire** a laughing stock (*Cf* **cùis 4, culaidh 4**); **2** a cause (*ie a principle, belief system &c*), **shaothraich i ann an adhbhar còraichean nam ban** she laboured in the cause of women's rights; **3** materials, **adhbhar bhròg** shoe-making materials, *Cf* **stuth 2**

adhbharaich *vt, pres part* **ag adhbharachadh,** cause, occasion, give rise to, **is i a' ghoirt a dh'adhbharaich bàs am measg an t-sluaigh** it is/was famine that caused death among the population

adhbrann, *gen* **adhbrainn,** *pl* **adhbrainnean** *nf* an ankle, *Cf* **caol na coise** (*see* **caol** *n* **3**)

a dh'ionnsaigh *prep see* **ionnsaigh 3**

a dhìth *adv see* **dìth 2**

adhlacadh, *gen* **adhlacaidh** *nm* **1** (*the act of*) burying, interring; **2** burial, a burial, an interment, a funeral, *Cf* **tiodhlacadh 2, tòrradh**

adhlaic *vt, pres part* **ag adhlacadh**, bury, inter, *Cf* **tiodhlaic 1**

adhradh, adhraidh, adhraidhean *nm*, worship, **dèan** *v* **adhradh** worship, **dèan/thoir** *v* **adhradh do Dhia** worship God

Afraga *nm* Africa

Afraganach, *gen & pl* **Afraganaich** *nm* an African, **Ban-Afraganach** *f* an African woman, *also as adj* **Afraganach** African

ag *with following verbal noun forms the pres part, eg* **ag èisdeachd** listening, *Note: before consonants usu* **a'**, *eg* **a' briseadh** breaking, **a' tionndadh** turning, *though note exception* **ag ràdh** saying; *Note:* **ag** *combines with the poss adjs* **mo, do, a** *&c to form the particles* **gam, gad, ga, gar, gur, gan/gam** *which express the object of the verb or the subject of a passive construction,* **tha iad gam bhrìodal** they're flattering/courting me, **bidh sinn gur faicinn!** we'll be seeing you! **bha a' bhò ga bleoghann** the cow was being milked

agad(sa), againn(e), agaibh(se) *prep prons see* **aig**

agair *vt, pres part* **ag agairt**, *similar uses to* **tagair**

agalladh, *gen* **agallaidh** *nm* (*media &c*) interviewing

agallaich *vt, pres part* **ag agalladh**, (*media &c*) interview

agallamh, agallaimh, agallamhan *nm* **1** (*media &c*) an interview; **2** conversation, **clasaichean agallaimh** conversation classes, *Cf* **còmhradh 1, conaltradh 1**

agam(sa) *prep pron see* **aig**

àgh *&* **àigh**, *gen* **àigh** *nm* **1** joy, *Cf* **gàirdeachas; 2** good fortune, *Cf more usu* **fortan, sealbh 1; 3** *in exclamation* **an ainm an àigh!** in heaven's name!

agh, aighe, aighean *nf* a heifer

aghaidh, aghaidhe, aghaidhean *nf* **1** a face, **aghaidh ri aghaidh** face to face, **air aghaidh na beinne** on the face of the mountain, *Cf* **aodann 1 & 2; 2** cheek, nerve, **nach (ann) airsan a tha an aghaidh!** hasn't he got a cheek! **abair aghaidh!** what a cheek! *Cf* **bathais 2; 3** *in expr* **an aghaidh** *prep* against, in the face of (*with gen*), **an aghaidh na gaoithe** against the wind, **chaidh e nam aghaidh** he went against me; **4** *in expr* **air aghaidh** *adv* forward(s), *Cf more usu* **air adhart** (*see* **adhart 2); 5** (*weather*) a front, **aghaidh bhlàth** a warm front

aghaidh-choimheach, aghaidh-coimhich, aghaidhean-coimheach *nf* (*fancy dress &c*) a mask, *Cf* **aodannan, masg**

aghann, aigh(ain)ne, aghannan *nf*, a pan, *esp* a frying pan

aghastar, aghastair, aghastaran *nm* a halter

àghmhor *adj* **1** pleasant, *Cf more usu* **taitneach, tlachdmhor** 1; **2** joyful, happy, *Cf* **aighearach, aoibhneach** 3

agus *also* **is** *or* **'s** *conj* **1** and, **rugadh agus thogadh mi an sin** I was born and brought up there, **tha mi sgìth; tha agus mise** I'm tired; so am I, *Note: often occurs as* **is** *or* **'s**, *esp in set phrases*, **m' athair 's mo mhàthair** my father and mother, **aran is ìm** bread and butter; **2** *in comp constructions* as, **chan eil mi cho òg agus/is a bha mi** I'm not as young as I was, **cho luath 's a b' urrainn dhomh** as quickly as I could, **dè cho fliuch 's a tha e?** how wet is it?; **3** *in concessive clauses* **air cho anmoch 's gu bheil e** however late it is/may be, **gabh e, beag 's gu bheil e** take it, small though it is; **4** *usu* **is** *or* **'s** (*trad*) *expressing simultaneity, & corres to Eng with, while, though &c as implied by the context*, **boireannach is triùir mhac aice** a woman with three sons, **cha chaidil iad 's an solas air** they won't sleep with the light on, **chaidil mi gu math is an solas air fad na h-oidhche** I slept well even though the light was on all night, **ghoid e e is ise ri thaobh** he stole it while (*or* even though) she was beside him, (*song*) **tè eile chan iarrainn 's tu beò** I wouldn't want any other woman as long as you live, **bha iad 's an gàirdeanan mun cuairt air a chèile** they had their arms around each other

a h-uile *adj see* **uile** 2

aibidil, aibidile, aibidilean *nf* an alphabet

aibidealach *adj* alphabetical, **òrdugh aibidealach** alphabetical order

aice(se) *prep pron see* **aig**

àicheadh, *gen* **àicheidh** *nm* **1** (*the act of*) denying, renouncing; **2** denial, a denial, **dèan** *v* **àicheadh** deny, *NB note the double neg* **cha dèan mi àicheadh nach do smaoinich mi** ... I won't deny that I thought ...; **3** renunciation, a renunciation (*of belief &c*)

àicheidh *vt, pres part* **ag àicheadh**, **1** deny, **ag àicheadh a chionta** denying his guilt; **2** deny, renounce, **ag àicheadh a chreideimh** denying/renouncing his faith

àicheil *adj* (*gram*) negative

aideachadh, aideachaidh, aideachaidhean *nm* **1** (*the act of*) confessing, admitting; **2** confession, a confession (*not in RC sense, see* **faoisid**), an admission (*of guilt &c*)

aidich *vti, pres part* **ag aideachadh**, confess, admit, **dh'aidich e a chionta** he confessed/admitted his guilt, **tha iad air aideachadh** they have confessed

aifreann, *gen* **aifrinn** *nm* (*relig*) a Mass

aig *prep, Note: the pers prons* **mi, thu, e** *&c combine with* **aig** *to form the prep prons* **agam(sa), agad(sa), aige(san), aice(se), againn(e), agaibh(se), aca(san)**, at me, you *&c, usu indicating possession (see 2);*

1 at, **aig an doras** at the door, **aig a' Mhòd** at the Mod, **aig baile** at home; 2 belonging to, in the possession of, **an cù aig Dòmhnall** Donald's dog, **a bheil teaghlach aig Iain?** does John have a family? **tha cù agam** I have a dog, **an cù aca** their dog, **Uilleam againn(e)** our William, **a bheil an iuchair agad?** have you got the key? **seo agad ugh** here's an egg (for you), *Cf* **le 4**; 3 *for mental and emotional states* **tha cuimhn' agam (ort &c)** I remember (you &c), **tha dùil agam (rithe &c)** I expect (her &c), **tha gaol agam (oirre &c)** I love (her &c); 4 *in expr* **tha agam (&c) ri … I (&c)** have to …, **bha bileag aice ri pàigheadh** she had a bill to pay, **tha aca ri goc a chàradh** they have to repair a tap, *Cf* **feudar 2, feum** *v* **1**; 5 *in expr* **dè a' Ghàidhlig a th 'agad air 'continental drift' (&c)?** what do you say in Gaelic for 'continental drift' (&c)?; 6 *misc idioms* **tha iad mòr aig a chèile** they're great friends, **chaidh agam air** I managed it; I got the better of him, **tha not agam air** he owes me a pound, **tha e ag obair aig an uachdaran** he's working for the landlord, **a' fuireach aig Ailig** staying (*ie* lodging) with Alec, **pòsta aig Peigi** married to Peggy, **bha i air a dearg-mhilleadh aig a màthair** her mother had got her completely spoiled, she'd been completely spoiled by her mother

aige(san) *prep pron see* **aig**

àigeach, *gen & pl* **àigich** *nm* a stallion

àigh *nm see* **àgh**

aighear, *gen* **aigheir** *nm* merriment, joy, cheerfulness

aighearach *adj* cheerful, merry, joyful, (*song*) **b' aighearach an-uiridh mi** merry was I last year, *Cf* **aoibhneach 3**

aighearachd *nf invar* cheerfulness, joyfulness

aigne *nf invar* 1 mind, *esp in expr* **air m' aigne/air d' aigne &c** on my/ your (&c) mind, *Cf* **aire 1, cùram 2, fa-near 1**; 2 character, disposition, *Cf* **mèinn 1, nàdar 2**

ailbhinn, *gen* **ailbhinne** *nf* flint, a flint

àile, *also* **àileadh, fàile & fàileadh,** *gen* **(f)àileidh,** *pl* **(f)àileachan, fàilean & fàilidhean** *nm* 1 air, atmosphere; 2 smell **bha droch àile a' tighinn às** *or* **bha droch àile dheth** it had a bad smell, *Cf* **boladh,** *& usu pleasant* **boltrach**

àileach *adj* 1 airy, 2 pertaining to the air or atmosphere

aileag, aileig, aileagan *nf* hiccups (*with the art*), **tha an aileag orm** I've got (the) hiccups

àill *nf invar* 1 (*trad*) desire, will, *now usu in expr* **'s àill leam (&c)** I (&c) desire, **'s àill leatha beartas** she desires wealth, *Cf* **iarr 1, miann 1**; 2 *in expr* **B' àill leibh/Bàillibh?** Pardon?, *Cf less polite* **dè an rud?** (*see* **rud 1**)

àilleag, àilleig, àilleagan *nf* **1** a jewel, (*song*) **àilleagan** (*dimin*) **nan gillean** a jewel among youths, *Cf* **leug, seud**; **2** a pretty girl

àillidh *adj* **1** shining, bright, resplendent, *Cf more usu* **boillsgeach, deàlrach 1**; **2** beautiful, *Cf more usu* **àlainn, bòidheach, sgèimheach**

ailm *see* **failm**

ailse & **aillse** *nf invar* cancer, **aillse sgamhanach** lung cancer

ailseag, ailseig, ailseagan *nf* a caterpillar

ailtire, ailtire, ailtirean *nm* an architect

ailtireachd *nf invar* architecture

aimhleas, *gen* **aimhleis** *nm* **1** (*trad*) misfortune, ruination, *Cf more usu* **creach** *n* **2, sgrios** *n*; **2** mischief, *Cf* **donas 1, olc** *n*

aimhreit, aimhreite, aimhreitean *nf* **1** disorder, a disorder, disturbance, a disturbance, trouble, *Cf* **trioblaid, ùpraid 2**; **2** (*hist*) **aimhreit an fhearainn** the 19th-century Land League agitation

aimhreiteach *adj* quarrelsome, turbulent, trouble-making, *Cf* **buaireasach**

aimsir, aimsire, aimsirean *nf* **1** (*occas*) time, *Cf more usu* **tìde 1, ùine 1**; **2** (*occas*) a season, *Cf* **ràith 1, tràth** *n* **1**; **3** (*more often*) weather, **droch aimsir** bad weather, *Cf* **sìde**

aimsireil *adj* **1** temporal; **2** climatic

ain- *a prefix corres to Eng* un-, *see examples below*, *Cf* **do-, mì-, neo-**

aindeoin *nf* **1** reluctance, unwillingness, *Cf opposite* **deòin**; **2** *usu in expr* **a dh'aindeoin** (*with gen*) in spite of, against the will of, **a dh'aindeoin na thuirt i** in spite of what she said, **a dh'aindeoin chùis** nonetheless, all the same, in spite of everything, **a dheòin no a dh'aindeoin** whether he was/is willing or not, (*prov*) **fear a chuirear a dh'aindeoin don allt, bristidh e na soithichean** a man sent unwilling to the burn will break the water jugs; **3** *also as conj* **a dh'aindeoin 's gu robh i sgìth** despite the fact that she was tired

aindeònach *adj* reluctant, unwilling, *Cf* **leisg** *adj* **2**

àineach & **àithneach** *adj* imperative, (*gram*) **am modh àineach** the imperative mood

aineolach *adj* **1** ignorant; **2** not knowledgeable, unfamiliar (**air** with), **aineolach air coimpiutairean** unfamiliar with computers, *Cf less usu* **ainfhiosrach**

aineolas, *gen* **aineolais** *nm* **1** ignorance; **2** unfamiliarity (**air** with)

ainfhios, *gen* **ainfhiosa** *nm* ignorance, *Cf more usu* **aineolas 1**

ainfhiosrach *adj* ignorant, *Cf more usu* **aineolach**

aingeal, aingil, ainglean *nm* an angel

aingidh *adj* wicked, *Cf more usu* **olc** *adj*

ainm, *gen* **ainme**, *pl* **ainmean** & **ainmeannan** *nm* a name, **dè an t-ainm a th' ort?** what's your name? **'s e Stiùbhart an t-ainm a th' orm** my name is Stewart, **ainm àite** a placename (*pl* **ainmean àite/ àiteachan**), (*excl*) **an ainm an duine mhaith!** in the name of the wee man!, *also in expr* **cuir** *v* **an** (&c) **ainm ri pàipear** sign a document

ainmeachadh, *gen* **ainmeachaidh** *nm* (*the act of*) naming, mentioning

ainmear, **ainmeir**, **ainmearan** *nm* (*gram*) a noun, **ainmear gnìomhaireach** a verbal noun

ainmeil *adj* famous, *Cf* **cliùiteach**, **iomraiteach**

ainmh- *prefix corres to Eng* zoo-, **ainmh-eòlas** *m* zoology

ainmhidh, **ainmhidhe**, **ainmhidhean** *nm* an animal, *Cf* **beathach**, **biast 1**

ainmich *vt*, *pres part* **ag ainmeachadh**, 1 name; 2 mention, **an tè a dh' ainmich mi roimhe** the woman I mentioned before, *Cf* **thoir iomradh air** (*see* **iomradh 1**)

ainmneach *adj* (*gram*) nominative, **an tuiseal ainmneach** the nominative case

ainneamh *adj* 1 (*trad*) unusual, scarce, *Cf* **tearc** & *more usu* **gann 1**; 2 (*trad*) *usu in expr* **is ainneamh a …** it's not often that …, **is ainneamh a chì thu a leithid** you won't often/you'll rarely see the likes of him/her/it

ainneart, *gen* **ainneirt** *nm* violence, *Cf* **fòirneart**

ainneartach *adj* violent

ainnir, **ainnire**, **ainnirean** *nf* a virgin, *Cf* **maighdeann 2**, **òigh 1**

ainnis, *gen* **ainnise** *nf* poverty, *Cf more usu* **bochdainn 1**

ainniseach *adj* poor, indigent, needy, *Cf* **bochd 1**, **easbhaidheach 1**, **uireasbhach 1**

aintighearn(a), **aintighearna**, **aintighearnan** *nm* a tyrant

aintighearnail *adj* tyrannical

aintighearnas, *gen* **aintighearnais** *nm* tyranny

air *prep* (*with dat*), *Note: the pers prons* **mi**, **thu**, **e** &c *combine with* **air** *to form the prep prons* **orm(sa)**, **ort(sa)**, **air(san)**, **oirre(se)**, **oirnn(e)**, **oirbh(se)**, **orra(san)** on me, you &c; 1 on, **air a' mhullach** on the roof, **cuir air an coire** put the kettle on, **air m' aire** on my mind; 2 *for phys*, *mental and emotional states*, **thàinig am pathadh orm** I grew thirsty, **tha smùid orra** they're drunk, **tha an cnatan oirre** she's got the cold, **tha mulad oirre** she's sad, **tha eagal orm** I'm afraid (*ie* I'm sorry to say …), **tha an t-eagal orm** I'm frightened; 3 *expressing disadvantage*, **ghoid e mo sgian orm** he stole my knife 'on me', **dè tha a' cur ort?** what's the matter with you? **gabh brath**

air cuideigin take advantage of somebody, **faigh spòrs air cuideigin** have fun at someone's expense; **4** on, about, **film air murtair** a film about a murderer, **òraid air feallsanachd** a lecture on philosophy, **cò air a tha thu a-mach?** what are you (going) on about?, *Cf* **mu 2 & 3**; **5** at, **air banais/tòrradh** at a wedding/a funeral, **tha iad math air iomain** they're good at shinty, **thug iad greis mu seach air an spaid** they each took a turn for a while at the spade; **6** during, in the course of, **bidh cèilidhean ann air a' mhìos seo** there'll be ceilidhs this month, **thig gam fhaicinn air an fheasgar** come to see me in the evening; **7** in exchange for, **reic air deagh phrìs** sell at a good price, **thug mi nota air** I paid/gave a pound for it; **8** however, **air cho bochd 's gu bheil e** however poor he might be; **9** by, judging by, **bha fhios aice air a ghuth gun robh e sgìth** she knew by his voice that he was tired; **10** *expr a completed action in the past*, **tha iad air falbh** they have gone, **bha mi air an doras a dhùnadh** I had closed the door, **tha iad air fhaicinn** they have seen him, **bha iad air am moladh** they had praised them, *also* they had been praised; **11** *misc idioms & exprs* **chaidh sinn air seachran** we got lost *or* went astray, **càite air an t-saoghal a bheil i?** where in the world is she? **cò tha sgìth? tha mise air aon** who's tired? I am for one, **bha iad air an dòigh** they were contented *or* delighted, **air an dòigh seo** in this way, **chan eil air sin ach sin fhèin** that's all there is to it, **chan eil cothrom air** there's nothing to be done about it/it can't be helped, **chan eil air ach (falbh &c)** there's nothing for it but (to leave &c), **tha nota agam ort** you owe me a pound, **mo mhallachd ort!** curse you! **air dheireadh** lagging behind, **thàinig i air deireadh** she came last, **air mo sgàth** for my sake, **air chor/ air dhòigh 's gun do chaochail iad** so that they died, **thug e Ameireaga air** he went off to America, **thoir an t-siteag ort** get out/outside! **air neo** or else, otherwise, **thig sinn air chèilidh oirbh** we'll come to 'ceilidh' on you/to visit you, **cùm ort** keep it up, keep going, **greas ort!** (*pl* **greasaibh oirbh**) hurry up! **a' coimhead a-mach air an uinneig** looking out (of) the window, **'s beag orm do cheòl** I don't think much of your music, **beag air bheag** little by little, **rug e air làimh oirre** he shook her hand; *Note:* **air** *sometimes causes aspiration/lenition in a following noun eg* **ceum air cheum** step by step

air(san) *prep pron see* **air**

air adhart *adv see* **adhart 2**

air aghaidh *adv see* **aghaidh 4**

air ais *adv* back, backwards, **cuir air ais e!** put it back! **chùm e air ais mi** he kept/held me back, he delayed me, **mìos air ais** a month back/ago, **ghabh e ceum air ais** he stepped back, *also* he took a retrograde step, **sùil air ais** a backward glance/look, *also* revision

air ball *adv* at once, immediately, *Cf* **bad 5**

air beulaibh *prep* in front of (*with gen*), **chì mi thu air beulaibh na h-eaglaise** I'll see you in front of the church, **air am beulaibh** in front of them, *Cf* **beulaibh, air cùlaibh, cùl 3**

air b(h)onn *adv see* **bonn 3**

air chall *adv see* **call 3**

airchealladh, *gen* **aircheallaidh** *nm* sacrilege

air chois *adv see* **cas** *n* 1 & 6

air choreigin *adj* some, some or other, **air dòigh air choreigin** somehow or other, **neach air choreigin** some person or other, **ann an àite air choreigin** somewhere or other, (in) some place or other

air cùl *prep see* **cùl 3**

air cùlaibh *prep* behind (*with gen*), **air cùlaibh na h-eaglaise** behind the church, **bha e air an cùlaibh** he was behind them, **dh'fhag mi/chuir mi air mo chùlaibh e** I left/I put it behind me, **thoir an aire air do chùlaibh** look/watch out behind you, *Cf* **air beulaibh, cùl 3, cùlaibh**

àird, àirde, àirdean *nf* **1** (*usu topog*) a height, a high place, *also in expr* **bha mi a' seinn (aig) àird mo chlaiginn** I was singing at the top of my voice; **2** a point, a promontory, *Cf* **rinn** *n* **2, rubha, sròn 2; 3** a compass point, a direction, (*Sc*) an airt, **an àird an iar** the East, **an àird an ear** the West; **4** *in expr.* **an àird** *adv* up, **cuiridh mi sgeilp an àird** I'll put a shelf up, **bha sanas an àird air a' chlàr** there was a notice up on the board, *Cf* **shuas, suas**

àirde *nf invar* **1** height, **dè an àirde a tha ann? tha sia troighean a dh'àirde ann** what height/how tall is he? he's six feet tall/in height, **tha troigh a dh'àirde ann** it's a foot tall/high; **2** (*hill, plane &c*) altitude; **3** (*musical note*) pitch

air do *conj* after, **air dhuinn am bealach a ruigsinn** after we had reached the top of the pass, *Cf* **an dèidh 2**

aire *nf invar* **1** mind, **tha rudeigin air a h-aire** there's something on her mind/preoccupying her, *Cf* **aigne 1, cùram 2, fa-near 1; 2** attention, *usu in phrase* **thoir** *v* **an aire** pay attention, notice, look after **cha tug e an aire don chàr** he paid no attention to/he ignored the car, *also* he didn't notice the car, *Cf* **fa-near 3, feart** *nf*, **for, suim 2; 3** care, *esp in expr* **thoir an aire (ort fhèin)!** take care (of yourself)!, **thoir an aire nach tuit thu** mind/watch you don't fall

aireachail *adj* attentive, *Cf* **faiceallach**

àireamh, àireimh, àireamhan *nf* a number, **àireamh a trì** number three, **àireamh fòn** a phone number, **àireamh mhòr bhoireannach** a large number of women

àireamhair, àireamhair, àireamhairean *nm* a *(pocket &c)* calculator

air èiginn *see* **èiginn 4**

air fad *adv see* **fad** *nm* **3**

air falbh *adv see* **falbh 1**

air feadh, *also* **feadh,** *prep* through, throughout, all over *(with gen)*, **air feadh an taighe** through/throughout the house, **bha glainneachan falamh air feadh an àite** there were empty glasses all over the place, **bha fàileadh air feadh an rùim** a scent filled the room, **air feadh an là** all through the day, all day, **chuir sin an ceòl air feadh na fìdhle!** that put the cat among the pigeons!

airgead, *gen* **airgid** *nm* **1** money, **airgead-pòcaid** pocket money, **airgead ullamh** ready money, cash, **tha e a' cosnadh mòran airgid** he's earning a lot of money, **'s e airgead mòr a tha sin!** that's a lot of money!; **2** silver, *(song)* **An Fhìdeag Airgid** The Silver Whistle, **bonn airgid** a coin, *also* a silver medal

airgeadach *adj* well-off, comfortably off, *Cf* **seasgair 2**

airidh *adj* worthy, deserving, **duine airidh** a worthy man, **airidh air moladh** worthy of praise, **bha sibh airidh air** you deserved it, *also* you were entitled to it, *(without prep)* **duais a b' airidh an t-ainm** a prize worthy of the name, *(trad)* **'s math an airidh** it's richly deserved, he (&c) richly deserves it, *Cf less usu* **toillteanach**

àirigh, àirighe, àirighean *nf* *(trad)* summer pasture(s), a sheiling, **bha na boireannaich air àirigh** the women were at the summer pastures, **bothan àirigh** a sheiling bothy, *Cf less usu* **ruighe 3**

air leth *adv see* **leth 2**

air muin *adv see* **muin 1 & 3**

àirneis *nf invar (coll)* **1** furniture, **àirneis taighe** household furniture, **ball àirneis** a piece/an item of furniture; **2** *(trad)* gear, accoutrements, trappings, *(theatre &c)* props, *Cf* **uidheam 2**

air neo *conj* or, or else, otherwise, **gabh do dhìnnear air neo chan fhaigh thu suiteis** eat your dinner or (else) you won't get any sweeties, **dùin an doras air neo gabhaidh sinn an cnatan** shut the door or we'll catch cold, *Cf* **no**

air sgàth *prep see* **sgàth** *n* **3**

airson *prep (with gen)* **1** for, **sgrìobh i aiste airson a bràthar** she wrote an essay for *(ie to oblige)* her brother, **na bi duilich air a son** don't be sorry for her *(Cf* **do** *prep* **3)**, **chaidh sinn don bhùth airson uighean** we went to the shop for eggs; **2** *of time* for, **ghabh i e air iasad airson**

dà sheachdain she borrowed it for two weeks; **3** for, for the sake of, **chaill e a bheatha airson a' Phrionnsa** he lost his life for the Prince, *Cf* **sgàth** *n* 3; **4** for, in support of, in favour of, ready or willing (*to do something*), **bha mi airson falbh** I was for leaving/felt like leaving/ was about to leave, **bhòt iad airson an riaghaltais** they voted for the government, **chan eil mi airson sin idir** I don't approve of/I'm not in favour of that at all, (*fam*) **a bheil thu airson pinnt?** are you for/do you fancy a pint?; **5** to, in order to (*less formal & trad than* **gus**), **chaidh mi don bhaile airson caraid fhaicinn** I went to town to see a friend, *Cf* **a-chum, gus** *conj*; **6** *in expr* **air a shon sin** in spite of that, for all that, *Cf* **aindeoin** 2

air thoiseach *adv see* **toiseach** 3

airtnealach *adj* (*trad, in songs &c*) weary, woeful, sorrowful, *Cf* **brònach, muladach, tùrsach**

aiseag, aiseig, aiseagan *nm* a ferry, (*trad*) a ferry crossing, **a' gabhail an aiseig** taking/crossing the ferry, **bàt'-aiseig** *m* a ferry boat, **aiseag-charbad** a car ferry

aiseal, aiseil, aisealan *nmf* an axle

aiseal *nm see* **asal**

aisean, *gen* **aisne,** *pl* **aisnean, aisnichean & asnaichean** *nm* a rib

aiseirigh *nf invar* **1** (*relig*) resurrection, a resurrection; **2** resurgence, revival, a revival, **aiseirigh na Gàidhlig** the resurgence of Gaelic, *Cf* **ath-bheothachadh** 2

Aisia *nf invar* Asia (*used with the art*), **thachair e san Aisia** it happened in Asia

Aisianach, *gen & pl* **Aisianaich** *nm* an Asian, *also as adj* **Aisianach** Asian

aisling, aislinge, aislingean *nf* a dream, a vision, **bha thu ag aisling** you were dreaming *or* seeing things, *Cf* **bruadar** 2

aiste(se) *prep pron see* **às**

aiste, aiste, aistidhean *nf* **1** (*school &c*) an essay; **2** (*journalism &c*) an article

àite, *gen* **àite,** *pl* **àiteachan, àitichean & àiteannan** *nm* **1** a place, **'s e àite brèagha a th' ann** it's a bonny/beautiful place, **bha a h-uile rud na àite fhèin** everything was in its (proper) place, **àite-coise** pedestrian crossing, **àite-fuirich & àite-còmhnaidh,** a dwelling, a dwelling place, accommodation, *Cf* **bad** 1, **ionad**; **2 an àite** *prep* instead of, in place of (*with gen*), **sìth an àite cogaidh** peace instead of war, **thàinig Iain na h-àite** Iain came in her place/instead of her

àiteach, *gen* **àitich** *nm* cultivation (*of land or crops*), **talamh àitich** arable/ cultivable land, *Cf* **àiteachadh** 1 & 2

àiteachadh, *gen* **àiteachaidh** *nm* **1** (*the act of*) cultivating (*land*); **2** cultivation (*of land*), *Cf* **àiteach**; **3** occupation, dwelling on (*land &c*), **luchd-àiteachaidh** *m coll* inhabitants, dwellers, *Cf* **còmhnaidh** 1

àiteachail *adj* agricultural

àiteachas, *gen* **àiteachais** *nm &* **àiteachd** *nf invar* agriculture, (*knowledge of*) farming

aiteal, *gen & pl* **aiteil** *nm* a glimpse, **fhuair iad aiteal den tìr** they got a glimpse of the land, **aiteal grèine** a glimpse/blink of sunshine, *Cf* **plathadh 1**

aiteamh, *gen* **aiteimh** *nm* a thaw, thawing, **an uair a thig an t-aiteamh** when the thaw comes

àiteigin *nm invar* some place, **chaill mi ann an àiteigin e** I lost it somewhere (or other)

aithghearr *adj* **1** short, brisk, quick, **sùil aithghearr air a' chleoc** a quick look at the clock; **2** (*manner &c*) abrupt, *Cf* **cas** *adj* **3**; **3** *esp in expr* **a dh'aithghearr** *adv* soon, shortly, **bidh sinn ann a dh'aithghearr** we'll be there soon

aithghearrachd *nf invar* **1** abbreviation, an abbreviation, *Cf* **giorrachadh 2**; **2** a short cut, **ghabh sinn aithghearrachd** we took a short cut; **3** *in expr* **an aithghearrachd** *adv* swiftly, promptly, 'sharpish', **sgrìobh e an litir an aithghearrachd** he wrote the letter in no time, *Cf* **grad 3**

aithisg, aithisge, aithisgean *nf* a report (*esp formal & written*), an account, *Cf* **aithris 1**

aithne *nf invar* **1** knowledge, acquaintance (*usu of people*); **2** *esp in expr* **cuir aithne air** get to know, get acquainted with; **3** *esp in expr* **an aithne dhuibh e (&c)? chan aithne** do you know him (&c)? no; *Cf* **eòlach 2, eòlas 3**

aithneachadh & faithneachadh, *gen* **(f)aithneachaidh** *nm* (*the act of*) knowing &c (*see senses of* **aithnich** *v*)

aithnich & faithnich, *vt, pres part* **ag aithneachadh & a' faithneachadh**, **1** know, recognise (*of people*), **aithnichidh sinn a-rithist sibh** we'll know/recognise you another time, (*prov*) **chan aithnichinn e ged thachradh e nam bhrochan orm** I wouldn't know him if I met him in my gruel; **2** know, experience, **cha do dh'aithnich ar sinnsearan na duilgheadasan a th' againn a-nis** our ancestors didn't know/experience the problems we have now

aithreachas, *gen* **aithreachais** *nm* (*relig*) repentance, **rinn i/ghabh i aithreachas** she repented

aithreachail *adj* repentant, remorseful

aithris *vt, pres part* **ag aithris**, **1** report or recount something; **2** recite, **dh'aithris i pìos bàrdachd** she recited a piece of poetry; **3** (*play &c*) rehearse

aithris, aithrise, aithrisean *nm* **1** a report, an account (*verbal or written*), tha *Aithris na Maidne* air an rèidio gach là 'Morning Report/ Bulletin' is on the radio every day, **beul-aithris** oral tradition, *Cf* **cunntas 4, iomradh 2; 2** recitation, a recitation; **3** (*play &c*) rehearsal, a rehearsal

àitich *vt, pres part* **ag àiteachadh, 1** cultivate (*land or crops*), *Cf* **obraich 2; 2** inhabit, dwell on, occupy (*land &c*), *Cf* (*vi*) **còmhnaich**

aitreabh, aitreibh, aitreabhan *nm* a building, a dwelling, *Cf more usu* **fàrdach 1, togalach**

àl, *gen* **àil** *nm* (*trad*) a litter, a brood, progeny, the young of a bird or mammal, *Cf* **cuain**

àlainn *adj* **1** lovely, fine, splendid, **abair bad àlainn!** what a lovely spot! **taigh àlainn** a lovely/fine house, *Cf* **àillidh 2, brèagha, grinn 1; 2** fine, grand, **bha sin dìreach àlainn!** that was just grand!, *Cf* **sgoinneil**

Alba, *gen* **Alba** *& trad gen* **Albann,** *trad dat* **Albainn** *nf* Scotland, **ann an Alba** *or* (*trad*) **ann an Albainn** in Scotland, **Gàidhlig na h-Alba** *or* (*trad*) **na h-Albann** the Gaelic of Scotland, Scottish/Scots Gaelic, **à Alba** *or* (*trad*) **à** (*also* **às**) **Albainn** from Scotland

Albais, *gen* **Albaise** *nf* the Scots language, Scots, *Cf* **A' Bheurla Ghallta** (*see* **Beurla 2**)

Albannach, *gen & pl* **Albannaich** *nm* a Scotsman, a Scot, **ban-Albannach** *f* a Scotswoman, *also as adj* **Albannach** Scottish, Scots

alcol, *gen* **alcoil** *nm* alcohol

allaban, *gen* **allabain** *nm* (*trad*) wandering, (*trad*) **rach air allaban** take to wandering, become a wanderer, *Cf* **fuadan 1**

allaidh *adj* wild (*ie not domesticated*), *usu in set compounds, eg* **madadh-allaidh** *m* a wolf (*Cf* **faol**), **damhan-allaidh** *m* a spider, *Cf* **fiadhaich 1**

allt, *gen & pl* **uillt** *nm* a mountain stream, a stream, a burn, *Cf* **abhainn, sruth** *n* **1**

alltan, *gen & pl* **alltain** *nm* (*dimin of* **allt**) a (*usu small*) stream, a water, (*stream name*) **alltan dubh** black water

alt, uilt, altan *nm* **1** (*anat*) a joint, **alt na h-uilne** the elbow joint; **2** a method, a way (*of doing something*), **cha robh an t-alt againn air eòin a ghlacadh** we didn't know the way to catch/the method/art of catching birds, **air alt 's gun** ... in such a way that ..., so that ..., *Cf* **dòigh 1, liut, seòl²** **1; 3** (*gram*) **an t-alt** the article; **4** *in expr* **an altan a chèile** *or* (*trad*) **an altaibh a chèile** together, **chan urrainn dha dà fhacal a chur an altaibh/an altan a chèile** he can't string two words together, *Cf* **an ceann a chèile** (*see* **ceann 3**)

altachadh, *gen* **altachaidh** *nm* grace *(before meals &c)*, **dèan** *v* **altachadh** say grace, *(prov)* **dh'ith e am biadh mun do rinn e an t-altachadh** he ate the food before he said the grace

altair, altarach, altairean *nf* an altar

altraim *vt, pres part* **ag altram(adh)/(as)**, **1** foster; **2** nurse *(esp a sick person)*, *Cf* **eiridnich**

altram, *gen* **altraim**, **1** fosterage, fostering; **2** nursing, **banaltram** *f* a nurse, **fear altraim** *m* a male nurse, **taigh altraim** *m* a nursing home, *Cf* **eiridinn**

am *poss adj see* **an** *poss adj*

am *art (for forms see table p 401)* the

àm, ama, amannan *nm* time, *Note: not used for clock time (see* **uair 1***)*; **bho àm gu àm** from time to time, **bha i bochd aig an àm** she was poorly at the time, **aig an àm seo den bhliadhna** at this time of the year, **thàinig i ron àm** she came early, **tha an t-àm againn falbh** it's time for us to go/leave, **bha an t-àm ann** it was high time/not before time, **san àm a dh'fhalbh** in the past, in olden times, **anns na h-amannan ùra/nodha seo** in these modern times, **aig amannan tha** *(or* **bidh***)* **e crosta, aig amannan eile tha** *(or* **bidh***)* **e solta** at times he's naughty, at other times he's good *(Cf* **uaireannan***)*

a-mach *adv* **1** out *(expressing motion)*, **leum iad a-mach às an trèan** they jumped out of the train, **sheall iad a-mach air an uinneig** they looked out of the window, **biadh a-mach à Tesco's** food from/out of Tesco's, **a-mach à seo (leat)!** out of here (with you), get out of here!, *Cf* **a-muigh; 2** *other idioms* **chaidh iad a-mach air a chèile** they fell out (with each other), **bha e (a' dol) a-mach air staid na dùthcha**, he was going on about the state of the country, **cha toigh leam an dol a-mach a th' aige** I don't like his manner/his behaviour/his 'carry on', **b' fheudar dhomh cur a-mach** I had to be sick/vomit, **a-mach air doras** out of doors

amadan, *gen & pl* **amadain** *nm* a fool, **'s e amadan a th' ann dheth** he's a fool, **abair amadan!** what a fool! **na dèan sin, amadain!** don't do that, you fool! *(also milder)* **tha fios gu bheil gaol agam ort, amadain!** of course I love you, silly!, *Cf* **òinseach**

amaideach *adj* foolish, silly, stupid, **duine/film amaideach** a stupid man/film, *Cf* **baoth, faoin 1, gòrach 1 & 2**

amaideas, *gen* **amaideis** *nm* foolishness, silliness, *Cf* **gòraiche 2**

a-màireach *adv* tomorrow, **nì mi a-màireach e** I'll do it tomorrow, **madainn a-màireach** tomorrow morning

amais *vti, pres part* **ag amas, 1** aim (*weapon &c*), **dh'amais mi air an damh** I aimed at the stag, *Cf* **cuimsich; 2** hit upon, find, come across, **dh'amais mi air deagh thàillear** I've found (&c) a good tailor, *Cf* **faigh 2, lorg 2, tachair 3**

amaiseach *adj* (*weapon, marksman*) accurate

amalach *adj* complicated, *Cf* **iomadh-fhillte** (*see* **fillte 2**)

amar, amair, amaran *nm* **1** a basin (*Cf* **mias 1**), a pool (*Cf* **linne 1**); **2** *now usu in compounds, eg* **amar-ionnlaid** a wash basin, **amar-snàimh** a swimming pool

amas, amais, amasan *nm* **1** (*the act of*) aiming &c (*see senses of* **amais** *v*); **2** (*weapons &c*) aim; **3** (*more generally*) an aim, an objective

am bitheantas *adv* usually, commonly, normally, generally, **am bitheantas bidh ìm buidhe** usually butter is yellow, *Cf* **an cumantas, tric 2**

am broinn *prep see* **broinn 2**

Ameireaga(idh) *nf* America

Ameireaganach, *gen & pl* **Ameireaganaich** *nm* an American, *also as adj* **Ameireaganach** American

am feasd *&* **am feast** *adv* ever, for ever, (*with verb in neg*) never, *Cf* much more *usu* **a-chaoidh, bràth 2 & 3, sìorraidh 2**

amh *adj* **1** raw, uncooked, **muilt-fheòil amh** raw mutton, **stuth amh** raw materials; **2** unripe, **ubhal amh** an unripe apple, *Cf* **an-abaich 1**

amha(i)ch, amhaiche, amhaichean *nf* **1** a neck, **ròpa mu amhaich** a rope around his neck, **bheir mi an ceann às an amhaich aige!** I'll wring his neck! **amhaich botail** neck of a bottle, *Cf* **muineal; 2** throat, **bha cnàimh aice na h-amhaich** she had a bone in her throat, *Cf* **sgòrnan**

a-mhàin *adv* **1** only (*more emph than* **ach 3 & 4**), **aon laogh a-mhàin** only one calf, **chan e a-mhàin gu bheil e gun airgead ach ...** it's not only that he's got no money but ... ; **2 ach a-mhàin** *prep* except, apart from, **cha robh duine beò ann ach mi-fhìn a-mhàin** there wasn't a living soul except myself; *Cf* **ach 3 & 4**

àmhainn, àmhainne, àmhainnean *nf* an oven

amharas, *gen pl* **amharais** *nm* suspicion, a suspicion, doubt, a doubt, *usu in expr* **tha amharas agam (agad** *&c*) I (you &c) suspect, **tha amharas agam gun deachaidh e a-null thairis** I suspect/(*Sc*) doubt he went abroad, *Cf* **teagamh 1**

amharasach *adj* suspicious, distrustful, doubting, *Cf* **teagmhach**

amharc, *gen* **amhairc** *nm* sight, view, *usu in exprs* **san amharc** in sight, **às an amharc** out of sight, *Cf more usu* **fradharc 2, sealladh 3**

amhran *see* **òran**

am measg *prep* among (*with gen*), **am measg an fhraoich** among the heather, **am measg an luchd-èisdeachd** among the listeners/ the audience, **tha tòrr dhaoine, is mise nam measg, den bheachd gu** … many people, myself among them, believe that …, *Cf less usu* **eadar 2**

a-muigh *adv* outside (*ie position*), **cà'il am bodach? tha e a-muigh** where's the old fellow? he's outside, **(air) an taobh a-muigh** (on) the outside, **a-muigh 's a-staigh** inside and out(side), (*more fig*) **oileanach an taobh a-muigh** an external student, *Cf* **a-mach 1**, **a-staigh**

an *art* (*for forms see table p 401*) the

an (**am** *before b, f, m & p*) *poss adj* their, **chaill iad an airgead** they lost their money, **chaill iad am pàrantan** they lost their parents, *Note: before a verbal noun the poss adj can express the object of the verb or the subject of a passive construction,* **chan urrainn dhomh am faicinn** I can't see them, **bha e gan leantainn** he was following them (*lit* he was at their following), **an dèidh am fuadach** after they were/had been exiled

an (**am** *before b, f, m & p*) *prep* **1** in (*mostly found in poetry & set phrases, & much less common than* **ann an**), **an treun a neirt** in his prime, at the height of his powers, **am beul na h-oidhche** at dusk, **an aithghearrachd** in a jiffy, **thèid mi an urras gu bheil e onarach** I guarantee/vouch that he is honest, **cuiridh mi an geall gur e slaightire a th' ann dheth!** I'll bet/wager he's a scoundrel!, *Cf* **ann an 1**; **2** *Note: the pers prons* **mi, thu, e** *&c combine with* **an** *to form the prep prons* **annam(sa), annad(sa), ann(san), innte(se), annainn(e), annaibh(se), annta(san)**, in me, you *&c, examples of use:- a) expressing identity* **is e sgrìobhadair a th' annam** I am a writer, **is e òinseach a th' annad** you are an idiot, **'s e poileasmain a th' annta** they are policemen, **is e là brèagha a th' ann!** it's a fine day! *b) expressing location, existence* **seo a' phoit, cuir an tì innte** here's the pot, put the tea in it, **is e inntinn mhath/sùilean gorma a th' innte** she's got a good mind/blue eyes, **a bheil Iain ann?** is Iain here/there/in? **creididh mi/tha mi a' creidsinn gu bheil taibhsean ann** I believe that there are ghosts (here) *or* I believe that ghosts exist; **3** *Note: the poss adjs* **mo, do, a, a, ar, ur, an** *combine with* **an** *to give* **nam, nad, na, na, nar, nur, nan** (*before b, f, m & p* **nam**) in my/your &c, *also found as* **na mo, na do** &c, *examples of use:-* **tha e nam phòcaid** it's in my pocket, **cur nad mhàileid e** put it in your bag, **chaidh e na shaighdear** he became a soldier, (*Sc*) he went for a sodger, **tha i na banaltram** she's a nurse, **bha sinn nar cadal** we were asleep/sleeping, (*bodily positions*) **a bheil sibh nur laighe?**

are you lying down/in bed? **tha iad nan seasamh** they are standing/standing up, **bha mi nam shuidhe** I was sitting/sitting down/seated; *Note:* **nam** *&c can often express more temporary situations than* **annam** *&c, eg Cf* **tha e na chìobair pàirt-ùine an-dràsta** he's a part-time shepherd just now, **'s e dotair a th' innte** she's a doctor (*ie permanently*); **4** *emphasising or 'highlighting' use of* **ann** *prep pron,* **is ann an-dè a thachair e** it's yesterday that it happened, **an ann le foill a cheannaich e e? is ann** is it/was it fraudulently that he bought it? yes, **an robh iad sgìth? cha robh, is ann leisg a bha iad!** were they tired? no, they were lazy (*emph*), *Note: this construction is used with adjs, advs & phrases, not with prons, nouns & proper nouns, contrast* **is e an trèana a chunnaic mi** it's/it was the train (*emph*) that I saw

an (**am** *before b, f, p & m*), *with neg v,* **nach**, *inter particle,* **an robh e ann?** was he there? **a bheil e ann?** is he there? **nach bi e ann?** won't he be there? **an do rinn iad e?** did they do it? **am faigh sinn e?** will we get it?

ana- (**an-** *before a vowel*) *a negativising prefix, but note that an identical prefix can also intensify the sense of the following word, eg* **ana-blasta** *adj* tasteless, insipid, **ana-cothrom** *f* disadvantage, unfairness, *but* **ana-chùram** *m* extreme anxiety, **anabarrach** *adj* exceeding, extreme

an-abaich *adj* **1** (*fruit &c*) unripe, *Cf* **amh 2**; **2** premature (*Cf* **mithich** *n*), **bha asaid an-abaich aice** she had a miscarriage, **bha breith an-abaich aice** she had an abortion

anabarrach *adj* **1** extreme; **2** *often used as adv* **bha am biadh anabarrach math** the food was extremely good/excellent, *Cf* **eagalach 3, uabhasach 2**

ana-cainnt, *gen* **ana-cainnte** *nf* abusive language

an aghaidh *prep see* **aghaidh 3**

anail, analach, anailean *nf* breath, a breath, **on a tharraing mi mo chiad anail** since I first drew breath, **bha i a' gearain fo a h-anail** she was grumbling under her breath, **leig d' anail!** get your breath back!, take a breather!, *Cf less usu* **deò 1**

anainn, anainne, *pl* **anainnean** *nf* eaves (*of building*)

an àite *prep see* **àite 2**

analachadh, *gen* **analachaidh** *nm* (*gram*) aspiration, lenition, *Cf* **sèimheachadh**

a-nall *adv* here (*ie movement*), hither, *Note: expressing point of view of person(s) towards whom the movement is made,* (*song*) **teann a-nall 's thoir dhomh do làmh** come hither/over here and give me your hand, (*song*) **thoir a-nall Ailean thugam** bring Alan over (here) to me (*Cf* **a-bhos, a-null, thall 1**), **a-null 's a-nall** hither and thither (*Cf* **thall 's a-bhos** – *see* **thall 1**), **bha sinn a' bruidhinn/a' còmhradh a-null 's a-nall** we were talking about this and that

anam, anma, anman *nm* a soul, (*trad*) **air m' anam**! upon my soul!

anart, anairt, anartan *nm* **1** (*the material*) linen, **lèine anairt** a linen shirt; **2** (*coll*) linen, **cuir** *v* **an t-anart sa phreas** put the linen in the cupboard, **anart bùird** table linen, **anart leapa** bed linen, (*trad*) **anart bàis** a shroud

an-asgaidh *adv see* **asgaidh 2**

an ath-bhliadhna *adv* next year

an ath-oidhch(e) *adv* tomorrow night

an ceann *prep see* **ceann 3**

an ceart(u)air *adv* just now (*used for immediate past, present & immediate future*), **bha e ann an ceartair** he was here just now, **tha mi trang an ceartair** I'm busy just now, **bidh mi agad an ceartair** I'll be with you in a moment, *Cf more usu* **an-dràsta**

an cèin *adv* abroad, *Cf more usu* **thall thairis** (*see* **thairis 1**)

an cois *prep see* **cas** *n* **4**

an comhair *prep* in the direction of (*with gen*), *usu* in phrases, *eg* (**thuit e &c**) **an comhair a chinn/an comhair a chùil** (he fell &c) head first/backwards, *see* **comhair 1**

an còmhnaidh *adv* always, **tha i còmhla ris an còmhnaidh** she's always with him, *Cf* **daonnan, sgur 2**

an-dè *adv* yesterday, **chunna mi an-dè i** I saw her yesterday

an dèidh *&* **às dèidh, 1** *prep* after (*with gen*), **an dèidh na stoirme** after the storm, **bhruidhinn e nam/nad** (*&c*) **dhèidh** he spoke after me/you (*&c*), **tha am poileas nan dèidh** the police are after them, **an dèidh sin 's na dhèidh** after all (is said and done), **tha thu ceàrr! 's an dèidh sin?** you're wrong! so?; **2 an dèidh do** *conj* after, **an dèidh dhomh an sgoil fhàgail chaidh mi nam shaighdear** after leaving/after I left school I became a soldier, *Cf* **air 11**; **3 an dèidh sin** *adv* nevertheless, however

an-diugh *adv* today, **madainn/feasgar an-diugh** this morning/afternoon, **bidh sin a' tachairt gu tric san là an-diugh** that often happens today/these days

an-dràsta (*&* **an-dràsda**) *adv* just now (*used for immediate past & present*) **bha e ann an-dràsta** he was here just now, **tha mi trang an-dràsta** I'm busy just now, **tha sinn ga dhèanamh an-dràsta fhèin** we're doing it this very instant/moment, **bha e agam an-dràsta fhèin** I had it just a moment ago, **an-dràsta 's a-rithist** now and again, from time to time, (*fam*) **tìoraidh an-dràsta** cheerio just now, (*less fam*) **mar sin leibh an-dràsta!** goodbye just now!, *Cf* **an ceart(u)air, a-nis(e)**

an ear *adv see* **ear**

an-earar *adv* the day after tomorrow

anfhann (**an-** *plus* **fann**) *adj* infirm, *Cf* **euslainteach** *adj*

annfhannachd *nf invar* infirmity, *Cf* **euslaint(e)**

an-fhoiseil *adj* restless, uneasy, *Cf* **anshocrach**

an iar *adv see* **iar**

an impis *prep* about to, on the point of, **an impis falbh** about to leave/go, **an impis an dùthaich fhàgail** on the point of leaving the country, *Cf* **beul 3, bi 11**

an-iochdmhor *adj* merciless, pitiless

a-nìos *adv* up, *Note: lit* 'from below', *expressing point of view of person(s) towards whom the ascent is made*, **thig a-nìos thugainn!** come up to us!, *Cf* **a-nuas, sìos, suas**

a-nis(e) *adv* now (*usu more permanent or lasting than* **an-dràsta**), **tha iad a' fuireachd ann an Canada a-nis** they're living in Canada now, **tha thu gun obair, dè a nì thu a-nis?** you've no job, what will you do now? **A-nis, a Dhonnchaidh** ... Now, Duncan ..., *Cf more transient* **an-ceart(u)air, an-dràsta**

an làthair *see* **làthair 2**

anmoch *adv* late, at a late hour, **anmoch san oidhche anmoch feasgar** late in the night/in the evening, *Cf* **fadalach 1** & *opposite* **moch**

annad(sa), annaibh(se), annainn(e), annam(sa) *prep prons see* **an** *prep* **2**

ann an (**ann am** *before b, f, m & p*) *prep, Note: this is a duplicated form of* **an** *prep*; **1** in, **dhùisg e ann an uaimh** he woke up in a cave, **bha an rùm ann am bùrach** the room was in a mess, **bidh mi an sin ann an tiotag** I'll be there in an instant, *Cf* **an** & **anns an** *preps*; **2** *expressing identity* **is e caraid dhomh a tha ann an Dòmhnall** Donald is a friend of mine, *Cf* **an** *prep* **2 a)**

annas, annais, annasan *nm* a rarity, a novelty, **o chionn ghoirid bha coimpiutairean nan annas fhathast** not long ago computers were still a novelty, **chan eil sinn air an t-annas a thoirt às fhathast** we haven't got used to it, the novelty of it hasn't worn off for us yet

annasach *adj* novel, unusual, odd, *Cf* **neònach, nuadh**

anns an, anns a', anns na, *the forms taken by the preps* **an** & **ann an** *when combined with the art (often shortened to* **san, sa, sna**), in the, **anns an taigh** *or* **san taigh** in the house, **anns a' bhaile** *or* **sa bhaile** in the town, **sna** *or* **anns na Stàitean Aonaichte** in the United States,

anns an dol seachad in passing, incidentally, **san t-sabhal** in the barn, *Note:* **anns** *can also occur as* **as**, *eg*, (*fam*) **bha mi as a' bhùth** I was in the shop; *note also exprs with seasons* **as t-earrach, as t-samhradh, as t-fhoghar** in (the) spring, in (the) summer, in (the) autumn (*but* **sa gheamhradh** in (the) winter), *Cf* **an** *prep*, **ann an**

ann(san) *prep pron see* **an** *prep* 2

annta(san) *prep pron see* **an** *prep* 2

a-nochd *adv* tonight

an sàs *see* **sàs**

an seo, ann an s(h)eo *advs see* **seo** *pron*

anshocair, anshocair, anshocran *nf* 1 unease, uneasiness; 2 discomfort

anshocrach *adj* uneasy, *Cf* **an-fhoiseil**

an sin, ann an s(h)in *advs see* **sin** *pron*

an s(i)ud, ann an s(h)ud, ann an s(h)iud *advs see* **siud** *pron*

an tòir air *see* **tòir** 2

an toiseach *adv see* **toiseach** 1

an uair a *&* **nuair a,** *conj* when (*not used in questions, Cf* **cuine**), (*song*) **nuair bha mi òg** (Màiri Mhòr) when I was young, **an uair a thig Uisdean bidh a h-uile duine ann** when Hugh comes everybody will be here

an uair sin *adv* then, **ghabh e pinnt is an uair sin drama** he had a pint and then a dram/a whisky, **gabhaidh mi mo dhìnnear 's an uair sin bidh mi a' coimhead an telebhisean** I'll have my dinner and then I'll be watching the television

a-nuas *adv* down, *Note: lit* 'from above', *expressing point of view of person(s) towards whom the descent is made*, **thig a-nuas thugainn!** come down to us! *Cf* **a-nìos, sìos, suas**

an-uiridh *adv* last year

a-null *adv* there (*ie movement*), thither, over, across, *Note: envisaged from the point from which the movement is made*, **thèid mi a-null do Ghlaschu** I'll go over/across to Glasgow (*Cf* **a-bhos, a-nall, thall** 1), **thèid sinn a-null thairis** we'll go abroad/overseas, **a-null 's a-nall** hither and thither (*Cf* **thall 's a-bhos** – *see* **thall** 1), (*fig*) **bha sinn a' còmhradh a-null 's a-nall** we were chatting about this and that

an urra *see* **urra**

ao- *prefix see* **eu-**

aobhar *nm see* **adhbhar**

aobrann *nmf see* **adhbrann**

aocoltach *adj* unlike, dissimilar, **tha na bràithrean aocoltach ri chèile** the brothers are unlike each other

aodach, aodaich, aodaichean *nm* 1 cloth, material, *Cf* **clò**[1] 1, **stuth** 1; 2 *more usu* clothes, clothing, **m' aodach** *or* **mo chuid aodaich** my clothes, **chuir i oirre a h-aodach/a cuid aodaich** she put on her clothes, she got dressed, **ball-aodaich** *m* a garment, a piece of clothing, **aodach-leapa** bed clothes, **aodach-oidhche** night clothes, **fo-aodach** underclothes, *Cf less usu* **trusgan** 1

aodann, aodainn, aodainnean *nm* 1 a face, **mhaisich i a h-aodann** she made up her face, **clàr an aodainn** the brow/forehead, **bhuail i e an clàr a aodainn** she struck him full in the face, *Cf* **aghaidh** 1; 2 (*topog*) a hillface, a hillslope, (*placename*) **An t-Aodann Bàn** Edinbane, the white/pale hillface, *Cf* **leathad, leitir, ruighe** 2

aodannan, *gen & pl* **aodannain** *nm* (*fancy dress &c*) a mask, *Cf* **aghaidh-choimheach, masg**

aoibhneach *adj* 1 pleasant, *Cf* **taitneach, tlachdmhor** 1; 2 glad, happy, *Cf* **sona, toilichte**; 3 joyful, *Cf* **àghmhor** 2, **aighearach**

aoidion, aoidiona, aoidionan *nm* (*tap &c*) a leak

aoidionach & **aoidion** *adj*, not waterproof or watertight, leaky

aoigh, aoigh, aoighean *nm* 1 a guest; 2 (*hotel &c*) a resident

aoigheachd, *nf* hospitality, **air aoigheachd aig teaghlach Sgitheanach** enjoying the hospitality of/as guests of a Skye family

aoigheil *adj* 1 generous; 2 hospitable; *Cf* **fial** 1

aoir, aoire, aoirean *nf* (*Lit &c*) satire, a satire

aois, aoise, aoisean *nf* 1 age, **dè an aois a tha Iain? tha e trì bliadhna a dh'aois** how old is Iain? he's three years old; 2 old age, **tha iad a' tarraing gu h-aois a-nis** they're getting on in years/getting quite old now

aol, *gen* **aoil** *nm* (*mineral*) lime

aom *vi, pres part* **ag aomadh**, 1 bend, incline (*phys*), *Cf* **crom** *v* 1, **fiar** *v* 1, **lùb** *v* 1; 2 tend, be inclined (*to do something*)

aomadh, *gen* **aomaidh** *nm* 1 bending, tending &c (*see senses of* **aom** *v*); 2 a tendency, an inclination, a trend, **aomadh eaconomach** an economic trend

aon *num adj* 1 one, **aon fhireannach is aon bhoireannach** one male and one female, one man and one woman, **thachair e aon là** it happened one day, **bidh smùid air gach aon là** he's drunk every single day; 2 *with art* the only, **is esan an t-aon mhac a th' aca** he's the only son they have; 3 *with art* the same, **bha sinn a' fuireachd san aon taigh** we were living in the same house, *in expr* (*trad*) **ag iomradh an aon ràimh** (*lit* rowing the same oar) pulling together, working together, co-operating, *Cf* **ceudna** 1

aon *nmf* 1 one, **cia mheud a th' agad? a h-aon** how many have you got? one, **ceithir fichead 's a h-aon** eighty-one, **cò a tha airson falbh? tha mise air aon!** who's for leaving? I am, for one!; 2 (*cards*) **an t-aon** the ace

aonach, aonaich, aonaichean *nm* (*topog*) an extensive upland moor, *cf* **mòinteach, monadh 1, sliabh 1**

aonachadh, *gen* **aonachaidh** *nm* 1 (*the act of*) uniting, combining; 2 (*pol*) coalition, a coalition

aonad, aonaid, aonadan *nm* (*maths &c*) a unit, **aonad tomhais** a unit of measurement, (*building &c*) **aonad mhàthraichean** a maternity unit

aona deug *num adj* eleventh, **an t-aona là deug den Ogmhios** the eleventh of June

aonadh, aonaidh, aonaidhean *nm* union, a union, a merger, **aonadh-cèaird** a trade(s) union, **na h-aonaidhean** the (Trades) Unions, **Aonadh Nàiseanta nam Maraichean** the National Union of Seamen, (*pol, law*) **An t-Aonadh** the Union (*between Scotland & England*), **Achd an Aonaidh** the Act of Union, **Aonadh na h-Eòrpa** the European Union

aonaich *vti, pres part* **ag aonachadh,** unite, combine, merge

aonan, merge *adj & pron* one, *similar uses to* **aon** *num adj* 1 *but can be more emphatic,* **aonan nota** one pound, **aonan dhiubh co-dhiù** one of them at least, *Cf more usu* **aon** *num adj* 1

aonar, *num gen* **aonair** *nmf, usu in phrase* **nam/nad** (*&c*) **aonar** 1 one person, **dhìrich i Everest na h-aonar** she climbed Everest alone/solo (*lit as one person*); 2 aloneness, the state of being by oneself, **tha i a' fuireachd na h-aonar** she is living alone/by herself

aonaran, aonarain, aonaranan *nm* a hermit, a recluse, a loner

aon(a)ranach *adj* 1 (*place*) lonely, desolate, deserted, *Cf* **fàs** *adj* 1, **uaigneach 2;** 2 (*person*) lonely, **bha iad a' faireachdainn aonaranach** they were feeling lonely, *Cf* **uaigneach 1**

aon(a)ranachd *nf invar* loneliness, desolation &c (*see senses of* **aonaranach** *adj*)

aon deug 1 *n* eleven, **cia mheud taigh a bh' ann? bha a h-aon deug** how many houses were there? eleven; 2 *adj* eleven, **aon chù deug** eleven dogs, **aon uair deug** eleven o'clock

aon-fhillte *adj* simple, uncomplicated, **buidheachas aon-fhillte** simple gratitude, *Cf* **sìmplidh 1 & 2**

aon-inntinneach *adj* unanimous, of one/the same mind

aon-sheasmhach *adj* (*equipment &c*) stand-alone

aonta & aontadh, *gen* **aontaidh**, *pl* **aontaidhean** *nm* agreement, assent, consent, an agreement, a settlement, **thàinig an dà riaghaltas gu aonta** the two governments came to an agreement/reached a settlement, **feumaidh sinn aonta a' bhaile fhaighinn** we must get the township's agreement/consent, *Cf* **còrdadh 2**

aontachadh, *gen* **aontachaidh** *nm* (*the act of*) agreeing &c (*see* **aontaich** *v*)

aontaich *vi*, *pres part* **ag aontachadh**, agree, **dh'aontaich iad le chèile** they agreed with each other, **chan eil mi ag aontachadh ris na molaidhean agaibh** I don't accept/agree to your proposals

aosmhor *adj* ancient, *Cf* **àrsaidh, sean 2**

aosta & aosda *adj* (*of people*) old, aged, **tha am pàrantan air fàs gu math aosta** their parents have grown quite old, *Cf* **sean 1**

aotrom *adj* 1 light, **bha na clachan aotrom a dh'aindeoin am meud** the stones were light in spite of their size; 2 light (*ie not serious*), **na h-òrain mhòra 's na h-òrain aotrom** the big/great/classic songs and the light songs, **a' bruidhinn mu rudan aotrom** talking about unimportant/trivial/flippant things

aotromachadh, *gen* **aotromachaidh** *nm* (*the act of*) lightening &c (*see senses of* **aotromaich** *v*)

aotromaich *vt*, *pres part* **ag aotromachadh**, 1 lighten, (*burden &c*) make light or lighter, alleviate; 2 (*ship &c*) unload, *Cf* **falmhaich 2**

aotroman, *gen & pl* **aotromain** *nm* (*anat*) a bladder

aparan, aparain, aparanan *nm* an apron

ar (**ar n-** *before a vowel*) *poss adj* our, **ar dachaigh** our home, **ar n-athair** our father, *Note: before a verbal noun the poss adj can express the object of the verb or the subject of a passive construction,* (*trad*) **rinn iad ar sgriosadh** they destroyed us/wrought our destruction, **chaidh ar moladh** we were praised, **an dèidh ar fògradh** after we were/had been driven out

àr, àir, àir *nm* slaughter, *Cf less strong* **marbhadh**

àra, àrann, àirnean *nf* (*anat*) a kidney, *Cf* **dubhag**

Arabach, *gen & pl* **Arabaich** an Arab, *also as adj* **Arabach** Arab, Arabic, **figearan** *m* **arabach** arabic numerals

àrach, *gen* **àraich** *nm* raising, upbringing, rearing, (*song*) **soraidh leis an àit' an d'fhuair mi m' àrach òg** (Màiri Mhòr) farewell to the place in which I was raised (*lit* got my raising) when young, *Cf* **togail**

àrachas, *gen* **àrachais** *nm* insurance, **àrachas beatha/nàiseanta** life/national insurance, **dìon/polasaidh** *m* **àrachais** insurance cover/policy, **tagairt àrachais** an insurance claim, *Cf* **urras 3**

àradh & **fàradh**, *gen* **(f)àraidh**, *pl* **(f)àraidhean** *nm* a ladder, **a' dìreadh àraidh** climbing a ladder

àraich *vt, pres part* **ag àrach**, raise, rear, bring up, **ag àrach cloinne/uan** raising/rearing children/lambs, *Cf* **tog 3**

àraid *adj* **1** particular, *see* **àraidh 1**; **2** peculiar, strange, unusual, **bha dìthis bhan aige, nach robh sin àraid?** he had two wives, wasn't that strange?, *Cf* **neònach**, & *stronger* **iongantach**

àraidh, *also* **àraid**, *adj* **1** particular, in particular, **'s e taigh àraidh a tha mi airson a cheannach** it's a particular house/one house in particular that I want to buy, *Cf* **sònraichte 1**; **2** exceptional, unusual, special, **'s e duine àraidh a bh' ann** he was an exceptional/unusual man, *Cf* **leth 2**; **3** *in expr* **gu h-àraid(h)** *adv* especially, particularly, **is toigh leam am foghar, is gu h-àraid(h) an t-Sultain** I like the autumn, and especially September, *Cf* **sònraichte 3** & *see* **seac**

àrainneachd *nf invar, with art* (*ecology*) **an àrainneachd** the environment

ar-a-mach *nm invar* rebellion, a rebellion, an uprising, **rinn an sluagh ar-a-mach an aghaidh an luchd-riaghlaidh** the people rebelled/rose up against their rulers (*Cf* **èirich 2**)

aran, *gen* **arain** *nm* bread, *Note: formerly restricted to home baked bread,* **lof** *being used for shop bread*

a-raoir *adv* last night, **feasgar a-raoir** last/yesterday evening, (*song*) **chan eil fios aig duin' air thalamh far an robh mi a-raoir** no-one on earth knows where I was last night

araon *adv* (*rather trad*) both, **araon air Ghàidhealtachd agus air Ghalltachd** both in Highlands and Lowlands, *Cf* **le chèile** (*see* **le 1**), **cuid 4**, **eadar 3**

arbhar, *gen* **arbhair** *nm* corn

àrc, **àirce**, **àrcan** *nf* cork, a cork, *Cf* **corcais**

Arcach, *gen* & *pl* **Arcaich** *nm* an Orcadian, *also as adj*, **Arcach** Orcadian, of, from or pertaining to Orkney

Arcaibh *nm* Orkney

ar (**leam/leat** &c) *defective verb* (*trad & formal*) (I/you &c) think, it seems (to me/you &c), **ar leam gu bheil e ro anmoch** I think/I consider that it is too late, *Cf more usu* **creid 2**, **saoil**

àrd *adj* **1** (*person, building, hill* &c) high, tall; **2** (*sounds*) loud, **tha an ceòl sin uabhasach àrd!** that music is terribly loud! *Cf trad* **labhar**; **3** *often as prefix* **àrd-** high, principal, supreme, **àrd-shagart** *m* a high priest, **àrd-chuidiche** *m* a principal assistant, **àrd-chumhachd** *mf* supreme power (& *see examples below*), *Cf* **prìomh**

àrdachadh, *gen* **àrdachaidh** *nm* **1** (*act of*) increasing &c (*see senses of* **àrdaich** *v*); **2** promotion, a promotion, a rise, **fhuair e àrdachadh** he got promotion, **fhuair sinn àrdachadh pàighidh** we got a pay rise

àrdaich *vt*, *pres part* **ag àrdachadh**, **1** increase, raise, **dh'àrdaich an luchd-stiùiridh turasdal an luchd-obrach** the management increased/raised the salary of the workforce; **2** promote, further, (*calque*) **àrdaich ìomhaigh na Gàidhlig** promote the image/raise the profile of Gaelic

àrdan, *gen* **àrdain** *nm* arrogance, pride (*usu excessive*), (*song*) **leis an àrdan nach d' rinn feum dhomh** through the pride that did me no good at all, *Cf* **pròis**, **uaibhreas 2**

àrdanach *adj* arrogant, (*usu excessively*) proud, *Cf* **dàna 4**, **uaibhreach 2**

àrd-doras, **àrd-dorais**, **àrd-dorsan** *nm* a lintel

àrd-easbaig, **àrd-easbaig**, **àrd-easbaigean** *nm* an archbishop

àrd-ìre *nf invar & adj* higher, high-grade, high-level, **rinn e Gàidhlig aig Ard-ìre** he did Higher Gaelic/Gaelic at Higher Grade, (*adjectivally*) **tha na sgoilearan a' feuchainn nan deuchainnean Ard-ìre aca** the pupils are taking/sitting their Higher Exams/their Highers, **foghlam àrd-ìre** Higher/Further (*ie Tertiary*) Education

àrd-ollamh, **àrd-ollaimh**, **àrd-ollamhan** *nm* a professor, *Cf less trad* **proifeasair**

àrd-sgoil, **àrd-sgoile**, **àrd-sgoiltean** *nf* a high school, a secondary school, **Ard-sgoil Phort Rìgh** Portree High School, **dh'ionnsaich iad Spàinnis anns an àrd-sgoil** they learnt/studied Spanish at secondary school

àrd-ùrlar, **àrd-ùrlair**, **àrd-ùrlaran** *nm* (*theatre, hall &c*) a stage, a platform

àrd-urram, *gen* **àrd-urraim** *nm* distinction, high honour, **ghabh i ceum le àrd-urram** she graduated with First Class Honours/with Distinction

a rèir *prep* **1** according to (*with gen*), **a rèir na mòr-chuid** in most people's opinion, according to the majority, **do gach fear a rèir a chomais** to each one according to his ability; **2** *adv* accordingly, **thug iad còig notaichean do Mhàiri agus don fheadhainn eile a rèir** they gave Mary five pounds and the others pro rata/accordingly; **3** *in expr* **a rèir choltais** apparently, seemingly, *see* **coltas 2**

a-rèist(e) *&* **a-rèisde** *adv* then, in that case, **cha do ghoid mise e! cò a ghoid e a-rèist?** I didn't steal it! who stole it then? *Cf* **ma 2**

argamaid, argamaide, argamaidean *nf* 1 an argument, a line of reasoning, **cha do lean mi an argamaid aice** I didn't follow/ understand her argument; 2 (*philo &c*) discussion, disputation; 3 (*more hostile*) arguing, an argument, *Cf* **trod 2**

argamaidich *vi, pres part* **ag argamaid**, argue

a-riamh *adv* 1 ever, always, (*poem*) **'s tha mo ghaol aig Allt Hallaig ... 's bha i riamh** (Somhairle MacGill-Eain) and my love is at the Burn of Hallaig ... and she has always been, *Cf* **daonnan**; 2 *more usu with a neg verb*, never, **an robh thu san Eipheit? cha robh a-riamh** have you been to Egypt? never, *Note: used only to refer to past time, for* ever & never *in the future Cf* **a-chaoidh 2, bràth 2 & 3, sìorraidh 2**

a-rithist *adv* again, **na dèan a-rithist e!** don't do it again! (*on parting*) **chì sinn a-rithist sibh!** we'll see you again! (*Cf* **fhathast 3**), (*calque*) **an-dràsta 's a-rithist** now and again, from time to time, occasionally

arm, *gen & pl* **airm** *nm* an army, **bha sinn san arm aig an àm sin** we were in the army at that time, (*song*) **nuair a thèid mi fhìn dhan arm, gheibh mi fèileadh 's sporan garbh** when I go to the army, I will get a kilt and a rough sporran, *Cf less usu* **armailt**

armachadh, *gen* **armachaidh** *nm* (*the act of*) arming

armachd *nf invar* armour

armaich *vt, pres part* **ag armachadh**, arm, **dh'armaich iad an sluagh airson a' chogaidh a bha a' tighinn** they armed the people for the coming war

armailt, armailte, armailtean *nm* an army, *Cf more usu* **arm**

armlann, armlainn, armlannan *nf* an armoury (*ie store for weapons*), an arsenal

arsa, *before a vowel usu* **ars,** *defective verb used after direct speech,* said, **'Gu sealladh orm!' ars Eòghann. 'Dè tha ceàrr ort?' arsa Tormod** 'Good Heavens/Good Grief!' said Ewan. 'What's the matter with you?' said Norman, *Note: used in speech and in writing to report conversations; more trad than* **can** & **abair**

àrsaidh *adj* ancient, **togalaichean/beul-oideas àrsaidh** ancient buildings/lore, *Cf* **aosmhor, sean 2**

àrsaidheachd *nf invar* 1 antiquarianism; 2 archaeology

àrsair, àrsair, àrsairean *nm* 1 an antiquarian; 2 an archaeologist

arspag *see* **farspag**

as (*for* **a is** that is) *see* **is** *v* 6

as *prep see* **anns an** *Note*

às *prep see* **à**

às(san), asad(sa), asaibh(se), asainn(e) *prep prons see* **à**

asaid, asaide, asaidean *nf* 1 (*gynaecology*) delivery, a delivery, childbirth, **asaid an-abaich** a miscarriage

às-aimsireil *adj* anachronistic

asal, asail, asalan *nf, also* **aiseal, aiseil, aisealan** *nm*, an ass; a donkey; **leth-asal** *f* a mule

asam(sa) *prep pron see* **à**

às aonais *prep* without, in the absence of (*with gen*), **às aonais chàirdean** without friends/relations, **tha mi brònach às d' aonais** I'm sad without you/in your absence, *Cf* **às eugmhais**, *&* **gun** *prep*

às dèidh *prep see* **an dèidh**

às eugmhais *prep* without, in the absence of, *Cf more usu* **às aonais** *which is used in a similar way,* *&* **gun** *prep*

asgaidh, asgaidhe, asgaidhean *nf* 1 a present, a gift, *Cf more usu* **tabhartas, tiodhlac;** 2 *usu in exprs* **an asgaidh** free, as a gift, *&* **saor 's an asgaidh** free, free of charge, **fhuair mi mo làithean-saora saor 's an asgaidh** I got my holidays completely free, *Cf* **saor** *adj* 3

asgair, asgair, asgairean *nm* (*orthography*) an apostrophe

às leth *prep see* **leth** 6 & 7

asta(san) *prep pron see* **à**

a-staigh *adv* in, *Note: traditionally* **a-staigh** *expresses 'position within' and* **a-steach** *'movement into', but this distinction is not always observed, Cf both* **thig a-steach!** *and* **thig a-staigh!** *for* come in/inside!; (*prov*) **cha robh thu a-staigh an uair a chaidh an ciall a roinn** you weren't in when sense was shared out, **bha an coitheanal a-staigh san eaglais** the congregation was inside the church, **taobh a-staigh is taobh a-muigh an togalaich** inside and outside the building, the inside/interior and the outside/exterior of the building, *Cf* **broinn** 2, **a-mach, a-muigh, a-steach**

astar, gen & pl astair *nm* 1 distance, a distance, **'s e astar math a tha sin** that's a good distance/a fair step; 2 speed, a speed, **ag itealaich aig astar gun tomhas** flying at an incalculable speed, **bha astar math aca** they were going at a good speed, **astar gun chiall** an insane speed, *Cf* **luas** 1

astarach *adj* fast, speedy, *Cf more usu* **luath** *adj* 1

a-steach *adv* 1 in, into, inside, *Note: traditionally* **a-staigh** *expresses 'position within' and* **a-steach** *'movement into', but this distinction is not always observed, Cf both* **thig a-steach!** *and* **thig a-staigh!** *for* come in/inside!; **chaidh sinn a-steach don eaglais** we went into the church, **cuir a'**

bhò a-steach don bhàthaich put the cow in/into the byre, *Cf* **a-staigh; 2** *also in expr* **thàinig e a-steach oirre (&c) gu** ... it occurred to her (&c) that ... , she (&c) realised that ...

Astràilia *nf invar* Australia

Astràilianach, *gen & pl* **Astràilianaich** *nm* an Australian, *also as adj* **Astràilianach** Australian

at *vi, pres part* **ag at** *&* **ag atadh,** swell, puff up, **tha mo shròn ag at/air at** my nose is swelling/is swollen, *Cf* **bòc 1, sèid 2**

at, at, atan *nm* swelling, a swelling, **tha at na mo ghlùin** I've a swelling in my knee, *Cf* **bòcadh 2**

atachas, *gen & pl* **atachais** *nm* (*fin*) inflation

atadh, *gen* **ataidh** *nm* (*the act of*) swelling &c (*see senses of* **at** *v*)

ataireachd *nf invar* swelling, a swell (*esp of sea*), (*song*) **an ataireachd àrd** the lofty swell, *Cf* **sumainn**

ath *adj* next, *precedes the noun* (*which is aspirated/lenited where possible*) *& is usu used with the art,* **an ath là/sheachdain/mhìos** (the) next day/week/month, **chaidh an obair a chur air ath là** the work was left till another day/put off, **bidh iad a' fuireachd an ath-dhoras** they'll be staying/living next door

àth, àtha, àthan *nf* a kiln

àth, àth, àthan *nm* a ford

ath- *prefix usu corres to Eng* re-, *see examples below*

ath- *prefix corres to Eng* after-, **ath-bhreith** *f* afterbirth, **ath-fhrithealadh** *m* aftercare, **ath-bhlas** *m* aftertaste

athach, *gen & pl* **athaich** *nm* a giant, *Cf more usu* **famhair 1**

athair, athar, athraichean *nm* **1** a father, **m' athair 's mo mhàthair** my father and (my) mother, **athair-cèile** a father-in-law, **bràthair d' athar** your uncle, **piuthar d' athar** your aunt (*ie on the father's side*); **2** a progenitor, a forefather, **ar n-athraichean** our forefathers

athaireil *adj* fatherly, paternal

athaiseach *adj* dilatory, tardy

ath-aithris *vt, pres part* **ag ath-aithris,** repeat, reiterate, **dh'ath-aithris e na naidheachdan air fad** he repeated/told again all the news

a thaobh *prep see* **taobh 5**

ath-aonachadh, ath-aonachaidh, ath-aonachaidhean *nm* **1** (*the act of*) reuniting, reunifying; **2** reunification, a reunification

ath-aonaich *vt, pres part* **ag ath-aonachadh,** reunite, reunify

atharrachadh, atharrachaidh, atharrachaidhean *nm* (*the act of*) changing, altering, varying; **2** change, a change, alteration, an alteration, a variation, **thàinig atharrachadh air** a change came over him, he changed, *Cf* **caochladh 2, mùthadh 2**

atharraich *vti, pres part* **ag atharrachadh**, change, alter, vary, **dh'atharraich mi mo chuid aodaich** I changed my clothes, **tha am baile air atharrachadh gu mòr** the township/town has changed greatly/considerably, *Cf* **caochail 1, mùth 1**

atharrais *vt, pres part* **ag atharrais**, copy, mimic, imitate, **atharrais air/ dèan atharrais air a' Phrìomhair** imitate the Prime Minister

atharrais *nf invar* **1** (*the act of*) copying &c (*see senses of* **atharrais** *v*); **2** imitation, an imitation, mimicry

ath-bheothachadh, *gen* **ath-bheothachaidh** *nm* **1** (*the act of*) reviving &c (*see senses of* **ath-bheothaich** *v*); **2** revival, a revival, **ath-bheothachadh cultair** a revival of culture, (*trad*) **rinn thu m' ath-bheothachadh** you revived me/brought me back to life; **3** (*hist*) **an t-Ath-bheothachadh** the Renaissance, **Linn an Ath-bheothachaidh** the Renaissance Period

ath-bheothaich *vt, pres part* **ag ath-bheothachadh**, revive, bring back to life, **molaidhean airson na mion-chànain ath-bheothachadh** proposals to revive the lesser-used languages

ath-chruthaich *vt, pres part* **ag ath-chruthachadh**, recreate

ath-chuairtich, *pres part* **ath-chuairteachadh**, recycle

athchuinge, athchuinge, athchuingean *nf* (*pol* &c) an entreaty, a petition, **chuir trì mìle neach an ainm ris an athchuinge** three thousand individuals signed the petition

ath-chuir, *pres part* **ag ath-chur**, (*hort*) replant, transplant

ath-dhìol *vt, pres part* **ag ath-dhìoladh**, repay, pay back, **ath-dhìolaidh mi a-màireach na tha agad orm** I'll pay back what I owe you tomorrow, *Cf* **dìoghail 1, pàigh** *v* **1**

ath-leasachadh, ath-leasachaidh, ath-leasachaidhean *nm* **1** (*the act of*) redeveloping, reforming; **2** redevelopment, a redevelopment, **ath-leasachadh nam bailtean mòra** (the) redevelopment of the big cities; **3** reform, a reform, **ath-leasachadh nan seann phoileasaidhean** (the) reform of the old policies; **4** (*hist, relig*) **an t-Ath-leasachadh** the Reformation

ath-leasaich *vt, pres part* **ag ath-leasachadh**, redevelop, reform, **feumaidh sinn am pàrtaidh ath-leasachadh** we need to reform the party

ath-nuadhachadh, *gen* **ath-nuadhachaidh** *nm* **1** (*the act of*) renewing &c (*see senses of* **ath-nuadhaich** *v*); **2** renewal, a renewal, renovation, a renovation

ath-nuadhaich *vt, pres part* **ag ath-nuadhachadh, 1** renew (*ie replace*), **b' fheudar dhuinn pìoban an uisge ath-nuadhachadh** we had to renew the water pipes; **2** renew, renovate; **3** renew, re-affirm, **dh'ath-nuadhaich iad an creideamh/an geallaidhean** they renewed their faith/their vows, **ath-nuadhaich fo-sgrìobhadh** renew a subscription

ath-sgrìobh *vt, pres part* **ag ath-sgrìobhadh**, re-write; copy (*a text &c*)

ath-sgrùdadh, ath-sgrùdaidh, ath-sgrùdaidhean *nm* **1** re-appraisal, re-assessment, a review, **sgrìobh i/rinn i ath-sgrùdadh mòr de sgrìobhaidhean nam bàrd** she wrote/carried out a major re-assessment/re-appraisal of the writings of the poets, **ath-sgrùdadh phoileasaidhean** a review of/a new look at policies; **2** (*education &c*) revision, **ath-sgrùdadh airson deuchainn(e)** revision for an exam

B

babag, **babaig**, **babagan** *nf* **1** a tassel; **2** a tuft, *Cf* **bad 2**

bàbhan, **bàbhain**, **bàbhanan** *nm* **1** a rampart, a bulwark, *Cf* **mùr**

babhstair, **babhstair**, **babhstairean** *nm* **1** a bolster, a large pillow, *Cf* **cluasag**; **2** a mattress

bac *vt, pres part* **a' bacadh**, prevent, obstruct, hinder, restrain, *Cf* **bacadh 3**

bac, *gen* **baca** & **baic**, *pl* **bacan** *nm* **1** a hindrance, a delay, an obstacle, *Cf more usu* **bacadh 2**; **2** a hollow or bend *esp on the body*, **bac na ruighe** the hollow/bend of the arm, **bac na h-iosgaid** the back of the knee; **3** a peat bank, *Cf* **poll 3**; **4** a sand bank

bacach, *gen* & *pl* **bacaich** *nm* a cripple, someone who is lame or who limps, *Cf* **crioplach**, **crùbach** *n*

bacach *adj* lame, crippled, **tha e bacach air aon chas** he's lame in one leg, **Eachann Bacach** Lame Hector (*a MacLean poet of the 17th century*), *Cf* **crùbach** *adj*

bacadh, **bacaidh**, **bacaidhean** *nm* **1** (*the act of*) preventing &c (*see senses of* **bac** *v*); **2** an obstacle, hindrance, a hindrance, restraint, prevention, delay, a delay, **is bacadh mòr an aois** old age is a great hindrance, *Cf less usu* **bac** *n* **2**, **cnap-starra** (*see* **cnap 1**); **3** *often in expr* **cuir** *v* **bacadh air** obstruct, prevent &c, **chuir a pàrantan bacadh air ar pòsadh** her parents obstructed/put obstacles in the way of our getting married, **chuir dìth airgid bacadh air a' ghnothach** lack of money held the business back

bacan, *gen* & *pl* **bacain** *nm* (*agric*) a hobble, a tether post, *Cf* **teadhair**, **feiste**

bachall, **bachaill**, **bachallan** *nm* a crozier, a (*cleric's*) staff

bachlach & **bachallach** *adj* (*of hair*) curled, curly, ringleted, (*song*) **b' e siud an cùl, seo an cùl bachallach** yonder, here, is the ringleted hair, *Cf* **camagach**

bachlag, **bachlaig**, **bachlagan** *nf* **1** a curl, a ringlet, *Cf* **camag 1**, **dual² 1**; **2** (*of plant &c*) a shoot, a sprout, *Cf* **gas**, **ògan**

bachlaich *vt, pres part* **a' bachlachadh**, curl, **bhachlaich an gruagaire m' fhalt** the hairdresser curled my hair, *Cf* **dualaich**

bad, **baid**, **badan** *nm* **1** a place, a spot, **bad grianach** a sunny spot, *Cf* **àite 1**, **ionad 1**; **2** a tuft, a bunch, **bad fraoich/fuilt/feòir** a tuft of heather/hair/grass, *Cf* **bagaid 2**; **3** a flock, a group, **bad ghobhar/ chaorach** a flock of goats/sheep (*ie in the concrete sense of a group together at one time*), *Cf* **buar**, **treud**; **4** a clump of trees, a thicket; **5** *in* *exprs* **anns a' bhad** immediately, this instant, **thig an seo anns a' bhad!** come here this instant! **bheir mi dhuibh an cofaidh anns a' bhad** I'll bring you your coffee right away, & (*calque*) **air a' bhad** on the spot, straight away, *Cf* **air ball**

badan, *gen & pl* **badain** *nm*, 1 *dimin of* **bad** little spot &c (*see senses of* **bad**); 2 a nappy

baga, *gen* **baga**, *pl* **bagannan** & **bagaichean** *nm* a hand-bag, (*paper, polythene, luggage &c*) a bag, *Cf more trad* **màileid**, **poca**

bagaid, **bagaide**, **bagaidean** *nf* a bunch, a cluster, **bagaid fhìon-dearcan** a bunch of grapes, **bagaid chnò** a cluster of nuts

bagair *vti, pres part* **a' bagairt** & **a' bagradh**, 1 threaten, **bhagair e orm** he threatened me, **bhagair iad mo mharbhadh** they threatened to kill me, **bha an abhainn a' bagairt cur thairis** the river was threatening to overflow, *Cf* **maoidh**; 2 (*vi*) bluster

bagairt, **bagairt**, **bagairtean** *nf* & **bagradh**, **bagraidh**, **bagraidhean** *nm* 1 (*the act of*) threatening, blustering (*see senses of* **bagair** *v*); 2 a threat, **bagairt cogaidh** a threat of war, (*prov*) **cha tèid plàsd air bagairt** you don't put a poultice on a threat (*roughly equivalent to* sticks and stones will hurt my bones but words will never harm me); 3 bluster

bàgh, *gen* **bàigh**, *pl* **bàghan** & **bàghannan** *nm* a bay, a cove, *Cf* **camas 1**, **òb**

bagradh *see* **bagairt**

bàidh, *gen* **bàidhe** *nf* 1 affection, fondness, (*song*) **cur mo chùil ri càirdean nochd am bàidh cho treun** as I turned away from (my) dear ones their great affection became evident, *Cf* **dèidh 2**, **spèis 2**; 2 a favour, an act of kindness, a good turn, **an dèan thu bàidh dhomh?** will you do me a favour?, *Cf* **fàbhar**, **seirbheis 2**

bàidheil & **bàigheil** *adj* kind, kindly (*person, act*), *Cf* **coibhneil**

baidhsagal, **baidhsagail**, **baidhsagalan** *nm* a bicycle, *Cf more trad* **rothar**

baile, **baile**, **bailtean** *nm* 1 a (crofting) township, **bha fang ùr aig a' bhaile** the township had a new fank/sheepfold, **clàrc a' bhaile** the township clerk; 2 *esp with* **beag**, a village, **baile beag Uige** the village of Uig, *Cf* **clachan 1** & **2**; 3 *esp with* **beag**, a small town, **baile beag Chuimrigh** the small town of Comrie; 4 **baile mòr** a town, a city, **chaidh iad a dh'fhuireach sa bhaile mhòr** they went to live in the town/city, **'s e baile mòr a th' ann an Glaschu** Glasgow is a big city (*Cf* **cathair 2**), **talla a' bhaile** the village/town/city hall; 5 *in expr* **aig baile** at home, **cà'il am bodach? chan eil e aig baile** where's the old fellow? he's not at home, *Cf* **taigh 2**

bailead, **baileid**, **baileadan** *nm* a ballad

baile-puirt, **baile-puirt**, **bailtean-puirt** *nm* a sea-port, **'s e baile-puirt a th' ann an Obar-Dheathain** Aberdeen is a sea-port

bàillidh, bàillidh, bàillidhean *nm* **1** (*law*) a bailiff; **2** (*civic admin &c*) a baillie; **3** a magistrate; **4** (*estate &c*) a factor, *Cf* **maor 1**

bàine *comp of* **bàn** *adj* whiter, whitest, **an t-aodann as bàine** the whitest face

bàinead, *gen* **bàineid** *nf* whiteness, fairness (*ie colouring*)

bàinidh *nf invar* **1** madness, fury, rage; **2** *esp in expr* **air bhàinidh** (*of person*) extremely angry, mad with rage, absolutely furious; *Cf* **boile**, **cuthach**

bainne, *gen* **bainne** *nm* milk

bàirlinn *nf invar* (*law*) **1** a summons; **2** an eviction order or notice

bàirneach, bàirnich, bàirnich *nf* **1** a barnacle; **2** a limpet

baist *vt*, *pres part* **a' baisteadh**, baptise, christen

Baisteach, Baistich, Baistich *nm* a Baptist

baisteadh, baistidh, baistidhean *nm* **1** (*the act of*) baptising or christening; **2** baptism, a baptism, a christening

bàl, *gen & pl* **bàil** *nm* a ball (*ie dance*), *Cf less formal* **danns(a)**

bàla, bàla, bàlaichean *nm* (*for games &c*) a ball

balach, *gen & pl* **balaich** *nm* **1** a boy, a lad, **cha robh aon bhalach aig an sgoil an-diugh** there wasn't a single boy at school today, **balach beag** a little/small/wee/young boy; **2** *affectionate or fam for a male of any age*, (*song*) **Balaich an Iasgaich** the fishing lads/boys, *expr admiration or irony* **nach esan am balach!** isn't he the boy/the boyo/the clever one/the rogue! *common as form of address* **thig a-steach is gabh drama, a bhalaich!** come inside and take a dram, boy!; *Cf* **gille 2** *&* **3**

balachan, *gen & pl* **balachain** *nm*, *dimin of* **balach**, a small boy, a wee boy

balbh *adj* **1** dumb, mute, **creutairean balbha** dumb animals/creatures; **2** silent, speechless, **bha e balbh ro fheirg na mnà aige** he was silent/speechless in the face of his wife's anger, **bog balbh** speechless, struck dumb, *Cf* **tosdach**; **3** (*place, scene &c*) quiet, silent, peaceful, *Cf more usu* **sàmhach, sìtheil 1**

balbhan, *gen & pl* **balbhain** *nm* a dumb person

balg *&* **bolg**, *gen & pl* **builg** *nm* **1** (*anat*) an abdomen, a belly, *Cf* **brù 2**, **stamag**; **2** a blister, **bha balg air mo làimh an dèidh dhomh fiodh a shàbhadh** I had a blister on my hand after sawing wood, *Cf* **leus 3**; **3** (*trad*) a bag

balgair, balgaire, balgairean *nm* **1** a fox, *Cf* **madadh 2**, **sionnach**; **2** a cunning person, a sly person, a rogue, *Cf* **slaightear**

balgam, balgaim, balgaman *nm* **1** a sip (*of liquid*), **balgam bùirn/uisge** a sip of water, *Cf* **drùdhag 2**; **2** a mouthful, a swig, **thug e balgam math às a' bhotal** he took a good swig from the bottle, *Cf* **sgailc** *n* **3, steallag**

balgan, *gen & pl* **balgain** *nm* a mushroom; a toadstool

balgan-buachair, *gen & pl* **balgain-buachair** *nm*, *also* **balg-bhuachair, balg-buachrach, balgan-buachrach** *nm*, the edible field mushroom

ball, *gen & pl* **buill** *nm* **1** (*anat*) a limb, an organ, **is e buill a th' ann an casan is gàirdeanan** legs and arms are limbs, **buill a' chuirp** the parts of the body, **ball-bodhaig** a (bodily) organ, **na buill-ghineamhainn** the reproductive/sexual organs, the genitals; **2** a member (*of organisation &c*) **a bheil thu nad bhall den Chomunn Ghaidhealach/de Chomann an Luchd-Ionnsachaidh?** are you a member of An Comunn Gaidhealach/of the Gaelic Learners' Association? **Ball Pàrlamaid** a Member of Parliament; **3** *used with coll nouns*, a piece of, an item of *&c*, **ball-acfhainn** a tool, a piece of equipment, **ball-airm** a weapon, **ball-àirneis** a piece/an item of furniture, **ball-aodaich** an item of clothing, a garment; **4** a rope (*esp part of ship's tackle*), *Cf* **ròp(a)**; **5** *in expr* **air ball** immediately, straight away, right away, *Cf similarly used* **bad 5**

balla, *gen* **balla**, *pl* **ballachan** & **ballaichean** *nm* a wall (*usu inner or outer wall of building but occas free-standing*), **ballachan cloiche** stone walls, *Cf* **gàrradh 1**

ballach *adj* (*cloth &c*) spotted, speckled, *Cf* **breac** *adj*, & *trad* **riabhach 1**

ball-basgaid, *gen & pl* **buill-basgaid** *nm* basketball, a basketball

ball-coise, *gen & pl* **buill-coise** *nm* football, a football, **ball-coise còignear** five-a-side football

ball-dòbhrain, *gen & pl* **buill-dòbhrain** *nm* a mole (*on skin*)

ball-lìn, *gen & pl* **buill-lìn** *nm* netball, a netball

ball-maise, *gen & pl* **buill-maise** *nm* an ornament, **bha tòrr bhall-maise aice air oir na h-uinneige** she had a lot of ornaments on the windowsill, **is seud-muineil mu h-amhaich na bhall-maise** with a necklace round her neck as an ornament

ballrachd, *gen* **ballrachd** *nf* (*abstr*) membership, (*coll*) a membership, **bhòtaidh a' bhallrachd airson atharrachaidhean** the membership/members will vote for changes, **bha ballrachd beatha aca** they had life membership

bàn[1] *adj* **1** fallow, **talamh bàn** fallow land; **2** (*paper &c*) blank

bàn[2] *adj* **1** white, fair (*in colouring*), **Dàibhidh Bàn** fair-haired David, **an cù bàn** the white dog, *Cf* **fionn, geal** *adj*; **2** *prefixed to other colours* light, pale, **bàn-dhearg** pale red, pink, **bàn-ghorm** pale/light blue

bana- & **ban-** *prefix, corres to Eng* female, woman, -ess, *see examples below*

bana-bhuidseach, bana-bhuidsich, bana-bhuidsichean *nf* a sorceress, a witch

banacharaid, banacharaide, banachàirdean *nf* **1** a (female *or* woman) friend or relative, **bha i na deagh bhanacharaid don mhnaoi agam** she was a good friend to my wife/of my wife's; **2** (*in corres*) **A Bhanacharaid**, Dear Madam, **A Mhàiri, a bhanacharaid** Dear Mary

bana-chliamhainn, bana-chleamhna, bana-chleamhnan *nf* a daughter-in-law

bànag, bànaig, bànagan *nf* a sea-trout, (*also coll*) **tha e mì-laghail lìontan a chur airson bànaig** it's illegal to set nets for sea-trout

bana-ghaisgeach, bana-ghaisgich, bana-ghaisgich *nf* a heroine

banail *adj* womanly, feminine, **dòighean banail** womanly/feminine ways, *Cf opposites* **duineil, fearail**

banais, bainnse, bainnsean *nf* a wedding, **bean** *f* **na bainnse** the bride, **fear** *m* **na bainnse** the groom, **cuirm** *f* **bainnse** a wedding reception, (*trad song*) **òlar am fìon air do bhanais** wine will be drunk at your wedding, *Cf* **pòsadh 2**

banaltram, banaltraim, banaltraman *nf* a nurse, **banaltram sgìreachd** a district nurse, *Cf* **bean-eiridinn** & *less trad* **nurs**

bana-mhaighistir-sgoile, bana-mhaighistir-sgoile, bana-mhaighistirean-sgoile a schoolmistress (*usu primary*)

bana-phrionnsa, bana-phrionnsa, bana-phrionnsan *nf* a princess

banarach, banaraich, banaraichean *nf* a milk-maid, a dairy-maid

banas-taighe *nm invar* housekeeping, the running of a house(hold), housewifery, home economics

banc & **banca**, *gen* **banca**, *pl* **bancaichean** & **bancan** *nm* a (*clearing, savings &c*) bank, **Banca Shrath Chluaidh** the Clydesdale Bank, **banca-siubhail** a mobile/travelling bank

bancair, bancair, bancairean *nm* a banker

bancaireachd *nf invar* banking

ban-dia, ban-dè, ban-diathan *nf* a goddess

ban-diùc, ban-diùc, ban-diùcan *nf* a duchess

bàn-ghlas *adj* (*complexion &c*) ashen

ban-ìompaire, ban-ìompaire, ban-ìompairean *nf* an empress, **b' e Bhictoria Ban-Iompaire nan Innseachan** Victoria was Empress of India

ban-leòmhann, *gen* & *pl* **ban-leòmhainn** *nf* a lioness

bann, bainne, bannan *nm* **1** a strip (*of material &c*), **chàirich e cas na spaide le bann teip** he mended the spade handle with a strip of tape, *Cf* **stiall** *n* 2; **2** a bandage; **3** a hinge; **4** (*fin*) a bond, **bann tasgaidh** an investment bond

banntach, banntaich, banntaichean *nm* a hinge, *Cf* **bann** 3, **lùdag** 2

ban(n)trach, ban(n)traich, ban(n)traichean *nf* **1** a widow, (*trad tale*) **Mac na Bantraich** the Widow's Son; **2** (*as nm*) a widower

ban-ogha, ban-ogha, ban-oghaichean *nf* a grand-daughter

bànrigh, bànrighe, bànrighrean *nf*, *also* **bànrighinn, bànrighinn, bànrighinnean** *nf*, a queen

ban-rùnaire, ban-rùnaire, ban-rùnairean *nf* a (female) secretary

baoghalta *adj* stupid, *Cf* **gòrach**

baoghaltachd *nf invar* stupidity, *Cf* **gòraiche**

baoit *nf invar*, *also* **baoiteag**, *gen* **baoiteige** *nf*, a fly, worm or other bait for fishing, *Cf* **maghar**

baoth *adj* foolish, silly, simple, **dh'ath-cheannaich am ministear baoth an t-each aige fhèin air an fhèill** the foolish minister bought back his own horse at the fair, *Cf* **amaideach, faoin** 1, **sìmplidh** 3

bàr, bàir, bàraichean *nm* (*hotel, pub &c*) a bar, **cuir na glainneachan falamh air a' bhàr** put the empty glasses on the bar, **Bàr na Camanachd** The Camanachd Bar (*in Portree*)

barail, baraile, barailean *nf* an opinion, **dè do bharail?** what's your opinion?, what do you think? **nam bharail-sa tha e sgriosail!** in my (*emph*) opinion it's dreadful!, *Cf* **beachd** 2

baraille, baraille, baraillean *nm* a barrel (*Cf* **tocasaid**), **baraille ola** a barrel of oil, **baraille gunna** a gun barrel

bàrd, *gen & pl* bàird *nm* a bard, a poet, (*title of anthology*) **Sàr Obair nam Bàrd Gàidhealach** The Master Work of the Gaelic Poets, *Cf* **filidh** 1

bàrdachd *nf invar* poetry, **sgrìobh e bàrdachd mun chogadh** he wrote poetry about the war, **rinn mi bàrdachd** I have written/I wrote poetry/a poem, **dh'ath-aithris e pìos bàrdachd leis fhèin** he recited a piece of his own poetry, *Cf* **dànachd, rann** 1

bàrdail *adj* poetic, bardic

bàrr, barra, barran *nm* **1** the top or uppermost surface of anything, **bàrr a' bhainne** the cream, the top of the milk, **air bàrr na talmhainn** on the surface of the earth, **cop air bàrr an leanna** foam on the top/surface of the beer, **a' seòladh air bàrr nan tonn** sailing on the crest of the waves, **thig** *v* **am bàrr** surface, come to the surface, (*abstr*) manifest itself/oneself, *Cf* **ceann as àirde** (*see* **ceann** 2), **mullach** 1, **uachdar** 1, 2 & 3; **2** (*agric &c*) a crop, **bàrr feòir/buntàta**

a crop of hay/potatoes, **prìomh bhàrr** a main crop; **3** *in expr* **thoir** *v* **bàrr air** top, cap or beat something, **tha do bhathais a' toirt bàrr air na chunnaic mi a-riamh** your cheek caps/beats anything I ever saw; **4** *in expr* **a bhàrr air**, *same as* **a bharrachd air** (*see* **barrachd 4**); **5** *in expr* **bhàrr** & **far** *prep* (*for* **de bhàrr**) from, from off, down from (*with gen*), **thug e leabhar bhàrr na sgeilp/a' bhùird** he took a book from the shelf/the table, **seiche bhàrr laoigh** hide from a calf, **chaidh e à sealladh mar sneachd bhàrr gàrraidh** he disappeared like snow off a dyke

Barrach, *gen* & *pl* **Barraich** *nm* someone from the Isle of Barra (**Barraigh** *f*), *also as adj* **Barrach** of, from or pertaining to Barra

barrachd *nf invar* **1** (*trad*) superiority; a surplus; **2** (*now usu*) more, **tha mi ag iarraidh barrachd!** I want (some) more! **barrachd ime/feòla** more butter/meat, *Cf* **tuilleadh 1**; **3** *in expr* **barrachd air** *prep* more than, **barrachd air dà fhichead** more than forty, **barrachd air na bha mi an dùil fhaicinn** more than I was hoping/expecting to see, (*prov*) **chì dithis barrachd air aon fhear** two will see more than one, *Cf* **còrr** *nm* **1**; **4** *in expr* **a bharrachd** (**air**) in addition (to), as well (as), besides, **chan eil mi ag iarraidh càil a bharrachd** I don't want anything else/another thing, **dithis neach-obrach a bharrachd** two more/additional/extra workers, **A bharrachd air sin** ... Moreover ..., Also ..., In addition ..., **cò na seinneadairean as toigh leat a bharrachd oirrese?** what/which singers do you like apart from/besides her?

barragach *adj* creamy, *Cf* **uachdarach 4**

barrall, barraill, barraillean *nm* a shoe-lace, *Cf* **iall**

bar(r)antas, bar(r)antais, bar(r)antasan *nm* **1** a pledge, a guarantee; **2** security (*for loan &c*); *Cf* **urras 1**

bas & **bois**, *gen* **boise**, *pl* **basan** & **boisean**, *nf* palm of the hand, **bas-bhualadh** *m* applause, clapping, **bhuail iad am basan** they applauded/clapped, (*prov*) **bonnach air bois, cha bhruich e is cha loisg** a bannock in the hand will neither cook nor burn (*roughly equivalent to* nothing ventured, nothing gained), *Cf* **glac** *n* **2**

bàs, *gen* **bàis** *nm* **1** death, **urras bàis** a death certificate, **ri uchd bàis** at the point of death, at death's door, **grèim-bàis** *m* death throe(s), (*poem*) **Glac a' Bhàis** (Somhairle MacGill-Eain) Death Valley, (*song title*) **Bàs an Eich** the death of the horse; **2** *in expr* **a' dol bàs** dying out, fading away, **tha na seann dòighean a' dol bàs** the old ways are dying out, (*as infinitive*) (*prov*) **faodaidh a' chaora dol bàs a' feitheamh ris an fheur ùr** the sheep may die waiting for the new grass; **3** *in expr* **faigh bàs** die, be killed, **am faigh a' Ghàidhlig bàs?** will Gaelic die? (*trad*) **fhuair e bàs le nàimhdean** he died at the hand of enemies

bàsachadh, *gen* **bàsachaidh** *nm* (*the act of*) dying

bàsaich *vi*, *pres part* **a' bàsachadh**, die, *Note: not used by some speakers when referring to humans, Cf* **bàs 3, caochail 2, siubhail 3**

basdalach *adj* (*of dress &c*) showy, flashy, garish

basgaid, basgaide, basgaidean *nf* a basket, **basgaid-sgudail** *&* **basgaid-truileis** waste-paper/rubbish basket, **cuir sa bhasgaid e!** put it in the (rubbish) basket!

bàsmhor *adj* **1** mortal, **do chorp bàsmhor is d' anam neo-bhàsmhor** your mortal body and your immortal soul; **2** deadly, fatal, *Cf* **marbhtach**

bàsmhorachd *nf invar* mortality, the state of being mortal

bata, bata, bataichean *nm* **1** a stick, *Cf* **maide 2; 2** (*also* **bata-coiseachd**) a walking stick

bàta, bàta, bàtaichean *nm* a boat, a ship, *Note: though* **bàta** *is masculine the pron* **i**, *she, is used,* (*song*) **chì mi am bàta 's i tighinn** I see the boat as she comes, **bàt'-aiseig** a ferry boat, **bàt'-iasgaich** a fishing boat, **bàta marsantachd** a merchant ship/vessel, **bàta-ràmh** a rowing boat (*Cf* **eathar**), **bàta-sàbhalaidh,** *&* **bàta-teasairginn,** a lifeboat, a rescue boat, **bàta-siùil** a sailing boat, **bàta-smùide** a steam-boat, (*song*) **Fear a' Bhàta** the Boatman, *Cf* **long, soitheach 2**

bàth *vt*, *pres part* **a' bàthadh, 1** drown, **bhàth e na piseagan** he drowned the kittens, **chaidh Uisdean a bhàthadh ann am boglaich** Hugh was drowned in a quagmire/a bog; **2** drown out, muffle (*sounds*)

bàthach, bàthcha, bàthchannan *nf &* **bàthaich, bàthaich, bàthaichean** *nm* a byre, a cow-shed

bàthadh, *gen* **bàthaidh** *nm* **1** (*the act of*) drowning &c (*see senses of* **bàth** *v*); **2** a drowning

bathais, bathais, bathaisean *nf* **1** a forehead, a brow, *Cf* **clàr 2, mala 2, maoil; 2** cheek, nerve, impudence, **nach ann airsan/aigesan a tha a' bhathais!** what a cheek/nerve he's got!, *Cf* **aghaidh 2**

bathar, *gen* **bathair** *nm coll* **1** goods, merchandise, wares, **bathar ri reic** goods/merchandise for sale, **bathar a-steach** imports, an import, **trèana bathair** a goods train; **2** (*IT*) **bathar cruaidh** hardware, **bathar bog** software

bàthte *adj* drowned (*see also* **dìle**)

beach, beacha, beachan *nm* **1** a bee (*Cf more usu* **seillean**), **beachlann** *m* a beehive; **2** a wasp, *Cf more usu* **speach**

beachd, beachda, beachdan *nm* **1** an idea, a thought (*also* **beachd-smuain**), **thàinig beachd(-smuain) thugam air sin** a thought/an idea occurred to me about that, *Cf* **smaoin; 2** *more usu* an opinion, **dè do bheachd air a' bhiadh?** what's your opinion/what do you think of the food? **thug mi seachad mo bheachd air na molaidhean aca** I gave my opinion of their proposals, **nam bheachd-sa, tha iad uabhasach math** in my opinion, they're extremely good, **tha sinn den bheachd gu** ... we are of the opinion that ..., **chan eil sinn den aon bheachd** we are not of the same opinion, **gabh** *v* **beachd air rudeigin** form an opinion on/observe something, *Cf* **barail; 3** *in expr* **bi am beachd a** ... be thinking of ..., be intending to ..., **dè a tha thu am beachd a dhèanamh a-nise?** what are you intending to do/thinking of doing now?; **4** *in expr* **rach** *v* **às mo (&c) b(h)eachd** go out of/lose my (&c) mind, *Cf* **ciall 2, rian 3**

beachdaich *vi, pres part* **a' beachdachadh**, consider, meditate, speculate (**air** about)

beachdail *adj* **1** observant, *Cf* **mothachail 1; 2** abstract, *Cf opposites* **nitheil, rudail; 3** self-satisfied, opinionated

beachd-smaoin(t)eachadh, *gen* **beachd-smaoin(t)eachaidh** *nm* **1** (*the act of*) meditating or contemplating; **2** meditation, a meditation, contemplation

beachd-smaoin(t)ich *vi, pres part* **a' beachd-smaoin(t)eachadh**, meditate, contemplate, **feallsanach a' beachd-smaointeachadh air ceist an uilc** a philosopher meditating on the problem of evil, *Cf less rigorous* **cnuasaich, meòmhraich**

beadaidh *adj* cheeky, impudent, pert, saucy, forward, *Cf* **dàna 3**

beag *adj, comp* **(n)as (&c) lugha, 1** small, little, wee, **balach beag** a little/ wee boy, **caileag bheag** a little/wee girl, **tuarastal beag** a small/ low salary, **ann an ùine bheag** in a short time/a little while, (*whisky*) **tè bheag** a wee one, a nip, **'s beag an ùidh a th' agam ann am poileataics** I'm not very interested in politics; **2** slight, light, **ceò beag air a' mhonadh** a slight/light mist on the hill, **bha uisge beag ann** it was raining slightly, **thàinig eagal beag orm** I grew a little bit afraid; **3** *as noun*, little, the least bit, few, **beag is beag** *or* **beag air bheag** little by little, **an d'fhuair thu a' bheag?** did you get some/any? (*with a neg sense*) **cha robh a' bheag de shiùcar sa phreas** there wasn't any/the least bit of sugar in the cupboard, **cha robh ach a' bheag de rùm sa bhàta** there was only the smallest amount of room in the boat, **tha glè bheag de chàirdean aige** he has very few friends, *Cf* **beagan** *n*; **4** *in expr* **rud beag** *adv* a bit, a wee bit, somewhat, **bha i rud beag sgìth** she was a bit/rather tired, *Cf* **beagan** *adv*, **rudeigin 2; 5** *in expr* **is beag orm (do chàr ùr &c)** I don't think much of/I don't like (your new car &c)

beagan *adv* a little, a bit, slightly, **tha i beagan nas sine na Màiri** she's a bit/slightly older than Mary, *Cf* **rudeigin 2, car** *n* **7, caran, rud beag** (*see* **beag 4**)

beagan, *gen* **beagain** *nm* a little, a bit of, a few, *can be used more positively than* **a' bheag** (*see* **beag 3**), **bha beagan siùcair sa phreas/beagan rùim sa bhàta** there was a bit of sugar in the cupboard/a little room in the boat, **chan eil ach beagan chàirdean aige** he only has a few friends, **a bheil airgead agad? tha beagan** have you any money? a little, **a' gluasad anns a' bheagan gaoithe** moving in the little wind (that there was)

beag-nàrach, also **beag-nàire**, *adj* shameless

beairt *see* **beart**

beairteach, beairteas *see* **beartach, beartas**

bealach, *gen & pl* **bealaich** *nm* **1** a mountain or hill pass, (*placename*) **Bealach na Bròige** the Pass of the Shoe (Ross-shire); **2** the top of a pass, **ràinig e am bealach** he reached the top of the pass/the col; **3** a detour, a round about way, **gabhaidh sinn bealach tron choille** we'll make/take a detour through the wood; **4 bealach goirid** a short cut

bealaidh *nm invar* (*bot*) broom

Bealltainn, *gen* **Bealltainne** *nf* May Day, the first of May, Beltane

bean, *gen* **mnà**, *dat* **mnaoi**, *pl* **mnathan** *nf* **1** a wife, **seo a' bhean agam** this is/here is my wife, (*song*) **a' bhean agam fhìn** my very own wife/that wife of mine, **bean-phòsta** a married woman, *also as form of address*, Mrs, **a Bhean-phòsta NicAoidh** (*voc*) Mrs MacKay; **2** (*trad*) a woman, (*song*) **a bhean** (*voc*) **ud thall a rinn an gàire** woman over there who laughed, *Cf* **boireannach, tè 2; 3** *in compounds & set exprs* woman, female, lady, **bean an taighe** lady of the house, housewife, landlady, *see further examples below*

bean *vi, pres part* **a' beantainn**, (*takes prep* **ri**) **1** touch, handle, meddle with, **na bean ris na buill-maise** don't touch/meddle with the ornaments, *Cf* **buin 3, làimhsich 1; 2 bean ri** brush against, *Cf* **suath 2; 3** deal with, touch upon, **bhean an òraid ris an t-suidheachadh ann an Afraga** the talk touched upon the situation in Africa

bean-bainnse, mnà-bainnse, mnathan-bainnse *nf* a bride, **bean na bainnse** the bride

bean-eiridinn, mnà-eiridinn, mnathan-eiridinn *nf* a nurse, *Cf more usu* **banaltram** *& less trad* **nurs**

bean-ghlùine, mnà-glùine, mnathan-glùine *nf* a midwife

beannachadh, beannachaidh, *pl* **beannachaidhean** *nm* **1** (*the act of*) blessing &c (*see senses of* **beannaich** *v*); **2** beatification; **3** a blessing, (*song*) **oir tha beannachadh Dhè agus sìth ann** for peace and God's blessing are there; **4** a greeting, a farewell, *Cf* **beannachd 4, soraidh**

beannachd, beannachd, beannachdan *nf* 1 a blessing, **mo bheannachd oirbh** my blessing on you, *Cf* **beannachadh 3**; 2 a blessing, a boon, (*trad*) **is i beannachd deagh shlàinte** good health is a blessing; 3 compliments, regards, **mo bheannachd don mhnaoi agad!** my compliments/regards to your wife!; 4 *on parting*, **beannachd leat/ leibh** goodbye!, *Cf* **mar 2, slàn 3, soraidh 1, tìoraidh**

beannaich *vti, pres part* **a' beannachadh,** 1 beatify; 2 bless; 3 (*vi*) **beannaich do chudeigin** greet someone

beannaichte *adj* blessed

bean-shìthe, mnà-sìthe, mnathan-sìthe *nf* a fairy woman, a female fairy

bean-taighe, mnà-taighe, mnathan-taighe *nf* 1 a housewife; 2 *with art* **bean an taighe** the woman/lady/mistress of the house, the lady householder, (*of lodgings, pub &c*) the landlady, (*song*) **a bhean an taighe** (*voc*) **dùin an seòmar, cha bhi aon dhen t-seòrsa leinn!** close up the room, Landlady, we won't have one of that sort among us!

bean-teagaisg, mnà-teagaisg, mnathan-teagaisg *nf* a (*female*) teacher (*usu secondary*)

bean-uasal, mnà-uaisle, mnathan-uaisle *nmf* 1 a noblewoman; 2 *as polite form of address* (*trad*) **A Bhean-Uasal** Madam

beàrn, *gen* **bèirn** *&* **beàirn,** *pl* **beàrnan** *nmf* a notch, gap, space or opening in anything, **tro bheàrnan sna neòil** through gaps in the clouds, *Cf* **fosgladh 2**

beàrnan-brìde, *gen & pl* **beàrnain-bhrìde** *nf* a dandelion

Beàrnarach, *gen & pl* **Beàrnaraich** *nm* someone from Bernera/Berneray (**Beàrnaraigh**), *also as adj* **Beàrnarach** of, from or pertaining to Berneray/Bernera

beàrr *vt, pres part* **a' bearradh,** 1 (*sheep &c*) shear, *Cf* **rùisg 2;** 2 (*more usu*) shave, **bheàrr am bearradair m' fheusag** the barber shaved my beard

bearradair, bearradair, bearradairean a barber *Cf less trad* **borbair**

bearradh, *gen* **bearraidh** *nm* (*the act of*) shaving, shearing

beart *&* **beairt,** *gen* **beairt,** *pl* **beartan** *&* **beairtean** *nf* 1 (*trad*) a deed, a feat, **droch-bheart** a vice, an evil deed, *Cf* **cleas 1, euchd 1, gnìomh;** 2 a machine, *Cf* **inneal;** 3 *esp* a (weaving) loom (*also* **beart-fhighe),** **bha a' bheart aige ann an seada air cùlaibh an taighe** his loom was in a shed behind the house

beartach *&* **beairteach** *adj* rich, wealthy, *Cf* **saidhbhir**

beartas *&* **beairteas,** *gen* **beartais** *&* **beairteis** *nm* riches, wealth, *Cf* **ionmhas 2, saidhbhreas, stòras**

beatha, beatha, beathannan *nf* 1 life, a life, **beatha chruaidh** a hard life, **bha e sona fad a bheatha** he was happy all his life, **chaith iad/chuir iad seachad am beatha san arm** they spent their lives in the army; 2 *in expr* **'s e do bheatha** you're welcome, **mòran taing! 's e ur beatha/do bheatha!** thank you very much! you're welcome!; 3 *in expr* **mar mo** (&c) **b(h)eatha** for dear life, **bha i a' ruith mar a beatha** she was running as fast as she could/for dear life/for all she was worth

beathach, beathaich, beathaichean *nm* a beast, an animal, *usu domestic, often cattle,* **a' togail/a' biathadh nam beathaichean** raising/ feeding the beasts/animals, (*wild*) **beathach-mara** a sea-creature, a marine animal, *Cf* **ainmhidh**

beathachadh, *gen* **beathachaidh** *nm* (*the act of*) feeding, maintaining (*see* **beathaich** *v*); 2 (*of livestock &c*) maintenance, keep

beathaich *vt, pres part* **a' beathachadh,** feed, maintain, (*prov*) **beathaich thusa mis' an-diugh is beathaichidh mise thus' a-màireach** you feed me today and I'll feed you tomorrow, *Cf* **biath**

beath-eachdraidh, beath-eachdraidhe, beath-eachdraidhean *nf* biography, a biography

beic, beice, beiceannan *nf* a curtsey, **dèan** *v* **beic** curtsey

bèicear, bèiceir, bèicearan *nm* a baker, *Cf more trad* **fuineadair**

Beilg *nf, with art,* **a' Bheilg** Belgium

Beilgeach, *gen & pl* **Beilgich** *nm* a Belgian, *also as adj* **Beilgeach** Belgian

being, beinge, beingean *nf* a bench (*ie seat*), *Cf* **furm 1**

beinn, *gen* **beinne,** *pl* **beanntan,** *gen pl* **beann** *nf* 1 *in mountain and hill names* Ben, **Beinn Nibheis** Ben Nevis, **Beinn Laoigh** Ben Lui; 2 a mountain, a ben, **a' streap beinne** climbing a mountain, **tìr nam beann àrda** the land of the high bens, (*song collection*) **Ceòl nam Beann** the music of the mountains, *Cf* **cnoc, mòinteach, monadh, sgùrr, tom, tulach**

beinn-theine, beinn-teine, beanntan-teine *nf* a volcano

beir *vti irreg* (*see tables p 405*), *pres part* **a' breith,** 1 (*vt*) bear, give birth to, **rug i nighean** she bore/had/gave birth to a daughter, (*song*) **'s ann an Ile (a) rugadh mi** it was in Islay that I was born, **rugadh is thogadh mi an sin** I was born and brought up there, **a' breith uighean** laying eggs, **a' breith cloinne/laoigh/uain** giving birth to children/a calf/ a lamb; 2 (*vi*) *with prep* **air,** overtake, catch up with, catch, **cha robh e luath gu leòr airson breith air a' chù** he wasn't fast enough to catch/catch up with the dog, **beiridh am poileas air ann an Lunnainn** the police will catch up with him in London; 3 (*vi*) *with prep* **air,** seize, take hold of, **rug mi air a' bhaga** I seized the bag, **beir air!** take hold of it!, *Cf* **gabh grèim air** (*see* **grèim 1**)

45

beireadh, beiream, beireamaid, beiribh, beiridh, beirinn *pts of irreg v* **beir** *see tables p 405*

beirm, *gen* **beirme** *nf* yeast

beò *adj* **1** alive, living, **chan fhaca sinn duine beò** we didn't see a living soul, (*fam*) **dè do chor? tha mi beò fhathast** how are you doing? I'm still in the land of the living, (*trad*) **ma mhaireas mi beò** if I survive/remain alive, if I'm spared, (*trad*) **cho fad 's as beò mi** as long as I live; **2** *used as noun* (*trad*) **rim** (&c) **b(h)eò** thoughout my (&c) life, all my (&c) life, **cha do dh'fhàg e an t-eilean ri bheò** he never left the island as long as he lived, *Cf* **beatha**, **maireann 2**, **saoghal 2**

beò-ghlacadh, beò-ghlacaidh, beò-ghlacaidhean *nm* obsession, an obsession

beòshlaint, beòshlainte, beòshlaintean *nf* a living, a livelihood, *Cf* **teachd-an-tìr**

beothachadh, *gen* **beothachaidh** *nm* (*the act of*) reviving &c (*see senses of* **beothaich** *v*)

beothaich *vti*, *pres part* **a' beothachadh**, revive, liven up, bring to life, animate, **tha na malairtean ùra a' beothachadh a' bhaile** the new businesses are livening up/reviving the town (*Cf* **ath-bheothaich**), **bheothaich mi an dèidh norraig** I revived after a snooze/nap

beothail *adj* lively, active, vivacious, **beothail a dh'aindeoin a h-aois** lively/active in spite of her age

beothalachd *nf invar* liveliness, vivacity

beuc *vi*, *pres part* **a' beucadh**, (*of humans & animals*) roar, bellow, *Cf* **geum** *v*, **nuallaich**

beuc, beuc, beucan *nm* (*of humans & animals*) a roar, a bellow, **leig e beuc às** he let out a roar/bellow, (*fig*) **beuc na mara** the roar of the sea, *Cf* **geum** *n*

beucadh, *gen* **beucaidh** *nm* (*the act of*) roaring, bellowing

beud, beud, beudan *nm* (*trad*) harm, loss, a blow, *usu in expr* **is mòr am beud (e)** it's a great shame/pity! (*Cf* **bochd 2**, **truagh 3**)

beul, *gen & pl* **beòil** *nm* **1** a mouth, **fosgail/dùin do bheul** open/shut your mouth, **làn-beòil bìdh** a mouthful of food, (*trad*) **air a** (&c) **b(h)eul fodha** face downwards, (*trad*) **chaochail iad/chaidh an tiodhlacadh air am beul fodha** they died/they were buried face downwards (*considered to be the most unfortunate form of death*), **beul na h-aibhne** the river mouth (*Cf* **bun 4**), **beul na h-uamha** the cave mouth, *Cf* (*fam*) **bus² 1, cab, gob 3; 2** (*trad*) *referring to the beginning or proximity of anything*, *esp* (**am**) **beul an là/na h-oidhche** (at) the onset of the day/the night; **3** (*as adv*) nearly, about, **beul a bhith deiseil** nearly ready, (*Cf more usu* **bi 11**), **beul ri dà mhìle leabhar**

almost/about two thousand books (*Cf more usu* **timcheall air** – *see* **timcheall 3**)

beulach *adj* **1** talkative, *Cf* **cabach**; **2** plausible, smooth-talking, *Cf* **beulchair**

beulaibh (*for* **beul-thaobh**) *nm invar* the front part of anything, *Cf* **cùlaibh** & *see also* **air beulaibh**

beul-aithris *nf invar* oral tradition, **chruinnich e òrain is sgeulachdan o bheul-aithris** he collected songs and stories from oral tradition, *Cf* **beul-oideachas, seanchas 1**

beulchair *adj* plausible, *Cf* **beulach 2**

beul-oideachas, *gen* **beul-oideachais** *nf,* & **beul-oideas,** *gen* **beul-oideis** *nf,* oral tradition, *Note: comparable to* **beul-aithris** *but with more emphasis on trad lore and learning as opposed to song, story &c*

beum, *gen* **beuma,** *pl* **beuman** & **beumannan** *nm* a stroke, a blow, *Cf more usu* **buille 1**

beurla *nf invar,* **1** (*originally*) a language; **2** (*now*) the English language, English, *often with the art,* **bhruidhinn e rinn anns a' Bheurla/ann am Beurla** he spoke to us in English, **chan eil facal Beurla agam** I don't have/speak a word of English, (*trad*) **luchd na Beurla** English speakers, English people, *also* non-Gaelic Scots, **Beurla Shasannach** the English of England, **Beurla Ghallta** Scots, Lowland Scots, **Beurla leathann** broad Scots (*Cf* **Albais**)

beus, beusa, beusan *nf* **1** moral character, virtue, *in pl* morals, **deagh-bheusan** virtuous morals; **2** behaviour, conduct, manners, **droch bheus** bad behaviour/manners, *Cf* **giùlan 3, modh 3**

beusach *adj* **1** (*morally, sexually &c*) modest, *Cf* **nàrach 2**; **2** moral, well-behaved, *Cf* **modhail**

beus-eòlas, *gen* **beus-eòlais** *nm* ethics

bha, bhathar, bheil, *pts of irreg v* **bi** *see tables p 414*

bhan, bhan, bhanaichean *nf* a van

bhàrr *prep see* **bàrr 5**

Bheunas *nf* the planet Venus

bheir, bheireadh, bheirinn *pts of irreg verbs* **beir** & **thoir** *see tables pp 405 & 413*

bheireas *pt of irreg v* **beir** *see tables p 405*

bhi, bhiodh, bhios, bhitheas, bhitheadh, bhitheamaid, bhithinn, *pts of irreg v* **bi** *see tables p 414*

bho & **o** *prep* from, *Note: the pers prons* **mi, thu, e** *&c combine with* **bho** *to form the prep prons* **bhuam(sa), bhuat(sa), bhuaithe(san), bhuaipe(se), bhuainn(e), bhuaibh(se), bhuapa(san);** *for senses & examples see* **o**

bhòt *vi, pres part* **a' bhòtadh**, vote, **cha do bhòt i san taghadh** she didn't vote in the election, **bhòt mise airson Lord Such** I (*emph*) voted for Lord Such, *Cf* **tagh 2**

bhuam(sa), **bhuat(sa)** &c *prep prons see* **bho**

bhur *see* **ur**

bi *vi irreg* be, *for forms see tables p 414, Note:* **bi** *cannot be used with a noun complement – Cf* **is boireannach i** she is a woman (*see irreg vb* **is**) *with* **tha i na ban-rùnaire** & **is e ban-rùnaire a tha innte** she is a secretary; **1** *with adj complement* **tha mi àrd/fadalach/tinn** I'm tall/late/ill; **2** *with adv* **chan eil i an seo/gu bochd/gu dòigheil** she isn't here/poorly/fine; **3** *with pres part* **cha robh e a' coiseachd/ag òl/a' sealltainn** he wasn't walking/drinking/looking; **4** *with* **ann**, *expressing existence, presence*, **bidh Iain ann** Iain will be here/there/present, **chan eil sìthichean ann!** there are no fairies, fairies don't exist!; **5** *in constr* **is e … a tha** (&c) **ann** *expressing identity, occupation, attributes &c*, **cò esan? is e Niall a th' ann** who's he? It's Neil, **is e duine comasach a bh' ann an Dòmhnall, 's e lannsair a bh' ann** Donald was an able man, he was a surgeon; **6** *with prep pron* **nam**, **nad** &c, *expr a (usu) more temporary state, position, occupation &c than* **5**, **an uair a bha i na caileig òig** when she was a young girl, **tha iad nan laighe** they're lying down, **cha bhi thu nad aonar** you won't be on your own; **7** *with* **ri**, **ris**, engaged in, up to, at, **dè tha thu ris?** what are you up to? **a bheil thu ri bàrdachd fhathast?** are you still writing poetry/at the poetry? **tha iad ri iasgach** they're fishing/at the fishing, *Note:* **ri** *is used after* **bi** *by some speakers as an alternative to* **ag/a'** *before the pres part*, **bha i ri seinn** she was singing; **8** *with* **air** & *the verbal noun or the infin expr a passive sense or a perfect/pluperfect tense*, **tha sinn air seinn** we have sung, **bha sinn air seinn** we had sung, **bha sinn air òrain a sheinn** we had sung songs, **bha an doras air a dhùnadh** the door had been closed; **9** *with* **aig** *indicates possession*, **cha bhi sgillinn ruadh agam/aig Màiri** I/Mary won't have a brass farthing; **10** *with* **aig … ri** *expresses obligation, tasks ahead*, **tha tòrr agam ri dhèanamh** I've got lots to do, **bha aig Peigi ri aran fhuineadh** Peggy had to bake bread; **11** *in expr* **gu(s) bhith** … nearly …, ready to … , **bha i gu bhith deiseil** she was nearly/almost ready, **tha iad gus falbh** they are ready to/about to leave; *Note: when* **bi** & **is** *can both be used* **is** *usu implies more permanence &/or emphasis, eg* **is math bùrn fuarain** spring water is good, **tha bùrn an fhuarain seo math** the water from this spring is good, **tha mi fèineil** I'm selfish, I'm being selfish, (*more emph*) **is fèineil mi** I'm (*inherently*) selfish

biadh, *gen* **bìdh** *&* **bidhe**, *pl* **biadhan** *nm* **1** food, **deasaich** *v* **biadh** prepare/cook food, **gabh do bhiadh!** eat your food/meal! **blasad** *m* **bìdh** *or* **grèim** *m* **bìdh** a bite to eat, **taigh-bìdh** *m* a restaurant, **thoir** *v* **biadh do na beathaichean** feed/fodder the animals; **2** a meal, *Cf* **diathad 1**, **lòn 2**

biadhlann, biadhlainn, biadhlannan *nf* a refectory, a canteen, a dining-hall

bian, *gen & pl* **bèin** *nm* **1** fur, a fur; **2** skin, a skin, hide, a hide, a pelt, *Cf* **seiche**

biast *&* **bèist**, *gen* **bèiste**, *pl* **biastan** & **bèistean** *nf* **1** a beast, an animal (*wild or domestic*), *Cf* **ainmhidh, beathach; 2** *as term of abuse* **'s e biastan a th' annta!** they're beasts/animals!, *Cf* **brùid 2**

biath *vt*, *pres part* **a' biathadh**, feed (*persons, stock &c*), *Cf* **beathaich**

biathadh, *gen* **biathaidh** *nm* (*the act of*) feeding (*see* **biath** *v*)

bìd *vt*, *pres part* **a' bìdeadh**, bite

bìd, bìde, bìdean *nm* **1** (*of bird*) a cheep, a chirp; **2** *of humans* (*fam*) a sound, a word, **cha duirt e bìd** he didn't say a word, **cha chluinn i bìd** she can't hear a sound/a thing, *Cf* **bìog, smid**

bìdeadh, bididh, bìdidhean *nm* **1** (*the act of*) biting (*see* **bìd** *v*); **2** a bite

bìdeag, bìdeig, bìdeagan *nf* **1** a fragment, a crumb, a morsel, a small piece of anything, *Cf* **criomag, mìr; 2** (*IT*) a bit

bidh *pt of irreg v* **bi** *see tables p 414*

bidse *nf invar* **1** a bitch; **2** *as oath/swear* (*fam/vulg*) **taigh na bidse!** sod it/bugger it!

bile, bile, bilean *nf* **1** a lip (*of mouth*), **a' bhile uachdarach/ìochdarach** the upper/lower lip, **thàinig faite-gàire bheag gu a bilean** a wee smile came to her lips, *Cf* **lip; 2** a rim, a lip (*of container &c*), *Cf* **iomall 2, oir** *n* **2**

bile, bile, bilean *nm* (*parliament*) a bill, *Cf* **achd**

bileag, bileig, bileagan *nf* **1** a petal; **2** a blade (*of grass*); **3** (*also* **bileag cunntais**), (*household &c*) an account, a bill, **bha bileag bheag agam ri phàigheadh** I had a wee bill to pay, *Cf* **cunntas 3; 4** a ticket, *Cf* **ticead; 5** a label; **6** a leaflet; a pamphlet

binid, *gen* **binide** *nf* rennet

binn *adj* **1** (*of sound*) sweet, **a guth binn** her sweet voice, (*song*) **bha na h-eòin air na crannaibh 's iad ri caithream gu binn** the birds were on the trees, singing away sweetly, *Note: not usu for smell or taste – see* **cùbhraidh, milis; 2** melodious, *Cf* **ceòlmhor**

binn, *gen* **binne** *nf* a judgement, a sentence, **thoir** *v* **a-mach binn** pronounce/give judgement, *Cf* **breith**[2]

binnean, *gen & pl* **binnein** *nm* a hilltop, a peak, a pinnacle

binneas, *gen* **binneis** *nm* (*of sounds*) sweetness

bìoball, *gen* **bìobaill**, *pl* **bìobaill** & **bìoblaichean** *nm* a Bible, **Am Bìoball** The Bible

bìoballach *adj* biblical

bìodach *adj* tiny, trifling, *Cf* **crìon** *adj* 1 & 2, **meanbh**, **suarach** 1

biodag, biodaig, biodagan *nf* a dirk, a dagger, (*trad*) **ag iomairt biodaig** wielding/using a dirk

biodh, *pt of irreg v* **bi** *see tables p 414*

bìog, bìoga, bìogan *nf* a cheep, a sound, *same uses as* **bìd** *n*

bìog *vi, pres part* **a' bìogail**, (*of bird*) chirp, cheep

biolar, *gen* **biolair** *nf* cress, water-cress

biona, biona, bionaichean *nmf* a bin, **cuir sa bhiona e!** bin it! **biona-stùir** a dustbin

bior, biora, bioran *nm* 1 a point (*of stick &c*); 2 a pointed object, *esp* a pointed stick, a goad, *Cf* **bioran, brod** n 1; 3 a prickle, a thorn, *Cf* **dealg** 1; 4 (*cookery*) **bior-ròstaidh** a spit

biorach *adj* 1 pointed, sharp, (*trad*) **claidheamh caol biorach** a pointed rapier, **maide biorach** a pointed/sharp stick, **sùil bhiorach** a sharp eye; 2 prickly, thorny

bioran, *gen & pl* **biorain** *nm* a stick, *esp* a pointed stick, **a' brosnachadh na sprèidhe le bioran** urging on the cattle/the stock with a stick, *Cf* **bior** 2, **brod** *n* 1

biorra-crùidein, biorra-crùidein, biorrachan-crùidein *nm* a kingfisher

biotais *nm sing & coll* beet, beetroot; **biotais (siùcair)** sugarbeet

birlinn, birlinn, birlinnean *nf* (*trad*) a galley, a birlinn, (*poem*) **Birlinn Chlann Raghnaill** The Galley of Clan Ranald

bith *nf invar* 1 life, existence, being, **thoir** *v* **rudeigin am bith** bring something into existence/into being, **a' dol à bith** passing out of existence, ceasing to be, **bith-eòlas** *m* biology (*lit* knowledge of life or being); 2 the world, the earth, *esp in exprs* **air bith** & **sam bith**, any, any at all (*lit* on earth, in the world), **cò air bith a bha sin?** whoever/who on earth was that? (*Cf* **fon ghrèin** – *see* **grian**), **bhiodh duine air bith/sam bith comasach air** anyone at all would be capable of it, **chan fhaca sinn duine sam bith** we didn't see anyone at all, **thoir dhomh leabhar – leabhar sam bith** give me a book – any book at all, (*emph*) **chan eil airgead agam, airgead sam bith** I've no money, no money at all (*Cf* **idir**); 3 *esp in expr* **às bith**

also **ge bith** (who-, what- &c) ever, **às bith cò a rinn e, às bith càite an d'fhuair thu e, tha e sgoinneil!** whoever made it, wherever you got it from, it's smashing/great!

bìth, *gen* **bìthe** *nf* **1** tar, tarmacadam, pitch; **2** gum

bith- *a prefix corres to Eng* ever-, **bith-bheò** *adj* ever-living, **bith-bhuan** *adj* eternal, everlasting, *Cf* **sìor-**

bitheadh, bitheam, bitheamaid, bithear *pts of irreg v* **bi** *see tables p 414*

bitheanta *adj* frequent, common, *Cf* **cumanta**

bitheantas *see* **am bitheantas**

bithibh, bithidh, bithinn *pts of irreg v* **bi** *see tables p 414*

bithis, bithis, bithisean *nf* (*joinery*) a screw, *Cf* **sgriubha**

bithiseach *adj* spiral

blais *vt, pres part* **a' blasad(h)**, taste, **bhlais e an càise ach cha do chòrd e ris** he tasted the cheese but he didn't like it

blàr, blàir, blàran *nm* **1** a plain, (*placename*) **Blàr Dhruiminn** Blair Drummond, the plain/level place of Drummond; **2** (*trad*) a battle, a battlefield, **blàr Chùil Lodair** the battle of Culloden, **air blàr Chùil Lodair** on the field/battlefield of Culloden

blas, *gen* **blais** *nm* **1** taste, flavour, **pògan air blas na meala** kisses tasting of honey, **tha droch bhlas air** it has a bad taste; **2** (*language*) accent, **tha blas na Beurla air a chuid Gàidhlig fhathast** there's an English accent/flavour to his Gaelic still

blasachadh, *gen* **blasachaidh** *nm* (*the act of*) flavouring

blasad(h), *gen* **blasaid(h)** *nm* **1** (*the act of*) tasting; **2** *usu in phrase* **blasad bìdh** a small amount of food, **gabhaidh mi/gheibh mi blasad bìdh** I'll take/get a bite to eat, *Cf* **grèim bìdh** (*see* **grèim 2**)

blasaich *vt, pres part* **a' blasachadh**, flavour, add flavour to something

blasmhor, *adj* full of flavour, delicious, *Cf* **blasta**

blasta & **blasda** *adj* tasty, full of flavour, **biadh/ubhal blasta** tasty food/a tasty apple, *Cf* **blasmhor**

blàth, blàith, blàthan *nm* **1** a bloom, a blossom, **blàth an ubhail** apple blossom, **preas fo bhlàth** a shrub in bloom/blossom/flower; **2** flower (*of smaller plants*), *Cf* **dìthean** & *more usu* **flùr**[2]

blàth *adj* **1** warm, **tha i blàth an-diugh** it's a warm day, **bainne blàth** warm milk; **2** (*of people, feelings &c*) warm, affectionate, tender, *Cf* **bàidheil, coibhneil**

blàth-chridheach *adj* tender-hearted, warm-hearted

blàthachadh, *gen* **blàthachaidh** *nm* (*the act & process of*) warming, warming up, **blàthachadh na cruinne** global warming

blàthaich *vt, pres part* **a' blàthachadh**, warm, warm up, *Cf* **teasaich**, **teòthaich**

blàths, *gen* **blàiths** *nm* warmth (*phys, & of affections &c*)

bleideag, bleideig, bleideagan *nf* a flake, **bleideagan sneachda/coirce/ siabainn** snowflakes/cornflakes/soapflakes

bleith *vt, pres part* **a' bleith**, 1 (*of grain*) grind, mill, **chaidh an t-arbhar a bhleith sa mhuileann** the corn was ground in the mill, *Cf* **meil**; 2 (*more generally*) grind, pulverise, *Cf more usu* **pronn** *v* 1

bleith, *gen* **bleithe** *nf* (*the act of*) grinding &c (*see senses of* **bleith** *v*)

bleoghain(n) *vt, pres part* **a' bleoghan(n)**, milk, **bhleoghainn a' bhanarach a' bhò** the dairymaid milked the cow

bleoghann *nf invar* (*the act of*) milking

bliadhna, *gen* **bliadhna**, *pl* **bliadhnachan** & **bliadhnaichean** *nf* a year, *Note: usu in singular after numerals*; **ceithir bliadhna a dh'aois** four years of age, **bliadhnachan air ais** years ago, **bha e san arm fad bhliadhnachan** he was in the army for years, **bidh sin a' tachairt gach bliadhna/a h-uile bliadhna** that happens each/every year, **Bliadhna Theàrlaich** the time of the Jacobite Rising of 1745– 6 (*lit* Charlie's Year), **ceann-bliadhna** *m* a birthday, **am bliadhna** *adv* this year, **chan eil biadh daor am bliadhna** food isn't dear this year, **an ath-bhliadhna** *adv* next year, **bliadhna-lèim** a leap year, **Bliadhna Mhath Ur (dhut/dhuibh)!** a Good/Happy New Year (to you)!

bliadhnach, *gen* & *pl* **bliadhnaich** *nm* a yearling

bliadhnail *adj* annual, yearly, **coinneamh bhliadhnail a' Chomuinn Ghaidhealaich** the annual meeting of An Comann Gaidhealach

blian *vi, pres part* **a' blianadh**, sunbathe, sun oneself, bask in the sun

blianadh, *gen* **blianaidh** *nm* (*the act of*) sunbathing &c (*see senses of* **blian** *v*)

blianna *see* **bliadhna**

bloigh & **bloidh**, *gen* **bloighe**, *pl* **bloighean** *nf* 1 (*trad*) half of something, *Cf more usu* **leth** 3; 2 a bit or piece of something, *Cf* **criomag, mìr, pìos** 1; 3 (*maths*) a fraction

bloighd, bloighd, bloighdean *nf* a fragment, a splinter, **bha am bata-coiseachd na bhloighdean** the walking stick was in splinters, *Cf* **sgealb** *n*, **spealg** *n*

bloinigean-gàrraidh, *gen* **bloinigein-gàrraidh** *nm* spinach

blonag, *gen* **blonaig** *nf* lard, fat

bò, *gen* **bà**, *dat* **boin** & **bò**, *pl* **bà**, *gen pl* **bò** *nf* a cow, **a' tionail/a' bleoghann bhò** herding/milking cows, **bò laoigh** a cow in calf, **bò bhainne** a milk cow, a milker, (*song*) **on a dh'fhàg mi i 'n Raineach nam bò** since I left her in Rannoch of the cattle, (*saying*) **bò mhaol odhar agus bò odhar mhaol** six and half a dozen, *Cf* **crodh, sprèidh**

bobhla, bobhla, bobhlaichean *nm* a bowl, *Cf more trad* **cuach**

boc, *gen* & *pl* **buic** *nm* **1** a male goat, a billygoat, *Cf* **gobhar**; **2** a buck, a roebuck, *Cf* **damh 1**

bòc *vi*, *pres part* **a' bòcadh**, swell, bloat, blister, *Cf more usu at v*, **sèid 2**

bòcadh, bòcaidh, bòcaidhean *nm* **1** (*the act of*) swelling &c (*see senses of* **bòc** *v*); **2** a swelling, *Cf at* *n*

bòcan, *gen* & *pl* **bòcain** *nm* **1** a spectre, an apparition, *Cf* **taibhse, tannasg**; **2** a bogy-man, (*Sc*) a bogle

bochd *adj* **1** poor, badly off, **fad làithean m' òige bha sinn bochd, bochd** all through my young days we were very, very poor, *Cf* **ainniseach**; **2** unfortunate, poor, **an duine bochd!** the poor man! **tha sin bochd** that's unfortunate/sad/a pity, *Cf* **duilich 4, truagh 3**; **3** not well, poorly, in a bad way, **ciamar a tha thu? chan eil ach bochd** how are you? I'm not too good at all, *also as adv* **gu bochd** poorly, **tha mi gu bochd** I'm poorly/in a bad way, *Cf* **tinn**

bochdainn, *gen* **bochdainne** *nf* **1** poverty, *Cf* **ainnis**; **2** misfortune, bad luck, *Cf* **dosgainn**

bocsa & **bogsa**, *gen* **bocsa**, *pl* **bocsaichean** *nm* **1** a box, **bocsa-fòn** a (tele)phone box *or* kiosk, **bocsa-litrichean** a letter box, a post box, **bocsa mhaidsichean** a match box, a box of matches, *Cf* **bucas**; **2** **bocsa** (*fam*) *for* **bocsa-ciùil**, *gen* **bocsa(-ciùil)**, *pl* **bocsaichean(-ciùil)** *nm* an accordeon, a box, **bha Phil Cunningham air a' bhocsa (-ciùil)** Phil Cunningham was on/was playing the box

bocsair, bocsair, bocsairean (*sport*) a boxer

bod, *gen* & *pl* **buid** & **boid** *nm* a penis, *Cf* **slat 4**

bodach, *gen* & *pl* **bodaich** *nm* (*fam*) **1** an old man, an old guy, an old fellow, **cà'il am bodach?** where's the old fellow? **Bodach na Nollaig(e)** Father Christmas, Santa Claus; **2** *sometimes more derog*, (*song*) **bodachan** (*dimin*) **le pinnt air, bidh e leis an daoraich** a little old man with a pint in him, he'll be drunk; **3** *not necessarily with implication of age*, **is esan bodach an airgid** he's the money man/the guy who looks after the money, **bodach nam bucaidean** the bucket man, the bin man, **bodach-sneachda** a snow man, **bodach-ròcais** a scarecrow, (*of husband*) **am bodach** the old man, my old man, *Cf* **cailleach**

bodhaig, bodhaige, bodhaigean *nf* a (*human*) body, *usu living*, *Cf* **colann, corp 1**

bodhair *vt, pres part* **a' bòdhradh**, deafen, make deaf

bodhar *adj* deaf

bodhar, bodhair, bodharan *nm* a deaf person, (*prov*) **cluinnidh am bodhar fuaim an airgid** (even) the deaf man will hear the sound of money

bòdhradh, *gen* **bòdhraidh** *nm* (*the act of*) deafening

bòdhran, bòdhrain, bòdhranan *nm* (*music*) a bodhran

bodraig *vti, pres part* **a' bodraigeadh**, 1 (*vt*) (*fam*) bother, **na bodraig mi!** don't bother me!, *Cf more trad* **sàraich**; 2 (*vi*) bother oneself, take the trouble, **an do dheasaich thu biadh dhomh? cha do bhodraig mi** did you prepare me some food? I didn't bother

bodraigeadh, *gen* **bodraigidh** *nm* (*the act of*) bothering

bog *vti, pres part* **a' bogadh**, 1 *vt* dip, soak, steep (*in liquid*); 2 *vi* (*movement*) bob, dip, (*of tail*) wag, **bha earball a' choin a' bogadh** the dog's tail was wagging

bog *adj* 1 soft, **stuth bog** soft material/fabric, **talamh bog** soft (*often* boggy) ground; 2 (*of character &c*) soft, **tha e bog on a mhill a mhàthair e** he's soft since his mother spoilt him, *Cf* **maoth 1**; 3 tender, **cridhe bog** a tender heart; 4 *in expr* **bog fliuch**, soaking wet, **bha sinn bog fliuch mus do sguir an t-uisge** we were soaking wet before the rain stopped; 5 moist, humid, *Cf* **tais**; 6 limp, flabby

bog, buig, bogachan *nf* 1 a bog, *Cf* **boglach, fèith(e)**; 2 *in expr* **air bhog** floating, afloat, **cuir** *v* **air bhog** launch, *Cf* **fleòdradh, flod**

bogachadh, *gen* **bogachaidh** *nm* (*the act of*) wetting &c (*see senses of* **bogaich** *v*)

bogadaich *nf invar* 1 a bouncing or bobbing movement; 2 *also as pres part* **a' bogadaich** bouncing, bobbing (**ri** against), jumping up and down

bogadh, *gen* **bogaidh** *nm* 1 (*the act of*) soaking &c (*see sense of* **bog** *v*); 2 *in expr* **cuir** *v* **aodach** (&c) **am bogadh** put clothes (&c) to soak/steep; 3 immersion, *also fig*, **bogadh cànain** language immersion, (*lang*) **cùrsa** *m* **bogaidh** an immersion course

bogaich *vti, pres part* **a' bogachadh**, 1 (*vt*) wet, make wet, *Cf* **fliuch** *v*; 2 (*vti*) soften, make or become soft

bogan, *gen & pl* **bogain** *nm* (*fam*) a penis

bogha, bogha, boghachan *nm* 1 a bow or curve in anything, a bulge, **tha bogha air a' bhalla** the wall has a bulge in it, *Cf* **lùb** *n* **1**; 2 an arch, a vault; 3 a bow (*ie weapon*); 4 a bow (*for violin &c*)

bogha-frois, bogha-fhrois, boghachan-frois *nm* a rainbow

boglach, boglaich, boglaichean *nf* a bog, soft or marshy ground, a swamp, **bha e an sàs ann am boglaich** he was stuck in a bog, *Cf* **bog** *n* 1, **fèith(e)**

bogsa *see* **bocsa**

bòid, bòide, bòidean *nf* 1 an oath, a vow, a solemn promise, *Cf less strong* **geall** *n* 2; 2 an oath, swearing, (*Sc*) a swear, *Cf* **droch cainnt** (*see* **cainnt** 2), **mionnan** 1 & 2

Bòideach, *gen & pl,* **Bòidich** *nm* a Bute man, someone from Bute (**Bòd**) *also as adj,* of from or pertaining to Bute

bòideachadh, *gen* **bòideachaidh** *nm* (*the act of*) vowing (*see* **bòidich** *v*)

bòidhchead *nf* beauty, loveliness, prettiness, *Cf* **maise**

bòidheach, *comp* **(n)as (&c) bòidhche,** *adj* beautiful, pretty, bonny, *esp of places, human females & other living things,* **àite bòidheach** a beautiful/bonny place, **caileag bhòidheach** a beautiful/bonny girl, (*song*) **isein bhòidhich tha ri siubhal null gud nead an Tìr an Fhraoich** O bonny wee bird travelling yonder to your nest in the Land of Heather, (*song*) **'s e Siabost as bòidhche** ... Siabost is the bonniest (place) ..., *Cf* **àlainn, brèagha, maiseach**

bòidich *vi, pres part* **a' bòideachadh,** vow

boile *nf invar* 1 madness; 2 frenzy, rage, passion, (*trad*) **boile chatha** battle frenzy, battle madness (*Cf* **misg chatha,** *see* **misg**); 3 *in expr* **air bhoile** in a frenzy, in a rage, **bha e air bhoile an dèidh dha obair a chall** he was mad/in a rage/furious after losing his job; *Cf* **bàinidh, cuthach**

boillsg *vi, pres part* **a' boillsgeadh,** gleam, flash, glitter, shine (*esp intermittently*), **bha an uamh a' boillsgeadh le òr** the cave was shining/glittering with gold, *Cf* **deàlraich** 2

boillsg, boillsge, boillsgean *nm* 1 a flash of light; 2 a gleam

boillsgeach *adj* gleaming, flashing, glittering, shining, *Cf* **deàlrach** 1

boillsgeadh, *gen* **boillsgidh** *nm* (*the act of*) gleaming, flashing &c (*see senses of* **boillsg** *v*)

boin *nf see* **bò**

boinne, *gen* **boinne,** *pl* **boinnean** & **boinneachan** *nmf* 1 a drop (*of liquid*), **boinne bainne** a drop of milk; 2 a very small quantity (*of liquid*), **chan eil boinne bùirn** (*or* **uisge**) **againn** we don't have a drop of water; *Cf* **boinneag, braon** *n* 1

boinneag, boinneige, boinneagan *nf* 1 a small drop, *Cf* **drùdhag** 1; 2 *in expr* **boinneag ri shròin** a drop on his nose

boireann *adj* female, feminine, **cù/each boireann** a female dog/horse, (*biol &c*) **an cineal boireann** the female sex/gender, (*gram*) **a' ghnè bhoireann** the feminine gender, **'s e facal boireann a th' ann an 'uiseag'** 'uiseag' is a feminine word, *Cf* **fireann**

boireannach, *gen & pl* **boireannaich** *nm* a woman, a (*human*) female, *Note: though* **boireannach** *is grammatically masculine the pronoun* **i** *is used*, **chuala mi boireannach is i a' seinn** I heard a woman singing, *Cf* **bean** *n* 2, **fireannach**, **tè** 2

boireannta *adj* effeminate

boiseag, boiseig, boiseagan *nf* 1 a slap or blow with the palm of the hand; 2 a palmful of anything

boiteag, boiteig, boiteagan *nf* a worm, *Cf* **cnuimh**

boladh, bolaidh, bolaidhean *nm* a smell (*pleasant or unpleasant*), an odour, a scent, a stink, *Cf* **àile** 2, **boltrach**, **tòchd**

bolgan, *gen* **bolgain**, *pl* **bolgain** & **bolganan** *nm* 1 (*hort*) a bulb; 2 a light bulb

boltrach, *gen & pl* **boltraich** *nm* a smell (*usu pleasant*), a scent, a perfume, *Cf* **àile** 2, **boladh**, **tòchd**

boma, boma, bomaichean *nm* a bomb, **leag** *v* **boma** drop a bomb

bonaid, bonaide, bonaidean *nmf* 1 a bonnet, **bonaid b(h)iorach** a Glengarry bonnet, **bonaid càir** a car bonnet; 2 (*headgear*) a cap

bonn, *gen & pl* **buinn** *nm* 1 the lowest part, base, foot or foundation of anything, **bonn taighe** foundations of a house, **bonn na coise/na bròige** the sole of the foot/of the shoe, **bonn na beinne** the foot/bottom of the mountain (*Cf* **bun** 1), **bonn-dubh** heel of the foot (*Cf more usu* **sàil**); 2 *esp* **bonn airgid** a coin, a piece of money, (*trad*) **bonn-a-sia** & **bonn-a-sè** (*orig*) sixpence Scots, (*subsequently*) a halfpenny; 3 a medal, **choisinn i am bonn airgid/òir aig a' Mhòd** she won the Silver/Gold Medal at the Mod, **bonn-cuimhne** a military medal, a medal for bravery, a commemorative medal; 4 *in expr* **thug iad na buinn asta** they took to their heels; 5 *in expr* **cuir** *v* **air b(h)onn** found, establish, set up, **chaidh an gnothach a chur air bonn le mo sheanair** the business was founded/set up by my grandfather, **tha a' chomhairle a' cur air bonn cròileagan tro mheadhan na Gàidhlig** the Council is setting up a Gaelic-medium playgroup, *Cf* **cas** *n* 5, **stèidhich**

bonnach, *gen & pl* **bonnaich** *nm* 1 a bannock; 2 a cake; 3 a scone (*Cf less trad* **sgona**); *Cf* **breacag**; 4 **bonnach-uighe** an omelette

borb *adj* wild, savage, barbarous, uncouth, **sluagh borb** a wild/savage people, **duine borb** a barbarous *or* uncouth man, **dòighean/dol a-mach borb** uncouth behaviour, *Cf* **garbh** 3, **garg**

borbair, borbair, borbairean *nm* a barber, *Cf more trad* **bearradair**

bòrd, *gen & pl* **bùird** *nm* 1 (*furniture*) a table, **bha sinn nar suidhe mun bhòrd** we were sitting round the table, **bòrd-iarnaigidh** an ironing-board, **bòrd-sgrìobhaidh** a writing table/desk; 2 (*joinery &c*) a board or plank of wood, *Cf* **clàr** 1, **dèile**; 3 (*in school &c*) a board, **bòrd-dubh** a blackboard, **bòrd-geal** a whiteboard, **bha liosta an àird air a' bhòrd** there was a list up on the (notice) board; **4** (*business, admin &c*) Board (*of Directors &c*), **Bòrd na Slàinte** the Health Board, **Bòrd nan Deuchainnean** the Examinations Board; **5** *in exprs* (*of boats &c*) **air bòrd** on board, *&* (**thuit e &c**) **far bòrd** (he fell &c) overboard, **bha sinn/chaidh sinn air bòrd na luinge** we were/we went on board the ship

bòst, bòsta, bòstan *nm* a boast, boasting, **dèan** *v* **bòst** boast

bòstail *adj* boastful, *Cf* **bragail**

botal *&* **buideal**, *gen & pl* **botail** *nm* a bottle, **botal fìon(a)** a bottle of wine *or* a wine bottle, **amhaich** *f* **botail** neck of a bottle, **botal-teth** a hot-water bottle

bòtann, bòtainn, bòtannan *nm* a boot, *usu* a Wellington boot, a wellie, *Cf* **bròg**

bothan, *gen & pl* **bothain** *nm* **1** a cottage; **2** a hut, a shed, *Cf less trad* **seada**; **3** a bothy, *esp* (*trad*) **bothan àirigh(e)** a sheiling bothy; **4** a shebeen (*a place where illicitly distilled whisky is/was drunk*), *Cf* **taigh dubh** (*see* **taigh 1**)

bracaist, bracaiste, bracaistean *nf* breakfast, **dè a ghabhas tu air/gu do bhracaist?** what will you have for your breakfast?

brach *vti*, *pres part* **a' brachadh**, **1** (*esp of beer, wine &c*) ferment; **2** (*vi*) (*of spot, boil*) gather, fill with pus

brachadh, brachaidh, brachaidhean *nm* **1** (*the act of*) fermenting (*see senses of* **brach** *v*); **2** fermentation; **3** pus, matter

bradan, *gen & pl* **bradain** *nm* a salmon, (*coll*) salmon

brag, *gen* **braig** *nm* a bang (*esp sharp not dull*), **rinn an dèile brag an uair a thuit i chun an ùrlair** the plank made a bang when it fell to the floor

bragail *adj* **1** boastful, *Cf* **bòstail**; **2** cheeky

braich, *gen* **bracha** *nf* malt, malted barley, (*trad*) **Mac na Bracha** Son of the Malt, *a nickname for malt whisky*

braid, *gen* **braide** *nf* theft, thieving, pilfering, stealing, *Cf* **goid** *n*, **mèirle**

bràigh, *gen* **bràighe** *&* **bràghad**, *pl* **bràigheachan** *nm* **1** the upper part of anything, **bràigh a' bhaile** the upper part of the township, the top of the town, **bràigh a' ghlinne** the head/the upper part of the glen, **bràigh a' chuirp** the upper part of the body, the chest area (*Cf more usu* **broilleach 2**), **losgadh-bràghad** heartburn; **2** *in placenames*, upland, *often rendered as* Brae(s), **Bràigh Dhùin** the Braes of Doune, **Bràigh Loch Abair** Brae Lochaber

bràigh, bràighe, bràighdean *nmf* a prisoner, a captive, *esp* a hostage, *Cf* **ciomach, prìosanach**

braighdeanas, *gen* **braighdeanais** *nm* captivity, imprisonment, **am braighdeanas** in captivity, *Cf* **ciomachas, daorsa, làmh 2, sàs 1**

braim, brama, bramannan *nm* breaking of wind, a fart, **leig e braim** he broke wind/farted

braisead, *gen* **braiseid** *nf* 1 (*of persons, behaviour*) hastiness, impetuosity; 2 (*of soldier &c*) intrepidity, boldness, *Cf* **dànadas 1**

bràiste, bràiste, bràistean *nf* a brooch

bràithreil *adj* brotherly, fraternal

bràmair, bràmair, bràmairean *nm* (*fam*) a girlfriend, *Cf* **car(a)bhaidh, leannan**

branndaidh *nf invar* brandy

braoisg, braoisge, braoisgean *nf* a grin *or* a grimace, **chuir i braoisg oirre** she grinned *or* she grimaced, *Cf* **bus² 2**

braoisgeil *adj* (*not usu complimentary*) grinning

braon *vi, pres part* **a' braonadh**, drizzle

braon, *gen & pl* **braoin** *nm* 1 a drop (*of liquid*), *Cf* **boinne 1**; 2 drizzle, *Cf* **ciùbhran 1**

bras *adj* 1 (*persons, behaviour*) hasty, impetuous, impulsive, *Cf* **cas** *adj* 3; 2 (*soldier &c*) intrepid, bold, *also* rashly bold, *Cf* **dàna 2**; 3 (*stream &c*) rushing, precipitous, *Cf* **cas** *adj* 2

brat, brata, bratan *nm* 1 a cover, a covering (*Cf* **còmhdach**), **brat-leapa(ch)** a bed cover, a coverlet, a quilt; 2 (*trad*) a cloak; 3 a mat, *also* **brat-ùrlair** & **brat-làir** a (*larger*) floor-covering, a carpet

bratach, brataich, brataichean *nf* a banner, a flag, colours (*of a regiment &c*), **a' Bhatach Shìth** the Fairy Flag (*of Dunvegan*), (*song*) **Mhic Iarla** (*voc*) **nam bratach bàna** O Son of the Earl of the white banners

bràth, *gen* **bràtha** *nm* 1 (*trad*) judgement, doom, **là a' bhràtha** judgement day, doomsday; 2 *esp in expr* **gu bràth** for ever, always, **bidh na beanntan ann gu bràth** the mountains will be there for ever/will always be there, (*more emph*) **gu sìorraidh bràth** for ever and ever; 3 **gu bràth** *with neg v* never, **cha bhruidhinn mi ris gu bràth (tuilleadh)** I'll never speak to him (again); *Cf* **a-chaoidh, sìorraidh 2**; *Note:* **gu bràth** *is used only to refer to future time, for 'ever', 'never' in the past see* **a-riamh**

brath *vt, pres part* **a' brathadh**, 1 betray, give away, inform on (*someone*); 2 give away (*a secret*)

brath, *gen* **bratha** *nm* 1 knowledge, information, *esp in exprs* **'s ann aig Dia tha brath!** God alone knows! & **aig Sealbh tha brath carson!** Heaven knows why!, *Cf more usu* **fios 1** & 2; 2 (unfair) advantage, **ghabh am fear-reic brath air** the salesman took advantage of him, *Cf* **fàth 3**; 3 betrayal, a betrayal

brathadair, brathadair, brathadairean *nm* **1** a betrayer, an informer; **2** a traitor

brathadh, *gen* **brathaidh** *nm* **1** (*the act of*) betraying &c (*see senses of* **brath** *v*); **2** treason

bràthair, bràthar, bràithrean *nm* a brother, **bràthair-athar** an uncle (*on father's side*), **bràthair-màthar** an uncle (*on mother's side*), **bràthair m' athar/mo mhàthar** my uncle, **bràthair-cèile** a brother-in-law

breab *vti, pres part* **a' breabadh, 1** kick; **2** stamp the foot, *Cf* **stamp** *v*

breab, breaba, breaban *nmf* a kick

breabadair, breabadair, breabadairean *nm* **1** one who kicks; **2** (*usu*) a weaver, one who works a loom, *Cf* **figheadair 1**; **3** a daddy-longlegs

breabadh, *gen* **breabaidh** *nm* (*the act of*) kicking &c (*see senses of* **breab** *v*)

breac *adj* speckled, spotted, variegated (*pattern, appearance, material &c*), (*more fig*) **tha an t-eilean breac le bailtean beaga** the island is dotted with villages, *Cf* **ballach** *&* *trad* **riabhach 1**

breac, *gen* *&* *pl* **bric** *nm* a trout

breac, *gen* **brice** *nf* (*with the art*) **a' bhreac** smallpox, **a' bhreac-òtraich** chicken-pox, **a' bhreac-sheunain** *&* (**am**) **breacadh-seunain** freckles

breacag, breacaig, breacagan *nf* **1** a cake; **2** a bannock; *Cf* **bonnach**

breacan, *gen* **breacain,** *pl* **breacain** *&* **breacanan** *nm* **1** (*trad*) a plaid, *Cf* **fèile 1**; **2** tartan cloth, **pìos breacain** a piece of tartan, (*song*) **soraidh leis a' bhreacan ùr** farewell to the fair tartan plaid; **3** a variegated pattern, **bha am fearann na bhreacan de fhraoch 's de raineach** the land was a patchwork of heather and bracken

breacanach *adj* tartan, of tartan, **aodach breacanach** tartan cloth, tartan clothing

breac-bhallach *adj* freckled

brèagha *adj* fine, lovely, beautiful, **là brèagha** a lovely/beautiful day, (*Sc*) a braw day, **sìde bhrèagha** fine/grand weather, **àite brèagha** a fine/bonny/lovely place, **nighean bhrèagha** a pretty/bonny/beautiful girl, *Cf* **àlainn, bòidheach, grinn 1** *&* **2**

brèaghachadh, brèaghachaidh, brèaghachaidhean *nm* **1** (*the act of*) embellishing, beautifying; **2** embellishment, an embellishment, *Cf* **sgeadachadh 2**

brèaghaich *vt, pres part* **a' brèaghachadh,** beautify, embellish, *Cf* **maisich 1, sgeadaich 1, sgèimhich**

Breatannach, *gen* *&* *pl* **Breatannaich** *nm* a British person, (*modern &* *hist*) a Briton, *also as adj* **Breatannach** British

brèid, brèide, brèidean *nm* 1 (*trad*) a kerchief worn formerly by married women; 2 a patch, **cuir brèid air seann bhriogais** put a patch on an old pair of trousers, *Cf* **tuthag**; 3 a cloth, (*Sc*) a clout, **brèid-shoithichean** a dish-cloth, *Cf* **clobhd, clùd 2**

breige, breige, breigichean *nf* a brick

brèige *adj* 1 false, deceitful, **leannan brèige** a deceitful lover, *Cf* **fallsa, meallta(ch)**; 2 false (*ie artificial*), **fear-brèige** *m* a puppet, **gruag-bhrèige** *f* a wig, *Cf* **fuadain**

breigire, breigire, breigirean *nm* a bricklayer

breisleach, *gen* **breislich** *nm* 1 confusion, **chuir am fuaim mòr am breisleach mi** the great noise confused me, *Cf* **buaireas 1, bruaillean**; 2 delirium

breisleachadh, *gen* **breisleachaidh** *nm* (*the act of*) confusing, raving &*c* (*see* **breislich** *v*)

breisleachail *adj* delirious, raving

breislich *vti, pres part* **a' breisleachadh,** 1 (*vt*) confuse, cause to be confused; 2 (*vi*) rave, talk irrationally, **bha i a' breisleachadh na cadal** she was raving/delirious in her sleep

breith[1], *nf invar* birth, a birth, **o là mo bhreith** since the day of my birth, **co-là-breith** a birthday (*Cf* **ceann-bliadhna**)

breith[2] *nf invar* a judgement, a decision, (*law*) a sentence, *usu in expr* **thoir** *v* **breith** pass judgement/sentence, give a decision, *Cf* **binn** *n*

breitheamh *see* **britheamh**

breithneachadh, *gen* **breithneachaidh** *nm* (*the act of*) judging &c (*see senses of* **breithnich** *v*)

breithnich *vti, pres part* **a' breithneachadh,** judge, assess, appraise

breug, brèige, breugan *nf* 1 a lie, **innis** *v* **breug** & **dèan** *v* **breug** lie, tell a lie; 2 *as excl* **breugan!** (*not necessarily in serious context*), **nach eil thu a' streap ris an dà fhichead? Breugan!** aren't you're getting on for forty? that's not true!, Rubbish!, Nonsense!

breugach *adj* lying, false, **faclan/briathran breugach** lying words, **duine breugach** a lying/mendacious man

breugaire, breugaire, breugairean *nm* a liar

breug-riochd, breug-riochda, breug-riochdan *nm* 1 disguise, a disguise; 2 camouflage

breun *adj* 1 putrid, corrupt, *Cf* **coirbte**; 2 filthy, disgusting, vile, *Cf* **grànda, sgreamhail, sgreataidh**

briathar, briathair, briathran *nm* 1 (*language*) a term, **is e 'sgaoileadh-cumhachd' am briathar a th' againn air 'devolution'** 'sgaoileadh-cumhachd' is the term we have/use for 'devolution', **briathran**

teicneolach technical terms; **2** *esp in pl*, words, statements, pronouncements, **briathran amaideach** foolish words/statements, **briathran ciallach** sensible words/statements, **cha chreid mi briathran luchd-poileataics** I don't believe politicians' words/statements, I don't believe what politicians say

briathrach *adj* wordy, verbose, *Cf* **faclach**

briathrachas, *gen* **briathrachais** *nm* **1** verbosity; **2** terminology

brìb *vt, pres part* **a' brìbeadh**, bribe

brìb, *gen* **brìbe**, *pl* **brìbean** & **brìbeachan** *nf* a bribe

brìbeadh, *gen* **brìbidh** *nm* (*the act of*) bribing

brìgh & **brìogh** *nf invar* **1** meaning, sense, (*dictionary title*) **Brìgh nam Facal** the Meaning/Sense of Words, *Cf* **ciall 3**, **seagh**; **2** virtue, quality, substance, essence of anything, **leabhar gun bhrìgh** a book without substance, **brìgh na feallsanachd aige** the essence of his philosophy; **3** (*plants, fruit &c*) pith, sap, juice, *Cf* **sùgh**; **4** strength, energy, **bha mi gun bhrìgh an dèidh na tubaiste** I had no strength/energy after the accident, *Cf* **lùth 3**, **neart**, **spionnadh**; **5** *prep* **do bhrìgh** because of, on account of, **do bhrìgh sin** because of that, for that reason, *Cf* **a chionn**, **sgàth 3**

brìghmhor & **brìoghmhor** *adj* **1** sappy, juicy, pithy, full of sap or juice or pith, *Cf* **smiorach**, **sùghmhor**; **2** energetic, zestful, full of zest or energy, *Cf* **lùthmhor 3**

brìodail *vt, pres part* **a' brìodal**, **1** caress, *Cf* **cnèadaich**; **2** flatter; **3** court, woo, *Cf* **dèan suirghe** (*see* **suirghe**)

brìodal, *gen* **brìodail** *nm* **1** (*the act of*) caressing &c (*see senses of* **brìodail** *v*); **2** endearments; **3** flattery, *Cf* **miodal**, **sodal**; **4** courtship, courting, wooing, *Cf* **leannanachd**, **suirghe**

briogais, **briogais**, **briogaisean** *nf* trousers, a pair of trousers, (*Sc*) breeks, (*song*) **chuir e bhriogais ghlas an gèill** he made the grey trousers compulsory, *Cf* **triubhas**

brìogh, **brìoghmhor** *see* **brìgh**, **brìghmhor**

briosgaid, **briosgaide**, **briosgaidean** *nf* a biscuit

brisg *adj* **1** crisp; **2** brittle

bris(t) *vti, pres part* **a' bris(t)eadh**, **1** break, smash, (*vi*) **bhris an uinneag** the window broke, (*vt*) **bhris i an lagh/an gealladh/an t-uaireadair** she broke the law/the promise/the watch, **brisidh an aimsir a-màireach** the weather will break tomorrow, **bhris iad a-mach às a' phrìosan** they broke out of prison, **brisidh e mo chridhe** it will break my heart, *Cf* **smuais**, **smùid** *v* **2**; **2** (*contract &c*) breach

briste *adj* broken, smashed, **tha an uinneag/mo chridhe briste** the window/my heart is broken

bris(t)eadh, *gen* **bris(t)idh** *nm* 1 (*the act of*) breaking, smashing, breaching; 2 bankruptcy; 3 (*of contract, conditions &c*) a breach; 4 *in expr* (*hist*) **Briseadh na h-Eaglaise** the Disruption

bris(t)eadh-cridhe, bris(t)idh-cridhe, bris(t)idhean-cridhe *nm* heart-break, a cause of heartbreak, (*poem*) **nist tha mi a' faicinn nad shùilean briseadh-cridhe na cùise** (Meg Bateman) now I see in your eyes the heart-break of the matter

bris(t)eadh-dùil, bris(t)idh-dùil, bris(t)idhean-dùil *nm* disappointment, a (cause of) disappointment, **is e bristeadh-dùil a bh' ann an toradh an taghaidh dha** the result/outcome of the election was a disappointment to/for him

bris(t)eadh-là, bris(t)idh-là, bris(t)idhean-là (*also* **bris(t)eadh an là**) *nm* daybreak, dawn, *Cf* **camhanach**

britheamh & **breitheamh**, *gen* **britheimh**, *pl* **britheamhan** *nm* a judge, **tha e na bhritheamh ann an Cùirt an t-Seisein/aig a' Mhòd Nàiseanta** he is a Judge in the Court of Session/at the National Mod

broc, *gen* & *pl* **bruic** *nm* a badger

brochan, *gen* & *pl* **brochain** *nm* porridge, gruel, (*song*) **brochan lom, tana lom, brochan lom sùghain** plain porridge thin and plain, plain sowans porridge, *Cf* **lite**

brod *vt*, *pres part* **a' brodadh**, 1 goad, drive on (*stock &c*), *Cf* **greas 2, iomain** *v* 1; 2 stimulate, encourage, stir up, *Cf* **brosnaich, spreig, stuig**

brod, bruid, brodan *nm* 1 (*a stick used as*) a goad, a prod, *Cf* **bioran**; 2 the best part of anything, the best example of anything, **brod a' bharra** the best part/the pick of the crop, **brod na croite** the best of crofts, an excellent croft, *Cf* **smior 2** & *opposite* **diù**

brodadh, *gen* **brodaidh** *nm* 1 (*the act of*) goading, driving &c (*see senses of* **brod** *v*); 2 (*also* **fèin-bhrodadh**) masturbation

bròg, bròige, brògan *nf* a shoe, a boot (*not a Wellington, Cf* **bòtann**), **bròg aotrom** a light shoe, **bròg-mhòr** *or* **bròg throm** a (*stout*) boot, **brògan ball-coise** football boots, **brògan tacaideach** nailed boots, (*Sc*) tackety boots, **bròg-eich** a horse-shoe (*Cf more trad* **crudha**), *Cf* **bòtann**

broilleach, *gen* **broillich**, *pl* **broilleachan** & **broillichean** *nm* 1 (*of male or female*) a breast, a bosom, (*song*) **cìochan corrach 's iad glè-gheal ann am broilleach na lèine** pointed breasts, and they so white, in the bosom of the shirt, *Cf* **com 1, uchd 1**; 2 a chest, the chest area, *Cf* **cliabh 4**

broinn, *dat of* **brù** (*see below*) *used as a nom*, *nf* 1 a belly, a womb, *Cf* **balg 1, machlag, maodal**; 2 the interior (*esp of a building*), *esp in exprs* **am broinn** in, inside, within, *and* **na** (&c) **b(h)roinn** inwards, in, **bha amar-snàimh am broinn an taighe** there was a swimming pool inside/within the house, **thuit am mullach na bhroinn** the roof fell in, *Cf* **taobh a-staigh** (*see* **taobh 1**)

bròn, *gen* **bròin** *nm* 1 sadness, sorrow, **adhbhar mo bhròin** the cause of/reason for my sadness, **tha mi fo bhròn** I am sorrowful/sad, *Cf* **mulad**; 2 mourning, **tha an teaghlach ri bròn** the family is in mourning, *Cf* **caoidh**

brònach *adj* sad, sorrowful, miserable, **òrain bhrònach** sad songs, **tha mi muladach brònach** I'm sad and miserable, *Cf* **dubhach 1, muladach, truagh 2, tùrsach**

brosnachadh, *gen* **brosnachaidh** *nm* 1 (*the act of*) encouraging &c (*see senses of* **brosnaich** *v*); 2 encouragement, stimulus, **feumaidh e brosnachadh mus dèan e a dhìcheall** he needs encouragement before he'll do his best, *Cf* **misneachadh 2**; 3 incitement, exhortation, (*trad*) **brosnachadh catha** incitement to battle, *Cf* **earalachadh 2**; 4 (*trad*) *the name of a class of martial bagpipe music*

brosnachail *adj* encouraging, **fear-teagaisg brosnachail** an encouraging teacher, *Cf* **misneachail 3**

brosnaich *vt*, *pres part* **a' brosnachadh**, encourage, urge on, arouse, inspire, *Cf* **brod** *v*, **misnich 2, spreig, stuig**

brot, brota, brotan *nm* broth, soup, *Cf trad* **eanraich**

broth, brotha, brothan *nm* a rash

brù, *gen* **bronn** *&* **broinne**, *dat* **broinn**, *pl* **brùthan** *nf* 1 a womb, **leanabh na broinn** a baby/child in her womb, *Cf* **broinn 1, machlag**; 2 a belly, **fhuair mi làn mo bhronn de bhiadh** I got a bellyful of food, *Cf* **balg 1, maodal, stamag**; 3 a bulge, **tha brù air a' bhalla** there's a bulge in the wall, the wall is bulging; 4 *see* **broinn**

bruach, bruaich, bruaichean *nf* a bank (*of a river, loch &c*), **bruach an lòin** the bank of the pond

bruadair *vi*, *pres part* **a' bruadar** & **a' bruadarachd**, dream, **bha mi a' bruadar ort a-raoir** I dreamt about you last night

bruadar, bruadair, bruadaran *nm* 1 (*the act of*) dreaming, **tha thu ri bruadar!** you're dreaming!; 2 a dream, *Cf* **aisling**

bruaillean, *gen* **bruaillein** *nm* trouble, confusion, upset (*esp moral &/or emotional*), *Cf* **breisleach 1, buaireas 1**

brùchd *vi*, *pres part* **a' brùchdadh**, 1 belch, *Cf* **rùchd** *v* 2; 2 burst out, **bhrùchd iad a-mach às an taigh-dhealbh** they burst out/came pouring out of the cinema, **bhrùchd na h-òganan ùra a-mach às an talamh** the new shoots burst out of the ground

brùchd, brùchda, brùchdan *nm* a belch, *Cf* **rùchd** *n* 2

brùchdadh, *gen* **brùchdaidh** *nm* (*the act of*) belching &c (*see senses of* **brùchd** *v*)

brù-dhearg, brù-dheirge, brù-dheargan *nm* a robin

bruich *vt, pres part* **a' bruich,** cook, boil (*esp food*), *Cf* **deasaich biadh** (*see* **biadh** 1)

bruich *nf invar* (*the act of*) boiling, cooking

bruich *adj* cooked, boiled

bruicheil *adj* (*of weather*) sultry, *Cf* **bruthainneach**

brùid, brùide, brùidean *nm* 1 (*trad*) a brute beast; 2 (*esp as term of abuse or condemnation*) a brute, a brutal person; *Cf* **biast** 1 & 2

brùidealachd *nf invar* brutality

brùideil *adj* (*person, act* &c) brutal

bruidhinn *vti, pres part* **a' bruidhinn,** speak, talk, converse, **bruidhinn ri cuideigin** talk to/converse with someone, **bruidhinn ri chèile** talk together/to each other, **bha sinn a' bruidhinn Frangais/ Gàidhlig** we were speaking French/Gaelic, **a' bruidhinn às beul a chèile** speaking with one voice/unanimously, *Cf less usu* **labhair**

bruidhinn, *gen* **bruidhne** *nf* 1 (*the act of*) speaking, talking, conversing; 2 talk, **aig deireadh na bruidhne** when all is said and done

bruidhneach *adj* talkative, fond of talking, chatty, *Cf* **còmhraideach**

bruis, bruise, bruisean *nf* a brush (*Cf more trad* **sguab** *n* 1), **bruis-aodaich** a clothes brush, **bruis-chinn** & **bruis-fhuilt,** a hair brush, **bruis-fhiaclan** a tooth brush, **bruis-pheant** a paint brush

bruisig *vt, pres part* **a' bruisigeadh,** brush, **bhruisig i a falt** she brushed her hair, *Cf more trad* **sguab** *v*

bruisigeadh, *gen* **bruisigidh** *nm* (*the act of*) brushing

brùite *adj* 1 bruised, crushed, broken, **tha mo chridhe briste brùite** my heart is broken and bruised; 2 oppressed, **sluagh brùite** an oppressed/downtrodden people

brùth *vt, pres part* **a' bruthadh,** 1 bruise; 2 push (*roughly*), shove, thrust, *Cf* **put** *v* 1, **sàth** 2, **spàrr** *v*

bruthach, bruthaich, bruthaichean *nmf* 1 a slope, a hillside, (*Sc*) a brae, **a' ruith ris a' bhruthaich** running uphill/against the slope/up the brae, **a' ruith leis a' bhruthaich** running downhill/with the slope/ down the brae, *Cf* **aodann** 2, **leathad, leitir, ruighe** 2; 2 a bank (*of a river, loch* &c), *Cf* **bruach**

bruthadh, *gen* **bruthaidh** *nm* 1 (*the act of*) bruising, pushing &c (*see senses of* **brùth** *v*); 2 (*esp science*) pressure, **bruthadh fala** blood pressure, **bruthadh an aile** atmospheric pressure

bruthadh an àile atmospheric pressure

bruthainneach *adj* (*of weather*) sultry, *Cf* **bruicheil**

bu *see* **is** *v*

buachaille, buachaille, buachaillean *nm* a cowherd, a herdsman, (*occas*) a shepherd, (*Sc*) a herd, (*placename*) **Buachaille Eite Mòr** the Big Herdsman of Etive

buachailleachd *nf invar* (*the act of*) herding or tending cattle

buachaillich *vt, pres part* **a' buachailleachd**, herd *or* tend cattle, (*song*) **na glinn san robh mi buachailleachd** the glens where I herded cattle

buachar, *gen* **buachair** *nm* cow-dung, *Cf* **innear**

buadh, buaidh, buadhan *nf* 1 a quality, a property, an attribute; a talent, an accomplishment, **buadhan nàdarra(ch)** natural qualities, **buadhan inntinn** intellectual/mental qualities *or* accomplishments, *Cf* **comas, tàlann; 2** virtue, goodness, excellence (*ie having ability to raise spirits or to nourish*) **tha buadh air an uisge-bheatha/air a' bhainne** whisky/milk has virtue/goodness in it, *Cf* **brìgh 2**

buadhair, buadhair, buadhairean *nm* (*gram*) an adjective

buadhmhor *adj* 1 effective, successful, *Cf* **èifeachdach; 2** victorious

buaic, buaice, buaicean *nf* a wick (*of lamp &c*), *Cf* **siobhag**

buaidh, buaidhe, buaidhean *nf* 1 victory, a victory, **bheir sinn buaidh orra** we will gain victory over them/defeat them; 2 success, **fhuair na h-iomairtean aige buaidh aig deireadh an là** his efforts gained success/were successful at the end of the day, *Cf* **soirbhich; 3** influence, **fo bhuaidh duine nimheil** under the influence of a venomous/pernicious man, *Cf* **cumhachd 1; 4** an effect, a consequence of something, **thoir** *v* **buaidh air** affect, have an effect on, **buaidh an taigh-ghlainne** the greenhouse effect, *Cf* **buil 1, èifeachd, toradh 2**

buail *vt, pres part* **a' bualadh, 1** hit, strike, **bha am balach bochd ga bhualadh leis na gillean mòra** the poor laddie was being hit by the big boys, **bhuail an t-itealan mullach an togalaich** the plane struck the top/roof of the building; 2 (*expr almost random appearance of something or someone*) **bhuail e a-steach do thaigh Sheumais** he dropped by at/dropped in to Seumas's house, **bhuail e na cheann pòg a thoirt dhi** it came into his head/occurred to him to give her a kiss

buaile, buaile, buailtean *nf* a sheep-fold, a cattle-fold, *Cf* **crò 1**

buailteach *adj* liable, apt, inclined, prone (**do** to), **buailteach do ghàire/do dh'fheirg** prone to laughter/to anger, **buailteach do chaochladh** prone/liable to change, **tha e buailteach airgead a chosg** he is liable to spend/waste money; 2 *also with prep* **air, tha sinn buailteach air fàs sgìth** we're apt to get tired; 3 *with conj* **gun, bha an t-sìde cheudna buailteach gun leanadh i** the same weather was liable/likely to continue; *Cf* **dual(t)ach**

buain *vt, pres part* **a' buain**, reap, cut, harvest (*crops*), (*prov*) **ge b' e nach cuir san là fhuar, cha bhuain san là theth** the man who (*lit* whoever) doesn't sow on the cold day will not reap/harvest on the hot day

buain, *gen* **buana** *nf* reaping, cutting, harvesting of crops, **buain an eòrna/an arbhair** the barley/the corn harvest, *Cf* **foghar 1**

buair *vt, pres part* **a' buaireadh**, 1 disturb, upset, trouble (*person, atmosphere &c*), **bhuair thu sìth nam beann** you have disturbed the peace of the mountains, **bhuair an droch naidheachd mi gu mòr** the bad news troubled/upset me greatly, **bhuair am fìon a smaointean** the wine troubled her thoughts; 2 tempt, **bhuair an Donas mi** the Evil One tempted me, *Cf* **meall** *v* 3, **tàlaidh 2**

buaireadair, buaireadair, buaireadaran *nm* a troublemaker

buaireadh, buairidh, buairidhean *nm* 1 (*the act of*) disturbing, tempting &c (*see senses of* **buair** *v*); 2 temptation, a temptation

buaireas, buaireis, buaireasan *nm* 1 trouble, confusion, anxiety, **chuir e buaireas ann an cridhe òg** he introduced (*moral*) confusion into a young heart, *Cf* **breisleach 1, bruaillean;** 2 turbulence, disorder, *Cf* **aimhreit 1**

buaireasach *adj* troublesome, annoying, disturbing, **leanabh buaireasach** a troublesome child, **neach buaireasach** a disruptive person/individual, **naidheachd bhuaireasach** disturbing news, *Cf* **aimhreiteach, draghail**

bualadh, *gen* **bualaidh** *nm* 1 (*the act of*) striking, hitting (*see senses of* **buail** *v*) **aig àm bualadh nan dòrn** at the time of fist blows/of the striking of fists; 2 a blow, *Cf* **beum, buille 1**

buan *adj* lasting, long-lasting, durable, **stuth buan** durable stuff/material, **bodach buan** a long-lived/tough old man, (*song*) **an ataireachd bhuan** the everlasting swell of the sea, *Cf* **maireannach**

buannachadh, *gen* **buannachaidh** *nm* (*the act of*) winning (*see senses of* **buannaich** *v*)

buannachd, buannachd, buannachdan *nf* 1 profit, gain, advantage, **là/obair gun bhuannachd** a fruitless day/task, *Cf* **tairbhe;** 2 (*fin*) profit, **chan eil an gnothach a' cosnadh buannachd sam bith** the business isn't making/earning any profit, (*prov*) **cha dèanar buannachd gun chall** profit is never made without some loss, *Cf less trad* **prothaid**

buannaich *vi, pres part* **a' buannachadh, 1** (*vi*) win, succeed, (*in race, battle, competition &c*), *Cf* **buinnig; 2** (*vt*) win, gain, acquire, **bhuannaich i bonn òir** she won a gold medal, **bhuannaich iad cliù** they won fame; **3** (*vt*) reach, (*Sc*) win to, **bhuannaich sinn am baile am beul na h-oidhche** we made it to/reached the village at dusk; *Cf* **buidhinn, coisinn 2**

buar, *gen & pl* **buair** *nm* a herd (*esp of cattle*), *Cf* **treud 1**

bucaid, bucaide, bucaidean *nf* **1** a bucket, *Cf* **peile** *& more trad* **cuinneag, cuman; 2** a dustbin, **cuir sa bhucaid e!** bin it!

bucas, *gen & pl* **bucais** *nm* a box, *Cf* **bocsa 1**

bugair, bugaire, bugairean *nm* (*fam, vulg*) a bugger, *usu in excls, eg* **na bugairean!** the buggers! **na bugair rudan!** the bloody things!

buideal *see* **botal**

buidhe *adj* **1** yellow, **buidhe-ruadh** auburn; **2** (*trad*) lucky, fortunate, *Cf more usu* **fortanach, sealbhach 1**

buidheach *adj* grateful, thankful, **tha mi buidheach airson ur cuideachadh** I am grateful for your help, **bi buidheach do do phàrantan!** be grateful to your parents!, *Cf* **taingeil**

buidheachas, *gen* **buidheachais** *nm* gratitude, *Cf* **taing 1**

buidheagan, *gen & pl* **buidheagain** *nf* an egg-yolk, the yolk of an egg

buidheann, buidhne, buidhnean *nmf* **1** a group, a band, a party (*of people*), a company (*of soldiers*), **buidheann (de) luchd-turais** a group/party of tourists, **buidheann-cluich(e)** a playgroup (*Cf* **cròileagan**), **buidheann-obrach** a working party, **buidheann-rannsachaidh** a research group/team, **buidheann-strì** a pressure group, *Cf* **còmhlan, cuideachd** *n* **3; 2** (*business*) a firm, a company, *Cf* **companaidh**

buidhinn *vti, pres part* **a' buidhinn**, win, *Cf similarly used* **buannaich**

buidhre *nf invar* (*abstr noun corres to* **bodhar**) deafness

buidseach, buidsich, buidsichean *nmf* a wizard, a sorcerer, a witch, a sorceress, **bana-bhuidseach** *f* a witch, a sorceress, *Cf* **draoidh 2**

bùidsear, bùidseir, bùidsearan *nm* **1** a butcher, *Cf more trad* **feòladair; 2** a butcher, someone thought of as murderous or brutal, (*hist*) **Am Bùidsear** 'Butcher' Cumberland, the Duke of Cumberland (*Commander of the Government forces in 1745–6*)

buige *nf invar* (*abstr noun corres to* **bog** *adj*) **1** softness (*phys, & of character &c*); **2** moistness; **3** humidity; **4** limpness

buil, *gen* **buile** *nf* **1** a consequence, a result, an effect, (*saying*) **an rud a nithear gu ceart, chithear a bhuil** when a thing is done properly the effect/result of it will be visible, *Cf* **buaidh 4, èifeachd, toradh 2; 2** completion, a conclusion, *esp in expr* **thoir** *v* **gu buil** complete, bring to a conclusion, achieve, implement, realise, **thoir pròiseact gu buil** complete a project, **cha tug thu càil gu buil a-riamh!** you never achieved anything! *or* you never saw anything through!, *Cf* **crìoch 1**

buileach *adj used as adv, also* **gu buileach** *adv,* completely, quite, entirely, **tha mi buileach cinnteach** I am quite sure (*Cf* **làn** *adj* 2), **chan eil i buileach deiseil** she's not quite ready, **gu buileach eadar-dhealaichte** completely/totally different, **nì mi an gnothach air gu buileach** I'll beat him completely, I'll get the better of him entirely, *Cf* **tur 2, uile gu lèir** (*see* **uile 4**)

buileann, builinn, buileannan *nf* a loaf (*of bread, sugar &c*), *Cf* **lof**

builgean, builgein, builgeanan *nf* a bubble

builgeanach *adj* bubbly, **'s toigh leam siaimpèan a chionn 's gu bheil e builgeanach** I like champagne because it's bubbly

builich *vt, pres part* **a' buileachadh**, bestow (**air** upon)

buille, buille, *pl* **buillean** *&* **builleannan** *nf* 1 a blow, a stroke, **buille chuip** a whip stroke, a stroke with a whip, *Cf* **beum, bualadh 2, stràc 1**; 2 emphasis, stress, importance, **bidh a' chompanaidh a' cur buille shònraichte air pongalachd** the company will place particular stress/importance on punctuality, *Cf* **cudthrom 2**; 3 (*speech, music, rhythm*) stress, a stress, a beat, **buille cridhe** a heartbeat, **ceithir buillean sa char** four beats to the bar, **anns an fhacal 'caraid' thig a' bhuille air a' chiad lide** in the word 'caraid' the stress comes on the first syllable; 4 (*sport*) a stroke

buin *vi, pres part* **a' buntainn**, 1 belong (**do & ri** to), **am buin e dhutsa?** does it belong to you (*emph*)? **às bith cò dha a bhuineas e** whoever it belongs to, *Cf* **bi aig** (*see* **aig 2**), **is le** (*see* **le 4**); 2 be related to, **buinidh iad do Chlann Dhòmhnaill** they belong to Clan Donald, they are MacDonalds, *Cf* **càirdeach**; 3 interfere with, meddle with, have to do with, (*prov*) **an rud nach buin dhut, na buin dha** do not interfere with something that doesn't concern you, *also with prep* **ri**, *Cf* **bean** *v* 1, **gnothach 4**

buinneach, *gen* **buinnich** *nf, with the art,* **a' bhuinneach** diarrhoea, *Cf* **sgàird, spùt 3**

buinnig *&* **buintig,** *vi, pres part* **a' buintig**, win, (*fam, calque*) **a bheil thu a' buintig?** are you winning/getting there?

buinteanas, buntainneas *&* **buntanas,** *gen* **buinteanais** *nm* link(s), connection(s) *esp with a particular place,* **bha buinteanas aige ris an Eilean Sgitheanach** he had Skye connections, he had (family) links with Skye

buirbe *nf invar* (*abstr noun corres to* **borb**), barbarity, wildness, savageness, uncouthness

bùirdeasach *adj* bourgeois

bumailear, bumaileir, bumailearan *nm* (*fam*) a fool, a blockhead, an oaf, an eejit, a no-user, *Cf* **stalcaire, ùmaidh**

bun, *gen* **buna** & **buin,** *pl* **buin** & **bunan** *nm* **1** the base, bottom or foot of anything, **bun na beinne** the foot of the mountain, *Cf* **bonn 1**; **2** *esp in expr* **bun-os-cionn** upside down, topsy-turvy, (*Sc*) tapsalteerie, **cuir** *v* **bun-os-cionn** turn upside down, upend, **bha seòmar mo mhic bun-os-cionn** my son's room was topsy-turvy/in a shambles (*Cf* **bùrach**), *Cf* **tro 2**; **3** a root, a source or an origin of something, **bun na craoibhe** the root (*or* the foot *or* the trunk) of the tree, **bun an uilc** the root/source of evil (*Cf* **freumh**), **bun-dealain** an electric socket, a power point, **bun-stuth** *m* basic/raw material(s); **4** (*topog*) mouth of a river or stream, (*placename*) **Bun Abha** Bonawe, the mouth of the River Awe, *Cf* **beul 1**

bunait, bunaite, bunaitean *nmf* the basis or foundation of anything (*esp abstr things*), **bunait a' chreideimh/na feallsanachd** the foundation/the fundamentals of religion/of philosophy, *Cf* **stèidh 2**, & *more con* **bonn 1**

bunai(l)teach *adj* **1** stable, steady, well founded, *Cf* **seasmhach 1**; **2** fundamental, radical, *Cf less usu* **bunasach 1**; **3** (*relig*) fundamentalist

bunasach *adj* **1** radical, fundamental, *Cf more usu* **bunaiteach 2**; **2** *esp in gram*, **an tuiseal bunasach** *the case in Gaelic corres to the nom <u>and</u> the acc in Eng, Latin &c*, the radical case

bun-os-cionn *see* **bun 2**

bun-sgoil, bun-sgoile, bun-sgoiltean *nf* a primary school

buntainn, *gen* **buntainne** *nm* (*the act of*) belonging, interfering with &c (*see senses of* **buin** *v*)

buntanas *see* **buinteanas**

buntàta *nm invar, sing* & *coll,* a potato, potatoes, **buntàta pronn** mashed potato(es)

bùrach, *gen* **bùraich** *nm* a mess, (*Sc*) a guddle, (*Highland Eng*) a b(o)urach, **an dèidh na h-imriche bha a h-uile càil ann am bùrach** after the flitting everything was in a mess/a guddle/a b(o)urach, *Cf* **bun 2, tro 2**

bùrn, *gen* **bùirn** *nm* water, *used by some speakers as alternative to* **uisge** *to refer to fresh running water, tap water &c, but not to salt water or rain,* (*prov*) **is tighe fuil na bùrn** blood is thicker than water, *Cf* **uisge 1**

burraidh, burraidh, burraidhean *nm* a fool, a blockhead, *Cf* **amadan, bumailear, ùmaidh**

bus[1], **bus**, **busaichean** *nm* a bus, **àite-stad bus** a bus-stop, **bha am bus làn** the bus was full, **tha am bus gun tighinn fhathast** the bus hasn't come/arrived yet

bus[2], **buis**, **busan** *nm* 1 (*derog*) a mouth, *Cf* **beul 1**, *&* (*fam*) **cab**, **gob 3**; 2 a grimace, a pout (*of anger, pique &c*), **chuireadh i bus oirre an uair a chàineadh a màthair i** she would grimace/pout when her mother gave her a row, *Cf* **braoisg**; 3 *in expr* (*fam*) **a-mach air a bhus le** ... overflowing with ..., *Cf* **cuir thairis** (*see* **thairis 1**)

bùth, *gen* **bùtha**, *pl* **bùthan**, **bùithean** *&* **bùithtean** *nmf* a shop, **bùth-èisg** a fish shop, **bùth-chungaidhean** a chemist's shop, a pharmacy, **bùth chiùird** a craft shop

C

cab, *gen & pl* **caib** *nm* (*fam*) a mouth, a gob, **duin do chab!** shut your mouth/your gob! *Cf* **beul 1** *&* (*fam*) **bus**² **1**, **gob 3**

cabach *adj* (*fam*) talkative, garrulous, apt to talk too much, *Cf* **beulach 1**, **gobach**

cabadaich, *gen* **cabadaiche** *nf* **1** chatter, chattering, (*Sc*) blether, *Cf* **cabaireachd**, **goileam**; **2** *used as a pres part*, **a' cabadaich** chattering, blethering

cabaireachd *nf invar, same senses as* **cabadaich**

càball, càbaill, càballan *nm* cable, a cable

cabar, *gen & pl* **cabair** *nm* **1** an antler, *esp in phrase* **cabair fèidh** a deer's antlers, *also* (*trad*) *a war cry of the Mackenzies and the name of a pipe tune*, *Cf* **crò(i)c**; **2** a pole, *esp* a rafter, **cabar-droma** (*also* **maide-droma**) a ridge pole (*of a house*); **3** (*Highland Games*) a caber

cabhag, *gen* **cabhaig** *nf* **1** haste, hurry, **na cùm air ais sinn, tha cabhag oirnn!** don't keep us back, we're in a hurry! **dèan** *v* **cabhag** hurry up, get a move on, **ann an cabhaig** in a hurry, *Cf less usu* **deann 2**; **2** *in expr* **cuir** *v* **cabhag air cuideigin** press, hurry someone, *Cf* **greas 2**

cabhagach *adj* **1** (*of person*) hurried, in a hurry; **2** (*of actions &c*) hurried, hasty; **3** urgent, pressing

cabhlach, cabhlaich, cabhlaichean *nm* a fleet (*trad of boats or ships, now also of vehicles, planes &c*), a navy, *Cf less usu* **loingeas 2**

cabhsair, cabhsair, cabhsairean *nm* a pavement, a causeway, (*Sc*) a causey

cabstair, cabstair, cabstairean *nm* a (*horse's*) bit

cac *vi, pres part* **a' cac** *&* **a' cacadh**, defecate

cac, *gen* **caca** *nm* **1** excrement; **2** (*fam, vulg*) crap, shit, cack, (*derog of person, action, statement &c*) **tòrr caca** a load of crap

caca *adj* (*fam*) nasty, unpleasant, 'yukky'

cacadh, *gen* **cacaidh** *nm* **1** (*the act of*) defecating; **2** defecation

càch, *gen* **càich** *&* **chàich** *pron* (*used of persons*) **1** the rest, others, other people, the others, **rinn i na b' fheàrr na càch** she did better than the rest/the others, **coltach ri càch** like the rest, like everybody else; **2** *in expr* **càch-a-chèile** each other, **a' faicinn càch-a-chèile** seeing each other, *Cf* **cèile 2**

cadal, *gen* **cadail** *nm* **1** (*the act of*) sleeping; **2** sleep, **dèan** *v* **cadal** sleep, go to sleep, **rach** *v* **a chadal** go to bed, **bha mi nam chadal/bha sinn nar cadal** I was/we were asleep/sleeping, **norrag** *f* **chadail** a wink of sleep, a nap, a snooze, **cha d'fhuair mi norrag chadail a-raoir** I didn't get a wink of sleep last night, **oidhche gun chadal** a sleepless night, **cadal sàmhach** peaceful sleep, **tha an cadal orm** I'm sleepy, **cadal math dhut!** sleep well!, **cadal-geamhraidh** hibernation, *Cf* **dùsal**, **norrag**, **suain** *n*; 3 *also in expr* **an cadal-deilgneach** pins and needles

cadalach *adj* sleepy

cafaidh, cafaidh, cafaidhean *nmf* a café

cagailt, cagailte, cagailtean *nf* a hearth, **na shuidhe ris a' chagailt** sitting beside the hearth/at the fireside, *Cf* **teallach**, **teinntean**

cagainn *vt, pres part* **a' cagnadh**, chew, gnaw, *Cf* **cnàmh** *v* 1, **creim** 2

cagair *vti, pres part* **a' cagar, a' cagarsaich** & **a' cagartaich**, whisper

cagar, cagair, cagairean *nm* 1 (*the act of*) whispering; 2 a whisper; 3 a secret, *Cf* **rùn** 5

cagnadh, *gen* **cagnaidh** *nm* (*the act of*) chewing, gnawing

caibe, caibe, caibeachan *nm* 1 a spade, *Cf more usu* **spaid**; 2 a mattock

caibeal, caibeil, caibealan *nm* a chapel

caibideil, caibideil, caibideilean *nmf* a chapter (*of book*), **caibideil a h-aon** chapter one

caidil *vi, pres part* **a' cadal**, sleep, **caidil gu math!** sleep well! *Cf* **dèan cadal** (*see* **cadal** 2)

càil, càile, càiltean *nf* (*trad*) desire, (*now esp for food*) appetite, an appetite, *also* **càil bidhe** (*lit* desire for food)

càil *nm invar* 1 a thing, **bha a h-uile càil troimh-chèile** everything was in a mess, *Cf* **dad** 1, **nì** *n* 1, **rud** 1, **sian** 3; 2 *with verb in neg* nothing, **chan eil càil againn ri dhèanamh** we've nothing to do, **cha robh càil ann** there was nothing there; 3 *in expr* **càil sam bith** anything, anything at all, **a bheil càil sa phreas? chan eil càil sam bith!** is there anything in the cupboard? there's nothing at all/not a thing! 4 *in expr* **càil a** (*for* **càil de**), any, *esp* **càil a dh'fhios** any information, knowledge, **a bheil càil a dh'fhios agad càit a bheil e?** have you any idea where he is? **chan eil càil a dh'fhios agam** I haven't the faintest idea/don't know anything about it

cailc, cailce, cailcean *nf* 1 (*the substance*) chalk; 2 (blackboard) chalk, a piece of (blackboard) chalk

caileag, caileige, caileagan *nf* 1 a (small) girl, a female child, (*Sc*) a lassie, *esp* **caileag bheag** a little girl, **an uair a bha mi nam chaileig (bhig) bha mi am bun-sgoil Phort-Rìgh** when I was a (little) girl I was at Portree Primary School; 2 (*a female up to the end of her teens approx*) a girl, (*Sc*) a lass, a lassie, **tha e daonnan an dèidh nan caileagan** he's always after/chasing the girls; *Cf* **clann-nighean**, **nighean**, **nìghneag**

cailin, cailin, cailinean *nf* (*trad*) a girl, a maid, (*song*) **mo chailin donn òg** my brown-haired young girl

caill *vti, pres part* **a' call, 1** lose, **chaill mi an t-uaireadair agam** I lost my watch, **chaill i a pàrantan ann an tubaist** she lost her parents in an accident, (*vi*) **chaill an sgioba ball-coise an-dè** the football team lost yesterday, (*fam*) **bha mi gus mo mhùn a chall leis cho èibhinn 's a bha e!** I was nearly wetting myself, he was so funny!; **2** miss, **chaill mi an trèana** I missed the train, **nach robh thu aig a' chèilidh? cha do chaill thu mòran!** weren't you at the ceilidh? you didn't miss much!

cailleach, cailliche, cailleachan *nf* **1** an old woman, (*Sc*) an old wifie; **2** (*not nec implying age*) a woman, a wifie, **bodach is cailleach nam faochagan** the guy/fellow and wifie who gather whelks, **cailleach nan cearc** the hen wife/wifie; **3** (*fam, of spouse*) **a' chailleach** the/my old woman; **4** a nun, *esp* **cailleach-dhubh**; **5** (*pej*) an old witch, an old hag; *Cf* **bodach**

cailleach-oidhche, caillich-oidhche, cailleachan-oidhche *nf* an owl, *Cf* **comhachag**

caime, caime, caimean *nf* curvature, a bend, a curve, *Cf* **lùb** *n* **1**

càin *vt, pres part* **a' càineadh, 1** scold, criticise, (*Sc*) give a row to, (*song*) **bhiodh m' athair 's mo mhàthair gam chàineadh gu bràth, nam pòsainn do leithid** my father and mother would be at me for evermore if I married the likes of you, *Cf* **cronaich, sàs 3; 2** slander

càin, *gen* **cànach** *&* **càine,** *pl* **càintean** *nf* taxation, tax, a tax, **leig** *v* **càin air an t-sluagh** tax the people/population, *Cf* **cìs**

cainb, *gen* **cainbe** *nf* **1** hemp, **lus-cainb** the cannabis plant; **2** canvas, *Cf less trad* **canabhas**

càineadh, *gen* **càinidh** *nm* **1** (*the act of*) scolding, criticising &c (*see senses of* **càin** *v*); **2** (verbal) abuse

caineal, *gen* **caineil** *nm* cinnamon

cainnt, cainnte, cainntean *nf* **1** speech, language (*in general & abstr sense*), **gun chainnt** not possessed of speech, unable to speak, **comas cainnte** the faculty of speech/language, the ability to speak, *Cf* **labhairt 1; 2** speech, language, tongue (*as used by a particular individual or group*), (*song*) **cainnt mo mhàthar, Gàidhlig Bharraigh** my mother tongue, the Gaelic of Barra (*Cf* **teanga 2, cànain, cànan**), (*song*) **bha mi eòlach air a cainnt** I was familiar with her speech/way of speaking, **droch cainnt** bad language, swearing, **dual-chainnt** (*also* **dualchainnt**) a dialect

caiptean, caiptein, caipteanan *nm* **1** (*of boat, plane, team &c*) a captain, a skipper, a master, *Cf* **sgiobair; 2** (*military rank*) a captain

càir *n see* **càrr**

càir *vt see* **càirich**

càirdeach *adj* related, kin (**do** to), **chan eil mi càirdeach dhut** I'm not related to you, *Cf* **buin** *v* **2**

càirdeas, *gen* **càirdeis** *nm* **1** family relationship, kinship, **càirdeas fala** blood relationship, **càirdeas pòsaidh** kinship by marriage (*Cf* **cleamhnas 1**); **2** friendship, ties of friendship, **an càirdeas eadar Alba is Canada** the ties between Scotland & Canada; *Cf* **dàimh 1**

càirdeil *adj* friendly

càirdineal, càirdineil, càirdinealan *nm* a Cardinal

càireas, *gen* **càireis** *nm* gum(s) (*ie of mouth*)

cairgein, *gen* **cairgein** *nm, also* **carraigean**, *gen* **carraigein** *nm*, edible seaweed, carrageen

càirich (*also* **càir**), *vt, pres part.* **a' càradh**, repair, mend, fix, (*Sc*) sort, **càirich do leabaidh** make your bed

cairt *also* **cart** *vt, pres part* **a' cartadh**, **1** tan (*leather*); **2** muck out, clean out (*byre &c*)

cairt[1], **cartach, cairtean** *nf* **1** card, **cairt-bhòrd** cardboard; **2** a card, **cairt Nollaig** a Christmas card, **cairt-chluiche** a playing card, **cairt-phuist** a postcard, **cairt-iasaid** & **cairt-creideis** a credit card; **3** a chart, **cairt-iùil** a sea-chart, a navigation chart; **4** (*hist &c*) a charter; **5** tree bark, *Cf* **rùsg**

cairt[2], **cartach, cairtean** *nf* a cart

cairteal, cairteil, cairtealan *nm* **1** a quarter (*usu for clock time*), **cairteal/ trì chairteil na h-uarach** a quarter/three quarters of an hour, **cairteal gu ceithir** a quarter to four, **cairteal an dèidh a deich** a quarter past ten, *Cf* **ceathramh**; **2** (*measure*) a quart

caisbheart, *gen* **caisbheirt** *nf* footwear

càise, càise, càisean *nmf* cheese, a cheese

caisead, *gen* **caiseid** *nm* steepness, a gradient

caisg *vti, pres part* **a' casgadh**, **1** (*vt*) prevent, stop, restrain, interrupt, staunch, *Cf* **bac** *v*, **bacadh 3**, **casg**, **stad** *n* **3**; **2** (*vi*) subside, abate, **chaisg an stoirm** the storm abated

Càisg, *gen* **Càisge** *nf, used with the art*, **a' Chàisg** Easter, **Diluain na Càisge** Easter Monday

caismeachd, caismeachd, caismeachdan *nf* **1** (*trad*) a call to arms, an alarm; **2** a march (*ie tune*), a martial song or piece of music; **3** (*the act of*) beating time, *also in expr* **cùm** *v* **caismeachd ri** keep time with

caisteal, caisteil, caistealan *nm* a castle

càite (*before a vowel* **càit**) *inter adv* where, **càit a bheil Iain? a bheil fios agad càit a bheil e?** where's Iain? do you know where he is?, *Note difference between* **càite** *and* **far a**, *eg* **an uair a gheibh mi a-mach càit a bheil e, thèid mi far a bheil e** when I find out where he is (*interrogative*), I'll go where he is (*non-interrogative*)

caith *vt, pres part* **a' caitheamh**, **1** *usu of clothing,* wear, wear out, (*trad wish or greeting – of new clothing*) **gum meal 's gun caith thu e** may you enjoy it and wear it, *Cf* **giùlain 2**; **2** (*of time*) spend, pass, (*song*) **chaith mi 'n oidhche cridheil coibhneil mar ri maighdeannan na h-àirigh** I spent the night in warm-hearted kindliness in the company of the sheiling maidens, *Cf* **seachad 2**; **3** (*esp of wealth, money*) waste, squander, consume, *Cf* **cosg** *v* **3**, **struidh**; **4** cast, throw, **fiodh air a chaitheamh don chladach** wood cast up onto the shore, *Cf* **tilg 1**

caitheadair, caitheadair, caitheadairean *nm* a consumer

caitheamh, *gen* **caitheimh** *nf* **1** (*the act of*) wearing, spending &c (*see senses of* **caith** *v*); **2** (*with the art*) **a' chaitheamh** tuberculosis, consumption; **3** (*business, fin &c*) consumption, **luchd-caitheimh** *m* consumers, **caitheamh ola** oil consumption

caithte *adj* **1** worn out, used up; **2** (*gram*) past, **an tràth caithte** the past tense

caith(t)each *adj* wasteful, extravagant, spendthrift, prodigal, *Cf* **struidheil**

Caitligeach, *gen & pl* **Caitligich** *nm* a Catholic, *also as adj* **Caitligeach** Catholic

càl, *gen & pl* **càil** *nm* cabbage, a cabbage, (*trad*) kail

cala(dh), cala(idh), calaidhean *nm* a harbour, *Cf* **acarsaid**, **port**[2]

càl-colaig, *gen & pl* **càil-cholaig** *nm* cauliflower, a cauliflower

calg, *gen* **cuilg** *nm* **1** a prickle, *Cf* **bior 3**, **dealg 1**; **2** a bristle, *Cf* **frioghan**

calg-d(h)ìreach *adv* directly, completely, *esp in expr* **calg-dhìreach an aghaidh** completely against, diametrically opposed to, dead against, **tha na pàrtaidhean calg-dhìreach an aghaidh a chèile** the parties are diametrically opposed to each other/in total disagreement, **tha mi calg-dhìreach na aghaidh** I am completely against him/it

call, *gen* **calla** *nm* **1** (*the act of*) losing, missing &c (*see senses of* **caill** *v*); **2** loss, a loss, (*book title*) **Call na h-Iolaire** The Loss of the Iolaire; **3** *in expr* **air chall** lost, **bha/chaidh sinn air chall** we were/got lost, *Cf* **seachran 2**; **4** a waste, **is e call a bh' ann** it was a waste, **call ùine/airgid** a waste of time/money, *Cf* **cosg** *n* **3**

calla & **callda** *adj* **1** tame; **2** domesticated

callachadh, *gen* **callachaidh** *nm* (*the act of*) taming, domesticating callaich, *vt, pres part* **a' callachadh**, 1 tame, *Cf* **ceannsaich 3**; 2 domesticate

callaid, callaide, callaidean *nf* 1 a hedge *Cf* **fàl 1**; 2 a fence, *Cf less trad* **feansa**

Callainn, *gen* Callainne *nf* (*trad*) *with art* New Year's Day, *see* **oidhche 2**

callda *see* calla

calltainn, *gen* calltainne *nm* (*bot*) hazel, **cnò challtainn** a hazelnut, *often in placenames as* cowden, colden

calma *adj* (*morally or phys*) stout, sturdy, robust, *Cf* **tapaidh 2**

calman, calmain & calmanan *nm* a dove, a pigeon

calpa¹, calpa, calpannan *nm* a calf (*of leg*)

calpa², calpa, calpannan *nm* (*fin*) capital

calpachas, *gen* calpachais *nm* capitalism

cam *adj* bent, curved, *Cf* **crom** *adj*, **fiar** *adj* 1, **lùbte**

cama-chasach *adj* bow-legged

camag, camaig, camagan *nf* 1 a curl, a ringlet, *Cf* **bachlag 1**, **dual² 1**; 2 (*typog*) a bracket

camagach *adj* (*of hair*) curled, in ringlets, *Cf* **bachlach**

caman, *gen* camain, *pl* camain & camanan *nm* 1 a shinty stick; 2 a golf club

camanachd *nf invar* shinty, *Cf* **iomain** *n*

camara, camara, camarathan *nm* a camera

camas, *gen* & *pl* camais *nm* 1 a bay, *Cf* **bàgh**, **òb**; 2 a curve or bend in a river

càmhal, *gen* & *pl* càmhail *nm* a camel

camhana(i)ch, *gen* camhanaich *nf* 1 dawn, *Cf* **bris(t)eadh-là**; 2 twilight, **camhana(i)ch an là** morning twilight, **camhana(i)ch na h-oidhche** evening twilight, *Cf* **duibhre**, **eadar-sholas**

campa, campa, campaichean *nm* a camp

campachadh, *gen* campachaidh (*the act of*) camping

campaich *vi, pres part* **a' campachadh**, camp

can *vti def pres part* **a' cantainn** & **a' cantail**, *for forms see table p 404*, 1 say, *used by some speakers instead of* **abair**, *mainly in imperative, fut, pres continuous, past continuous and conditional*, **canaidh mi seo ribh** ... I'll say this to you ... , **can a-rithist e** say it again, (*name of Gaelic course*) **Can Seo** Say This *also in expr* **mar a chanas iad** as they say, *esp after using Eng words or phrases*, **tit for tat**, **mar a chanas iad sa Bheurla** tit for tat, as they say in English, *Cf* **abair 1**; 2 *in expr* **can air** say for, **dè a chanas sibh ri 'spade' sa Ghàidhlig?** what do you say in Gaelic for 'spade'?, *Cf* **aig 5**; **3** *in expr* **can ri** (*of people, places*) call, **Dàibhidh Bàn, mar a chanadh iad ris** Fair-haired Davie, as they called him/used to call him

cana, cana, canaichean *nm* a can, a tin (*for drinks, food &c*), *Cf* **canastair**

canabhas, *gen* **canabhais** *nm* **1** canvas, *Cf* **cainb 2**; **2** (*painting*) a canvas

canach, *gen* **canaich** *nm* **1** (*bot*) bog-cotton; **2** cotton, *Cf* **cotan**

cànain, cànaine, cànainean *nf &* **cànan**, *gen & pl* **cànain** *nm* a language, (*song*) **Cànan nan Gàidheal** (Murchadh MacPhàrlain) the language of the Gaels, **cànain** *or* **cànainean cèin** foreign languages, **mion-chàna(i)n** *&* **càna(i)n b(h)eag** a minority language, a lesser-used language, (*IT*) **cànan (prògramaidh)** a (programming) language, *Cf* **cainnt 2**

cànanach *adj* **1** linguistic, pertaining to language(s); **2** *in adj exprs* **dà-chànanach** bilingual, **trì-chànanach** trilingual, **ioma-chànanach** multilingual, polyglot

cànanaiche, cànanaiche, cànanaichean *nm* a linguist

canastair, canastair, canastairean *nm* a can, a tin (*for drinks, food &c*), *Cf* **cana**

Canèidianach, *gen & pl* **Canèidianaich** *nm* a Canadian, *also as adj* **Canèidianach** Canadian

cantainn, *gen* **cantainne** *nm* (*the act of*) saying &c (*see senses of* **can** *v*)

caochail *vi, pres part* **a' caochladh**, **1** change, alter, **bha i air caochladh gu mòr** she had changed/altered greatly, *Cf* **atharraich, mùth 1**; **2** (*of persons*) die, pass away, *Cf* **bàsaich, siubhail 3**

caochladh, caochlaidh, caochlaidhean *nm* **1** (*the act of*) changing, dying &c (*see senses of* **caochail** *v*); **2** change, alteration, a change, an alteration, *Cf* **atharrachadh 2**; **3** a variety, *esp with gen pl* a variety of, various, **ann an caochladh àiteachan** in various places

caochlaideach *adj* **1** variable, changeable, **sìde chaochlaideach** changeable/unsettled weather; **2** (*of people, fate &c*) fickle, volatile, moody, apt to change, (*song*) **tha an saoghal caochlaideach na dhòigh** the world is fickle in its conduct/ways, *Cf* **carach 2, cugallach 2**

caog *vi, pres part* **a' caogadh**, blink, wink, *Cf more usu* **priob**

caogad, caogaid, caogadan *nm* **1** (*trad*) the number fifty; **2** (*trad*) a group of fifty men; *Cf* **leth-cheud**

caogadh, *gen* **caogaidh** *nm* (*the act of*) blinking, winking, *Cf more usu* **priobadh 1**

caoidh *vi, pres part* **a' caoidh**, **1** lament, mourn, grieve, *Cf* **bròn 2, caoin** *v* **1**; **2** moan, *Cf* **caoin** *v* **2**

caoidh, *gen* **caoidhe** *nf* **1** (*the act of*) lamenting, mourning &c (*see senses of* **caoidh** *v*); **2** lamentation

caoimhneas, caoimhneil *see* **coibhneas, coibhneil**

caoin *vi, pres part* **a' caoineadh**, **1** lament, mourn, *Cf* **bròn 2, caoidh** *v* **1**; **2** weep, cry, wail, moan, *Cf* **guil**

caoineadh, *gen* **caoinidh** *nm* (*the act of*) lamenting, weeping &c (*see senses of* **caoin** *v*)

caol *adj* **1** narrow, thin, slender, **sràidean caola** narrow streets, (*trad*) **claidheamh caol** a rapier, (*trad*) **an taigh caol** the narrow house, the grave, (*Gaelic spelling rule*) **leathann ri leathann is caol ri caol** broad (vowel) next to broad and slender next to slender, *Cf* **cumhang 1**; **2** *of people* thin, skinny, lanky, **bodach fada caol** a tall lanky old guy, *Cf* **seang, tana 1**

caol, *gen* **caoil**, *pl* **caoil** & **caoiltean** *nm* **1** a strait, narrows, a narrow place in a river or arm of the sea, (*Sc*) a kyle, **chaidh iad tarsainn air a' chaol** they crossed the narrows, (*placenames*) **An Caol** Kyle of Lochalsh, **Na Caoil Bhòdach** Kyles of Bute, *Cf* **caolas**; **2** the narrow part of anything, *esp in exprs* **caol an dùirn** the wrist, **caol na coise** the ankle (*Cf* **adhbrann**), **caol an droma** the small of the back

caolan, *gen* **caolain**, *pl* **caolain** & **caolanan** *nm* an intestine, a gut, (*vulg*) **chuir mi a-mach rùchd mo chaolanan** I spewed my guts up, **beul a' chaolain** *m* the duodenum, *Cf* **greallach, innidh, mionach 1**

caolas, *gen* & *pl* **caolais** *nm* a strait, narrows, (*Sc*) a kyle, kyles, *Cf* **caol** *n* **1**

caol-shràid, caol-shràide, caol-shràidean *nf* a vennel, a wynd, an alley, a lane, *Cf* **lònaid**

caomh *adj* **1** dear, beloved, *Cf* **ionmhainn**; **2** *esp in expr* **is caomh leam** (*&c*) I (&c) like (*used by some, esp Lewis speakers, as equivalent to* **is toigh le**), **is caomh leis ceòl traidiseanta** he likes traditional music, **cha chaomh leatha creamh** she doesn't like garlic, *Cf* **toigh**

caomhain *vt, pres part* **a' caomhnadh**, save, economise on, be thrifty with, **caomhain gus a-màireach e** save it till tomorrow, **a' caitheamh airgid gun chaomhnadh** spending money unsparingly, *Cf* **glèidh 2, sàbhail 3**

caomhnadh, *gen* **caomhnaidh** *nm* (*the act of*) saving, economising &c (*see senses of* **caomhain** *v*)

caon *adj* wily, cunning, *Cf more usu* **carach 1, fiar** *adj* **4, seòlta 1**

caora, *gen* **caorach**, *dat* **caora**, *pl* **caoraich**, *gen pl* **caorach** *nf* a sheep, a ewe, **rùisg** *v* **na caoraich** shear the sheep, **caora uain** a ewe in lamb

caorann, *gen* **caorainn** *nf* (*bot*) a rowan, a mountain ash

car, cuir, caran *nm* **1** a twist, a turn, (*prov*) **an car a bhios san t-seann mhaide, is deacair a thoirt às** the twist that is in the old stick is hard to get out (*roughly equivalent to* you can't teach an old dog new tricks); **2** a (circular) movement, a turn, a spin, **bheir mi car a-muigh** I'll take a stroll/a 'turn' outside, **cuir car den chuibhle!** give the wheel a turn/a spin! **cuir car den bhrot!** give the soup a stir! **car a' mhuiltein** a somersault, **a' dol car mu char leis a' bhruthaich** rolling over and over down the brae; **3** a movement, *esp in expr* **cuir** *v* **car de** move, **na cuir car dheth!** don't move/upset it! **cuir car dhìot!** move yourself, get a move on!, *Cf* **caraich, gluais 1**; **4** a trick, *esp in expr* **thoir** *v* **an car às** trick, cheat, **thug iad an car aiste** they tricked her, (*prov*) **cha tugadh an donas an car às** the devil couldn't cheat him, *Cf* **cleas 2, meall** *v* **1**; **5** *in expr with a superlative* **aig a' char as miosa/lugha (&c)** at worst/least (&c), **aig a' char as mò cha chaill sinn ach fichead nota** at most we will only lose twenty pounds; **6** *in expr* **a' chiad char sa mhadainn** first thing in the morning; **7** *as adv* a bit, rather, **car anmoch** rather late, (*song*) **ged tha mi car sgìth** though I'm a bit tired, *Cf* **beag 4, beagan** *adv*, **caran, rudeigin 2**

car *prep* (*with dat*) during, for, **car mìosa** for a month, **bha sinn ann an Glaschu car uair** we were in Glasgow for a while/a time, *Cf* **fad** *n* **2**

càr, càir, càraichean *nf* a car, *Cf trad* **carbad**

car(a)bhaidh, car(a)bhaidh, car(a)abhaidhean *nf* (*fam*) a boyfriend, *Cf* **bràmair, leannan**

carach *adj* **1** wily, sly, crafty, cunning, up to tricks, *Cf* **caon, fiar** *adj* **4, seòlta 1**; **2** changeable, unreliable, *Cf* **caochlaideach 2, cugallach 2**

carachadh, *gen* **carachaidh** *nm* (*the act of*) moving, *Cf* **gluasad 1**

carachd *nf invar* wrestling

caractar, caractair, caractairean *nm* (*play &c*) a character, *Cf less usu* **pearsa 2**

càradh, *gen* **càraidh** *nm* **1** (*the act of*) repairing, mending &c (*see senses of* **càirich** *v*); **2** a repair, **luchd-càraidh** repairers; **3** (*trad*) state, condition, **is truagh mo chàradh** sad is my condition, *Cf now more usu* **cor 1, staid**

caraich *vti, pres part* **a' carachadh,** move, **na caraich am bòrd!** don't move the table! **na caraich bhon bhòrd!** don't move from the table, *Cf* **car** *n* **3, gluais 1**

caraiche, caraiche, caraichean *nm* a wrestler

càraid, càraide, càraidean *nf* **1** a pair, a brace, a couple, **càraid (phòsta)** a married couple, *Cf* **dithis 2**; **2** a pair of twins, **caora chàraid** a sheep with twin lambs

caraid, caraid, càirdean *nm* **1** a friend, (*Note: in this sense, the pl can be* **caraidean**), **tha thu nad dheagh charaid dhomh** you're a good friend to me/of mine, (*prov*) **cha chall na gheibh caraid** what a friend gets is no loss, **banacharaid** a female/woman friend, **Caraid nan Gàidheal** The Friend of the Gael (*the Rev Norman MacLeod 1783–1862*); **2** a relative, *esp in pl*, **tha mo chàirdean air fad ann an Steòrnabhagh** all my relatives/folks/family are in Stornoway; **3** (*corres*) **A Charaid** Dear Sir, **A Chàirdean** Dear Sirs, **A Sheumais, a charaid** Dear James/Hamish, **A Bhanacharaid** Dear Madam, **A Mhòrag, a bhanacharaid** Dear Morag, *Cf* **còir** *adj* 2

caran *adv* (*dimin of* **car** *n*) a little, a bit, (*Sc*) a wee bit, **tha thu caran fadalach!** you're a wee bit late! **bha sinn caran sgìth** we were a bit tired, *Cf* **beag** 4, **beagan** *adv*, **car** *n* 7, **rudeigin** 2

carbad, carbaid, carbadan *nm* a vehicle, a conveyance, a carriage, (*trad*) a motorcar (*Cf* **càr**), (*trad*) **carbad iarainn** a railway train (*Cf* **trèana**), **carbad-eiridinn** an ambulance, **carbad-smàlaidh** a fire engine, **carbad-adhair** an aircraft, **carbad-speura** a spacecraft

cargu & **carago**, *gen* **carago**, *pl* **caragothan** *nm* a cargo, *Cf more trad* **luchd**[1]

càrn *vt*, *pres part* **a' càrnadh**, heap, pile up, accumulate, **càrn** *v* **maoin is airgead** accumulate possessions and money, **càrn am buntàta air an làr** heap the potatoes on the ground, *Cf* **cruach** *v*

càrn, *gen* **càirn** & **cùirn**, *pl* **càirn** & **cùirn** *nm* **1** a cairn, a heap of stones, (*trad*) **cuiridh sinn clach air a chàrn** we will put a stone on his cairn, we will remember him/honour his memory, **càrn-cuimhne** a monument; **2** (*topog*) a hill (*often stony*)

càrnadh, *gen* **càrnaidh** *nm* (*the act of*) heaping, accumulating &c (*see senses of* **càrn** *v*)

càrnaid, càrnaide, càrnaidean *nf* a carnation

càrnan[1], *gen* **càrnain**, *pl* **càrnain** & **càrnanan** *nm* (*dimin of* **càrn** *n*) a small cairn, a small heap of stones

càrnan[2], **càrnain, càrnanan** *nm* a cockroach

càrr, *gen* **càrra** *nf*, *also* **càir**, *gen* **càire** *nf*, **1** a scab; **2** dandruff

carragh, carraigh, carraighean *nf* **1** a rock, a pillar (*of rock*); **2** a standing stone, *Cf* **gallan, tursa**

carraig, carraige, carraigean *nf* a rock (*often by the sea*)

carraigean *see* **cairgein**

carson *inter adv* why, **carson a dh'fhalbh e?** why did he leave? **chan eil Màiri ag obair, carson a tha sin?** Mary's not working, why's that? **na faighnich carson** don't ask why

cartadh, *gen* **cartaidh** *nm* (*the act of*) tanning, mucking out &c (*see senses of* **cairt** *v*)

carthannachd *nf invar* & **carthannas**, *gen* **carthannais** *nm* **1** (*trad*) kindness, (Christian) charity, (*poem*) **Spiorad a' Charthannais** The

Spirit of Charity, *Cf* **seirc 2**; **2** charity (*ie charitable giving and the work of charities*), **buidheann-charthannachd** a charity, a charitable organisation, *Cf* **dèirc**

cas, *gen* **coise,** *dat* **cois,** *pl* **casan** *nf* **1** a foot, **ball-coise** football, a football, (*command to dog*) **cùl mo chois!** *also* **rim chois!** heel! **de chois** on foot, **thèid mi ann dhem chois** I'll go there on foot, I'll walk there, **air mo** (*&c*) **chois** up, up and about, **nach tràth a bha thu air do chois an-diugh!** weren't you up and about early today!; **2** a leg, **thoir do chasan leat!** (*lit* take your legs/feet with you) get out, take yourself off! **caol mo choise** my ankle (*Cf* **adhbrann**), **cas-lom** & **casruisgte,** barefoot, *also* barelegged; **3** a handle, **cas na spaide** the spade handle, **cas sgeine** a knife handle; **4** *also in expr* **an cois** near, accompanying, associated with, **caora is uan na cois** a ewe with a lamb at foot, **cha tàinig iad nam chois** they didn't come with me, **bochdainn agus na duilgheadasan a thig na cois** poverty and its associated difficulties, (*also in corres*) **an cois na litreach** enclosed with the letter, **cuir** *v* **rudeigin an cois** enclose something, *Cf* **lùb** *n* **3**; **5** *in expr* **cuir** *v* **air chois** found, set up, organise, *Cf* **bonn 5, stèidhich**

cas *adj* **1** steep, **leathad cas** a steep slope, **bruthach c(h)as** a steep brae; **2** precipitous, fast-flowing (*burn, current &c*); **3** (*of person*) irritable, hasty, impetuous, *Cf* **aithghearr 2, bras 1**

càs, càis, càsan *nm* a difficulty, a predicament, *esp* **(ann an) cruaidh-chàs** (in) serious difficulty, (in) an extreme predicament

casad, casaid, casadan *nm* a cough (*the action and the ailment*), **rinn i casad** she coughed

casadaich *vi, pres part* **a' casadaich,** cough

casadaich *nf invar* **1** (*the act of*) coughing; **2** a cough; *Cf* **casad**

casa-gobhlach *adj & adv* astride, **casa-gobhlach air a' chathair/air an stairsnich** astride the chair/the threshold, **a' marcachd casa-gobhlach** riding astride

casaid, casaide, casaidean *nf* a complaint (*esp official, legal*), an accusation, **dèan** *v* **casaid** make/bring a complaint, make an accusation, **rinn e casaid orm/nam aghaidh** he accused me, **fear-casaid** & **neach-casaid** an accuser, a prosecutor, **Fear-casaid/ Neach-casaid a' Chrùin** the Procurator Fiscal, the Crown Prosecutor, **tha e fo chasaid muirt** he is accused of murder

cas-chrom, cois(e)-cruim(e), casan-croma *nf* (*trad*) a foot plough

casg, *gen* **caisg** *nm* prevention, restraint, **cuir** *v* **casg air** stop, prevent, restrain, *Cf* **casgadh 2**

casgadh, *gen* **casgaidh** *nm* **1** (*the act of*) subsiding, preventing &c (*see senses of* **caisg** *v*); **2** prevention, restraint, interruption, *Cf* **casg**

casgair *vt, pres part* a' casgairt & a' casgradh, slay, slaughter, massacre, butcher, *Cf* marbh *v*, murt *v*

casgairt *nf invar, also* casgradh, *gen* casgraidh *nm*, 1 (*the act of*) slaying &c (*see senses of* casgair *v*); 2 slaughter, butchery, massacre, a massacre, *Cf* murt *n*

casgan, *gen* casgain, *pl* casgain & casganan *nm* 1 (*on wheel &c*) a brake; 2 a condom

casg-gineamhainn *nm invar* 1 contraception; 2 a contraceptive

cat, *gen & pl* cait *nm* a cat, cat-fiadhaich a wild cat

cath, *gen* catha, *pl* cathan & cathannan *nm* a battle, warfare, (*trad dance*) cath nan coileach the battle of the cocks, the cockfight, (*trad*) misg catha (*also* mire catha) battle frenzy (*lit* battle drunkenness), *Cf* blàr 2, cogadh

càth, *gen* càtha *nf* chaff, *Cf* moll

cathadh, cathaidh, cathaidhean *nm* 1 a snowdrift, (*poem*) An Cathadh Mór (Aonghas MacNeacail) (*translated as*) The Great Snow Battle; 2 cathadh-mara sea-spray

cathag, cathaig, cathagan *nf* a jackdaw

cathair, cathrach, cathraichean *nf* 1 a chair, cùl cathrach a chair back, cathair-ghàirdeanach an armchair, cathair-chuibhle a wheelchair, *Cf less trad* sèithear; 2 a big city, a cathedral city, cathair-eaglais a cathedral

cath-bhuidheann, cath-bhuidhinn, cath-bhuidhnichean *nf* a batallion

cead *nm invar* 1 permission, leave, (*trad*) le ur cead by your leave, with your permission, thug mi cead dhaibh falbh I gave them permission to leave/go; 2 a permit, a licence, cead-dràibhidh a driving licence, cead-dol-thairis a passport; 3 farewell, leave, a leave-taking, ghabh sinn ar cead dhiubh we took our leave of them/bade them farewell, (*poem*) Cead Deireannach nam Beann The Last Farewell to the Mountains, taking leave of the mountains for the last time

ceadach *adj* tolerant

ceadachadh, *gen* ceadachaidh *nm* (*the act of*) permitting, licensing &c (*see senses of* ceadaich *v*), bòrd *m* ceadachaidh a licensing board

ceadachail *adj* permissive

ceadachas, *gen* ceadachais, *nm* (*of attitude &c*) tolerance

ceadaich *vti, pres part* a' ceadachadh, 1 permit, allow, (*song*) Nan Ceadaicheadh an Tìde Dhomh If Time Would Allow Me, *Cf* leig 1; 2 license, grant or issue licences

ceadaichte *adj* allowed, permitted, permissible, licit

ceàird, ceàirde, ceàirdean *nf* a trade, a craft, **fear-ceàirde** a skilled tradesman, a craftsman, an artisan

cealg, *gen* **ceilge** *nf* deceit; hypocrisy, *Cf* **foill 1**

cealgach *adj* deceitful, hypocritical

cealgair(e), cealgair(e), cealgairean *nm* a deceiver, a cheat, a hypocrite, *Cf* **mealltair**

cealla, cealla, ceallan *nf* (*biol*) a cell

ceanalta *adj* kind, gentle, pretty, comely, (*song*) **chunnaic mi caileag a bha ceanalta grinn** I saw a girl who was comely and neat, *Cf* **eireachdail, grinn 2**

ceangail *vt, pres part* **a' ceangal,** tie, link, join, unite, connect (**ri** to), **cheangail e iallan a bhrògan** he tied his shoe laces, **ceangail ri chèile** join together

ceangal, ceangail, ceanglaichean *nm* **1** (*the act of*) tying, linking &c (*see senses of* **ceangail** *v*); **2** (*abstr & con*) a connection, a link, a bond, **bha dlùth-cheangal aca ris a' Ghàidhealtachd** they had a close link with the Highlands, **chan fhaic mi an ceangal eadar an dealbh 's na faclan** I don't see the connection between the picture and the words, *Cf* **dàimh 2**

ceann, *gen & pl* **cinn** *nm* **1** a head, **bha a ceann goirt** her head ached/ was sore, (*song*) **ged tha mo cheann air liathadh** though my head has turned grey, **ceannruisgte** bare-headed; **2** the end of anything, **ceann an rathaid** the end of the road, **bho cheann gu ceann** from end to end, **phòs iad aig a' cheann thall** they married in the end/ eventually, **ceann as àirde/as ìsle (a' mhullaich &c)** the top/ bottom (of the roof &c), (*IT*) **ceann-obrach** a (computer) terminal; **3** *in expr* **an ceann** *prep* after, in (*of time*), **an ceann greiseig** in/after a little while, (*of time & space*) **an ceann a chèile** together, one after the other, in succession, **chan urrainn dha dà fhacal a chur an ceann a chèile** he can't string/put two words together, **trì tubaistean an ceann a chèile** three accidents one after the other/ in succession/in a row (*Cf* **sreath 3**); **4** *in expr* **ag obair** (*&c*) **air a cheann fhèin** working (*&c*) on his own account/for himself

ceannach, *gen* **ceannaich** *nm, also* **ceannachd** *nf invar,* **1** (*the act of*) buying, purchasing, trading; **2** trade, commerce, *Cf* **malairt 1**

ceannaich *vt, pres part* **a' ceannach(d),** buy, purchase, **ceannaich air deagh phrìs** buy at a good price

ceannaiche, ceannaiche, ceannaichean *nm* **1** a purchaser; **2** (*more usu*) a merchant

ceannard, ceannaird, ceannardan *nm* **1** a leader, a chief, a commander; **2** a boss (*of firm &c*)

ceannbheart, *gen* **ceannbheairt** *nf* headgear

ceann-bliadhna, *gen & pl* **cinn-bliadhna** *nm* a birthday, **bha ceann-bliadhna agam an-dè** it was my birthday yesterday, *Cf* **co-là-breith**

ceann-cinnidh, *gen & pl* **cinn-chinnidh** *nm also* **ceann-feadhna**, *gen & pl* **cinn-fheadhna** *nm* a clan chief, **ceann-cinnidh nan Dòmhnallach** chief of the MacDonalds

ceann-là, *gen & pl* **cinn-là** *nm* a (*calendar*) date

ceann-làidir *adj* headstrong

ceann-naidheachd, *gen & pl* **cinn-naidheachd** *nm* (*news*) a headline

ceann-pholan, **ceann-pholain**, **ceann-pholanan** *nm also* **ceann-simid**, **ceann-simide**, **ceann-simidean** *nm* a tadpole

ceannsachadh, *gen* **ceannsachaidh** *nm* **1** (*the act of*) conquering, quelling &c (*see senses of* **ceannsaich** *v*); **2** conquest, repression

ceannsaich *vt, pres part* **a' ceannsachadh**, **1** conquer, overcome (*army, enemy &c*); **2** (*people, emotions &c*) quell, master, control, repress, **cheannsaich am poileas an aimhreit** the police quelled/controlled the disturbance, **cheannsaich mi m' fhearg** I controlled/mastered my anger, *Cf* **mùch 3**; **3** (*animal &c*) tame, *Cf* **callaich 1**

ceannsal, *gen* **ceannsail** *nm* rule, authority, subjugation, **fo cheannsal a nàmhaid** under his enemy's rule, *Cf* **smachd**

ceannsalach *adj* **1** authoritative, commanding; **2** dictatorial, domineering

ceann-simid *see* **ceann-pholan**

ceann-suidhe, *gen & pl* **cinn-suidhe** *nm* a president (*of firm, company, also of country*)

ceann-uidhe, *gen & pl* **cinn-uidhe** *nm* a destination, **'s e Glaschu mo cheann-uidhe** Glasgow's my destination

ceap, *gen* **cip**, *pl* **ceapan** & **ceapannan** *nm* **1** a block *or* lump of anything, **ceap mòna/fiodha** a block *or* a lump of peat/wood, *Cf* **cnap 1**; **2** (*also* **ceap-bròige**) a cobbler's last; **3** a cap (*ie headgear*), *Cf* **bonaid 2**

ceapach, *gen & pl* **ceapaich** *nm* (*hort*) a plot, a bed

ceapaire, **ceapaire**, **ceapairean** *nm* a sandwich

cearb, **cirbe**, **cearban** *nf* **1** a rag, *Cf* **luideag**; **2** a defect, a fault

cearbach *adj* **1** (*person, action*) clumsy, awkward; **2** ragged, untidy, tatty, *Cf* **luideach**

cearbair(e), **cearbair(e)**, **cearbairean** *nm* an awkward *or* clumsy person, a bungler, *Cf* **uaipear**

cearc, **circe**, **cearcan** *nf* **1** a (*domestic*) hen; **2** a female game bird, **cearc ruadh** a red grouse

cearcall, *gen* **cearcaill**, *pl* **cearcaill** & **cearcallan** *nm* a circle, a ring, **a' dannsadh ann an cearcall** dancing in a circle/a ring, (*song*) **Cearcall a' Chuain** The Circle of the Ocean

cearclach *adj* circular

ceàrd & **cèard**, *gen* **ceàird** & **ciùird**, *pl* **ceàrdan** *nm* **1** a tinker; **2** (*usu in compounds*) a smith, **ceàrd-airgid** a silversmith, **òr-cheàrd** a goldsmith, **ceàrd-copair** a coppersmith, *Cf* **gobha**

ceàrdach, **ceàrdaich**, **ceàrdaichean** *nf* a smithy, a blacksmith's shop; a forge

ceàrn, *gen* **ceàrnaidh**, *pl* **ceàrnaidhean** & **ceàrnan** *nm* an area, a district, a corner, **sa cheàrn seo den dùthaich** in this part/corner of the country, **ceàrnaidhean iomallach** remote areas/districts, *Cf* **sgìre 1, tìr 3**

ceàrnach *adj* square

ceàrnag, **ceàrnaig**, **ceàrnagan** *nf* **1** (*geometry*) a square; **2** a square (*in a town &c*), **Ceàrnag Shomhairle** Somerled Square

ceàrnagach *adj* square, **meatair ceàrnagach** a square metre

ceàrr *adj* wrong, **bha mi cinnteach gun robh mi ceart, ach bha mi ceàrr** I was sure I was right, but I was wrong, **fada ceàrr** far wrong, **tha rudeigin ceàrr air mo dhruim** there's something wrong with my back; **2** left, **mo làmh cheàrr** my left hand, *Cf* **clì**

ceàrraiche & **ceàrraiche**, *gen* **ceàrraiche**, *pl* **ceàrraichean** *nm* a gambler

ceart *adj* **1** right, correct, exact, **tha thu pòsta a-nis, a bheil sin ceart?** you're married now, is that right? **tha na cunntasan/na freagairtean ceart** the accounts/the answers are correct, **ann an ceart-mheadhan a' bhaile** right in the centre/in the exact centre of the town, *as excl* **ceart ma-tha!** right then!; **2** just, right, **binn cheart** a just sentence, **duine ceart** a just/upright man, **cuir** *v* **ceart na tha ceàrr** put right what is wrong; **3** same, very, **Iain bràthair Mòraig, a bheil thu a' minigeadh? an ceart duine!** Iain, Morag's brother, do you mean? the very man!/the very same!, **ach feumaidh mi ràdh aig a' cheart àm ...** but I have to say at the same time ..., *Cf* **aon 3, ceudna 1, dearbh** *adj* **1, fèin 5; 4** right, right-hand, *Cf more usu* **deas 2; 5** *as adv* **a cheart cho** just as, every bit as, **tha margarain a cheart cho math ri ìm** margarine is just as good as butter; **6** *used as noun*, right, **cho ceart ri ceart** as right as can be, perfectly correct, (*prov*) **thèid neart thar ceart** might before right, *Cf* **ceartas, còir** *n* **4**

ceartachadh, **ceartachaidh**, **ceartachaidhean** *nm* **1** (*the act of*) correcting, marking &c (*see senses of* **ceartaich** *v*); **2** correction, a correction; *Cf* **comharrachadh**

ceartaich *vt, pres part* **a' ceartachadh**, correct, rectify, put right, (*teacher &c*) mark, **bha i a' ceartachadh obair a sgoilearan** she was correcting/marking her pupils' work, *Cf* **comharraich 2**

ceartas, *gen* **ceartais** *nm* justice, right, *Cf* **còir** *n* **4**, **ionracas 2**

ceartuair *see* **an ceartuair**

ceart-uilinn, ceart-uilinn, ceart-uilnean *nf* a right angle

ceas, ceasa, ceasaichean *nm* a suitcase, *Cf* **baga, màileid**

ceasnachadh, ceasnachaidh, ceasnachaidhean *nm* **1** (*the act of*) question-ing &c (*see senses of* **ceasnaich** *v*); **2** a questionnaire, *Cf* **ceisteachan**; **3** interrogation, an interrogation; **4** a quiz

ceasnachail *adj* inquisitive, *Cf* **faighneach**

ceasnaich *vti, pres part* **a' ceasnachadh**, **1** question; **2** interrogate; **3** (*relig*) catechise

ceathach, *gen & pl* **ceathaich** *nm* mist, (*poem*) **Oran Coire a' Cheathaich** Song to the Misty Corrie, *Cf more usu* **ceò 1**

ceathrad, ceathraid, ceathradan *nm* the number forty (*in alt numbering system*), *Cf* **dà fhichead** (*see* **fichead**)

ceathramh *num adj* fourth, **an ceathramh fear** the fourth man/one, **ceathramh deug** fourteenth

ceathramh, ceathraimh, ceathramhan *nm* **1** a quarter, a fourth part of anything, (*placename*) **An Ceathramh Cruaidh** Kerrycroy, the hard quarter (*ie division of land*); **2** (*of time*) a quarter (of an hour), **ceathramh gu sia** a quarter to six, *Cf* **cairteal 1**

ceathrar *nm invar* (people numbering) four, a foursome, *takes the gen*, **bha ceathrar mhac aice** she had four sons, **tha ceathrar mun bhòrd** there are four people round/at the table

cèic, cèice, cèicean *nf* cake, a cake

cèidse, cèidse, cèidsichean *nf* a cage

ceil *vt, pres part* **a' ceileadh**, **a' cleith** & **a' ceiltinn**, hide, conceal (**air** from), **ceil an fhìrinn air do mhàthair!** hide the truth from your mother!, *Cf* **falaich**

cèile *nmf invar* **1** a spouse, a wife, a husband, **a chèile** his spouse/wife, **a cèile** her spouse/husband, *Cf* **bean 1, duine 4**; **2** a counterpart, a fellow, *esp in exprs based on* **a chèile**, each other, **phòg iad a chèile** they kissed each other, **a' bruidhinn ri chèile** talking to each other, **tha na bràithrean thar a chèile** the brothers are at loggerheads/ have fallen out with each other, **tha sinn mòr aig a chèile** we are good friends (with each other); **3** *for* **le chèile** *see* **le 1**

ceileadh, *gen* **ceilidh** *nm, also* **ceiltinn** *nf invar* & **cleith**, *gen* **cleithe** *nmf* **1** (*the act of*) hiding, concealing; **2** concealment, a hiding place; *Cf* **falach**

ceileir *vi, pres part* **a' ceileireadh**, **1** sing like a bird, warble; **2** sing sweetly

cèilidh, cèilidh, cèilidhean *nmf* **1** a visit (*to someone's house*), **thàinig i a chèilidh oirnn a-raoir** she came to visit us/to ceilidh on us last night, *Cf* **tadhal 2**; **2** a ceilidh, **bidh cèilidh ann an talla a' bhaile an ath-oidhch'** there'll be a ceilidh in the village hall tomorrow night

cèilidheach *adj* companionable, sociable, fond of company

ceilp, *gen* **ceilpe** *nf* (*trad*) kelp, (*hist*) **losgadh** *m* **na ceilpe** kelp burning

Ceilteach, *gen & pl* **Ceiltich** *nm* a Celt, *also as adj* **Ceilteach** Celtic, **na cànainean Ceilteach** the Celtic languages

ceiltinn *n & pres part, see* **ceil** *v*, **ceileadh** *n*

ceimig, ceimig, ceimigean *nf* a chemical substance, a chemical

ceimigeachd *nf invar* chemistry

ceimigear, ceimigeir, ceimigearan *nm* a chemist (*not a pharmacist – see* **cungaidh 3**)

cèin *adj* **1** foreign, **dùthaich/cànain chèin** a foreign country/language, **an cèin** *adv* abroad; **2** distant, faraway, *Cf* **cian** *adj* **1**

cèir, *gen* **cèire** *nf* wax, **cèir-chluaise** ear-wax

cèis, cèise, cèisean *nf* **1** a frame, **cèis dealbha/baidhsagail** a picture/bicycle frame, **cèis streap** a climbing frame, *Cf* **frèam**; **2** (*also* **cèis litreach**) an envelope

cèiseag, cèiseig, cèiseagan *nf* a cassette, *Cf* **teip 2**

ceist, ceiste, ceistean *nf* **1** a question, a query, **chuir e ceist dhoirbh orm** he asked me a difficult question; **2** a problem, a question, a point at issue, **a bheil e ro chosgail? 's e sin a' cheist!** is it too costly? that's the question/the point/the problem!

ceisteachan, *gen & pl* **ceisteachain** *nm* a questionnaire, *Cf* **ceasnachadh 2**

ceistear, ceisteir, ceistearan *nm* **1** a questioner, an interrogator; **2** a question-master; **3** (*relig*) a catechist

Cèitean, *gen* **Cèitein** *nm* the month of May, *usu with art* **an Cèitean** May, *also adjectivally* **air madainn Chèitein** on a May morning, *Cf less trad* **Màigh**

ceithir *n & num adj* four, **ceithir coin** four dogs, **cia mheud a th' ann? a ceithir** how many are there? four, **ceithir-chuibhleach** *adj* four-wheeled, **ceithir-chasach** *adj & nm* (a) quadruped, **dà-chasach** *adj & nm* (a) biped

ceithir-deug *n & adj* fourteen

ceò, ceò, ceothannan *nm* **1** mist, a mist, a haze, **Eilean a' Cheò** The Misty Isle (Skye), **bha na beanntan fo cheò** the mountains were in/covered in mist, *Cf* **ceathach 1**; **2** fog, a fog; **3** smoke, *Cf* **toit 2**

ceòl, *gen* **ciùil** *nm* music, **luchd-ciùil** musicians, **còmhlan-ciùil** a band, a group, **bocsa-ciùil** an accordeon, **inneal-ciùil** a musical instrument, **ceòl na mara** the music/song of the sea, **ceòl mòr** the 'great music' or classical music of the Highland bagpipe, **ceòl beag** light music, dance music (for the pipes), **cuir** *v* **an ceòl air feadh na fìdhle** put the cat among the pigeons

ceòlmhor *adj* musical, harmonious, melodious, tuneful, *Cf* **binn** *adj* 2, **fonnmhor**

ceòthach *also* **ceòthar** *adj* 1 misty, covered in mist, hazy; 2 foggy

ceud, **ceud**, **ceudan** *nm* a hundred, **ceud duine** a/one hundred people, **thàinig iad nan ceudan** they came in their hundreds, hundreds of them came, **iomadh ceud bliadhna** many hundreds of years, **a ceithir** (*&c*) **às a' cheud** four (*&c*) percent, **ceud taing!** thanks a lot! (*trad greeting*) **ceud mìle fàilte!** a hundred thousand welcomes!

ceudameatair, ceudameatair, ceudameatairean *nm* a centimetre

ceudamh *num adj* hundredth

ceudna *adj* 1 same, very, **chunnaic mi srainnsear an-dè is chunnaic mi an srainnsear ceudna an-diugh** I saw a stranger yesterday and I saw the same stranger today, **an e Seòras a th' ann? an duine ceudna!** is it George? the very man!, *Cf more usu* **aon** 3, **ceart** 3, **dearbh** *adj* 1; 2 *also in expr* **mar an ceudna** similarly, likewise, also, too, **bha mi math air dannsadh, mo phiuthar mar an ceudna** I was good at dancing, my sister likewise/too, *Cf* **cuideachd** *adv*

ceum, *gen* **ceuma** & **cèim**, *pl* **ceuman** & **ceumannan** *nm* 1 (*in walking &c*) a step, a pace, **ghabh i ceum air adhart** she took a step/pace forwards, she stepped forward, **ceum air cheum** step by step; 2 a footstep **chuala mi ceumannan fad air falbh** I heard footsteps far away; 3 a step (*of staircase &c*) **a' dol suas na ceumannan** going up the steps; 4 a (university) degree, **thug i a-mach ceum** she graduated (*Cf* **ceumnaich** 2)

ceumnachadh, ceumnachaidh, ceumnachaidhean *nm* 1 (*the act of*) pacing, graduating (*see* **ceumnaich** *v*); 2 (*ed*) (also **ceumnachd** *nf invar*) graduation, a graduation

ceumnaich *vi*, *pres part* **a' ceumnachadh**, 1 pace; 2 (*ed*) graduate, *Cf* **ceum** 4

ceus *vt*, *pres part* **a' ceusadh**, crucify

ceusadh, ceusaidh, ceusaidhean *nm* crucifixion, a crucifixion

cha (*before a vowel, or fh followed by a vowel*, **chan**), *neg particle expressing concepts* 'not', 'No', **cha robh sinn ann** we weren't there, **cha toigh leatha ìm** she doesn't like butter, **a bheil thu sgìth? chan eil** are you tired? No *or* I'm not, **an sibhse Ailean? cha mhì** are you Alan?

No *or* I am not, **an d'fhuair thu an duais? cha d'fhuair** did you get the prize? No *or* I didn't

chaidh *pt of irreg v* **rach** *see tables p 410*

chì, chitheadh, chithinn *pts of irreg vb* **faic** *see tables p 408*

chluinn, chluinneadh, chluinneas, chluinninn, chluinntinn *pts of irreg v* **cluinn** *see tables p 406*

cho *adv* **1** so, **bha e cho trang!** he was so busy! **chan eil mi cho math an-diugh** I'm not so good today; **2** *in comparisons* **cho ... sin** as ... as that, **cha robh e cho math sin** he wasn't that good/as good as that, **chan eil mi cho aosta sin!** I'm not that old!; **3** *in comparisons* **cho ... ri** as ... as, **cho mòr ri taigh** as big as a house, **cho beag ri a trì** as few as three; **4** *in comparisons involving a verb* **tha mi (a cheart) cho luath 's a bha mi a-riamh** I'm (just) as fast as I ever was, **chan eil an aimsir cho math agus a chleachd i (a bhith)** the weather isn't as good/so good as it used to be; **5** *in questions* **dè cho ... 's/ agus ... ?** how ... ?, *eg* **dè cho fada 's a bhios sibh a' fuireach againn?** how long will you be staying with us? **dè cho trom agus a tha e?** how heavy is it?

chuala *pt of irreg v* **cluinn** *see tables p 406*

chuca, chugad, chugam, chugainn, chugaibh, chuice, chuige *prep prons, & **chun** *prep, see* **gu**[1] *prep* **1 & 2**

chum *see* **a chum**

chunna, chunnaic *pts of irreg v* **faic** *see tables p 408*

ciad *adj* first, *with art,* **a' chiad leasan** the first lesson, **a' chiad turas** the first time, **anns a' chiad àite ...** in the first place

ciadameatair, ciadameatair, ciadameatairean *nm* a centimetre

ciad-fhuasgladh, *gen* **ciad-fhuasglaidh** *nm (medical)* first aid

ciall, *gen* **cèille,** *dat* **cèill & ciall,** *pl* **ciallan** *nf* **1** sense, good sense, **briathran làn cèille** words full of good sense, *Cf* **toinisg, tuigse 1; 2** reason, mind *(ie sanity),* **chaill mi mo chiall** I've lost my mind/ my reason, **tha i gu bhith às a ciall le iomagain** she's nearly out of her mind with worry, *Cf* **reusan, rian 3; 3** meaning, sense, *(trad & emph)* **gu dè as ciall dhut?** what on earth/whatever do you mean? **faclan gun chiall** meaningless words, *also* senseless words, *Cf* **brìgh 1, seagh; 4** *excl* **a chiall!** goodness! good heavens!

ciallach *adj* sensible, *Cf* **toinisgeil 1, tuigseach 1, tùrail**

ciallaich *vt, pres part* **a' ciallachadh,** mean, **dè a tha thu a' ciallachadh?** what do you mean? **dè a tha am facal seo a' ciallachadh?** what does this word mean? *Cf* **minig** *v*

ciamar *inter adv* how, **ciamar a tha thu an-diugh?** how are you today? **ciamar a chaidh dhut?** how did you get on? **chan eil fhios agam ciamar a rinn e e** I don't know how he did it

cia mheud & **co mheud**, *inter adv* how many, how much, *Note: takes a sing noun*, **cia mheud duine a bha ann?** how many people were there?

cian *adj* **1** distant, remote (*in time or space*), *Cf* **cèin, iomallach; 2** long, weary, (*poetry collection*) **An Rathad Cian** (Ruaraidh MacThòmais) The Long/Weary (*or* Distant) Road

cian, *gen* **cèin** *nm* distance, remoteness (*in time or space*), (*song*) **'s cian nan cian bho dh'fhàg mi Leòdhas** it is a very long time (*lit* the age of the ages) since I left Lewis

cianail *adj* **1** sad, *Cf* **brònach, muladach; 2** plaintive, melancholy; **3** terrible, *as intensifying element* (*also* **cianail fhèin**) **tha e cianail (fhèin) mòr** it's very big indeed/terribly big, *Cf* **eagalach 3, uabhasach 2**

cianalach *adj* sad, *esp through homesickness*

cianalas, *gen* **cianalais** *nm* **1** sadness, *Cf* **bròn, mulad; 2** homesickness; **3** nostalgia

ciar *vi, pres part* **a' ciaradh**, darken, grow dark, **mus do chiar am feasgar** before the evening grew dark, before dusk fell, *Cf* **doilleirich**

ciar *adj* **1** (*of persons*) dark, dusky, swarthy, *Cf* **lachdann 2; 2** (*of atmosphere, setting*) dark, gloomy, *Cf* **doilleir; 3** (*of colour*) dun, *Cf* **odhar 1; 4** *in expr* **is** *v* **ciar leam** ... I take a dim view of ... , *Cf* **beag 5**

ciatach *adj* **1** pleasant, attractive, agreeable, *Cf* **taitneach, tarraingeach; 2** *in expr* **bu chiatach air** ... he ought to/should ... , *Cf more usu* **còir** *n* **1**

cidhe, cidhe, cidhean *nm* a quay, a pier

cidsin, cidsin, cidsinean *nm* a kitchen

cileagram, cileagraim, cileagraman *nm* a kilogram, a kilo

cilemeatair, cilemeatair, cilemeatairean *nm* a kilometre

cill, *gen* **cille**, *pl* **cillean** & **cilltean** *nf* **1** (*trad*) a cell of a saint, monk or hermit, a holy site associated with such a saint &c, (*placenames*) **Cill Aonghais** Killanish, the cell or church of (St) Angus, **Cille Mhoire** Kilmore, Kilmuir, Mary's church; **2** (*trad*) a kirkyard, a burial ground, *Cf* **clachan 3, cladh**

cineal, cineil, cinealan *nm* **1** race, a race, **dàimh-chinealan** *f* race relations; **2** a species, *Cf* **gnè 2, seòrsa 2**

cinealtach *adj* racist, racialist

cinealtas, *gen* **cinealtais** *nm* racism, racialism

cinn *vi, pres part* **a' cinntinn**, grow, increase, multiply, (*trad*) **chinn a shliochd** his progeny increased, *Cf* **fàs** *v* **2, meudaich**

cinneadail *adj* clannish

cinne-daonna *see* daonna

cinneach, *gen & pl* cinnich *nm* a heathen

cinneadh, cinnidh, cinnidhean *nm* 1 (*in Scotland & Ireland*) a clan, ceann-cinnidh a clan chief, the head of a clan, fear-cinnidh a (fellow) clansman, *also* a (male) namesake, bean-chinnidh a (fellow) clanswoman, *also* a (female) namesake, *Cf* clann 2, fine 2; 2 (*in general*) a race, a tribe, a people, *esp of real or supposed common ancestry*; 3 a surname, one's second *or* family name, dè an cinneadh a th' agad? what's your surname/second name?, *Cf more usu* sloinneadh 2

cinneas, *gen* cinneis *nm* growth (*abstr & con*), cinneas eaconomach economic growth, *Cf* fàs *n*

cinnt, *gen* cinnte *nf* certainty, a certainty

cinnteach *adj* certain, sure, confident, a bheil thu cinnteach gun tig i? tha mi làn-chinnteach às! are you certain/sure she'll come? I'm quite certain/sure of it, *Cf more trad* deimhinne

cinntinn *nm invar* (*the act of*) growing &c (*see senses of* cinn *v*)

cìobair, cìobair, cìobairean *nm* a shepherd, (*song*) Duanag a' Chìobair The Shepherd's Song

cìoch, cìche, cìochan *nf* 1 a (*woman's*) breast; 2 a nipple; 3 *in expr* cìoch an t-slugain the uvula

cìochag, cìochaig, cìochagan *nf* a valve

ciomach, *gen & pl* ciomaich *nm* a prisoner, a captive, a detainee, *Cf* prìosanach

ciomachas, *gen* ciomachais *nm* imprisonment, captivity, detention, *Cf* bràighdeanas, daorsa, làmh 2, sàs 1

cion *nm invar* 1 a lack, a want, a shortage, cion-fala anaemia, cion-ùidhe apathy, (*song*) Cion a' Bhuntàta The Lack of Potatoes, the potato shortage, *Cf* dìth 1, easbhaidh, gainne; 2 desire, a desire (*for something or someone*), mo chion ort fhèin my desire for you, *Cf more usu* miann 1 & 2

cionn, chionn *see* a chionn, o chionn, os cionn

ciont(a), cionta, ciontan *nm* 1 guilt; 2 a guilty action, a sin, a transgression, a fault, *Cf* peacadh

ciontach *adj* guilty, *Cf* coireach *adj* 1

ciontach, *gen & pl* ciontaich *nm* a guilty person, an offender, *Cf* coireach *n*, eucorach

ciontachadh, *gen* ciontachaidh *nm* (*the act of*) offending &c (*see senses of* ciontaich *v*)

ciontaich *vi, pres part* a' ciontachadh, offend, commit an offence, commit a guilty action, sin, transgress, *Cf* peacaich

ciora, ciora, *pl* **cioran** & **ciorachan** *nf, an affectionate word for a lamb or sheep,* **trobhad, a chiora bheag!** come to me, little sheep!

ciorram, ciorraim, ciorraman *nm* disability, a disability, a (*phys*) handicap, **cuibhreann-ciorraim** *m* a disability allowance

ciorramach, *gen* & *pl* **ciorramaich** *nm* a disabled person, a handicapped person, **na ciorramaich** the disabled

ciorramach *adj* disabled, (*phys*) handicapped

ciotach *adj* left-handed, (*hist*) **Colla Ciotach** Colkitto (left-handed Colla)

cipean, cipein, cipeanan *nm* **1** a stake, *Cf less trad* **post**; **2** a tether post, *Cf* **bacan**

cìr *vt, pres part* **a' cìreadh,** comb, **cìr d' fhalt anns a' bhad!** comb your hair this instant! (*trad*) **cìr do cheann** comb your hair

cìr, cìre, cìrean *nf* **1** a (*hair*) comb; **2** (*also* **cìr-mheala**) a honeycomb; **3** cud, **a' cnàmh na cìre** (*of animals*) chewing the cud, (*fam, of humans*) talking things over, chewing the fat, talking of this and that

cìreadh, *gen* **cìridh** *nm* (*the act of*) combing

cìrean, *gen* **cìrein,** *pl* **cìrein** & **cìreanan** *nm* **1** a comb or crest of a cock or game bird; **2** a crest of a clan or other group or body, *Cf* **suaicheantas 1**

cìs, cìse, cìsean *nf* taxation, a tax, **a' chìs-chinn** the poll tax, *Cf* **càin**

ciste, ciste, cisteachan *nf* (*furniture &c*) a chest, **ciste anairt** a linen chest, **ciste-càir** a car boot, **ciste-laighe** a coffin

ciùb, ciùb, ciùban *nm* a cube

ciùbach *adj* cubic

ciùbhran & **ciùthran,** *gen* & *pl* **ciùbhrain,** *also* **cunthrach,** *gen* & *pl* **cunthraich,** *nm* **1** drizzle, *Cf* **braon 2**; **2** a shower of rain, *Cf* **fras** *n* **1**

ciudha, ciudha, ciudhaichean *nf* a queue

ciùin *adj* mild, gentle, quiet, calm, **madainn chiùin** a calm/still morning, **oiteag chiùin** a gentle/mild breeze, (*trad*) **maighdeann chiùin** a gentle maiden, *Cf* **sàmhach 2, sèimh 1**

ciùineachadh, *gen* **ciùineachaidh** *nm* (*the act of*) quietening &c (*see senses of* **ciùinich** *v*)

ciùineas, *gen* **ciùineis** *nm* calm, calmness, quiet, quietness, tranquility, *Cf* **sàmhchair 2**

ciùinich *vti, pres part* **a' ciùineachadh,** quieten, calm, calm down, pacify, still, soothe, *Cf* **sìthich 1** & **2, socraich 1, tàlaidh 3**

ciùraig *vt, pres part* **a' ciùraigeadh,** cure (*bacon, fish &c*)

ciùrr *vt, pres part* **a' ciùrradh,** **1** (*phys*) hurt intensely, pain, torture, *Cf* **cràidh, goirtich**; **2** harm, injure (*someone's feelings, situation &c*)

ciùrradh, ciùrraidh, ciùrraidhean *nm* **1** (*the act of*) hurting, harming &c (*see senses of* **ciùrr** *v*); **2** a hurt, *Cf* **creuchd**

ciùrrte *adj* hurt, injured (*phys or emotionally*)

ciuthrach, ciùthran *see* **ciùbhran**

clabar-snàimh, clabair-snàimh, clabaran-snàimh *nm* a flipper (*as worn by divers &c*)

clabhstair, clabhstair, clabhstairean *nm* a cloister

clach *vt, pres part* **a' clachadh**, stone, pelt with stones

clach, cloiche, clachan *nf* **1** stone, a stone, **thilg e clach orm** he threw a stone at me, **ballachan cloiche** stone walls, **Clach Sgàin** *also* **Clach na Cineamhainn** the Stone of Destiny/of Scone, **clach chuimhne** *or* **clach chuimhneachain** a memorial, a memorial stone, a monument, **clach phlumaise/shirist** a plum/cherry stone, **clach-mheallain** a hailstone, **clach-mhuilinn** a millstone, **clach-iùil** a magnet, **clach uasal** a precious stone, **clach na sùla** the eyeball, the apple of the eye; **2** a stone (*ie measure of weight*), **clach bhuntàta** a stone of potatoes; **3** a testicle, *Cf* **magairle**

clachach *adj* stony

clachadh, *gen* **clachaidh** *nm* (*the act of*) stoning, pelting with stones

clachair, clachair, clachairean *nm* a mason, a stonemason

clachan, *gen & pl* **clachain** *nm* **1** (*trad*) a village with a parish church, (*Sc*) a kirktoun; **2** a hamlet; **3** (*trad*) a kirkyard, a cemetery, *Cf* **cill 2**, **cladh**

clach-bhalg, clach-bhuilg, clach-bhalgan *nf* **1** a rattle (*ie toy &c*); **2** a scrotum

clach-ghràin, *gen* **cloich-gràin** *nf* granite

cladach, cladaich, cladaichean *nm* a shore, a beach, a stony beach, *usu of sea, but also of loch*, (*prov*) **is lom an cladach air an cunntar na faochagan** it's a bare beach on which the whelks can be counted, *Cf* **tràigh** *n* **1**

cladh, *gen* **cladha** *&* **claidh**, *pl* **cladhan** *nm* a churchyard, a kirkyard, a cemetery, *Cf* **cill 2**, **clachan 3**

cladhach, *gen* **cladhaich** *nm* (*the act of*) digging

cladhaich *vi, pres part* **a' cladhach**, **1** dig, *Cf* **ruamhair 1**; **2** (*fig*) **fiosrachadh a chladhaich i à leabhraichean** information she dug out of books

cladhaire, cladhaire, cladhairean *nm* a coward, *Cf* **gealtaire**

cladhaireach *adj* cowardly, *Cf* **gealtach**

clag, *gen & pl* **cluig** *nm* a bell

clagarsaich *nf invar* **1** a clinking, a rattling (*as of glasses &c*); **2** *as pres part*, **a' clagarsaich** clinking, rattling

claidheamh, claidheimh, claidhnean *nm* a sword, **claidheamh leathann** a broadsword, **claidheamh dà-làimh** a two-handed sword, *Note: the latter of these is properly referred to in Gaelic as* **claidheamh mòr** *but both it and the broadsword can be found as* 'claymore' *in Sc/Eng*, **claidheamh caol** a rapier

claidheamhair, claidheamhair, claidheamhairean *nm* a swordsman

claigeann, claiginn, claignean *nm* a skull, *also in expr* (**aig**) **àird mo** (**&c**) **c(h)laiginn** at the top of my (&c) voice, **bha i a' seinn àird a claiginn** she was singing at the top of her voice

clàimhean, clàimhein, clàimheanan *nm* (*on door &c*) a latch

clais, claise, claisean *nf* **1** a ditch, a trench, *Cf* **dìg; 2** a drain, *Cf* **drèana; 3** (*agric*) a furrow, *Cf* **sgrìob 2; 4** a groove

claisneachd & **claisteachd**, *nf invar* the faculty of hearing, **tha mi a' call mo chlaisneachd** I'm losing my hearing

clamhan, *gen & pl* **clamhain** *nm* a buzzard

clann, *gen* **cloinne** *nf coll* **1** children, **càraid gun chlann** a childless couple, **clann bheaga** little children, **dithis chloinne** two children, *Note:* **clann** *is sing but with coll or pl sense*, **duine cloinne**, *a child, can be more strictly and logically used to refer to individual children*, **cia mheud duine cloinne a th' agaibh? aon duine cloinne** how many children do you have? one child; **2** a clan, the descendants of the real or supposed progenitor of a clan, **Clann Dòmhnaill** Clan Donald, the MacDonalds, **Clann 'Ic Leòid** Clan MacLeod, (*trad*) **Clann a' Cheò** the Children/Clan of the Mist *a nickname for the MacGregors, Cf* **cinneadh 1, fine 2**

clann-nighean, *gen* **cloinn-nighean** *nf coll* **1** girl children; **2** girls *up to and incl late teens approx*; **3** young women of a variety of ages, *eg in expr* (*trad*) **clann-nighean an sgadain** the herring girls/lasses

claoidh *vt, pres part* **a' claoidh** & **a' claoidheadh**, (*of people*) **1** exhaust, wear out, *Cf* **sgìthich; 2** vex, weary, harass, *Cf* **sàraich 2**

claoidh *nf invar*, & **claoidheadh** *gen* **claoidhidh** *nm*, (*the act of*) exhausting, vexing &c (*see senses of* **claoidh** *v*)

claoidhte *adj* tired out, worn out, exhausted

claon, *vti, pres part* **a' claonadh**, **1** slope, incline; **2** go astray, lead astray; **3** (*vt*) pervert, *Cf* **coirb** *v*, **truaill 3; 4** veer, move obliquely

claon *adj* **1** awry, oblique, askew, (*Sc*) squint, *Cf* **fiar** *adj* **2; 2** sloping; **3** perverse

claonadh, *gen* **claonaidh** *nm* **1** (*the act of*) inclining &c (*see senses of* **claon** *v*); **2** a slant, a slope, an incline; **3** obliqueness; **4** a squint, *Cf* **fiaradh 2, spleuchd** *n* **2**; **5** perversion, a perversion; **6** prejudice, bias, discrimination

clàr, **clàir**, **clàran** *nm* **1** *used for many types of smooth, level surface, esp wooden*, a board, a plank, a table, *Cf more usu* **bòrd 2, dèile**; **2 clàr aodainn** a brow, a forehead, *esp in expressions* **bhuail i e an clàr aodainn** she struck him full in the face, (*fig*) **dh' innis mi an fhìrinn dhi an clàr a h-aodainn** I told her the truth to her face; **3** (*in book &c*) a table, a list, a register, **clàr-innse** a table/list of contents, **clàr-amais** an index, **clàr ainmean/dhaoine** a list of names/people, **clàr an luchd-taghaidh** the register of electors, **clàr-gnothaich** an agenda, **clàr-ama** a timetable, **clàr-oideachais** a curriculum, (*IT*) **clàr ruith** a flow chart, *Cf less trad* **liosta**; **4** a map (*also* **clàr-dùthcha**), **clàr den Eilean Sgitheanach** a map of Skye, *Cf* **mapa**; **5** a (gramophone) record, a recording, **inneal-chlàr** a record player; **6** *misc uses*, (*med*) **clàr sgiorrte** a slipped disc (*IT*) a disc, **meanbh-chlàr** a compact disc, (*IT*) **clàr cruaidh/sùbailte** a hard/floppy disc, (*IT*) **clàr-inneal** *m* a disc drive, (*IT*) **clàr iùil** a menu, (*oil industry*) **clàr tollaidh/ola** a drilling/an oil platform, **clàr seòlaidh** a signpost, a direction board, **clàr-iarrtais** an application form

clàrachadh, *gen* **clàrachaidh** *nm* (*the act of*) recording, registering (*see* **clàraich** *v*)

clàraich *vti, pres part* **a' clàrachadh**, **1** (*on paper, electronically &c*) register, record; **2** (*at college &c*) register, enrol

clàrc, *gen & pl* **clàirc** *nm* a clerk, *esp* (*crofting*) **clàrc a' bhaile** the township/grazings clerk, *Cf more trad* **clèireach 2**

clàr-fhiacail, **clàr-fhiacail**, **clàr-fhiaclan** *nf* (*tooth*) an incisor

clàrsach, **clàrsaich**, **clàrsaichean** *nf* a harp, *esp* a Celtic harp, a clarsach, (*poetry collection*) **Creachadh na Clàrsaich** (Ruaraidh MacThòmais) the plundering of the harp, *Cf less usu* **cruit 1**

clàrsair, **clàrsair**, **clàrsairean** *nm* a harper, *Cf less usu* **cruitear**[1]

clas, **clas**, **clasaichean** *nm* (*school &c*) a class, **cò an clas sa bheil thu?** which class are you in? **tha clas agam an-dràsta** I have a class just now

clasaigeach *adj* classical, **ceòl clasaigeach** classical music, **eachdraidh chlasaigeach** classical history

cleachd *vti, pres part* **a' cleachdadh**, **1** (*vt*) use, **cha chleachd mi salann sa chidsin** I don't use salt in the kitchen, *Cf less usu* **gnàthaich 1**; **2** (*vt*) accustom, get used to, **cleachd thu fhèin ris an fhuachd!** accustom yourself/get used to the cold!, *Cf less usu* **gnàthaich 2**; **3**

(*vi*) *in the past tense* used to, was/were accustomed to, **chleachd mi a bhith droch-nàdarach** I used to be bad-tempered, *in comp expr* **is/agus a chleachd** as it (*&c*) used to, **chan eil iad cho fàilteach 's a chleachd iàd a bhith** they're not so/as welcoming as they used to be, **cha tèid sinn ann cho tric agus a chleachd sinn** we don't go as often as we used to, *Cf* **àbhaist 2**

cleachdadh, cleachdaidh, cleachdaidhean *nm* 1 (*the act of*) using &c (*see senses of* **cleachd** *v*); 2 a custom, a habit, a practice, **bha na chleachdadh agam a bhith a' coiseachd a h-uile là** it used to be a habit of mine to walk every day; 3 (*musical instrument &c*) practice, (*prov*) **is e an cleachdadh a nì teòma** practice makes perfect; 4 (*IT*) *in pl* **cleachdaidhean** applications

cleachdte *adj* used, accustomed (**ri** to), **dh'fhàs i cleachdte ris aig a' cheann thall** she got/grew used to it/him in the end, **chan eil mi cleachdte ris a' bhiadh a tha seo** I'm not used to this food

cleamhnas, *gen* **cleamhnais** *nm* 1 relationship by marriage, *Cf* **càirdeas pòsaidh** (*see* **càirdeas 1**); 2 sex, sexual relations, intercourse, *Cf* **feis(e)**

cleas, cleasa, cleasan *nm* 1 (*trad*) a feat, an exploit, **Cù Chulainn nan cleas** Cuchulainn of the exploits, *Cf* **euchd 1**; 2 (*now usu*) a trick, a joke, **rinn iad cleas orm** they played a trick/a joke on me, *Cf* **car** *n* 4; 3 a conjurer's trick; 4 (*children &c*) play, playing, *Cf more usu* **cluich** *n* 1;

cleasachd *nf invar*, 1 (*usu of children*) play, (*the action of*) playing, *Cf more usu* **cluich** *n*; 2 conjuring; 3 juggling

cleasaich *vi, pres part* **a' cleasachd**, (*of children*) play, *Cf more usu* **cluich** *v*

cleasaiche, cleasaiche, cleasaichean *nm* 1 (*film, theatre*) an actor, a player, *Cf less trad* **actair**; 2 a comedian, a comic, a clown; 3 a conjurer; 4 a juggler

cleas-chluich, cleas-chluiche, cleas-chluichean *nf* a comic film or play, a comedy

clèir, *gen* **clèire** *nf* 1 (*coll*) clergy; 2 (*Presbyterian churches*) a Presbytery

clèireach, *gen & pl* **clèirich** *nm* 1 (*trad*) a clergyman, *Cf* **ministear 1**, **pears-eaglais, sagart**; 2 a clerk, *Cf less trad* **clàrc**; 3 a Presbyterian

clèireach *adj* presbyterian, **an Eaglais Chlèireach** the Presbyterian Church, **an Eaglais Shaor Chlèireach** the Free Presbyterian Church

clèireachail *adj* clerical, **luchd-obrach clèireachail** clerical staff

cleith *n & pres part, see* **ceil** *v*, **ceileadh** *n*

cleòc, cleòca, cleòcan *nm* a cloak

cleoc *see* gleoc

clì *adj* left, **mo chas chlì** my left foot, **air a làimh chlì** on his/her left, *Cf* **ceàrr 2**

CLI *nm, the acronym of* **Comann an Luchd-Ionnsachaidh**, the Gaelic Learners' Association

cliabh, *gen & pl* clèibh *nm* **1** (*trad*) a pannier (*for a horse or pony*); **2** (*trad*) a creel (*for carrying peats &c*); **3** a creel (*to set for crabs &c*), **cliabh ghiomach** a lobster creel, a lobsterpot; **4** a (*human*) chest, a thorax, *Cf* **broilleach 2**; **5** (*mus notation*) a stave

cliamhainn, cleamhna, cleamhnan *nm* a son-in-law, **bana-chliamhainn** *f* a daughter-in law

cliath *vti, pres part* **a' cliathadh**, (*agric*) harrow

cliath, clèithe, cliathan *nf* **1** a grating, a grid, **cliath-uinneig** a lattice, window bars, **cliath-theine** a fire grate, **cliath chruidh** a cattle grid (*maps*) **ceàrnag clèithe** a grid square; **2** (*agric*) a harrow

cliatha(i)ch, cliathaich, cliathaichean *nf* a side, **tha pian agam nam chliathaich** I've a pain in my side, **dhìrich sinn cliathach na beinne** we climbed the side of the mountain, *Cf more usu* **taobh 1**

cliathan, cliathain, cliathanan *nm* (*anat*) a sternum, a breastbone

clìomaid, clìomaide, clìomaidean *nf* climate, a climate

clis *adj* nimble, agile, swift; *also* sudden, **Na Fir Chlis** Aurora Borealis, the Northern Lights, *also the name of a sadly defunct Gaelic theatre company*, *Cf* **lùthmhor 1**

cliseachd *nf invar* nimbleness, quickness, agility, *Cf* **lùth 2**

clisg, *pres part* **a' clisgeadh**, start, jump (*through fear or surprise*), **chlisg e** he jumped/started

clisgeach *adj* **1** jumpy, nervy, nervous, on edge; **2** timid; *Cf* **sgeunach**

clisgeadh, clisgidh, clisgidhean *nf* **1** (*the act of*) starting, jumping &c (*see senses of* **clisg** *v*); **2** a start, a jump, a fright, a shock, **chuir thu clisgeadh orm!** you gave me a start/a fright, you made me jump/ startled me

clisgear, clisgeir, clisgearan *nm* (*gram*) an exclamation, an interjection

clisg-phuing, clisg-phuinge, clisg-phuingean *nf* (*typog*) an exclamation mark

cliù *nm invar* **1** fame, reputation, a reputation, renown, glory, (*prov*) **is buaine cliù na saoghal** reputation (*ie* honour) lasts longer than life, **choisinn e cliù ann an saoghal na poileataics** he won fame/ made a reputation in the world of politics, **choisinn an rèiseamaid cliù sa bhlàr** the regiment won glory in the battle (*Cf* **glòir 2**); **2** praise, (*song*) **fàilte, fàilte, mùirn is cliù dhut!** welcome, welcome, love and praise to you!, *Cf* **luaidh** *n* **2**, **moladh**

cliùiteach *adj* famous, celebrated, renowned, *Cf* **ainmeil, iomraiteach**

clò[1], *gen* **clòtha**, *pl* **clòitean** & **clòithean** *nm* **1** cloth, woven material, *Cf* **aodach 1**; **2** woollen cloth, tweed, **Clò Mòr** *also* **Clò na Hearadh** & **An Clò Hearach** Harris Tweed

clò[2] & **clòdh**, *gen* **clòdha**, *pl* **clòdhan** *nm* **1** print, **cuir** *v* **leabhar (&c) an clò** to print/bring out/publish a book (&c), **nochd a' bhàrdachd aige an clò an-uiridh** his poetry appeared in print last year (*Cf* **clò-bhuail, foillsich 1**), **ùr on chlò** newly published, hot off the presses, **mearachd clò** a printing error, a misprint; **2** a printing press; **3** a publishing house, an imprint, **Clò Ostaig** the Ostaig Press

clòbha, clòbha, clòbhan *nf* a clove

clobha, clobha, clobhan *nm* tongs

clòbhar, *gen* **clòbhair** *nm* clover, *Cf more trad* **seamrag 2**

clobhd, clobhda, clobhdan *nm* a cloth (*for cleaning &c*), *Cf* **brèid 3, clùd 2**

clobhsa, clobhsa, clobhsaichean *nm* (*in tenement &c*) a close

clò-bhuail *vt, pres part* **a' clò-bhualadh**, print, **air a chlò-bhualadh le … printed by …**

clò-bhuailte *adj* printed, **clò-bhuailte le A Learmonth 's a Mhac Sruighlea** printed by A Learmonth & Son Stirling

clò-bhualadair, clò-bhualadair, clò-bhualadairean *nm* **1** a printer; **2** a printing firm

clò-bhualadh, clò-bhualaidh, clò-bhualaidhean *nm* **1** (*the act of*) printing; **2** a publication, an imprint, **Clò-bhualaidhean Gairm** Gairm Publications

cloc *see* **gleoc**

clò-chadal, *gen* **clò-chadail** *nm* dozing, a doze, **chaidh mi nam chlò-chadal** *or* **thàinig clò-chadal orm** I dozed off/dropped off

clochar, clochair, clocharan *nm* a convent

clòdh *see* **clò**[2]

cloga(i)d, clogaide, clogaidean *nm* a helmet, **clogad-dìona** a crash helmet, a hard hat

clòimh, *gen* **clòimhe** *nf* wool, **aodach clòimhe** woollen clothing, *Cf* **olann**

clòimhteachan, *gen* & *pl* **clòimhteachain** *nm* an eiderdown

closach, closaich, closaichean *nf* **1** a dead body (*usu not human*), *Cf* **corp 2**; **2** a carcase (*ie to be prepared by butcher*)

clòsaid, clòsaide, clòsaidean *nf* a closet

clò-sgrìobh *vti, pres part* **a' clò-sgrìobhadh**, type, use a typewriter

clò-sgrìobhadair, clò-sgrìobhadair, clò-sgrìobhadairean *nm* a typewriter

clò-sgrìobhadh, clò-sgrìobhaidh, clò-sgrìobhaidhean *nm* 1 (*the act of*) typing; 2 typescript, a typescript

clò-sgrìobhaiche, clò-sgrìobhaiche, clò-sgrìobhaichean *nm* a typist

clua(i)n, *gen* **cluaine,** *pl* **cluainean** & **cluaintean** *nf* a meadow, a pasture, *Cf* **dail 1, faiche, ionaltradh 2**

cluaineas, *gen* **cluaineis** *nm* retirement, **thàinig e air ais bho chluaineas** he came out of retirement, **peinnsean** *m* **cluaineis** a retirement pension

cluaran, cluarain, cluaranan *nm* a thistle, *Cf* **fòghnan**

cluas, cluaise, cluasan *nf* 1 an ear, (*song*) **toirm mum chluais** a din about my ear, **cluas-fhail** *f* an ear-ring, **cèir-chluaise** *f* ear-wax, **grèim-cluaise** *m* earache, **tolladh-chluasan** *m* ear-piercing; 2 a handle of a vessel or container, (*Sc*) a lug

cluasag, cluasaig, cluasagan *nf* a pillow, *Cf* **babhstair**

club, club, clubaichean *nm* a club (*ie association*), *Cf* **comann 1**

clùd, clùid, clùdan *nm* 1 a rag, *Cf* **luideag;** 2 a cloth, (*Sc*) a clout, *Cf* **brèid 3, clobhd**

cluich *vti, pres part* **a' cluich(e),** play, **cha bhi mi a' cluich sa mhaidse an-diugh** I won't be playing in the match today, **cluich ball-coise/ rugbaidh** play football/rugby, **bidh sinn a' cluich (an aghaidh) Rangers** we'll be playing (against) Rangers, **tha a' chlann a' cluich sa ghàrradh** the children are playing in the garden (*Cf less usu* **cleasaich**), **cluich Hamlet air an àrd-ùrlar** play Hamlet on the stage, **cò tha a' cluich a' bhocsa/air a' bhocsa?** who's playing/playing on the accordeon?

cluich & **cluiche,** *gen* **cluiche,** *pl* **cluichean** & **cluicheannan** *nm* 1 play, (*the activity of*) playing, *Cf less usu* **cleas 4;** 2 a game, **cluich-bùird** a board game, *Cf less trad* **geama 1**

cluicheadair, cluicheadair, cluicheadairean *nm* 1 a player (*of a game, instrument*); 2 (*on stage, screen*) a player, an actor, *Cf more usu* **actair**

cluinn, *vt irreg* (*see tables p 406*), *pres part* **a' cluinntinn,** hear, **chuala mi gun robh thu tinn** I heard you were ill, **cha chluinn e bìd/guth** he can't hear a thing/a sound, **'s math a bhith a' cluinntinn bhuat!** it's good to be hearing from you!

cluinneadh, cluinneam, cluinneamaid, cluinnibh *pts of irreg v* **cluinn** *see tables p 406*

cluinntinn *nf invar* (*the act of*) hearing

cnag *vti, pres part* **a' cnagadh,** 1 (*vi*) crunch (*ie make a crunching noise*), **bha am mol a' cnagadh fo chasan** the shingle was crunching beneath his feet; 2 (*vti*) bang, knock

cnag, cnaig, cnagan *nf* **1** a bang, a knock; **2** a peg, **cnag-aodaich** a clothes peg; **3** a knob, *Cf* **cnap 2**; **4** a plug (*for sink, container &c*); **5** *in expr* **cnag na cùise**, the nub/crux of the matter, the fundamental issue, the crucial question, **am bi clann bheaga a' togail na Gàidhlig aig an taigh? 's e sin cnag na cùise** are small children picking up Gaelic at home? that's the crucial question

CNAG *n, the acronym of* **Comunn na Gàidhlig**, the Gaelic Association, *a body set up to promote the language and its culture*

cnag-dealain, cnaig-dealain, cnagan-dealain *nf* an electric plug, a power plug, *Cf* **bun-dealain** (*see* **bun 3**)

cnàimh, *gen* **cnàmha**, *pl* **cnàmhan** & **cnàimhean** *nm, also* **cnàmh, cnàimh, cnàmhan** *nm*, bone, a bone, **cnà(i)mh an droma** the backbone, the spine, **cnà(i)mh an uga** the collarbone

cnàimhneach, *gen* & *pl* **cnàimhnich** *nm* a skeleton

cnàimhseag, cnàimhseig, cnàimhseagan *nf* acne; a blackhead

cnàmh *vt, pres part* **a' cnàmhadh** & **a' cnàmh**, **1** chew, masticate; **2** digest; **3** *in expr* **a' cnàmh na cìre**, (*of animals*) chewing the cud, (*fam, of humans*) talking things over, chewing the fat, talking of this and that; *Cf* **cnuas**

cnàmh¹ *nm see* **cnàimh**

cnàmh², *gen* **cnàimh** *nm* potato blight, *Cf* **gaiseadh**

cnàmhach *adj* bony

cnàmhadh, *gen* **cnàmhaidh** *nm* (*the act of*) chewing &c (*see senses of* **cnàmh** *v*)

cnàmh-loisg *see* **loisg 1**

cnap, cnaip, cnapan *nm* **1** a block *or* a lump *or* a chunk of anything, *Cf* **ceap 1**, **geinn 1**; **2** a knob, a boss, *Cf* **cnag 3**; **3** a small (lumpy) hill, *Cf* **meall** *n* **2**

cnapach *adj* lumpy, knobby, nobbly

cnap-starra(dh) (*lit*) an obstruction, a barrier, an obstacle (*Cf* **bacadh 2**), (*fig*) a stumbling block

cnatan, *gen* & *pl* **cnatain** *nm* a cold, (*Sc*) the cold, *used with the art*, **tha an cnatan a' tighinn orm** I'm getting a/the cold, *Cf* **fuachd 2**

cnead, cneada, cneadan *nm* a groan (*of pain or grief*), **rinn i cnead** *or* **leig i cnead (aiste)** she groaned/let out a groan

cnèadachadh, *gen* **cnèadachaidh** *nm* (*the act of*) caressing &c (*see senses of* **cnèadaich** *v*)

cnèadaich & **cniadaich** *vt, pres part* **a' cnèadachadh**, caress, fondle, stroke affectionately or amorously, **bha e a' cnèadachadh a fuilt** he was stroking her hair

cneutag, cneutaig, cneutagan, *nf* a small ball (*for ball games, esp shinty*) cniadaich *see* cnèadaich

cnò, *gen* cnò & cnotha, *pl* cnothan *nf* 1 (*bot*) a nut, cnò Fhrangach &
gall-chnò a walnut, cnò-challtainn a hazelnut, cnò-thalmhainn a
peanut, cnò-bhainne & cnò-còco a coconut; 2 (*engin &c*) a nut, cnò
is crann a nut and (a) bolt

cnoc, *gen* & *pl* cnuic *nm* a hill, *usu small to medium-sized*, mullach nan
cnoc the top of the hills, *in placenames usu rendered as* Knock, An
Cnoc Liath Knocklea, the grey hill, *Cf* beinn 2, mòinteach, monadh,
sgùrr, tom, tulach

cnocach *adj* hilly, sgìre chnocach a hilly area/district, *Cf* monadail

cnocan, *gen* & *pl* cnocain (*dimin of* cnoc) *nm* a small hill, a hillock, *Cf*
tulach

cnòthach *adj* (*taste &c*) nutty

cnuas & cnuasaich, *vti, pres part* a' cnuasa(cha)dh, 1 chew (*food*); 2 (*vi*)
(*ideas, topics &c*) chew over, reflect, ruminate, think, contemplate,
ponder, (air on, about, upon) bha e a' cnuasachadh air na thubhairt
i ris he was turning over in his mind/thinking over what she (had)
said to him; *Cf* cnàmh *v*

cnuasaich *see* cnuas

cnuimh, cnuimhe, cnuimhean *nf* 1 a maggot, a grub; 2 a worm, cnuimh-
thalmhainn an earthworm, *Cf* boiteag

cò *inter pron, Note: in some constrs the v* is *can be understood as implicitly*
following cò *eg* cò esan? who's he?; *Note: in senses 4, 5 & 6 the accent*
is usu omitted; 1 (*of persons only*) who, *in direct questions* cò a rinn e?
who did it? *in indirect questions* chan eil fhios 'am cò a th' ann I
don't know who it is, is coma leam cò ris a bha i a' bruidhinn I
don't care who she was talking to; 2 (*of persons & things*) which, what,
cò na seinneadairean as fheàrr leat? which are the singers you like
best? cò na leabhraichean a tha thu airson fhaighinn air iasaid?
which/what books would you like/do you want to borrow? cha
robh mi cinnteach cò aca (*also* cò dhiubh) a phòsainn I wasn't sure
which of them I would marry, (*prov*) chan eil fios cò as glice – fear
a chaomhnas no fear a chaitheas there's no knowing which is wiser
– a man who saves or a man who spends; 3 *in expr* cò … às …?
where … from?, cò às a tha thu?, where are you from? cò às a nochd
esan? where did he (*emph*) appear/spring from?; 4 *in exprs* co aca &
co-dhiù *conj* whether, tha thu ciontach co-dhiù a ghoid thu e no
nach do ghoid you're guilty whether you stole it or not; 5 *in expr*
co-dhiù anyway, in any case, at least, fuirich ma thogras tu, tha
mise a' falbh co-dhiù! stay if you like/want, I'm leaving anyway/
in any case, bha dà mhìle ann co-dhiù there were two thousand
there at least/anyway, tha mi coma co-dhiù I don't mind/care
either way, I'm indifferent; 6 co mheud *see* cia mheud

co- *a prefix often corres to Eng* co-, con-, fellow-, *also found in older spellings as* **comh-** *&* **coimh(-)**; **co-** *does not usu change the basic sense of the word it precedes, but it stresses mutuality, reciprocity, co-operation &c; see examples below*

co-aimsireil *adj* **1** contemporary, living at the same time; **2** belonging to the present time

co-alta (*also* **co-dhalta**), *gen* **co-alta**, *pl* **co-altan** *nmf* a foster brother or sister

co-aois *&* **comhaois**, *gen* **co-aois**, *pl* **co-aoisean** *nm* a person of roughly the same age as another, a contemporary, **bha Iain Mac a' Ghobhainn is Domhnall MacAmhlaigh nan co-aoisean** Iain Crichton Smith and Donald MacAulay were contemporaries

co-aoiseach *adj* having roughly the same age as another

co-aontachadh, *gen* **co-aontachaidh** *nm* **1** (*the act of*) consenting &c (*see senses of* **co-aontaich** *v*); **2** agreement, an agreement, accord, an accord

co-aontaich *vti, pres part* **co-aontachadh**, **1** *vi* be in agreement, consent, come together in agreement, combine; **2** *vt* consent to, agree to

cobhair, *gen* **cobhrach** *&* **coibhre** *nf* **1** help, aid, relief, **bàta-coibhre** a life boat (*Cf* **bàta-teasairginn**), **an dèan thu cobhair orm?** will you help me? *Cf more general* **cuideachadh** 2; **2** *as excl* **cobhair orm!** help!

cobhar, *gen* **cobhair** *nm* foam, froth, *Cf* **cop**

cobhartach, *gen* **cobhartaich** *nmf* booty, plunder; prey

co-bhualadh, co-bhualaidh, co-bhualaidhean *nm* **1** (*the act of*) colliding; **2** collision, a collision, an impact

co-bhuail *vi, pres part* **a' co-bhualadh**, collide

còc *nm invar* (*fuel; also the drink*) coke

còcaire, còcaire, còcairean *nm* a cook, a chef, **ban-chòcaire** *f* a (female) cook *or* chef

còcaireachd *nf invar* cooking, cookery

cochall, *gen* *&* *pl* **cochaill** *nm* **1** (*of a seed &c*) a husk, (*peas, beans*) a shell, *Cf* **plaosg**; **2** (*headgear*) a hood

co-cheangail *vt, pres part* **a' co-cheangal**, link, connect, tie together

co-cheangailte *adj* linked together, connected, **tha blàthachadh na cruinne is a' chlìomaid co-cheangailte ri chèile** global warming and the climate are linked to one another

co-cheangal, co-cheangail, co-cheanglaichean *nm* **1** (*the act of*) linking &c; **2** linkage, a link, connection, a connection, **co-cheangal smaointean** association of ideas

co-chomann, *gen* *&* *pl* **co-chomainn** *nm* **1** a community, a commune; **2** (*business*) a co-operative, **co-chomann chroitearan** a crofters' co-operative, **Co-chomann Stafainn** Staffin Co-operative, *Cf* **co-obrachadh** 3

co-chòrd, *vi, pres part* **a' co-chòrdadh**, agree mutually, come to a mutual agreement

co-chòrdadh, co-chòrdaidh, co-chòrdaidhean *nm* 1 (*the act of*) agreeing &c (*see senses of* **cò-chòrd** *v*); 2 concord, agreement, an agreement, an accord, a treaty, an alliance

co-chothrom, *gen* **co-chothruim** *nm* balance, equilibrium

co-chruinnich *vti, pres part* **a' co-chruinneachadh**, gather together, assemble, collect (*people & things*)

co-chruinneachadh, co-chruinneachaidh, co-chruinneachaidhean *nm* 1 (*the act of*) gathering &c (*see senses of* **co-chruinnich** *v*); 2 assembly, an assembly, a gathering, a convention, **Co-chruinneachadh Ughdarrasan Ionadail na h-Alba** the Convention of Scottish Local Authorities; 3 (*Lit*) a collection, a compilation, an anthology, **co-chruinneachadh de sgeulachdan goirid** a collection of short stories

còco *nm invar* cocoa

còd *nm invar* (*cypher &c*) code, a code, (*IT*) **còd dà-fhillte** binary code, (*IT*) **còd inneil** machine code

co-dhèanta *adj* composed, made up, assembled, put together

co-dhiu *adv & conj see* **cò 4 & 5**

co-dhlùthaich *vti, pres part* **a' co-dhlùthachadh**, condense

co-dhùin *vti, pres part* **a' co-dhùnadh**, 1 (*process, meeting &c*) conclude, bring to a conclusion, end; 2 come to a decision, come to a conclusion, decide

co-dhùnadh, co-dhùnaidh, co-dhùnaidhean *nm* 1 (*the act of*) concluding, ending &c (*see senses of* **co-dhùin** *v*); 2 a conclusion, an end, an ending, (*song*) **nì mi nis co-dhùnadh is bheir mi an dàn gu crìch** now I will conclude and bring the song to an end; 3 a decision, a conclusion, **cha tàinig na comhairlichean gu co-dhùnadh** the councillors didn't reach a decision/come to a conclusion

co-èigneachadh, *gen* **co-èigneachaidh** *nm* 1 (*the act of*) forcing, compelling; 2 compulsion

co-èignich *vt, pres part* **a' co-èigneachadh**, force, compel, **cho-èignich a chàirdean e sin a dhèanamh** his friends forced/compelled him to do that, *Cf* **thoir 4**

cofaidh, cofaidh, cofaidhean *nm* coffee, a coffee, **a bheil thu ag iarraidh cofaidh?** do you want/would you like a coffee?

co-fhoghlam, *gen* **co-fhoghlaim** *nm* co-education

co-fharpais (*also* **farpair**), *gen* **co-fharpaise**, *pl* **co-fharpaisean** *nf* a competition, **co-fharpaisean a' Mhòid** the Mod competitions co-fhlaitheachd *nf invar* 1 a republic; 2 republicanism; 3 *in expr* **a' Cho-Fhlaitheachd Bhreatannach** the British Commonwealth (*cf next*)

co-fhlaitheas, co-fhlaitheis, co-fhlaitheasan *nm* a confederation (*of countries*), **An Co-fhlaitheas** the (British) Commonwealth

co-fhoghar, co-fhoghair, co-fhoghairean *nm* a consonant, *Cf* **connrag, consan**

co-fhreagair *vti, pres part* **a' co-fhreagairt**, match, correspond, cause to match or correspond (**do** to)

co-fhreagairt, co-fhreagairte, co-fhreagairtean *nf* 1 (*the act of*) matching &c (*see senses of* **co-fhreagair** *v*); 2 (*general incl letter-writing*) correspondence

co-fhulangach *adj* sympathetic, compassionate

co-fhulangas, *gen* co-fhulangais *nm* sympathy, fellow-feeling

cofhurtachadh, *gen* cofhurtachaidh *nm* (*the act of*) comforting, consoling

cofhurtachd *nf invar* 1 consolation, comfort (*spiritual, emotional*); 2 (*phys*) comfort

cofhurtaich *vt, pres part* **a' cofhurtachadh**, comfort, console, *Cf* **faothaich, furtaich**

cofhurtail *adj* comfortable, **a bheil thu cofhurtail? a bheil a' chathair sin cofhurtail gu leòr?** are you comfortable? is that chair comfortable enough?, *Cf* **seasga(i)r 1**

cogadh, cogaidh, cogaidhean *nm* war, warfare, a war, **An Cogadh Mòr** The Great War, **A' Chiad Chogadh, An Darna Cogadh** the First (World) War, the Second (World) War, **cuimhneachan-cogaidh** *m* a war-memorial, **rinn iad cogadh** they made/waged war

cogais, cogaise, cogaisean *nf* conscience, a conscience, **bha mo chogais gam shàrachadh fad na h-oidhche** my conscience was tormenting me all night

co-ghin *vi, pres part* **a' co-ghineadh**, mate, have sexual intercourse, copulate, *Cf* **cuplaich, muin 4**

co-ghineadh, *gen* co-ghinidh *nm* 1 (*the act of*) mating &c (*see senses of* **co-ghin** *v*); 2 copulation, intercourse, *Cf* **cuplachadh 2**

co-ghnìomhair, co-ghnìomhair, co-ghnìomhairean *nm* (*gram*) an adverb

coibhneas, *gen* coibhneis *nm* kindness, kindliness

coibhneil *adj* kind, kindly, (*song*) **chaith mi an oidhche cridheil coibhneil mar ri màighdeannan na h-àirigh** I spent the night in warm-hearted kindliness in the company of the sheiling maidens, *Cf* **bàidheil**

coidse *nf invar* (*transport*) a coach

còig *n & num adj* the number five, five, **còig mionaidean** five minutes

còig-deug *n & adj* fifteen, **còig mionaidean deug** fifteen minutes

còigeamh *adj* fifth

còigeamh-deug *adj* fifteenth, **an còigeamh là deug den Ogmhios** the fifteenth of June

còignear *nm invar* (people numbering) five, a fivesome, *takes gen pl* **còignear mhinistearan** five ministers

coigreach, *gen & pl* **coigrich** *nm* 1 a foreigner, an alien, *Cf* **eilthireach 1, Gall 1**; 2 a stranger, *Cf* **coimheach** *n* 2, **srainnsear 1**; 3 an incomer, *Cf* **seatlair, srainnsear 2**

coileach, *gen & pl* **coilich** *nm* a cock (*male domestic fowl or game bird*), **coileach dubh** a blackcock, a male black grouse, **coileach-coille** a woodcock, **coileach-gaoithe** a weathercock

coilean & **coimhlion** *vt, pres part* **a' coileanadh**, accomplish, achieve, complete, *Cf* **thoir gu buil** (*see* **buil 2**), **crìochnaich**

coileanadh, *gen* **coileanaidh** *nm* (*the act of*) accomplishing &c (*see senses of* **coilean** *v*)

coileanta *adj* 1 accomplished, achieved, finished; 2 perfect (*not usu in moral sense, Cf* **foirfe**), (*gram*) **an tràth coileanta** the perfect tense

coilear, coileir, coilearan *nm* a collar

coill *nf invar* 1 guilt, sin; 2 *in expr* **bha e fon choill** he was outlawed/an outlaw

coille, coille, coilltean *nf* a wood, a forest, (*poem*) **Coilltean Ratharsair** (Somhairle MacGill-Eain) The Woods of Raasay, **coille-uisge** a rainforest

coilleag, coilleig, coilleagan *nf* a cockle, *Cf* **srùban**

coillear, coilleir, coillearan *nm* 1 a forestry worker; 2 a woodcutter

coillteachadh, *gen* **coillteachaidh** *nm* afforestation

coimeas *vt, pres part* **a' coimeas**, compare, liken, *Cf* **dèan coimeas eadar** (*see* **coimeas** *n* 2)

coimeas, *gen* **coimeis** *nf* 1 (*the act of*) comparing, likening; 2 comparison, resemblance, **dèan** *v* **coimeas eadar dà rud** compare two things; 3 *esp in expr* **an coimeas ri** compared to, in comparison to, **is tana bainne an coimeas ri uachdar** milk is thin in comparison to/compared to cream, *Cf* **seach 2, taca 2**; 4 a match, the like(s) of, an equal, (*trad*) **chan fhaca mi a choimeas a-riamh** I never saw the like of him/it, I never saw his/its equal, *Cf* **leithid, samhail**

coimeasach *adj* 1 comparable; 2 (*gram*) comparative, **buadhair coimeasach** an adjective of comparison, a comparative adjective

coimeasgaich *see* **co-mheasgaich**

coimheach *adj* 1 strange, foreign, unfamiliar, (*prov*) **a h-uile cù air a'
chù choimheach** all dogs against/down on the strange dog,
aghaidh choimheach a mask (*ie disguise for face*)

coimheach, *gen & pl* **coimhich** *nm* 1 a foreigner; 2 a stranger; *Cf more
usu* **coigreach** *n*, **eilthireach, Gall, srainnsear**

coimhead *vti, pres part* **a' coimhead**, 1 (*vt*) watch, **coimhead film/TV**
watch a film/TV, **coimheadaidh mi dol fodha na grèine** I will
watch the sunset; 2 (*vi*) look (**air** at), **coimhead oirre** look at her, **a'
coimhead air dealbhan** looking at pictures/photos, *Cf* **seall 1**; 3
(*vi*) *in exprs* **coimhead ri** expect, **tha sinn a' coimhead ri stoirmean**
we're expecting storms (*Cf* **dùil1 2, sùil 3**), & (*calque*) **coimhead
air adhart gu/ri** look forward to, **bha iad a' coimhead air adhart
chun/ris an fhoghair** they were looking forward to the autumn;
4 (*vi*) (*calque*) look (*ie appear*), **tha sin a' coimhead math!** that
looks/is looking good!

coimhead, *gen* **coimhid** *nm*, (*the act of*) watching, looking &c (*see senses
of* **coimhead** *v*), **luchd coimhid** *m* watchers, onlookers, spectators,
(*TV &c*) viewers

coimhearsnach, *gen & pl* **coimhearsnaich** *nm* a neighbour, *Cf more usu*
nàbaidh

coimhearsnachd *nf invar* a neighbourhood, *Cf* **nàbaidheachd**

coimheatailt, coimheatailte, coimheatailtean *nf* (*metals*) an alloy

coimh-leapach *also* **coileapach**, *gen & pl* **coi(mh)leapaich** *nm* a
mistress, a live-in lover, a (sexual) partner, (*Sc*) a bidie-in

coimhlion *see* **coilean**

coimisean, coimiseain, coimiseanan *nm* a commission, **Coimisean nan
Croitearan** the Crofters Commission, **Coimisean na Roinn Eòrpa**
the European Commission

coimpiuta(i)r, coimpiutair, coimpiutairean *nm* a computer, *Cf more
trad, less usu* **rianadair 2**

coineanach, *gen & pl* **coineanaich** *nm* a rabbit, *Cf less trad* **rabaid**

còinneach, *gen* **còinnich** *nf* (*bot*) moss

coinneachadh, *gen* **coinneachaidh** *nm* (*the act of*) meeting &c (*see senses
of* **coinnich** *v*)

coinneal, coinnle, coinnlean *nf* a candle

coinneamh, coinneimh, coinneamhan *nf* 1 (*business, societies &c*) a
meeting, **coinneamh bhliadhnail** an annual meeting; 2 *in expr* **mu
choinneimh** opposite, facing, **bha mi nam shuidhe mu coinneimh**
I was sitting opposite/facing her, *Cf* **comhair 2**; 3 *in expr* **an
coinneimh** towards, to meet, **rachamaid nan coinneimh** let's go
to meet them, *Cf* **ionnsaigh 3**

coinnich *vi, pres part* **a' coinneachadh,** 1 meet, congregate, come together, **bidh sinn a' coinneachadh ann an talla a' bhaile** we'll be meeting in the town/village hall, *Cf more usu* **cruinnich** 1; 2 *in expr* **coinnich ri** meet (*by chance or by arrangement*), **'s ann sa phàirc a choinnich mi riutha** it was in the park that I met them, *Cf* **tachair** 3, 4 & 5

coinnleir, coinnleir, coinnlearan *nm* a candlestick, a candle holder

co-ionann & **co-ionnan,** *adj* identical, equal, the same, equivalent **tha bùrn agus uisge co-ionann (ri chèile)** 'bùrn' and 'uisge' are the same (as each other), (*maths*) **tha x uiread x (or x air iomadachadh le x) co-ionann ri** x^2 x times x equals x^2, *Cf* **ionann**

còir, *gen* **còire** & **còrach,** *pl* **còraichean** *nf* 1 an obligation, a (*usu moral*) duty, *esp in expr* **bu chòir dhomh** (&c) I (&c) should, I (&c) ought, **bu chòir dhut sgrìobhadh thuice an-diugh** you should/ought to write to her today, **bu chòir dhomh a bhith a' falbh** I ought to be going/leaving, *in neg,* **cha bu chòir dhomh** (&c) I (&c) shouldn't, I (&c) ought not to, **cha bu chòir dhut goid/smocadh** you shouldn't steal/smoke, **chan eil e cho math agus bu chòir** it's not as good as it should be; 2 a right, what is just or fitting, **Còraichean Daonna** Human Rights, **chan eil còir aig a' Chomhairle an taigh-òsta agam a dhùnadh** the Council has no right to close my hotel, **dh'athdhìol e e, mar bu chòir** he repaid it, as was only right/as was fitting; 3 *esp in expr* **tuilleadh 's a' chòir** more than enough, too much, far too much, **an robh biadh gu leòr agaibh aig a' phàrtaidh? bha tuilleadh 's a' chòir againn!** did you have plenty food at the party? we had more than enough!; 4 justice, right, (*trad*) **a' seasamh na còrach** maintaining/standing up for justice, *Cf* **ceartas, ionracas** 2

còir *adj* 1 (*trad*) *of people* decent, worthy, kindly, (*prov*) **duine còir an rathaid mhòir is bèist mhòr a-staigh** a fine fellow when he's out and about and a monster at home; 2 (*esp in corres*) dear, **A Dhòmhnaill chòir** Dear Donald, *more personal &/or affectionate than* **A Dhòmhnaill a charaid** (*see* **caraid** 3)

coirb *vt, pres part* **a' coirbeadh,** corrupt, *Cf* **claon** *v* 3, **truaill** 3

coirbte *adj* corrupt, corrupted

coirce *nm invar* oats, **aran-coirce** oatmeal bread, **min-choirce** *f* oatmeal

coire, coire, coireannan *nf* 1 a wrong, an offence, *Cf* **eucoir** 2; 2 blame, **cuir** *v* **coire air duine eile** blame/lay blame on someone else (*Cf* **coirich**), *Cf* **cron** 2 & *less usu* **lochd** 1

coire, coire, coireachan *nm* 1 a kettle, **cuir air an coire!** put the kettle on!; 2 (*trad*) a cauldron; 3 (*topog*) a corrie

coireach *adj* **1** guilty, at fault, (*trad*) **is e Seumas as** (*for* **a is**) **coireach** James is guilty/to blame/at fault, *Cf* **ciontach** *adj*; **2** responsible, the reason or explanation for (*often without implication of guilt or blame*), **tha an gàrradh a' coimhead uabhasach math am bliadhna, cò as coireach ri sin?** the garden's looking great this year, who's responsible for that?, to whom do we owe that? **dè as coireach nach eil duine beò air an t-sràid an-diugh?** what's the explanation/ reason for there being nobody on the street today?

coireach, *gen & pl* **coirich** *nm* a guilty person, an offender, *Cf* **ciontach** *n*, **eucorach**

coirich *vti, pres part* **a' coireachadh**, blame, *Cf* **coire** *nf* 2

coireachadh, *gen* **coireachaidh** *nm* (*the act of*) blaming

coiseachd *nf invar*, walking, the act of walking, **an dèidh pìos math coiseachd ràinig sinn am bàgh** after a good bit of walking we reached the bay

coisich *vi, pres part* **a' coiseachd**, walk, **choisich mi romham fad an là** I walked on/onwards all day

coisiche, coisiche, coisichean *nm* **1** a walker; **2** a pedestrian

coisinn *vt, pres part* **a' cosnadh**, **1** earn, **tha mi a' cosnadh airgid mhòir a-nis** I'm earning big money now; **2** win, gain, **choisinn i cliù air an àrd-ùrlar** she won fame on the stage, **cha do choisinn mi duais aig a' Mhòd** I didn't win a prize at the Mod, *Cf* **buannaich** 2

còisir *&* **còisir-chiùil**, *gen* **còisre(-ciùil)** *&* **còisire(-ciùil)**, *pl* **còisirean (-ciùil)** *nf* a choir, **Còisir Ghàidhlig Shruighlea** Stirling Gaelic Choir

coisrig *vt, pres part* **a' coisrigeadh**, **1** consecrate (*a church &c*) (**do** to); **2** devote (**do** to), **choisrig e a bheatha do dh'adhbhar na saorsa** he devoted his life to the cause of freedom; **3** (*book, music &c*) dedicate (**do** to)

coisrigeadh, coisrigidh, coisrigidhean *nm* **1** (*the act of*) consecrating &c (*see senses of* **coisrig** v); **2** consecration, a consecration, dedication, a dedication

coisrigte *adj* sacred, consecrated, **abhlan coisrigte** a consecrated (communion) wafer

coitcheann *adj* **1** communal, shared, public, common, **amar-snàimh coitcheann** public baths/swimming pool, **Am Margadh Coitcheann** The Common Market, *Cf* **poblach**; **2** general, **foghlam-eòlas coitcheann** general knowledge, general education, **taghadh-pàrlamaid coitcheann** a general election, **stailc choitcheann** a general strike

coiteachadh, *gen* **coiteachaidh** *nm* (*the act of*) pressing &c (*see senses of* **coitich** *v*)

coitheanal & **coithional**, *gen* **coitheanail**, *pl* **coitheanalan** *nm* a (church) congregation

coitich *vt, pres part* **a' coiteachadh**, press, urge, encourage (*someone to do something*), *Cf* **spreig, stuig**, & *more usu* **brosnaich**

col, *gen* **cola** *nm* incest

colach *adj* incestuous

co-labhairt *nf invar* a conference, a symposium, (*business &c*) a seminar, *Cf* **còmhdhail**

co-là-breith, co-là-breith, co-làithean-breith *nm* a birthday **tha co-là-breith agam an-diugh** it's my birthday today, *Cf* **ceann-bliadhna**

cola-deug *nm invar* a fortnight, **bidh sinn air ais an ceann cola-deug** we'll be back in/after a fortnight, **tha mi a' falbh airson cola-deug** I'm going away for a fortnight, **bidh mi air falbh fad cola-deug** I'll be away for a (whole) fortnight

colaiste & **colaisde**, *gen* **colaisde**, *pl* **colaisdean** *nmf* a college, **colaiste phrìobhaideach** a private college

colann, *gen* **colainn** & **colna**, *pl* **colainnean** *nf* a body, *Cf more usu* **bodhaig, corp 1**

colbh, *gen* & *pl* **cuilbh** *nm* 1 (*architecture*) a column, a pillar; 2 (*newspaper*) a column

Col(l)ach, *gen* & *pl* **Col(l)aich** *nm* someone from Coll (**Col(l)a**), *also as adj* **Col(l)ach** of, from or pertaining to Coll

collaidh *adj* 1 sensual, carnal, *Cf* **feòlmhor 2**; 2 lewd, *Cf more usu* **drabasta, draosta**

coltach *adj* 1 likely, probable, **tha e coltach gun tig i** it's likely that she'll come, she'll probably come; 2 *in expr* **coltach ri** *prep* like, similar to, resembling, **chan eil i coltach ri a bràthair** she's not like her brother, **bha a ghuth coltach ri guth ròcais** his voice was like a rook's voice, **bha na togalaichean air fad coltach ri chèile** all the buildings were alike/resembled each other

coltachadh, *gen* **coltachaidh** *nm* (*the act of*) comparing, likening (**ri** to)

coltachd *nf invar* likelihood, possibility, probability

coltaich *vt, pres part* **a' coltachadh**, compare, liken (**ri** to)

coltas, *gen* **coltais** *nm* 1 appearance, look, **tha coltas saighdeir ort** you look like a soldier, **cha do chaidil mi idir a-raoir, tha a choltas (sin) ort!** I didn't sleep at all last night, you look like it!, *Cf* **dreach 1**; 2 *esp in expr* **a rèir c(h)oltais** by the look of it, judging by appearances, seemingly, apparently, **chaill e obair, a rèir coltais** he lost his job, it seems, **a rèir choltais bidh stoirm ann a dh'aithghearr** it looks as if/by the look of it there'll be a storm soon

com, *gen & pl* **cuim** *nm* **1** a bosom (*male or female*), the chest area (*Cf* **broilleach 1, uchd 1**), **thig nam chom!** come to my arms!, come and let me hug you! (*Cf* **achlais 2**); **2** a trunk (*of a human body*), the chest cavity, **a chridhe a' bualadh na chom** his heart beating in his chest/bosom

coma *adj* indifferent, unconcerned, of no concern, **is coma sin** that doesn't matter, that's of no concern (*Cf* **diofar 2**), **coma leat!** don't worry!, never mind!, **thig an saoghal gu crìch a-màireach! tha mise coma, is coma leam an tig no nach tig** the world ends tomorrow! I (*emph*) don't care/mind, I don't care if it ends or not, *also more emph* **coma co-dhiù** indifferent either way, **ge b' e cò a bhuannaich, tha mi coma co-dhiù** whoever won, I don't care either way

comain, comain, comainean *nf* **1** an obligation, a debt (*moral, not fin*), **fo chomain aig cuideigin** under an obligation to someone; **2** *esp in expr* **(fada) nad (&c) c(h)omain** (very much) obliged to you (&c), **chuidich sibh gu mòr sinn, tha sinn fada nur comain** you helped us greatly, we are very much obliged to you

comanachadh, comanachaidh, comanachaidhean *nm* **1** (*the act of*) taking (Holy) Communion, going to the Lord's Table; **2** (Holy) Communion, *Cf* **òrdugh 4**; **3** the Communion season, *Cf* **òrdugh 4**

comanaich *vi, pres part* **a' comanachadh**, take (Holy) Communion, go to the Lord's Table

comanaiche, comanaiche, comanaichean *nm* a communicant, someone taking (Holy) Communion/going to the Lord's Table

comann (*also found as* **comunn**), *gen & pl* **comainn** *nm* **1** an association, a society, a club, **Comann Gàidhlig Ghlaschu** The Gaelic Society of Glasgow, **comann togalaich** a building society, **chuir sinn air bonn comann airson dheugairean** we set up/started a club for teenagers; **2** a commune, a community; **3** company, fellowship, society, **is toigh leam comann na h-òigridh** I like the company of young people, *Cf* **conaltradh 2** *& more usu* **cuideachd** *n* **1**

comar, comair, comaran *nf* a confluence of rivers, burns, *esp in place-names*, **Comar nan Allt** Cumbernauld, the confluence of the burns

comas, comais, comasan *nm* ability, capacity, faculty, power, **comas bruidhne** power/faculty/capacity of speech, ability to speak, **comas inntinn** intellectual ability/powers, **rinn i na bha na comas** she did what she could/what she was capable of, *also in expr* **thar mo chomais** beyond my ability/capacity/power, **na (h-)iarr sin orra, tha e thar an comasan** don't ask that of them, it's beyond their capabilities,

comasach *adj* able, capable (**air** of), **duine comasach** an able/a capable man, **chan eil mi comasach air mìorbhailean a dhèanamh** I'm not capable of performing miracles

comataidh, comataidh, comataidhean *nf* a committee

combaist, combaiste, combaistean *nf* a compass

co-measgaich *see* **co-mheasgaich**

comhachag, comhachaig, comhachagan *nf* an owl, *esp* a barn owl, *Cf* **cailleach-oidhche**

comhair *nf invar* **1** a direction (*in which something, & esp someone, faces or moves*), *esp in exprs* **thuit** (*&c*) **e an comhair a chinn, an comhair a chùil, an comhair a thaoibh** he fell (*&c*) headlong/head first, backwards, sideways, (*of vehicle &c*) **an comhair a thoisich** front end first, forwards; **2** *in expr* **fa chomhair** *prep* opposite, in front of, before (*with the gen*), **stad e fa mo chomhair** he stopped opposite/ in front of me, *Cf* **mu choinneimh** (*see* **coinneamh 2**)

comhairle, comhairle, comhairlean *nf* **1** advice, a piece of advice, **thoir** *v* **comhairle air/do** advise, give advice to, **rinn ur comhairle feum mòr dhomh** your advice did me a great deal of good/was very useful to me, **fear-comhairle** *&* **neach-comhairle** *m* an adviser, *also in expr* **ann an iomadh-chomhairle (dè a dhèanainn &c)** in a quandary/undecided (what I would do &c); **2** (*elected or appointed body*) a Council, **Comhairle Ealain na h-Alba** The Scottish Arts Council, *esp a local authority council* **comhairle-sgìre** a district council, **comhairle-roinne** a regional council, **taigh-comhairle** a council house, *Cf* **ùghdarras 2**

comhairleach, *gen & pl* **comhairlich** *nm* an adviser

comhairleachadh, *gen* **comhairleachaidh** (*the act of*) advising

comhairlich *vt, pres part* **a' comhairleachadh**, advise, *Cf* **thoir comhairle air/do** (*see* **comhairle 1**)

comhairliche, comhairliche, comhairlichean *nm* a (local authority) councillor

comhaois, comhaoiseach *see* **co-aois, co-aoiseach**

comharrachadh, *gen* **comharrachaidh** *nm* **1** (*the act of*) marking &c (*see senses of* **comharraich** *v*); **2** (*teacher &c*) correction (*of work*), marking, *Cf* **ceartachadh 2**

comharra(dh), comharraidh, comharraidhean *nm* **1** a mark, **fhuair Eilidh deagh chomharran san sgoil an-dè** Eilidh got good marks at school yesterday, **comharradh cluaise** an ear-mark (*on livestock*), **comharradh-stiùiridh** a landmark (*for navigation, Cf* **iùl 3**); **2** a sign, a mark, a symbol, **is e deagh/droch chomharradh a tha sin!** that's a good/bad sign! **comharradh urraim** a mark/sign of respect, **comharradh inbhe** a status symbol, **comharradh-ceiste** a question mark; **3** a mark (*left by someone or something*), *Cf* **lorg** *n* **2, làrach 1; 4** (*med*) a symptom; **5** *in expr* (*maps*) **comharradh-clèithe** a grid reference

comharraich *vt, pres part* **a' comharrachadh**, **1** mark, put a mark on; **2** (*teacher*) mark, correct (*work*), *Cf* **ceartaich**; **3** mark, observe (*anniversaries &c*)

comhart, comhairt, comhartan *nm* a bark (*of dog*)

comhartaich *vi, pres part* **a' comhartaich**, bark (*as dog*), *Cf* **tabhannaich** *v*

còmhdach, còmhdaich, còmhdaichean *nm* a cover, a covering, **còmhdach leapa/leapach** a bed cover, **còmhdach ùrlair** a floor covering (*Cf* **brat 1**)

còmhdaich *vt, pres part* **a' còmhdachadh**, cover

còmhdaichte *adj* covered

còmhdhail, còmhdhalach, còmhdhailean *nf* a congress, a conference, *Cf* **co-labhairt**

co-mheasgaich, *also* **co-measgaich** & **coimeasgaich**, *vti, pres part* **a' co-m(h)easgachadh**, mix, blend, intermix, mingle, intermingle, amalgamate, merge

co-m(h)easgachadh, *gen* **co-m(h)easgachaidh** *nm* (*the act of*) mixing &c (*see senses of* **co-mheasgaich** *v*); **2** a blend, a mixture

co mheud *see* **cia mheud**

còmhla *adv* **1** together, **thig** *v* **còmhla** come together, congregate, unite, assemble, **thàinig an dà thaobh còmhla airson co-labhairt** the two sides came together for a conference, *Cf* **co-chruinnich, tional 1**; **2** **còmhla ri** *prep* with, along with, together with, **is toigh leam a bhith còmhla riut** I like being with you, **tha iad uile a' fuireach còmhla ri chèile** they're all living together, *Cf* **cuide ri, le 1, mar 5**

còmhla(dh), *gen* **còmhla** & **còmhlaidh**, *pl* **còmhlan, còmhlaidhean** & **còmhlaichean** *nmf* (*trad*) a door, *ie the leaf of a door* (**doras**, *now used for door* <u>and</u> *doorway, was trad the door opening/doorway*), (*song*) **biodh e muigh air cùl na còmhla** let him be outside behind the door, *Cf* **doras 1** & **2**

còmhlan, *gen* & *pl* **còmhlain** *nm* a band, a group (*of people*), **còmhlan actairean** a troupe of actors, **còmhlan-ciùil** (*mus*) a band, a group, **còmhlan shaighdearan** a company of soldiers, *Cf* **buidheann 1, cuideachd** *n* **3**

còmhnaich *vi, pres part* **a' còmhnaidh**, live, dwell, inhabit, reside, (*Sc*) stay, **a' còmhnaidh anns an sgìre** dwelling/living/staying in the district, *Cf* **fuirich 2**

còmhnaidh, còmhnaidhe, còmhnaidhean *nf* **1** (*the act of*) dwelling &c (*see senses of* **còmhnaich** *v*), **cead còmhnaidh** a residence permit; **2** *esp in compounds* **àite-còmhnaidh** a dwelling place, an abode, **gun àite-còmhnaidh seasmhach** of no fixed abode, **taigh-còmhnaidh**

a dwelling house; **3** *in expr* **an còmhnaidh** *adv* always, **tha i an sàs annam an còmhnaidh airson an gàrradh a sgioblachadh** she's always on at me to tidy the garden, *Cf* **daonnan**

còmhnard *adj* flat, level, even, smooth (*ground, surface &c*); horizontal, *Cf* **rèidh 1**

còmhnard, còmhnaird, còmhnardan *nm* **1** a plain, a piece of level ground, *Cf* **blàr 1; 2** (*railway &c*) a platform

còmhradh, còmhraidh, còmhraidhean *nm* **1** conversation, talk, chat, a conversation, a talk, a chat, **dèan** *v* **còmhradh** talk, converse, chat, **rinn sinn còmhradh beag an-dè** we had a wee chat yesterday, **bonn còmhraidh** a bit of conversation, a chat, **cuspair a' chòmhraidh againn** the subject of our conversation, *Cf less usu* **agallamh 1, conaltradh 1; 2** *occas used as pres part eg* **a' còmhradh a-null 's a-nall** talking/chatting of this and that

còmhrag, còmhraig, còmhragan *nf* combat, conflict, fighting, a combat, a conflict, a fight, **còmhrag-dithis** a duel, *Cf more usu* **sabaid** *n*

còmhraiteach *adj* talkative, fond of talking, chatty, *Cf* **bruidhneach**

còmhstri, còmhstri, còmhstrithean *nf* **1** strife, conflict; **2** competition, rivalry

com-pàirt, com-pàirte, com-pàirtean *nf* **1** participating share; **2** (*mus*) accompaniment, an accompaniment

com-pàirteachadh, *gen* **com-pàirteachaidh** *nm* (*the act of*) communicating, accompanying &c (*see senses of* **com-pàirtich** *v*)

com-pàirtich *vti, pres part* **a' com-pàirteachadh, 1** communicate (*information &c*); **2** participate, take part; **3** (*mus*) accompany

companach, *gen & pl* **companaich** *nm* **1** a companion, a comrade, a pal, *Cf* **caraid 1; 2** a colleague, an associate, *Cf* **co-obraiche; 3** (*trad, affectionate*) a husband, **bha i ag ionndrain a companaich** she was missing her husband, *Cf* **cèile 1, duine 4**

companaidh, companaidh, companaidhean *nmf* (*commerce &c*) a firm, a company, **na companaidhean mòra eadar-nàiseanta** the big international companies

companas, *gen* **companais** *nm* companionship

comraich, comraiche, comraichean *nf* sanctuary, a place of sanctuary, *Cf* **tèarmann**

còn, còn, cònaichean *nm* (*geometry &c*) a cone

conaire, conaire, conairean *nf* a rosary, *Cf* **paidirean 1 & 2**

conaltrach *adj* (*of person*) social, sociable, *Cf more usu* **cuideachdail**

conaltradh, *gen* **conaltraidh** *nm* **1** conversation, *Cf* **agallamh 2 & more usu còmhradh 1; 2** company, *Cf* **comann 3, cuideachd** *n* **1; 3** sociability; **4** communication

conasg, *gen* **conaisg** *nm* (*bot*) gorse, (*Sc*) whins

con(a)stabal, con(a)stabail, conastabalan *nm* (*crofting*) a land/township constable

connadh, *gen* **connaidh** *nm coll* fuel

connadh-làmhaich, *gen* **connaidh-làmhaich** *nm coll* munitions, ammunition

connlach, *gen* **connlaich** *nf coll* straw, fodder

connrag, connraig, connragan *nf* a consonant, *Cf* **consan, fuaimreag**

connsachadh, *gen* **connsachaidh** *nm* **1** (*the act of*) arguing &c (*see senses of* **connsaich** *v*); **2** an argument, a dispute, a squabble, *Cf* **tuasaid 1**

connsachail *adj* quarrelsome, argumentative, disputatious

connsaich *vi, pres part* **a' connsachadh**, **1** argue, row, squabble, quarrel, **bidh iad ri connsachadh gun sgur** they're continually squabbling/rowing, *Cf* **argamaid 3, troid**; **2** (*less confrontational, philo &c*) argue, dispute, debate

connspaid, connspaide, connspaidean *nf* dispute, a dispute, controversy, a controversy, wrangling, contention

connspaideach *adj* **1** disputatious, litigious; **2** contentious, controversial

con(n)traigh, con(n)traighe, con(n)traighean *nf* a neap tide, the lowest tide, (*poetry collection*) **Reothairt is Contraigh** (Somhairle MacGill-Eain) Spring tide and Neap tide

consal, consail, consalan *nm* a consul

consan, *gen & pl* **consain** *nm* a consonant, *Cf* **connrag, fuaimreag**

co-obrachadh, co-obrachaidh, co-obrachaidhean *nm* **1** (*the act of*) co-operating, working together; **2** co-operation; **3** a co-operative, *Cf* **co-chomann 2**

co-obraich & **co-oibrich** *vi, pres part* **a' co-obrachadh**, co-operate, work together

co-obraiche (*also* **co-oibriche**), *gen* **co-obraiche**, *pl* **co-obraichean** *nm* **1** one who co-operates or collaborates with others; **2** a fellow worker, a colleague, *Cf* **companach 2**

co-ogha, *gen* **co-ogha**, *pl* **co-oghachan** & **co-oghaichean** *nm* (*trad*) a cousin, *Note:* 'cousin' *is used in Gaelic by many speakers*

cop, *gen* **coip** & **cuip** *nm* foam, froth, *Cf* **cobhar**

copach *adj* frothy, foaming

copag, copaig, copagan *nf* (*bot*) a dock, (*Sc*) a docken

copan, copain, copanan *nm* a (drinking) cup, *Cf* **cupa, cùp**

copar, *gen* **copair** *nm* copper, **ceàrd-copair** *m* a coppersmith

cor, coir, cuir *nm* **1** a condition, a state, **chunnaic mi cor truagh nam fògarrach** I saw the pitiful state of the refugees, *esp in expr* (*fam*) **dè do chor?** how are you doing?, how are you? (*lit* what is your condition?), *Cf less trad* **staid**; **2** a condition, an eventuality, a circumstance, **air chor** on condition, **gheibh thu e air chor 's gum pòs thu mi** you'll get it on condition that you marry me (*Cf* **cumha** *nf*, **cùmhnant 2**), **na buin dha air chor sam bith!** don't touch it under any circumstances!; **3** a method, a manner, *esp in expr* **air chor is gu/nach** ... so that ... (*lit* in such a manner that), **ghlas e an doras air chor is nach b' urrainn dhomh faighinn a-steach** he locked the door so that I couldn't get in, *Cf similarly used* **dòigh 5**

còrcair & **corcair** *adj* purple, *Cf* **purpaidh**

corcais, corcais, corcaisean *nf* cork, (*esp*) a bottle cork, **tarraing** *v* **corcais** draw/pull a cork, *Cf* **àrc**

còrd, *gen* & *pl* **cùird** *nm* cord, a cord, line, a line (*of a thickness between string and rope*)

còrd *vi, pres part* **a' còrdadh**, **1** agree with, be agreeable to, please, get on with, **a' còrdadh ri chèile** getting on (well) with each other; **2** *followed by* **ri**, **còrd** *is commonly used to express the idea* enjoy, **ciamar a tha sin a' còrdadh ribh?** how are you enjoying that? **cha do chòrd an ceòl rium idir** I didn't enjoy the music at all

còrdadh, còrdaidh, còrdaidhean *nm* **1** (*the act of*) agreeing &c (*see senses of* **còrd** *v*); **2** agreement, an agreement, an understanding, **thàinig iad gu còrdadh** they reached an agreement/an understanding, **bha droch chòrdadh eatarra** they were on bad terms; **3** a contract, *Cf* **cùmhnant 1**

còrn, *gen* & *pl* **cùirn** *nm* **1** (*trad*) a drinking horn; **2** (*mus*) a horn; **3** a corn (*on foot*)

Còrnach, *gen* & *pl* **Còrnaich** *nm* a Cornishman, someone from Cornwall (**a' Chòrn**), *also as adj* **Còrnach** Cornish

còrnair, còrnair, còrnairean *nm* a corner, (*short story*) **Granny anns a' Chòrnair** Granny in the Corner, *Cf more trad* **cùil 1, oisean, uileann 2**

corp, *gen* & *pl* **cuirp** *nm* **1** a body (*of any living creature*), **buill a' chuirp** the parts of the body, **corp is anam** body and soul; **2** a dead (*human*) body, a corpse, **fhuair iad a chorp dà là an dèidh a bhàis** they found his body/corpse two days after his death, *Cf* **marbhan**

corpailear, corpaileir, corpailearan *nm* (*army &c*) a corporal, **bha e na chorpailear sna Seaforths** he was a corporal in the Seaforths

corp-eòlas, *gen* **corp-eòlais** *nm* anatomy

corp-làidir *adj* able-bodied, (*bodily*) strong

corporra *adj* bodily, corporal, corporeal

còrr *nm invar* 1 *in expr* **còrr is**, more than, **tha iad còrr is fichead mìle air falbh** they're more than twenty miles away; 2 *with art* **an còrr** the rest, **dh'ith mise mo leòr, an gabh thusa an còrr?** I've eaten my fill/had enough, will you take the rest?; 3 *with art* **an còrr**, anything else, **thubhairt i, 'Obh! Obh!', ach an uair sin cha tubhairt i an còrr** she said, 'Dear oh dear', but then she didn't say anything else, **cha robh an còrr ann ach sin** that's all there was to it, there was no more to it than that

còrr *adj* odd (*ie not even*), **àireamh chòrr** an odd number, *Cf* **cothrom** *adj*

corra *adj* odd, occasional, **corra dhuine** the odd person, **gabhaidh mi corra phinnt còmhla ris na co-obraichean agam** I have the odd/occasional pint with my workmates/the people from work

corra-biod *nm invar, in expr* **air mo (&c) c(h)orra-biod** on tiptoe, on the tip of my (&c) toes

corrach *adj* 1 unsteady, unstable, *Cf more usu* **critheanach 2, cugallach 1**; 2 (*terrain &c*) steep, rough

corrag, corraig, corragan *nf* a finger, *Cf* **meur 1**

corra-ghritheach, corra-grithich, corrachan-gritheach *nf* a heron, (*poem*) **thàinig corra-ghritheach ghiùigeach, sheas i air uachdar tiùrra** (Somhairle MacGill-Eain) a demure heron came, and stood on top of sea-wrack

corran, *gen & pl* **corrain** *nm* 1 a sickle; 2 a crescent

còs, còis, còsan *nm* (*topog*) a hollow, *Cf more usu* **lag** *n*, **sloc 1**

còsach *adj* hollow

cosamhlachd, cosamhlachd, cosamhlachdan *nf* a parable

cosg *vt, pres part* **a' cosg & a' cosgadh**, 1 cost, **dè a chosgas briogais ùr? cosgaidh i dà fhichead not** what will some new trousers cost? they'll cost forty pounds; 2 spend, **bidh ise a' cosnadh airgid 's bidh esan ga chosg** she earns money and he spends it; 3 waste, **cosg airgead** waste money, *Cf* **caith 3**

cosg *nm invar* 1 (*also* **cosgadh**, *gen* **cosgaidh**) (*the act of*) costing &c (*see senses of* **cosg** *v*); 2 cost, *Cf* **cosgais 1, pris**; 3 a waste, **cosg airgid/tìde** a waste of money/time, *Cf* **call** *n* 4

cosgail *adj* expensive, dear, costly, **'s e stuth cosgail a tha sin!** that's expensive stuff!, *Cf* **daor**

cosgais, cosgaise, cosgaisean *nf* 1 cost, the monetary cost of anything, **cosgais bith-beò** the cost of living, *Cf* **cosg** *n* 2; 2 *in pl* costs, expenses, **dh'fhàillig an gnothach air sgàth chosgaisean àrda** the business failed because of/on account of high costs, **cosgaisean siubhail** travelling costs/expenses

co-sheirm, *gen* **co-sheirme** *nf* (*music*) harmony

co-shìnte *adj* parallel, **loidhnichean co-shìnte** parallel lines

cosnadh, cosnaidh, cosnaidhean *nm* **1** (*the act of*) earning, winning &c (*see senses of* **coisinn** *v*); **2** (*abstr*) employment, a job, **ionad cosnaidh** (*also* **ionad obrach**) a job centre, **gun chosnadh** unemployed, without work/a job, *Cf* **dreuchd, obair 4**; **3** (*con*) work, **am beagan cosnaidh a rinn iad** the little work that they did, *Cf* **obair 1**; **4** earnings, *Cf more usu* **pàigh, tuarasdal**

costa, costa, costaichean *nm* a coast, *Cf* **oirthir**

còta, còta, còtaichean *nm* a coat, **còta-mòr** an overcoat, a greatcoat, **còta-leapa** a dressing gown, a housecoat, **còta-bàn** a petticoat, **còta-froise** a raincoat

cotan, *gen* **cotain** *nm* cotton

cothrom, cothruim, cothroman *nm* **1** a chance, an opportunity, **an do ghlan thu na h-uinneagan? cha d'fhuair mi an cothrom fhathast** did you clean the windows? I didn't get the chance yet, **cothroman air foghlam àrd-ìre** opportunities for higher education, (*prov*) **far am bi càil bidh cothrom** where there's a will there's a way, **gabh** *v* **cothrom air** take advantage of (*not nec unfairly* – *Cf* **brath** *n* 2, **fàth** 3), (*trad expr*) **cothrom na Fèinne** a sporting chance, fair odds; **2** *in expr* **chan eil cothrom air** there's nothing to be done, it can't be helped, **ma tha sin an aghaidh nan riaghailtean, chan eil cothrom air** if that's against the regulations, it can't be helped; **3** *in expr* **air chothrom a (dhol a-mach &c)** able/fit to (go out &c), *Cf* **comasach**; **4** equilibrium, balance, *Cf* **meidh 2**; **5** a pair of scales, a balance, *Cf* **meidh 1**

cothrom *adj* even (*ie not odd*), **àireamh chothrom** an even number, *Cf* **còrr** *adj*

cothromach *adj* fair, just, decent, reasonable, **tuarasdal cothromach** a decent/reasonable salary, **duine cothromach** a fair/decent man, **breith chothromach** a just/fair decision, *Cf* **dìreach 2, reusanta 2**

cothromachadh, *gen* **cothromachaidh** *nm* (*the act of*) weighing, balancing

cothromaich *vt, pres part* **a' cothromachadh**, weigh, balance

co-thuit *vi, pres part* **a' co-thuiteam**, coincide

co-thuiteamas, co-thuiteamais, co-thuiteamasan *nm* coincidence, a coincidence, **abair co-thuiteamas!** what a coincidence!

cràbhach *adj* devout, pious, very religious, *Cf* **diadhaidh**

cràbhadh, *gen* **cràbhaidh** *nm* piety, devoutness, *Cf* **cùram 3, diadhachd 3**

crac, *also* **craic**, *gen* **craice** *nf* (*fam*) chat, conversation, 'crack'

cràdh, *gen* **cràidh** *nm* 1 (*the act of*) paining, torturing &c (*see senses of* **cràidh** *v*); 2 (*mental or phys*) pain, anguish, suffering, torture, torment, **cuir** *v* **an cràdh** torture, put to torture (*Cf* **cràidh** *v*); *Cf* **ciùrradh**

craiceann, *gen* **craicinn** & **craicne**, *pl* **craicnean** *nm* skin, a skin

cràidh *vt, pres part* **a' cràdh**, pain, torture, torment (*mentally or phys*), **bha pian is dòrainn ga chràdh** pain and grief were tormenting him, *Cf* **ciùrr, goirtich**

crài(dh)teach *adj* grievous, painful, causing grief or pain (*mentally or phys*), **cuimhneachan cràiteach** a painful reminder, *Cf* **dòrainneach**

cràin, cràine, cràintean *nf* a sow, *cf* **cullach, muc, torc**

crann, *gen* & *pl* **crainn** & **croinn** *nm* 1 a tree, *now usu restricted to tree names, eg* **crann-fìogais** *m* a fig tree, **crann-fìona** *m* a vine, *Cf more usu* **craobh;** 2 a (ship's) mast; 3 a bar (*of wood, metal*), **crann-tarsainn** a crossbar, (*trad*) **cuir** *v* **an crann air an doras** bar the door; 4 a plough, **crann-sneachda** a snow plough, (*astronomy*) **An Crann-arain** The Plough; 5 (*engin*) a bolt, **cnò is crann** a nut and bolt; 6 (*also* **crann-togail**) a crane (*for lifting*), a derrick; 7 *in expr* **crann-ola** an oil rig (*also* an olive tree!); 8 (*heraldry &c*) a saltire, a St Andrew's cross, **An Crann** the Saltire; 9 *also in expr* **cuir** *v* **crainn** (*pl*) draw lots, toss a coin (*to decide something*), **chuir iad crainn feuch cò a phàigheadh** they drew lots/tossed a coin to see who would pay

crannag, crannaig, crannagan *nf* 1 a pulpit, *Cf more usu* **cùbaid;** 2 a milk churn, *Cf* **muidhe;** 3 (*hist*) a crannog, an artificial island

crann-ceusaidh, *gen* & *pl* **crainn-cheusaidh** & **croinn-cheusaidh** *nm* a cross (*for crucifixion*), **An Crann-Ceusaidh** Our Lord's Cross, *Cf* **crois 2**

crannchur, crannchuir, crannchuran *nm* 1 the casting or drawing of lots, **an crannchur nàiseanta** the national lottery, **crannchur-gill** a raffle; 2 (*trad*) one's fate, one's lot, **mas e sin mo chrannchur** if that is my fate/lot, *Cf* **dàn¹ 1**

crann-sgaoilidh, *gen* & *pl* **crainn-sgaoilidh** *nm* (*radio, TV*) a transmitter, a radio or television mast

craobh, craoibhe, craobhan *nf* a tree, **craobh mheas** a fruit tree, (*song*) **Craobh nan Ubhal** the Apple Tree, *Note:* **craobh-** *can be prefixed to the name of a species to give the tree name eg* **craobh-challtainn** a hazel tree, **craobh-dharaich** an oak tree; *Cf less usu* **crann 1**

craobh-sgaoil *vti, pres part* **a' craobh-sgaoileadh**, 1 (*trad*) diffuse, propagate; 2 (*more recently*) broadcast, transmit (*by radio or TV*), **'s e seo Rèidio Alba, a' craobh-sgaoileadh air feadh na dùthcha** this is Radio Scotland, broadcasting/transmitting throughout the country

craobh-sgaoileadh, *gen* **craobh-sgaoilidh** *nm* **1** (*the act of*) diffusing, broadcasting &c (*see senses of* **craobh-sgaoil** *v*); **2** (*radio, TV*) a broadcast, a transmission, *Cf* **prògram**

craos, craois, craosan *nm* **1** (*pej when of humans*) a mouth, a wide or gaping mouth, (*of animal*) a maw; **2** gluttony, *Cf* **geòcaireachd**

craosach *adj* **1** gluttonous, *Cf* **geòcach**; **2** having a wide or gaping mouth

craosaire, craosaire, craosairean *nm* a glutton, *Cf* **geòcaire**

crasg, craisg, crasgan *nf* a crutch (*ie walking aid*), *Cf* **croitse**

crasgag & **crosgag**, *gen* **crasgaig**, *pl* **crasgagan** *nf* a starfish

crath *vti, pres part* **a' crathadh**, **1** (*deliberately*) shake, wave, brandish, **chrath e a cheann** he shook his head, **crath dhìot an cadal!** wake up!, look lively! (*lit* shake the sleep from you!), **bha a' chlann a' crathadh rithe** the children were waving to her (*Cf* **smèid 2**), **chrath e a dhòrn** he shook/brandished his fist, **cù a' crathadh earbaill** a dog wagging its tail; **2** (*vt*) sprinkle, shake (*on or over something*), **crath salann air an iasg** sprinkle salt on the fish

creach *vti, pres part* **a' creachadh**, **1** rob, plunder, *Cf* **spùill**; **2** ruin, bring ruin upon (*someone*), *Cf* **sgrios** *v*

creach, creiche, creachan *nf* **1** (*trad, hist*) booty, plunder *often stolen cattle in particular*; **2** a disaster, destruction, ruin or ruination befalling someone, *esp in excl expressing surprise or dismay* **O mo chreach!** Good Heavens!, Dear me!, *also* (*stronger*) **O mo chreach-sa (a) thàinig!** Good gracious me!, Mercy me!, Good grief! &c (*lit* O my very destruction has come!), *Cf* **sgrios** *n*

creachadh, *gen* **creachaidh** *nm* (*the act of*) robbing, ruining &c (*see senses of* **creach** *v*)

creachan, creachain, creachanan *nm* a scallop, **slige** *f* **chreachain** a scallop shell

crèadh, *also* **criadh** & **crè**, *gen* **creadha** & **creadhadh** *nf* clay

crèadhadair, crèadhadair, crèadhadairean *nm* a potter

crèadhadaireachd *nf invar* pottery

creag, creige, creagan *nf* **1** a rock, a crag, an outcrop of rock, a cliff, (*placename*) **Creag an Iubhair** Craignure, the rock or crag of the yew tree; **2** a hill (*usu rocky*)

creagach *adj* rocky, craggy

creamh, *gen* **creamha** *nm* garlic, **creamh-gàrraidh** a leek, (*coll*) leeks

creapan, *gen* & *pl* **creapain** *nm* (*trad*) a stool, *Cf* **furm 2**, **stòl**

creathail, *gen* **creathaile** & **creathlach**, *pl* **creathailean** *nf* a cradle

creid *vti, pres part* **a' creidsinn** & **a' creids**, **1** believe, **cha bu mhise a ghoid e! chan eil mi gad chreidsinn** it wasn't me who stole it! I don't believe you, **chan eil mi a' creidsinn anns na**

sìthichean I don't believe in fairies; **2** *with double neg constr and understated positive sense* **cha chreid mi nach eil** (&c) I wouldn't be surprised if it is (&c), **am faigh i duais? cha chreid mi nach fhaigh** will she get a prize? I wouldn't be surprised if she does, *more emph* **bidh mi air an daoraich a-nochd! cha chreid mi nach bi!** I'll be drunk tonight! I'm sure you will!/I know fine you will!

creideamh, creideimh, creideamhan *nm* **1** belief, a belief; **2** faith, religious belief, a faith, a creed, a religion, **daoine gun chreideamh** people without faith, unbelievers, **an creideamh Ioslamach** the Islamic faith/religion

creideas, *gen* **creideis** *nm* **1** trust; **2** belief; **3** *in expr* **thoir** *v* **creideas do** believe, trust, **thubhairt e gun tigeadh e agus tha mi a' toirt creideas dha** he said he would come and I believe/trust him, **an toir thu creideas dhomh? cha toir!** will you/do you trust me? no!; *Cf* **earb, earbsa**

creidsinn *nm invar* (*the act of*) believing &c (*see senses of* **creid** *v*)

creim *vti, pres part* **a' creimeadh, 1** nibble, pick (*at food*), *Cf* **pioc 2; 2** gnaw, *Cf* **cagainn**

creimeadh, *gen* **creimidh** *nm* (*the act of*) nibbling &c (*see senses of* **creim** *v*)

crèis, *gen* **crèise** *nf* grease, fat, (*Sc*) creesh, *Cf* **geir 2, saill** *n*

crèiseach *adv* greasy, fatty

creithleag, creithleig, creithleagan *nf* a cleg, a horsefly

creuchd, creuchda, creuchdan *nf* a wound, a hurt, *Cf* **ciùrradh 2, leòn** *n*, **lot** *n*

creud, creuda, creudan *nf* (*relig &c*) a creed

creutair, creutair, creutairean *nm* a creature, **is creutairean daoine agus beathaichean** people and animals are creatures, **tha e gun sgillinn ruadh, an creutair bochd** he hasn't a penny to his name, the poor creature/soul, (*Cf* **truaghan**)

criathar, criathair, criatharan *nm* a sieve, a riddle

criathraich *vt, pres part* **a' criathradh** & **a' criathrachadh**, sieve, sift, riddle

cridhe, cridhe, cridheachan *nm* a heart, **buille** *f* **cridhe** a heartbeat, **tinneas** *m* **cridhe** heart disease, a heart ailment, **clisgeadh** *m* **cridhe** a heart attack, **bris(t)eadh-cridhe** *m* heartbreak, (*trad*) **a charaid** (&c) **mo chridhe** my dear friend (&c); **2** courage, heart, **cha robh iad air a shon agus cha robh a** (*for de*) **chridhe agam na rachadh nan aghaidh** they didn't approve and I hadn't the heart/courage to go against them, *Cf* **misneach**

cridhealas, *gen* **cridhealais** *nm* heartiness, jollity, merriment, hilarity, conviviality (*sometimes with implication of intoxication*), (*song*) **siud far an robh cridhealas!** that was where conviviality was to be found!

cridheil *adj* (*person, atmosphere &c*) hearty, cheery, jovial, **fàilte chridheil** a hearty welcome

crìoch, crìche, crìochan *nf* 1 the end or completion of something, **aig a' chrìch** at the end, **thàinig a' choinneamh gu crìch** (*dat*) the meeting came to an an end, (*song*) **aig crìch mo là** at the end of my days/ life, **cuir** *v* **crìoch air** finish, complete, **chuir i crìoch air an nobhail aice a-raoir** she finished her novel last night; 2 a boundary, a border, a frontier, a limit, (*Sc*) a march, **is e seo crìoch an fhearainn agam** this is the boundary/march of my land, **crìoch na sgìre** the parish boundary, **Na Crìochan** *or* **Crìochan Shasainn** The Borders, **Na Crìochan-Grèine** The Tropics, **crìoch astair** a speed limit

crìoch(n)ach *adj* finite, **neo-chrìoch(n)ach** infinite

crìochnachadh, *gen* **crìochnachaidh** *nm* (*the act of*) finishing &c (*see senses of* **crìochnaich** *v*)

crìochnaich *vt, pres part* **a' crìochnachadh**, finish, end, complete, *Cf* **cuir crìoch air** (*see* **crìoch 1**)

crìochnaichte *adj* finished, completed, *Cf* **coileanta 1**

criomag, criomaige, criomagan *nf* a bit, a piece, a crumb of anything, **bha na dèideagan aice a' dol nan criomagan** her toys were falling to pieces/dropping to bits, (*title of newspaper column*) **Criomagan** Bits and Pieces, Odds and Ends

crìon *vti, pres part* **a' crìonadh**, wither, dry up, fade, fade away, *Cf* **searg**

crìon *adj* 1 tiny, *Cf* **meanbh, mion 1**; 2 petty, mean, trifling, insignificant, *Cf* **suarach 1**; 3 withered, dried up, wizened

crìonadh, *gen* **crìonaidh** *nm* (*the act of*) withering &c (*see senses of* **crìon** *v*)

crìoplach & **cripleach**, *gen* & *pl* **crìoplaich** *nm* a cripple, *Cf more usu* **bacach** *n*, **crùbach** *n*

crios, criosa, criosan *nm* a belt, a band, **tha mo chrios ro theann** my belt's too tight, **crios-sàbhalaidh**, *also* **crios-teasairginn**, a lifebelt, **crios-muineil** a neckband, a necklace, **crios-rubair** a rubber band

Crìosdachd *nf invar, with art* **A' Chrìosdachd** Christendom

Crìosdaidh, Crìosdaidh, Crìosdaidhean *nm* a Christian

Crìosdaidheachd *nf invar* Christianity

Crìosdail *also* **Crìosdaidh**, *adj* Christian, **An Eaglais Chrìosdail** the Christian Church

Crìosdalachd *nf invar* Christian behaviour and beliefs, way of life characteristic of a Christian

criostal, criostail, criostalan *nm* crystal, a crystal

cripleach *see* **crioplach**

crith *vi, pres part* **a' crith**, tremble, shiver, shake, quake, *Cf more usu* **bi air chrith** (*see* **crith** *n* 1)

crith, crithe, crithean *nf* 1 (*the act of*) trembling, shaking &c (*see senses of* **crith** *v*), *esp in expr* **air chrith** *adv* trembling, shaking, shivering, **bha e air chrith leis an fhiabhras** he was shaking/trembling with the fever, **rach** *v* **air chrìth** start to tremble, shake &c; 2 a tremble, a tremor, a quake, a shake, a shiver (*through fear, cold, illness &c*), **crith-thalmhainn** an earthquake

critheanach *adj* 1 liable to shake or tremble; 2 shaky, unsteady, (*Sc*) shooglie, *Cf* **cugallach** 1; 3 liable to give one the shivers, scary

crò, *gen* **cròtha**, *pl* **cròitean** & **cròthan** *nm* 1 a pen, a fold (*for livestock esp sheep*), *Cf* **buaile**; 2 **crò snàthaid**, the eye of a needle

croch *vt, pres part* **a' crochadh**, 1 hang, **croch am murtair gu h-àrd!** hang the murderer high!, **chrochadh na dealbhan aige san taisbeanlann** his pictures were hung in the art gallery

crochadair, crochadair, crochadairean *nm* 1 a hangman; 2 a hanger, (*also* **crochadair-còta**) a coat hanger

crochadh, *gen* **crochaidh** *nm* 1 (*the act of*) hanging (*see* **croch** *v*), (*trad, hist*) **am maide-crochaidh** *lit* the hanging stick, *a piece of wood hung as a punishment around the neck of a child caught speaking Gaelic at school*; 2 *in expr* **an crochadh** *adv* (*of objects*) hanging, **seann chòta an crochadh air cùl dorais** an old coat hanging behind a door; 3 *in expr* **an crochadh air** *prep* depending on, **am bi thu a' ceannachd an taighe? bidh sin an crochadh air a' phrìs** will you be buying the house? that will depend on the price

crochte *adj* hung, hanged, hanging

crodh, *gen* **cruidh** *nm* cattle, stock, livestock (*esp cattle*), (*song*) **ged nach eil mo chrodh air bhuailidh** though I have no cattle in the fold, **crodh-bainne** milking cows, dairy cows, *Cf* **bò**, **sprèidh**

crò-dhearg *adj* crimson

cròg, cròige, c’ògan *nf* 1 (*of animal*) a paw, *Cf* **màg**, **spòg** 1; 2 (*of humans*) a large hand, (*derog*) a clumsy hand, a paw, a (great) fist, **bha am botal a' coimhead beag sa chròig mhòir aige** the bottle looked small in his great fist

crò(i)c, *gen* **cròice**, **cròicean** *nf* a deer's antler, *Cf* **cabar** 1

croich, croiche, croichean *nf* 1 gallows, a gibbet; 2 *in excl* (**òrd** &c) **na croiche!** the damned/bloody (hammer &c)!, *Cf* **bugair**, **galla** 2

cròileagan, *gen & pl* **cròileagain** *nm* a playgroup

crois, croise, croisean *nf* **1** a cross, **chuir e crois air a' phàipear o nach robh sgrìobhadh aige** he put a cross on the paper, as he couldn't write, **crois rathaid** a cross-roads; **2** (*relig*) a cross, a crucifix, **rinn e comharradh na croise** he made the sign of the cross, he crossed himself, *Cf* **crann-ceusaidh**

croit & **cruit**, *gen* **croite**, *pl* **croitean** *nf* **1** a croft, **bhiodh e a' togail bheathaichean 's a' cur eòrna air a' chroit aige** he used to rear animals and sow barley on his croft, *Cf* **lot** *nf*; **2** a hump (*on the back*)

croitear & **cruitear**, *gen* **croiteir**, *pl* **croitearan** *nm* a crofter, **Aonadh nan Croitearan** The Crofters' Union

croitse, croitse, croitseachan *nf* a crutch (*ie walking aid*), *Cf* **crasg**

crom *vti*, *pres part* **a' cromadh**, **1** (*vt*) bend, incline, bow, stoop, **chrom i a ceann** she bent/bowed her head, *Cf* **crùb** 2, **lùb** *v* 1; **2** (*vi*) *in expr* **crom air an obair** set to work, get stuck in; **3** (*vti*) bend, curve, *Cf* **lùb** *v* 1; **4** (*vti*) descend, climb down, **chrom e bhon asail** he climbed/got down from the donkey's back, **chrom e leis a' chreig** he climbed down the rock, *Cf* **teirinn** 1 & 2

crom *adj* bent, crooked, curved, **bata crom** a bent/crooked stick, (*poem*) **dìreach an druim, crom an ceann** (Somhairle MacGill-Eain) straight their backs, bent their heads, **crom-chasach** bandy-legged, *Cf* **cam, fiar** *adj* 1, **lùbte**

cromadh, *gen* **cromaidh** *nm* (*the act of*) bending &c (*see senses of* **crom** *v*)

cromag, cromaig, cromagan *nf* **1** a hook, a clasp, a clip, *Cf* **dubhan**; **2** a (shepherd's) crook, a cromag; **3** (*typog*) a comma, **cromagan turrach** inverted commas

cron, *gen & pl* **croin** *nm* **1** harm, injury (*not usu phys*), **dèan** *v* **cron air cuideigin** harm/injure someone; **2** fault, blame, **'s ann ortsa a tha a chron** it's with you that the blame for it lies, it's you who are to blame for it, **faigh** *v* **cron do chuideigin** blame someone; *Cf* **coire** *nf* & *less usu* **lochd**

cronachadh, *gen* **cronachaidh** *nm* (*the act of*) chiding, scolding, rebuking (*see* **cronaich** *v*)

cronaich *vt*, *pres part* **a' cronachadh**, chide, scold, rebuke, *Cf* **càin** *v* 1

cronail *adj* harmful, hurtful, injurious

crònan, *gen* **crònain** *nm* **1** (*a low, continuous, usu musical sound*) humming, buzzing (*eg of insects*), murmuring (*eg of voices, water*), purling, purring, *Cf* **torman**; **2** belling, bellowing (*of red deer stags*), *Cf* **dàmhair** 1

crost(a) & **crosda**, *adj* **1** cross, irritable, grumpy, grouchy, *Cf* **diombach** 1, **gruamach** 4; **2** (*usu of child*) naughty, badly behaved, peevish

crotach *adj* hump-backed

crotal, *gen* **crotail** *nm* (*bot*) lichen

cruach *vt*, *pres part* **a' cruachadh**, heap, pile, stack, *Cf* **càrn** *v*

cruach, cruaiche, cruachan *nf* 1 a heap, a pile, *esp* a stack, a rick (*esp of peats, hay, corn &c*), *Cf less usu* **dùn** 1, **tudan** 1; 2 (*topog*) a hill (*usu conical*)

cruachan, cruachain, cruachanan *nm dimin of* **cruach** *n*, little heap &c, *see senses above*

cruachann, cruachainn, cruaichnean *nf* (*anat*) a hip

cruadal, *gen* **cruadail** *nm* 1 adversity, hardship, a tight corner, *Cf* **cruaidh-chàs** 2; 2 hardihood, intrepidity, courage

cruadalach *adj* 1 difficult, dangerous (*situation &c*); 2 (*of person*) bold, hardy, intrepid, *Cf* **cruaidh** *adj* 3, **fulangach** 1

cruadhaich *vti*, *pres part* **a' cruadhachadh**, harden, solidify

cruadhachadh, *gen* **cruadhachaidh** *nm* (*the act of*) hardening, solidifying

cruaidh, *gen* **cruaidhe** *nf* steel, *Cf* **stàilinn**

cruaidh *adj* 1 hard, (*song*) **bheir mi às a' ghreabhal chruaidh do mo luaidh teachd-an-tìr** I will win from the hard gravel a living for my love, **obair chruaidh** hard work; 2 (*of person, situation*) cruel, harsh, hard, **tìr chruaidh** a hard/harsh land, **cruaidh-chridheach** hard-hearted; 3 (*usu of person*) hardy, tough, *Cf* **cruadalach** 2, **fulangach** 1

cruaidh-chàs, cruaidh-chàis, cruaidh-chàsan *nm* 1 an emergency, a sudden crisis; 2 a difficult, dangerous, dicy situation, a tight corner, *Cf* **cruadal** 1, **staing**

cruan, *gen* **cruain** *nm* enamel

cruas, *gen* **cruais** *nm* 1 hardness; 2 harshness, cruelty; 3 hardiness, hardihood, toughness, endurance, *Cf* **fulang** 3

crùb *vi*, *pres part* **a' crùbadh**, 1 crouch, squat, (*Sc*) coorie, *Cf* **dèan crùban** (*see* **crùban**); 2 stoop, bend, *Cf* **crom** *v* 3; 3 cringe, *Cf* **strìochd** 2; 4 crawl, *Cf* **snàig** 1

crùbach *adj* lame, *Cf* **bacach** *adj*

crùbach, *gen & pl* **crùbaich** *nm* a lame person, *Cf* **bacach** *n*, **crioplach**

crùbadh, *gen* **crùbaidh** *nm* (*the act of*) crouching &c (*see senses of* **crùb** *v*)

crùbag, crùbaig, crùbagan *nf* a crab, *Cf smaller* **partan**

crùbagan *nm in exprs* **bha e na chrùbagan** he was crouched down, **chaidh iad nan crùbagan** they crouched down, *Cf* **crùban**

crùban, *gen* **crùbain** *nm* a crouch, a squat, a crouching or squatting position, *esp in exprs* **dèan** *v* **crùban** crouch, squat, **rinn e crùban san oisean** he crouched down in the corner, & **na c(h)rùban** crouching, in a crouch, squatting, **bha iad nan crùban air bruaich na h-aibhne** they were crouched on the river bank, *Cf* **crùbagan**

crùdh *vt, pres part* **a' crùidheadh**, shoe (*a horse*), *Cf* **cuir crudha air** (*see* **crudha**)

crudha, cruidhe, cruidhean *nm* a horseshoe, **cuir crudha air** shoe (*horse*) *Cf less trad* **bròg-eich** (*see* **bròg**)

cruineachd *see* **cruithneachd**

cruinn *adj* 1 round, circular, spherical, **tha bàla, ubhal agus planaid cruinn** a ball, an apple and a planet are round/spherical; 2 (*sums &c*) accurate, *Cf* **grinn 4**; 3 assembled, gathered, **bha an coitheanal cruinn san eaglais** the congregation was assembled in the church

cruinne (*m*), *gen* **cruinne** (*f*), *pl* **cruinnean** (*m*) *nmf* 1 roundness; 2 a sphere, a globe, **leth-chruinne** a hemisphere; 3 (*with art*) **an cruinne** the world, the earth, the globe, **crìoch na cruinne** the end of the world, **uachdar na cruinne** the surface of the globe, (*football &c*) **Cuach na Cruinne** the World Cup, *Cf* **cruinne-cè 1, saoghal 1, talamh 1**

cruinneachadh, cruinneachaidh, cruinneachaidhean *nm* 1 (*the act of*) gathering &c (*see senses of* **cruinnich** *v*); 2 a gathering, an assembly (*of people*); 3 a collection (*of objects*), an anthology (*of writing*); *Cf* **co-chruinneachadh**

cruinne-cè (*m*), *gen* **cruinne-cè** (*f*), *nmf, used with art*, **an cruinne-cè**, 1 the world, the earth, *Cf* **cruinne 3, saoghal 1, talamh 1**; 2 the universe, *Cf* **cruitheachd, domhan**

cruinneil *adj* global, **blàthachadh cruinneil** global warming

cruinn-eòlas, *gen* **cruinn-eòlais** *nm* geography, *Cf* **tìr-eòlas** (*see* **tìr 2**)

cruinnich *vti, pres part* **a' cruinneachadh**, 1 (*of people*) gather, assemble, collect, come or bring together, **bha an sluagh a' cruinneachadh** the people were gathering, **chruinnich e a' chlann san leabhar-lann** he assembled the children in the library, *Cf* (*vi*) **coinnich, thig còmhla** (*see* **còmhla** *adv* 1); 2 gather, collect (*objects*), pick (*flowers &c*); 3 gather, round up (*livestock*), **a' cruinneachadh nam bò** gathering the cattle, *Cf* **tionail 2, tru(i)s 3**

cruinn-leum, cruinn-lèim, cruinn-leuman *nm* a standing jump

crùisgean, crùisgein, crùisgeinean *nm* (*trad*) an oil lamp, a cruisie

cruit[1], cruite, cruitean *nf* 1 a harp (*Cf more usu* **clàrsach**), **cruit-chòrda** a harpsichord

cruit[2] *see* **croit**

cruitear[1], cruiteir, cruitearan *nm* a harper, *Cf more usu* **clàrsair**

cruitear[2] *see* **croitear**

cruitheachd, cruitheachd, cruitheachdan *nf* creation, a creation, **a' Chruitheachd** Creation, the World, the Universe (*Cf* **cruinne-cè**)

cruithear, cruitheir, cruithearan *nm* a creator, **an Cruithear** the Creator, God

Cruithneach, *gen & pl* **Cruithnich** *nm* (*hist*) a Pict

cruithneachd & **cruineachd** *nf invar* wheat

crùn *vt, pres part* **a' crùnadh**, crown (*a monarch &c*)

crùn, crùin, crùintean *nm* a crown

crùnadh, crùnaidh, crùnaidhean *nm* 1 (*the act of*) crowning, **chaidh a chrùnadh** he was crowned; 2 a coronation

cruth, *gen* **crutha**, *pl* **cruthan** & **cruthannan** *nm* 1 a shape, a form, a figure, an appearance or aspect (*of a person &c*), **rinn iad a-mach a cruth san dorchadas** they made out her form/appearance in the darkness, **cruth-tìre** landscape, *Cf* **cumadh 2, dealbh** *n* 5; 2 (*Lit &c*) form, **cuspair is cruth** matter and form

cruthachadh, *gen* **cruthachaidh** *nm* 1 (*the act of*) creating, creation

cruthachail *adj* creative

cruthaich *vt, pres part* **a' cruthachadh**, create

cù, *gen & pl* **coin**, *gen pl* **con** *nm* a dog, **cù-chaorach** a sheepdog, *Cf obs* **madadh 1**

cuach, cuaich, cuachan *nf* 1 a bowl; 2 (*as trophy &c*) a cup, a quaich

cuagach *adj* 1 bent, twisted; 2 lame, limping, *Cf* **bacach, crùbach** *adjs*

cuaille, cuaille, cuaillean *nm* a cudgel, a club, a bludgeon

cuain, cuaine, cuainean *nf* (*of animals*) a litter, *Cf* **àl**

cuairt, cuairte, cuairtean *nf* 1 a circuit, a cycle, a round, an orbit, **cuairt na grèine** the sun's orbit, **cuairt a' phosta** the postman's round, **cuairt goilf** a round of golf, **cuairt-rathad** *m* a ring road; 2 a stroll, a walk, **tha iad a' gabhail cuairt a-muigh** they're taking a stroll/walk/turn outside, *Cf* **car** *n* 2; 3 a trip, an excursion, a tour, **thèid sinn air chuairt do na h-eileanan** we'll go on a trip/tour to the islands, *Cf* **sgrìob 3, turas 1** & 2; 4 *in expr* **mun cuairt** *also* **mu chuairt** *adv* about, around, **tha an cnatan a' dol mun cuairt** the cold's going around, *Cf* **timcheall 1**; 5 *in expr* **mun cuairt air** *prep* around, **bha seallaidhean brèagha fada mun cuairt oirre** there were fine views all around her, *Cf* **timcheall 2** & 3

cuan, cuain, cuantan *nm* a sea, an ocean, **an Cuan Sgìth(e)** the Little Minch, **an Cuan Siar** the Atlantic, (*song*) **slighe cuain eadar mi 's m' eudail** a sea journey between me and my darling, (*prov*) **a' dèanamh cuain mhòir de chaolas cumhang** making a great ocean of a narrow strait

cuaraidh, cuaraidh, cuaraidhean *nmf* a (stone-) quarry

cuaran, *gen* **cuarain**, *pl* **cuarain** & **cuaranan** *nm* a light shoe, a sandal

cuartachadh & **cuairteachadh**, *gen* **cuartachaidh** *nm* 1 (*the act of*) surrounding &c (*see senses of* **cuartaich** *v*); 2 circulation (*of blood, air &c*)

cuartaich & **cuairtich** *vt, pres part* **a' cuartachadh**, 1 surround, enclose, encircle, *Cf* **iadh**; 2 (*movement*) circle (around); circulate

cùbaid, cùbaide, cùbaidean *nf* a pulpit

cubhaidh *adj* fitting, befitting, (*trad*) **rinn thu do dhleasdanas, mar bu chubhaidh dhut** you did your duty, as was fitting for you

cùbhraidh *adj* (*of smells*) sweet, fragrant, (*song*) **fàile cùbhraidh an fhraoich tighinn thar mullach nam beann** the fragrant scent of the heather coming over the mountain tops

cucair, cucair, cucairean *nf* a cooker, **cucair gas** a gas cooker, **cucair dealain** an electric cooker

cùdainn, cùdainn, cùdainnean *nf* a large tub, (*trad, hist*) **Clach na Cùdainn** the washtub stone (*a stone in Inverness where women used to rest their washtubs*)

cudthrom & **cudrom**, *also* **cuideam**, *gen* **cudthruim** *nm* 1 weight, a weight, **b' fheudar dhomh cudthrom a chur orm** I had to put on weight, **bha i a' giùlan cudthruim mhòir** she was carrying a great weight, **cileagram de chudthrom** a kilogram in weight, **cuir cudthrom eile air a' chothrom** put another weight on the scales; 2 importance, stress, emphasis, **leigidh a' chompanaidh cudthrom mòr air trèanadh a luchd-obrach** the company lays great importance/stress on training its workforce, *Cf* **buille 2**

cudthromach *also* **cudromach** *adj* 1 (*phys*) heavy, *Cf more usu* **trom 1**; 2 (*in abstr sense*) weighty, important, serious, **gnothaichean cudthromach** serious/weighty matters, **duine mòr cudthromach** a big important man, (*ironic*) a big-wig, a big shot

cugallach *adj* 1 unsteady, shaky, wobbly, (*Sc*) shooglie, **bòrd cugallach** a wobbly table, **cugallach air a chasan** unsteady on his feet, *Cf* **critheanach 2**; 2 (*in abstr sense*) shaky, dodgy, precarious, unreliable, **na buin ris a' ghnothach ud, tha e gu math cugallach** don't get involved in yon affair/business, it's pretty dodgy/shaky, (*trad*) **is cugullach an saoghal** the world is precarious/unreliable

cuibhle *also* **cuibheall**, *gen* **cuibhle**, *pl* **cuibhlean** & **cuibhlichean** *nf* a wheel, (*Cf more trad* **roth**), **cuibhle-stiùiridh** a steering wheel

cuibhreach, cuibhrich, cuibhrichean *nm* a chain, *Cf* **slabhraidh**

cuibhreachadh, *gen* **cuibhreachaidh** *nm* (*the act of*) chaining (*see* **cuibhrich** *v*)

cuibhreann, *gen* **cuibhrinn**, *pl* **cuibhrinnean** & **cuibhreannan** *nmf* 1 a portion, a share, *Cf* **cuid 1, roinn** *n* 1; 2 (*fin*) an allowance; 3 an instalment

cuibhrich *vt, pres part* **a' cuibhreachadh**, chain, chain up, put in chains

cuibhrig, cuibhrige, cuibhrigean *nmf* a quilt, a coverlet

cuid, codach, codaichean *nf* **1** a share, a portion, a part, **tha fichead nota againn, sin agad do chuid-sa dheth** we've twenty pounds, there's your (*emph*) share of it, (*prov*) **feumaidh an talamh a chuid fhèin** the earth (*ie* grave) must have its due share, (*trad*) **mo chuid den t-saoghal** my share of worldly goods, my possessions, **bha cuid den chirc nach deachaidh ithe** there was part of the chicken that wasn't eaten, **mòr-chuid** a greater part, (*people*) a majority, **a' mhòr-chuid de a bheatha** most/the greater part of his life, **tha a' mhòr-chuid air a shon** the majority/most people are in favour of it, **leth-chuid** a half, a half share, **cia mheud a tha thu ag iarraidh? a leth-chuid** how many do you want? half, **a' chuid as lugha/as motha** the smallest/biggest part, *also in expr* **cuid oidhche** a night's lodging/accommodation, **fhuair sinn ar cuid oidhche** (*or* **fhuair sinn cuid na h-oidhche**) **aig an taigh-òsta** we were put up for the night at the hotel, *Cf* **cuibhreann 1, roinn** *n* **1**; **2** *with following gen noun*, what one possesses or has acquired of anything, **ar cuid mhac** our sons, **mo chuid aodaich** my clothes/clothing, **càit an do thog thu do chuid Gàidhlig?** where did you learn/pick up your Gaelic?, (*can be derog, dismissive*) **còmhlan-ciùil 's an cuid fuaim** a band with their noise/din; **3** (*of people*) some, **tha cuid dhiubh a' cumail a-mach gu bheil e às a rian, tha a' chuid eile coma co-dhiù!** some of them are making out that he's out of his mind, the rest/the others don't care! *Cf* **feadhainn 1**; **4** *in expr* **an dà chuid** both, **leann no uisge-beatha? an dà chuid!** beer or whisky? both! **chan fhaodar an dà chuid dràibheadh agus òl** you/one can't/it's not permitted to both drink and drive, *Cf* **dara 3, gach 3**; **5** *in expr* **aon chuid ... no** neither ... nor, **cha phòs e aon chuid Mòrag no Màiri** he'll marry neither Morag nor Mary; **6** *in expr* **an dara cuid ... no** either ... or, **gabhaidh sinn an dara cuid trèana no bus** we'll take either a train or a bus

cuideachadh, *gen* **cuideachaidh** *nm* **1** (*the act of*) helping &c (*see senses of* **cuidich** *v*); **2** help, assistance, aid, **mòran taing airson do chuideachaidh** many thanks for your help, **làmh chuideachaidh** a helping hand, *Cf* **cobhair 1**

cuideachail *adj* helpful

cuideachd, cuideachd, cuideachdan *nf* **1** company, society, **nam chuideachd** in my company, **is toigh leis cuideachd na h-òigridh** he likes the company/society of young people, *Cf* **comann 3, conaltradh 2**; **2** one's companions, (*trad*) one's people, one's followers, (*song*) **mo chuideachd air m' fhàgail** my people/followers having left me, *Cf* **muinntir 1**; **3** a group, a company, **cuideachd shaighdearan** a company of soldiers, *Cf* **buidheann 1, còmhlan**

cuideachd *adv* also, too, as well, **an do dh'fhalbh Eòghann? dh'fhalbh, agus Iain cuideachd** has Ewan left? yes, and Iain too, *Cf* **ceudna 2**

cuideachdail *adj* sociable, fond of company, *Cf less usu* **conaltrach**

cuideigin *nmf invar* someone, somebody, **tha cuideigin air tighinn a-steach** someone's come in, *Cf* **duine 2**

cuide ri *prep* with, along with, together with, (*song*) **an uair a bha mi ann an Ile, bha Catrìona cuide rium** when I was in Islay, Catriona was with me, *Cf more usu* **còmhla 2, le 1**

cuidhteag & **cùiteag**, *gen* **cuidhteig**, *pl* **cuidhteagan** *nf* a whiting

cuidhteas, cuidhteis, cuidhteasan *nm* **1** a receipt (*for money &c*); **2** *in expr* **faigh** *v* **cuidhteas** get rid/shut of, **fhuair sinn cuidhteas na loidsearan mu dheireadh thall** we got rid of the lodgers at last

cuidich *vti, pres part* **a' cuideachadh**, help, assist, **cuidich iad**, (*more trad*) **cuidich leotha**, help them

cuidiche, cuidiche, cuidichean *nm* a helper, **cuidiche taighe** a home help

cùil, cùile, cùiltean *nf* **1** a corner (*esp internal*), **na shuidhe sa chùil** sitting in the corner (*Cf* **oisean** & *less trad* **còrnair**), (*calque*) **ann an cùil-chumhang** in a tight corner/a fix; **2** a nook, (*Sc*) a neuk, a tucked away part of a place or building, (*placename*) **Cùil na Muice** Cuilmuick, pig neuk

cuilbheart, cuilbheirt, cuilbheartan *nf* a trick, a wile, a plot, a stratagem, *Cf* **innleachd 4**

cuilc, cuilce, cuilcean *nf* **1** a reed; **2** cane, a cane, **cuilc Innseanach** bamboo

cuileag, cuileig, cuileagan *nf* a fly, a house-fly, **meanbhchuileag** a midge

cuilean, cuilein, cuileanan *nm* **1** (*dog*) a pup, a puppy; **2** (*fox, beur, liun, seal &c*) a cub, a whelp, a pup

cuileann, *gen* **cuilinn** *nm* holly

cuimhne *nf invar* memory (*incl IT*), remembrance, **chan eil cuimhne agam**, *also* (*trad*) **cha chuimhne leam**, I don't remember, **mas math mo chuimhne** if I remember rightly, **chaidh e às mo chuimhne** I forgot/have forgotten it, (*song*) **a' cur nam chuimhne nuair bha mi òg** reminding me of when I was young, (*IT*) **cuimhne bhuan** ROM

cuimhneachadh, *gen* **cuimhneachaidh** *nm* (*the act of*) remembering

cuimhneachan, *gen* & *pl* **cuimhneachain** *nm* **1** a memorial, a commemoration; **2** a remembrance, a souvenir, a keepsake; **3** a memorandum

cuimhnich *vti, pres part* **a' cuimhneachadh**, remember

cuimir *adj* **1** (*report, document &c*) succinct; **2** (*person, figure &c*) neat, trim, shapely, tidy, **calpa cuimir** a shapely/well-turned calf, *Cf* **grinn 3, sgiobalta 2, snasail**

Cuimreach, *gen & pl* **Cuimrich** *nm* a Welshman, someone from Wales (**a' Chuimrigh**), *also as adj* **Cuimreach** Welsh

cuimseachadh, *gen* **cuimseachaidh** *nm* (*the act of*) aiming

cuimsich *vti, pres part* **a' cuimseachadh**, aim (*gun &c*), *Cf* **amais 1**

cuine *&* **cuin** *inter adv* when, **cuin a bha sin?** when was that? **cuine bhios a' bhracaist deiseil?** when will the breakfast be ready?

cuing[1], **cuinge, cuingean** *nf* a yoke, (*fig*) **fo chuing an aintighearna** beneath the tyrant's yoke

cuing[2], *gen* **cuinge** *nf* (*with art*) **a' chuing** asthma, *Cf* **sac 2**

cuingealaich *&* **cuingich** *vt, pres part* **a' cuingealachadh** *&* **a' cuingeachadh**, restrict, limit, narrow down, **air a chuingealachadh gu còig mionaidean** restricted/limited to five minutes

cuinneag, cuinneige, cuinneagan *nf* a bucket, a pail, *esp* a milking pail, *Cf* **cuman** *& less trad* **bucaid 1, peile**

cuinn(l)ean, cuinn(l)ein, cuinn(l)eanan *nm* a nostril

cuip *vt, pres part* **a' cuipeadh**, whip, *Cf* **sgiùrs**

cuip, *gen* **cuipe**, *pl* **cuipean** *&* **cuipeachan** *nf* a whip, *Cf* **sgiùrsair**

cuipeadh, *gen* **cuipidh** *nm* (*the act of*) whipping

cuir *vti, pres part* **a' cur**, *there are very many idioms & expressions using this verb and only a selection can be given here*, **1** *involving the notions* put, place, set, **cuir gual air an teine** put coal on the fire, **cuiridh mi sa phreas e** I'll put it in the cupboard, **cuir rudeigin air an spàrr** stow/store something away, **cuir ort** (*more trad* **cuir umad**) **do chuid aodaich** put your clothes on, **cuir dhìot do chòta** (&c) take your coat (&c) off, **cuir air an solas** put the light on, **cuir air an teine** light the fire, **cuir às an solas/an teine** put the light/the fire out, **cuir an cèill** put into words, express, **cuir Beurla air Gàidhlig** translate Gaelic into English, **cuir às do rudeigin no chuideigin** put an end to/destroy something or someone, **cuir rudeigin air ath là** put something off (till another day), **cuir mu seach** put by, save, keep, **cuir an suarachas** belittle, **cuir gnothach** (&c) **air chois** set up/start up/found a business (&c), **chuir iad orm/chuir iad às mo leth nach robh mi onarach** they accused me of not being honest, **cuir aithne/eòlas air cuideigin** get to know/ get acquainted with someone, **cuir dragh air** worry/trouble (someone), **cuiridh mi (an) geall nach bi (an t-)uisge ann** I bet it won't rain, **cuir seachad ùine** spend/pass time, **tha e a' cur (an t-sneachda)** it's snowing, **cuir sìol** sow seed, **cuir buntàta** plant potatoes, **dè a tha a' cur ort?** what's wrong/the matter with you?, **chuir mi romham a' bhùth a dhùnadh** I decided to close the shop, **cuir an ceòl air feadh na fìdhle** set/put the cat among the pigeons, **chuir seo gu smaoineachadh mi** this set me thinking; **2** *involving the notions* send, bring, turn, **cuir air falbh** send away, **cuir a dh'iarraidh** send for, **chuir mi litir thugad** I sent you a letter, **chuir i a-mach a dìnnear** she brought up her dinner, **bha am ministear a' cur dheth** the minister was talking away/was in full flow, **cuir fios thuige** (&c) let him (&c) know/send him (&c) word, **chuir Gairm a-mach leabhar ùr** Gairm brought out/published a new book, **cha do chuir e suas no sìos mi** it didn't worry/affect/bother me in the least, **bha e gus mo chur dhìom fhìn** it was nearly driving me demented/out of my mind, **cuir fodha bàta** sink a boat, **cuir thairis** overflow, **chuir e nam aghaidh** he opposed me, **cò ris nach cuireadh e a làmh?** what couldn't he turn his hand to? **cuir mo** (&c) **c(h)ùl ri** turn my (&c) back on, leave, forsake, abandon, **cuir prìosanach** (&c) **mu sgaoil** set free/release a prisoner (&c)

cuireadh, cuiridh, cuiridhean *nm* an invitation, **cuireadh gu banais** an invitation to a wedding, **thoir** *v* **cuireadh do chuideigin** invite someone, *Cf* **iarr 3, iarraidh 3**

cuirm, cuirme, cuirmean *nf* a feast, a banquet (*Cf* **fèis 2, fleadh**), **cuirm-chnuic** a picnic, **cuirm-chiùil** a concert

cuirmeach *adj* festive

cùirt, cùirte, cùirtean *nf* **1** a (royal &c) court; **2** a law court (*also* **cùirt-lagha**)

cùirtean, cùirtein, cùirteanan *also* **cùirtear, cùirteir, cùirtearan** *nm* a curtain

cùirteil *adj* **1** courteous, *Cf* **modhail**; **2** courtly

cùis, cùise, cùisean *nf* **1** a matter, an affair, a business, **ciamar a chaidh a' chùis?** how did the matter/affair go/turn out? **cnag na cùise** the nub/crux of the matter, the fundamental issue, the crucial question, **aig crìch na cùise** in the end, finally, *in expr* (*in argument, discussion &c*) **chan e sin a' chùis!** that's not the point!, *Cf* **gnothach 2**; **2** (*in pl*) matters, things, **tha cùisean gu math dripeil an-dràsta** things are pretty busy just now; **3** (*legal*) a case (*also* **cùis-lagha**), a lawsuit, **chaidh a' chùis na h-aghaidh** the case went against her; **4** a cause, a reason, a butt, an object, **cùis mo bhròin** the cause of/reason for my sadness, **bha iad nan cùis-mhagaidh an dèidh sin** they were a laughing-stock/a butt of ridicule after that, **cùis-ghearain** a cause for complaint, a grievance, *Cf* **adhbhar 1, culaidh 4**; **5** *in expr* **dèan** *v* **a' chuis air** manage (*a task &c*), get the better of *or* defeat (*someone*), *Cf* **gnothach 6, uachdar 5**; **6** *in expr* **nì sin a' chùis!** that'll do!, that'll do the job/trick!, *Cf* **gnothach 7**

cùis-bheachd, cùis-bheachd, cùis-bheachdan *nf* an abstraction, an abstract idea

cùisear, cùiseir, cùisearan *nm* (*gram*) a subject, *Cf* **cuspair 4**

cuisle, cuisle, cuislean *nf* **1** a vein, *Cf less usu* **fèith 3** ; **2** (*also* **cuisle mhòr**) an artery, **a' chuisle-chinn** the aorta; **3** a pipe, **cuisle-chiùil** a flute, *Cf next*

cuislean, cuislein, cuisleanan *nm* a flute

cùiteag *see* **cuidhteag**

cùl, cùil, cùiltean *nm* **1** (*trad*) the back or nape of the neck, the hair on the nape, the hair of the head in general, **Gàidheal gu chùl** a Gael/ Highlander through and through, every bit a Gael/Highlander; **2** *more generally* a back (*of human, animal, object &c*), **chuir mi mo chùl ris** I turned my back to/on him, **cùl na làimhe** the back of the hand, **cùl na h-amhaich** the back of the neck, **shad e an cùl na làraidh e** he shoved it in the back of the lorry, *Note:* **druim** *is used for the phys human back*; **3** *in expr* **air cùl** *prep* behind (*with gen*), **air cùl na h-eaglaise** behind the church, *Cf* **air cùlaibh**

cùlaibh (*for* **cùl-thaobh**) *nm invar* the back part of anything, **cùlaibh air beulaibh** back to front, vice versa, *Cf* **beulaibh** *& see* **air cùlaibh**

culaidh, culaidhe, culaidhean *nf* **1** (*trad*) a garment, *Cf* **ball-aodaich** (*see* **aodach 2**); **2** (*also* **culaidh-aodaich**) a suit of clothes, *Cf* **deise, trusgan 2**; **3** (*theatre, party &c*) a costume, **culaidh-choimheach** a fancy dress costume; **4** an object, a butt (*of emotions, reactions &c*), **culaidh-fharmaid** an object of envy, **culaidh-mhagaidh** an object of mockery, a butt of ridicule, *Cf* **adhbhar 1, cùis 4**

cùlaist, cùlaiste, cùlaistean *nf* a scullery, a back kitchen, a utility room

cularan, cularain, cularanan *nm* a cucumber

cùl-chàin *vt, pres part* **a' cùl-chàineadh**, slander, back-bite

cùl-chàineadh, *gen* **cùl-chàinidh** *nm* **1** (*the act of*) slandering; **2** slander, back-biting, calumny

cullach, *gen & pl* **cullaich** *nm* **1** a boar, a male (domestic) pig; **2** a wild boar; *Cf* **cràin, muc, torc**; **3** a male cat, a tom-cat

cùl-mhùtaire, cùl-mhùtaire, cùl-mhùtairean *nm* a smuggler

cùl-mhùtaireachd *nf invar* smuggling

cultar, cultair, cultaran *nm*, *&* **cultur, cultuir, culturan** *nm*, (*mental, artistic*) culture, a (*national &c*) culture, **cultur na Gàidhlige** Gaelic culture

cum *vt, pres part* **a' cumadh**, shape, form, fashion, **chum e ìomhaigh às a' chloich** he formed/fashioned an image/a figure out of the stone, *Cf* **dealbh** *v* **2**

cùm *vt, pres part* **a' cumail,** 1 keep, hold, hold on to, **cùm seo dhomh gu Dihaoine** keep this for me until Friday, **an cùm a' mhàileid sin mo chuid aodaich air fad?** will that bag hold all my clothes? **cùm grèim air rudeigin** keep a grip on/keep hold of something, **cumaibh air ais!** keep back! **cha chùm mi air ais sibh** I won't keep/ hold you back, I won't delay you, *Cf* **glèidh 1;** 2 continue, keep (on), *(calque)* **ciamar a tha thu a' cumail?** how are you keeping? **tha mi a' cumail beò** I'm surviving/still in the land of the living, **cùm ort!** keep going!, keep at it!, *(work, a task &c)* **cùm ris!** stick at it!, persevere!, don't give up!; 3 *(misc senses)* **cha do chùm sinn a' Bhliadhna Ur an-uiridh** we didn't keep/observe New Year last year, **cùm suas** keep, maintain, support, **tha teaghlach agam ri chumail suas** I have a family to support, **cùm a-mach** assert, maintain, claim, make out, **tha iad a' cumail a-mach gun tig an saoghal gu crìch a-màireach** they are making out that the world will end tomorrow

cumadh, cumaidh, cumaidhean *nm* 1 *(the act of)* shaping &c *(see senses of* **cum** *v)*; 2 a shape, a form, **rinn iad a-mach a chumadh san dorchadas** they made out his/its shape in the darkness, **chunnaic mi clach air chumadh eich** I saw a stone in the shape of a horse, *Cf* **cruth 1, dealbh 5**

cumail, *gen* **cumalach** *nf (the act of)* keeping &c *(see senses of* **cùm** *v)*

cuman, *gen & pl* **cumain** *nm (trad)* a pail, a bucket *esp for milking, Cf* **cuinneag** *& less trad* **bucaid 1, peile**

cumanta *adj* common, frequently met with, **facal cumanta** a common word, *Cf* **àbhaisteach, gnàthach**

cumantas, *gen* **cumantais** *nm* the quality of being common or usual, normality, *esp in exprs* **an cumantas** *adv* usually, commonly, normally (*Cf* **am bitheantas**), & **às a' chumantas** *adv* out of the ordinary, out of the common run of things, *(calque)* **chan eil mòran aca an cumantas** they haven't much in common

cumha, cumha, cumhachan *nm (trad) esp as genre of poetry or music,* a lament, an elegy, *Cf* **marbhrann**

cumha, cumha, cumhachan *nf* 1 *(trad, esp in contracts &c)* a stipulation, a condition; 2 *also in expr* **air chumha is gu ...** on condition that ..., as long as ..., provided that ...; *Cf* **cor 2, cùmhnant 2**

cumhach *adj (gram)* conditional, **an tràth cumhach** the conditional tense

cumhachd *nmf invar* 1 *(mainly abstr, pol, military &c)* power, might, force, influence, **cumhachd na h-Iompaireachd Ròmanaich** the might of the Roman Empire

cumhachdach *adj* 1 powerful, mighty; 2 influential

cumhang *adj* **1** narrow, *Cf more usu* **caol 1**; **2** (*people, attitudes*) limited, narrow, narrow-minded

cùmhnant, cùmhnaint, cùmhnantan *nm* **1** (*legal, official, fin &c*) a covenant, a contract, a bargain, *Cf* **cunnradh**; **2** *also in expr* **air a' chùmhnant seo** on this condition, *Cf* **cor 2, cumha** *nf* **1** & **2**

cunbhalach *adj* **1** even, regular, constant, firm, steady; **2** tidy

cungaidh, cungaidh, cungaidhean *nf* **1** (*trad*) stuff, materials, ingredients; **2** (*trad*) a tool, an implement; **3** (*also* **cungaidh-leighis**) a medicine, a (medical) drug, **bùth-chungaidh** a chemist's shop, a pharmacy, **fear/neach-chungaidhean** a pharmacist, a (pharmaceutical) chemist

cunnart, cunnairt, cunnartan *nm* danger, risk, a danger, a risk, **(ann) an cunnart** in danger, at risk, endangered, **cuir** *v* **cuideigin/ rudeigin an cunnart** endanger/put at risk someone/something, **cunnart bàis** danger/risk of death, mortal danger, *Cf* **gàbhadh 1**

cunnartach *adj* dangerous, risky, hazardous, *Cf usu stronger* **gàbhaidh**

cunnradh, cunnraidh, cunnraidhean *nm* **1** a covenant, a contract, an agreement, *Cf more usu* **cùmhnant 1**; **2** (*business, fin*) a bargain, a deal

cunnt *vti, pres part* **a' cunntadh**, count, **a' cunntadh chaorach** counting sheep, **chan urrainn do mo bhràthair beag cunntadh fhathast** my wee brother can't count yet, **chan eil Teàrlach ann ach chan eil esan a' cunntadh** Charles/Charlie isn't here but he doesn't count

cunntadh, *gen* **cunntaidh** & **cunntais**, *gen* **cunntais**, *nm* (*the act of*) counting

cunntas, cunntais, cunntasan *nm* **1** arithmetic; **2** a (bank &c) account, **tha cunntas agam aig a' Bhanca Rìoghail** I have an account at the Royal Bank, **cunntas tasgaidh/sàbhalaidh** an investment/ savings account; **3** an account, an invoice, a bill **chuir an grosair cunntas thugainn** the grocer sent us an account/bill, *Cf more fam* **bileag 3**; **4** a written or verbal account, a narration, a description, **sgrìobh e cunntas (air) a bheatha fhèin** he wrote an account of his own life, **cunntas-beatha** a CV; **5** (*sports, games*) a score, *Cf* **sgòr**

cunntasachd *nf invar* accountancy, accounting

cunntasair, cunntasair, cunntasairean *nm* an accountant

cuntair, cuntair, cuntairean *nm* (*shop &c*) a counter, (*song*) **chosg mi de dh'airgead aig cuntair a' bhàir a cheannaicheadh trì taigheanòsta** I spent/squandered as much money at the bar counter as would buy three hotels/pubs

cùp, cùpa, cùpannan *nm* a cup, *Cf* **copan, cupa**

cupa, cupa, cupannan *nm* a cup, *Cf* **copan, cùp**

cupan, cupain, cupanan *nm* a small cup (*dimin of* **cupa**), **nach gabh sibh cupan teatha?** won't you have a wee cup of tea?

cuplachadh, *gen* **cuplachaidh** *nm* **1** (*the act of*) copulating &c (*see senses of* **cuplaich** *v*); **2** copulation

cuplaich *vi, pres part* **a' cuplachadh,** copulate, couple, mate, have sexual intercourse, *Cf* **co-ghin, muin 4**

cùpon, cùpoin, cùponan *nm* a coupon, a voucher

cur, *gen* **cuir** *nm* (*the act of*) placing, putting, sending &c, (*see senses of* **cuir** *v*)

curach, curaich, curaichean *nf* **1** (*trad, hist*) a curach *or* curragh, a coracle, *a light, usu round, boat of timber or wattle covered with hide,* **curach Innseanach** a canoe

curaidh, curaidh, curaidhean *nm* a hero, *Cf* **gaisgeach, laoch, seòd**

cùram, cùraim, cùraman *nm* **1** care, responsibility, **air cùram Dhòmhnaill** in Donald's care/charge, under Donald's responsibility, *Cf* **uallach 2, urra 2; 2** anxiety, preoccupation, **fo chùram** anxious, worried, (*song*) **tha i daonnan air mo chùram anns gach nì** she is always on my mind in every situation, *Cf* **iomagain 1; 3** (*Presbyterianism*) conversion, becoming very devout or religious, *esp in expr* **ghabh e (&c) an cùram** he (*&c*) became converted/ became very devout, (*Highland Eng*) he's (*&c*) got the cùram

cùramach *adj* **1** careful, cautious, acting responsibly, *Cf* **faiceallach; 2** anxious, prone to anxiety or worry, *Cf* **iomagaineach 1**

cur na mara *nm invar* sea-sickness, *Cf* **tinneas-mara** (*see* **tinneas**)

curran, *gen* **currain,** *pl* **currain** *&* **curranan** *nm* a carrot

curracag, curracaig, curracagan *nf* a lapwing, a peewit, a green plover, (*Sc*) a peesie, *Cf* **adharcan-luachrach**

cùrsa, cùrsa, cùrsaichean *nm* **1** (*academic &c*) a course, **rinn mi cùrsaichean sa Ghàidhlig agus sa Bheurla anns an oilthigh** I did/ took courses in Gaelic and English at University, (*lang teaching*) **cùrsa bogaidh** an immersion course; **2** a course, a direction of travel, *Cf* **iùl 1, seòl² 2**

cùrsair, cùrsair, cùrsairean *nm* (*IT &c*) a cursor

cur-seachad, cuir-seachad, cur-seachadan *nm* a hobby, a pastime, a (leisure) pursuit, **is e ball-coise an cur-seachad as fheàrr leam/as fheàrr a th' agam** football is my favourite hobby/pastime

cùrtair *see* **cùirtean**

cus, *gen* **cuis** *nm* an excess, too much, **dh'òl mi cus a-raoir!** I drank too much last night! **cus bruidhne** too much talking

cusbainn *nf invar* customs (*ie levying of import duty*), **cìs-chusbainn** *f* customs duty

cusp, cusp, cuspan *nf* a chilblain

cuspair, cuspair, cuspairean *nm* **1** a subject, a topic, **cuspair a h-òraid** the subject of her talk; **2** (*school &c*) a subject, **b' e ceimigeachd an cuspair a b' fheàrr leis** chemistry was his favourite subject; **3** (*trad*) an object (*of emotion &c*), **cuspair a ghràidh** the object of his love; **4** (*gram*) an object (*of a verb*), *Cf* **cùisear**; **5** (*Lit, art &c*) a subject, subject matter, **cuspair is cruth** matter and form

cut *vti, pres part* **a' cutadh**, gut (*esp fish*)

cutair, cutair, cutairean *nm* a gutter (*esp of fish*)

cuthach, *gen* **cuthaich** *nm* **1** madness, insanity; **2** rage, fury, extreme anger, **chaidh e air chuthach** he went mad/insane, *also* he went mad (*with rage*), he became furious, **ghabh e an cuthach (dearg)** he went mad with rage; *Cf* **bàinidh, boile**

cuthag, cuthaig, cuthagan *nf* a cuckoo

D

dà *n & adj* **1** two (*takes the dat, aspirates/lenites following noun*), **dà chù** two dogs, **dà chloich** two stones, **uair no dhà** a time or two, once or twice, *also* an hour or two; **2** *in compound adjs & nouns* two-, bi-, *eg* **dà-chànanach** *adj* bilingual, **dà-shùileach** *adj* two-eyed, **creutair dà-bheathach** an amphibious creature (*Cf* **muir-thìreach**), **dà-thaobhach** *adj* bilateral, (*IT*) **dà-fhillte** *adj* binary

dachaigh & **dachaidh**, *nf invar* a home, one's home, **1** (*one's dwelling*) **am faic thu an taigh ud thall? 's e sin mo dhachaigh** do you see the house over yonder? that's my home, (*house name*) **Ar Dachaigh** Our Home, *Cf* **baile 5**, **taigh 2**; **2** (*district, country &c one belongs to*) (*song*) **eilean beag Leòdhais, dachaigh nan seòid** the little isle of Lewis, home of heroes, *Cf* **dùthaich 3**; **3** *as adv expressing movement* **dhachaigh** home, homewards, **tha mi a' falbh/a' dol dhachaigh** I'm away/going home

dad *nf invar* **1** a thing, anything, **chan eil dad agam** I haven't a thing/ anything, *Cf* **càil 1 & 2**, **nì** *n* **1**, **rud 1**, **sian 3**; **2** *also in expr* **dad ort!** never mind, don't worry!

dadaidh, dadaidh, dadaidhean *nm* (*fam*) Daddy, a Daddy, *Cf* **athair**, **mamaidh**

dadam, *gen & pl* **dadaim** *nm* **1** an atom; **2** a tiny piece of anything

dà-dheug *n & adj* twelve, **dà uair dheug** twelve o'clock

daga & **dag**, *gen* **daige**, *pl* **dagan** & **dagaichean** *nm* a handgun, a pistol, a revolver

dail, dalach, dailean *nf* a meadow (*Cf* **clua(i)n**); a haugh (*Cf* **innis** *n* **2**)

dàil, dàlach, dàlaichean *nf* **1** delay, a delay, **thig dhachaigh gun dàil** come home without delay, *Cf* **maille 2**; **2** *in expr* **cuir** *v* **dàil ann/air** delay, **chuir an aimsir dàil anns a' chùis** the weather delayed the business/matter, *Cf* **cùm air ais** (see **cùm 1**); **3** (*fin*) credit, **ceannaich** *v* **air dàil** buy on credit/hire purchase

dàimh *nmf invar* **1** a relationship, ties (*of kinship, friendship*), **an dàimh eadar an dà theaghlach** the relationship/ties between the two families, *Cf* **càirdeas**; **2** (*in general*) a connection, a tie, a link (**ri** with), **cha robh dàimh agam ris a' chompanaidh sin** I had no connection with that firm, *Cf* **buinteanas**, **ceangal 2**

dàimheach *adj* relative, (*gram*) **mion-fhacal/mìrean dàimheach** a relative particle

daingeann *adj* (*structure, building &c*) firm, solid, *Cf* **teann** *adj* **2**

daingneach, daingnich, daingnichean *nf* a fort, a fortress, a stronghold, a (*fortified*) castle, *Cf* **dùn 2**

daingneachadh, *gen* **daingneachaidh** *nm* (*the act of*) fortifying, confirming &c (*see senses of* **daingnich** *v*)

daingnich *vt, pres part* **a' daingneachadh**, **1** (*structure, building &c*) fortify, strengthen, consolidate, make firm or solid; **2** (*truths, principles &c*) confirm, prove, **dhaingnich i a creideamh le a bhith a' dol na caillich dhuibh** she confirmed her faith by becoming a nun, *Cf* **dearbh** *v* **1**

dàir, *gen* **dàra** *nf* (*of cattle*) breeding, coupling, **crodh-dàra** breeding *or* calving cattle, **bò fo dhàir** a cow in season, a bulling cow

dall *adj* blind, **an Clàrsair Dall** the Blind Harper (*a 17th–18th century poet*)

dall, *gen & pl* **doill** *nm* a blind person, (*prov*) **chì sinn, mar a thuirt an dall** we'll see, as the blind man said

dall *vt, pres part* **a' dalladh**, blind

dalladh, *gen* **dallaidh** *nm* (*the act of*) blinding, *state of* (blindness)

dàmais *nf invar* (*game*) draughts, **bòrd-dàmais** *m* a draught board

damh, *gen & pl* **daimh 1** *nm* a stag (*usu red deer*), *Cf* **boc 2**, **eilid**; **2** an ox; **3** a bullock

dàmhair, dàmhair, dàmhairean *nf* **1** rutting of red deer, rutting time or season; **2** (*with art*) **An Dàmhair** October

damhan-allaidh, *gen & pl* **damhain-allaidh** *nm* a spider

dàn[1], *gen* **dàin** *nm* **1** fate, destiny, **na cuir an aghaidh dàin!** don't oppose/go against fate!; **2** *in expr* **an dàn do** fated, destined, ordained (*for someone*), **ghabh e ris na bha an dàn dha** he accepted his fate/what fate had ordained for him

dàn[2], *gen* **dàin**, *pl* **dàna** & **dàin** *nm* **1** a poem, (*title of poem sequence*) **Dàin do Eimhir** (Somhairle MacGill-Eain) Poems to/for Eimhir, *Cf* **bàrdachd, rann 1**; **2** (*trad*) a song, (*song*) **nì mi nis co-dhùnadh is bheir mi an dàn gu crìch** I'll conclude now and bring the song to an end, **dàn spioradail** a spiritual song, a hymn (*Cf* **laoidh 2**); *Note: before the 20th century the distinction between poem and song hardly existed in Gaelic culture*

dàna *adj* **1** bold, daring, intrepid, *Cf* **gaisgeil**; **2** rashly brave, *Cf* **bras 2**; **3** impudent, *Cf* **ladarna**; **4** arrogant, *Cf* **àrdanach, uaibhreach 2**

dànachd *nf invar* poetry, verse, *Cf more usu* **bàrdachd, rann 1**

dànadas, *gen* **dànadais** *nm* **1** boldness, daring, intrepidity; **2** impudence; **3** arrogance

danns *vti, pres part* **a' dannsa(dh)**, dance

dannsa, dannsa, dannsaichean *nm* a dance (*individual dance and social event*), **bidh cèilidh agus dannsa ann a-nochd** there'll be a ceilidh-dance tonight

dannsadh, *gen* **dannsaidh** *nm* (*the act of*) dancing, **an toigh leat dannsadh? cha toil!** do you like dancing? no!

dannsair, dannsair, dannsairean *nm* a dancer

daoimean, daoimein, daoimeanan *nm* a diamond

daoine *see* **duine**

daolag, daolaig, daolagan *nf* a beetle, **daolag-bhreac-dhearg** a ladybird

daonna *adj* human, *usu in expr* **an cinne-daonna** *m* humanity, human-kind, mankind, the human race, *Cf* **mac-an-duine** (*see* **duine 3**)

daonnan *adv* always, constantly, *Cf similarly used* **an còmhnaidh, fad na h-ùine** (*see* **ùine 1**)

daor *adj* dear, expensive, costly (*opposite of* **saor**), (*song*) **'s daor a cheannaich mi 'n t-iasgach** I paid dearly for the fishing, *Cf* **cosgail**

daorach, *gen* **daoraich** *nf* 1 drunkenness, intoxication, *esp in exprs* **tha an daorach air** & **tha e air an daoraich** & **tha e leis an daoraich** he's drunk, **ceann daoraich** *m* a hangover, *Cf* **misg, smùid** *n* 3; 2 (*trad*) a drinking spree, (*pibroch*) **An Daorach Mhòr** The Big Spree

daorachail *adj* intoxicating

daorsa *nf invar* captivity (*opposite of* **saorsa**), *Cf more usu* **braighdeanas, ciomachas, làmh 2, sàs 1**

dara & **dàrna** *adj* 1 second, **an dara là den mhìos** the second day of the month; 2 (*when in contrast to* **eile**) one, **tha an dara mac dèanadach ach tha am fear eile leisg** one son is industrious but the other one is lazy, *in expr* **cuir** *v* **an dara taobh** put to one side, set aside; 3 *in expr* **an dara cuid**, either, **thoir dhomh an dara cuid feòil no iasg** give me either meat or fish

darach, *gen* & *pl* **daraich** *nm* oak

dara-deug *adj* twelfth, **an dara là deug** the twelfth day

da-rìribh & **da-rìreadh** *adv* 1 *in expr* (**cha robh iad &c**) **ann an da-rìribh** (they weren't &c) serious/in earnest, they didn't mean it, *see* **fealla-dhà** & *Cf less usu* **stòlda 2**; 2 *often in expr* **math dha-rìribh** very good indeed, excellent, extremely good, *Cf* **eagalach 3, uabhasach 2**

dàrna *see* **dara**

dà-sheaghach *adj* ambiguous

dàta *nm invar* data, information, (*IT*) **stòr-dàta** *m* a database

dath *vt, pres part* **a' dathadh**, 1 colour; 2 dye; *Cf* **cuir dath air** (*see* **dath** *n*)

dath, datha, dathan *nm* 1 colour, a colour, **dè an dath a th' air a' chòta?** what colour's the coat? **cuir** *v* **dath air** colour, dye, **dath-lipean** lipstick, **dath-dhall** *adj* colour blind, **dath-bhacadh** *m* a colour bar; 2 dye, a dye

dathte *adj* coloured; dyed

dè *pron* 1 what, **dè an t-ainm a th' oirbh?** what's your name?, **dè a tha a' tachairt?** what's happening? **dè am math a bhith bruidhinn!** what's the good/use of talking! **dè do bheachd?** what do you think?, **Dè an rud?** What?, Pardon? (*Cf more polite* **B' àill leibh?** – *see* **àill** 2), **dè na tha e?** how much is it?, (*in indirect questions*) **chan eil fhios 'am dè a nì mi** I don't know what I'll do; 2 *in constr* **dè cho … agus/'s a … ?** how … ?, **dè cho feumail 's a tha e?** how useful is it?; 3 (*trad, now more emph*) **gu dè** what, whatever, **gu dè as ciall dhut?** whatever do you mean?

de & **dhe** *prep* (*with the dat, aspirates/lenites following consonant*), Note: *the pers prons* **mi**, **thu**, **e** *&c combine with* **de** *to form the prep prons* **dhìom(sa)**, **dhìot(sa)**, **dheth(san)**, **dhith(se)**, **dhinn(e)**, **dhibh(se)**, **dhiubh(san)**, of/from me, you &c; 1 of, **a' chuid as mò dheth** most of it, **aig an àm seo den bhliadhna** at this time of the year, **am ficheadamh là den mhìos** the twentieth of the month, **làn de bhainne** full of milk, **fear de na bh' ann** one of those who were there, **amadan de dhuine** a fool of a man, *sometimes occurs as* **a**, **chan eil càil a dh'fhios agam** I haven't the faintest idea (*lit* I have nothing of knowledge), **fear dhiubh sin** one of those; 2 of (*ie made of*), **bràiste de dh'airgead** a brooch of silver; 3 of, out of, (*song*) **dèan am foghar den gheamhradh** make autumn (out) of winter; 4 from, off, **cuir dhìot do chòta** take your coat off, **tog** *v* **clachan den làr** lift stones from the ground; 5 *in expr* **ullamh de** finished with, **bha am poileas ullamh de a cheasnachadh** the police had finished questioning him

deacair *adj* hard, difficult, abstruse, **leabhar deacair** a difficult book (*ie to understand*), *Cf* **doirbh**, **duilich** 1

deach, **deachaidh** *pts of irreg v* **rach** (*see tables p 410*)

deachd *vti*, *pres part* **a' deachdadh**, dictate (*letter &c*)

deachdadh, **deachdaidh**, **deachdaidhean** *nm* 1 (*the act of*) dictating; 2 dictation, a dictation

deachdaire, **deachdaire**, **deachdairean** *nm* (*pol &c*) a dictator

deagh *adj* (*precedes & aspirates/lenites the noun*) 1 good, **is e deagh sheinneadair a th' ann** he's a good singer, (*corres &c*) **leis gach deagh dhùrachd!** with best wishes! (*lit* with every good wish), **tha e air a dheagh dhòigh** he's pleased/delighted, **tha mi ann an deagh thriom** I'm in good trim; 2 *also in compounds eg* **deagh-thoil** *f* good will, **deagh-chridheach** *adj* good-hearted, **deagh-bheusan** *f* (good) morals; 3 *as adv* well, **tha e air a dheagh chumadh/dhèanamh** (&c) it's well shaped/made (&c); *Cf* **math** & *opposite* **droch**

dealachadh, dealachaidh, dealachaidhean *nm* **1** (*the act of*) parting &c (*see senses of* **dealaich** *v*), **thug i nota dha anns an dealachadh** she gave him a pound on parting/as they parted; **2** separation, a separation, **dealachadh-pòsaidh** a divorce, *Cf* **sgaradh 3**; **3** segregation

dealaich *vti, pres part* **a' dealachadh**, **1** part, separate, segregate, (**ri** from), **dhealaich na càirdean ri chèile** the friends parted/separated, **cha dealaich thu bho chuid airgid e!** you won't part him from his money!, **dhealaich am bàs iad** death parted them; **2** (*elec &c*) insulate

dealan, *gen* **dealain** *nm* electricity, **Bòrd an Dealain** the Electricity Board, (*song*) **solas an dealain** the electric light, **dealan-uisge** hydroelectricity, *Cf* **cumhachd 2**; **2** *gen* **dealain** *used as adj* electric, electronic, **teine** *m* **dealain** an electric fire, (*IT*) **post** *m* **dealain** electronic mail, e-mail

dealanach, *gen & pl* **dealanaich** *nm* lightning

dealanach *adj* electronic

dealanaich *vt, pres part* **a' dealanachadh**, electrify (*not in fig sense*)

dealanair, dealanaire, dealanairean *nm* an electrician

dealan-dè, dealain-dè, dealanan-dè *nm* a butterfly

dealasach *adj* eager, zealous, *Cf* **deònach, èasgaidh**

dealbh *vt, pres part* **a' dealbhadh**, **1** picture (*mentally*), imagine, **tachartas nach b' urrainn dhut a dhealbhadh** an event you couldn't imagine; **2** make, shape, construct, *Cf* **cum**; **3** design, plan (*technical & artistic objects*), **dealbh innealan** design machines

dealbh, *gen* **dealbha** & **deilbh**, *pl* **dealbhan, deilbh** & **dealbhannan** *nmf* **1** a picture, **taigh-dhealbh** a picture house, a cinema; **2** a painting; **3** a photograph, **tog** *v* **dealbh** take a photograph; **4** a drawing, **dealbh-èibhinn** a cartoon; **5** a form, a shape, a figure, **rinn mi a-mach dealbh duine/dealbh taighe san dorchadas** I made out the shape/figure of a man/the shape/form of a house in the darkness, *Cf* **cruth 1, cumadh 2**; **6** *also in compounds eg* **dealbh-chluich** a (stage) play, **dealbh-chumadh** a (*usu technical*) plan or diagram

dealbhadh, *gen* **dealbhaidh** *nm* (*the act of*) picturing, shaping, planning &c (*see senses of* **dealbh** *v*), **cead** *m* **dealbhaidh** planning permission

dealg, deilg, dealgan *nf* **1** a prickle, a thorn, *Cf* **bior 3**; **2** a thorn (*ie the plant*); **3** a skewer; **4** a pin, *Cf more usu* **prìne**

deàlrach *adj* **1** shining, radiant, *Cf* **boillsgeach**; **2** shiny

deàlradh, *gen* **deàlraidh** *nm* **1** (*the act of*) shining &c (*see senses of* **deàlraich** *v*); **2** radiance

deàlraich *vi, pres part* **a' dcàlradh,** (*of lights*) **1** shine, *Cf* **soillsich 2; 2** flash, glitter, *Cf* **boillsg**

dealt, *gen* **dealta,** *nmf* dew, (*song*) **dealt na h-oidhche a' sileadh coibhneis** the dew of the night shedding kindliness, *Cf* **driùchd**

deamhais, deamhais, deamhaisean *nmf* a pair of shears

deamhan, *gen & pl* **deamhain** *nm* a demon, *Cf* **diabhal**

dèan *vt irreg* (*see tables p 407*), *pres part* **a' dèanamh, 1** do, **dèan do dhleastanas** do your duty, **na dèan sin!** don't do that! **rinn mi mo dhìcheall** I did my best, **nach math a rinn thu!** well done!, didn't you do well! **nì sin an gnothach** that will do!, that's just the job; **2** make, **nì mi silidh a-màireach** I'll make jam tomorrow, (*poem*) **ma bha siud an dàn dhaibh, dhèanadh iad daoine** (Ruaraidh MacThòmais) if that was their fate, they would make men, **rinn iad adhartas** they made progress, **rinn e air a' bhàta** he made for the boat; **3** (*art &c*) compose, **rinn mi bàrdachd/òran** I've made/composed some poetry/a song; **4** (*trad*) *as auxiliary verb with poss adj & verbal noun* **rinn iad ar sgriosadh/ar sàbhaladh** (&c) they ruined/saved (&c) us (*lit* they did our ruining/our saving &c); **5** *other common exprs* **dèan cabhag!** hurry up! **dèan cadal!** go to sleep! **dèan suidhe** be seated **nì e feum dhut** it will do you good

dèanadach *adj* industrious, hardworking, active, *Cf* **dìcheallach, gnìomhach**

dèanadas, *gen* **dèanadais** *nm* industry, industriousness, *Cf* **gnìomhachas 1**

dèanadh, dèanaibh, dèanainn, dèanam, dèanamaid *pts of irreg v* **dèan** *see tables p 407*

dèanamh, *gen* **dèanaimh** *nm* **1** (*the act of*) doing, making &c (*see senses of* **dèan** *v*); **2** one's form, figure, build, constitution, **'s e iasg is min-choirce a thug an deagh dhèanamh dhaibh** it's fish and oat-meal that gave them their fine build/constitution

deann, deanna, deannan *nf* **1** (*trad*) force, impetus; **2** haste, speed, *usu in expr* **na dheann** rushing, in (great) haste, **chaidh iad dhachaigh nan deann** they rushed home, *Cf* **cabhag 1; 3 deann-ruith** *same as* **dian-ruith** (*see* **dian 3**)

deanntag *see* **feanntag**

dèanta & dèante *adj* made, done, completed, **duine dèanta** a grown man (*Cf* **foirfe**), **dèanta ri cogadh** raised/trained to war

dearbh *vt, pres part* **a' dearbhadh, 1** prove, demonstrate, **dearbh a chionta/gu bheil Dia ann** prove his guilt/that there is a God; **2** test, put to the test, try, *Cf* **deuchainn 2, feuch 2**

dearbh *adj* **1** very, same, exact, **an e Tormod a tha a' tighinn? an dearbh dhuine!** is it Norman who's coming? the very man! **'s e òrd an dearbh rud a bha dhìth orm** a hammer was the very/exact thing I needed, *Cf* **ceart 3, ceudna 1, fèin 5**; **2** *as adv* **gu dearbh** indeed, certainly, definitely, really, **a bheil thu sgìth? tha gu dearbh!** are you tired? I certainly am! **tha e beartach! a bheil gu dearbh?** he's rich! is he really? is he indeed?

dearbhadh, dearbhaidh, dearbhaidhean *nm* **1** (*the act of*) proving &c (*see senses of* **dearbh** *v*); **2** proof, a proof, evidence, a piece of evidence (**air** of), **dearbhadh air a chionta** proof/evidence of his guilt, *Cf* **fianais 2, teisteanas 1**; **3** a test, a trial, **dearbhaidhean air càr ùr** tests on/trials of a new car

dearc, dearc, dearcan *nf, also dimin* **dearcag, dearcaig, dearcagan** *nf,* a berry, *Cf* **sùbh**

dearg *adj* **1** red (*usu for a brighter red than* **ruadh**), **frìde dhearg** red corpuscle, **brù-dhearg** a robin, **dearc dhearg** a redcurrant; **2** *with other colours* reddish-, reddy-, **dearg-dhonn** reddish-brown; **3** *as pej intensifying element* complete, utter, **dearg amadan** *m* an utter fool; **4** *as adv* completely, utterly, **tha i air a dearg mhilleadh** she's utterly spoilt, **dearg rùisgte** stark naked

deargad, deargaid, deargadan *nf &* **deargann, deargainn, deargannan** *nf,* a flea, (*poem*) **Deargadan na Pòlainn** the Fleas of Poland

deargnaich *vt, pres part* **a' deargnachadh,** make *or* colour red, redden

dearmad, dearmaid, dearmadan *nm* **1** (*the act of*) neglecting, omitting (*see senses of* **dearmaid** *v*); **2** neglect, negligence, omission, **peacaidhean dearmaid** sins of omission; **3** *also in exprs* **cuir** *v* **rudeigin air dhearmad** neglect to do something, **leig** *v* **rudeigin/ cuideigin air dhearmad** neglect something/someone, *Cf* **dearmaid** *v* **1 & 2**

dearmadach *adj* neglectful, negligent

dearmaid *vt, pres part* **a' dearmad, 1** omit *or* neglect (*to do something*); **2** neglect (*something or someone*)

deàrrs *vi, pres part* **a' deàrrsadh,** *also* **deàrrsaich** *vi, pres part* **a' deàrrsachadh,** shine, (*often of sun*) **chan eil a' ghrian a' deàrrs(ach)adh** the sun's not shining

deas *nf invar & adj* **1** south, **an àird(e) deas** south (*ie the compass direction*), **Uibhist a Deas** South Uist, **a' fuireach/a' dol mu dheas** living in/ going to the south, **oiteag on deas** a breeze from the south, **an taobh deas den dùthaich** *also* **taobh a deas na dùthcha** the southern part/the south of the country, **tha Ceann Rois deas air Peairt** Kinross is south of Perth; **2** *in expr* **an làmh dheas,** right, **tha a' bhùth air an làimh dheis** (*dat*) the shop is on the right(-hand side),

Cf less usu **ceart 4; 3** ready, **a bheil thu deas?** are you ready? *also* have you finished?, *Cf more usu* **deiseil 1 & 2, ullamh 1 & 2; 4** (*of person, action*) active, quick, prompt, **rinn e gu deas e** he did it promptly, *Cf* **clis, ealamh**

deasachadh, *gen* **deasachaidh** *nm* **1** (*the act of*) preparing &c (*see senses of* **deasaich** *v*); **2** preparation; **3** editing, **fear-deasachaidh** *m* an editor

deasaich *vt, pres part* **a' deasachadh, 1** prepare, get ready, **deasaich biadh** prepare/cook food, *Cf* **ullaich 1; 2** (*publishing &c*) edit

deasbad, deasbaid, deasbadan *nmf* **1** discussion, a discussion, debate, a debate

deasg, deasga, deasgan *nm* a desk

deas-ghnàth, deas-ghnàith, deas-ghnàthan *nm* ceremony, a ceremony

deatach, deataiche, deataichean *nf* fumes, gas, smoke, vapour, **cuir** *v* **deatach** emit/give out fumes, *Cf* **smùid** *n* **3**

deatamach *adj* crucial, essential, *Cf* **riatanach**

deich *n invar & adj* ten

deicheach *adj* decimal

deichead, deicheid, deicheadan *nm* ten years, a decade

deicheamh, *gen* **deicheimh** *nm* a decimal

deicheamh *adj* tenth

deichnear *nmf invar* (*people numbering*) ten, **deichnear mhac** ten sons

dèideadh, *gen* **dèididh** *nm* toothache, (*used with art*) **tha an dèideadh orm** I've got (the) toothache

dèideag, dèideig, dèideagan *nf* **1** a toy; **2** a pebble

dèidh, dèidhe, dèidhean *nf* **1** a wish, a desire, *Cf more usu* **miann 1, rùn 3, togradh 2; 2** fondness, *Cf* **rùn 1, spèis 1**

dèidheil *adj* fond (**air** of), keen (**air** on), **ro dhèidheil air deoch-làidir** over-keen on drink, **bha i dèidheil orm** she was fond of me, *Cf* **measail 2**

deidhinn *see* **mu 3**

deifrichte *adj see* **diof(a)rach**

deigh *see* **eigh**

deilbh *v & n same as* **dealbh** *v & n*

dèile, *gen* **dèilidh**, *pl* **dèilean** & **dèileachan** *nf* a (wooden) board, a plank, *Cf* **bòrd 2, clàr 1**

dèilig *vi, pres part* **a' dèiligeadh**, deal (**ri** with), **dèiligidh mi ris a-màireach** I'll deal with it tomorrow

deimhinn(e), *also* **deimhinnte** *adj* sure, certain, **bidh (an t-)uisge ann, tha mi deimhinne** it'll rain, I'm certain, *Cf more usu* **cinnteach**

dèine, *nf invar* (*abstr n corres to* **dian**) eagerness, keenness, fervour, ardour

dèirc, dèirce, dèircean *nf* charity, alms, charitable gifts, *Cf* **carthannachd 2**

dèirceach *adj* charitable, apt to give charitably

dèirceach, *gen & pl* **dèircich** *nm* a beggar, someone dependent on charity

deireadh, deiridh, deiridhean *nm* 1 end *usu of period of time*, **deireadh a' mhìosa** the end of the month, **aig deireadh an là** at the end of the day, in the end, finally, *Cf* **ceann 2**; 2 *in expr* **air dheireadh** *adv* behind, lagging behind; 3 *in expr* (**thàinig i &c**) **air deireadh** *adv* (she came &c) last, *also* late, **còig mionaidean air deireadh** five minutes late; 4 *in expr* **mu dheireadh** *adj* last, *adv* at last, **'s e seo an cothrom mu dheireadh a gheibh thu** this is the last opportunity you'll get, **sguir an t-uisge mu dheireadh (thall)** the rain stopped at (long) last

deireannach *adj* last, final, **air an là dheireannach** on the last day, (*song*) **Cead Deireannach nam Beann** The Final Farewell to the Mountains, *Cf less emph* **mu dheireadh** (*see* **deireadh 4**)

deisciobal, *gen & pl* **deisciobail** *nm* a disciple

deise, deise, deiseachan *nf* a suit (*of clothes*), *Cf* **culaidh 2, trusgan 2**

deiseil *adj* 1 ready, **tha am biadh deiseil** the food's ready, **tha mi deiseil** I'm ready, *Cf* **ullamh 1** *& less usu* **deas 3**; 2 having finished (*a task &c*), **a bheil thu deiseil fhathast?** have you finished yet? **deiseil dhe a bhreacaist** having finished his breakfast, **chan eil iad deiseil den fòn** they haven't finished with the phone, *Cf* **ullamh 2**; 3 handy (*ie convenient*) **bidh sin deiseil dhut** that'll be handy for you, *Cf* **ullamh 3**; 4 *as adv* clockwise, *Cf opposite* **tuathal 1**; 5 *as adv* (*trad*) sunwise (*opposite of Sc* widdershins), *Cf opposite* **tuathal 2**

deò *nf invar* 1 breath, a breath, **deò gaoithe** a breath of wind (*Cf* **ospag 2**), *Cf more usu* **anail**; 2 life, the breath of life, **fhad 's a bhios an deò annam** as long as there's life in me/breath in my body, *Cf* **rong** *nf*

deoch, dighe, deochannan *nf* 1 a drink (*of any liquid*), **deoch bhainne/ uisge** a drink of milk/of water; 2 an alcoholic drink, drink, *also more specifically* **deoch-làidir** strong drink, alcoholic drink, **thoir** *v* **dhomh deoch** give me a drink, (*prov*) **an uair a bhios an deoch a-staigh bidh a' chiall a-mach** when drink's in sense is out, **tha e measail air an deoch** he's fond of the drink/booze, (*trad*) **deoch-an-dorais** a 'Jock and Doris', a parting drink, 'one for the road', **tinneas** *m* **na dighe** alcoholism

deoghail *vi, pres part* **a' deoghal**, suck

deoghal, *gen* **deoghail** *nm* (*the act of*) sucking

deòin, *gen* **deòine** *nf* consent, willingness, *usu in expr* **a dheòin no a dh'aindeoin** willing(ly) or not, willy-nilly, *Cf opposite* **aindeoin 1**

deònach *adj* willing, prepared (*to do something*), **chan eil iad deònach** (*more trad* **deònach air**) **a dhèanamh** they're not willing/prepared to do it, *Cf* **airson 4**, **toileach 1** *& opposite* **aindeònach**

deuchainn, deuchainne, deuchainnean *nf* 1 (*ed &c*) an examination, a test, **feuch/suidh** *v* **deuchainnean** sit *or* take exams; 2 a test, a trial, **chuir iad na h-innealan ùra gu deuchainn** they tried out/ tested the new machines, *Cf* **dearbh** *v* 2, **feuch 2**; 3 (*science &c*) an experiment, **deuchainn-lann** *m* a laboratory; 4 a trying time or experience, a trial, **'s e deuchainn a bh' ann an tinneas mo mhàthar dhomh** my mother's illness was a trial for me

deudach *adj* dental, *Cf* **fiaclach 3**

deug *num suffix in numbers 11 to 19*, **a h-aon deug** eleven, **sia cait dheug** sixteen cats

deugaire, deugaire, deugairean *nm* a teenager, *Cf* **òigear**

deur, *gen & pl* **deòir** *nm* a tear, a teardrop, (*song*) **'s na deòir a' sileadh** with the tears flowing

deurach *adj* tearful, weeping, *Cf* **silteach**

dha, *with sing art* **dhan**, *prep used by some speakers for* **do**, to, **a' dol dhan bhùth** going to the shop, *see* **do** *prep*

dha *&* **dhà** *prep pron see* **do** *prep*

dhachaigh *adv see* **dachaigh 3**

dhaibh *prep pron see* **do** *prep*

dhèanadh, dhèanainn *pts of irreg v* **dèan** *see tables p 407*

dheth *adv* off, (*calques*) **tha an dealan dheth** the electricity's off, **cuir dheth an rèidio** turn the radio off, **tha an t-uachdar a' dol dheth** the cream's going off

dheth *prep pron see* **de** *prep*

dhi, dhomh, dhuibh, dhuinn, dhut *prep prons see* **do** *prep*

dhibh, dhinn, dhìom, dhìot, dhith, dhiubh *prep prons see* **de** *prep*

dia, dè, diathan *nm* 1 **Dia**, God; 2 a god, **diathan nan Ròmanach** the gods of the Romans, **ban-dia** *f* a goddess; 3 (*excl after a sneeze*) **Dia leat!** Bless you!

diabhal, diabhail, diabhail & **diabhlan** *nm* 1 a devil, *Cf* **deamhan**; 2 **an Diabhal** the Devil

diabhlaidh *adj* diabolical, devilish, fiendish

diadhachd *nf invar* 1 godhead, the quality of being a god; 2 theology; 3 godliness, devoutness, piety, *Cf* **cùram 3**, **cràbhadh**

diadhaidh *adj* devout, pious, godly, *Cf* **cràbhach**

diallaid *see* dìollaid

dia-mhaslachadh, *gen* dia-mhaslachaidh *nm* blasphemy, *Cf* toibheum

dian *adj* (*trad*) 1 eager, fierce, keen (*pursuit, fighting, endeavour &c*); 2 intense, fervent, ardent (*persons, emotions, deeds*); 3 dian-ruith & deann-ruith *m* a headlong rush, dh'fhalbh e na dhian-ruith he left in a headlong rush/at full speed

Diardaoin *nm invar* Thursday

dias, dèise, diasan *nf* an ear of corn

diathad, diathaid, diathadan *nf* 1 a meal, *Cf* biadh 2, lòn¹ 2; 2 *with art* an diathad dinner, *Cf more usu* dìnnear

dibhearsan, *gen* dibhearsain *nm* fun, entertainment, *Cf* spòrs 2

dìblidh *adj* vile, abject

dìcheall, *gen* dìchill *nm* 1 (*trad*) diligence, effort, application, *Cf* dèanadas, gnìomhachas 1; 2 *now usu in expr* rinn mi mo (&c) dhicheall (air ...) I (&c) did my (&c) best (to ...)

dìcheallach *adj* diligent, hardworking, conscientious, *Cf* dèanadach, gnìomhach

dì-cheannachadh, *gen* dì-cheannachaidh *nm* 1 (*the act of*) beheading, decapitating; 2 decapitation

dì-cheannaich *vt, pres part* a' dì-cheann(ach)adh, behead, decapitate

dì-chuimhnich *see* dìochuimhnich

Diciadain *nm invar* Wednesday

Didòmhnaich *nm invar* Sunday, *trad used by Catholic communities, Cf* Sàbaid

difir *see* diofar

dìg, dìge, dìgean *nf* a ditch, *Cf* clais 1

Dihaoine *nm invar* Friday, feasgar Dihaoine Friday afternoon/evening

dìle, *gen* dìleann & dìlinn *nf* 1 heavy rain, a deluge, a downpour, bha dìle bhàthte ann it was bucketing down/raining cats and dogs; 2 a flood, *Cf* tuil

dìleab, dìleib, dìleaban *nf* a legacy (*lit or fig*), heritage, a heritage, dìleab na h-eachdraidh the legacy of history

dìleas *adj* faithful, trusty, loyal (*also popular as a dog's name*)

dìlseachd *nf invar* loyalty, faithfulness

Diluain *nm invar* Monday

Dimàirt *nm invar* Tuesday

dìmeas *nm invar* contempt, disrespect, (*poem*) Alba fo dhìmeas (Meg Bateman) Scotland despised

dìnichean *npl* jeans

dinn *vti, pres part* **a' dinneadh**, stuff, cram, *Cf* **sàth 2**

dìnnear, dìnnearach, dìnnearan *nf* dinner, **dè a th' againn gu/air ar dìnnear?** what have we got/what are we getting/having for our dinner? **àm dìnnearach** dinner time, *Cf more trad* **diathad 2**

dìobair *vt, pres part* **a' dìobradh**, desert, abandon, **dhìobair e a' bhean aige** he deserted his wife, *Cf* **fàg, trèig**

dìobhair *vti, pres part* **a' dìobhairt**, vomit, throw up, be sick, sick up, *Cf* **sgeith, tilg 3**

dìobhairt *nm invar* **1** (*the act of*) vomiting &c (*see senses of* **dìobhair** *v*); **2** vomit, sick (*ie the substance*)

dìobradh, *gen* **dìobraidh** *nm* (*the act of*) deserting, abandoning

dìochuimhne *nf invar* **1** forgetfulness; **2** the state of being forgotten, oblivion, *esp in expr* **rach** *v* **air dìochuimhne** be forgotten, pass into oblivion

dìochuimhneach *adj* forgetful

dìochuimhneachadh, *gen* **dìochuimhneachaidh** *nm* (*the act of*) forgetting

dìochuimhnich *&* **dì-chuimhnich**, *vt, pres part* **a' dìochuimhneachadh**, forget

diofar, *gen* **diofair** *nm, also* **difir** *nm invar &* **deifir**, *gen* **deifire** *nf*, **1** difference, a difference **dè an diofar a tha eadar A agus B?** what's the difference between A and B?, *Cf* **eadar-dhealachadh 2**; **2** importance, *esp in exprs* **chan eil diofar ann!** *&* **chan eil e gu diofar!** it's not important!, it doesn't matter!, it makes no difference!

diof(a)rach, *also* **deifrichte** *&* **diofaraichte**, *adj* different, *Cf* **eadar-dhealaichte**

diog, diog, diogan *nm* (*clock time*) a second, *Cf* **tiota 1**

diogail *vti, pres part* **a' diogladh**, tickle, *Cf vi* **tachais 2**

diogalach *adj* ticklish

dìoghail *&* **dìol** *vt, pres part* **a' dìo(gh)ladh**, **1** repay (*esp loan, debts*); **2** take revenge, get one's own back, pay someone back

dìoghaltas, *gen* **dìoghaltais** *nm* revenge, vengeance

dìo(gh)ladh, *gen* **dìo(gh)laidh** *nm* **1** (*the act of*) repaying &c (*see senses of* **dìoghail** *v*); **2** payment, a payment

dìoghras, *gen* **dìoghrais** *nm* zeal, enthusiasm

dìol *see* **dìoghail**

dìolain *adj* bastard, illegitimate, **duine/neach dìolain** a bastard

dìollaid *&* **diallaid**, *gen* **dìollaide**, *pl* **dìollaidean** *nf* a saddle

diomb *&* **diumb** *nm invar* indignation, displeasure (*esp towards another person*)

diombach & **diumbach** *adj* **1** out of sorts, in a dark mood or temper, *Cf* **crost(a) 1**, **dubhach 1**, **gruamach 4**; **2** indignant, disgruntled, put out

diombuan *adj* transient, fleeting, ephemeral, *Cf* **siùbhlach 3**

dìomhain *adj* **1** vain, empty, without substance, **cur-seachadan dìomhain** vain/pointless pastimes, *Cf* **faoin 2**; **2** idle (*ie lazy*), *Cf* **leisg 1**; **3** idle (*ie unoccupied, unemployed*), *Cf* **tàmh** *n* **3**

dìomhair *adj* **1** secret, private (*ie confidential*); **2** mysterious

dìomhanas, **dìomhanais**, **dìomhanasan** *nm* vanity, **dìomhanas nan dìomhanas** vanity of vanities, *Cf* **faoineas 2**

dìon *vt, pres part* **a' dìon** & **a' dìonadh**, shelter, protect

dìon, *gen* **dìona** *nm* protection, shelter, **fo dhìon an rìgh/a' chaisteil** protected by the king/the castle, *Cf* **fasgadh**, **tèarmann**

dìonach *adj* **1** sheltering, safe, secure; **2** leakproof, waterproof, rainproof, (*house, ship &c*) wind and watertight

dìonadh, *gen* **dìonaidh** *nm* (*the act of*) sheltering, protecting

dìorrasach *adj* keen, tenacious, stubborn

dìosail *nm invar* diesel

dìosgan, *gen* **dìosgain** *nm, also* **dìosgail** *nf invar*, **1** a creaking, crunching, grating or squeaking noise; **2** *also as pres part* **a' dìosgail** creaking &c

diosgo *nm invar* a disco

dìreach *adj* & *adv* **1** straight, **seas dìreach** stand (up) straight, **loidhne dhìreach** a straight line, (*song*) **'s fheudar dhomh fhìn a bhith gabhail dhachaigh dìreach** I must be going straight home; **2** upright, just, **duine dìreach** an upright man, *Cf* **ionraic 2**; **3** (*as adv*) just, (*calques*) **bhiodh sin dìreach sgoinneil!** that would be just great! **tha e dìreach an dèidh falbh** he's just left, (*Sc*) he's just after leaving; **4** *as excl expr agreement* **dìreach!** exactly!, quite!, just so!

dìreachadh, *gen* **dìreachaidh** *nm* (*the act of*) straightening &c (*see senses of* **dìrich**[1] *v*)

dìreadh, *gen* **dìridh** *nm* (*the act of*) climbing, *Cf* **streap(adh)**

dìrich[1] *vti, pres part* **a' dìreachadh**, straighten, make or become straight

dìrich[2] *vt, pres part* **a' dìreadh**, climb (*hill &c*), *Cf* **streap**

Disathairne *nm invar* Saturday

dìsinn *nm* & **dìsne** *nmf, gen* **dìsne**, *pl* **dìsnean**, a die, *pl* dice (*ie for gaming &c*)

dìt *vt, pres part* **a' dìteadh**, condemn, **dhìt iad ar dol-a-mach** they condemned our conduct, **dìt gu bàs** condemn/sentence to death

dìteadh, dìtidh, dìtidhean *nm* **1** (*the act of*) condemning, sentencing; **2** condemnation, a condemnation

dìth, *gen* **dìthe** *nm* **1** a lack, a want, a deficit, **dìth cleachdaidh** lack of practice, **dìth cèille** a lack of common sense; **2** *often in expr* **a** (*for* **de**) **dhìth** lacking, wanting, needed, **tha biadh a dhìth** food is lacking/in short supply, **dè tha a dhìth oirbh?** what do you want/ need? (*in shop &c*) what would you like?, what are you wanting? **tha còta a dhìth orm** I need/want a coat, **cha tèid sinn a dhìth** we won't go short, *Cf* **easbhaidh**

dìthean, dìthein, dìtheanan *nm* a flower, *Cf* **blàth** *n* **2**, **flùr**²

dithis, dithis, dithisean *nf* (*usu used of people only*) **1** two, a twosome (*with gen pl*) **bha dithis aig a' bhòrd** there were two people at the table, **dithis shaighdearan** two soldiers, **an dithis agaibh** both/ the two/the pair of you; **2** a couple, a pair, **bha iad nan suidhe nan dithisean** they were sitting in pairs/couples, *Cf* **càraid 1**

dìthreabh, dìthreibh, dìthreabhan *nf* a desert, a wilderness, *Cf more usu* **fàsach**

diù *nm invar* the worst, the worst thing, (*proverb*) **diù an domhain droch bhean** the worst thing in the world (is) a bad wife, **diù nan dreuchdan** the worst of jobs/professions, *Cf opposites* **brod** *n* **2**, **smior 2**

diùc, diùc, diùcan *nm* a duke, **ban-diùc** *nf* a duchess

diùid *adj* shy, bashful, timid, *Cf* **nàrach 2**

diùide *nf invar* bashfulness, shyness, timidity, *Cf* **nàire 2**

diùlt *vti, pres part* **a' diùltadh, 1** refuse, **dhiùlt sinn biadh** we refused food, **dhiùlt an athair an leigeil air falbh** their father refused to let them go, **a' diùltadh èirigh** refusing to get up; **2** deny, disown, **cha diùlt i a nighean fhèin** she won't deny/reject/disown her own daughter

diùltadh, *gen* **diùltaidh** *nm* **1** (*the act of*) refusing, denying &c (*see senses of* **diùlt** *v*); **2** refusal, a refusal

diumb, diumbach *see* **diomb, diombach**

Diùrach, *gen & pl* **Diùraich** *nm* someone from Jura (**Diùra**), *also as adj* **Diùrach** of, from or pertaining to Jura

dleas, dleasa, dleasan *nm* **1** *same as more usu* **dleasdanas**; **2** a due, a right, an entitlement, **dleas ùghdair** (*book &c*) royalties,

dleastanas, *also* **dleasdanas** *&* **dleasnas**, *gen* **dleas(ta)nais**, *pl* **dleas(ta)nasan** *nm* duty, a duty, **rinn iad an dleastanas** they did their duty

dlighe *nf invar* **1** a right, one's due

dligheach *adj* lawful, rightful, legitimate

dlùth *adj* **1** close, near, adjacent, **dlùth ri chèile** close to each other, **dlùth air a' bhaile** close to the village/township, **dlùth-cheangal** *nm* a close link (**ri** with, **eadar** between), *Cf more usu* **faisg**; **2** (*hair, woodland, crowd &c*) thick, dense, closely packed, *Cf* **dòmhail 2, tiugh 1**

dlùthachadh, *gen* **dlùthachaidh** *nm* (*the act of*) approaching &c (*see senses of* **dlùthaich** *v*)

dlùthaich *vi*, *pres part* **a' dlùthachadh**, approach, come near, draw close (**ri** to), **bha sinn a' dlùthachadh ris a' mhuir** we were nearing/ drawing near to the sea

dlùths *nm invar* density

do *poss adj, sometimes as* **t'** *before a vowel or before* **fh** *followed by a vowel*, your (*corres to the sing/fam pron* **thu**), **gabh do dhìnnear** take/eat your dinner, **'s math d' fhaicinn!** it's good to see you!, *Cf* **ur**

do *verbal particle used in some neg & inter contexts*, **cha do rinn mi e** I didn't do it, **an do dh'fhalbh i?** did she leave? **nach d'fhuair sibh iad?** didn't you find/get them? **càit an do rugadh e?** where was he born?

do *prep* (*takes the dat, aspirates/lenites a following cons*), *Note: the pers prons* **mi, thu** *&c combine with* **do** *to form the prep prons* **dhomh(sa), dhu(i)t(sa), dha(san), dhi(se), dhuinn(e), dhuibh(se), dhaibh(san)** to/for me, you &c; **1** to, **thoir do dh'Iain e** give it to Iain, **innis do Mhàiri e** tell it to Mary, **dè a thachair dhut?** what happened to you?; **2** to (*phys movement*) *Note: in this usage* **do** *can appear as* **a**, *and* **don** *&* **do na** *can appear as* **dhan** *&* **dha na**; **a' dol do** (*or* **a**) **Ghlaschu** going to Glasgow, **thèid mi don** (*or* **dhan**) **eaglais** I'll go to the church, **sgrìob do na** (*or* **dha na**) **h-eileanan** a trip to the islands, **cuir màileid dhan chàr** put a bag in the car, **tilg clach dhan loch** throw a stone in(to) the loch; **3** for, **nì mi sin dhut** I'll do that for you, **ciamar a chaidh dhuibh?** *or more trad* **ciamar a dh'èirich dhuibh?** how did you get on? (*lit* how did it go/turn out for you?); **4** *misc usages* **tha e na dheagh charaid dhomh** he's a good friend of mine/to me, **co-ogha dhomh** a cousin of mine, **cha b' aithne dha i** he didn't know her, **an urrainn dhaibh a dhèanamh?** can they do it? **b' fheudar do Sheumas falbh** James had to leave, **air dha am bealach a ruigsinn ...** on (his) reaching/when he reached the top of the pass ..., **an dèidh dhomh mo shùilean a dhùnadh** after I closed/had closed my eyes

do- *a prefix corres to Eng* un-, in-, im-, *eg* **do-àireamh** *adj* innumerable, uncountable, **do-dhèanta** *adj* impossible, **do-labhairt** *adj* unspeakable, *Cf* **ain-, mì-, neo-**

dòbhran, *gen & pl* **dòbhrain** *nm* an otter

do bhrìgh *see* **brìgh 5**

dòcha *comp adj* **1** (*trad*) more likely, probable; **2** *now in expr* **'s dòcha!** *adv* perhaps!, maybe!, *also* probably!; **3** *also as conj* **'s dòcha gun tig e a-màireach** maybe he'll come tomorrow, *Cf* **faod 2, teagamh 2**

dòchas, dòchais, dòchasan *nm* **1** hope, a hope, **'s e sin mo dhòchas** that is my hope (*Cf* **dùil**[1] **1,** *less usu in this sense*), **gun dòchas** hopeless, without hope, *also in expr* **cuir** *v* **dòchas ann an** put one's hope in (*something, someone*); **2** *often in expr* **an dòchas** (*lit* in hope), **tha mi an dòchas nach tig i** I hope she won't come, **bidh là math ann, tha mi an dòchas** it'll be a good day, I hope

do(c)tair, do(c)tair, do(c)tairean *nm* a (*medical*) doctor, *Cf trad* **lighiche**

dòigh, dòighe, dòighean *nf* **1** a way, a manner (*of doing something*), **dèan e air an dòigh seo** do it (in) this way, **dòigh-beatha** a way of life, a lifestyle, *Cf less usu* **modh 1, nòs 2**; **2** *in pl* ways, manners, customs, **chan eil iad cleachdte ri ar dòighean** they aren't used to our ways; **3** a (*good, proper*) state, condition or situation, **bha a h-uile rud air dòigh** everything was in good order/as it should be, **cuir** *v* **air dòigh** put in order, organise, sort (out); **4** form, a mood, a state of mind, **bha Murchadh air a (dheagh) dhòigh** Murdo was on good form/in fine fettle, *also* very pleased (with himself), (*fam*) **dè an dòigh (a th' ort)?** how are you doing?, *Cf* **cor 1, fonn 2, gean, gleus** *n* **2**; **5** *in expr* **air dhòigh is gu/nach ... ** *conj* so that, in such a way that, **bhruidhinn e air dhòigh 's nach cuala mi e** he spoke so that/in such a way that I didn't hear him, *Cf similarly used* **air chor is gu** (*see* **cor 3**)

dòigheil *adj* **1** well-ordered, proper, in good order; **2** *esp as adv*, **rinn e gu dòigheil e** he did it properly/well, **ciamar a tha thu? tha gu dòigheil** how are you? I'm fine

dòil *nm invar* dole, unemployment benefit, (*Sc*) broo

doille *nf invar* blindness

doilleir *adj* dark, gloomy, obscure, dim (*opposite of* **soilleir**), *Cf* **ciar** *adj* **2, dorch(a)**

doilleirich *vti, pres part* **a' doilleireachadh**, become or make dark, darken, dim, obscure (*opposite of* **soilleirich**), *Cf* **ciar** *v*

doimhne *nf invar, usu with art* **an doimhne** the Deep

doimhneachd *nf invar* depth

doimhnich *vti, pres part* **a' doimhneachadh**, deepen

doineann, doininn, doineannan *nf* a storm, a tempest, a hurricane, *Cf* **gailleann, sian 1, stoirm 1**

doirbh *adj* difficult, hard (*opposite of* **soirbh**), **ceist dhoirbh** a difficult question/problem, **tha sin uabhasach doirbh a ràdh** that's terribly hard to say, *Cf* **deacair, duilich 1**

doire, *gen* **doire**, *pl* **doirean** & **doireachan** *nmf* a grove, a thicket, a small wood, (*poetry collection*) **Clàrsach an Doire** (Niall MacLeòid) the harp of the grove, *can occur in placenames as* Derry, *Cf* **bad 4**

dòirt *vti, pres part* **a' dòrtadh**, *of liquids* **1** (*vt*) pour; **2** (*vi*) flow, pour down, **uisge a' dòrtadh tron mhullach** water pouring through the roof; **3** (*vt*) spill, shed, (*song*) **dhòirt iad fhuil mu làr** they spilled / shed his blood upon the ground

dol *nm invar* (*the act of*) going, happening, becoming, &c, &c (*see senses of* **rach** *v*)

dolair, dolair, dolairean *nm* a dollar

dol-a-mach *nm invar* **1** behaviour, conduct, way of carrying on, **cha toigh leam an dol-a-mach (a th') aice** I don't like the way she behaves/carries on, *Cf* **giùlan 3**; **2** *in expr* **sa chiad dol-a-mach** at first, initially, in the first instance

dòlas, *gen* **dòlais** *nm* **1** grief, *Cf sometimes less strong* **bròn, mulad**; **2** *as excl* **an dòlas!** 'woe is me'!, how terrible!, good grief!

dol-às *nm invar* (*means of*) escape, a way out, **cha robh dol-às againn a-nis ach** ... there was no way out/escape for us now except ...

dòmhail & **dùmhail**, *adj* **1** (*places, buildings, gatherings &c*) crowded, congested, packed; **2** (*trees, hair, vegetation &c*) thick, dense, *Cf* **dlùth 2, tiugh 1**

domhainn *adj* **1** deep, **uisge domhainn** deep water, **eu-domhainn** shallow; **2** (*fig*) deep, profound, **leabhar domhainn** a profound book

domhan, *gen* **domhain** *nm, with art*, **an domhan** the universe, **An Treas Domhan** the Third World, *Cf* **cruinne-cè 2**

dona *adj, comp* **(n)as** (&c) **miosa**, bad, **tha siùcar dona dhut** sugar's bad for you, **gille dona** a bad/naughty boy (*Cf* **crost(a)**), **ciamar a tha thu? chan eil gu dona, chan eil mi cho dona 's a bha mi** how are you? not bad, I'm not as bad as I was, **ciamar a chaidh dhut? cha deach ach gu dubh dona!** how did it go? just terrible!; **2** *occas* (*trad*) unlucky, unfortunate

donas, *gen* **donais** *nm* **1** badness, evil, mischief, *Cf stronger* **olc** *n*; **2** *with art* **an Donas** the Devil, the evil one, *excl* **mac an donais!** the devil!, damn it!, (*prov*) **cha d'fhuaradh an Donas a-riamh marbh air cùl gàrraidh** the Devil was never found dead behind a dyke

donn *adj* **1** brown, **brat-ùrlair donn** a brown carpet, **dubh-dhonn** dark brown, (*song*) **eilean beag donn a' chuain** the little brown island of the ocean (Lewis); **2** brown-haired, (*song*) **an tèid thu leam, mo nighean donn?** will you go with me, my brown-haired lass?

donnal, donnail, donnalan *nm* a howl (*esp of dog*)

donnalaich, *gen* **donnalaiche** *nf* howling

dòrainn, dòrainne, dòrainnean *nf* anguish, torment, (deep) sorrow

dòrainneach *adj* anguished, (*emotionally*) tortured, pained, **sgeulachd dhòrainneach** a painful/harrowing/tragic story, *Cf* **cràidhteach**

doras, dorais, dorsan *nm* **1** (*trad*) a doorway, *see* **còmhla(dh)**; **2** a door, **an doras mòr** the main/front door, **làmh an dorais** the door handle, **deoch-an-dorais** a 'Jock and Doris', a parting drink, **a' fuireach an ath-dhoras** living next door

dorch(a) *adj* dark, **neul dorcha** a dark cloud, (*story anthology*) **Dorcha tro Ghlainne** Through a Glass Darkly, (*hist*) **na Linntean Dorcha** the Dark Ages, *Cf* **doilleir**

dorchadas, *gen* **dorchadais** *nm* darkness

dòrlach, *gen & pl* **dòrlaich** *nm* a fistful, a handful

dòrn *vt*, *pres part* **a' dòrnadh**, thump

dòrn, *gen & pl* **dùirn** *nm* a fist, (*poem*) **san taigh-òsda an àm nan dòrn a bhith gan dùnadh** (Somhairle MacGill-Eain) in the pub at the time of (the) fists being clenched

dorsair, dorsair, dorsairean *nm* a doorman, a porter, a janitor, a concierge, *Cf* **portair 2**

dos, *gen* **dois**, *pl* **dois** & **dosan** *nm* **1** a bush, *Cf* **preas¹**; **2** a drone of a bagpipe

dosgainn, dosgainn, dosgainnean *nf* calamity, a calamity, misfortune, a misfortune

dotair *see* **do(c)tair**

dòth *vt*, *pres part* **a' dòthadh**, scorch, singe, burn

dòthadh, *gen* **dòthaidh** *nm* (*the act of*) scorching &c (*see senses of* **dòth** *v*)

drabasta & **drabasda** *adj* obscene, lewd, *Cf* **draosta**

drabastachd & **drabasdachd** *nf invar* smut, obscenity, lewdness, *Cf* **draostachd, rabhd 2**

dràbhail *adj* grotty, *Cf* **grodach, mosach 1**

drabhair, drabhair, dràbhraichean *nm* a drawer

dràc, dràic, dràcan *nm* a drake, *Cf* **ràc** *n*

dragh, dragha, draghannan *nm* **1** trouble, bother, **chan eil mi airson dragh a chur oirbh** I don't want to bother you/put you to any trouble (*Cf* **bodraig**); **2** annoyance, **tha fuaim a' chiùil sin a' cur dragh orm** the noise of that music is annoying me; **3** worry, anxiety, **gabh/dèan** *v* **dragh** worry, get worried, **tha dìth airgid a' dèanamh dragh dhomh** lack of money is causing me worry, *Cf* **iomagain 1**

draghail *adj* worrying, troublesome, annoying (*person, situation*)

dràibh *vti*, *pres part* **a' dràibheadh**, *also* **dràibhig** *vti*, *pres part* **a' dràibhigeadh**, drive (*a vehicle*)

dràibhear, dràibheir, dràibhearan *nm* a driver (*of a vehicle*)

dràibhig *see* **dràibh**

dràm, drama, dramannan *nm, also* **drama, drama, dramaichean** *nm,* (*fam*) a dram, a drink of whisky, **an gabh thu drama?** will you take a dram?

dràma, dràma, dràmathan *nm* drama, a drama (*play or crisis*), **bidh i a' teagasg dràma** she teaches drama

dranndail *nf invar, also* **dranndan**, *gen & pl* **dranndain** *nm,* (*of dog &c*) snarling, a snarl, growling, a growl, **rinn an cù dranndan** the dog snarled/growled, *Cf* **grànsgal**

dranndanach *adj* **1** (*esp dog*) apt to snarl or growl; **2** (*people*) snappy, irritable, (*Sc*) crabbit

draoidh, draoidh, draoidhean *nm* **1** (*trad, hist*) a druid; **2** a wizard, a sorcerer, a magician, *Cf* **buidseach**

draoidheachd *nf invar* wizardry, sorcery, magic

draoidheil *adj* magic, magical

draosta *adj* smutty, lewd, obscene, *Cf* **drabasta**

draostachd *&* **draosdachd** *nf invar* smut, obscenity, lewdness, *Cf* **drabastachd, rabhd 2**

drathais *&* **drathars** *nf pl invar* **1** pants, knickers; **2** underpants

dreach, dreacha, dreachan *nm* **1** (*phys*) appearance, aspect, **air dhreach taibhse** with the appearance of/looking like a ghost, *Cf* **coltas 1; 2** complexion, *Cf* **fiamh 1, snuadh 2, tuar**

dreag, dreige, dreagan *nf* a meteor

dreallag, dreallaige, dreallagan *nf* a (*child's*) swing

drèana, drèana, drèanaichean *nf* **1** a drain; **2** a drainage ditch, *Cf* **clais 1 & 2, dìg**

dreasa, dreasa, dreasaichean *nf* a dress

dreasair, dreasair, dreasairean *nm* (*furniture*) a dresser

dreathan-donn, dreathain-duinn, dreathain-donna *nm* a wren

dreuchd, dreuchd, dreuchdan *nf* a job, an occupation, a profession, a career, *usu non-manual work*, **leigidh mi dhìom mo dhreuchd an ath-bhliadhna** I'll give up my job/I'll retire next year, *Cf* **cosnadh 2, obair 4**

dreuchdail *adj* professional **1** (*relating to a job or profession*) **briathrachas dreuchdail** professional terminology; **2** (*working for payment*) **seinneadair dreuchdail** a professional singer; *Cf* **proifeiseanta**

driamlach, driamlaich, driamlaich(ean) *nmf* a fishing line

drile, drile, drilichean *nf* a drill, an auger, *Cf more trad* **snìomhair(e)**

drioftair, drioftair, drioftairean *nm* (*fishing*) a drifter

drip, *gen* **dripe** *nf* bustle, the state of being busy, *Cf* **sàs 2**

dripeil *adj* busy, **tha cùisean garbh dripeil an-dràsta** things are hell of a busy just now, *Cf* **trang**

dris, drise, drisean *nf* the bramble, the brier, the blackberry (*ie the plant,* *Cf* **smeur** *n*)

drithleann, *gen & pl* **drithlinn** *nm* a sparkle, a flash

dr(i)ùchd, dr(i)ùchd, dr(i)ùchdan *nmf* dew, (*song*) **is an sliabh fo dhriùchd** and the hill with dew upon it, *Cf* **dealt**

dròbh, dròibh, dròbhan *nm* (*hist*) a drove (of cattle)

dròbhair, dròbhair, dròbhairean *nm* (*hist*) a cattle drover

droch *adj* 1 bad, (*precedes the noun, which it aspirates/lenites*) **droch aimsir** *or* **droch shìde** bad weather, **droch anail** bad breath, halitosis, **tha an togalach ann an droch staid** the building's in a bad state/ condition; 2 (*also in compounds*) bad-, ill-, *eg* **droch-chainnt** *f* bad language, swearing, (*trad*) **an droch-shùil** *f* the evil eye, **droch-nàdarrach** *adj* ill-/evil-natured, ill-/evil-tempered; *Cf* **dona 1** *&* *opposite* **deagh**

drochaid, drochaide, drochaidean *nf* a bridge, **Drochaid an Eilein Sgitheanaich** the Skye Bridge

droga, droga, drogaichean *nf* a drug (*medical, illegal &c*)

drùchd *see* **dr(i)ùchd**

drùdhag, drùdhaig, drùdhagan *nf* 1 a drop (*of liquid*), *Cf* **boinneag 1**; 2 a small sip, **nach gabh thu drùdhag tì?** won't you take a drop of tea?, *Cf* **balgam 1**

druid, druid, druidean *nf* a starling, (*song*) **thig an smeòrach, thig an druid, thig gach eun a dh'ionnsaigh nid** the thrush will come, the starling will come, each bird will make for its nest

drùidh *vti, pres part* **a' drùidheadh,** 1 penetrate to the skin, *esp in expr* **dhrùidh an t-uisge orm/oirnn (&c)** the rain soaked me/us (*&c*) to the skin; 2 affect, make an impression on, 'get to', **cha do dhrùidh an naidheachd oirre** the news didn't affect/'get to' her/made no impression on her

drùidheadh, *gen* **drùidhidh** *nm* 1 (*the act of*) penetrating &c (*see senses of* **drùidh** *v*); 2 an effect, an impression (*made on someone*)

drùidhteach *adj* impressive

druim, droma, dromannan *nm* 1 a back (*ie considered as part of a human or animal body*, *Cf* **cùl 2, muin 1**), **air do dhruim dìreach** flat on your back, **tha mo dhruim goirt** my back aches/is sore, (*trad*) **bha ultach a droma aice** she had as much as she could carry (*lit* her back's load), **caol** *m* **an droma** the small of the back, **cnà(i)mh** *m* **an**

droma the backbone/spine; **2** (*topog*) a ridge, *usu in placenames as* Drum-

drùis, *gen* **drùise** *nf* lust, lechery, *Cf* **miann 2**

drùiseach *adj* & **drùiseil** *adj* lustful, lecherous, randy

druma, **druma**, **drumaichean** *nmf* (*mus*) a drum

duais, **duais**, **duaisean** *nf* **1** (*trad*) wages, reward (*for services &c performed*), *Cf usu* **pàigh** *n*, **tuarasdal**; **2** (*now usu*) a prize, an award, **choisinn i duais aig a' Mhòd** she won a prize at the Mod

dual[1], **duail**, **dualan** *nm* (*trad*) **1** what might be expected of one because of one's descendance, one's character considered as inherited, (*prov*) **bu dual dha sin** that was to be expected of him (*ie him being the man he is*), **bu dual dha/bàrdachd bho thaobh athar** he inherited a talent for poetry from his father's side of the family (*lit* poetry was hereditary for him from his father's side); **2** a hereditary right, a birthright, (*song*) **MacGriogair à Ruadhshruth dam bu dual bhith 'n Gleann Lìobhann** MacGregor of Roro whose birthright it was to be in Glen Lyon; *Cf* **dualchas 2**, **dùthchas**

dual[2], **duail**, **dualan** *nm* **1** a curl, lock or ringlet of hair, *Cf* **bachlag 1**, **camag 1**; **2** (*in hair, rope &c*) a plait

dualach *see* **dual(t)ach**

dualachadh, *gen* **dualachaidh** *nm* (*the act of*) curling &c (*see senses of* **dualaich** *v*)

dualaich *vt*, *pres part* **a' dualachadh**, **1** curl (*hair*), *Cf* **bachlaich**; **2** twist, plait (*hair, rope &c*)

dualchainnt, **dualchainnte**, **dualchainntean** *nf* a dialect

dualchas, *gen* **dualchais** *nm* **1** heritage (*esp cultural*), tradition; **2** (*trad*) one's character or characteristics (*with a suggestion of hereditary influence*), one's inheritance, what one is, what might be expected of one, or what one might be entitled to, by reason of one's descent, **is e a dhualchas a bhith àrdanach** it's in his char-acter/nature to be proud, *Cf* **dual**[1], **dùthchas 2**

dualchasach *adj* **1** traditional, **ceòl** *m* **dualchasach** traditional music

dual(t)ach *adj* natural, inherent, innate, in one's nature or temperament (*with a suggestion of hereditary influence*), **tha e dualtach dhut a bhith ag innse bhreugan!** it's in your nature/just like you/typical of you to tell lies! **tha iad dualach a bhith spìocach** they are inclined to be stingy/mean, *Cf* **buailteach**

duan, *gen* & *pl* **duain** *nm* **1** a poem, *Cf more usu* **dàn**[2] **1**; **2** *esp as dimin* **duanag**, **duanaig**, **duanagan** *nf*, a song, **Duanag a' Chìobair** The Shepherd's (little) Song

dùbailte *adj* double, dual, **gunna dùbailte** a double-barrelled shotgun, **rathad dùbailte** a two-lane road

dubh *adj* **1** black, **bha an oidhche cho dubh ri gual** the night was as black as coal, **boireannach dubh** a black woman, (*mus*) **dubh-nota** *m* a crotchet; **2** *with other colours*, dark, **dubh-ghorm** dark blue; **3** *of colour of human hair, colour of coat, feathers &c of other creatures*, black, dark, **boireannach dubh** a black-haired/dark-haired woman, **coileach dubh** a blackcock; **4** *as intensifying element*, very, extremely, **tha e leisg agus dubh leisg!** he's utterly lazy!, (*also* **gu dubh**) **ciamar a chaidh dhuibh? cha deachaidh ach gu dubh dona!** how did it go? it went absolutely terribly!

dubh, *gen* **duibh** *nm* **1** the colour black, (*story anthology*) **An Dubh is an Gorm** The Black and the Blue; **2** ink, *Cf less trad* **inc**; **3** pupil (*of the eye*)

dubh *vti, pres part* **a' dubhadh, 1** blacken, make black, become black; **2** **dubh às** *vt*, erase; black out, blot out

dubhach *adj* **1** sad, gloomy, (*song*) **chan eil adhbhar (a) bhith dubhach no sgìth ann** there's no reason to be gloomy or weary there, *Cf* **smalanach** (*see* **smalan**); **2** moody, in a bad mood, **nach tusa tha dubhach an-diugh!** aren't you the moody one today!, *Cf* **diombach 1**

dubhadh, dubhaidh, dubhaidhean *nm* **1** (*the act of*) blackening &c (*see senses of* **dubh** *v*); **2** (*astronomy*) an eclipse, **dubhadh na grèine/na gealaich** an eclipse of the sun/of the moon

dubhag, dubhaig, dubhagan *nf* (*anat*) a kidney, *Cf* **àra**

dubh-aigeann *nm invar* **1** the deep, the ocean; **2** an abyss

dubhairt, duirt, *pts of irreg v* **abair** (*see tables p 403*)

dubhan, *gen & pl* **dubhain** *nm* a hook (*for fastenings, hanging objects, fishing, &c*), *Cf* **cromag 1**

dubhar, *gen* **dubhair** *nm* shade, shadow, **thàinig iad gu stad fo dhubhar nam ballachan** they came to a halt in the shade/shadow of the walls, *Cf* **sgàil(e) 1**

Dùbhlachd & **Dùdlachd** *nf invar, with the art*, **an Dùbhlachd** December

dùbhlan & **dùlan**, *nm* a challenge, *also in expr* **thoir** *v* **dù(bh)lan do** challenge, defy, **thug e dùlan dhomh an fhìrinn innse** he challenged/defied me to tell the truth

dùblaich *vti, pres part* **a' dùblachadh**, (*numbers, quantities &c*) double

dùdach, dùdaiche, dùdaichean *nmf* & **dùdag, dùdaig, dùdagan** *nf* **1** a bugle; **2** a hooter, a siren

Dùdlachd *see* **Dùbhlachd**

duibhre *nf invar* dusk, evening twilight, *Cf* **camhanaich**, **eadar-sholas**

duibhreachadh, *gen* **duibhreachaidh** *nm* (*the act of*) shading &c (*see senses of* **duibhrich** *v*)

duibhrich *vti, pres part* **a' duibhreachadh**, shade, darken, eclipse, *Cf* **sgàil** *v*

dùil[1], **dùile, dùilean** *nf* **1** hope, a hope, (*trad song*) **gun dùil ri tilleadh** without hope of returning, *Cf more usu* **dòchas 1** *&* **2**; **2** expectation, an expectation, **dùil-aoise** life expectancy, **tha dùil agam gun tig e** I expect he'll come, **tha dùil agam rithe** I expect her, **chan eil mi an dùil gun tèid aige air** I don't expect he'll manage it, *Cf* **sùil 3, sùilich**

dùil[2], *gen* **dùile**, *pl* **dùil(t)ean**, *gen pl* **dùl** *nf* **1** (*trad*) a creature, a created being, **Rìgh nan Dùl** the King/Lord of the Universe/of Creation, God; **2** (*chemistry &c*) an element

duileasg, *gen* **duilisg** *nm* (*bot*) dulse

duilgheadas, duilgheadais, duilgheadasan *nm* a difficulty, a problem, **tha duilgheadasan againn a thaobh airgid** we've got difficulties where money is concerned, **cha bhi sin na dhuilgheadas dhàsan** that won't be a problem for him (*emph*), **duilgheadasan sòisealta** social problems

duilich *adj* **1** difficult, hard (*to solve*), **ceist dhuilich** a difficult question/ problem, *Cf* **deacair, doirbh**; **2** difficult, hard (*to bear*), (*poem*) **is duilich leam do dhol air ais a dh'Eirinn** (Meg Bateman) hard for me is your going back to Ireland, *Cf* **cruaidh** *adj* **2**; **3** sorry, **tha mi duilich!** I'm sorry!, (*calque*) **bha i a' faireachdainn duilich air a son fhèin** she was feeling sorry for herself; **4** *in expr* **tha sin duilich!** that's a pity/shame!, *Cf more usu* **bochd 2, truagh 3**

duilleach, *gen* **duillich** *nm* foliage

duilleachan, *gen & pl* **duilleachain** *nm* (*publicity &c*) a leaflet

duilleag, duilleige, duilleagan *nf* **1** a leaf (*of tree, plant*); **2** a sheet (*of paper*); **3** (*also* **taobh-duilleige** *m*) a page (*of a book &c, abbrev* **d**, *pl* **dd**, *& * **td**, *pl* **tdd**), **Na Duilleagan Buidhe** The Yellow Pages

dùin *vti, pres part* **a' dùnadh**, **1** close, shut, **dùin an doras!** shut the door! **bha a' bhùth a' dùnadh** the shop was closing, (*vulg*) **dùin do chab!** shut your gob! **dhùin an uinneag le brag** the window shut with a bang; **2** bring or come to a close, **dùinidh am fear-cathrach a' choinneamh aig sia uairean** the chairman will close the meeting at six o'clock

duine, duine, daoine *nm* **1** a man, **an uair a bhios mi nam dhuine** ... when I'm a man ... (*Cf* **inbheach** *n*), **is duine Iain** Ian is a man, **duine-uasal** (*origin of Sc* duniewassal) a nobleman, a gentleman, *Cf* **fear** *which stresses male gender more*; **2** a person (*regardless of gender*), someone, somebody, anyone, anybody, **a bheil duine ann?** is there anyone there/in? (*Cf* **cuideigin**), **cha robh duine beò air an rathad** there was no-one/wasn't a living soul on the road, **duine sam bith** anyone at all, **a h-uile duine** everyone, everybody, **chuireadh e**

iongnadh air duine it would amaze one/you/(*Sc*) a body, *Cf* **neach 1**; **3** a human being, a man (*ie member of mankind*), *also in expr* **mac an duine** humanity, humankind (*Cf* **cinne-daonna** – *see* **daonna**); **4** a husband, **an duine agam** my husband, (*Sc*) my man, *Cf* **bodach 3**, **cèile 1**, **companach 3**; **5** *in pl* people, folk, **mòran dhaoine** many people, **na daoine-sìth** the fairies, fairy folk; **6** *in pl* one's people, relatives, folks, **tha buinteanas aig mo dhaoine ris an Eilean Dubh** my people/folks have links with the Black Isle, (*song*) **gun duine de mo dhaoine ris am faod mi mo ghearan** without anyone of my people/kin to whom I might make my complaint, *Cf less usu* **muinntir 1**; **7** *in excl* **dhuine! dhuine!** oh dear! oh dear!

duinealas, *gen* **duinealais** *nm* **1** manliness; **2** decisiveness, firmness of character

duineil *adj* **1** manly, having manly qualities, *Cf* **fearail**, **smiorail 2**, **tapaidh 2**; **2** (*of woman*) mannish; **3** (*of both sexes*) decisive, enterprising, resourceful, firm (*in actions, character*)

dùinte *adj* **1** (*buildings, objects &c*) closed, shut; **2** (*of persons*) reserved, withdrawn, introvert, *Cf* **fad(a) 4**

dùisg *vti, pres part* **a' dùsgadh**, **1** wake up, waken, awaken, **dhùisg mi aig a sia** I woke up at six, **dùisg mi an ceann dà uair a thìde** wake me in/after two hours, (*poem*) **dùisg suas, a Ghàidhlig!** Gaelic, awake!; **2** *as noun in expr* **nam (&c) d(h)ùisg** awake, **chan eil iad nan dùisg** they're not awake, *Cf* **dùsgadh 2**

Duitseach, *gen & pl* **Duitsich** *nm* a Dutchman, someone from the Netherlands, *also as adj* **Duitseach** Dutch

dùlan *see* **dùbhlan**

dùmhail *see* **dòmhail**

dùn, *gen* **dùin**, *pl* **dùin** & **dùintean** *nm* **1** a heap, a pile, *Cf* **cruach** *n* **1**, **tòrr 1**; **2** (*trad*) a (*usu fortified*) castle, a fortress, (*song*) **chaidh Mac-alla às an dùn** Echo left the castle (*ie it fell silent*), *Cf* **daingneach**; **3** a (*Pictish or Iron Age*) hill fort; **4** (*topog*) a hill (*usu rounded & suitable for fortification*), occurs in placenames as **Dun-**

dùnadh, **dùnaidh**, **dùnaidhean** *nm* **1** (*the act of*) closing, shutting; closure, a closure; **2** (*Lit, music*) a cadence, a fall

dùnan, *gen & pl* **dùnain** *nm*, *dimin of* **dùn**, **1** a small hill; **2** a dung-heap, a manure heap, a midden, *Cf* **òtrach**, **siteag**

dùr *adj* **1** stubborn, obstinate, (*Sc*) thrawn, *Cf* **rag 2**, **rag-mhuinealach**; **2** (*Sc*) dour

dùrachd, **dùrachd**, **dùrachdan** *nm* **1** (*trad*) earnestness, seriousness, sincerity; **2** (*now usu*) an expression of good will, a good wish, (*radio programme*) **dùrachdan** greetings, good wishes, *Cf more trad* **soraidh**

2; 3 *formulae closing letter &c* **le dùrachd** yours sincerely, **le deagh dhùrachd** with compliments, **leis gach deagh dhùrachd** with best wishes/kindest regards

dùrachdach *adj* **1** serious, earnest; **2** eager, fervent, keen, *Cf* **dealasach, dian 1 & 2**

dùraig *vi, pres part* **a' dùraigeadh**, dare (*to do something*), **bha an stoirm cho garbh 's nach do dhùraig sinn an taigh fhàgail** the storm was so wild we didn't dare leave the house

durcan, *gen & pl* **durcain** *nm* a pine cone, a fir cone

dùrdail, *gen* **dùrdaile** *nf* (*of doves, pigeons*) cooing, **dèan** *v* **dùrdail** coo

dùsal, *gen & pl* **dùsail** *nm* slumber, light sleep, a snooze, a nap, a drowse, **dèan** *v* **dùsal** snooze, take a snooze/nap, *Cf* **cadal 2, norrag, suain** *n*

dusan, *gen & pl* **dusain** *nm* **1** a dozen; **2** (*fam*) twelve, **dusan bliadhna a dh'aois** twelve years old

dùsgadh, *gen* **dùsgaidh** **1** (*the act of*) awakening, waking up &c (*see senses of* **dùisg** *v*); an awakening; **2** an awakened state, *esp in expr* **tha mi nam dhùsgadh** I am awake, **bha i na leth-dhùsgadh** she was half-awake, *Cf* **dùisg 2**; **3** religious revival

duslach, *gen* **duslaich** *nm* **1** dust, *Cf* **dust, stùr**; **2** mortal remains

dust *nm invar* dust, *Cf* **duslach, stùr**

dustach *adj* dusty

dustair, dustair, dustairean *nm* a duster

dùthaich, dùthcha, dùthchannan *nf* **1** a country, a land, **dùthaich chèin** a foreign country, *Cf* **tìr 2**; **2** a land, a territory, a country (*associated with a particular clan, group, individual &c*), (*trad*) **dùthaich MhicAoidh** the Mackay country/lands (*in Sutherland*); **3** one's homeland *or* home district, (*song*) **O mo dhùthaich, 's tu th' air m' aire** O my homeland, it is you who are on my mind; **4** country (*as opposed to town*), countryside, **bha sinn a' fuireach air an dùthaich** we lived/were living in the country, (*formerly*) **Ughdarras Dùthcha na h-Alba** the Countryside Commission for Scotland

dùthchas, *gen* **dùthchais** *nm* **1** (*trad*) the ancestral land(s) of a clan or an individual, (*prov*) **cha bhi dùthchas aig mnaoi no aig sagart** a woman and a priest have no homeland, *Cf* **dùthaich 2**; **2** (*trad*) one's cultural inheritance or heritage, what one is by reason of the place one belongs to, *Cf* **dualchas 2**

dùthchasach *adj* **1** native, indigenous, aboriginal

E

e *pron m sing, emph form* **esan,** he, him, (**e** *only, representing nm*) it, **chunnaic e e** he saw him/it, **is esan a rinn e,** *or* **'s e esan a rinn e** he (*emph*) did it; *also impersonal* it, **is e mo bràthair a dh'fhalbh** it's my brother who left

eabar, *gen* **eabair** *nm* mire, mud, sludge, silt, **bha a chasan a' dol fodha san eabar** his feet were sinking into the mire, *Cf* **poll 1**

Eabhra *nf invar* (*lang*) Hebrew

eacarsaich, eacarsaiche, eacarsaichean *nf* (*phys, ed &c*) exercise, an exercise

each, *gen & pl* **eich** *nm* a horse, **each dìollaid** a saddle horse, a riding horse, **each-obrach** a workhorse, (*trad*) **each-uisge** a kelpie, a water-horse

each-aibhne, *gen & pl* **eich-aibhne** *nm* a hippopotamus

eachdraiche, eachdraiche, eachdraichean *nm* a historian

eachdraidh, eachdraidhe, eachdraidhean *nf* history, **eòlach air eachdraidh na dùthcha** familiar with the country's history, **rinn i eachdraidh aig an/anns an oilthigh** she did history at university

eachdraidheil *adj* historical, pertaining to history or its study

eaconamachd *nf invar* economics

eaconomaidh, eaconomaidh, eaconomaidhean *nm* an economy, **eaconomaidh na dùthcha** the country's/the national economy

eaconomair, eaconomair, eaconomairean *nm* an economist

Eadailteach, *gen & pl* **Eadailtich** *nm* an Italian, *also as adj* **Eadailteach** Italian

Eadailt *nf, with art,* **an Eadailt** Italy

Eadailtis *nf invar, with art,* (*lang*) **an Eadailtis** Italian

eadar *prep* **1** between, *Note:* **eadar** *combines with the pl pers prons* **sinn, sibh, iad** *to give the prep prons* **eadarainn, eadaraibh, eatarra** *also* **eatorra,** between us/you/them, **thàinig i eadarainn** she came between us, **tha iad a' fuireach eadar Port Rìgh agus Dùn Bheagain** they stay between Portree and Dunvegan, *also in expr* **eadar-dhà-lionn** undecided, hesitating; neither one thing nor another; **2** among, **a bheil dotair eadaraibh?** is there a doctor among you?, *Cf more usu* **am measg; 3** both, *Note: in this usage* **eadar** *aspirates/lenites both words qualified, Cf* **thàinig iad, eadar bheag agus mhòr** they came, both small and great, *and* **tha e eadar beag agus mòr** he is between small and big/neither small nor big, *Cf* **cuid 4, gach 3; 4** *in compounds* inter-, **eadar-ùine** *f* an interval, an interlude, **eadar-phòsadh** *m* intermarriage, *see further examples below*

eadarach *adj* interim, temporary, stop-gap, **beart** *m* **eadarach** an interim measure

eadar-aghaidh, eadar-aghaidhe, eadar-aghaidhean *nf* (*IT &c*) an interface

eadar-dhealachadh, eadar-dhealachaidh, eadar-dhealachaidhean *nm* **1** (*the act of*) differentiating, distinguishing; **2** a difference, **dè an t-eadar-dhealachadh eadar** … **?** what's the difference between …?, *Cf* **diofar 1**; **3** differentiation, a distinction, **cha dèan mi eadar-dhealachadh eadar saorsa is neo-eisimealachd** I make no distinction/don't differentiate between freedom and independence

eadar-dhealaich *vt, pres part* **ag eadar-dhealachadh**, differentiate, distinguish, *Cf* **eadar-dhealachadh 3**

eadar-dhealaichte *adj* distinct, separate, **tha an dà cheist gu tur eadar-dhealaichte** the two questions/matters are totally distinct/separate, *Cf less strong* **diof(a)rach**

eadar-lìon, eadar-lìn, eadar-lìontan *nm, usu with art*, (*IT*) **an t-eadar-lìon** the internet

eadar-nàiseanta *adj* international

eadar-sholas, *gen & pl* **eadar-sholais** *nm* morning or evening twilight, *Cf* **camhana(i)ch 2, duibhre**

eadar-theangachadh, eadar-theangachaidh, eadar-theangachaidhean *nm* **1** (*the act of*) translating; translation; **2** a translation

eadar-theangaich *vt, pres part* **ag eadar-theangachadh**, translate (**do** into), *Cf* **cuir Beurla air Gàidhlig**, *see* **cuir 1**

eadar-theangair, eadar-theangair, eadar-theangairean *nm* a translator

eadh *obs neut pron see* **seadh** *adv*

eadhon *adv* even, **cha robh eadhon dà nota agam** I didn't even have two pounds, *Cf* **fiù** *n* **2**, **uiread 3**

eadradh, eadraidh, eadraidhean *nm* milking, *esp in expr* **crodh-eadraidh** milk/milch cows

eag, eige, eagan *nf* a nick, a notch, an indentation

eagal *& occas* **feagal**, *gen* **(f)eagail** *nm* **1** fear, fright, **bha an t-eagal oirre ron mhèirleach** she was afraid of the robber, **bha eagal mo bheatha orm** I was scared stiff/to death, **gabh** *v* **eagal** become afraid, take fright, **cuir** *v* **eagal air cudeigin** frighten someone, (*expr polite regret*) **chan eil fhios 'am, tha eagal orm** I don't know, I'm afraid, *Cf less usu* **fiamh 2**; **2** *in conj* **air eagal 's gu** lest, for fear, in case, **gabh greum air an fhàradh air eagal 's gun tuit mi** get hold of the ladder in case/for fear I fall, *Cf* **fios 5, mus 2**

eagalach *adj* **1** fearful, prone to fear; **2** terrible, awful, dreadful (*now usu with attenuated sense*), **ciamar a chaidh an dealbh-chluich? bha e dìreach eagalach!** how did the play go? it was just dreadful!, *Cf* uabhasach 1; 3 *also as adv* **bha na h-actairean eagalach math!** the actors were awfully/terribly good!, *Cf* **uabhasach 2**

eaglais, eaglaise, eaglaisean *nf* a church (*ie building & institution*), **cathair-eaglais** *f* a cathedral, **Eaglais na h-Alba** the Church of Scotland

eala, eala(dh), ealachan *nf* a swan, (*song*) **An Eala Bhàn** The White Swan

èalaidh *vi, pres part* **ag èala(i)dh, 1** creep, *Cf* **snàig 2; 2** creep or sneak away (*from gathering &c*), **bha iad ag èalaidh dhachaigh** they were sneaking/creeping off home, *Cf* **siolp**

ealain, ealaine, ealainean *nf* art, a branch of the arts, **is e tè de na h-ealainean a th' ann am bàrdachd** poetry is one of the arts, **Comhairle nan Ealain an Albainn** *also* **Comhairle Ealain na h-Alba** the Scottish Arts Council, **neach-ealain** *m* an artist

ealamh *adj* quick, nimble, swift (*in performing tasks &c*), *Cf* **clis, deas 4**

ealanta *adj* **1** artistic; **2** expert, *Cf* **teòma 1**

ealantach, *gen & pl* **ealantaich** *nm* an expert, *Cf* **eòlaiche 1**

eallach, *gen & pl* **eallaich** *nm* (*lit & fig*) a burden, a load, (*song*) **is trom an t-eallach an gaol** love is a heavy burden, *Cf* **uallach 1, ultach 1**

ealt(a), ealta, ealtan *nf* a flock (*of birds*)

ealtainn, ealtainne, ealtainnean *nf* a razor

eanchainn, eanchainne, eanchainnean *nmf* **1** (*anat*) brain, a brain, (*fam*) **chuir e an eanchainn às** he brained him; **2** a brain, brains, mental or intellectual ability, **tha eanchainn mhath innte** she's got a good brain, *Cf* **inntinn 1**

eanraich, *gen* **eanraiche** *nf* (*trad*) soup, broth, *Cf* **brot**

ear *nf invar* east, **on ear** from the east, **an ear air Eden** east of Eden, **gaoth às an ear** a wind from/out of the east, **gaoth an ear** an easterly wind, *Note that* **an** *of* **an ear** *does not behave as an article in the following exprs* **an àird(e) an ear** the east (*ie compass direction*), **an taobh an ear** the east coast/east side of the country, **a' dol an ear** going east, *see* **sear** *& Cf* **deas 1, iar, siar, tuath**[1]

earalachadh, earalachaidh, earalachaidhean *nm* **1** (*the act of*) exhorting &c (*see senses of* **earalaich** *v*); **2** an exhortation, *Cf* **brosnachadh 3; 3** a caution, a warning, *Cf* **rabhadh**

earalaich *vt, pres part* **ag earalachadh, 1** exhort, *Cf* **brosnaich; 2** caution, warn (**air** about)

earalas, *gen* **earalais** *nm* caution, foresight (*in case of trouble*), *esp in expr* **cuir** *v* **air earalas** forewarn, put on (his &c) guard, *Cf* **faiceall**

earb *vti, pres part* **ag earbsa(dh), 1** (*vi*) trust (*with prep* **à, às**) **cha robh iad ag earbsadh às na nàbaidhean aca** they didn't trust their neighbours, *Cf* **creideas 3; 2** (*vt*) entrust oneself, rely on (*with prep* **ri**) **na h-earb thu fhèin riutha** don't entrust yourself to/rely on them, *also* don't confide in them

earb(a), earba, earbaichean *nf* a roe-deer, **boc-earba** *m* a roe-buck

earball, *gen & pl* **earbaill** *nm* a tail, **cù a' crathadh earbaill** a dog wagging its tail, **earball daimh** ox-tail

earbsa *nf invar* trust, confidence, reliance, **cuir** *v* **earbsa ann an rudeigin** trust/put one's trust in something, rely on something, **chan eil earbsa aca annaibh** *or* **asaibh** they don't trust you, *Cf* **creideas 1 & 3**

earbsach *adj* **1** trusting; **2** trustworthy, *Cf* **urrasach**

eàrlas, *gen & pl* **eàrlais** *nm* (*fin*) an advance, **thug am foillsichear eàrlas dha** the publisher gave him an advance

earrach, *gen & pl* **earraich** *nm* (*the season*) spring, **as t-earrach** in (the) spring

earrann, earrainn, earrannan *nf* a part, a piece, a section (*of something*), (*fin*) a share, **margadh nan earrannan** the stock market, **a' chiad earrann den nobhail aice** the first part of her novel, *Cf* **pàirt 1**, **roinn** *n* **2**

earranta *adj* (*business*) limited, **companaidh earranta** a limited company, **Birlinn Earranta** Birlinn Limited

eas, easa, easan *nm* a waterfall, falls, a cascade, (*prov*) **cha tèid stad ort nas mò na air eas na h-aibhne** you don't stop any more than the waterfall in the river, *Cf* **leum-uisge, linne 3, spùt** *n* **2**

eas- *a prefix implying negation, eg* **eascaraid** *m* a foe (*lit* a non-friend), *can corres to Eng* in-, un-, dis- &c, *eg* **eas-umhail** *adj* insubordinate, disobedient, irreverent, **eas-urramach** *adj* dishonourable, *Cf* **eu-, mi-, neo-**

easag, easaig, easagan *nf* a pheasant

eas-aonta, eas-aonta, eas-aontan *nf* disagreement, discord, dissent, **dh'èirich eas-aonta mhòr eadar na ministearan** there arose considerable disagreement/dissent among/between the ministers

easbaig, easbaig, easbaigean *nm* a bishop, **àrd-easbaig** an archbishop

Easbaigeach, *gen & pl* **Easbaigich** *nm* an Episcopalian, *also as adj* **Easbaigeach 1** Episcopalian; **2** episcopal

easbhaidh, easbhaidhe, easbhaidhean *nf* lack, want, need, a deficiency or deficit, *esp in expr* **a** (*for* **de**) **dh'easbhaidh** lacking, wanting, missing, **dè (a) tha a dh'easbhaidh orra?** what do they lack/want/need?, **bha còmhdach an leabhair a dh'easbhaidh** the cover of the book was missing, *Cf more usu* **dìth**

easbhaidheach *adj* **1** needy, in need, *Cf* **feumach**; **2** lacking, wanting, in short supply, *Cf* **dìth 2**

èasgaidh *adj* (*of persons*) active, willing, keen, prompt, obliging (*with implication of ability, handiness*), **èasgaidh gus a dhèanamh** willing/keen to do it, **èasgaidh gu èirigh sa mhadainn** keen to get up in the morning, *Cf* **dealasach, deas 4, deònach**

easgann, easgainn, easgannan *nf* an eel

eatarra, eatorra *prep prons see* **eadar**

eathar, eathair, eathraichean *nmf, also* **eithear, eitheir, eithrichean** *nmf*, a small boat, *also specifically* a rowing boat, (*saying*) **eathar ùr is seana chreagan** a new boat and old rocks, *Cf* **geòla**

èibh *v see* **èigh** *v*

èibhinn *adj* funny, amusing, **dealbh-èibhinn** *nmf* a cartoon (*single sketch, strip cartoon or animated film*), *Cf less usu* **àbhachdach**

èibhleag, èibhleige, èibhleagan *nf* an ember, a cinder, **bheothaich i èibhleagan an teine** she revived/stirred up the embers of the fire

èideadh, èididh, èididhean *nm* dress (*esp a particular mode of dress*), a garb, a uniform, (*song*) **chuir e bhrìogais ghlas an gèill gus an t-èideadh seo (a) thoirt bhuainn** he made the grey breeks compulsory in order to take this garb/dress away from us, **an t-èideadh Gàidhealach** the garb of the Gael, Highland dress

eidheann, *gen* **eidhne** *nf* ivy

èifeachd *nf invar* an effect, a consequence, **gun èifeachd** without effect, of no avail, *Cf* **buaidh 4, buil 1, toradh 2**

èifeachdach *adj* **1** effective, *Cf* **buadhmhor**; **2** efficient

Eigeach, *gen & pl* **Eigich** *nm* someone from Eigg (**Eilean Eige**), *also as adj* **Eigeach** of, from or pertaining to Eigg

èigh & **èibh** *vi, pres part* **ag èigheach(d)**, shout, cry, call, *Cf* **gairm** *v* **1**, **glaodh** *vi*

èigh, èighe, èighe(ach)an *nf* a shout, a cry, *Cf* **gairm** *n* **3**, **glaodh** *n*

eigh, *gen* **eighe** *nf, also* **eighre,** *gen* **eighre** *nf, also* **deigh,** *gen* **deighe** *nf*, ice

eighe, eighe, eigheachan *nf* (*metalwork &c*) a file

èigheachd *nf invar* (*the act of*) shouting, crying, calling

eighre *see* **eigh**

-eigin *a suffix corres to Eng* some-, **rudeigin** something, **latheigin** one day, some day, **tha cuideigin air a thighinn a-steach** someone's come in, **chaill mi ann an àiteigin e** I lost it somewhere, **chì mi uair no uaireigin thu** I'll see you sometime or other, **latheigin** one day, one of these days

èiginn *nf invar* **1** difficulty, trouble, a difficult situation, an emergency, **tha mi ann an èiginn** (*also* **nam èiginn**) I'm in trouble/in a fix (*Cf more con* **staing**), **itealan ann an èiginn os cionn a' phuirt-adhair** an aeroplane in difficulty/difficulties above the airport, **doras-èiginn** an emergency exit; **2** necessity; **3** violence, *esp in expr* **thoir** *v* **air èiginn** rape, *also* take (*something*) by force; **4** *in expr* **air èiginn** hardly, scarcely, barely, with difficulty, **'s ann air èiginn a dh'fhosgail e a shùil** it was with difficulty that he opened his eye, *also* he barely opened his eye, *Cf* **gann 2**

èigneachair, èigneachair, èigneachairean *nm* a rapist, a ravisher

èignich *vt, pres part* **ag èigneachadh**, rape, ravish

eil *pt of irreg vb* **bi** (*see tables p 414*)

Eilbheiseach, *gen & pl* **Eilbheisich** *nm* someone from Switzerland (**an Eilbheis** *f*), *also as adj* **Eilbheiseach** Swiss

èildear, èildeir, èildearan *nm* a (church) elder, *Cf more trad* **foirfeach**

eile *adj* other, another, else, **b' fheàrr leam leabhar eile** I'd prefer another (*ie different*) book, **cha ghabh mi pinnt eile** I won't take another (*ie additional*) pint, **air an dara làimh … ach air an làimh eile …** on the one hand … but on the other hand …, (*set expr*) **mar a thuirt am fear eile** as someone once said, **rud eile** another thing, something else, (*set expr*) **agus rud eile dheth …** and another thing …, **cò eile a bh' ann?** who else was there? **chan eil mi ag iarraidh càil eile** I don't want another thing/anything else (*Cf* **barrachd 4**)

èile, èileadh *see* **fèileadh**

eilean, eilein, eileanan *nm* an island, **air/**(*more usu*) **anns an eilean** on the island, **Na h-Eileanan Siar** The Western Isles, **Comhairle nan Eilean Siar** the Western Isles Council, **Eilean Fraoich** Isle of Heather (*ie Lewis*), *often prefixed to island name in gen or adj form* **Eilean Mhuile/An t-Eilean Muileach** Mull, **Eilean Leòdhais** Lewis, *Cf less usu* **innis** *n* **1**

eileanach, *gen & pl* **eileanaich** *nm* an islander

eilid, èilde, eil(i)dean *nf* a hind (*of red or roe deer*), *Cf* **boc 2, daimh 1, earb(a)**

eilthireach, *gen & pl* **eilthirich** *nm* **1** someone from another country, a foreigner, *Cf* **coigreach 1; 2** an exile, *esp* (*trad, hist*) *a Highlander who emigrated as a result of the Clearances*, an emigrant, an émigré, *Cf* **fògrach 2, fuadan 2; 3** a pilgrim

einnsean, einnsein, einnseanan *nm* an engine, **einnsean càir** a car engine, **einnsean-smàlaidh** a fire engine

Eipheiteach, *gen & pl* **Eipheitich** *nm* an Egyptian, *also as adj* **Eipheiteach** Egyptian

Eiphit *nf invar, with art,* **an Eiphit** Egypt

eireachdail *adj* handsome, graceful, elegant, *Cf* **gasta 1**, **grinn 1**

eireag, eireig(e), eireagan *nf* a pullet, (*port à beul*) **b' fheàrr leam fhìn gum beireadh an tèile 'màireach dhe na h-eireagan** I would dearly like the other one of the pullets to lay tomorrow

Eireannach, *gen & pl* **Eireannaich** *nm* an Irishman, *also as adj* **Eireannach** Irish

èirich *vi, pres part* **ag èirigh**, **1** rise, arise, get up (*from bed, sitting position &c*), stand up, **dh'èirich mi anmoch an-dè** I got up late yesterday, **dh'èirich e na sheasamh** he stood up/rose to his feet, **dh'èirich i air a leth-uilinn** she raised herself up onto one elbow; **2** rise up, rebel, revolt, **èirichibh suas an aghaidh nan aintighearnan!** rise up against the tyrants!, *Cf* **ar-a-mach**; **3** happen, befall, **dè a dh'èirich dha?** what happened to him? *or* what became of him? (*Cf* **tachair 1**), **ciamar a dh'èirich dhaibh?** how did they get on? **'s math a dh'èireas dha mura tèid a mharbhadh** it will go well with him/he'll be lucky if he isn't killed (*Cf* **rach 2**)

eiridinn *nm invar* (*trad*) nursing, care of the sick, **taigh-eiridinn** *m* a hospital (*Cf less trad* **ospadal**), an infirmary, **carbad-eiridinn** *m* an ambulance, *Cf* **altram 2**

eiridnich *vt, pres part* **ag eiridneachadh**, nurse, tend (*the sick*), *Cf* **altraim 2**

èirig, èirige, èirigean *nf* a payment (*in reparation for something*), *esp* a ransom

Eirinn, *gen* **Eireann** *nf* Ireland, **Gàidhlig na h-Eireann** Irish Gaelic

Eirisgeach, *gen & pl* **Eirisgich** *nm* someone from Eriskay (**Eirisgeigh**), *also as adj* **Eirisgeach** of, from or pertaining to Eriskay

eirmseach *adj* **1** witty; **2** sharp, smart, intelligent

èisd *&* **èist** *vi, pres part* **ag èisdeachd**, listen (**ri** to), **ag èisdeachd ris na h-òrain** listening to the songs

èisdeachd *nf invar* (*the act of*) listening

eisimeil, *gen* **eisimeile** *nf*, dependence, *esp in expr* **an eisimeil** (*with gen*) dependent on, **bha a' chompanaidh an eisimeil an luchd-earrann aice** the company was dependent on its shareholders, *also with prep* **air**, **an eisimeil air a bràthair** dependent on her brother

eisimealach *adj* dependent (**air** on), **neo-eisimealach** *adj* independent

eisimealachd *nf invar*, dependence, **neo-eisimealachd** independence, *Cf* **eisimeil**

eisimpleir, eisimpleir, eisimpleirean *nm* an example, *esp in expr* **mar eisimpleir** for example (*abbrev* **m. e.**)

eist *see* ist

èist *see* èisd

eitean, *gen* eitein & eitne, *pl* eitnean *nm* 1 a kernel, eitean cnotha a nut kernel; 2 a core, eitean ubhail an apple core

eòlach *adj* 1 knowledgeable, familiar (with), conversant (with), duine eòlach a knowledgeable man, eòlach air coimpiutairean familiar / conversant with computers, bha an t-each eòlach air an rathad dhachaigh the horse knew the way home, *Cf* fiosrach; 2 (*of people*) acquainted, tha iad eòlach air a chèile they're acquainted (with one another), 's e sin Uisdean, a bheil thu eòlach air? that's Hugh, do you know him?; *Cf* aithne 1, 2 & 3

eòlaiche, eòlaiche, eòlaichean *nm* 1 an expert, *Cf* ealantach; 2 a scientist; 3 a savant, a scholar

eòlas, eòlais, eòlasan *nm* 1 knowledge, tha e làn eòlais air filmichean he's full of knowledge about films; 2 (*in compounds*) a branch of knowledge, bith-eòlas biology, eòlas-leighis medicine, eòlas-inntinn psychology, luibh-eòlas botany; 3 acquaintance, familiarity, (*trad*) tìr m' eòlais the land I am familiar with / know best (*ie* my homeland *or* home district), cuir *v* eòlas air cuideigin get to know / get acquainted with someone, luchd-eòlais acquaintances, *Cf* aithne 1

eòrna *nm invar* barley, eilean an eòrna the barley island, Tiree, (*song*) gealach abachaidh an eòrna, bheir i sinne Leòdhas dhachaigh the barley-harvest moon will get us home to Lewis, (*prov*) cha dèan làmh glan eòrna clean hand(s) won't make barley

Eòrpach, *gen* & *pl* Eòrpaich *nm* a European, *also as adj* Eòrpach European

Eòrpa *nf invar* Europe, *more usu* an Roinn-Eòrpa Europe, the continent of Europe

esan *see* e

eu-, *occas* ao-, *a negating prefix, can corres to Eng* in-, un-, dis-, -less, *eg* eu-coltach *adj* unlikely, improbable; dissimilar, eu-dòchas *m* hopelessness, eu-domhainn *adj* shallow, (*of person &c*) superficial, *Cf* eas-, mi-, neo-

euchd, euchd, euchdan *nm* 1 (*trad*) a feat, a deed, an exploit (*of heroes &c*), *Cf* cleas 1; 2 (*now more usu*) an achievement

eucoir, eucorach, eucoirean *nf* 1 a crime; 2 a wrong, rinn iad eucoir orm they wronged me, *Cf* coire 1

eu-coireach *adj* innocent, blameless

eucorach, *gen* & *pl* eucoraich *nm* a criminal

eud (*also* iad) *nm invar* 1 jealousy (*often sexual*), *Cf* farmad; 2 zeal

eudach (*also* **iadach**) *adj* jealous, (*song*) **A' Bhean Eudach** The Jealous Woman

eudach (*also* **iadach**), *gen* **eudaich** *nm* jealousy (*usu sexual*), *also used as pres part*, **bha i ag eudach ris mu bhoireannaich eile** she was jealous about him and other woman, (*lit* she was showing/feeling jealousy towards him concerning other women)

eudail *occas* **feudail**, *gen* **eudail** & **eudalach**, *pl* **eudailean** *nf* **1** (*trad*) treasure, cattle, valuable possessions; **2** *now usu in affectionate address or excl* **m' eudail!** my darling! (*less intimate*) (my) dear! (*to children*) pet!, love!, precious!; *Cf* **ulaidh**

eudmhor *adj* jealous

eug *vi, pres part* **ag eugadh**, (*trad*) die, *Cf more usu* **bàsaich, caochail, siubhail**

eug, *gen* **èig** *nm* (*trad*) death, *Cf more usu* **bàs**

eugmhais *see* **às eugmhais**

eun, *gen* & *pl* **eòin** *nm* a bird, **eun-eòlas** *m* ornithology, **eòin-mhara** sea birds, **eòin-àir** birds of prey, **eòin-uisge** waterfowl, (*prov*) **ge beag an t-ugh, thig eun às** though the egg is small, a bird will come out of it

eunlaith *nf pl coll* birds, **ealt eunlaith** a flock of birds

euslaint(e), **euslainte**, **euslaintean** *nf* illness, ill-health, *Cf* **anfhannachd, tinneas**

euslainteach *adj* ill, unhealthy, in bad health, sick, *Cf* **anfhann, tinn**

euslainteach, *gen* & *pl* **euslaintich** *nm* an invalid, a patient, **eiridnich** *v* **na h-euslaintich** tend/care for the sick/ill

F

fàbhar, fàbhair, fàbharan *nm* a favour, **rinn e fàbhar dhut** he did you a favour, *Cf* **bàidh 2, seirbheis 2**

fàbharach *adj* favourable, propitious

faca *pt of irreg v* **faic** (*see tables p 408*)

fabhra, fabhra, fabhran *nm* **1** an eyelash, *Cf* **rosg**²; **2** an eyelid

facal, *gen* **facail**, *pl* **facail** & **faclan** *nm* **1** a word (*written or spoken*), **is e facal boireann a tha ann an 'eaglais'** 'eaglais' is a feminine word, **thubhairt i facal no dhà anns a' Ghàidhlig** she said a word or two/a few words in Gaelic, **cha do bhruidhinn sinn facal Gàidhlig air a' bhàt'-aiseig** we didn't speak a word of Gaelic on the ferry, **an toir thu dhomh d' fhacal (air)?** will you give me your word (on it)/swear (to it)? **2** a saying, **is e facal a th' ann an 'is tighe fuil na bùrn'** 'blood is thicker than water' is a saying, *Cf* **ràdh 1, seanfhacal**

fa chomhair *see* **comhair 2**

faclach *adj* wordy, verbose, *Cf* **briathrach**

facladair, facladair, facladairean *nm* (*IT*) a word processor

facladaireachd *nf invar* (*IT*) word processing

faclair, faclair, faclairean *nm* a dictionary, **am faclair as ainmeile sa Ghàidhlig, 's e am fear aig Dwelly** the most famous dictionary in Gaelic is Dwelly's one

faclaireachd *nf invar* lexicography

facs, facsa, facsaichean *nm* (*IT*) a fax, **inneal** *m* **facsa** a fax machine

fad, *gen* **faid** *nm* **1** (*spatial*) length, **mìle a** (*for* **de**) **dh'fhad** a mile long/ in length, **tha dà throigh de dh'fhad ann** it's two feet long, **dh'itealaich e air fad an taighe** it flew the length of the house, **cuir** *v* **rudeigin am fad** lengthen something, **a' dol am fad** getting longer, *Cf less usu* **faide**; **2** length (*of time*), *prepositional use corres to Eng* for, whole, all, **bha sinn sa bhaile mhòr fad cola-deug** we were in the town for a fortnight (*lit* the length of a fortnight), **fad na h-ùine** the whole/all the time, **bha mi bochd fad mo bheatha** I was poor my whole/all my life, **bidh mi nam dhùisg fad na h-oidhche** I'll be awake the whole night; **3** *in expr* **air fad** *adv* all, the whole, completely, **chaidh na taighean air fad a losgadh** all the houses were burned, **sgrios iad an dùthaich air fad** they ravaged the whole country, **mhill e air fad e** he spoiled it completely; **4 fhad is a** *conj* while, **fhad 's a bha i anns an Fhraing dh'ionnsaich i an Fhraingis** while she was in France she learnt French

fàd, fàid, fàdan *nm* a (single) peat (*also* **fàd mònach**), *Cf* **fòid 3**

fad(a) *adj* **1** (*spatially*) long, a long way, far, (*of people*) tall, **druim fada** a long ridge, **dè cho fada 's a tha e?** how long is it? *or* how far is it? (*song*) **'s fhada bhuam Grìminis** a long way/far from me is Griminish, (*prov*) **fada bhon t-sùil, fada bhon chridhe** what the eye doesn't see the heart doesn't grieve over, **tìr fad' air falbh** a faraway/distant land, **boireannach fada caol** a tall lanky woman, **còta/film làn-fhada** a full-length coat/film; **2** long (*in time*), **bha na làithean fada dhuinn** the days were long for us, **na bi fada!** don't be long! **'s ann o chionn fhada a thachair sin** it's long ago/a long time ago that that happened, **is fhada o nach fhaca mi thu** it's a long time since I saw you, long time no see, **chan fhad thuige a-nis** it won't be long now; **3** *in comparative exprs* **fada nas fheàrr, fada nas sine** far better, much older, *Cf* **mòran 3**; **4** *in expr* **fad' às** (*of persons*) distant, remote, withdrawn (*Cf* **dùinte 2**), *also* preoccupied, absent-minded; **5** *in compounds* long-, *eg* **fad-fhulangachd** *f* long-suffering, **fad-shaoghalach** *adj* long-lived

fadachd *nf invar*, *also* **fadal**, *gen* **fadail** *nm*, **1** longing, yearning, nostalgia for *or* feeling of missing a place, person or thing, **thàinig fadachd orm ris** a longing/nostalgia came over me for it/him; **2** weariness, tedium, boredom, impatience (*for something to be finished*), **bha fadachd orm fhad 's a bha e a' bruidhinn** I was bored/impatient all the time he was talking, **gabh** *v* **fadachd** grow weary

fadalach *adj* **1** late (*ie after the appropriate moment*), tardy, **bha mi fadalach, bha a h-uile duine air falbh** I was late, everyone had left, *Cf* **deireadh 3**; **2** tedious, boring, long drawn out, **òraid fhadalach** a boring/long drawn out talk, *Cf* **liosda, màirnealach 2, slaodach 2**

fàg *vt*, *pres part* **a' fàgail**, **1** leave, quit, abandon, (*songs*) **a' fàgail Steòrnabhaigh** leaving Stornoway, **on dh'fhàg thu mi 's mulad orm** since you left me with sadness upon me, **càit na dh'fhàg thu an fhichead gini?** where did you leave the twenty guineas?; **2** leave in a particular state, make, cause to be, (*song*) **dh'fhàg thu tana-ghlas mo shnuadh** you made my complexion pale and wan, **dh'fhàg an turas sgìth iad** the journey made/left them tired

fàgail, fàgaile *nf* (*the act of*) leaving, quitting &c (*see senses of* **fàg** *v*)

faic *vt irreg* (*see tables p 408*), *pres part* **a' faicinn**, see, **chan fhaic mi càil** I can't see anything, (*song*) **chì mi 'm bàta 's i tighinn** I see the boat approaching, **bidh sinn ga fhaicinn gu math tric** we see him pretty often, **chì sinn** we'll see

faiceall, *gen* **faicill** *nf* care, caution, circumspection, *Cf* **earalas**

faiceallach *adj* careful, cautious, prudent, circumspect, **bi faiceallach!** be careful! *Cf* **cùramach 1**

faiceadh, faiceam, faiceamaid *pts of irreg v* faic *see tables p 408*

faiche, faiche, faichean *nf* a meadow, a grass park, a lawn, *Cf* clua(i)n, dail 1, lòn² 3

faicinn *nf invar* (*the act of*) seeing, **'s math d' fhaicinn** it's good to see you

faicsinneach *adj* 1 visible, *Cf less usu* lèirsinneach 1; 2 conspicuous

faide *nf invar* length, *Cf more usu* fad 1

fàidh, fàidhe, fàidhean *nm* (*Bibl, trad*) a prophet, a seer, (*poem*) **A' Cluich air Football le Fàidh** (Ruaraidh MacThòmais) Playing Football with a Prophet, *Cf* fiosaiche 1

fàidheadaireachd, fàidheadaireachd, fàideadaireachdan *nf* prophecy, a prophecy, *Cf* fàisneachd

faidhle, *gen* faidhle, *pl* faidhlean & faidhlichean *nm* (*IT*) a file

faigh *vt irreg* (*see tables p 409*), *pres part* **a' faighinn** & **a' faotainn**, 1 get, obtain, **faigh iasg on bhan** get/fetch some fish from the van, (*song*) **gu dè nì mi mur faigh mi thu?** what will I do if I don't get you?, (*prov*) **cha d'fhuair droch bhuanaiche a-riamh deagh chorran** bad reaper never got good sickle, **cha d'fhuair mi an obair ud** I didn't get yon job, **fhuair i duais** she got/won a prize (*Cf* coisinn 2); 2 find, **fhuair i sgillinn air a' chabhsair** she found a penny on the pavement, **gheibh sibh san taigh-òsta e** you'll find him in the pub, *Cf* lorg *v* 2; 3 **faigh a-mach** find out, discover, **fhuair iad a-mach gun robh e briste** they found out that he was broke/bankrupt; 4 *in expr* **faigh seachad air** (**opairèisean** &c) get over, recover from (an operation &c); 5 *in expr* **faigh air** manage to, **gheibh mi air tilleadh ann uair no uaireigin** I'll manage to go back there some time or other, *Cf* rach 5

faigheadh, faigheam, faigheamaid *pts of irreg v* faigh *see tables p 409*

faighean, faighein, faigheanan *nm* a vagina, *Cf* pit 1, ròmag

faighinn *nf invar* & faotainn *nf invar* (*the act of*) getting, finding &c (*see senses of* faigh *v*)

faighneach & faighneachail *adj* inquisitive, enquiring, *Cf* ceasnachail

faighneachd *nf invar* (*the act of*) asking, enquiring

faighnich *vi*, *pres part* **a' faighneachd**, ask, enquire, **faighnich de Mhòrag** ask Morag, **dh'fhaighnich i an robh beatha air Mars** she asked whether there was life on Mars, *Cf less usu* feòraich

fail, faile, failean *nf* (*agric*) a sty

failc *vti*, *pres part* **a' failceadh**, bathe, *Cf* ionnlaid, nigh

fàile & fàileadh *see* àile

faileas, faileis, faileasan *nm* **1** a shadow, **laigh a faileas orm** her shadow fell on me; **2** reflection, **chì mi faileas na gealaich air uachdar an locha** I can see the reflection of the moon on the surface of the loch

faileasach *adj* shadowy

failich *see* **fairtlich**

faillean, faillein, failleanan *nm* an eardrum

fàillig *vti, pres part* **a' fàilligeadh**, fail, **fàillig deuchainn** fail an exam

fàilligeadh, fàilligidh, fàilligidhean *nm* **1** (*the act of*) failing; **2** a failing, a deficiency; **3** failure, a failure

fàillinn, fàillinne, fàillinnean *nf* **1** a failing, a fault, a blemish (*in personality &c*), *Cf* **meang 1**; **2** weakening, falling off, deterioration, (*song*) **chan eil fàillinn san teangaidh aig a' bhean agam fhìn!** there's no deterioration in the tongue of my very own wife!; **3** failure

failm & **ailm**, *gen* **(f)ailme**, *pl* **(f)ailmean** *nf* a boat's tiller

failmean & **falman**, *gen* **failmein**, *pl* **failmeanan** *nm* a kneecap

fail-mhuc, fail-mhuc, failean-mhuc *nf* a pigsty

fàilte, fàilte, fàiltean *nf* **1** a welcome, **cuir** *v* **fàilte air cuideigin** welcome someone (*Cf* **fàiltich**), **fàilte oirbh don bhaile!** welcome to the village! **fhuair sinn fàilte chridheil** we got a hearty welcome (*Cf* **gabhail 4**), (*trad*) **ceud mìle fàilte!** a hundred thousand welcomes!, (*hotel &c*) **an t-ionad fàilte** reception, the reception desk, *Cf less usu* **furan**; **2** a greeting, a salute; **3** (*pibroch*) a salute, **Fàilte an t-Siosalaich** Chisholm's Salute

fàilteach & **fàilteachail** *adj* welcoming, hospitable

fàilteachadh, *gen* **fàilteachaidh** *nm* (*the act of*) welcoming, greeting, saluting

fàiltich *vt, pres part* **a' fàilteachadh**, welcome, salute, greet, *Cf more usu* **cuir fàilte air** (*see* **fàilte 1**)

fàiltiche, fàiltiche, fàiltichean *nm* (*hotel &c*) a receptionist

faing & **fang**, *gen* **fainge**, *pl* **faingean** *nmf* **1** a sheepfold, (*Sc*) a (sheep-) fank; **2** the activity and occasion of gathering, dipping, shearing &c carried out at the sheep-fank, **bidh faing ann a-màireach** there'll be a fank tomorrow

fàinne, fàinne, fàinneachan *nmf* a ring (*esp for finger*), **fàinne-pòsaidh/ fàinne-pòsta** a wedding ring, **fàinne gealladh-pòsaidh** an engagement ring

fàinne-solais, fàinne-solais, fàinneachan-solais *nf* a halo

fairche, fairche, fairchean *nm* a mallet

faire, faire, fairean *nf* 1 (*the action of*) guarding, watching, **dèan**/**cùm** *v* **faire** be on guard, keep watch, keep a look-out, **faire na h-oidhche** the night watch (*abstr*); 2 (*coll, con*) a guard, **cuir** *v* **faire air** put a guard on it, **fear-faire** *m* a (*single*) guard, a member of the guard, *Cf* **freiceadan**

fàire, fàire, fàirean *nf* 1 a horizon, a skyline, **air fàire** on the horizon; 2 *in expr* **faigh** *v* **fàire air** spot, catch sight of (*usu at a distance or on horizon*)

faireachdainn, faireachdainne, faireachdainnean *nf* 1 (*the act of*) feeling, smelling (*see* **fairich** *v*); 2 (*phys*) feeling, a feeling, sensation, a sensation, *Cf* **mothachadh 2**; 3 (*emotional, mental*) a feeling, *in pl* feelings

fàireag, fàireig, fàireagan *nf* (*anat*) a gland, **fàireag-fhallais** a sweat gland

fairge, *gen* **fairge,** *pl* **fairgeachan** & **fairgeannan** *nf* (*trad, in poetry &c*) an ocean, a sea, (*song*) **air luing mhòir air bhàrr na fairge** on a great ship on the crest of the ocean, *Cf* **sàl 2** & *more usu* **cuan, muir**

fairich *vti, pres part* **a' faireachdainn** & **a' faireachadh,** 1 (*vti*) feel (*phys*), **fairich fuachd is teas** feel cold and heat, **ciamar a tha thu a' faireachdainn an-diugh?** how are you feeling/how do you feel today?; 2 (*vi*) feel (*emotionally, mentally*), **a' faireachdainn diombach** feeling disgruntled; 3 (*vt*) smell, **am fairich thu ceò na mòna/boladh an èisg?** can you smell the peat reek/the smell of the fish?

fairtlich, *also* **failich,** *vi, pres part* **a' fairtleachadh** *also* **a' failicheadh,** overcome, *esp in expr* **fairtlich air** get the better of, defeat, baffle (*something, someone*), **bha mi airson a' bheinn a dhìreadh ach dh'fhairtlich i orm** I wanted to climb the mountain but it defeated/got the better of me *or* I failed, **fairtlichidh sinn air an nàmhaid** we will overcome/defeat the enemy

faisg *adj* near, close (**air** to), **faisg air a chèile** close together, **tha àm na Nollaige faisg a-nis** Christmas time is near now, *Cf less usu* **dlùth 1**

fàisg *vt, pres part* **a' fàsgadh,** compress, press, squeeze, wring

faisge *nf invar* nearness, closeness

fàisneachd *nf* prophecy, a prophecy, *Cf* **fàidheadaireachd**

faite, faite, faitichean *nf* a smile, *now esp as* **faite-gàire** *f* a smile, **dèan** *v* **faite-gàire** smile (*Cf* **faitich**), *Cf* **fiamh-gàire** (*see* **fiamh 3**), **snodha-gàire**

fàitheam, fàitheim, fàitheaman *nm* a hem (*on material or garment*)

faitich *vi, pres part* **a' faiteachadh,** smile

fàl, *gen* & *pl* **fàil** *nm* 1 a hedge, *Cf* **callaid;** 2 a turf, a sod, a divot, *Cf* **fòid 1**

falach, *gen* **falaich** *nm* hiding, the act of hiding, concealment, **am falach** in hiding, **rach** *v* **am falach** go into hiding, **àite-falaich** *m* a hiding-place, **cuiridh mi am falach thu** I will hide/conceal you, **falach-fead** *m* hide-and-seek

falachd *nf invar* a feud

falaich *vti, pres part* **a' falach** *&* **a' falachadh**, hide, conceal, secrete, *Cf more usu* **rach/cuir am falach** (*see* **falach**)

falaichte *adj* hidden, concealed, secret, (*song*) **chuir iad a ghleann falaicht' mi** they sent me to a hidden glen

falamh *adj* 1 empty, **tha na glinn/mo stamag falamh** the glens are/my stomach is empty, *Cf* **fàs** *adj* 1, *less usu in this sense*; 2 hollow

fal(a)mhachd *nf invar* emptiness; a void, a vacuum, *Cf* **fànas** 2

falbh *vi, pres part* **a' falbh**, 1 leave, go (away), depart, **dh'fhalbh iad an-dè** they left/went away yesterday, **tha i air falbh** she's left/gone, she's away, **ceart! tha mi (a') falbh** right! I'm going, I'm off, I'm away, *imper also occurs as* **thalla!**, **f(h)albh/thalla don bhùth dhomh** away you go to the shop for me, (*eg to dog*) **falbh/thalla dhachaigh!** away/get off home!; 2 *in expr* **falbh a dh'iarraidh rudeigin** go to fetch/get something

fallain *adj* 1 (*persons*) sound, healthy, well, able-bodied, (*song*) **fallainn gum bi thu!** may you be safe and sound/in perfect health! **ràinig sinn an cala slàn is fallain** *or* (*trad*) **gu slàn fallain** we reached the harbour safe and sound/in one piece; 2 wholesome, health-giving, **biadh fallain** wholesome/healthy food; *Cf* **slàn** 1 & 2

fallas, *gen* **fallais** *nm* sweat, perspiration, **tha mi a' cur fallas dhìom** *or* **tha fallas orm** *or* **tha mi nam fhallas** I'm sweating

fallasach *adj* sweaty

fallsa *adj* false, deceitful, *Cf* **brèige** *adj* 1, **meallta(ch)**

falmadair, falmadair, falmadairean *nm* a helm (*of boat*)

falmhachadh, *gen* **falmhachaidh** *nm* (*the act of*) emptying, unloading

falmhaich *vti, pres part* **a' falmhachadh**, 1 empty, make empty, become empty; 2 unload, *Cf* **aotromaich** 2

falt, *gen* **fuilt** *nm* hair (*of human head*), *Cf* **gruag** 1

famh, faimh, famhan *nmf* a mole (*ie the animal*)

famhair, famhair, famhairean *nm*, *also* **fuamhaire, fuamhaire, fuamhairean** *nm*, 1 a giant, *Cf less usu* **athach**; 2 (*trad*) a champion, a hero, *Cf usu* **curaidh, gaisgeach**

fan *vi, pres part* **a' fantainn, a' fantail** *&* **a' fanachd**, 1 wait (**air** for), stay, **fan thusa an seo!** you wait/stay here! **bha mi a' fantainn ort** I was waiting for you/(*Sc*) on you, *Cf* **feith** 1, **fuirich** 1; 2 live, stay, **fan aig cuideigin** stay/lodge with someone, *Cf* **fuirich** 2

fanaid, *gen* **fanaide** *nf* **1** mockery, ridicule (*of person, his/her possessions &c*), *esp in expr* **dèan** *v* **fanaid air** mock, ridicule, scoff at, make fun of, *Cf* **magadh 2** & *less usu* **àbhacas 2**; **2** *also found as pres part* **bha iad a'/ri fanaid air a chuid aodaich** they were making fun of his clothes; *Cf* **mag** *v*

fànas, fànais, fànasan *nm* **1** space (*ie extra-terrestrial*), **fànas-long** *f* a spaceship, **linn an fhanais** the space age, *Cf* **speur 3**; **2** a void, *Cf* **falamhachd**

fa-near *adv* **1** *in expr* **fa-near dhomh** (*&c*) on my (*&c*) mind, (*song*) **an uair (a) bhios mi leam fhìn bidh tu tighinn fa-near dhomh** when I'm alone you come into my thoughts, *Cf* **aigne 1, aire 1, cùram 2**; **2** *expr intention, inclination,* **bha e fa-near dhi an taigh a sgioblachadh rud beag** it was on her mind/she was minded/had a mind to tidy the house a wee bit, *Cf* **beachd 3**; **3** *as noun, in expr* **thoir** *v* **fa-near (do)** notice, *Cf* **aire 2, mothaich 1**

fang *see* **faing**

fann *adj* (*phys*) weak, feeble, faint, **guth fann** a weak/feeble voice, *Cf* **lag** *adj*

fannachadh, *gen* **fannachaidh** *nm* (*the act of*) weakening &c (*see senses of* **fannaich** *v*)

fannaich *vti, pres part* **a' fannachadh**, **1** weaken, make or become weak, feeble or faint, *Cf more usu* **lagaich**; **2** (*vi*) faint, *Cf* **fanntaig 2, laigse 2, neul 3**

fanntaig *vi, pres part* **a' fanntaigeadh**, faint, *Cf* **fannaich 2, laigse 2, neul 3**

faobhar, faobhair, faobharan *nm* an edge (*of blade, tool &c*), **faobhar gearraidh** a cutting edge

faobharachadh, *gen* **faobharachaidh** *nm* (*the act of*) sharpening (*see* **faobharaich** *v*)

faobharaich *vt, pres part* **a' faobharachadh**, sharpen, put an edge on (*blade, tool &c*), *Cf* **geuraich**

faochadh *see* **faothachadh**

faochag, faochaig, faochagan *nf* (*Sc*) a whelk, (*Eng*) a winkle, (*prov*) **is lom an cladach far an cunntar na faochagan** it's a bare beach on which the whelks can be counted

faod *vti def, no pres part,* **1** may, can, might (*ie be permitted, allowed to – for can physically see* **urrainn**), **am faod sinn falbh? faodaidh** may/ can we go? yes, **chan fhaodar smocadh** smoking not allowed, no smoking, **dh'fhaodadh e a bhith gu bheil beatha air Mars** it could/ might be that there is life on Mars, **faodaidh gu bheil e tinn** he may/might be ill, perhaps he's ill; **2** *past part* **faodte** *in adv & conj*

(is) ma(th) dh'fhaodte, *also* **is mathaid**, maybe, perhaps, possibly, **bidh là brèagha ann, ma dh'fhaodte** it'll be a fine day, perhaps, **ma dh'fhaodte nach cuir i** maybe it won't snow, *Cf* **dòcha 2** & **3**, & *less usu* **teagamh 2**

faoighe *nf invar* (*trad*) cadging, thigging, begging for gifts of food &c, *now in expr* **dèan faoighe** *v* beg

faoileag, faoileig, faoileagan *nf* a seagull

faoilidh *adj* **1** hospitable, generous, *Cf* **fial 1**; **2** frank (*in nature, speech* &c), *Cf* **fosgailte 3**

Faoilleach, *gen* **Faoillich** *nm*, *also* **Faoilteach**, *gen* **Faoiltich** *nm*, *with art* **am Faoilleach, am Faoilteach**, **1** (*trad*) the last two weeks of January and the first two weeks of February, approximately; **2** (*now*) January, **am ficheadamh là den Fhaoilteach** the 20th of January

faoin *adj* **1** silly, empty-headed, foolish, brainless, *Cf* **amaideach, baoth**; **2** vain, futile, **ionnsaighean faoin mhic-an-duine** the vain/futile endeavours of mankind, *Cf* **dìomhain 1**

faoineas, *gen* **faoineis** *nm* **1** silliness, foolishness, vacuity; **2** vanity, futility, *Cf* **dìomhanas**

faoinsgeul, *gen* & *pl* **faoinsgeòil** *nm* **1** a myth, a legend, *Cf* **fionnsgeul**

faoisid, faoiside, faoisidean *nf* confession, a confession, (*rel*) **dèan** *v* **faoisid** make confession, *Cf* **aideachadh 2**

faoisidich *vti, pres part* **a' faoisidich**, confess, *Cf* **dèan faoisid** (*see* **faoisid**)

faol, *gen* & *pl* **faoil** *nm* a wolf, *Cf* **madadh 3**

faotainn *see* **faigh** & **faighinn**

faothachadh & **faochadh**, *gen* **fao(tha)chaidh** *nm* **1** (*the act of*) alleviating &c (*see senses of* **faothaich** *v*); **2** relief, respite, alleviation (*of pain, suffering*), **thàinig faothachadh air** he experienced some respite, his suffering/pain lessened, *Cf* **furtachd**

faothaich *vti, pres part* **a' fao(tha)chadh**, alleviate, relieve, bring or experience relief or respite (*of pain, suffering*), *Cf* (*vi*) **furtaich**, (*vt*) **lasaich 2**

far *prep see* **bàrr 5**

far a *conj* where, *Note: used in non-interrogative contexts* (*Cf interrogative* **càite**); **gheibh thu e far na dh'fhàg thu e** you'll find it where you left it

faradh, faraidh, faraidhean *nm* (*transport* &c) **1** a fare; **2** a freight charge, carriage, haulage (*ie the charges*)

fàradh *see* **àradh**

far-ainm, *gen* **far-ainme**, *pl* **far-ainmean** & **far-ainmeannan** *nm* a nickname, *Cf* **frith-ainm**

faram, *gen* **faraim** *nm* loud noise, a loud noise (*of various kinds*), *Cf* **fuaim, gleadhraich, toirm**

faramach *adj* noisy, loud, *Cf* **fuaimneach**

farchluais, *gen* **farchluaise** *nf* eavesdropping

fàrdach, fàrdaich, fàrdaichean *nf* **1** a dwelling, a house, *Cf more usu* **taigh 1**; **2** a lodging, *Cf more usu* **lòistinn**

farmad, *gen* **farmaid** *nm* envy, **dèan/gabh** *v* **farmad ri cuideigin** feel envious of/envy someone, (*song*) **cha bhi agad eud no farmad ri luchd-cruit ged tha iad ainmeil** you will have no (need to feel) jealousy or envy towards crofter folk, though they are famous (*for being well-off!*)

farmadach *adj* envious

farpais *see* **co-fharpais**

farpaiseach, *gen & pl* **farpaisich** *nm* a competitor, an entrant, a participant (*in a competition*)

farranaich *vt, pres part* **a' farranachadh**, **1** tease, *Cf* **tarraing** *v* **6**; **2** vex

farsaing *adj* **1** wide, broad, *Cf* **leathann**; **2** *also in expr* **fad' is farsaing** *adv* far and wide, **sgaoil a cliù fad' is farsaing** her fame spread far and wide

farsaingeachd *nf invar* **1** breadth, width, *Cf* **leud**; **2** extent, area; **3** *in expr* **san fharsaingeachd** generally, in general, broadly speaking, by and large, on the whole, **san fharsaingeachd tha a' mhòr-chuid na aghaidh** generally speaking the majority are against it/him

farspag & arspag, *gen* **(f)arspaig**, *pl* **(f)arspagan** *nf* a great black-backed gull, **farspag bheag** a lesser black-backed gull

fàs *vi, pres part* **a' fàs**, **1** grow (*of crops &c*), **'s e eòrna a tha a' fàs ann an sheo** it's barley that's growing here; **2** grow (*ie increase in size*) **tha am balach a' fàs gu math luath** the boy's growing pretty quickly, *Cf* **cinn, meudaich**; **3** grow, become, **dh'fhàs iad sgìth dheth** they grew/became tired of it/him

fàs, *gen* **fàis** *nm* **1** (*the act of*) growing, becoming (*see* **fàs** *v*); **2** (*of crops &c, con & abstr*) growth, *Cf* **cinneas**

fàs *adj* **1** empty, *Cf* **falamh 1**; **2** waste, uncultivated, barren, **talamh fàs** waste ground *or* uncultivated ground

fàsach, fàsaich, fàsaichean *nmf* **1** a desert, **fàsaichean Afraga** the deserts of Africa; **2** a wilderness, a deserted place or area, (*song*) **Coille an Fhàsaich** the wood in (*lit* of) the wilderness/the deserted place; *Cf less usu* **dìthreabh**

fàsachadh, *gen* **fàsachaidh** *nm* **1** (*the act of*) emptying, depopulating &c (*see senses of* **fàsaich** *v*); **2** clearance, depopulation

fàsaich *vt, pres part* **a' fàsachadh**, **1** empty; **2** (*hist, esp with ref to the Highland Clearances*) depopulate, clear (*a district &c of people*)

fàsail *adj* desolate (*not used of people*), **tìr fhàsail** a desolate land

fasan, fasain, fasanan *nm* fashion, a fashion, **san fhasan, às an fhasan** in fashion, out of fashion, **fasan ùr** a new fashion

fasanta *adj* fashionable, modish, **seann-fhasanta** old-fashioned

fasdachadh, fasdaich, fasdaidhear *see* **fastachadh, fastaich, fastaidhear**

fasgach *adj* **1** sheltering, **coille fhasgach** a sheltering wood; **2** sheltered, **bad fasgach** a sheltered spot

fasgadh, fasgaidh, fasgaidhean *nm* shelter, a shelter, protection, **gabh** *v* **fasgadh on dìle** take shelter from the downpour, *Cf* **dìon** *n*

fàsgadh, *gen* **fàsgaidh** *nm* (*the act of*) compressing &c (*see senses of* **fàisg** *v*)

fasgain *vt, pres part* **a' fasgnadh**, winnow (*grain*)

fastachadh, fasdachadh *&* **fastadh**, *gen* **fastachaidh** *&* **fastaidh** *nm* (*the act of*) hiring &c (*see senses of* **fastaich** *v*)

fastaich, *also* **fasdaich** *&* **fastaidh**, *vt, pres part* **a' fastachadh** *&* **a' fastadh**, hire, employ, take on (*workers*)

fastaidhear *&* **fasdaidhear**, *gen* **fastaidheir**, *pl* **fastaidhearan** *nm* an employer

fàth *nm invar* **1** a cause, a reason, **fàth mo mhulaid** the cause of my sadness, **fàth magaidh** a cause/object of mockery, *Cf more usu* **adhbhar 1, cùis 4**; **2** an opportunity, **fàth airson spòrs** an opportunity for some fun, *Cf more usu* **cothrom 1**; **3** *in expr* **gabh** *v* **fàth air** take (unfair) advantage of, *Cf* **brath** *n* **2**

fathann, *gen & pl* **fathainn** *nm* a rumour, **bha fathann mun deidhinn a' dol timcheall** a rumour about them was going round/circulating, **sgeul no fathann cha robh air Murchadh** there was neither news nor rumour concerning Murdo, there was no trace of Murdo

feabhas, *gen* **feabhais** *nm* improvement, excellence, superiority, *esp in expr* **rach** *v* **am feabhas** improve, get better, **chaidh an t-euslainteach am feabhas** the invalid got better/recovered, **tha na seirbheisean ionadail a' dol am feabhas** the local services are improving

feachd, feachd, feachdan *nf* (*trad*) an army, a host, a force, **Feachd an Adhair** the Air Force, (*calque*) **feachd obrach/oibre** a work force, *Cf* **armailt** *& more usu* **arm**

fead, fead, feadan *nf* **1** a whistle (*the noise not the instrument*), **rinn mi fead** *or* **leig mi fead (asam)** I whistled (*ie a single whistle*); **2** *also for more continuous whistling*, **fead na gaoithe** the whistling of the wind

fead *vi, pres part* **a' feadail**, whistle, **bha am balach beag a' feadail** the wee boy was whistling

feadag, feadaige, feadagan *nf* **1** a whistle (*ie penny whistle, Irish flute &c*), **ghabh e port air an fheadaig** he played a tune on the whistle, *Cf* **fìdeag; 2** a plover

feadaireachd *nf invar, also* **feadalaich** *nf invar, &* **feadarsaich** *nf invar*, **1** whistling (*ie with mouth, usu continuous, Cf* **fead** *n*), **chuala sinn feadaireachd** we heard whistling; **2** (*the act or art of*) playing a whistle

feadan, feadain, feadanan *nm* **1** a bagpipe chanter; **2** *objects of tubular shape such as* a tube, a pipe (*Cf* **pìob 1**), a spout

feadh *see* **air feadh**

feadhainn, *gen* **feadhna** *nf* **1** some, some people, **tha feadhainn air a shon, tha feadhainn eile na aghaidh** some (people) are in favour, others are against, *Cf* **cuid 3; 2** *with art*, **tha an fheadhainn seo a' dol dhachaigh** these/these ones/this group are going home, (*also of objects*) **tha an fheadhainn a th' air an sgeilp briste** the ones that are on the shelf are broken

feagal *see* **eagal**

feàirrde *adj* (*trad*) better, made better, *now esp in expr* **is fheàirrde e** (*&c*) he (*&c*) is the better for, **b' fheàirrde sinn cuairt bheag** we'd be/we were the better for a wee stroll, a wee stroll would do us good/did us good, **'s fheàirrd' thu Guinness** you're better for a Guinness, Guinness is good for you, *Cf* **feum** *n* **4** *& opposite* **miste**

fealladh, feallaidh, feallaidhean *nm* (*sports & games*) a foul, foul play

fealla-dhà *nf invar* joking, a joke, a jest, **chan ann ri fealla-dhà a tha mi!** I'm not joking! **eadar fealla-dhà is da-rìribh** half in jest, half joking(ly), *Cf* **da-rìribh 1, fìor 4**

feall-fhalach, feall-fhalaich, feall-fhalaichean *nm* an ambush

feallsanach, *gen & pl* **feallsanaich** *nm* a philosopher

feallsanachd, feallsanachd, feallsanachdan *nf* **1** philosophy, a philosophy, **feallsanachd Aristotle** the philosophy of Aristotle; **2** the rationale or thinking behind something, (*ed*) **feallsanachd a' chùrsa** the course rationale

feamainn, *gen* **feamann** *&* **feamnach**, *nf* (*the generic name for*) sea-weed

feamainn *vt, pres part* **a' feamnadh**, manure (*with seaweed*), **a' feamnadh an fhearainn** manuring the land

feannag¹, feannaige, feannagan *nf* a crow, **feannag dhubh** a carrion crow, **feannag ghlas** a hooded crow, (*Sc*) a hoodie

feannag², feannaige, feannagan *nf* a rig or ridge of land (*for cultivation*), (*trad, hist*) a lazy bed

feanntag, feanntaige, feanntagan *nf*, & **deanntag, deanntaige, deanntagan** *nf*, a nettle

feansa, feansa, feansaichean *nmf* (*agric &c*) a fence, *Cf* **callaid 2**

fear, *gen & pl* **fir** *nm* **1** a man, **tha fear agus boireannach/tè a' tighinn** there's a man and a woman coming, **fear an taighe** the man of the house *or* the landlord (*of pub &c*) *or* the MC/compère (*at a ceilidh &c*), **thug fear Caimbeulach dhomh e** a Campbell/a man of the name of Campbell/some Campbell guy gave me it, *Cf* **duine** *which stresses male gender less, Cf also* **fireannach; 2** *in numerous compounds, corres to Eng* -man, -er, -ian *&c, eg* **fear-labhairt** a spokesman, **fear-siubhail** a traveller, **fear-ciùil** a musician, **fear-stiùiridh** a director, **fear-ealain** an artist, *Cf* **neach**; *Note: the pl of such nouns is usu* **luchd(-ciùil** &c) *see* **luchd**[2]; **3** *representing a m sing n*, one, **seo leabhraichean, gabh fear no dhà dhiubh** here are some books, take one or two of them, **cò am fear as fheàrr leat?** which one do you prefer? *Note: in this usage the pl can be supplied by* **an fheadhainn**, ones (*see* **feadhainn 2**); *Cf* **tè 1**

fearail *adj* manly, of manly character, **feartan/giùlan fearail** manly characteristics/conduct, *Cf* **duineil 1, tapaidh 2**

fearalachd *nf invar* manliness, *Cf* **duinealas 1**

fearann, *gen* **fearainn** *nm* ground, land, **àitich** *v* **am fearann** cultivate/till the land, **pìos fearainn** a piece of ground/land, *Cf* **talamh 3, tìr 4**

fearas-feise *see* **feis(e)**

fear-brèige, *gen & pl* **fir-bhrèige** *nm* a puppet

fearg, *gen* **feirge** *nf* anger, ire, wrath, **thàinig fearg oirre** she grew angry, **chuir i fearg air** she made him angry

feargach *adj* angry

feàrna *nf invar* alder

feàrr *adj* **1** (*trad*) better, best (*comp of* **math** *adj*); **2** *now usu with v* is, **am fear as** (*for* **a is**) **fheàrr** the best one/man, **tha A nas fheàrr na B** A is better than B, **'s e Ailean as fheàrr a bhitheas** Alan will be best, **mar a b' fheàrr a chaidh aige** as best he could, **b' fheàrr leam càise** I would prefer/rather have cheese; **3** *in expr* **b' fheàrr dhomh** (&c) ... I (&c) had better ..., **b' fheàrr dhut fuireach** you'd better stay, you'd be better staying, **b' fheàrr dhuibh a bhith a' falbh** you'd better be going

feart & **feairt,** *gen* **feirt,** *pl* **feartan** *nf* attention, heed, *esp in expr* **thoir** *v* **fea(i)rt air** pay attention to, heed, *Cf* **aire 2, for**

feart, fearta, feartan *nm* an inherent quality, an attribute, a characteristic, **gheibh sinn mòran fheartan bhor sinnsirean** we get many characteristics from our forebears/ancestors

feasgar, *gen* **feasgair**, *pl* **feasgaran** & **feasgraichean** *nm* **1** afternoon, evening, **feasgar an-dè** yesterday afternoon, **feasgar math!** good afternoon! *or* good evening! **air an fheasgar** in/during the afternoon/evening, **bidh sinn ann feasgar** we'll be there in the afternoon/evening; **2** (*with times*) pm, **seachd uairean feasgar** seven in the evening, seven pm

fèath, **fèatha**, **fèathan** *nmf* (*of weather*) calm, a calm, **thàinig fèath air a' bhàta** the boat was becalmed

fèichear, **fèicheir**, **fèichearan** *nm* a debtor

fèile & **èile**, *gen* **(f)èile**, *pl* **(f)èileachan** *nm*, *also* **(f)èileadh**, **(f)èilidh**, **(f)èileachan** *nm*, **1** a kilted plaid, (*trad*) **fèileadh** *or* **fèileadh-mòr** *the earlier form of this dress, stretching from the shoulder to the knee or calf;* **2** **fèileadh** *or* **fèileadh-beag** the kilt, *the later form of kilted plaid, either (trad) passing between the legs, or as the modern kilt,* (*song*) **èileadh beag os cionn mo ghlùin ann am pleataibh dlùth mun cuairt** a kilt above my knee in close enfolding pleats; *Cf* **breacan 1**

fèill, **fèille**, **fèill(t)ean** *nf* **1** (*trad*) a feast, a festival, **latha-fèille** a feast day, **An Fhèill Brìde** the Feast of St Bride/Bridget, Candlemas; **2** a fair (*trad often linked to a saint's day*), (*song*) **nam faicinn air an fhèill thu, an Glaschu no 'n Dùn Eideann** if I should see you at the fair, in Glasgow or in Edinburgh; **3** a market, a sale (*esp of livestock*), **fèill uan** a lamb sale, *Cf* **margadh 1**; **4** (*economics, business*) demand, a market, **am bi fèill air?** will there be a market/demand for it? *Cf* **margadh 2**; **5** a fair (*ie rides, amusements &c*)

fèin *reflexive pron* (*usu aspirated/lenited as* **fhèin**, *after* **mi** & **sinn** *usu becomes* **fhìn**) **1** *corres to Eng* -self, **am fear a thug buaidh air fhèin, thug e buaidh air nàmhaid** the man who has conquered himself has conquered an enemy, **chunnaic e e fhèin san sgàthan** he saw himself in the mirror, **bha i ga tiormachadh fhèin** she was drying herself, **thoir an aire ort fhèin** take care of yourself, **rinn Ealasaid fhèin a' chèic** Ealasaid herself made the cake, **air mo shon fhìn** ... for my part ..., as for myself ..., **'s math thu fhèin!** well done!, good for you! **leam fhìn** by myself, *Note: in direct address* **thu fhèin** & **sibh fhèin** *are more polite than* **thusa** & **sibhse**; **2** *emphasising identity*, **rinn mi fhìn e** I (*emph*) did it, **tha mi gu math, ciamar a tha thu fhèin?** I'm well, how are you (*emph*)/how's yourself? **nach aithnich thu mi? 's mi fhìn a th' ann!** don't you know me? It's me (*emph*)!, *Cf emph prons* **mise, thusa** &c; **3** own, **an taigh aige fhèin** his own house, **bhris e a chas fhèin** he broke his own leg; **4** even, **thàinig an t-eagal air Calum fhèin** even Calum grew afraid, **chaill mi am barrall fhèin às mo bhròig** I lost even the lace/I lost the very lace out of my shoe, *Cf* **eadhon, fiù** *n* **2**; **5** same, very (same), **sin an duine fhèin a chunna mi an-dè** there's the very (same) man

I saw yesterday, *Cf* **aon 3**, **ceart 3**, **ceudna 1**, **dearbh** *adj 1*; **6** *as emphasising element*, **bha an ceòl uabhasach fhèin math** the music was very good indeed/really excellent, **cianail fhèin fada** exceedingly long; **7** *as noun* **am fèin** the self, the ego, (*poem*) **Eadh is Fèin is Sàr-Fhèin** (Somhairle MacGill-Eain) Id and Ego and Super-Ego; **8** *in compound nouns & adjs, eg* **fèin-riaghladh** *m* self-government, **fèin-fhrithealadh** *m* self-service, **fèin-spèis** *f* self-love, self-importance, **fèin-mheas** *m* self-respect, **fèin-mholadh** *m* conceit (*lit* self-praise), **fèin-mhurt** *m* suicide, **fèin-fhoghainteach** *adj* self-sufficient, **fèin-chùiseach** *adj* selfish

fèin-eachdraidh, fèin-eachdraidhe, fèin-eachdraidhean *nf* autobiography, an autobiography

fèin-ghluaiseach *adj* (*machine &c*) automatic

fèinealachd *nf invar* selfishness

fèineil *adj* selfish, *Cf* **fèin-chùiseach** (*see* **fèin 8**)

fèis, *also* **fèisd** *&* **fèist**, *gen* **fèis(d)e**, *pl* **fèis(d)ean** *nf* **1** a festival, **fèis litreachais/chiùil** a literature/a music festival, *Cf* **mòd 2**; **2** a feast, a banquet, *Cf* **cuirm, fleadh**

feis(e), *gen* **feise** *nf* sex, sexual intercourse, **fearas-feise** homosexuality, *Cf* **cleamhnas 2**

feiste, feiste, feistean *nf* a tether

fèistear, fèisteir, fèistearan *nm* an entertainer

fèisteas, *gen* **fèisteis**, *nm* entertainment

feith *vi, pres part* **a' feitheamh**, **1** wait (**air** *&* **ri** for), **a' fèitheamh ris a' bhus** waiting for the bus, *Cf* **fan 1**; **2** stay, remain, *Cf more usu* **fuirich 1**

fèith, fèithe, fèithean *nf* **1** a muscle; **2** a sinew; **3** a vein, *Cf more usu* **cuisle 1**

fèith(e), fèithe, fèithean *nf* a bog, a marsh, *Cf* **bog** *n* **1**, **boglach**

fèitheach *adj* **1** muscular; **2** sinewy

feitheamh, *gen* **feithimh** *nm* (*the act of*) waiting &c (*see senses of* **feith** *v*)

feòil, *gen* **feòla(dh)** *nf* **1** meat, **feòil-caorach** *&* **muilt-fheòil** mutton, **feòil-muice** *&* **muic-fheòil** pork, **mairt-fheòil** beef; **2** flesh

feòladair, feòladair, feòladairean *nm* a butcher, *Cf less trad* **bùidsear 1**

feòlmhor *adj* **1** fleshy; **2** sensual, carnal, fleshly, *Cf* **collaidh 1**

feòlmhorachd *nf invar* sensuality

feòrag, feòraig, feòragan *nf* a squirrel

feòrachadh, *gen* **feòrachaidh** *nm* (*the act of*) asking

feòraich *vi, pres part* **a' feòrachadh**, ask, *Cf more usu* **faighnich**

feuch & **fiach**, *vti, pres part* **a' feuch(d)ainn**, **1** try, attempt, **feuchaidh mi ri/ris an doras fhosgladh** I'll try to open the door, **dh'fheuch iad ri ar togail** they attempted to lift us, **bi math! feuchaidh mi** be good! I'll try, **feuch deuchainn** attempt/take/sit an exam; **2** try, try out, test, **feuch an leann a tha seo** try/taste this beer, **feuch ris** give it a try, try it out, *Cf* **dearbh** *v* 2, **deuchainn** 2; **3** *as imperative*, try, see, **feuch gum bi sibh ann ron àm** see that you're/try to be there early, **feuchaibh a bheil am buntàta deiseil** see if the potatoes are done/ready, **fosgail an doras feuch a bheil an t-uisge ann fhathast** open the door to/and see if it's still raining (*Cf* **ach** 5); **4** (*trad*) **feuch!** behold!, lo!

feudail *see* **eudail**

feudar *n* **1** (*trad*) ability, possibility, *Cf* **urrainn** 1; **2** *now in expr* **'s fheudar dhomh** (*&c*) I (*&c*) must, **'s fheudar/b' fheudar dhi sgur** she has to/ had to stop, (*song*) **'s fheudar dhomh fhìn a bhith gabhail dhachaigh dìreach** I must be getting straight home, *Cf* **feum** *v* 1, **aig** 4

feum *vti defective, no pres part*, **1** must, have to, **feumaidh mi aideachadh gu** ... I have to/must admit that ..., **am feum sibh falbh?** must you/do you have to go? **feumaidh (e bhith) gu bheil stailc ann** there must be a strike, it must be that there's a strike, *Note: the past tense of this verb can be supplied by* **b' fheudar dhomh** (*&c*) I (*&c*) had to (*see* **feudar** 2); *Cf* **aig** 4; **2** (*vt*) need, **feumaidh e beagan sgioblachaidh fhathast** it needs a bit of tidying up yet, **feumaidh mi airgead!** I need money!, *Cf* **feum** *n* 2

feum, *gen* **feuma** & **fèim** *nm* **1** need, **is e feum bìdh a thug air a bhith a' goid** it's need of food that made him steal, *Cf* **dìth** 1; **2** *esp in expr* **tha feum agam** (*&c*) **air** ... I (&c) need ..., **tha feum aca air comhairle** they need advice *Cf* **feum** *v* 2; **3** use, good, **dè am feum a bhith a' bruidhinn?** what's the good/use of talking? (*Cf* **math** *n*), **chan eil feum anns an inneal seo** this machine's no good/ useless, **duine/obair gun fheum** a useless man/job, **cuir** *v* **gu feum** use, **dèan** *v* **feum de** use, utilise, make use of; **4** *in expr* **dèan** *v* **feum (do)** do good (to), *also* be useful (to), **nì na saor-làithean feum dhuibh** the holidays will do you good (*Cf* **feàirrde**), **dhèanadh siosar feum an-dràsta** scissors would be useful/come in handy just now (*Cf* **feumail** 1)

feumach *adj* **1** needy, in need, *Cf* **easbhaidheach** 1; **2** *in expr* **feumach air** in need of, **tha mi feumach air fois** I need some peace, **feumach air leasachadh** in need of improvement

feumail *adj* **1** useful, handy, **bhiodh siosar feumail an-dràsta** scissors would be useful/handy just now, **bha do chomhairle feumail dhomh** your advice was useful to me, *Cf* **feum** *n* 4; **2** needful, necessary, *Cf stronger* **deatamach**, **riatanach**

feur, *gen* **feòir** *nm* **1** grass; **2** hay

feurach *adj* grassy, covered with grass

feurach, *gen* **feuraich** *nm* grazing, pasture

feuraich *vt, pres part* **a' feurachadh**, graze, pasture, put (*cattle &c*) out to graze, (*song*) **sprèidh a-mach gam feurach(adh) madainn ghrianach chiùin** cattle out grazing/put out to graze on a mild sunny morning

feusag, feusaig, feusagan *nf* a beard

feusgan, *gen & pl* **feusgain** *nm* a mussel

fhad is a *conj see* **fad** *n* **4**

f(h)asa *see* **furasta**

fhathast *adv* **1** yet, **cha do sguir an t-uisge fhathast** the rain hasn't stopped yet, **a bheil a' bhracaist deiseil? chan eil fhathast** is breakfast ready? not yet, **nì sinn a' chùis air fhathast** we'll get the better of it/crack it yet; **2** still, **tha an t-uisge ann fhathast** it's still raining; **3** again, **chì mi fhathast sibh** I'll see you again, I'll be seeing you (*similar to* au-revoir), I'll see you later, **dèan fhathast e!** do it again!, *Cf* **a-rithist**

fheàrr *see* **feàrr**

fhèin, fhìn *see* **fèin**

fhuair *pt of irreg v* **faigh** *see tables p 409*

fiabhras, fiabhrais, fiabhrasan *nm* fever, a fever, **am fiabhras dearg/ buidhe** scarlet/yellow fever

fiacail(l), fiacla, fiaclan *nf* a tooth, **clàr-fhiacail** an incisor, **fiacail-chùil** a molar, **fiacail-forais & fiacail a' ghliocais** a wisdom tooth, **sgrùdadh** *m* **fhiacail** a dental check-up/examination, **fiacail sàibh** a tooth of a saw

fiach *vti see* **feuch**

fiach *adj* worth, worthwhile, of value, *usu in expr* **is/b' fhiach (do)** is/ was worth (to), **aon uair eile? chan fhiach e!** one more time? it's not worth it! **rud as fhiach fhaicinn** a thing worth seeing, **an fhiach seo dhut? chan fhiach** is this of value/worth anything to you? no, **airson na 's fhiach e** for what it's worth, **duine nach fhiach tromb gun teanga** a worthless/good for nothing man (*lit* not worth a jew's harp without a tongue)

fiach, fèich, fiachan *nm* **1** value, worth, **thoir dhomh fiach dà nota dheth** give me two pounds-worth of it, *Cf* **luach 1**; **2** debt, a debt, **dìoghail** *v* **fiach** repay a debt, (*Bibl*) **maith dhuinn ar fiachan** forgive us our debts, (*prov*) **cha tèid fiach air beul dùinte** a closed mouth doesn't run into debt; **3** *exprs with* **fiachaibh** (*obs dat pl*), (*formal*) **tha e mar fhiachaibh orm facal no dhà a ràdh** it is incumbent upon me to say a few words, **chuir iad mar fhiachaibh orm an dreuchd a ghabhail** they obliged me/made me feel obliged to accept the post, **tha mi fo fhiachaibh dhaibh** I'm indebted to them (*not nec financially, Cf* **comain 2**)

fiachaibh *see* **fiach** *n* 3

fiaclach *adj* **1** toothed; **2** toothy; **3** dental, *Cf* **deudach**

fiaclair(e), **fiaclaire**, **fiaclairean** *nm* a dentist, **ionad** *m* **fiaclaire** a dental surgery

fiadh, *gen & pl* **fèidh** *nm* a deer

fiadhaich *adj* **1** wild (*ie not domesticated*), **cat** *m* **fiadhaich** a wildcat, *Cf* **allaidh**; **2** (*fam*) angry, furious, **bha mi fiadhaich an dèidh na thuirt e rium** I was wild/furious after what he said to me; **3** (*fam*) wild (*ie given to uninhibited behaviour, heavy drinking &c*), **'s e duine fiadhaich a th' ann dheth, ceart gu leòr!** he's a wild man, right enough!

fial & **fialaidh** *adj* **1** generous, open-handed, hospitable, *Cf* **faoilidh** 1; **2** tolerant, easy-going, liberal

fiamh, *gen* **fiamha** *nm* **1** hue, tinge, tint, complexion, *Cf* **dreach** 2, **snuadh** 2, **tuar**; **2** fear, *Cf more usu* **eagal** 1; **3** a (*transient*) look, an expression (*on face, in eye*), **fiamh-ghàire**, *also* **fiamh a' ghàire**, a smile (*lit a look of laughter, Cf* **faite**, **snodha-gàire**), *Cf more permanent* **gnùis**

fianais, **fianais**, **fianaisean** *nf* **1** the act or fact of witnessing something; **2** evidence, witness, testimony, **fear-fianais** & **neach-fianais** *m* a witness (*at scene of crime, trial*), **thoir** *v* **fianais** give evidence, testify, *Cf* **dearbhadh** 2, **teisteanas** 1; **3** sight, **bha/thàinig e am fianais** he was/he came in sight, **à fianais** out of sight (*Cf* **fradharc** 2 & *more usu* **sealladh** 3), **bha sinn am fianais an eilein** we were in sight of the island; **4** (*trad*) presence, **nam fianais** in their presence, **a-mach às m' fhianais!** out of my presence/sight!, *Cf* **làthair** 1

fiar & **fiaraich** *vti, pres part* **a' fiaradh**, **1** bend, become or make curved, *Cf* **crom** *v* 3, **lùb** *v* 1; **2** slant

fiar *adj* **1** bent, crooked, *Cf* **cam**, **crom**, **lùbte**; **2** slanting, aslant, oblique, (*Sc*) squint, *Cf* **claon** *adj* 1; **3** (*of eyes*) squinting, having a squint, **seall** *v* **fiar** squint, **fiar-shùileach** *adj* squint-eyed; **4** wily, cunning, *Cf* **caon**, **carach** 1, **seòlta** 1

fiaradh, *gen* **fiaraidh** *nm* **1** (*the act of*) bending &c (*see senses of* **fiar** *v*); **2** a squint (*in eye*), *Cf* **claonadh** 4, **spleuchd** *n* 2; **3** a slant, **air fhiaradh** slanting, at a slant, at an angle, (*Sc*) squint

fichead, **fichid**, **ficheadan** *nm* twenty, a score, *takes the nom sing* (*radical*) *of the noun*, **fichead sgillinn/bliadhna** twenty pence/years, **dà fhichead** forty

ficheadamh *adj* twentieth

fìdeag, fìdeig, fìdeagan *nf* a whistle, (*song*) **cò (a) sheinneas an fhìdeag airgid?** who will sound the silver whistle?, *Cf* **feadag 1**

fidheall, *gen* **fìdhle,** *dat* **fidhill,** *pl* **fìdhlean** *nf* a fiddle, a violin, **port** *m* **air an fhidhill** a tune on the fiddle, **cuir** *v* **an ceòl air feadh na fìdhle** put the cat among the pigeons

fìdhlear, fìdhleir, fìdhlearan *nm* a fiddler, a violinist

fidir *vt, pres part* **a' fidreadh,** sympathise with, appreciate, comprehend, (*prov*) **chan fhidir an sàthach an seang** the well-fed don't sympathise with the hungry, (*song*) **chan fhidir thu idir mar tha mise led ghràdh** you don't appreciate at all the state I'm in through loving you

fìge *see* **fìogais**

figear, figeir, figearan *nm* (*arith &c*) a figure, a digit, a numeral, *Cf* **àireamh**

figearail *adj* (*IT &c*) digital, **gleoc/sealladh figearail** a digital clock/display

figh *vti, pres part* **a' fighe(adh),** 1 weave; 2 knit

fighe *nf invar* 1 weaving, **beart-fhighe** *f* a weaving loom; 2 knitting, **bior-fighe** *m* a knitting needle

figheachan, *gen & pl* **figheachain** *nm* a pigtail, a pony-tail (*on head*)

figheadair, figheadair, figheadaran *nm* 1 a weaver, *Cf* **breabadair 2**; 2 a knitter

fighte *adj* 1 woven; 2 knitted

fileanta *adj* 1 eloquent, articulate, good at expressing oneself; 2 (*now esp*) good at speaking a language, fluent, **tha i fileanta sa Ghàidhlig** she's fluent in Gaelic/speaks Gaelic fluently

fileantach, *gen & pl* **fileantaich** *nm* 1 someone fluent in a language; 2 (*esp*) a native speaker, **clas nam fileantach** the native speakers' class

filidh, filidh, filidhean *nm* 1 (*trad*) a poet, *Cf* **bàrd**; 2 **filidh aig Sabhal Mòr Ostaig** writer-in-residence at Sabhal Mòr Ostaig

fill *vt, pres part* **a' filleadh,** 1 (*paper*) fold; 2 (*cloth*) fold, pleat; 3 (*hair &c*) braid, plait; 4 (*material, parcel &c*) wrap (up), roll (up), *Cf more usu* **paisg**

filleadh, *gen* **fillidh,** *pl* **filltean** & **filleachan** *nm* 1 (*the act of*) folding, pleating, plaiting; 2 a fold, a pleat, a plait

fillte *adj* 1 folded, pleated, plaited; 2 *in compounds eg* **trì-fillte** *adj* folded three times, threefold, triple, three-ply, **iomadh-fhillte** *adj* complex, complicated, manifold

film, film, filmichean *nm* (*cinema, TV &c*) film, a film

fine, fine, fineachan *nf* **1** a tribe; **2** *esp* a (Highland) clan, *(song)* **òran nam fineachan a fhuair am fearann air ais** the song of the clans who got their land back, *Cf* **cinneadh 1, clann 2**

fiodh, *gen* **fiodha** *nm* wood, timber, **pìos fiodha** a piece of wood, **taigh fiodha** a wooden house, *Cf* **maide 1** *which is usu wood when shaped, fashioned &c*

fiodhrach, *gen* **fiodhraich,** *nm* timber, wood (*not shaped, finished &c*)

fìogais, fìogais, fìogaisean *nf, also* **fìge, fìge, fìgean** *nf,* a fig, **crann** *m* **fìogais** a fig-tree, *(song)* **gur mìlse na fìogais a pòg** sweeter than a fig is her kiss

fiolan, fiolain, fiolanan *nm, also* **fiolan-gobhlach, fiolain-ghobhlaich, fiolanan-gobhlach** *nm,* an earwig, *Cf* **gobhlag 2**

fìon, *gen* **fìona** *nm* wine, **crann-fìona** *m* a vine, **fìon-dhearc** *f* a grape, **fìon-geur** *m* vinegar

fionn *adj* (*trad*) white, *often in placenames as* Fin-, *Cf* **bàn**² **1, geal** *adj*

fionnach *adj* hairy, rough, shaggy, *Cf* **molach, ròmach 1**

fionnadh, *gen* **fionnaidh** *nm coll* hair (*of animal*)

fionnan, *gen* **fionnain,** *pl* **fionnain** & **fionnanan** *nm* a vine, *Cf* **crann-fìona** (*see* **fìon**)

fionnan-feòir, *gen* & *pl* **fionnain-fheòir** *nm* a grasshopper

fionnar *adj* **1** (*weather*) cool, fresh, **2** (*welcome, attitude &c*) cool, cold, off-hand, **fhreagair i gu fionnar** she answered coolly/coldly

fionnarachadh, *gen* **fionnarachaidh** *nm* **1** (*the act of*) cooling &c (*see senses of* **fionnaraich** *v*); **2** refrigeration

fionnaraich *vti, pres part* **a' fionnarachadh,** cool, refrigerate, make or become cool

fionnsgeul, *gen* & *pl* **fionnsgeòil** *nm* a legend, a myth, *Cf* **faoinsgeul 2**

fìor *adj* **1** true, **tha am fathann/an sgeul fìor** the rumour/story is true; **2** true, real, genuine (*precedes the noun*), **'s e fìor Albannach a th' ann** he's a real/true Scot, **fìor òr** real gold; **3** *emphasising,* **bha am biadh fìor mhath** the food was very/truly/really good, **am Fìor Urramach Uilleam Caimbeul** the Very/Right Reverend William Campbell, *Cf* **garbh 4, glè, uabhasach 2; 4** *in expr* **mas fhìor** kidding, pretending, **thuirt mi gun robh mi gu bhith ann am film ach cha robh mi ach mas fhìor** I said I was to be in a film but I was only kidding

fìoreun, *gen* & *pl* **fìoreòin** *nm* (*trad*) an eagle, *Cf usu* **iolaire**

fios, *gen* **fiosa** *nm* **1** knowledge, **chan eil fios càit a bheil e** no-one knows/it's not known where he is, **gun fhios do Mhàiri** without Mary's knowledge, unknown to Mary; **2** *esp in expr* **tha fios agam (&c)** I (*&c*) know (*of facts, information*), *often aspirated/lenited eg* **chan**

eil fhios agam I don't know (it *understood*), *lit* I do not have its knowledge, **air na bha a dh'fhios aca** as far as they knew, **cha robh mi air fhaicinn bho nach b' fhios cuin** I hadn't seen him since Heaven knows when; **3** information, word, a message, news, (*song*) **thoir am fios seo thun a' bhàird** give this information/message to the poet, tell the poet this, **cuir fios orra** send (word) for them, **chuir sinn fios thuige** we sent him word/let him know; **4** *in expr* **tha fios** obviously, of course, naturally, **bidh sin saor 's an asgaidh, tha fios** that will be free of charge, of course/naturally, **a bheil thu toilichte? tha fios gu bheil!** are you pleased? of course I am!; **5** *in expr* **gun fhios nach** *conj* lest, in case, **chuir e pìos na phoca gun fhios nach tigeadh an t-acras air** he put a piece in his pocket in case he should grow hungry, *Cf* **eagal 2, mus 2**

fiosaiche, fiosaiche, fiosaichean *nm* **1** (*trad*) a prophet, a soothsayer, a seer, *Cf* **fàidh; 2** a fortune teller

fiosrach *adj* (well-)informed, knowledgeable (**air** about), *Cf* **eòlach 1**

fiosrachadh, fiosrachaidh, fiosrachaidhean *nm* information (*coll*), a piece of information, **bu toigh leam fiosrachadh fhaighinn air a' chompanaidh** I'd like to receive information about the company/firm, (*IT*) **teicneolas** *m* **fiosrachaidh** information technology

fir-chlis *see* **clis**

fireann *adj* masculine, male, **cat fireann** a male cat, a tomcat, (*gram*) **facal/ainmear fireann** a masculine word/noun, *Cf* **fireannta**

fireann-boireann *adj* androgynous, hermaphrodite

fireannach, *gen & pl* **fireannaich** *nm* a man, a male, **fireannaich air an làimh dheis is boireannaich air an làimh chli, mas e ur toil e!** men on the right and women on the left, please!, *Cf* **fear 1**

fireannta *adj* (*of living things*) masculine, of the male gender, *Cf* **fireann**

fìrinn, fìrinne, fìrinnean *nf* truth, **'s e an fhìrinn a th' aige** he's telling the truth, **leis an fhìrinn innse, chan eil fhios 'am** to tell the truth, I don't know, (*of devout person*) **tha e/i làn den Fhìrinn** he/she is full of the (*scriptural*) Truth

fìrinneach *adj* **1** (*of person*) truthful; **2** true (*ie factual*)

fitheach, *gen & pl* **fithich** *nm* a raven

fiù *adj corres to Eng* worth, *takes v* **is**, **chan fhiù e deich sgillin** it's not worth 10p, **chan fhiù i a màthair** she's not worth/the equal of her mother, she's not the woman her mother was

fiù *nm invar* **1** worth, value, **sgrìobhaidhean gun fhiù** worthless writings, *Cf* **luach 1; 2** *in expr* **fiù agus/is** even, as much as, **cha robh fiù is pìos arain air fhàgail** there wasn't even/as much as a piece of bread left (*Cf* **uiread 3**), **cha do rinn iad fiù agus sùil a**

thoirt oirnn they didn't even/didn't so much as look at us, *Cf* **eadhon**

fiùdalach *adj* feudal

flaitheas, *gen* **flaitheis** *nm* heaven, paradise, *Cf* **nèamh 1**, **Pàrras**

flanainn, flanainne, flanainnean *nf* 1 flannel; 2 a (face &c) flannel

flat, flat, flataichean *nm* a saucer, (*Sc*) a flat, *Cf* **sàsar**

flath, *gen* **flaith**, *pl* **flathan** & **flaithean**, *nm* 1 (*trad*) a king, prince or ruler; 2 a noble, *Cf* **uasal** *n* 1

flathail *adj* 1 princely; 2 noble, *Cf* **uasal** *adj* 1

fleadh, fleadha, fleadhan *nm* a feast, a banquet, *Cf* **cuirm**, **fèis 2**

fleasgach, *gen* & *pl* **fleasgaich** *nm* 1 (*trad*) a young man, a youth, a stripling, *Cf* **òganach**; 2 (*now usu*) a bachelor, **seann fhleasgaich** old bachelors

fleisg, fleisge, fleisgean *nf* (*elec*) flex, a flex

fleòdradh, *gen* **fleòdraidh** *nm* the act of floating, buoyancy, *esp in expr* **(tha am ball &c) air fleòdradh** (the ball &c is) floating, *Cf* **bog** *n* 2, **flod**

flin, flinne *nm invar* sleet

fliuch *adj* wet, **tha mi bog fliuch** I'm wet through/soaking wet, (*of weather*) **tha i fliuch, fliuch!** it's gey wet!

fliuch *vt, pres part* **a' fliuch(d)adh**, wet, make wet, **chuir an t-uisge thairis, a' fliuchadh a h-uile càil** the water overflowed, wetting everything, **chaidh a fhliuchdadh chun na seiche** he got soaked to the skin, (*fam*) **fliuch do ribheid!** wet your whistle!

fliuch(d)adh, *gen* **fliuch(d)aidh** *nm* (*the act of*) wetting (*see* **fliuch** *v*)

flod, *gen* **floda** *nm* the state of being afloat, **air flod** afloat, floating, **cuir** *v* **air flod** float, launch, *Cf* **bog** *n* 2, **fleòdradh**

flùr[1], **flùir, flùraichean** *nm* a flower, *Cf less usu* **blàth** *n* 2, **dìthean**

flùr[2], *gen* **flùir** *nm* flour, *Cf* **min** *n* 2

flùranach *adj* flowery, covered in flowers

fo *prep, aspirates/lenites following noun* & *takes the dat, Note: the pers prons* **mi, thu, e** &c *combine with* **fo** *to form the prep prons* **fodham(sa), fodhad(sa), fodha(san), foidhpe(se)** *or* **foipe(se), fodhainn(e), fodhaibh(se), fòdhpa(san)** *or* **fòpa(san)** under/beneath me, you &c; 1 under, beneath, below, **fon uachdar** below the surface, **fo chraoibh** under a tree, **chaidh am bàta fodha** the boat went under/sank, (*fig*) **chaidh a' chompanaidh fodha** the company failed/folded, **fo smachd** under control; 2 *in compounds, corres to Eng* sub-, under-, infra-, *eg* **fo-aodach** *m* underwear, underclothes, **fo-chomataidh** *f* a sub-committee, **fo-thiotalan** *mpl* subtitles, **fo-mhothachail** *adj* subconscious, **fo-dhearg** *adj* infra-red; 3 influenced *or* affected by, suffering from (*emotions, situations &c*), **fo eagal** afraid, **fo mhulad** sad, afflicted with sadness, **fo chomain** under/ having an obligation

fòd *see* **fòid**

fodar, *gen* **fodair** *nm* fodder

fodha, fodhad, fodhaibh, fodhainn, fodham, fòdhpa *prep prons see* **fo** *prep*

fògair *vt, pres part* **a' fògradh** *&* **a' fògairt**, (*mainly trad & hist, referring to the Highland Clearances*) banish, exile, expel, drive out, **dh'fhògradh an sluagh às a' ghleann** the people were driven/ banished from the glen, **chaidh am fògradh** they were exiled/ expelled, *Cf* **fuadaich 2**

fògairt *see* **fògradh**

fògarrach *see* **fògrach**

foghain *vi, pres part* **a' fòghnadh**, suffice, be enough, do, **am foghain sin?** will that be enough/do? (*saying*) **fòghnaidh na dh'fhòghnas** enough is enough, enough is as good as a feast, (*to children &c*) **fòghnaidh siud!** that's enough!, that will do! **chan fhòghnadh leis gun mise dhol còmhla ris** he wouldn't be satisfied unless/until I went with him

foghar, foghair, fogharan *nm* **1** (*trad*) harvest, harvest time, **foghar an eòrna** the barley harvest, *Cf* **buain** *n*; **2** autumn, fall, (*novel title*) **Deireadh an Fhoghair** (Tormod Caimbeul) The End of Autumn, **as t-fhoghar** in autumn

foghlaim *vt, pres part* **a' foghlam**, educate, *Cf* **teagaisg 2**

foghlaimte *adj* educated, learned, *Cf* **ionnsaichte**

foghlam, *gen* **foghlaim** *nm* **1** (*the act of*) educating; **2** education, learning, scholarship, **foghlam fo-sgoile** pre-school/nursery education, **foghlam inbhidh** adult education, **foghlam tro meadhan na Gàidhlig** Gaelic-medium education, **roinn an fhoghlaim** the education department, *Cf* **ionnsachadh 2, oideachas 1**

fòghnadh, *gen* **fòghnaidh** *nm* sufficiency, a sufficiency, enough, *Cf more usu* **leòr 1**

fòghnan, fòghnain, fòghnanan *nm* a thistle, (*song*) **Fòghnan na h-Alba** the Thistle of Scotland, *Cf* **cluaran**

fògrach *&* **fògarrach**, *gen & pl* **fòg(ar)raich**, *nm* **1** an exile, a fugitive, a refugee; **2** *esp with reference to Highland Clearances*, someone cleared from his/her home district, *Cf* **eilthireach 2, fuadan 2**

fògradh, *gen* **fògraidh** *nm, also* **fògairt** *nm invar*, **1** (*the act of*) banishing &c (*see senses of* **fògair** *v*); **2** exile, banishment, *Cf* **fuadan 2**

fòid *&* **fòd**, *gen* **fòide**, *pl* **fòidean** *nf* **1** turf, a turf, a sod, (*trad*) **an uair a bhios mi fon fhòid** when I'm beneath the sod/in my grave, *Cf* **fàl**

2, ploc 1; 2 a clod *or* clump of earth, *Cf* **ploc**; **3** a (single) peat (*occas m in this sense*), (*song*) **gun solas lainnteir (= lanntair) ach ceann an fhòid** (Màiri Mhòr) with the (burning) end of the peat as my only lamp light, *Cf* **fàd**

foidhpe *prep pron see* **fo** *prep*

foighidinn, *gen* **foighidinne** *nf* patience, **mì-fhoighidinn** impatience

foighidneach *adj* patient, **mì-fhoighidneach** impatient

foileag, foileig, foileagan *nf* a pancake

foill, *gen* **foille** *nf* **1** deceit, *Cf* **cealg, mealladh 2; 2** cheating, **tha iad ri foill!** they're cheating! **fear-foille** *m* a cheat, **rinn thu foill orm** you cheated me; **3** fraud, deception, **a' faighinn bathair le foill** obtaining goods fraudulently

foilleil *adj* **1** deceitful; **2** fraudulent

foillseachadh, *gen* **foillseachaidh** *nm* **1** (*the act of*) publishing, revealing *&c* (*see senses of* **foillsich** *v*); **2** publication; **3** revelation, disclosure

foillsear, foillseir, foillsearan *nm* (*IT*) a monitor

foillsich *vt, pres part* **a' foillseachadh 1** publish, bring out (*books &c*), *Cf* **cuir an clò** (*see* **clò² 1**); **2** reveal, disclose (*facts &c*)

foillsichear, foillsicheir, foillsichearan *nm* a publisher

foinne, foinne, foinnean *nm* a wart

foi(dh)pe *prep pron see* **fo** *prep*

foirfe *adj* perfect (*usu morally, Cf* **coileanta 2**), **duine foirfe** a man without fault, *also* a full-grown man (*Cf* **dèanta**)

foirfeach, *gen & pl* **foirfich** *nm* an elder (*of church*), *Cf less trad* **èildear**

foirmeil *adj* formal, **tha mi a' cur fios thugaibh gu foirmeil gu ...** I am informing you formally that ..., **cainnt fhoirmeil** formal language/ speech

fòirneart, *gen* **fòirneirt** *nm* violence, oppression, force, **fear-fòirneirt** an oppressor, *Cf* **ainneart**

fois, *gen* **foise** *nf* **1** rest, peace (*ie tranquility*), (*story collection*) **Gun Fhois** (Eilidh Watt) Without Peace/rest, (*esp of dead*) **tha iad aig fois a-nise** they are at peace/rest now, *Cf* **sìth** *n* **2; 2** rest, leisure, relaxation, ease, **gabh** *v* **fois** have a rest, take a break, *Cf* **tàmh 3**

fo-lèine, fo-lèine, fo-lèintean *nf* a vest

follais *nf invar* evidentness, obviousness, clarity, openness, *esp in exprs* **am follais** *adv* obvious, clear, evident, **thoir** *v* **am follais** bring into the open, bring to light, expose, **thig** *v* **am follais** come to light, become apparent

follaiseach *adj* 1 evident, obvious, clear, apparent, **tha e follaiseach nach eil e ciontach** it's obvious he's not guilty, *Cf* **soilleir 2**; 2 public (*esp of knowledge, information &c*), **rannsachadh follaiseach** a public enquiry, **coinneamh fhollaiseach** a public meeting, *Cf* **fosgailte 2**

fòn, fòn, fònaichean *nmf* 1 a phone, a telephone, **bha mi a' bruidhinn ris air a' fòn** I was talking to him on the phone, **dè an àireamh-a'-fòn agad?** what's your phone number?; 2 a phone call, *in expr* **chuir e fòn thuice** he phoned her, he gave her a call

fòn *vi, pres part* **a' fònadh**, *also* **fònaig** *vi, pres part* **a' fònaigeadh**, phone, telephone, **dh'fhòn e thuice** he phoned her

fonn, *gen & pl* **fuinn** *nm* 1 a tune, an air, a melody, **air fonn 'Fill-ò-ro'** (*words to be sung*) to the tune of 'Fill-ò-ro', (*song*) **togaidh sinn fonn air eilean beag donn a' chuain** we will raise a tune to the little brown island of the ocean (*Lewis*), *Cf* **port**[1]; 2 a mood, frame of mind, *esp in expr* (*fam*) **dè am fonn?** how are you?, how are you doing?, *Cf* **dòigh 4, gean, gleus**

fonnmhor *adj* tuneful, melodious, *Cf* **ceòlmhor**

fòpa *prep pron see* **fo** *prep*

for *nm invar* attention, notice, heed, concern, **gun for a thoirt air** without paying attention/heed to it, **gun for aige ach air a ghnothaichean fhèin** with concern for nothing but his own affairs, *Cf* **aire 2, feart** *nf*

fo-rathad, fo-rathaid, fo-rathaidean *nm* an underpass, a subway

forc(a), *gen* **forca,** *pl* **forcan & forcaichean** *nf* a (*table*) fork, **forc agus sgian** a fork and a knife, *Cf* **greimire 1**

fòrladh, *gen* **fòrlaidh** *nm* (*army &c*) furlough, leave

forsair, forsair, forsairean *nm* a forester, a forestry worker

fortan, *gen* **fortain** *nm* fortune, luck, **fortan leat!** good luck! **deagh/droch fhortan** good/bad luck, (*song*) **Cuibhle an Fhortain** The Wheel of Fortune, *Cf* **àgh 2, dàn**[1] **1, sealbh 1**

fortanach *adj* lucky, fortunate, *Cf* **sealbhach 1** *& less usu* **buidhe 2**

for-thalla, for-thalla, for-thallachan *nm* a foyer (*of public building*)

fosgail *vti, pres part* **a' fosgladh**, open, **fosgail an doras!** open the door! **dh'fhosgail an doras** the door opened, **tha a' bhùth a' fosgladh** the shop's opening

fosgailte *adj* 1 open, opened, **uinneag fhosgailte** an open window, **tha a' bhùth/a' choinneamh fosgailte** the shop/meeting is open; 2 public, **coinneamh fhosgailte** a public/an open meeting, *Cf* **follaiseach 2**; 3 (*character &c*) open, frank, *Cf* **faoilidh 2**

fosgladh *gen* **fosglaidh** *nm* 1 (*the act of*) opening; 2 an opening, a gap, an aperture, *Cf* **beàrn**; 3 an opening, a chance, an opportunity, *Cf* **cothrom 1**

fosglair, fosglair, fosglairean *nm* (*tins, bottles &c*) an opener

fo-sgrìobhadh, fo-sgrìobhaidh, fo-sgrìobhaidhean *nm* **1** a postscript, a PS; **2** (*magazine &c*) a subscription

fo-shlighe, fo-shlighe, fo-shlighean *nf same as* **fo-rathad**

fradharc *&* **radharc**, *gen* **(f)radhairc** *nm* **1** eyesight, vision, *Cf* **lèirsinn 1**; **2** sight, view, **san (fh)radharc** in sight/view, **às an (fh)radharc** out of sight/view, *Cf* **fianais 3, sealladh 3**

Fraingis *nf, with the art,* (*lang*) **an Fhraingis** French

Frangach, *gen & pl* **Frangaich** *nm* a Frenchman, a French person, *also as adj,* **Frangach** French

fraoch, *gen* **fraoich** *nm* heather, heath, ling (*ie the plants*), **coileach-fraoich** *m* a heather-cock, a (male) grouse

fraoidhneas, fraoidhneis, fraoidhneasan *nm* a fringe (*on material, hair &c*)

fras, froise, frasan *nf* **1** a shower (*of rain, sleet, snow*), **bogha-frois** *m* a rainbow, *Cf* **meall** *n* **3**; **2** (*coll*) seed, *Cf more usu* **sìol 1**

fras *vi, pres part* **a' frasadh**, rain lightly, shower

frasair, frasair, frasairean *nm* a (*bathroom*) shower

freagair *vti, pres part* **a' freagairt**, **1** answer, reply, **nach freagair thu mi?** won't you answer me? **cha do fhreagair e fhathast** he hasn't replied yet; **2** suit, **chan eil an ad sin a' freagairt ort!** that hat doesn't suit you! **cha fhreagair dhomh a bhith nam thàmh** it doesn't suit me to be unoccupied/idle, **a bheil an obair a' freagairt dhut?** is the job suiting you?, *Cf* **thig 4**; **3** match, correspond to, (*prov*) **freagraidh a' bhriogais don mhàs** the breeks will match the backside

freagairt, freagairt, freagairtean *nf* **1** (*the act of*) answering &c (*see senses of* **freagair** *v*); **2** an answer, a reply, **cha d'fhuair mi freagairt** I didn't get/haven't got a reply, **bheir sinn freagairt dhaibh a dh'aithghearr** we'll reply to you/give you an answer soon

freagarrach *adj* suitable, appropriate, fitting, **cha robh an taigh freagarrach dha** the house wasn't suitable for him, **àite freagarrach airson snàimh** a place suitable for swimming/a swim

frèam, frèama, frèamaichean *nm* a frame, a framework, *Cf* **cèis 1**

freasdail *&* **freastail**, *vti, pres part* **a' freasdal**, attend, serve, wait on (*someone*), **freasdail don bhòrd** wait/serve at table, *Cf* **fritheil**

freasdal *&* **freastal**, *gen* **freasdail** *nm* **1** (*the act of*) attending, serving, waiting (*on someone*); **2** service, attendance, *Cf* **frithealadh 1**; **3** providence, *Cf* **sealbh 2**

freiceadan, freiceadain, freiceadanan *nm* a watch, a guard (*sing & coll*), **freiceadan-oirthire** a coast guard, **Am Freiceadan Dubh** The Black Watch, **freiceadan cloinne** a babysitter, a child minder, *Cf* **faire 2**

freumh, **freumha**, **freumh(aiche)an** *nm* a root, **freumh craoibh** a tree root, **thug e na h-eileanan air, an tòir air a fhreumhaichean** he went off to the islands, in search of his roots

frìde, **frìde**, **frìdean** *nf*, *also* **meanbh-fhrìde** *nf*, an insect

frids, **frids**, **fridsichean** *nm* a fridge, a refrigerator, *Cf less usu* **fuaradair**

frighig *vt*, *pres part* **a' frighigeadh**, fry, *Cf* **ròist 2**

frioghan, *gen & pl* **frioghain** *nm* a bristle (*esp on body of animals*), *Cf* **calg 2**

frionasach *adj* 1 worried, upset, fretful; 2 irritable, touchy, *Cf* **frithearra**; 3 (*situations &c*) vexing, annoying, niggling, irritating, upsetting, **bidh iad a' cur cheistean frionasach orm gun sgur** they're constantly asking me niggling questions

frìth, **frìthe**, **frìthean** *nf* 1 (*trad*) a deer forest, (*placename*) **Achadh na Frìthe** Achnafrie, the field of the deer forest; 2 moor, moorland, *Cf more usu* **mòinteach**, **sliabh 1**

frith-ainm, *gen* **frith-ainme**, *pl* **frith-ainmean** & **frith-ainneannan** *nm* a nickname, *Cf* **far-ainm**

frithealadh, *gen* **frithealaidh** *nm* 1 (*the act of*) serving, attending; waiting (*at table &c*), service, attendance (*on someone*), **luchd-frithealaidh** *m coll* attendants, **gille-frithealaidh** *m* a waiter, **caileag-fhrithealaidh** *f* a waitress, *Cf* **freasdal 1**; 2 attendance (*at an event &c*)

frithearra *adj* touchy, peevish, *Cf* **frionasach 2**

fritheil *vti*, *pres part* **a' frithealadh**, serve, wait on, attend, *Cf* **freasdail**

frith-rathad, **frith-rathaid**, **frith-rathaidean** *nm* a path, a footpath, a track

froca & **froga**, *gen* **froca**, *pl* **frocaichean** *nm* a frock

fuachd, **fuachd**, **fuachdan** *nmf* 1 cold, coldness, **chan fhuiling mi fuachd a' gheamhraidh** I can't stand/bear the cold of winter; 2 *with art*, **am fuachd** a cold, (*Sc*) the cold, **tha am fuachd aice** she's got a/the cold, *Cf* **cnatan**

fuadachadh, *gen* **fuadachaidh** *nm*, *also* **fuadach**, **fuadaich**, **fuadaichean** *nm*, banishing, banishment, clearance, driving or being driven away (*esp in relation to the Highland Clearances*), (*song*) **òigridh ghuanach tha nis air fuadach** happy-go-lucky young folk who are now banished/driven away, (*hist*) **na Fuadaichean** the (Highland) Clearances, *Cf* **fògradh 2**, **fuadan 2**

fuadaich *vt*, *pres part* **a' fuadachadh** & **a' fuadach**, 1 chase, chase away, **dh'fhuadaich an cù an sionnach** the dog chased away the fox; 2 *esp in relation to the Highland Clearances*, clear, banish, drive away, *Cf* **fògair**

fuadain *adj* false, artificial, synthetic, **fiaclan fuadain** false teeth, dentures, *Cf* **brèige** *adj* 2

fuadan, *gen* **fuaidain** *nm* 1 wandering, **air fhuadan** *adv* wandering, astray, *Cf* **allaban, seachran** 1; 2 exile, **fear-fuadain** *m* an exile, (*song*) **is cianail dùsgadh an fhir-fhuadain, 's e sìor-ionndrain tìr a bhruadair** sad is the waking of the exile forever longing for the land he sees in his dream, **cù fuadain** a stray dog, *Cf* **fògradh** 2

fuaigh & **fuaigheil** *vti, pres part* **a' fuaigheal**, sew, stitch, seam

fuaigheal, *gen* **fuaigheil**, *nm* 1 (*the act of*) sewing, stitching, seaming; 2 a piece of sewing; 3 a seam

fuaighte *adj* 1 sewn, stitched; 2 connected

fuaim, fuaime, fuaimean *nmf* (*the general word for*) noise, sound

fuaimeadair, fuaimeadair, fuaimeadairean *nm* a megaphone

fuaimneach *adj* noisy, *Cf* **faramach**

fuaimnich *vt, pres part* **a' fuaimneachadh**, (*lang*) pronounce

fuaimneachadh, *gen* **fuaimneachaidh** (*lang*) pronunciation, a pronunciation

fuaimreag, fuaimreig, fuaimreagan *nf* a vowel, *Cf* **connrag, consan**

fual, *gen* **fuail** *nm* urine, *Cf* **mùn**

fuamhaire *see* **famhair**

fuar *adj* 1 (*phys*) cold, **là fuar** a cold day, **tha am brochan a' fàs fuar!** the porridge is getting cold!; 2 (*emotionally &c*) cold, impersonal, unfeeling, **bodach fuar** a cold chiel, **is i fàilte fhuar a gheibh thu an sin!** it's a cold welcome you'll get there!; *Cf* **fionnar** 2, **fuaraidh, leth-fhuar**

fuarachadh, *gen* **fuarachaidh** *nm* (*the act of*) cooling &c (*see senses of* **fuaraich** *v*)

fuaradair, fuaradair, fuaradairean *nm* a refrigerator, a fridge, *Cf more usu* **frids**

fuaraich *vti, pres part* **a' fuarachadh**, cool, chill, make or become cold or colder, *Cf* **meilich**

fuaraidh *adj* (*lit & fig*) cool, chill, chilly, *Cf* **fionnar, leth-fhuar**

fuaran, *gen* **fuarain**, *pl* **fuarain** & **fuaranan** *nm* a spring, a well (*usu in its natural state*), *Cf* **tobar** 1 & 2

fuasgail *vt, pres part* **a' fuasgladh**, 1 release, set free, liberate, *Cf* **saor** *v* 1, **sgaoil** *v* 2, **sgaoil** *n*; 2 untie, loosen, undo, disentangle, **fuasgail snaidhm/barrall** untie a knot/a shoelace, *Cf* **lasaich** 1; 3 solve, resolve, **fuasgail tòimhseachan-tarsainn** solve a crossword

fuasgladh, *gen* **fuasglaidh** *nm* 1 (*the act of*) releasing, loosening, solving &c (*see senses of* **fuasgail** *v*); 2 a solution, a resolution (*to problem &c*), **ceist gun fhuasgladh** an unsolved/unresolved problem

fuath, fuatha, fuathan *nf* hate, hatred, loathing, *Cf* **gràin 1**

fuathach *adj* hateful, loathsome, detestable, *Cf* **gràineil 1**

fuathachadh, *gen* **fuathachaidh** *nm* (*the act of*) hating, loathing, detesting

fuathaich *vt, pres part* **a' fuathachadh,** hate, loathe, detest, *Cf* **tha gràin agam air** (*see* **gràin 1**)

fùdar, fùdaraich *see* **pùdar, pùdaraich**

fuidheall & **fuigheall,** *gen* **fuighill,** *nm* 1 a relic, a remnant, a remainder, a residue, leavings, what is left (*after some activity, operation &c*), **fhuair esan a roghainn dheth, fhuair mise am fuidheall** he got his pick of it, I got what was left/the leavings, *Cf less usu* **iarmad; 2** (*arith, fin*) a balance, a remainder

fuighleach, *gen* **fuighlich** *nm* rubbish, refuse, *Cf more usu* **sgudal 1**

fuil, *gen* **fola** & **fala,** *nf* blood, gore, **tha an fhuil a' tighinn às** it's bleeding, **caill** *v* **fuil** bleed, **dòrtadh-fala** *m* bloodshed, **càirdeas-fala** *m* kinship, blood relationship, (*saying*) **is tighe fuil na bùrn** blood is thicker than water

fuilear *adv* 1 (*trad*) too much; 2 *now in expr* **chan fhuilear dhut** you need ... (at least), *lit* it is not too much for you, **chan fhuilear dha cola-deug dheth** he needs (at least) a fortnight off

fuiling & **fulaing** *vti, pres part* **a' fulang,** 1 (*vi*) suffer, **cha do dh'fhuiling e an uair a bha e tinn** he didn't suffer when he was ill; 2 (*vt*) bear, stand, put up with, endure, abide, (*Sc*) thole, **chan fhuilinginn a dhèanamh** I couldn't bear to do it, **b' fheudar dhaibh fuachd is acras fhulang** they had to put up with/endure cold and hunger, **chan urrainn dhomh a fulang!** I can't stand/abide her!

fuil-mìos, *gen* **fala-mìos,** *nf* menstruation, a period

fuil(t)each *adj* bloody, gory, **cath fuilteach** a bloody battle

fuiltean, fuiltein, fuilteana *nm* a (single) hair (*of the head*), **fuilteana do chinn** the hairs of your head, *Cf* **ròineag**

fuin *vt, pres part* **a' fuine(adh),** 1 bake; 2 knead (*dough*)

fuineadair, fuineadair, fuineadairean *nm* a baker, *Cf less trad* **bèicear**

fuineadh, *gen* **fuinidh** *nm* 1 (*the act of*) baking, kneading; 2 (*a batch of*) baking

fuireach(d), *gen* **fuirich** *nm* 1 (*the act of*) staying, waiting &c (*see senses of* **fuirich** *v*); 2 (*in compounds*) **àite-fuirich** *m* a dwelling place, accommodation, **taigh-fuirich** *m* a dwelling house; *Cf* **còmhnaidh 1** & **2**

fuirich *vi, pres part* **a' fuireach(d),** 1 stay, remain, **fuirich thusa far a bheil thu!** you stay where you are! *Cf* **fan 1;** 2 live, dwell, (*Sc*) stay, **bha sinn a' fuireach ann an Ile aig an àm** we were living in Islay at the time, **a' fuireach aig Calum** staying/lodging with Calum,

Cf **còmhnaich, fan 2; 3** wait, **fuirich (ort)!** wait! **chan fhuirich sinn rithe** we won't wait for her, **thachair sin** ... , **fuirich ort** ... , **ann an Steòrnabhagh** that happened ... , wait a minute/let me see now ... , in Stornoway

fùirneis, fùirneis, fùrneisean *nf* a furnace

fulaing *see* **fuiling** & **fulang**

fulang, *gen* **fulaing** *nm* **1** (*the act of*) suffering, bearing &c (*see senses of* **fuiling** *v*); **2** suffering (*through pain &c*); **3** endurance, hardiness, toughness, capacity for bearing suffering and hardship, *Cf* **cruas 3**

fulangach *adj* **1** capable of bearing suffering and hardship, hardy, tough, long-suffering, *Cf* **cruadalach 2, cruaidh** *adj* **3**; **2** passive, (*gram*) **an guth fulangach** the passive voice

fulmair, fulmaire, fulmairean *nm* a fulmar

furachail *adj* **1** watchful, observant, alert, attentive, vigilant; **2** attentive (*to task, someone's needs &c*)

furan, *gen* & *pl* **furain** *nm* hospitality, a welcome, (*trad*) **fàilte is furan** welcome and hospitality

furasda & **furasta,** *comp* **(n)as** (&c) **fhasa,** *adj* easy, **obair/ceist fhurasta** an easy job/question, **bidh sin nas fhasa** that will be easier, **b' e an rud a b' fhasa tilleadh** the easiest thing was to come back, *Cf* **soirbh**

furm, fuirm, fuirm(ean) *nm* **1** a form, a bench (*ie seat*), *Cf* **being**; **2** a stool

furtachadh, *gen* **furtachaidh** *nm* (*the act of*) consoling &c (*see senses of* **furtaich** *v*)

furtachd *nf invar* consolation, relief (*from pain, worry &c*), comfort, solace, **furtachd air a dhòrainn** comfort/relief for his anguish, *Cf* **faothachadh 2, sòlas 1**

furtaich *vi, pres part* **a' furtachadh,** (*with prep* **air**) console, relieve (*from pain, worry &c*), comfort, bring solace, **furtaichidh sinn oirbh** we will comfort/console you, *Cf* **faothaich**

G

gabaireachd *see* **gobaireachd**

gabh *vt, pres part* **a' gabhail**, *Note: there are many idioms & expressions with this verb and only a selection can be given here;* **1** *corres to the notion* take, **gabh àite** take place, **gabh a-steach** take in, include, **gabh cupan tì** take/have a cup of tea, **ghabh mi mo dhìnnear mu thràth** I've already taken/had my dinner, **gabh mo leisgeul** excuse me (*lit* take/accept my excuse), **gabh comhairle** take counsel, get advice, **gabh truas de chuideigin/ri cuideigin** take pity on someone, **gabh eagal** take fright, become afraid, **ghabh na saighdearan e** the soldiers took/captured him, **ghabh sinn an cnatan** we took/caught the cold, **gabh d' anail** take a breather/a rest (*Cf* **leig d' anail** – *see* **leig 3**), **gabhaidh an talla trì cheud duine** the hall will take/hold 300 people, **gabh cead de** take leave of, (*prov*) **bidh teine math an sin an uair a ghabhas e** that will be a good fire when it takes hold/kindles, **gabh gnothach os làimh** take a matter in hand; **2** *corres to the notion* go, **ghabh i an rathad** *also* **ghabh i roimhpe** she went her way/set off, **ghabh iad chun a' mhonaidh** they went to/made for the hill, **ghabh i ris an leabaidh** she took/went to her bed, **ghabh e san nèibhidh** he went into/joined the navy; **3** *corres to the notions* give, perform, deliver, **gabh òran!** give us/sing a song! **gabh port air an fhidhill!** give us/play a tune on the fiddle!; **4** *corres to the notion* can, **cha ghabh sin a dhèanamh** that can't be done, **tha an àmhainn cho teth 's a ghabhas** the oven's as hot as can be/as hot as possible; **5** *misc exprs* **gabh gnothach ri rudeigin** interfere in/meddle in something, **na gabh gnothach ris!** don't have anything to do with him/it!, **na gabh ort!** don't let on!, **ghabh iad ris an t-suidheachadh ùr** they accepted the new situation, **dè tha a' gabhail riut?** what's troubling you/wrong with you?, **ghabh iad dha chèile** they set about each other

gàbhadh, gàbhaidh, gàbhaidhean *nm* **1** danger, a danger, peril, a peril, **ann an gàbhadh** in danger/peril, *usu stronger than* **cunnart**; **2** a crisis, *Cf* **cruaidh-chàs**

gàbhaidh *adj* dangerous, perilous, *Cf usu less strong* **cunnartach**

gabhail, gabhalach, gabhalaichean *nmf* **1** (*the act of*) taking &c (*see senses of* **gabh** *v*); **2** a lease, **thug an t-uachdaran seachad tuathanas air gabhail** the landlord leased (out) a farm; **3** a course, a bearing, a tack (*of boat*), *also fig in expr* **chuir thu às mo ghabhail mi** you made me lose my drift/wander from the point (*also* you disappointed me); **4** a welcome, a reception, **dè seòrsa gabhail a fhuair sibh?** what sort of a reception/welcome did you get?, *Cf* **fàilte 1**

gabhal *see* **gobhal**

gabhaltach *adj* infectious, catching, **tinneasan gabhaltach** infectious diseases, **a bheil e gabhaltach?** is it catching?

gabhaltas, *gen* **gabhaltais** *nm* 1 a piece of rented land; 2 a tenancy

gach *adj* 1 each, every, **fhuair gach gille dà nota** each boy got two pounds, **leis gach deagh dhùrachd** with every good wish, *Cf* **uile** 1; 2 (*more emph*) **gach aon** every single, **gach uile** each and every, **bha an t-uisge ann gach aon là** it rained every single day, **bidh i an sàs annam mu gach uile nì** she's on at me about each and every thing; 3 *in expr* **gach cuid** both, **thoir dhomh gach cuid siùcar is salann** give me both sugar and salt, *Cf* **cuid 4, dara 3**

gad, goid, gadan *nm* a supple stick, a withy, a switch

gad *conj see* **ged**

gadaiche, gadaiche, gadaichean *nm* a thief, a robber, *Cf* **mèirleach**

gagach *adj* stammering, stuttering, **bruidhinn** *v* **gagach** stutter, stammer

gagachd *nf invar* stammering, stuttering, a stammer, a stutter

gagaire, gagaire, gagairean *nm* a stammerer, a stutterer

Gaidheal & **Gàidheal**, *gen* & *pl* **Gaidheil** *nm* 1 someone of Goidelic race, a Gael, (*song*) **Cànan nan Gàidheal** the tongue/language of the Gaels; 2 a Highlander; 3 *restricted by some to those who speak Gaelic, sometimes including fluent non-native speakers*

Gaidhealach & **Gàidhealach**, *adj* 1 (*trad*) belonging or pertaining to the Gaels; 2 *now usu* Highland, **An Comunn Gaidhealach** The Highland Association, **Geamannan Gaidhealach** Highland Games

Gaidhealtachd & **Gàidhealtachd**, *nf invar, with art* **a' Ghàidhealtachd** the Highlands, **Roinn na Gàidhealtachd** Highland Region, **air (a') Ghàidhealtachd** in the Highlands

Gàidhlig, *gen* **Gàidhlig(e)** *nf* (*lang*) Gaelic, **tha Gàidhlig agam** I speak Gaelic, **cuir Gàidhlig air Beurla** put/translate English into Gaelic, *often with art*, **bruidhinn Gàidhlig/sa Ghàidhlig** speaking (in) Gaelic, **Comunn na Gàidhlig** the Gaelic Association, **luchd na Gàidhlig** Gaelic people, Gaelic speakers, *also as adj* **is e facal Gàidhlig a th' ann** it's a Gaelic word

gail *see* **guil**

gailbheach *adj* (*sea, weather*) stormy

gaileiridh & **gailearaidh**, *gen* **gaileiridh**, *pl* **gaileiridhean** *nm* an art gallery, *Cf more trad* **taisbean-lann**

gailleann, gaillinn, gailleannan *nf* a storm, a tempest, *Cf* **doineann, sian 1, stoirm 1**

gainmheach, *gen* **gainmhich** *nf* sand, **gainmheach an fhàsaich** the desert sand(s), **pàipear-gainmhich** *m* sandpaper

gainmheil *adj* sandy

gainne *nf invar, also* **gainnead** *nm invar*, scarcity, *Cf* **cion 1**

gàir *vi, pres part* **a' gàireachdainn**, laugh, *Cf* **dèan gàire** (*see* **gàire**)

gàir, gàir, gàirean *nm* a cry, a call, an outcry

gairbhe *nf invar, also* **gairbhead**, *gen* **gairbheid** *nm* (*abstr nouns corres to* **garbh**), roughness, coarseness, wildness

gàirdeachas, *gen* **gàirdeachais** *nm* joy, gladness, rejoicing, **dèan** *v* **gàirdeachas** rejoice (**ri** *at*), *Cf* **àgh 1**

gàirdean, gàirdein, gàirdeanan *nm* an arm (*of person, chair*)

gàire *nmf invar* a laugh, laughter, **cò a tha a' dèanamh gàire?** who's laughing?

gàireachdainn *nf invar* **1** (*the act of*) laughing; **2** laughter, *Cf* **gàire**

gairge *nf invar* (*abstr noun corres to* **garg**) **1** fierceness, ferocity; **2** wildness, unruliness

gairm *vi, pres part* **a' gairm**, **1** call, cry, **a' gairm ri chèile** calling to each other, (*fig*) **ghairm iad oirre sin a dhèanamh** they called on her to do that, *Cf* **èigh** *v*, **glaodh** *vi*; **2** (*cock &c*) crow; **3** *in expr* **gairm cogadh** declare war

gairm, gairme, gairmean(nan) *nf* **1** (*the act of*) calling, crying, crowing; **2** a crow (*ie the sound*), **gairm coilich** a cock-crow; **3** a cry, a call, **gairm-chogaidh** a warcry (*Cf* **sluagh-ghairm 1**), *Cf* **èigh** *n*, **glaodh**[1] *n*; **4** a proclamation; **5 Gairm** *the Gaelic quarterly magazine*

gairmeach *adj* (*gram*) vocative, **an tuiseal gairmeach** the vocative case

gàirnealair, gàirnealair, gàirnealairean *nm* a gardener

gàirnealaireachd *nf invar* gardening

gaiseadh, *gen* **gaisidh** *nm, with art* **an gaiseadh** potato blight, *Cf* **cnàmh**[2]

gaisge *nf invar, also* **gaisgeachd** *nf invar*, (*esp phys*) bravery, valour, heroism, *Cf* **dànadas 1**

gaisgeach, *gen & pl* **gaisgich** *nm* a hero, a champion, *Cf* **curaidh, laoch, seòd**

gaisgeil *adj* (*esp phys*) heroic, brave, *Cf* **dàna 1**

gal *see* **gul**

galan, galain, galanan *nm* a gallon

galar, galair, galaran *nm* a disease, an illness, a malady, (*song*) **is trom an galar an gaol** love is a heavy malady/affliction, *Cf* **tinneas**

Gall, *gen & pl* **Goill** *nm* **1** (*trad*) a non-Gael, a foreigner, *Cf* **coigreach 1**; **2** *now usu* a Lowlander, a Lowland Scot, **tìr nan Gall** the Lowlands (*Cf* **Galldachd**); **3 Innse Gall** *fpl* the Hebrides

galla, galla, gallachan *nf* **1** a bitch; **2** *as a swear*, damned, bloody, **càr** (*&c*) **na galla!** bloody car (*&c*)! **taigh na galla dhaibh!** damn them!, sod them!

gallan, *gen* **gallain**, *pl* **gallain** & **gallanan** *nm* a standing stone, *Cf* **carragh 2**, **tursa**

Gallda *adj* Lowland, **A' Bheurla Ghallda** (*lang*) Lowland Scots, **air a' Mhachair Ghallda** in the Lowlands

Galldachd *nf invar, with art*, **a' Ghalldachd** the Lowlands, **air a' Ghalldachd** in the Lowlands, *Cf* **machair 2**

gàmag, gàmaig, gàmagan *nf* (*music*) an octave

gamhainn, *gen* & *pl* **gamhna** & **gaimhne** *nm* a stirk, a six-month or year-old calf

gamhlas, *gen* **gamhlais** *nm* malice, ill-will, spite

gamhlasach *adj* malevolent, spiteful

gann *adj* **1** scarce, scant(y), sparse, short, in short supply, **bha airgead gann air a' mhìos sin** money was in short supply/scarce that month, **bàrr gann** a sparse/scanty crop; **2** *in expr* **is gann** scarcely, hardly, barely, **is gann a rinn sinn a-mach dè a bha e ag ràdh** we barely/scarcely made out what he was saying (*Cf* **èiginn 4**), **is gann a chì thu a leithid** it's rare that you'll see/you'll hardly ever see the likes of him (*Cf* **ainneamh 2**)

gaoid, gaoide, gaoidean *nf* a blemish, a defect, a flaw, *Cf more usu* **fàillinn 1**, **meang 1**

gaoir, gaoire, gaoirean *nf* **1** a cry (*usu of pain, anguish &c*), (*poem*) **Gaoir na h-Eòrpa** (Somhairle MacGill-Eain) Europe's Anguished Cry; **2** a thrill, **cuir** *v* **gaoir air** thrill, give a thrill to

gaoisid & **gaosaid**, *gen* **gaoiside** *nf* **1** hair (*of animals*); *esp* horsehair; **2** pubic hair, *Cf* **ròm**

gaol, *gen* **gaoil** *nm* **1** love, (*song*) **thig trì nìthean gun iarraidh, an t-eagal, an t-iadach 's an gaol** three things come unsought, fear, jealousy and love, **tha i ann an gaol** she's in love, **gaol na h-òige** young love, **mo chiad ghaol** my first love, **thug mi mo ghaol dhut 's mi òg** I gave my love to you when I was young, **tha gaol agam ort** I love you, *Cf* **gràdh 1** *which can be less intimate*; **2** *in vocative expr* **a ghaoil** (my) love, (my) dear, (my) darling, *Cf* **a ghràidh** (*see* **gràdh 2**) *which can be less intimate*

gaolach *adj* **1** loving, affectionate, *Cf* **gràdhach**; **2** beloved, dear;

gaoth, *gen* **gaoithe**, *pl* **gaothan** & **gaoithean** *nf* **1** wind, a wind, (*prov*) **an nì a thig leis a' ghaoith, falbhaidh e leis an uisge** what comes with the wind will go with the rain (easy come, easy go), **a' ghaoth an iar** the west wind, **tha gaoth ann** it's windy; **2** *with art*, **a' ghaoth** (intestinal) wind, flatulence

gaothach, *also* **gaothar**, *adj* **1** windy; **2** flatulent

gaotharan, gaotharain, gaotharanan *nm* a fan, **gaotharan teasachaidh** a fan heater

gàradh *see* **gàrradh**

garaids, garaids, garaidsean *nf* a garage (*household garage, service station &c*)

garbh *adj* **1** (*phys*) rough, wild, rugged, harsh, **oidhche gharbh** a wild/rough night, **allt garbh** a wild/impetuous stream, **tìr gharbh** a wild/rugged/harsh/land, wild &c country, *can occur in placenames as* garve-, *Cf* **cruaidh** *adj* **2**; **2** coarse, rough (*to the senses*) **stuth garbh** coarse/rough material, **guth garbh** a harsh/hoarse voice; **3** vulgar, uncouth, coarse, **duine garbh** a coarse/vulgar man, (*also a wild man or a harsh man*), *Cf* **borb**; **4** *as intensifying adv* very, terribly, dreadfully, **tha cùisean garbh dripeil an-dràsta** things are terribly/hell of a busy just now, *Cf* **glè**, **uabhasach 2**

garg *adj* **1** fierce, ferocious; **2** wild, turbulent, unruly, **sluagh garg** a wild/turbulent people, *Cf* **borb**

gàrradh & **gàradh**, *gen* **gàrraidh**, *pl* **gàrraidhean** *nm* **1** a wall (*not of buildings*), a stone dyke, *Cf* **balla**; **2** a garden, *Cf* **lios 1**

gartan, *gen* **gartain**, *pl* **gartain** & **gartanan** *nm* a garter

gas, *gen* **gaise**, *pl* **gasan** & **gaisean** *nf* (*of plants*) a stalk, a stem, a shoot, *Cf* **bachlag 2**, **ògan**

gasda & **gasta**, *adj* **1** handsome, fine, splendid, **bha na saighdearan a' coimhead gasda** the soldiers looked fine/splendid (*Cf* **eireachdail**), **duine calma gasda** a sturdy handsome man; **2** (*fam*) great, fine, **bha sin dìreach gasda!** that was just great!, *Cf* **glan** *adj* **2**, **sgoinneil**

gath, **gatha**, **gathan(nan)** *nm* **1** *a small sharp point such as* a dart, a sting, a barb, **gath speacha** a wasp's sting, **cuir** *v* **gath ann** sting (*Cf* **guin** *v*); **2** a spear, a javelin, *Cf* **sleagh**; **3** a ray, a beam, **gath solais** a light ray, a ray/beam of light, **gath-grèine** a sunbeam, *Cf* **leus 1**

ge *conj* **1** (*trad*) though, *Cf* **ged**; **2** *now usu in expr* **ge b 'e** whatever, however &c, **ge b 'e cò a dh'innis e dhut, chan eil e fìor!** whoever told you it, it isn't true! **ge b 'e cuin a ràinig iad** ... whenever they arrived ... , (*prov*) **ge b 'e mar a bhios an t-sian, cuir do shìol anns a' Mhàrt** whatever the weather may be, sow your seed in March

gèadh, *gen* & *pl* **geòidh** *nmf* a goose

geal *adj* white, **dubh is geal** black and white, **duine geal** a white man (*Cf* **duine bàn** a fair-haired/blonde man), *Cf* **bàn**[2] **1** & *trad* **fionn**

geal, *gen* **gil** *nm* the white part of anything, **geal na sùla** the white of the eye

gealach, gealaich, gealaichean *nf, with art,* **a' ghealach** the moon, **gathan na gealaich** the rays of the moon, **gealach an abachaidh** the harvest moon, **làn-ghealach** a full moon

gealachadh, *gen* **gealachaidh** *nm* (*the act of*) whitening, bleaching

gealagan, *gen & pl* **gealagain** *nm* an egg white, the white of an egg

gealaich *vti, pres part* **a' gealachadh, 1** whiten, make or become white; **2** bleach, *Cf* **todhair 2**

gealbhonn, gealbhuinn, gealbhonnan *nm* a sparrow

geall *vti, pres part* **a' gealltainn**, promise, pledge, vow, **gheall e dhomh nach dèanadh e a-rithist e** he promised me he wouldn't do it again

geall, *gen & pl* **gill** *nm* **1** a bet, a wager, **bùth** *f* **gheall** a betting shop, **cuir** *v* **geall (air each &c)** bet, put/lay/place a bet (on a horse &c), **cuiridh mi an geall nach tig e** I bet he won't come; **2** a promise, a pledge, *Cf more usu* **gealladh**

gealladh, geallaidh, geallaidhean *nm* a promise, a pledge, a vow, **thoir** *v* **gealladh** promise, vow, make a promise, **thoir gealladh dhomh gun sgrìobh thu thugam** promise me you'll write to me (*Cf* **geall** *v*), (*song*) **gur òg thug mi mo ghealladh dhut** I gave you my promise when I was young, **gealladh-pòsaidh** an engagement, a betrothal, **thug iad gealladh-pòsaidh dha chèile an-dè** they got engaged yesterday, **tìr a' gheallaidh** the promised land

gealltainn *nm invar* (*the act of*) promising &c (*see senses of* **geall** *v*)

gealltanach *adj* promising, **cluicheadair/oileanach gealltanach** a promising player/student

gealtach *adj* cowardly, fearful, timid, *Cf* **cladhaireach**

gealtaire, gealtaire, gealtairean a coward, *Cf* **cladhaire**

geama, *gen* **geama**, *pl* **geamannan** *&* **geamaichean** *nm* **1** a game (*of any kind*), *Cf* **cluich** *n* **2; 2** *esp football,* a game, a match, **am bi thu a' dol dhan gheama?** will you be going to the game/match?, *Cf* **maidse 2**

geamair, geamair, geamairean *nm* a gamekeeper

geamhradh, geamhraidh, geamhraidhean *nm* winter, a winter, **sneachd a' gheamhraidh** the winter snow

gean, *gen* **geana** *nm* a mood, a humour, a frame of mind, **deagh/droch ghean** a good/bad mood, **dè an gean a th' air a' bhodach an-diugh?** what sort of mood/frame of mind's the old fellow in today?, *Cf* **dòigh 4, fonn 2, gleus** *n* **2, sunnd 2**

geanmnachd *nf invar* chastity

geanmnaidh *adj* chaste

geansaidh, geansaidh, geansaidhean *nm* a jersey, a jumper, a pullover, (*Sc*) a gansey

gèar *nf invar, also* **gìodhar, gìodhair, gìodhraichean** *nm*, a gear (*ie in machinery*)

gearain *vi, pres part* **a' gearan, 1** complain, grumble, moan (**air** about), **gearain ris a' mhanaidsear** complain to the manager, **cha leig thu a leas a bhith a' gearan fad na h-ùine!** you needn't bother grumbling/moaning all the time! **dè a tha thu a' gearan?** what ails you?, what's wrong with you?

gearan, gearain, gearanan *nm* **1** (*the act of*) complaining &c (*see senses of* **gearain** *v*); **2** a complaint, a grumble; **3** (*med*) a complaint, *Cf* **galar, tinneas**

gearanach *adj* complaining, grumbling, querulous, apt to grumble or complain, apt to moan and groan

gearastan & **gearasdan**, *gen* **gearastain**, *pl* **gearastanan** *nm* a garrison, (*placename*) **An Gearasdan** Fort William

Gearmailt *nf invar, with art,* **a' Ghearmailt** Germany

Gearmailteach, *gen* & *pl* **Gearmailtich** *nm* a German, *also as adj* **Gearmailteach** German

Gearmailtis *nf invar, with art,* **a' Ghearmailtis** (*lang*) German

geàrr *vt, pres part* **a' gearradh**, **1** cut, **geàrr sìos craobhan** cut down trees, **ghearr e a ghlùn** he cut his knee; **2** castrate, **tha iad a' gearradh nan uan** they are castrating the lambs, *Cf* **spoth**

geàrr, gearra, gearran *nf* a hare, *Cf* **maigheach**

geàrr *adj* **1** short, **an ùine gheàrr** in a short time, shortly, *Cf more usu* **goirid 1**; **2** *in compounds* short-, *eg* **geàrr-chasach** *adj* short-legged, **geàrr-sgrìobhadh** *m* shorthand, **geàrr-shealladh** *m* short-sightedness

gearradh, gearraidh, gearraidhean *nm* **1** (*the act of*) cutting, **gearradh an fheòir** mowing/cutting the hay/grass; **2** a cut, **bha gearradh aige na ghlùin** he had a cut in his knee; **3** sarcasm; **4** *in pl* (financial) cuts, **chaill e obair air sgàth nan gearraidhean** he lost his job on account of the cuts

Gearran, *gen* **Gearrain** *nm, with art,* **an Gearran** February

gearran, *gen* & *pl* **gearrain** *nm* **1** a gelding; **2** a garron (*a type of horse trad used in the Highlands & Islands for work and riding*)

geas, *gen* **geasa** & **geis**, *pl* **geasan** *nf*, **1** enchantment, a charm, a spell, *Cf* **ortha, seun 1**, **2** *in expr* **fo gheasaibh** (*obs dat pl*) spellbound, under a spell, enchanted, bewitched

geata, geata, geataichean *nm* a gate

ged, *also* **gad**, *conj* though, although, (*song*) **ged nach eil sinn fhathast pòst', tha mi 'n dòchas gum bi** though we are not yet married, I am hopeful that we will be, **cha do sguir i den obair ged a bha i claoidhte** she didn't stop work although she was exhausted, **chì mi e cho math 's ged a b' ann an-dè a bh' ann** I can see it/him as well as though it were yesterday, *Cf trad* **ge 1**

ged-thà *see* **ge-tà**

gèile, *gen* **gèile**, *pl* **gèilean** & **gèiltean** *nm* a gale

gèill *vi, pres part* **a' gèilleadh**, yield, surrender, submit, give in, **ghèill an t-arm gu lèir (dha)** the entire army surrendered (to him), **ghèill e do/ro na h-argamaidean aca** he gave in to/in the face of their arguments, *Cf* **strìochd 1**

gèilleadh, *gen* **gèillidh** *nm* **1** (*the act of*) yielding &c (*see senses of* **gèill** *v*); **2** submission

geimheal, geimheil, geimhlean *nm* a shackle, a fetter

geimhlich *vt, pres part* **a' geimhleachadh**, shackle, fetter

geinn, geinne, geinnean *nm* **1** a chunk of anything, *Cf* **cnap 1**; **2** a wedge, (*prov*) **'s e geinn dheth fhèin a sgoltas an darach** it's (only) a wedge of itself that will split the oak

geir, *gen* **geire** *nf* **1** suet; **2** fat, *Cf* **crèis, saill** *n*

gèire *nf invar* (*abstr noun corres to* **geur** *adj*) sharpness, bitterness, harshness &c (*see senses of* **geur**)

geòcach *adj* gluttonous, greedy (*for food*), *Cf* **craosach**

geòcaire, geòcaire, geòcairean *nm* a glutton, *Cf* **craosaire**

geòcaireachd *nf invar* gluttony, greed (*for food*), *Cf* **craos 2**

geodha, geodha, geodhaichean *nmf* a cove, a narrow bay, *Cf less specialised* **camas**

geòla, geòla(dh), geòlachan *nf* a yawl, a small boat, *Cf* **eathar**

geòlas, *gen* **geòlais** *nm* geology

ge-tà & **ged-thà** *adv* though, **thug iad gealladh-pòsaidh dha chèile; cha do phòs iad, ge-tà** they got engaged; they didn't get married, though/(*Sc*) but

geug, gèige, geugan *nf* a branch (*of tree*), *Cf* **meur 3**

geum *vi, pres part* **a' geumnaich**, (*cattle*) bellow, low, moo, (*humans &c*) bellow, **bha sprèidh a' geumnaich** cattle were lowing, *Cf* **beuc** *v*

geum, *gen* **geuma** & **gèime**, *pl* **geuman** *nm* (*cattle*) bellowing, a bellow, lowing, mooing, (*humans &c*) bellowing, a bellow, **leig e geum às** he let out a bellow, *Cf* **beuc** *n*

geur *adj* **1** sharp, having a sharp blade or point, **sgian gheur** a sharp knife; **2** (*of faculties*) sharp, **sùil/cluas gheur** a sharp eye/ear, **tha e geur na inntinn** he's mentally sharp/quick/alert; **3** (*phys sensation*) bitter, sharp, biting, harsh, **gaoth gheur** a bitter/biting/ (*Sc*) snell wind, **blas geur** a bitter/sharp taste, *Cf* **searbh 1**; **4** (*temperament, words &c*) acerbic, sarcastic, sharp, bitter, sardonic, **teanga gheur** a sharp/cutting tongue, **briathran geura** bitter/ sarcastic/cutting remarks, *Cf* **guineach 1** & **2, searbh 3**

geurachadh, *gen* **geurachaidh** *nm* (*the act of*) sharpening

geuraich *vt, pres part* **a' geurachadh**, sharpen, *Cf* **faobharaich**

geur-chùiseach *adj* (*mentally*) smart, shrewd, quick, subtle, *Cf* **toinisgeil 2**

gheibh, gheibheadh, gheibhinn *pts of irreg v* **faigh,** *see tables p 409*

giall, *gen* **gialla** & **gèille,** *pl* **giallan** *nf* a jaw, *Cf* **peirceall 1**

gibht, gibht, gibhtean *nf* a gift, a present, *Cf more trad* **tabhartas, tiodhlac**

Giblean, *gen* **Giblein** *nm, also* **Giblinn,** *gen* **Giblinne** *nf, with art,* **an Giblean/a' Ghiblinn** April

gidheadh *adv* (*trad*) nevertheless, yet, nonetheless, however

gilb, gilbe, gilbean *nf* a chisel, *Cf* **sgeilb**

gile *nf invar, also* **gilead,** *gen* **gilid** *nm,* (*abstr nouns corres to* **geal**) whiteness

gille, gille, gillean *nm* **1** (*trad*) a servant (*Cf Sc* gillie), *in surnames as* Gil-, *eg* Gilchrist *from* **gille Chrìosd** servant/follower of Christ; **2** (*a young male from, say, 4 or 5 to, say, mid-twenties approx*) a boy, a lad, a youth, a young man, **tha na gillean a' cluich ball-coise** the lads are playing football, **a bheil teaghlach agaibh? tha triùir ghillean is dithis nighean againn** do you have a family? we have three boys and two girls, **seana-ghille** a (*usu middle-aged or elderly*) bachelor (*Cf* **fleasgach 2**); **3** (*fam*) *address to male of any age,* **a ghille** (*voc*) boy, lad, **tha thu ceart, a ghille!** (*or shortened to* **'ille**) you're right, boy!; *Cf* **balach**

gille-brì(gh)de, gille-bhrì(gh)de, gillean-brì(gh)de *nm* an oyster-catcher

gin *vti, pres part* **a' gineadh** *also* **a' gineamhainn 1** (*vt*) (*Bibl*) beget, conceive, **agus ghin Noah triùir mhac** and Noah begat three sons, **an nì a tha air a ghineamhainn innte** that which has been conceived in her; **2** (*vi*) breed, conceive, bear offspring, **tha an crodh a' gineadh** the cattle are breeding

gin *pron* any, *with neg v* none, **bha e ag iarraidh tairngean ach cha robh gin agam** he was wanting nails but I hadn't any/I had none, **a bheil gin chèisean-litreach againn?** have we any envelopes?

gine, gine, gineachan *nf* (*biol*) a gene

gineadair, gineadair, gineadairean *nm* (*elec*) a generator

gineal, gineil, ginealan *nmf* offspring, race, progeny, *Cf* **clann 2, sìol 3, sliochd**

ginealach, *gen* & *pl* **ginealaich** *nm* **1** a generation (*of a family*), **bha dà ghinealach den teaghlach agam ann an Canada** two generations of my family were in Canada; **2** *a whole group living in a society at the same time, or of approx the same age,* **ginealach nan Trì-ficheadan** the Sixties generation, **ginealach an donais** the wicked generation

gineamhainn *nm invar* **1** (*the act of*) begetting, breeding &c (*see senses of* **gin** *v*), **na buill-ghineamhainn** *mpl* the reproductive organs, the genitals; **2** conception, **casg-gineamhainn** *m* contraception, a contraceptive

ginean, ginein, gineanan *nm* a foetus

ginideach *adj* **1** (*gram*) genitive, **an tuiseal ginideach** the genitive case; **2** *also as noun, with art*, **an ginideach**, *gen* **a' ghinidich** *nm* the genitive

ginidich *vi, pres part* **a' ginideachadh**, germinate

giodar, *gen* **giodair** *nm* sewage

gìodhar *see* **gèar**

giomach, *gen & pl* **giomaich** *nm* a lobster

gioma-goc, gioma-goc, gioma-gocan *nm* a piggy-back (*Sc* cuddy-back) ride

gionach *adj* **1** greedy (*for wealth, food*), *Cf* **sanntach**; **2** keen, ambitious, 'hungry' (*for success*)

gionaiche *nm invar* **1** greed (*for wealth, food*), *Cf* **sannt**; **2** ambition

giorrachadh, giorrachaidh, giorrachaidhean *nm* **1** (*the act of*) shortening &c (*see senses of* **giorraich** *v*); **2** curtailment, abbreviation, an abbreviation, abridgement, an abridgement

giorrad, *gen* **giorraid** *nm* shortness

giorraich *vt, pres part* **a' giorrachadh**, shorten, abbreviate, abridge, curtail

gìosg *vt, pres part* **a' gìosgail**, gnash, **bha e a' gìosgail fhiaclan** he was gnashing his teeth

giùlain *vt, pres part* **a' giùlan**, **1** carry, transport, **bha e a' giùlan bùird** he was carrying a table, **bha an làraidh a' giùlan guail** the lorry was carrying/transporting coal; **2** (*occas*) wear (*clothing*); **3** behave, **cha robh e ga ghiùlan fhèin uabhasach math** he wasn't behaving (himself) terribly well

giùlan, giùlain, giùlanan *nm* **1** (*the act of*) carrying &c (*see senses of* **giùlain** *v*), **fear-giùlain** *m* a carrier, a bearer; **2** transport, **dòighean giùlain** means/modes of transport; **3** behaviour, conduct, **is beag orm do ghiùlan** I don't think much of your conduct/behaviour, *Cf* **dol-a-mach 1**; **4** carriage, deportment, bearing, *Cf* **gluasad 3**

giùran, giùrain, giùranan *nm* a gill (*of fish*)

giuthas, *gen* **giuthais** *nm* pine, a pine or fir tree, a Scots pine, a spruce tree, **giuthas Lochlannach** Norway spruce

giùthsach, *gen & pl* **giùthsaich** *nf* a pine wood or forest

glac *vt, pres part* **a' glacadh**, catch, capture, apprehend, trap, seize, grasp, snatch, **glac iasg** catch/trap fish, **ghlac am poileas e** the police caught/apprehended him, **cha do ghlac sinn am plèana** we didn't catch the plane, *Cf* **beir 2 & 3**, **gabh grèim air** (*see* **grèim 1**), **greimich**

glac, glaice, glacan *nf* **1** a (*usu small or narrow*) valley, a hollow, (*poem*) **Glac a' Bhàis** (Somhairle MacGill-Eain) Death Valley, *Cf* **gleann**, **lag** *n*; **2** a palm, the hollow of a hand, *Cf more usu* **bas**

glacadh, *gen* **glacaidh** *nm* **1** (*the act of*) catching, capturing &c (*see senses of* **glac** *v*); capture, seizure (*not med*), **an dèidh a ghlacadh** after capturing him *or* after he had been captured *or* after his capture; **2** a grasp, *Cf* **grèim 1**

glacte *adj* caught, captured, trapped, seized, *Cf* **sàs 1**

glagadaich, *gen* **glagadaiche** *nf* a clattering, clanging, clashing or rattling noise

glaine *nf invar* (*abstr noun corres to* **glan** *adj*) cleanliness

glainne & **gloinne,** *gen* **glainne,** *pl* **glainneachan** & **glainnichean** *nf* **1** glass, a glass, **taigh-glainne** a greenhouse, a glasshouse, (*story collection*) **Dorcha tro Ghlainne** Through a Glass Darkly, **glainne-sìde** a barometer; **2** *in pl* **glainneachan** & **glainnichean** glasses, spectacles, *Cf more trad* **speuclairean**

glais *vt, pres part* **a' glasadh,** lock, **glais an doras** lock the door

glaiste *adj* locked, (*song*) **an seòmraichean glaiste le claspaichean iarainn** in rooms locked with iron clasps

glam & **glamh** *vt, pres part* **a' glam(h)adh,** gobble, devour, 'wolf', **na glam do bhiadh!** don't gobble/wolf down your food!

glan *vt, pres part* **a' glanadh,** clean, cleanse, purge

glan *adj* **1** clean, **tubhailte ghlan** a clean towel, **a bheil do làmhan glan?** are you hands clean!; **2** fine, grand, **a bheil mi gad chumail air ais? fuirich an sin, a bhalaich, tha thu glan** am I keeping you back? stay there boy, you're fine

glanadh, *gen* **glanaidh** *nm* (*the act of*) cleaning &c (*see senses of* **glan** *v*)

glaodh *vi, pres part* **a' glaodha(i)ch,** call, cry, shout, yell, bawl, *Cf* **èigh** *v*, **gairm** *v* **1**

glaodh *vt, pres part* **a' glaodhadh,** glue

glaodh[1]**, glaoidh, glaodhan** *nm* a call, a cry, a shout, a yell, *Cf* **èigh** *n*, **gairm** *n* **3**, **sgairt**[2] **1**

glaodh[2]**, glaoidh, glaodhan** *nm* glue

glaodhadh, *gen* **glaodhaidh** *nm* (*the act of*) glueing

glaodha(i)ch *nm invar* (*the act of*) calling, crying &c (*see senses of* **glaodh** *vi*)

glaodhaire, glaodhaire, glaodhairean *nm* a loudspeaker, a public address system, a tannoy

glaodhan, *gen* **glaodhain** *nm* **1** pulp, pith, **glaodhan-fiodha** wood pulp; **2** (*flour & water*) paste

glas, glaise, glasan *nf* (*on door &c*) a lock

glas *adj* **1** grey, (*song*) **chuir mi bhriogais ghlas fom cheann** I put the grey breeks about me, **glas-neulach** *adj* pale-faced, wan, pasty, pallid, *Cf* **liath** *adj*; **2** green, **tulaichean glasa** green hillocks, *Cf* **gorm 2, uaine**

glas-làmh, glais-làmh, glasan-làmh *nf* a handcuff

glasraich *nf invar, sing & coll,* a vegetable, vegetables, greens

glè *adv* very, (*aspirates/lenites following consonant*), **bha sin glè mhath** that was very good, **rinn i glè luath e** she did it very quickly, *Cf* **fìor 3, garbh 4, uabhasach 2**

gleadhar, gleadhair, gleadharan *nm* uproar, an uproar, *Cf* **othail, ùpraid 1**

gleac *vi, pres part* **a' gleac(adh), 1** fight, struggle (**ri** with, against), *Cf* **strì** *v*; **2** wrestle

gleac, *gen* **gleaca** *nm* **1** a struggle, a fight, *Cf* **strì** *n* 2; **2** wrestling

gleacadair, gleacadair, gleacadairean *nm* a wrestler

gleacadh, *gen* **gleacaidh** *nm* (*the act of*) struggling, fighting, wrestling

gleadhraich, gleadhraich, gleadhraichean *nf* **1** a loud rattling or clattering noise, a clamour, a din; **2** the noise of loud talking or chattering

gleann, *gen* **glinn(e),** *pl* **glinn** & **gleanntan** *nm* a glen, a valley

glèidh *vt, pres part* **a' gleidheadh, 1** keep, hold, retain, have custody of, *Cf* **cùm 1; 2** save (*money &c*), *Cf* **caomhain(n), sàbhail 3; 3** keep, preserve, save, conserve, (*phys*) **tha iad gan gleidheadh ann an taigh-tasgaidh** they're being kept/conserved in a museum, (*spiritually*) **gleidhidh Dia sinn** God will preserve/save us (*Cf* **sàbhail 2**)

gleidheadh, *gen* **gleidhidh** *nm* (*the act of*) keeping, saving &c (*see senses of* **glèidh** *v*)

glèidhte *adj* kept, held, saved &c (*see senses of* **glèidh** *v*), (*copyright*) **na còraichean uile glèidhte** all rights reserved

glèidhteach *adj* conservative

glèidhteachas, *gen* **glèidhteachais** *nm* conservation, **neach-glèidhteachais** *m* a conservationist, **glèidhteachas nàdair** nature conservancy, conservation

gleoc, *also* **cloc** & **cleoc,** *gen* **gleoca,** *pl* **gleocaichean** *nm* a clock, *Cf* **uaireadair 2**

gleus *vt, pres part* **a' gleusadh, 1** get ready, prepare, put in good order or trim; **2** (*machines &c*) adjust, service; **3** (*music*) tune, *Cf* **gleus** *n* 3

gleus, *gen* **gleusa** & **gleois,** *pl* **gleusan** & **gleois** *nmf* **1** (*of objects*) order, condition, trim, **air (deagh) ghleus** in good order/trim/nick, **cuir** *v* **air ghleus** get ready, put in trim *or* good order; **2** (*of people*) mood, humour, trim, **air (deagh) ghleus** in good trim, in a good mood, **gleus inntinn** a frame of mind, *Cf* **dòigh** 4, **fonn, gean**; 3 (*music*) a key; tune, tuning, **air (deagh) ghleus** in tune, well tuned, **cuir** *v* **air ghleus** tune (*Cf* **gleus** *v* 3)

gleusadh, *gen* **gleusaidh** *nm* (*the act of*) preparing, adjusting &c (*see senses of* **gleus** *v*)

gleusda & **gleusta**, *adj* 1 ready, prepared, in good trim *or* order, (*music*) tuned, in tune; 2 (*people*) in good trim, in a good mood *or* humour, *Cf* **dòigh** 4; 3 (*people*) handy, clever, resourceful, skilled, **gleusda ann an làimhseachadh nan arm** skilled in the handling of weapons

glic *adj* 1 wise, full of wisdom; 2 clever, mentally able; 3 sensible, *Cf* **ciallach**

gliocas, *gen* **gliocais** *nm* 1 wisdom; 2 cleverness

gliog, glioga, gliogan *nm* a drip, dripping (*ie the sound*), **gliog an uisge is e a' tuiteam on mhullach** the drip of water as it falls from the roof

gliong, glionga, gliongan *nm, also* **gliongartaich** *nm invar*, a clinking, tinkling *or* jingling noise

gloc *vi, pres part* **a' glocail**, cackle

gloc, *gen* **gloic** *nm, also* **glocail** *nf invar*, a cackle, cackling, *Cf* **gogail**

glòir *nf* **glòir(e)** & **glòrach** 1 (*spiritual*) glory, (*hymn*) **tha do rìoghachd làn de ghlòir** thy kingdom is filled with glory; 2 fame, honour, *Cf* **cliù** 1

glòirich *vt, pres part* **a' glòireachadh**, glorify

glòir-mhiann, *gen* **glòir-mhianna** *nmf* ambition, an ambition, **is e a' ghlòir-mhiann (a tha) agam a bhith nam phrìomhaire** it's my ambition to be prime minister

glòir-mhiannach *adj* ambitious

glòrmhor *adj* glorious, magnificent, *Cf* **greadhnach, òirdheirc**

gluais *vti, pres part* **a' gluasad**, 1 (*phys*) move, **ghluais i an càr** she moved the car, **ghluais an talamh** the earth moved (*Cf* **caraich**), **ghluais an t-arm chun a' bhaile** the army moved towards the town; 2 (*emotionally*) move, touch, affect, stir, (*prov*) **an nì nach cluinn cluas, cha ghluais e cridhe** what (the) ear doesn't hear will not affect (the) heart, (*song*) **ghluais ar buadhan nàdair ann an gràdh dha chèil'** our natural feelings moved/stirred in mutual affection, **chaidh mo ghluasad** I was moved

gluasad, gluasaid, gluasadan *nm* 1 (*the act of*) moving, affecting &c (*see senses of* **gluais** *v*); 2 (*phys*) motion, mobility, movement, a movement, a gesture, **bha sinn gun ghluasad** we were motionless, **chuala mi gluasad san dorchadas** I heard a movement in the darkness, **taigh-gluasaid** a mobile home; **3** a gait, **tha gluasad cearbach aice** she has an awkward gait, *Cf* **giùlan 4**; **4** agitation, emotional arousal

gluasadach *adj* (*phys & emotionally*) capable of moving

glug, gluig, glugan *nm* gurgling, a gurgle, a gulp, a gulping noise, **glug caoinidh** a sob

glugan, glugain, gluganan *nm* gurgling, a gurgle

glumag, glumaig, glumagan *nf* **1** a pool *esp in a river or stream*, *Cf* **linne 1, lòn² 1**; **2** a puddle, *Cf* **lòn² 2**

glùn, glùin(e), glùin(t)ean *nmf* a knee, **fèileadh-beag os cionn mo ghlùin** the kilt abune ma knee, **lùbadh na glùine** bending the knee (*esp in prayer*), **bean-ghlùine** *f* a midwife

gnàth, gnàtha, gnàthan(nan) *nm, also* **gnàth(a)s,** *gen* **gnàthais** *nm,* **1** a custom, a practice, a habit, a usage (*trad*) **mar bu ghnàth leis** as was his custom/habit, **a rèir gnàthan na dùthcha** in accordance with the customs of the country, *Cf* **àbhaist 1, cleachdadh 2, dòigh 2, nòs 1**; **2** a convention, **gnàth litreachail** a literary convention

gnàthach *adj* customary, normal, usual, habitual, routine, *Cf* **àbhaisteach, cumanta**

gnàthaich *vt, pres part* **a' gnàthachadh, 1** use, *Cf more usu* **cleachd 1**; **2** accustom, *Cf* **cleachd 2**; **3** behave towards, use, treat, **is dona a ghnàthaich e a' bhean aige** he behaved badly towards his wife, *Cf* **làimhsich 2**

gnè *nf invar* **1** a kind, a sort, **nithean de gach gnè** things of all kinds, *Cf more usu* **seòrsa 1**; **2** (*biol*) a species, **gnè nan gobhar** the goat species, *Cf* **cineal 2, seòrsa 2**; **3** a sex, a gender, **daoine den dà ghnè** people of both sexes, (*gram*) **a' ghnè bhoireann/fhireann** the feminine/masculine gender

gnè(i)theach *&* **gnè(i)theasach** *adj* sexual, pertaining to sexuality or gender

gnìomh, gnìomh, gnìomhan *nm* **1** action, an action, a deed, an act, **cuir** *v* **an gnìomh** put into action, practise (*theory, precept &c*), **fear gnìomha** *m* a man of action, **droch ghnìomh** a bad deed/action; **2** (*esp IT*) a function, a process, **iuchair-gnìomha** *f* a function key, **gnìomh-inneal** *m* a processor, **gnìomh bodhaig** a bodily function

gnìomhach *adj* active, enterprising, hardworking, industrious, *Cf* **dèanadach, dìcheallach**

gnìomhachadh, *gen* **gnìomhachaidh** *nm* (*the act of*) acting, carrying out *&c* (*see senses of* **gnìomhaich** *v*), (*IT*) **gnìomhachadh-dàta** data processing

gnìomhachail *adj* industrial, *Cf* **tionnsgalach 2**

gnìomhachas, *gen* **gnìomhachais** *nm* **1** industry, industriousness, *Cf* **dèanadas**; **2** business, a business, **chuir e gnìomhachas ùr air chois** he set up a new business, **cairt-ghnìomhachais** *f* a business card, **raon** *m* **gnìomhachais** a business park, an industrial estate, *Cf* **gnothach 1**, **malairt 1**; **3** an industry, **gnìomhachas an dealain/a' bhìdh** the electricity/food industry

gnìomhaich *vti*, *pres part* **a' gnìomhachadh**, **1** (*vi*) act; **2** (*vt*) effect, carry out, execute (*a task, process &c*)

gnìomhaiche, **gnìomhaiche**, **gnìomhaichean** *nm* **1** an executive; **2** an activist

gnìomhair, **gnìomhair**, **gnìomhairean** *nm* (*gram*) a verb, **gnìomhairean (neo-)riaghailteach** (ir)regular verbs

gnog *vt*, *pres part* **a' gnogadh**, **1** knock, (*Sc*) chap, **gnog an doras/an uinneag** chap/knock at the door/window; **2 gnog an ceann** nod the head

gnogadh, *gen* **gnogaidh** *nm* **1** (*the act or noise of*) knocking; **2** a knock (*on door &c*); **3 gnogadh cinn** a nod of the head

gnothach, **gnothaich**, **gnothaichean** *nm* **1** (*commerce*) business, a business, **fear-gnothaich** a businessman, **dèan** *v* **gnothach ri** do/transact business with, **dh'fhàillig an gnothach aige** his business failed, **chaidh e don Fhraing air ceann gnothaich** he went to France on business, *Cf* **gnìomhachas 2**, **malairt 1**; **2** a matter, a business, an affair, **'s e droch ghnothach a bh' ann!** it was a bad business!, **chan e sin do ghnothach-sa** that's no business/affair of yours, *Cf* **cùis 1**; **3** an errand, **dh'fhalbh am balach air gnothach** the boy went on an errand; **4** *in expr* **gabh gnothach ri** interfere/meddle in *or* with, *or* get involved in, have anything to do with, **na gabh gnothach ri sin!** don't meddle in that! *or* don't have anything to do with that! *Cf* **buin** *v* **3**; **5** *in expr* **a dh'aon ghnothach** *adv* expressly, deliberately, specially, on purpose, specifically, **sgrìobh mi an litir a dh'aon ghnothach gus a' chùis a thoirt gu ceann** I wrote the letter expressly to bring the matter to an end, *Cf* **rùn 4**; **6** *in expr* **dèan** *v* **an gnothach air** get the better of, defeat, *Cf* **cùis 5**, **uachdar 5**; **7** *in expr* **nì sin an gnothach!** that'll do!, that'll do the trick/job!, *Cf* **cuis 6**

gnù *adj* surly, sullen, *Cf* **mùgach 2** *& more usu* **gruamach 1**

gnùis, **gnùise**, **gnùisean** *nf* one's face, one's facial appearance or habitual expression, one's complexion, *Cf more temporary* **fiamh 3**, **tuar**

gob, *gen & pl* **guib** *nm* **1** a beak, a bill (*of bird*); **2** the point or (sharp) end of anything, **gob rubha/snàthaid/prìne** the point of a headland/needle/pin; **3** (*vulg*) a gob, a mouth, **dùin do ghob!** shut your mouth/gob!, *Cf* **beul 1**, **bus**[2] **1**, **cab**

gobach *adj* prattling, chattering, *Cf* **cabach**

gobaireachd *also* **gabaireachd** *nf invar* prattle, chatter, prattling, chattering, **chuala sinn gobaireachd na cloinne** we heard the children's prattling, *Cf* **cabadaich, goileam**

gobha, gobhainn, goibhnean *nm* a (black)smith, *Cf* **cèard 2**

gobhal & **gabhal**, *gen* **gobhail** & **goibhle**, *pl* **goibhlean** *nm* 1 a fork (*ie angle where two lines join*), an object so shaped (*NB not a table fork, see* **forc, greimire**, *nor a farm or garden fork, see* **gobhlag, gràpa**), **gobhal san rathad** a fork in the road, **gobhal-gleusaidh** a tuning-fork, **gobhal baidhsagail** the fork of a bicycle; 2 the crutch (*ie at the groin*), **gobhal briogais** the crutch of a pair of trousers

gobhar, *gen* **goibhre** & **gobhair**, *pl* **goibhrean, gobhraichean** & **gobhair** *nmf* a goat, *Cf* **boc 1**

gobhlach *adj* forked, **earball gobhlach** a forked tail, **dealanach gobhlach** forked lightning

gobhlag, gobhlaig, gobhlagan *nf* 1 a (two-pronged) fork, a pitch-fork, a hay-fork, *Cf* **gràpa**; 2 an earwig, *Cf* **fiolan**

gobhlan-gaoithe, gobhlain-ghaoithe, gobhlanan-gaoithe *nm* a swallow (*ie the bird*)

goc, *gen* **goca**, *pl* **gocan** & **gocaichean** *nm* a tap, a stopcock, a faucet, (*Sc*) a toby, *Cf* **tap**

gogail *nf invar* cackling, clucking (*of hen*), (*prov*) **gogail mhòr is ugh beag** a great deal of cackling and a little egg, *Cf* **gloc** *n*

goid *vt*, *pres part* **a' goid**, steal, pinch, thieve, **ghoid iad càr** they stole a car

goid, *gen* **goide** *nf* 1 (*the act of*) thieving, stealing, pinching, **a bheil thu ri goid a-rithist?** are you at your thieving again?; 2 theft; *Cf* **braid, mèirle**

goil *vti*, *pres part* **a' goil**, 1 (*of liquids*) boil; 2 (*fig*) **bha an loch a' goil le iasg** the loch was seething/(*Sc*) hotchin with fish

goile, goile, goilea(cha)n *nf* a stomach, *Cf more usu* **stamag**

goileach *adj* boiling

goileam, *gen* **goileim** *nm* prattle, tittle-tattle, chatter, *Cf* **cabadaich, gobaireachd**

goireas, goireis, goireasan *nm* 1 a resource, an amenity, a facility, **ionad-ghoireasan** *m* a resource centre, **tha goireasan gu leòr aig a' chlub shòisealta** the social club has lots of facilities/resources; 2 a convenience, *in pl* **na goireasan** the conveniences, the toilets, *Cf* **taigh-beag** (*see* **taigh 3**)

goireasach *adj* convenient, handy, *Cf* **deiseil 3, ullamh 3**

goirid (*comp* **(n)as** (*&c*) **giorra**) *adj* 1 short, brief, **sgeulachd ghoirid** a short story, **tha na làithean a' fàs goirid** the days are getting short,

cuairt ghoirid a brief tour, *Cf* **aithghearr** 1; 2 (*as n*) **o chionn ghoirid** a short time ago, recently, **an ceann ghoirid** in/after a short time; *Cf less usu* **geàrr** *adj* 1

goirt *n see* **gort(a)**

goirt *adj* 1 painful, hurting, (*Sc*) sore, **ceann goirt** a sore head, a headache, **tha mo dhruim goirt** my back hurts/is sore, *Cf* **pianail**; 2 sour, **bainne/uachdar goirt** sour milk/cream; 3 bitter, severe, sore, **deuchainn ghoirt** a sore/severe trial, **àmhghar goirt** bitter distress, *Cf* **crài(dh)teach**

goirteachadh, *gen* **goirteachaidh** *nm* (*the act of*) hurting, causing pain

goirtich *vt, pres part* **a' goirteachadh**, hurt, cause pain to (*usu phys*), *Cf* **ciùrr**

goistidh, goistidh, goistidhean *nm* 1 a godfather; 2 a sponsor (*of sporting or cultural event &c*); 3 a gossip

gòrach *adj* 1 stupid, *Cf* **baoghalta**; 2 foolish, silly, daft, *Cf* **amaideach, baoth**

gòraiche, *nf invar* 1 stupidity; 2 foolishness, folly, silliness, *Cf* **amaideas**

gorm *adj* 1 blue, **adhar gorm** a blue sky, (*song*) **Teàrlach òg nan gorm-shùl meallach** young Charles (*ie Edward Stewart*) of the bewitching blue eyes; 2 green, **feur gorm** green grass (*a more intense green than* **glas**), *Cf* **glas** *adj* 2, **uaine**

gort(a), *gen* **gorta** *nf* famine, a famine, **a' ghort mhòr** the great famine, the great hunger

gràbhail *vt, pres part* **a' gràbhal(adh)**, engrave

grad *adj* 1 sudden, **lasair/fuaim ghrad** a sudden flash/noise, *Cf* **obann**; 2 quick, sharp, agile, alert, **gluasadan grada** quick movements, **bha i grad na h-inntinn** she was mentally quick/alert, *Cf* **deas** 4, **luath** *adj* 2; 3 *as adv* **gu grad** suddenly, quickly, shortly, **dh'èirich e gu grad** he rose suddenly, **bidh e deiseil gu grad** it will be ready/finished shortly (*Cf* **a dh'aithghearr**)

gràdh, *gen* **gràidh** *nm* 1 love, affection, **tha gràdh agam ort!** I love you! **thug i a gràdh dha** she gave her love to him, *Cf* **gaol** 1; 2 *in voc expr* **a ghràidh**, (my) love, (my) dear, *Note: can be used more widely than* **a ghaoil** (*see* **gaol** 2), *which tends to be a mode of address for lovers & close family*

gràdhach *adj* loving, affectionate, *Cf* **gaolach** 1

graf, grafa, grafaichean *nm* a graph

gràg, gràig, gràgan *nm* a croak, a caw

gràgail *nf invar* (*the act & sound of*) croaking, cawing, **dèan** *v* **gràgail** croak, caw

graide *nf invar* (*abstr noun corres to* **grad**) suddenness, quickness &c (*see senses of* **grad**)

gràin, *gen* **gràine** *nf* **1** hate, hatred, abhorrence, loathing, **tha gràin agam orra** I hate/loathe/detest them, *Cf* **fuath**; **2** disgust, *Cf* **sgreamh**

gràineag, gràineig, gràineagan *nf* a hedgehog

gràineil *adj* **1** hateful, loathsome, abhorrent, detestable, *Cf* **fuathach**; **2** disgusting, vile, *Cf* **grànda 2, sgreamhail**

gràinne, gràinne, gràinnean *nf* a (*single*) grain (*of a cereal*)

gràinneach *adj* granular

gràinnean, gràinnein, gràinneanan *nm* a grain, **gràinnean salainn/ siùcair** a grain of salt/sugar

gràisg, gràisge, gràisgean *nf* a crowd (*derog*), a mob, a rabble, *Cf* **prabar**

gràisgealachd *nf invar* vulgarity, uncouthness, yobbishness, loutishness

gràisgeil *adj* vulgar, uncouth, yobbish, loutish

gram, grama, graman *nm* a gram(me) **ceud gram de shiùcar** a hundred grams of sugar

gramail & **greimeil** *adj* persistent, resolute

gràmar, *gen* **gràmair** *nm* grammar, **leabhar** *m* **gràmair** a grammar book

gràmarach *adj* grammatical, pertaining to grammar

gràn, *gen* & *pl* **gràin** *nm* **1** a cereal, a cereal crop, a grain crop; **2** (*coll*) grain (*from cereal crops*)

granaidh, granaidh, granaidhean *nf* (*fam*) a granny, a grandmother, (*story*) **Granaidh anns a' Chòrnair** (Iain Mac a' Ghobhainn) Granny in the Corner

grànda & **grannda** *adj* **1** ugly; **2** vile, *Cf* **gràineil 2, sgreamhail**

gràpa, gràpa, gràpan *nm* a fork (*usu 4 or more prongs, for farm or garden*), (*Sc*) a graip, *Cf* **gobhlag 1**

gràs, gràis, gràsan, *nm* **1** grace, graciousness, **gun ghràs** graceless, **gràsmhor** gracious; **2** (*spiritual*) grace, **gràs Dhè** God's grace, divine grace

greadhnach *adj* gorgeous, magnificent, splendid, *Cf* **glòrmhor, òirdheirc**

greallach, *gen* **greallaiche** *nf* entrails, intestines, innards (*esp of animals*), *Cf* **caolan, innidh, mionach 1**

greannach *adj* **1** ill-tempered, (*Sc*) crabbit, *Cf* **crost(a) 1, diombach 1, gruamach 4**; **2** (*of weather*) gloomy, threatening

greannmhor *adj* cheerful, joyful, (*song*) **is os mo chionn sheinn an uiseag ghreannmhor** (Màiri Mhòr) and above my head sang the joyful skylark, *Cf* **àghmhor**

greas *vti, pres part* **a' greasad, 1** (*trad*) (*vi*) hurry, make haste, **ghreas mi orm** I hurried/made haste, *now usu in imperative* **greas ort!** *pl* **greasaibh oirbh!** hurry up! **bu chòir dhaibh greasad orra** they ought to hurry, *Cf* **dèan cabhag** (*see* **cabhag 1**); **2** (*vt*) hurry, drive *or* urge on (*people, animals*), *Cf* **cabhag 2, iomain** *v* **1**

grèata, **grèata**, **grèataichean** *nm* a grate, grating

greideal, *gen* **greideil** & **greidealach**, *pl* **greidealan** *nf* (*baking*) a griddle, a gridiron, (*Sc*) a girdle

Grèig *nf, with art*, **a' Ghrèig** Greece

greigh, **greighe**, **greighean** *nf* a herd, a flock (*of animals*), *esp* a stud of horses

greigheach *adj* gregarious

grèim, **greime**, **greimean(nan)** *nm* **1** a grip, a grasp, a hold, **gabh** *v* **grèim air rudeigin** take hold of/grip/grasp/grab/seize something (*Cf* **greimich**), **bha grèim aice air làimh air** she was holding/gripping his hand, **bha e an grèim** he was held (*ie in captivity*); **2** a bite, a bit, *esp in expr* **grèim bìdh** a bite, a morsel, **tha mi airson grèim bìdh a ghabhail** I fancy getting/having a bite to eat, **cha d'fhuair sinn grèim bìdh fad an latha** we didn't get a bite to eat all day, *Cf* **blasad 2**; **3** (*needlework*) a stitch

greimeil *see* **gramail**

greimich *vi, pres part* **a' greimeachadh**, (*with prep* **ri** *or* **air**) seize, grasp, *Cf more usu* **gabh grèim air** (*see* **grèim 1**), **glac** *v*

greimire, **greimire**, **greimirean** *nm* a (table) fork, **sgian is greimire** a knife and (a) fork, *Cf* **forc(a)**; **2** pliers

greis, **greise**, **greisean** *nf* a while, a time, **fad/car/airson greis** for a while/a time, **o chionn ghreis** a while ago, (*trad*) **greis air seinn/pìobaireachd** a while (spent) singing/piping, *Cf* **greiseag**, **treis**

grèis, *gen* **grèise** *nf* needlework, embroidery (*ie the activity*), **obair-ghrèise** *nf is the product*

greiseag, **greiseig**, **greiseagan** *nf* (*dimin of* **greis**) a short *or* little while, (*Sc*) a whilie, *Cf* **greis**, **treis**, **ùine ghoirid** (*see* **ùine 2**)

Greugach, *gen* & *pl* **Greugaich** *nm* a Greek, *also as adj* **Greugach** Greek

Greugais *nf invar, with art* **a' Ghreugais** (*language*) Greek

greusaiche, **greusaiche**, **greusaichean** *nm* a shoemaker, a shoe-repairer, a cobbler

grian, **grèine**, **grianan** *nf, with art* **a' ghrian** the sun, **solas** *m* **na grèine** sunlight, **gathan** *mpl* **na grèine** the sun's rays, **gath-grèine** *f* a sunbeam, **èirigh** *f* **na grèine** sunrise, **dol fodha** *m*/**laighe** *mf* **na grèine** sunset, **gabh** *v* **a' ghrian** sunbathe, **beum-grèine** *m* sunstroke, **càite fon ghrèin a bheil e?** where on earth (*lit* beneath the sun) is he?

grinn *adj* **1** elegant, fine (*in appearance*), **aodach grinn** fine/elegant clothing, *Cf* **eireachdail**, **brèagha**; **2** pretty, *Cf* **bòidheach**; **3** neat, *Cf* **cuimir 2**, **sgiobalta 2**, **snasail**; **4** accurate, correct, **tomhas grinn** an accurate/correct measurement/calculation, *Cf* **cruinn 2**

grinneal, *gen* **grinneil** *nm* **1** gravel, *Cf* **morghan**; **2** bottom of sea, river or well, *Cf* **grunnd 1**

grinneas, *gen* **grinneis** *nm* elegance, neatness, fineness

grìogag, grìogaig, grìogagan *nf* a bead (*on necklace &c*)

Grioglachan, *gen* **Grioglachain** *nm*, *with art* **an Grioglachan** the Pleiades

Griomasach, *gen & pl* **Griomasaich** *nm* someone from Grimsay (**Griomasaigh**), *also as adj* **Griomasach** of, from or pertaining to Grimsay

grìos, grìosa, grìosachan *nm* a grill (*ie for cooking*)

grìosaich *vt, pres part* **a' grìosachadh**, (*cookery*) grill

griù(th)lach & **griù(th)rach**, *gen* **griùlaich** *nf*, *with art* **a' ghriùlach** (the) measles, **tha e sa ghriùlaich** he has (the) measles

grod *vti, pres part* **a' grodadh**, rot, putrefy, *Cf* **lobh**

grod *adj* rotten, rotted, putrid, *Cf* **lobhte**

grodach *adj* (*fam*) grotty, (*fam, calque*) **grodach-coimhead** *adj* grotty-looking, *Cf* **dràbhail**

grodadh, *gen* **grodaidh** *nm* **1** (*the act of*) rotting, putrefying; **2** rot, putrefaction; *Cf* **lobhadh**

gròiseid, gròiseide, gròiseidean *nf* a gooseberry, (*Sc*) a groset

grosair, grosair, grosairean *nm* a grocer

gruag, gruaig, gruagan *nf* **1** hair, a head of hair (*human*), (*song*) **thug thu ghruag far mo chinn** you caused my hair to fall (*lit* took the hair from my head), *Cf more usu* **falt**; **2** a wig (*also* **gruag-bhrèige**)

gruagach, gruagaich(e), gruagaichean *nf* (*now mostly in love songs*) a maid, a virgin, a girl *or* young woman, (*song*) **Gruagach Og an Fhuilt Bhàin** The Fair-haired Young Maid/Girl, *Cf* **maighdeann 1, nighean, nìghneag**

gruagaire, gruagaire, gruagairean *nm* a hairdresser

gruaidh, gruaidhe, gruaidhean *nf* a cheek, **bha dath nan ròsan air a gruaidh** her cheek was the colour of roses, *Cf* **pluic**, & *trad* **lethcheann 1**

gruaim, *gen* **gruaime** *nf* **1** gloom, gloominess, melancholy, **is tu a dh'fhàg mi fo ghruaim** it's you who plunged me into gloom/left me melancholy, *Cf* **bròn 1, mulad**; **2** scowling, a scowl, frowning, a frown, **chuir i gruaim oirre** she scowled/frowned, *Cf* **mùig, sgraing**; **3** sulkiness, a sulk, *Cf* **mùig**; **4** grumpiness, ill-humour, **fo ghruaim** gloomy, in an ill humour

gruamach *adj* **1** gloomy, melancholy, morose, sullen, surly, **stuadhan gruamach** surly/sullen waves, **aghaidh ghruamach** a gloomy/morose face, *Cf* **brònach, dubhach, gnù, muladach**; **2** scowling, frowning; **3** sulky, sulking; **4** grumpy, grouchy, ill-humoured, *Cf* **crost(a) 1, diombach 1, greannach 1**

grùdair(e), grùdaire, grùdairean *nm* a brewer; a distiller

grùdaireachd *nf invar* brewing; distilling

grùid, *gen* **grùide,** *nf* 1 lees, dregs, grounds, sediment (*in liquids*); 2 *in expr* **taigh-grùide** *m* a brewery

grunn, *gen* **gruinn** *nm* 1 a crowd, a group, **grunn dhaoine** a crowd of people; 2 (*fam*) many, a lot of, lots of, **chuir mi seachad grunn bhliadhnachan an sin** I spent a fair number of years there, *Cf* **iomadach, iomadh 1, mòran 1, tòrr 2**

grunnan, grunnain, grunnanan *nm* (*dimin of* **grunn**) a group, a small number, a few (*persons or things*)

grunnd, *gen* **gruinnd** & **grunnda,** *pl* **grunndan** *nm* 1 the base, bed, bottom *or* ground of anything, **grunnd na mara** the bottom of the sea, the sea-bed, **grunnd glinne** a valley bottom, *Cf* **bonn 2, grinneal 1, ìochdar;** 2 (*occas*) ground (*ie land*), (*song*) **Flòdaigearraidh sgiamhach, càit 'eil d' fhiach de ghrunnd?** lovely Flodigarry, where is your equal as a piece of ground?, *Cf* **fearann, talamh 3**

grùnsgal, *gen* **grùnsgail** *nm* growling, a growl, *Cf* **dranndail**

gruth, *gen* **grutha** *nm* (*dairying*) curd(s), crowdie, *Cf* **slaman**

grùthan, grùthain, grùthanan *nm* (*anat*) a liver (*usu of animal*), *Cf* **adha**

gu 1 *a particle placed before an adj to form an adv, eg* **gu mòr** greatly, **gu tric** frequently, often, **gu mì-fhortanach** unfortunately, **tha mi gu math** I'm well, **tha i gu bochd** she's poorly; 2 (*trad*) *found before first of a pair of adjectives, eg* **bha iad gu muladach brònach** they were sad and melancholy

gu[1] & **gus** *prep* 1 to, up to, towards, *Note: the pers prons* **mi, thu, e** &c *combine with* **gu** *to form the prep prons* **thugam(sa), thugad(sa), thuige(san), thuice(se), thugainn(e), thugaibh(se), thuca(san)** (*also* **chugam(sa), chugad(sa)** &c), to me, you &c; **cuiridh mi leabhar thuice** I'll send a book to her, **chaidh e gu Glaschu** he went to (*ie to the outskirts of*) Glasgow (*Cf* **chaidh e do Ghlaschu** he went to (*ie into*) Glasgow); *Note:* **gu** *plus the art becomes* **chun** *or* **thun** *prep* (*with gen*), **chaidh e chun a' bhaile** he went to the town, *or* he went towards the town, *Cf* **ionnsaigh 3;** 2 (*occas for time*) **chan fhad' thuige a-nis** it won't be long now (*lit* not long to/until it), **cha do thachair e chun a seo** it hasn't happened up to now/so far/until now, *Cf* **gu ruige 2;** 3 to, for (*with implication of intention*), **thig gam** (*for* **gu mo**) **fhaicinn** come to see me (*lit* to *or* for my seeing), **thàinig e dhachaigh gu biadh** he came home to eat (*lit* to food), *Cf* **airson 5;** 4 on the point of, about to, almost, nearly, **tha mi gu bhith deiseil** I'm almost/just about ready (*ie up to the point of being ready*), **tha sinn gu falbh** we're (just) about to go, **bha e gus a mhùn a chall ag èisteachd riutha** he was nearly wetting himself listening to them

gu² & **gus 1** *prep* until, till (*with dat*), **fanaidh sinn gu sia uairean** we'll wait/stay till six o'clock, **chan urrainn dhomh a ghleidheadh gus a-màireach** I can't keep/save it until tomorrow; **2** *in forms* **gus an, gus am, gus nach,** *conj* until, **cha deasaich mi am biadh gus an tig thu dhachaigh** I won't get the meal ready until you come home, **cosnaidh mi airgead gus am bi gu leòr againn dheth** I'll earn money until we've got enough of it, **cùm e gus nach bi feum agad air** keep it until you don't need it

gual, *gen* **guail** *nm* coal

gualan, gualain, gualanan *nm* carbon

gualann & **gualainn,** *gen* **gualainn** & **guailne,** *pl* **guailnean** & **guaillean** *nf* a shoulder, **poca air a ghualainn** a sack on his shoulder, **gualainn ri gualainn** shoulder to shoulder, *Cf less usu* **slinnean; 2** a shoulder of a hill, **leig/ghabh iad an anail an uair a ràinig iad gualann na beinne** they took a rest/a breather when they reached the shoulder of the mountain

gual-fiodha, *gen* **guail-fhiodha** *nm* charcoal

guanach *adj* **1** giddy, scatter-brained, skittish, **na h-èildean guanach** the giddy/skittish hinds, **caileag ghuanach** a giddy/scatter-brained girl, **òigridh ghuanach** happy-go-lucky young folk; **2** coquettish

guanag, guanaig, guanagan *nf* **1** a giddy or scatter-brained girl; **2** a coquettish girl

gu buileach *see* **buileach**

gucag, gucaig, gucagan *nf* **1** (*botany*) a bud; **2** a bubble

gucag-uighe, gucaig-uighe, gucagan-uighe *nf* an egg-cup

gu dè *see* **dè 3**

gu dearbh *adv* **1** certainly, definitely, indeed, **a bheil thu gu math? tha gu dearbh!** are you well? I certainly am!, I am indeed! **am bi thu ann? bithidh gu dearbh!** will you be there? definitely! *Cf* **fios 4; 2** *as intensifying element* **gu dearbh fhèin** extremely, **bha sin gu dearbh fhèin math** that was extremely good/very good indeed, *Cf* **uabhasach 2**

guga, guga, gugaichean *nm* a young gannet or solan goose (*trad gathered from cliffs & stacks for food*), *Cf* **sùlaire**

guidh *vi, pres part* **a' guidhe, 1** beg, beseech, entreat, plead, pray, **tha mi a' guidhe ort fuireach!** I'm begging/pleading with you to stay!, **ghuidh e oirnn a leigeil ma sgaoil** he begged us to let him go/set him free; **2** wish (*a situation, benefit &c upon someone*), **guidhidh mi mallachd air** I wish a curse on him, **a' guidhe Nollaig Chridheil dha** wishing him a Happy Christmas, **guidheam slàint' is sonas dhut** I wish you health and happiness; **3** (*relig*) pray, *Cf more usu* **dèan ùrnaigh** (*see* **ùrnaigh**)

guidhe, guidhe, guidheachan *nmf* **1** (*the act of*) beseeching, praying &c (*see senses of* **guidh** *v*); **2** an entreaty, a plea; **3** a wish, **droch ghuidhe** an ill wish; **4** (*relig*) a prayer, *Cf more usu* **ùrnaigh**

guidheam *obs & trad present, see* **guidh** *v*

guil *vi, pres part* **a' gul**, *also* **gail** *vi, pres part* **a' gal**, weep, cry, (*poem*) **Eirinn a' Gul** Ireland Weeping, *Cf* **caoin 2**

guilbneach, *gen & pl* **guilbnich** *nmf* a curlew

guin *vt, pres part* **a' guineadh**, sting, **ghuin speach mi** a wasp stung me, *Cf* **cuir gath ann** (*see* **gath 1**)

guin, guin, guinean *nm* **1** a sting (*part of bee &c*), *Cf* **gath 1; 2** a sting (*ie the wound inflicted*); **3** a pang

guineach *adj* **1** sharp, bitter, acerbic (*remarks, character &c*); **2** stinging, cutting, wounding, hurtful (*remarks &c*); *Cf* **geur 4, searbh 3**

guineadh, *gen* **guinidh** *nm* (*the act of*) stinging

guir *vti, pres part* **a' gur** (*vi, of hen &c*) brood, (*vti*), hatch (*eggs*)

guirean, guirein, guireanan *nm* a pimple, a pustule, a spot, (*Sc*) a plouk

gul, *gen* **guil** *nm*, *also* **gal**, *gen* **gail** *nm*, (*the act of*) weeping, crying (*see* **guil** *v*)

gu lèir *adv with adjectival force*, entire, complete, whole, **chaidh an t-arm gu lèir an sàs** the entire/complete/whole army was captured, *Cf* **fad 3**

gu leòr *see* **leòr 2**

gu leth *see* **leth 3**

gum *see* **gun** *conj*

gùn, gùin, gùintean *nm* a gown, **gùn-oidhche** a nightgown

gun *conj*, **gum** *before b, f, m & p, also in forms* **gu, nach** & (*with v* is) **gur** & **guma** (*see examples*), that, **tha mi toilichte gun tàinig sibh** I'm glad (that) you came, **'s cinnteach gu bheil i air chall** it's certain/definite that she's lost, **chan eil mi airson gum bi thu nad aonar** I don't want you to be on your own, **thuirt iad nach robh iad deiseil** they said (that) they weren't ready, **an e òr a th' ann? cha chreid mi gur e** is it gold? I don't think (that) it is, I don't think so, (*trad*) *expr wishes &c* (*prov*) **guma fada bhios tu beò agus ceò bhàrr do thaighe!** (*also* **guma fada bèo thu is ceò as do thaigh**) lang may ye live an yer lum(b) reek!, (*song*) **fallain gum bi thu** may you be in good health

gun *prep* (*takes nom, aspirates/lenites except for d, n & t*) **1** without, **gun fhois** without peace/rest, **càraid gun chlann** a childless couple, **thig gun dàil** come without delay, (*prov*) **fainne mun mheur 's gun snàithne mun mhàs** a ring around the finger and not a stitch about the bum (*corres to Sc* fur coat an nae knickers), *Cf* **às aonais;** **2** *in neg verbal expressions* **dh'iarr e orm gun a bhith mì-mhodhail** he asked me not to be rude, **cha b' urrainn dhi gun a bhith a' gàireachdainn** she couldn't help laughing, **tha am bus gun tighinn** the bus hasn't come, (*calque*) **gun ach beagan dhiubh ainmeachadh** to name but a few of them; **3** *in conj* **gun fhios nach** in case *see* **fios 5**

gunna, gunna, gunnaichean *nm* a gun

gunnair, gunnair, gunnairean *nm* a gunner

gurraban, *gen* **gurrabain** *nm* crouching, a crouch, a crouching position, *Cf* **crùbagan, crùban**

gu ruige *prep* (*with nom*) **1** (*of distance, space*) up to, as far as, **chaidh iad romhpa gu ruige an druim** they went on as far as the ridge, **thàinig na tuilltean gu ruige an taigh** the floods came (right) up to the house; **2** (*of time*) up to, until, **cha do rinn sinn mearachdan gu ruige seo** we haven't made any mistakes so far/up to now, **bidh sinn trang gu ruige a' Bhliadhna Ur** we'll be busy until/(right) up to New Year

gus, *also in forms* **gus am, gus an, gus nach,** *conj* to, in order to, so that, **cheannaich i sguab gus an taigh a ghlanadh** she bought a broom (in order) to clean the house (*Cf* **a-chum 1**), **fhuair e obair bheag gus am biodh airgead-pòcaid aige** he found a little job so that he would have some pocket money, **seo an seòladh againn gus an urrainn dhut an taigh a lorg** here's our address so that you can find the house, **thug a màthair pìos dhi gus nach biodh an t-acras oirre** her mother gave her a piece so that she wouldn't be hungry, *Cf* **dòigh 5, los 2** & *less trad* **airson 5**

gus, gus an, gus nach *prep* & *conj* until, *see* **gu²**

guth, gutha, guthan *nm* **1** a voice, **guth binn** a sweet voice, **ann an guth ìosal** in a low voice; **2** news, a word, **ciamar a chaidh do Chalum? cha chuala mi guth mu dheidhinn** how did Calum get on? I haven't heard a thing/a word/any news about him, *Cf* **fios 3; 3** a mention, **tha na peuran pailt am bliadhna, gun ghuth air na h-ùbhlan** pears are plentiful this year, not to mention/never mind apples, **thoir** *v* **guth air rudeigin** mention something, *Cf* **iomradh 1**

gu tur *see* **tur 2**

H

hàidraidean, *gen* **hàidraidein** *nm* hydrogen

halò *excl* hello, hullo

heactair, heactair, heactairean *nm* a hectare

Hearach (*also* **Tearach**), *gen & pl* **Hearaich** *nm* someone from Harris, *also as adj* **Hearach** of, from or pertaining to Harris

Hearadh *nf invar*, *with art*, **Na Hearadh** Harris, the Island of Harris

heileacopta(i)r, heileacoptair, heileacoptaran *nm* a helicopter

Hiort (*also* **Hirt** & **Tirt**) *nf invar* St Kilda

Hiortach (*also* **Hirteach** & **Tirteach**), *gen & pl* **Hiortaich** *nm* a St Kildan, someone from St Kilda, *also as adj* **Hiortach** of, from or pertaining to St Kilda

hò-ro-gheallaidh *nm invar* **1** (*fam*) a boisterous party, ceilidh or get-together &c, a 'knees-up', a hoolie; **2** *in expr* (*fam*) **cha toir mi hò-ro-gheallaidh air** I don't give a damn/a fig/a bugger for it/him

I

i *pron f sing, emph form* **ise**, she, her, (*representing nf*) it, **chunnaic i i** she saw her/it, **bha ad agam uaireigin ach chaill mi i** I had a hat once but I lost it

iad *n, see* **eud**

iad *pron m & f pl, emph form* **iadsan**, they, them

iadach *adj & noun see* **eudach**

iadh & **iath** *vt, pres part* **ag iadhadh**, surround, circle, enclose, **dh'iadh na saighdearan e** the soldiers surrounded him

iadh-shlat & **iath-shlat**, *gen* **iadh-shlait** *nf* honeysuckle

iall, èille, iallan *nf* a thong, a (dog's) lead *or* leash, a strap, a strop, **iall bròige** a shoe-lace (*Cf* **barrall**)

ialtag, ialtaig, ialtagan *nf* a bat (*ie the animal*)

iar *nf invar* west, **tha sinn a' dol an iar** we're going west(wards), (*story collection*) **Oiteagan on Iar** Breezes from the West, *Note that* **an** *of* **an iar** *does not behave as an article in the following exprs* **an àird(e) an iar** the west (*ie compass direction*), **an taobh an iar** the west coast/ west side of the country, **Na h-Eileanan an Iar** The Western Isles, *see* **sear** & *Cf* **deas 1, ear, siar, tuath**[1]

iar- 1 *a prefix corres to* Eng under-, vice-, deputy, (*Sc*) depute, *eg* **iar-chlèireach** *m* an under-secretary, **iar-stiùiriche** *m* a deputy director, **iar-cheann-suidhe** *m* a vice-president (*of company*); **2** *also* post-, *eg* **iar-cheumnaiche** *m* a postgraduate; **3** (*family relationships*) great-, **iar-ogha** *m* a great-grandchild

iarann, iarainn, iarannan *nm* **1** iron, (*song*) **seòmraichean glaiste le claspaichean iarainn** rooms locked with clasps of iron; **2** (*household*) an iron

iargalt(a) *adj* churlish, surly, *Cf* **gnù, mùgach**

iarla, iarla, iarlan *nm* an earl, (*song*) **mhic iarla nam bratach bàna o** son of the earl of the white banners

iarmad, iarmaid, iarmadan *nm* a remnant, a residue, *Cf more usu* **fuidheall 1**

iarmailt, iarmailt, iarmailtean *nf, with art,* **an iarmailt** the firmament, the sky, the skies, the heavens, *Cf* **nèamh 2, speur 2**

iarnaich *vti, pres part* **ag iarnachadh**, *also* **iarnaig** *vti, pres part* **ag iarnaigeadh**, iron (*clothes &c*)

iarnachadh *gen* **iarnachaidh** *nm, also* **iarnaigeadh** *gen* **iarnaigidh** *nm*, **1** (*the act of*) ironing; **2** (*a batch of*) ironing

iar-ogha *see* **iar- 3**

iarr *vt, pres part* **ag iarraidh**, 1 want, require, **a bheil thu ag iarraidh cofaidh?** do you want/would you like a/some coffee? **bha a' chlann ag iarraidh orm piseag a cheannach** the children wanted me to buy a kitten, *Cf* **dìth 2, miannaich 1, togair 1**; 2 ask, ask for, request, demand, **dh'iarr iad àrdachadh pàighidh** they asked for/demanded a pay rise, **dh'iarr i orm an doras a dhùnadh** she asked me to shut the door; 3 ask, invite, **chan iarr sinn oirbh a thighinn a-steach** we won't ask/invite you to come in, **dh'iarr iad mi gu pàrtaidh** they asked/invited me to a party (*Cf* **thoir cuireadh do** (*see* **cuireadh**)); 4 *in expr* **rach** *v* **a dh'iarraidh rudeigin** go to/and get something, go to/and fetch something

iarraidh, iarraidh, iarraidhean *nm* 1 (*the act of*) wanting, asking &c (*see senses of* **iarr** *v*); 2 a request, *Cf more usu* **iarr(a)tas 1**; 3 an invitation, (*song*) **thig trì nithean gun iarraidh** ... three things come unasked/uninvited ..., *Cf more usu* **cuireadh**

iarr(a)tas, iarr(a)tais, iarr(a)tasan *nm* 1 a request, a demand, *Cf less usu* **iarraidh 2**; 2 an application (*for job &c*), **foirm** *m* **iarr(a)tais** an application form

iasad, iasaid, iasadan *nm* borrowing, a loan, **iasad banca** a bank loan, **gabh/faigh** *v* **rudeigin air iasad** borrow something, get something on loan, **faigh/thoir** *v* **iasad de rudeigin** get/give a loan/a lend of something, borrow/lend something, (*prov*) **cha bhi each-iasaid sgìth a-chaoidh** a borrowed horse never gets tired

iasg (*sing & coll*), *gen & pl* **èisg** *nm* fish, a fish, **is toigh leam iasg** I like fish, (*prov*) **glac thusa foighidinn is glacaidh tu iasg** catch yourself some patience and you'll catch fish

iasgach, *gen* **iasgaich** *nm* 1 (*the act & activity of*) fishing (*deep sea & inshore*), **tha a h-athair ris an iasgach** her father's a fisherman/at the fishing, **bàta-iasgaich** *m* a fishing-boat; 2 (*as hobby &c*) fishing, angling, **slat-iasgaich** *f* a fishing rod

iasgaich *vt, pres part* **ag iasgach(d)**, fish, **nam bhalach bhithinn ri/ag iasgach fad na h-ùine** as a boy I'd be fishing all the time,

iasgair, iasgair, iasgairean *nm* a fisher, an angler, a fisherman

iath *see* **iadh**

idir *adv* 1 at all, (*usu with neg verb*) **a bheil thu sgìth? chan eil idir!** are you tired? not at all!, not in the least!, *often duplicated for emphasis* **cha dèan sin a' chùis idir idir!** there's no way that will do/suffice!; 2 *in emph question* **càit idir an deach e?** where on earth did he go? *Cf* **fon ghrèin** (*see* **grian**), **air an t-saoghal** (*see* **saoghal 1**)

ifrinn, ifrinn, ifrinnean *nf* hell, a hell, *Cf less usu* **iutharn(a)**

ifrinneach *adj* hellish, infernal

ighne, ighnean *see* **nighean**

Ile *nf invar* Islay, (*song*) **'s ann an Ile ghorm an fheòir a rugadh mi 's a thogadh mi** it was in green grassy Islay that I was born and raised

Ileach, *gen & pl* **Ilich** *nm* someone from Islay, *also as adj* **Ileach** of, from or pertaining to Islay

ìm, *gen* **ime** *nm* butter, (*prov*) **bu dual don bhlàthaich tòchd an ime** it's only to be expected that buttermilk should smell of butter

imcheist, imcheist, imcheistean *nf* **1** anxiety, **fo imcheist** *adv* anxious, *Cf* **cùram 2, iomagain 1; 2** perplexity, doubt, a dilemma, **an/fo imcheist** *adv* perplexed, in doubt, in a dilemma, **cuir** *v* **an imcheist** perplex

imcheisteach *adj* **1** anxious, worrying, perplexed, perplexing, *Cf* **an/fo imcheist** (*see* **imcheist 1**), **iomagaineach**

imich *vi, pres part* **ag imeachd, 1** depart, leave, go, *Cf more usu* **falbh 1; 2** go, journey, move (*from one place to another*), (*song*) **'s mi ri imeachd nam aonar anns an òg-mhadainn Mhàirt** as I walked out alone in the morning freshness of March, *Cf more usu* **rach 1, triall**

imleag, imleige, imleagan *nf* a navel, a belly-button

imlich *vt, pres part* **ag imlich,** lick, lap

imlich, *gen* **imliche** *nf* **1** (*the act of*) licking, lapping; **2** a lick

imnidh, *gen* **imnidhe,** *also* **iomnaidh** *gen* **iomnaidhe,** *nf* solicitude, anxiety, *Cf* **iomagain 2**

impidh, impidhe, impidhean *nm* persuasion, entreaty, urging, *esp in expr* **cuir** *v* **impidh air** persuade, urge, entreat, **chuir iad impidh orm mo dhreuchd a leigeil dhìom** they urged me to give up my job/to retire

impidheach *adj* persuasive, urging

ìmpireil *adj* imperial

impis *see* **an impis**

imrich *vi, pres part* **ag imrich(d)** *&* **ag imreacheadh, 1** move house, (*Sc*) flit, *Cf* **imrich** *n* **2; 2** migrate

imrich, imriche, imrichean *nf* **1** (*the act of*) moving (*house &c*), (*Sc*) flitting; **2** a removal a flitting, **dèan** *v* **imrich** move house, (*Sc*) flit (*Cf* **imrich** *vi* **2**); **2** migration

inbhe, inbhe, inbhean *nf* **1** (*in hierarchy, progression &c*) rank, dignity, status, a rank, a level (*of rank, attainment, ability*), **mòr-inbhe** eminence, high rank or attainment, **comharradh inbhe** a status symbol, *Cf* **ìre 1; 2** adulthood, maturity, the state of being grown up/fully grown, **thig** *v* **gu inbhe** grow up, reach adulthood, *Cf* **ìre 2**

inbheach *adj* adult, grown-up, fully grown, mature, **oileanach** *m* **inbheach** a mature student

inbheach, *gen & pl* **inbhich** *nm* an adult, a grown-up, a fully grown individual

inbheil *adj* eminent, high-ranking

inbhidh *adj* adult, **foghlam inbhidh** adult education

inbhidheachd *nf invar* puberty

inbhir, inbhir, inbhirean *nm* a confluence, the place where water-courses meet or a watercourse joins a loch &c, the mouth of a watercourse, *now in placenames, occurring as* Inver-, Inner-, **Inbhir Nis** Inverness, the mouth of the River Ness; *also* an estuary

inc *nmf invar* ink, *Cf* **dubh** *n* 2

ìne, ìne, ìnean, *also* (*more trad*) **iong(n)a, ingne, ingnean,** *nf* 1 a nail (*of finger, toe*), (*prov*) **is ann air ìnean a dh'aithnichear duine-uasal** it's by his nails that a gentleman/nobleman can be recognised; 2 a claw, a talon (*of birds*), *Cf* **spuir**; 3 a hoof (*of horse, cattle &c*), *Cf* **ladhar**

inneal, inneil, innealan *nm* 1 a machine, **inneal-nighe** & **inneal-nigheadaireachd** a washing machine, *Cf* **beart** 2; 2 *for devices of various kinds eg* **inneal-smàlaidh** a fire extinguisher, **inneal-clàir** a record-player, **inneal-ciùil** a musical instrument; 3 a tool, an implement, *Cf* **ball-acainn** (*see* **acainn** 1)

innealach *adj* mechanical

innean, innein, inneanan *nm* an anvil

inneir & **innear,** *gen* **innearach** *nf* (*agric*) dung, manure, (*prov*) **dùnan math innearach, màthair na ciste-mine** a good heap of dung, the mother of the meal-kist, *Cf* **buachar, todhar**

innidh *nf invar* a bowel, bowels, innards, intestines, *Cf* **caolan, greallach, mionach** 1

innis *vti, pres part* **ag innseadh** & **ag innse,** (*with prep* **do**) tell, inform, relate, recount, **mar a dh'innis mi dhuibh** as I told you, **innis dhomh mu dheidhinn!** tell me about it/him! **innsidh mi na tha a dh'fhios agam** I'll tell/relate what I know, **leis an fhìrinn innse, cha robh e cho math sin** to tell the truth, it wasn't that good, **innis sgeulachd** tell a story

innis, innse, innsean *nf* 1 an island, *Cf more usu* **eilean**; 2 low-lying ground or meadowland, *esp near water*, (*Sc*) a haugh, (*song*) **innis nam bò** the haugh of the cattle; 3 *in expr* **Innse Gall** *fpl* the Hebrides

innleachadh, *gen* **innleachaidh** *nm* (*the act of*) inventing, conceiving, contriving &c (*see senses of* **innlich** *v*)

innleachd, innleachd, innleachdan *nf* 1 ingenuity, invention, an invention, (*prov*) **nì airc innleachd** necessity is the mother of invention, *Cf* **tionnsgal** 2; 2 artfulness, resourcefulness, cunning; 3 intelligence, *Cf* **inntinn** 1, **tuigse** 1; 4 a stratagem, a plot, a plan, a ploy, **ro-innleachd** a strategy, *Cf* **cuilbheart; 5** a (*mechanical*) device, a machine, *Cf more usu* **inneal 1** & **2**

innleachdach *adj* **1** ingenious, inventive, *Cf* **tionnsgalach 1; 2** artful, resourceful, adroit, cunning, *Cf* **carach 1; 3** intelligent, *Cf* **tuigseach 1**

innleadair, innleadair, innleadairean *nm* an engineer, a mechanic, **innleadair-dealain** an electrical engineer, **innleadair-thogalach** a civil engineer

innleadaireachd *nf invar* engineering

innlich *vt, pres part* **ag innleachadh**, invent, devise, plan, plot, hatch (*a plot &c*), contrive, conceive, create, engineer (*a plan, a stratagem, a mental or mechanical device of some kind*), **dh'innlich e inneal ùr airson arbhar a bhuain** he invented/devised/conceived a new machine for harvesting corn, **innlich cuilbheart** conceive/devise a trick/a stratagem, *Cf* **cruthaich, dealbh** *v* **3, tionnsgail**

Innseachan *nmpl, with art,* **Na h-Innseachan** India

innse(adh), *gen* **innsidh** *nm* (*the act of*) telling, informing &c (*see senses of* **innis** *v*)

Innseanach, *gen & pl* **Innseanaich** *nm* someone from India, an Indian, *also as adj* **Innseanach** Indian

innte(se) *prep pron see* **an** *prep* **2**

inntinn, inntinn, inntinnean *nf* **1** mind (*as seat of knowledge & intelligence*), intellect, **tha inntinn mhath aice** she's got a good mind, **comas** *m* **inntinn** mental/intellectual ability, mental powers, intellectual capacity, *Cf* **eanchainn 2; 2** mind (*as seat of memory, feeling &c*), **bha i rud beag sìos na h-inntinn** she was a bit down/a bit depressed

inntinneach *adj* **1** interesting, **leabhar/cuspair/duine inntineach** an interesting book/subject/man; **2** (*also* **inntinneil**) intellectual, mental, to do with the mind

inntrig *vi, pres part* **ag inntrigeadh**, enter, go in

inntrigeadh, inntrigidh, inntrigidhean *nm* **1** (*the act of*) entering; **2** (*mainly abstr*) entrance, entry, access, **deuchainn** *f* **inntrigidh** an entrance exam/test, **còir** *f* **inntrigidh** right of entry/access

ìobair *vt, pres part* **ag ìobradh,** (*relig*) sacrifice, offer (up) as a sacrifice

ìobairt, ìobairte, ìobairtean *nf* (*relig*) a sacrifice, a sacrificial offering

ìoc *vti, pres part* **ag ìocadh,** pay, *Cf more usu* **pàigh** *v* **1**

ìoc, *gen & pl* **ìce** *nm* payment, a payment, *Cf more usu* **dìo(gh)ladh 2, pàigheadh**

iochd *nf invar* compassion, mercy, clemency, pity, *Cf* **tròcair, truacantas, truas**

ìochdar, ìochdair, ìochdaran *nm* (*opposite of* uachdar), bottom, base, foundation, lowest part of anything, am beul-ìochdair the lower lip, *Cf* bonn 1

ìochd(a)rach *adj* (*opposite of* uachdarach), 1 lower, nether, bottom; 2 inferior; *Cf* (n)as (&c) ìsle (*comp of* ìosal)

ìochdaran, *gen & pl* ìochdarain *nm* (*opposite of* uachdaran), 1 an inferior, a subordinate, an underling; 2 (*of monarchy &c*) a subject

ìochdaranachd *nf invar* inferiority

iochdmhor *adj* merciful, compassionate, *Cf* tròcaireach, truacanta

ìocshlaint, ìocshlainte, ìocshlaintean *nf* a medicine, a remedy, *Cf* leigheas 2

iodhal, iodhail, iodhalan *nm* an idol, *Cf* ìomhaigh 3

iodhlann, iodhlainn, iodhlannan *nf* (*agric*) a corn-yard, a stackyard

iolach, *gen & pl* iolaich *nf* a shout, a cheer, dèan/tog *v* iolach shout, cheer, *Cf more usu* èigh *n*, glaodh[1] *n*

iolair(e), iolaire, iolairean *nf* an eagle, iolair(e) bhuidhe a golden eagle

iolra, iolra, iolran *nm, also as adj* iolra, (*gram*) plural, a plural, ainmear iolra a plural noun

ioma- *a prefix corres to Eng* multi-, poly-, *eg* ioma-chànanach *adj* multilingual, polyglot, (*IT &c*) ioma-mheadhan *adj* multimedia, ioma-thìreach *adj* multinational, ioma-phòsadh *m* polygamy, ioma-sheòrsach *adj* heterogenous, *Cf* iomadh 2

iomadach *adj* many, many a, *Note: precedes the noun, which is in the nom sing* (*radical*); rinn mi iomadach uair e I did it often/many a time, rudan de dh'iomadach seòrsa things of many kinds, all sorts of things, *Cf less usu* iomadh 1

iomadaich, *pres part* ag iomadachadh, *vt* (*maths*) multiply (le by)

iomadh *adj* 1 many, many a, *Note: precedes the noun, which is in the nom sing* (*radical*); dh'fheuch iomadh duine e many a man/many men tried it, iomadh là many a day, many days, *Cf more usu* iomadach; 2 *occas in compound adj eg* iomadh-fhillte complex, complicated, manifold, *Cf* ioma-

iomagain, iomagaine, iomagainean *nf* 1 anxiety, worry, fo iomagain anxious, worried, troubled, *Cf* cùram 2, dragh 3, imcheist 1; 2 solicitude, *Cf* imnidh

iomagaineach *adj* 1 worried, anxious, prone to worry or anxiety, *Cf* cùramach 2; 2 worrying, causing worry or anxiety, *Cf* draghail; *Cf* imcheisteach

iomain *vt, pres part* ag iomain, 1 drive, drive on, urge on (*esp livestock*), *Cf* greas 2; 2 drive, propel (*machinery &c*), stuth-iomain propellant, dh'iomaineadh an t-inneal le smùid the machine was driven by steam; 3 propel (*a ball in a game, esp shinty*); 4 (*as vi*) play a ball game (*esp shinty*), **bha na gillean ag iomain** the lads were playing shinty

iomain, *gen* **iomaine** *nf* shinty, *Cf* **camanachd**

iomair *vti, pres part* **ag iomramh**, row (*a boat*), **ag iomramh an aon ràimh** pulling/working together, co-operating, (*lit* rowing/pulling the same oar)

iomair *vt, pres part* **ag iomairt**, use, employ, wield (*weapon, tool &c*), **ag iomairt ùird/bhiodagan** wielding a hammer/dirks, *Cf more usu* **cleachd 1, làimhsich 3**

iomairt, iomairte, iomairtean *nf* **1** (*the act of*) using, employing, wielding (*see* **iomair** *vt*); **2** an effort, an endeavour, a struggle (*in aid of something, to achieve something*), a campaign, **Iomairt na Gàidhealtachd** Highlands and Islands Enterprise

iomall, iomaill, iomallan *nm* **1** an edge, a border, a margin, an extremity, a limit, a verge, a fringe, a periphery, **iomall na coille** the edge of the wood, **iomall na dùthcha** the limits/fringes of the country, **iomall a' bhaile** the suburbs/outskirts of the town, **fearann iomaill** marginal land, *Cf* **crìoch 2, oir** *n* **1**; **2** a rim, a lip (*of jug &c*), **iomall na poite** the rim of the pot, *Cf* **oir** *n* **2**

iomallach *adj*, remote, isolated, distant, on the margins, peripheral, **ceàrnaidhean iomallach** remote areas/districts

iomchaidh & iomchuidh *adj* **1** suitable, *Cf more usu* **freagarrach**; **2** fitting, decent, proper, *Cf* **cothromach**

iomchair *vt, pres part* **ag iomchar**, bear, carry, transport, *Cf more usu* **giùlain 1**

iomchar, *gen* **iomchair** *nm* **1** (*the act of*) bearing &c (*see senses of* **iomchair** *v*), **fear-iomchair** *m* a bearer, *Cf more usu* **giùlan**; **2** comportment, behaviour, conduct, *Cf more usu* **dol-a-mach, giùlan**

ìomhaigh, ìomhaigh, ìomhaighean *nf* **1** an image or physical representation of something or someone (*in art, sculpture &c*), a likeness; **2** a visual image (*in mirror, lens &c*); **3** (*relig*) an image, an idol, *Cf* **iodhal**; **4** (*publicity &c*) an image, a profile, **leasaich** *v* **ìomhaigh na companaidh** improve the company's image, **tog** *v* **ìomhaigh a' phàrtaidh** raise the party's profile; **5** (*Lit*) an image

iomlaid, iomlaid, iomlaidean *nf* **1** (*trad*) exchange, barter, *Cf more usu* **malairt 2**; **2** *now usu* change (*ie money*), **iomlaid nota** change for a pound, **iomlaid à nota** change from a pound, **thug mi dà nota dha ach cha d'fhuair mi iomlaid** I gave him two pounds but I didn't get any change

iomlan *adj* **1** (*abstr & con*) complete, entire, whole, absolute, **chan eil a' charragh iomlan** the stone isn't complete, *Cf* **slàn 4**; **2** *as adv* **gu h-iomlan** absolutely, entirely, fully, completely, quite, *Cf* **buileach, tur 2**

iomlan, *gen* **iomlain** *nm* all *or* the whole of anything, **a bheil thu ag iarraidh an iomlain (dheth)?** do you want all/the whole of it?

iomnaidh *see* **imnidh**

iompachadh, iompachaidh, iompachaidhean *nm* **1** (*the act of*) converting, persuading &c (*see senses of* **iompaich** *v*); **2** (*esp relig*) conversion, a conversion

iompachan, *gen & pl* **iompachain** *nm* (*relig &c*) a convert, a neophyte

iompaich *vt, pres part* **ag iompachadh**, **1** (*relig*) convert, **chaidh a h-iompachadh** she was converted, *Cf* **cùram 3**; **2** persuade, cause someone to change his/her opinion or mind, *Cf* **cuir impidh air** (*see* **impidh**)

ìompaire, ìompaire, ìompairean *nm* an emperor, **ban-ìompaire** *f* an empress

ìompaireachd, ìompaireachd, ìompaireachdan *nf* empire, an empire

iomradh, iomraidh, iomraidhean *nm* **1** mentioning, a mention, an allusion, a reference (**air** to), **cha tug e iomradh air an teaghlach aige** he didn't mention his family, *Cf* **guth 3**; **2** a report, an account, a commentary, **tha iomradh air an stailc sa phàipear-naidheachd** there's an account of the strike in the paper, *Cf* **aithris** *n* **1**

iomraiteach *adj* (*esp persons*) well-known, celebrated, famous, renowned, notorious, *Cf* **ainmeil, cliùiteach**

iomrall, iomraill, iomrallan *nm* **1** error, a mistake, an error, *Cf more usu* **mearachd**; **2** wandering, straying, **air iomrall** *adv* astray, wandering, *Cf* **seachran 1**; **3** *in expr* **rach** *v* **air iomrall** go astray (*phys, morally*), *also* make a mistake, err, go wrong

iomrallach *adj* mistaken, wrong, erroneous, *Cf* **mearachdach**

iomramh, *gen* **iomraimh** *nm* (*the act of*) rowing (*a boat*) (*see* **iomair** *vti*)

ion- **1** *a prefix corres to Eng* -able, -ible, *eg* **ion-ithe** *adj* eatable, edible, **ion-dhèanta** *adj* feasible, possible, practicable, *Cf* **so-**; **2** *occas corres to Eng* worthy of, fit for, *eg* **ionmholta** *adj* praiseworthy

ionad, ionaid, ionadan *nm* **1** (*trad*) a place, a spot, *Cf* **àite 1, bad 1**; **2** (*now often*) a building where a particular activity is based or administered, a centre, an agency; **ionad-latha** (*pensioners &c*) a day centre, **ionad-obrach** a job centre, *also* (*IT*) a work station, **ionad-slàinte** a health centre, **ionad-spòrsa** a sports centre/complex, **ionad-stiùiridh** a management centre, **Ionad airson Eòlas-dìona** Centre for Defence Studies, *Cf* **taigh 3**; **3** (*IT*) a site, **ionad eadar-lìn** an internet site

ionadail *adj* local, **ùghdarras** *m* **ionadail** a local authority, **eachdraidh** *f* **ionadail** local history

ionaltair *vi, pres part* **ag ionaltradh**, (*livestock*) graze

ionaltradh, ionaltraidh, ionaltraidhean *nm* **1** (*the act of*) grazing; **2** grazing (*ie land*), pasture, a pasture, *Cf* **clua(i)n**

ionann & **ionnan** *adj* same, alike, similar, identical, *takes the v* **is**, **is ionann X is Y** X equals Y, **chan ionann thusa is mise** you and I are not the same/are different, **cha b' ionnan an uair a bha sinn òg** it wasn't the same when we were young, *in expr* **ionnan agus** just/ exactly like, the same as, identical with, *Cf* **co-ionann, coltach 2**

ionga *see* **ìne**

iongantach *adj* strange, surprising, amazing, wonderful, marvellous, phenomenal, *Cf* **mìorbhaileach**, & *less strong* **neònach**

iongantas, iongantais, iongantasan *nm* **1** amazement, wonder, **gabh** *v* **iongantas** be amazed; **2** a wonder, an amazing thing or event, a phenomenon, *Cf* **mìorbhail 1**; *Cf less strong* **iongnadh 1**

iongna *see* **ìne**

iongnadh, iongnaidh, iongnaidhean *nm* **1** a surprise, a surprising *or* amazing thing, a wonder, a marvel, *esp in expr* **chan iongnadh** ... no wonder ..., **chan iongnadh sin** that's no wonder/not surprising, **chan iongnadh gu bheil e toilichte!** no wonder he's pleased!; **2** surprise, amazement, wonder, **gabh** *v* **iongnadh** be surprised/ amazed, **chuir e iongnadh orm** it surprised/amazed me, **mòr-iongnadh** astonishment; *Cf stronger, less usu* **iongantas**

ionmhainn *adj* (*trad*) (*term of endearment*) dear, precious, darling, beloved, **a leannan ionmhainn** her darling (*&c*) sweetheart, *Cf* **còir** *adj* **2, gaolach 2**

ionmhas, ionmhais, ionmhasan *nm* **1** treasure, *Cf* **ulaidh 1**; **2** wealth, riches, *Cf* **beartas, saidhbhreas, stòras**

ionmhasair, ionmhasair, ionmhasairean *nm* a treasurer

ionnan *see* **ionann**

ionnanach *adj* equal, identical (*Cf more usu* **ionann**), (*sport*) **geama** *m* **ionnanach** a draw, a drawn game

ionndrainn *vt, pres part* **ag ionndrainn**, miss, long for, feel the absence or lack of, (*song*) **a' sìor-ionndrainn tìr a bhruadair** eternally longing for/missing the land he dreams of, **tha mi gad ionndrainn** I miss/am missing you

ionnlad, *gen* **ionnlaid** *nm* (*the act of*) washing or bathing, ablution(s), **mias** *f* **ionnlaid** a wash basin, **seòmar/rùm** *m* **ionnlaid** a bathroom

ionnlaid *vti, pres part* **ag ionnlad**, wash, bathe, *Cf* **failc, nigh**

ionnsachadh, *gen* **ionnsachaidh** *nm* **1** (*the act of*) learning, studying &c (*see senses of* **ionnsaich** *v*); **2** learning (*ie knowledge, scholarship*), *Cf* **foghlam 2, oideachas 1**

ionnsaich *vti, pres part* **ag ionnsachadh, 1** learn, **cha do dh'ionnsaich mi mòran anns an sgoil** I didn't learn much at school, **ionnsaich**

mu dheidhinn learn/find out about it; **2** learn, study (*a particular subject &c*), **bidh sinn ag ionnsachadh na Gàidhlig aig a' cholaiste** we'll be studying Gaelic at college; **3** (*occas*) teach, train, instruct, *Cf usu* **teagaisg**

ionnsaichte *adj* educated, trained, *Cf* **foghlaimte**

ionnsaigh, ionnsaigh, ionnsaighean *nmf* **1** an attack, an assault, **fear-ionnsaigh** *m* an attacker/assailant, **thoir** *v* **ionnsaigh air cuideigin** attack/assault someone, (*legal*) **droch ionnsaigh** assault, an assault; **2** an attempt, an effort, a try, (*Sc*) a shot, **thoir** *v* **ionnsaigh eile** have another try/attempt/shot (**air** at), *Cf* **oidhirp 1**; **3** *in prep* **a dh'ionnsaigh** to, towards, *with gen*, **a dh'ionnsaigh a' bhaile** to/towards the town(ship), **bha am balach a' ruith dha h-ionnsaigh** the boy was running towards her, *Cf* **gu**[1] **1**

ionns(t)ramaid, ionns(t)ramaide, ionns(t)ramaidean *nf* an instrument (*esp music*, *Cf* **inneal-ciùil** – *see* **inneal 2**)

ionracas, *gen* **ionracais** *nm* **1** honesty, *Cf* **onair 3**; **2** justice, justness, righteousness, *Cf* **ceartas, còir** *n* **4**

ionraic *adj* **1** honest, *Cf* **onarach 3**; **2** just, righteous, *Cf* **ceart 2, dìreach 2**

ìoran(t)as, *gen* **ìoran(t)ais** *nm* irony

ìoranta *adj* ironic(al)

iorghail, iorghail, iorghailean *nf* tumult, a tumult, *Cf* **gleadhar, othail, ùpraid 1**

iorghaileach *adj* tumultuous

Iosa *nm invar* Jesus

ìosal & **ìseal** *adj* (*opposite of* **uasal**), *comp* **(n)as** (&c) **ìsle**, **1** (*phys*) low, **cnoc ìosal** a low hill, **taigh ìosal air a thogail** a low-built house; **2** (*status &c*) low, lowly, humble, *Cf* **iriosal 1**; **3** (*sound*) low, quiet, **ann an guth ìosal** in a low/quiet voice, **os ìosal** *adv* quietly, *also* secretly, privately, covertly

Ioslamach *adj* Islamic, *Cf* **Mohamadanach**

Iosrael & **Israel**, *nf invar* Israel

Iosralach, *gen* & *pl* **Iosralaich** *nm*, *also* **Israeleach**, *gen* & *pl* **Israelich**, *nm*, an Israeli, (*Bibl, hist*) an Israelite, *also as adj* **Iosralach** & **Israeleach** Israeli, of, from or pertaining to Israel

ìota(dh), *gen* **ìotaidh** *nm* thirst, *Cf* **tart** & *more usu, less strong*, **pathadh**

ìotmhor *adj* parched, dry, very thirsty, *Cf* **tartmhor**

ìre *nf invar* **1** a degree, a level, a stage (*of progress, development, ability &c*), **foghlam (aig) àrd-ìre** higher/tertiary/further education, **duine aig ìre na h-obrach** a man up to the job; **2** maturity, **thig** *v* **gu ìre** come to/reach maturity, become full-grown, *Cf* **inbhe 2**; **3** *in expr* **an ìre mhath** *adv* quite, pretty, fairly, **bha sinn an ìre mhath sgìth** we were quite/pretty/fairly tired (*Cf* **gu math** – *see* **math 4**), *also* just about, pretty well, more or less, **tha an geamhradh an ìre mhath seachad** the winter's pretty well/just about over (*Cf* **bi 11**); **4** *in expr* **gu ìre bhig** almost, nearly, all but, **chaill sinn am bus gu ìre bhig** we almost/all but missed the bus, *Cf* **mòr 5**

iriosal *adj* **1** (*status &c*) humble, lowly, *Cf* **ìosal 2**; **2** humble (*ie self-effacing*), *Cf* **umha(i)l 1**

irioslachadh, irioslachaidh, irioslachaidhean *nm* **1** (*the act of*) humbling, humiliating; **2** humiliation, a humiliation; *Cf* **ìsleachadh, ùmhlachadh**

irioslachd *nf invar* **1** lowliness, humble status; **2** humility, *Cf* **ùmhlachd 1**

irioslaich *vt, pres part* **ag irioslachadh**, humble, humiliate, *Cf* **ùmhlaich 2**

iris, iris, irisean *nf* a periodical, a magazine, a (*literary &c*) quarterly, *Cf* **ràitheachan**

is (*inter* **an**, *neg* **cha(n)**, *neg inter* **nach**, *past & conditional* **bu**) *v irreg & defective*, is, are, was, were, would be, **1** *as a copula linking nouns, prons*, **is duine mi** I am a man, **an ise Iseabail?** is she Isabel?, **b' iadsan an fheadhainn a rinn e** they were the ones who did it, (*trad*) **is meatailt copar** copper is a metal; **2** *when linking a noun &c and an adj* **is** *often implies a more permanent quality or greater emphasis than* **bi**, (*trad*) **is searbh fìon-geur** vinegar is bitter, **is fèineil mi!** I'm (so) selfish! *Note:* **is** + *an adj is common in set phrases & exprs, eg* **is toigh leam** I like, **b' fheàrr leam** I preferred/I'd prefer, **is truagh sin!** that's a shame! **is coma leis** he doesn't mind, **'s math seachad e** it's good that it's finished/over; **3** *introducing a rel clause*, **an tusa a sgrìobh e? cha mhi!** was it you who wrote it? no! **nach iadsan a thèid ann?** isn't it they who'll go?, **a bheil thu deiseil? is mi a tha!** are you ready? I certainly/sure am! **nach math a rinn thu!** didn't you do well!, well done!; *Note: before nouns* **is e, b' e, chan e** (*&c*) *is used*, **is e am bodach a chaill e** it's the old man who lost it, **nach e a cèile a chaochail?** isn't/wasn't it her husband who died?; **4** *when introducing an adj or adv constr* **is** (*&c*) **ann** (*often emph*) *is used*, **'s ann aosta a tha i** she's old (*lit* it's old that she is), **an ann a-màireach a chì sinn i? chan ann** is it tomorrow we'll see her? no; **5 is** *with* **gun** *conj becomes* **gur**, *conj*, that it (*&c*) is, **an e saor a th' ann? cha chreid mi gur e** is he a joiner, I don't think (that) he is, *see also* **gun** *conj*; **6** *introducing a comp or superlative*, **as** (*for* **a is**), *in past tense* **a bu, am fear as sine** the oldest one, **am peann a b' fheàrr a bh' agam** the best pen I had; *Cf* **bi**

is *conj see* **agus**

ìsbean, ìsbein, ìsbeanan *nm* a sausage

ìseal *see* **ìosal**

isean, isein, iseanan *nm* **1** a chick, a chicken, a young bird; **2** a baby mammal, **isean cait** a kitten (*Cf usu* **piseag**); **3** *a term for a child* (*sometimes affectionate*), **droch isean** a brat, a naughty, unruly or badly brought-up child

ìsleachadh, *gen* **ìsleachaidh** *nm* **1** (*the act of*) lowering, degrading &c (*see senses of* **ìslich** *v*); **2** abasement, humiliation, a humiliation, *Cf* **ùmhlachadh 2**

ìslich *vti, pres part* **ag ìsleachadh**, become or make low or lower (*phys & fig*), degrade, debase, demote, humble, humiliate

is mathaid (gu) *adv & conj see* **faod 2**

isneach, isnich(e), isnichean *nf* a rifle, *Cf usu, less trad,* **raidhfil**

ist *pl* **istibh**, *also* **èist** *pl* **èistibh**, *excl* hush! be quiet! (*Sc*) wheesht!, *Cf* **sàmhach 1**

ite, ite, itean *nf* **1** a feather, *Cf* **iteag 1**; **2** a fin (*of fish*)

iteach, *gen* **itich** *nm* plumage

iteach *adj* feathered, having feathers, *Cf* **iteagach**

iteachan, *gen* **iteachain**, *pl* **iteachain** *&* **iteachanan** *nm* a bobbin, a spool

iteag, iteig, iteagan *nf* (*dimin of* **ite**) **1** a (small) feather; **2** flight, flying, *esp in expr* **air iteig** flying, on the wing, **rach** *v* **air iteig** fly (*Cf* **itealaich, sgiathaich**)

iteagach *adj* feathered, having feathers, *Cf* **iteach**

itealaich *vi, pres part* **ag itealaich** *&* **ag itealachadh**, fly, *Cf* **rach air iteig** (*see* **iteag 2**), **sgiathaich**

itealan, *gen & pl* **itealain** *nm* an aeroplane, a plane, an aircraft, *Cf less trad* **plèana**

iteileag, iteileig, iteileagan *nf* a kite (*ie the flying structure*)

ith *vti, pres part* **ag ithe(adh)**, eat

iubhar, iubhair, iubharan *nm* yew (*wood & tree*), *also* **craobh-iubhair** *f* a yew tree

iuchair, iuchrach, iuchraichean *nf* a key (*for locking, winding up, typing &c*)

Iuchar, *gen* **Iuchair** *nm, with art,* **an t-Iuchar** July

Iùdhach, *gen & pl* **Iùdhaich** *nm* a Jew, *also as adj* **Iùdhach** Jewish

iùil-tharraing, *gen* **iùil-tharrainge** *nf* magnetism

iùil-tharraingeach *adj* magnetic

iùl, iùil, iùilean *nm* (*trad*) **1** (*of boat &c*) a course, *Cf more usu* **cùrsa 2**, **seòl**² **2**; **2** guidance, **neach-iùil** *m* (*person*) a guide, *Cf more usu* **treòrachadh 2**; **3** a landmark (*ie for nagivation*), *Cf* **comharradh-stiùiridh** (*see* **comharradh 1**)

L

là & **latha**, *gen* **là** & **latha**, *pl* **làithean, lathachan** & **lathaichean** *nm* a day, **làithean na seachdain** the days of the week, **dè an là a th' ann?** what day is it? **co-là-breith** a birthday (*Cf* **ceann-bliadhna**), **là-breith** a date of birth, **latha-fèille** a (public) holiday, a feast-day, **làithean-saora** & **saor-làithean** holidays, **a dh'oidhche 's a là** by night and by day, **chunna sinn an là roimhe e** we saw him the other day, **chì mi latha no latha-eigin thu** I'll see you some day or other/ one of these days, **cuir** *v* **rudeigin air an ath là** put something off (till another day), (*trad*) **nach oirnn a thàinig an dà là!** what a change has come upon us! (*trad*) **là-luain** doomsday, Nevermas (*a day that will never come*), (*trad song*) **gu là-luain cha ghluaisear mis'** I will not be moved until doomsday

labhair *vi, pres part* **a' labhairt**, speak, talk, *Cf more usu* **bruidhinn** *v*

labhairt *nf invar* **1** (*the act of*) speaking, talking, **fear-labhairt** a speaker, *more usu* a spokesman, *Cf* **bruidhinn** *n* **1**; **2** speech, **comas** *m* **labhairt** faculty/power of speech, *Cf* **cainnt 1**

labhar *adj* loud, *Cf more usu* **àrd** *adj* **2**

lach, lacha, lachan *nf* a (*usu* wild) duck, *Cf* **tunnag**

lachdann *adj* **1** dun, tawny, khaki, *Cf* **odhar 1**; **2** swarthy, *Cf* **ciar** *adj* **1**

ladar, ladair, ladaran *nm* **1** a ladle, a large spoon, (*song*) **gabh an ladar no an taoman** take the ladle or the baling dish (*ie any expedient that comes to hand*), *Cf* **liagh 1, spàin**; **2** a scoop, *Cf* **liagh 2**

ladarna *adj* bold, shameless, audacious, bare-faced, impudent, *Cf* **dàna 3**

ladhar, *gen* **ladhair** & **ladhra**, *pl* **ladhran** *nm* a hoof, *Cf* **ìne 3**

lag *adj* weak, feeble, **bha mi lag leis an acras** I was weak with/from hunger, **bha i lag na h-inntinn** she was feeble-minded, *Cf* **fann**

lag, *gen* **laig** & **luig**, *pl* **lagan** *nmf* (*body, topog &c*) a hollow, a pit, (*Sc*) a howe, a den, **lag na h-achlaise** the armpit, (*placename*) **Lag a' Mhuilinn** Lagavulin, mill hollow, *Cf* **còs, glac 1, sloc 1**

lagaich *vti, pres part* **a' lagachadh**, weaken, grow or make weak or weaker, enfeeble, debilitate, *Cf less usu* **fannaich 1**

lagachadh, *gen* **lagachaidh** *nm* (*the act of*) weakening &c (*see senses of* **lagaich** *v*)

lag-chùiseach *adj* unenterprising, unadventurous, **duine lag-chùiseach** a stick-in the mud

lagh, lagha, laghannan *nm* (*jurisprudence, science &c*) law, a law, **an aghaidh an lagha** against the law, **fear-lagha** *m* a lawyer, a solicitor

laghach *adj* (*esp of people*) nice, kind, *Cf* **lurach**, **snog 2**

laghail *adj* lawful, legal, **mì-laghail** unlawful, illegal

laghairt, laghairt, laghairtean *nmf* a lizard

Laideann, *gen* **Laidinne** *nf* Latin

Laidinneach *adj* Latin

làidir *adj*, Note: *as well as the regular comp* **(n)as** (&c) **làidire**, *stronger*, **(n)as** (&c) **treise** *or* **treasa** (*see* **treun** *adj*) *is also used*, 1 strong, physically powerful, **gàirdean** *m* **làidir** a strong arm, **corp-làidir** *adj* able-bodied, strong in body, *Cf* **neartmhor**; 2 potent, strong, **deoch** *f* **làidir** strong/potent drink, alcoholic drink, intoxicating liquor

laigh *vi*, *pres part* **a' laighe**, 1 (*of people &c*) lie (down), **laigh sìos** lie down (*esp for sleep*) **tha sinn a' dol a laighe** we're going to bed; 2 land, settle, lie, come to rest, perch, **laigh a' phlèana** the plane landed, **gach rud air an laigheadh a shùil** each thing his eye would rest/light/settle upon; 3 decline, subside, go down, set, **tha a' ghaoth a' laighe a-nis** the wind's subsiding now, **laigh a' ghrian** the sun set/went down

laighe *nmf invar* 1 (*the act of*) lying (down), landing &c (*see senses of* **laigh** *v*); 2 a recumbent position, **tha i na laighe** she's lying down, **figear na laighe** a reclining/recumbent figure

laigse, laigse, laigsean *nf* 1 weakness, infirmity, debility; 2 a faint, a fainting fit, **chaidh mi an laigse** I fainted, *Cf* **fannaich 2**, **fanntaig**, **neul 3**

làimhseachadh, *gen* **làimhseachaidh** *nm* 1 (*the act of*) feeling, handling, treating &c (*see senses of* **làimhsich** *v*); 2 treatment, behaviour, conduct (*towards another person, animal &c*), **droch-làimhseachadh** ill-treatment, *also* (physical) abuse

làimhsich *vt*, *pres part* **a' làimhseachadh**, 1 feel, finger, touch, handle (*person. objects &c*), *Cf* **bean** *v* 1; 2 treat, behave towards (*esp persons*), *Cf* **gnàthaich 3**; 3 handle, wield (*tool, weapon &c*), *Cf* **iomair** *vt*; 4 handle, manage (*situation &c*), *Cf* **dèilig (ri)**

laimrig, laimrige, laimrigean *nf* a quay, a landing-place

lainnir, *gen* **lainnire** *nf* (*of light*) a glint, a glitter, a sparkle; brilliance, radiance

lainnireach *adj* sparkling, brilliant, radiant, *Cf* **boillsgeach**

làir(e), *gen* **làiridh** & **làireadh**, *pl* **làiridhean** *nf* a mare

làirne-mhàireach & **làrna-mhàireach** *adv* (on) the morrow, the next *or* following day, **bha i tinn air an oidhche ach bha i gu dòigheil làirne-mhàireach** she was ill in/during the night but she was fine the next/following day

làitheil *adj* daily, everyday

làmh, *gen* **làimh(e)**, *dat* **làimh**, *pl* **làmhan** *nf* **1** a hand, (*song*) **thoir dhomh do làmh** give me your hand, **air an làimh chlì** on the left(-hand side), **cha do rug e air làimh orm** he didn't shake hands with me, he didn't shake my hand, **crathadh-làimhe** *m* a handshake, **ghabh sinn làmh an uachdair orra** we got the upper hand of them, **gabh obair** (&c) **os làimh** undertake/take on work (&c); **2** captivity, arrest, **cuir** *v* **an làimh** capture, arrest, (*trad song*) **tha mis' an làimh** I am a prisoner/captive, *Cf* **braighdeanas, ciomachas, daorsa, sàs 1**; **3** a handle, *Cf* **cas** *n* **3**

làmhainn, làmhainn, làmhainnean *nf* a glove, *Cf* **miotag 1**

làmh-lèigh, làmh-lèigh, làmh-lèighean *nm* a surgeon

làmh-sgrìobhadh, làmh-sgrìobhaidh, làmh-sgrìobhaidhean *nm* handwriting

làmh-sgrìobhainn, làmh-sgrìobhainn, làmh-sgrìobhainnean *nmf* a manuscript

làmhthuagh, làmhthuaigh, làmhthuaghan *nf* a hatchet, a chopper

lampa, lampa, lampaichean *nmf* a lamp, *Cf* **lanntair, leus**

làn *adj* **1** full, **botal làn bainne/làn de bhainne** a bottle full of milk, **leth-làn** half full, **film làn-fhada** a full length film, **làn-chumhachd** *m* full power/authority, **làn-thìde** *adj* full-time, **bha làn-fhios agam nach robh e fìor** I was fully aware that it wasn't true (*lit* I had full knowledge); **2** *as adv* fully, completely, **tha sinn làn-chinnteach** we're quite/completely certain, *Cf* **buileach**

làn, *gen & pl* **làin** *nm* **1** fullness, a fill, as much as will fill something, **làn beòil** a mouthful, **làn dùirn** a handful, a fistful (*Cf* **dòrlach**), **làn spàine** a spoonful, **fhuair mi mo làn de bhrot** *or* **fhuair mi làn mo bhroinn de bhrot** I got my fill of/a bellyful of soup (*Cf* **leòr 1, sàth** *n*); **2** (*also* **làn-mara**, *gen & pl* **làin-mhara** *nm*) a (high) tide, *Cf* **muir-làn, seòl-mara** (*see* **muir**), **tràigh** *n* **2**

langa, langa, langan *nf* (*fish*) ling, a ling

lànachd *nf invar* fulness

langanaich *vi, pres part* **a' langanaich**, (*cattle & esp deer*) bellow, low, (*song*) **bhiodh na fèidh a' langanaich** the deer would be bellowing, *Cf* **beuc** *v*, **geum** *v*, **nuallaich**

langasaid, langasaide, langasaidean *nf* a sofa, a couch, *Cf* **sòfa**

lann[1], *gen* **lanna** & **lainne**, *pl* **lannan** *nf* **1** a blade, **lann sgeine** a knife blade, **tharraing e a lann** he drew his blade/sword; **2** (*fish, reptile*) a scale

lann[2], **lainn, lannan** *nf* **1** an enclosure, an enclosed piece of ground; **2** a fence, *Cf more usu* **feansa**; **3** (*in compounds*) a repository, a place where objects are kept, a place where a particular activity is carried out, **leabharlann** a library, **obair-lann** & **deuchainn-lann** a laboratory, **cainnt-lann** a language laboratory, **biadh-lann** a refectory, **taisbean-lann** an art gallery, an exhibition hall

lanntair, lanntair, lanntairean *nmf* a lantern, *Cf* **lampa, leus**

laoch, *gen* & *pl* **laoich** *nm* a hero, a warrior, *Cf* **curaidh, gaisgeach**

laochan, *gen* & *pl* **laochain** *nm* (*dimin of* **laoch**), a little/wee hero, *now esp a term of endearment applied to a young boy*, **ciamar a tha thu andiugh, a laochain?** how are you today, (my) wee hero?

laogh, laoigh, laoghan *nm* 1 a calf, **laoigh-fheòil** *f* veal; 2 (*as voc term of endearment*) **a laoigh!** (my) love!, (my) dear!, *Cf* **eudail 2, gaol 2, gràdh 2, luaidh** *nmf*

laoidh, laoidhe, laoidhean *nmf* 1 a song, a poem, a lay, *Cf* **dàn**² 1 & 2, **duan 1**; 2 a hymn; 3 an anthem

lapach *adj* 1 numb; 2 weak, feeble, *Cf more usu* **fann, lag** *adj*

làr, làir, làran *nm* 1 (the) ground, (*song*) **dhòirt iad fhuil mu làr** they spilled his blood upon the ground, **sìnte air an làr** stretched out on the ground; 2 a floor, *Cf* **ùrlar 1**

làrach, làraich, làraichean *nf* 1 a trace or vestige of something, a mark, a scar, (*of building*) a ruin (*Cf* **tobhta**), **cha do dh'fhàg e làrach** it didn't leave a trace, *also in expr* **an làrach nam bonn** immediately, on the spot (*lit* in the sole prints), *Cf* **comharra(dh) 3, lorg** *n* 2; 2 a site (*of something past or to come*), **làrach taighe** a site for a house

làraidh, làraidh, làraidhean *nf* a lorry

las *vti, pres part* **a' lasadh**, 1 (*vt*) light, set fire to, kindle, ignite (*candle, fire &c*), **las toitean** light a cigarette, *Cf* **leig 8, loisg 1**; 2 (*vi*) blaze, flame, burn brightly, flare up; 3 (*vi*) (*fig*) light up, **bhiodh aodann a' lasadh** his face would light up

lasachadh, *gen* **lasachaidh** *nm* (*the act of*) loosening &c (*see senses of* **lasaich** *v*)

lasadair, lasadair, lasadairean *nm* a match (*for lighting*), *Cf less trad* **maids 1**

lasadh, *gen* **lasaidh** *nm* (*the act of*) lighting, blazing &c (*see senses of* **las** *v*)

lasaich *vt, pres part* **a' lasachadh**, 1 (*fastenings &c*) loosen, slacken, *Cf* **fuasgail 2**; 2 ease (*suffering &c*), *Cf* **faothaich**

lasair, *gen* **lasrach** & **lasair**, *pl* **lasraichean** *nf* 1 a flame, flames, (*song*) **Glaschu a' dol na lasair** Glasgow going up in flames, (*fig, situation &c*) **cuir** *v* **lasair ri** inflame; 2 a flash

lasanta *adj* 1 inflammable; 2 (*person*) passionate, hot-blooded, easily inflamed

lasgan, *gen & pl* **lasgain** *nm* (*of noise, emotion &c*) a burst, an outburst, **lasgan gàire** a burst/peal of laughter, **lasgan feirge** a fit/outburst of anger

lasrach *adj* flaming, flashing, blazing, **teine** *m* **lasrach** a blazing fire, **sùilean** *fpl* **lasrach** flashing eyes

lastaic & **lastaig** *nf invar* elastic

latha *see* **là**

làthair, *gen* **làthaire** *nf* 1 presence, **a-mach às mo làthair (leat)!** out of my presence/sight (with you)! *Cf* **sealladh 3, fradharc 2; 2** the fact of being present, **an làthair** present, there, **bha mi eòlach air na bha an làthair** I knew those who were present/there, **cùm** *v* **às an làthair** keep out of sight, keep away

làthaireachd *nf invar* presence, **neo-làthaireachd** absence

le *prep* (*takes the dat*), *before art* **leis**, *Note: the pers prons* **mi, thu, e** *&c combine with* **le** *to form the prep prons* **leam(sa), leat(sa), leis(-san), leatha(se), leinn(e), leibh(se), leotha(san)** with me, you &c; **1** with, along with (*Note: referring to people* **còmhla ri** *is more usu/polite than* **le**), (*corres &c*) **le deagh dhùrachd** with compliments, **air falbh leis a' ghaoith** gone with the wind, (*song*) **an tèid thu leam, mo nighean donn?** will you go with me, my brown-haired lass? (*song*) **nuair a bhios mi leam fhìn** when I am alone/by myself, **le chèile** together, *also* both, **dh'fhalbh iad le chèile** they left together *or* they both left, **beannachd/slàn leat!** goodbye (*lit* a blessing/health be with you), *Cf* **còmhla 2** & *less usu* **cuide ri, maille ri, mar 5; 2** with (*expr means*), **bhuail e le òrd e** he struck it with a hammer; **3** (*expr agent*) by, **chaidh a mharbhadh le peilear** he was killed by a bullet, **sgeulachd air a sgrìobhadh le ban-sgrìobhadair** a story written by a woman writer, **faigh** *v* **le foill** obtain fraudulently/by fraud; **4** belonging to, **cò leis a tha seo? 's ann leamsa a tha e** who does this belong to? it's mine, it belongs to me, (*pibroch*) **is leamsa an gleann** the glen is mine, *Cf* **aig 2; 5** *in numerous verbal exprs conveying emotion, attitude &c, eg* **is toigh leam e** & (*esp in Lewis*) **is caomh leam e** I like it, **is duilich leam e** I find it difficult *or* it is hard/painful for me, **is math leam e** I find/think it good, **b' fhada leam e** it seemed/was long/tedious for me; **6** *expr motion*, (**choisich i** *&c*) **leis a' bhruthaich** (she walked *&c*) down/with the slope (*Cf* **ris a' bhruthaich** up/against the slope), **leis an t-sruth** downstream, with the current; **7** *in adv expr* **leis (a) sin** whereupon, thereupon, at that, **dhùin am bàr, is leis a sin chaidh e dhachaigh** the bar closed, and at that he went home, *Cf* **an uair sin, sin** *pron* **4; 8** *in expr* **leis cho ... is ...** with it being so ..., **chan fhaic mi thu leis cho dorch 's a tha e** I can't see you with it being so dark

leabaidh, *gen* **leapa(ch)**, *pl* **leapannan** & **leapaichean** *nf* a bed, **bha iad san leabaidh** they were in bed, **aodach** *m* **leapa** bedclothes

leabhar, **leabhair**, **leabhraichean** *nm* a book, **leabhar-latha** a diary, a journal, **leabhar-mìneachaidh** a manual

leabharlann, **leabharlainn**, **leabharlannan** *nmf* a library

leabhrachan, **leabhrachain**, **leabhrachanan** *nm* & **leabhran**, **leabhrain**, **leabhranan** *nm* a booklet, a pamphlet, a brochure, a manual

leabhran *see* **leabhrachan**

leac, **lic(e)**, **leacan** *nf* 1 (*topog*) a slab or ledge of natural stone or rock, an expanse of flat stone or rock; 2 (*masonry &c*) a slab or flat piece of (*usu dressed*) stone, **leac uaighe** a tombstone, a gravestone, **leac-ùrlair** a paving/flooring stone

leacach *adj* flat, slab-like

leacag, **leacaig**, **leacagan** *nf* a tile (*ie earthenware &c*)

leag *vt*, *pres part* **a' leagail**, 1 (*building, tree, opponent &c*) knock down, throw down, demolish, fell, **leag gu làr** raze to the ground; 2 lower, bring *or* let down, **leag e an uinneag** he lowered/let down the window; 3 lay down, put down, **leag leacagan air ùrlar** lay tiles on a floor; 4 drop, **leag boma** drop a bomb

leagail, *gen* **leagalach** *nf* (*the act of*) knocking down, lowering &c (*see senses of* **leag** *v*)

leagh *vti*, *pres part* **a' leaghadh**, 1 melt, thaw; 2 dissolve (*in liquid*)

leaghadh, *gen* **leaghaidh** *nm* (*the act or process of*) melting, thawing, dissolving

leamh *adj* exasperating, vexing, galling

leamhach *adj* insipid

leamhachadh, *gen* **leamhachaidh** *nm* (*the act of*) exasperating &c (*see senses of* **leamhaich** *v*)

leamhaich *vt*, *pres part* **a' leamhachadh**, exasperate, plague, get on someone's nerves, *Cf* **sàraich** 2

leamhan, *gen* **leamhain** & **leamhna** *nm* elm

leam(sa) *prep pron see* **le**

lean *vti*, *pres part* **a' leantainn** & **a' leantail**, 1 follow, **thog e air is ise ga leantainn** off he went with her following him, **ionnsaich na faclan a leanas** learn the following words; 2 follow, understand, **a bheil sibh gam leantainn?** are you following/understanding me?, *Cf* **tuig**; 3 continue, persevere, keep *or* go on, **an lean an droch aimsir?** will the bad weather continue/go on? **bha e sgìth den dreuchd aige ach lean e air** he was tired of his job but he kept on/persevered, **lean ort!** keep going!, *Cf* **cùm** 2; 4 (*lit & fig*) stick, adhere (**ri** to), **lean a' chuileag ris a' bhalla** the fly stuck to the wall

leanabail *adj* childish, juvenile, infantile

leanaban, leanabain, leanabanan *nm* (*dimin of* **leanabh**), a baby, a small child, an infant, *Cf* **leanabh, naoidhean, pàiste**

leanabas, *gen* **leanabais** *nm* childhood

leanabh, leanaibh, leanaban *nm* a baby, a child, an infant, *Cf* **leanaban, naoidhean, pàisde**

leanailteach *adj* **1** continuous, incessant; **2** sticky, adhesive

leann, leanna, leanntan *nm* beer, ale

leannan, leannain, leannanan *nm* a lover, a sweetheart, a boyfriend, a girlfriend, *Cf* (*fam*) **bràmair,** (*fam*) **car(a)bhaidh**

leannanach *adj* amorous, fond of the opposite sex

leannanachd *nf invar* courtship, courting, *Cf* **suirghe**

leannra, leannra, leannran *nm* sauce (*ie for food*), *Cf* **sabhs**

leantainneach *adj* **1** continuing, continuous, **measadh** *m* **leantainneach** continuous assessment, **pàipear** *m* **leantainneach** continuous paper/stationery; **2** persevering, enduring, lasting, **stòras** *m* **leanntainneach** a renewable resource

leas, *nm invar* **1** (*trad*) benefit, profit, advantage, improvement; **2** *now esp in expr* **cha leig/ruig mi** (&c) **a leas** ... I (&c) don't need to ..., **cha leig thu (a) leas tighinn còmhla rinn** you don't need to come with us, there's no point in your coming with us, **am faigh mi fàinne dhut? cha leig thu a leas!** will I get you a ring? you don't need to/you needn't bother!, *Cf* **feum** *v* **2, feum** *n* **2**

leas- *prefix* (*in family relationships*) step-, **leas-bhràthair** a step-brother

leasachadh, leasachaidh, leasachaidhean *nm* **1** (*the act of*) improving, developing &c (*see senses of* **leasaich** *v*); **2** improvement, an improvement, development, a development, **bòrd** *m* **leasachaidh** a development board, **tìr fo leasachadh** a developing country, **tabhartas** *m* **leasachaidh** an improvement grant; **3** a remedy, a means of putting something right, **cha robh leasachadh air a' chùis ach** ... there was no remedy for the matter except ..., **foghlam/ obair leasachaidh** remedial education/work, *Cf* **cothrom** *n* **2** ; **4** (*agric*) manure, fertiliser, *Cf* **mathachadh**

leasaich *vt, pres part* **a' leasachadh, 1** improve, develop, **tha mi airson mo chuid Gàidhlig a leasachadh** I want to improve my Gaelic, **bidh a' chomhairle a' leasachadh meadhan a' bhaile** the council will be improving/developing the town centre; **2** remedy, rectify, reform, put right; **3** (*agric*) manure, fertilise (*ground*), *Cf* **mathaich, todhair 1**

leasaiche, leasaiche, leasaichean *nm* a therapist, **leasaiche cainnt** a speech therapist

leasan, leasain, leasanan *nm* a lesson

leasbach, *gen & pl* **leasbaich** *nf* a lesbian, *also as adj* **leasbach** lesbian

leat(sa), leatha(se) *prep prons see* **le**

leathad, leathaid, leathaidean *nm* a slope, a hillslope, a hillside, **leathaidean casa** steep hillsides, *common in placenames as* Le(a)d-, *eg* **An Leathad Beag** Ledbeg, little hillslope, *Cf* **aodann 2, bruthach 1, leitir**

leathann *adj* broad, wide, (*placename*) **An t-Ath Leathann** Broadford, *Cf* **farsaing 1** *& opposite* **caol** *adj* 1

leathar, *gen* **leathair** *&* **leathrach** *nm* leather, **seacaid** *f* **leathair** a leather jacket

leatrom, *gen* **leatruim** *nm* pregnancy

leibh(se) *prep pron see* **le**

leig *vt, pres part* **a' leigeil** *&* **a' leigeadh**, 1 let, permit, allow, **cha do leig e dhomh/leam a cheannachd** he didn't let me buy it, *Cf* **ceadaich 1**; 2 leave, entrust, **leig leathase am pàiste a thogail** leave it to her to bring up the child; **3 leig** *&* **leig às** let go, drop, release, let off, let slip, (*trad*) **leig às na coin** let slip the dogs, **leig saighead** loose/fire an arrow, **leig e às braim** he farted, let off a fart, **leig iad sgreuch (asta)** they let out a yell, **leig d' anail!** take a breather!; **4 leig le** leave alone, let be, **leig leatha** let her alone, let her be, *also* let her get on with it; **5 leig de** *&* **leig seachad** stop, cease, give up, relinquish, **leig mi seachad smocadh** I've given up smoking, **leig am bodach dheth an obair** the old fellow gave up his job *or* retired; **6 leig air** pretend, make out, **leig na saighdearan orra gun robh iad nan sìobhaltairean** the soldiers pretended/made out they were civilians; **7 leig air** give something away, let on, **chuir iad ceistean gu leòr ach cha do leig sinn oirnn** they asked lots of questions but we didn't let on/give the game away; **8 leig na theine** set on fire, *Cf* **las 1, loisg 1**; **9** *for* **leig (a) leas** *see* **leas 2**

leigeadh, *gen* **leigidh** *nm*, *also* **leigeil**, *gen* **leigealach** *nf*, (*the act of*) letting, dropping &c, (*see senses of* **leig** *v*)

leigheas, leigheis, leigheasan *nm* 1 (*the act & process of*) healing (*see* **leighis** *v*), **leigheas inntinn** psychiatry; 2 a cure, a remedy, a medicine, **leigheas air a ghalar** a cure for his malady, **leigheas chasad** cough medicine, (*after drink*) **leigheas na pòit** the hair of the dog, *Cf* **ìocshlaint**

leighis *vt, pres part* **a' leigheas**, cure, heal, *Cf* **slànaich**

lèine, lèine, lèintean *nf* a shirt

leinn(e) *prep pron see* **le**

lèir *adj* **1** (*trad*) visible, clear, plain, evident, obvious; **2** *esp in expr* (*rather trad*) **is lèir dhomh** (*&c*) I (*&c*) see, **cha lèir dhomh an fhàire** I can't see the horizon, **bu lèir dha gun robh e air chall** it was clear/plain *&c* to him/he could see that he was lost; *Cf* **faicsinneach 1**, **follaiseach 1**, **soilleir 2**

lèir-chlaisneach *adj* audio-visual

lèirmheas *nm invar* a review (*of book &c*), a critique

lèirsinn *nf invar* **1** sight, eyesight, vision, *Cf more usu* **fradharc 1**; **2** insight, perceptiveness, *Cf more usu* **tuigse 1**

lèirsinneach *adj* **1** visible, *Cf more usu* **faicsinneach 1**; **2** perceptive, *Cf more usu* **mothachail 1**, **tuigseach 1**

leis, leise, leisean *nf* a thigh, *Cf more usu* **sliasaid**

leis(san) *prep pron see* **le**

leisg *adj* **1** lazy, idle, indolent, slothful, **bu chòir dhomh am mullach a chàradh ach tha mi ro leisg** I ought to mend the roof but I'm too lazy, *Cf less usu* **dìomhain 2**; **2** reluctant, loth, unwilling, *esp in expr* **is leisg leam** (*&c*) I (*&c*) am loth/reluctant/unwilling, I (&c) hesitate (to), **bu leisg leatha an teallach fhàgail** she was reluctant to leave the fireside, *Cf* **ain-deònach**

leisg(e), *gen* **leisge** *nf* **1** laziness, idleness, indolence, sloth, (*prov*) **cha dèan làmh na leisge beairteas** the lazy hand will not earn riches; **2** reluctance, **bha leisg orm falbh** I was reluctant to leave

leisgeadair, leisgeadair, leisgeadairean *nm* a lazy *or* idle person, a lazybones

leisgeul, leisgeil, leisgeulan *nm* an excuse, a pretext, *also in exprs* **gabh mo leisgeul!** excuse me! pardon me!, **dèan** *v* **leisgeul** apologise

leiteas, leiteis, leiteisean *nf* a lettuce

lèith, lèithe, lèithean *nf* (*anat*) a nerve

leitheach *adv* half, semi-, **leitheach làn** half full, **leitheach-slighe eadar Port Rìgh is Dùn Bheagain** halfway between Portree and Dunvegan

leithid, leithide, leithidean *nf* the like of someone or something, *usu with poss adj*, **cha robh a leithid ann a-riamh** his/her like never existed, **a leithid sin** the like(s) of that, such a thing/one as that, **chan aithne dhomh a leithid de dhuine** I don't know such a man/ a man the like of him, *Cf* **coltas, mac-samhail 2, samhail, seòrsa**

leitir, leitire, leitirean *nf* a slope (*often near water*), *now usu in placenames*, *eg* **Leitir Choill** Letterchall, wood slope, *Cf* **aodann 2, leathad, ruighe 2**

Leòdhasach, *gen & pl* **Leòdhasaich** *nm* someone from (the Isle of) Lewis (**Leòdhas** *or* **Eilean Leòdhais**), *also as adj*, **Leòdhasach** of, from or pertaining to Lewis

leòghann, *gen & pl* **leòghainn** *nm, also* **leòmhann**, *gen & pl* **leòmhainn** *nm*, a lion

leòinteach, *gen & pl* **leòintich** *nm* a casualty, a victim (*of accident &c*), **na leòintich** the injured, the wounded, the casualties

leòm, *gen* **leòim(e)** *nf* pride, conceit, 'side', affectation, *Cf more usu* **àrdan**, **mòrchuis**, **pròis**

leòman, *gen & pl* **leòmain** *nm* a moth

leòmhann *see* **leòghann**

leòn *vt, pres part* **a' leònadh**, (*phys or emotionally*) wound, hurt, injure, *Cf* **ciùrr 1 & 2**, **lot** *v*

leòn, **leòin**, **leòntan** *nm* (*phys or emotional*) a wound, a hurt, an injury, (*song*) **'s e an gunna caol a rinn mo leòn** it's the fowler's gun that caused my hurt, *Cf* **ciùrradh 2**, **creuchd**, **lot** *nm*

leònadh, *gen* **leònaidh** *nm* (*the act of*) wounding, hurting, injuring

leònta *&* **leònte**, *adj* wounded, hurt, injured

leòr *nf invar* **1** enough, a sufficiency, **fhuair mi mo leòr de dh'òrain a-raoir** I got (more than) enough songs/all the songs I could take/ my fill of songs last night, *Cf* **làn** *n* **1**, **sàth** *n*; **2** *esp in expr* **gu leòr** enough, sufficient, plenty (*Cf* **pailteas**), **a bheil gu leòr bìdh agad?** have you enough food? **tha gu leòr ann a tha den bheachd sin** there are plenty of/a good many people around who think that, **tha trioblaid gu leòr againn aig an taigh** we've plenty/a lot of trouble at home, **ceart gu leòr!** right enough!, quite right! (*also*) OK!

leotha(san) *prep pron see* **le**

leth *nm invar* **1** (*trad*) a side, **cuir** *v* **airgead air leth** put money aside/on one side, **leth ri** *prep* next to, beside, **rach** *v* **às leth cuideigin** side with someone, **chaidh i às an leth** she sided with them/took their part, *Cf* **taobh 3**; **2** *as adv expr* **air leth** (*lit*) apart, *also* exceptional, excellent, outstanding, special, **duine air leth** a man apart *or* an outstanding man, **bha sin air leth math** that was extremely/ especially good, *Cf* **anabarrach 2**, **fìor 3**; **3** a half, **an leth eile** the other half, **mìle/dusan gu leth** a mile and a half/a dozen and a half, **leth uair** *&* **leth-uair** half an hour, **leth-bhotal** half a bottle, a half bottle, **leth mar leth** half and half, **leth an t-samhraidh/a' gheamhraidh** mid-summer/winter (*ie the half-way point*); **4** *often used adverbially* **leth-shean** middle-aged (*lit* half old), **leth-mharbh** half dead, *Cf* **leitheach**; **5** one of a pair, **leth-aon** *&* **leth-chàraid** a twin, (*trad*) *often of parts of the body* **dh'èirich i air a leth-uilinn** she rose up onto one elbow, **air leth-chois** on one leg; **6** *in expr* **às leth** *prep* on behalf of, **is ann às mo leth a rinn e e** it was on my behalf/for me that he did it, *Cf* **airson 3**, **sgàth** *n* **3**; **7** *in expr* **cuir** *v* **às leth** accuse, attribute, **chuir iad às mo leth gun robh mi leisg**

they accused me of being/made out that I was lazy (*Cf* **tilg 2**), **na cuiribh am fathann às mo leth-sa** don't attribute the rumour to me; **8** *in expr* **fa leth** *adv* separate, **nochd na h-òrain mu dheireadh aige ann an leabhar fa leth** his last songs appeared in a separate book

lethbhreac, lethbhric, lethbhreacan *nm* **1** (*trad*) a like, a fellow, an equal, a match, (*prov*) **gheibh Gàidheal fhèin a lethbhreac** even a Gael will meet his match, *Cf* **coimeas 4, leithid, mac-samhail 2, samhail, seis(e)**; **2** a copy, a reproduction (*of book, picture &c*), a duplicate, a transcript; **3** *now esp* an individual copy (*of a book, newspaper &c*)

lethcheann, *gen & pl* **lethchinn** *nm* **1** (*trad*) a cheek, *Cf more usu* **gruaidh, pluic**; **2** the side of the head, the temple, **buille air a lethcheann** a blow on the side of his head

leth-cheud *&* **lethcheud,** *gen* **leth-cheud,** *pl* **leth-cheudan** *nm* fifty (*lit* half a hundred), *takes nom sing* (*radical*) **leth-cheud boireannach** fifty women, **rugadh e sna leth-cheudan** he was born in the fifties, *Cf* (*trad*) **caogad**

leth-chuid, leth-chodach, leth-chodaichean *nf* a half, a half share, **cia mheud a tha thu ag iarraidh? a leth-chuid** how many do you want? half

leth-fhuar *adj* (*lit & fig*) tepid, lukewarm, **fhuair sinn fàilte leth-fhuar** we got a lukewarm/half-hearted welcome, **brot leth-fhuar** lukewarm broth, *Cf* **fionnar 2, fuaraidh**

leud, *gen* **leòid** *nm* breadth, width, *Cf* **farsaingeachd 1**

leudachadh, leudachaidh, leudachaidhean *nm* **1** (*the act of*) extending &c (*see senses of* **leudaich** *v*); **2** extension, an extension, enlargement, an enlargement, expansion, an expansion

leudaich *vti, pres part* **a' leudachadh,** extend, enlarge, widen, broaden, expand, **chaidh an rathad a leudachadh** the road was widened

leudaichte *adj* **1** extended, enlarged, widened, broadened, expanded; **2** (*occas*) flattened, **bha a shròn leudaichte ris an lòsan** his nose was flattened against the window pane

leug, lèig, leugan *nf* a jewel, *Cf* **seud**

leugh *vti, pres part* **a' leughadh,** read, **an do leugh thu an leabhar ùr aige?** have you read his new book?

leughadair, leughadair, leughadairean *nm* a reader

leughadh, *gen* **leughaidh** *nm* (*the act of*) reading, a reading

leum *vti, pres part* **a' leum** *also* **a' leumadh, a' leumnaich** *&* **a' leumadaich, 1** jump, leap, skip, spring, **leum am balla** jump (over) the wall; **2** (*of nose*) bleed, **tha mo shròn a' leum** my nose is bleeding

leum, lèim, leuman(nan) *nm* **1** (*the act of*) jumping &c (*see senses of* **leum** *v*); **2** a jump, a leap, a skip, a spring, *Cf* **sùrdag**

leum-sròine, lèim-sròine, leumannan-sròine *nm* a nose bleed

leum-uisge, lèim-uisge, leumannan-uisge *nm* a waterfall, *Cf more usu* **eas, linne 3, spùt** *n* 2

leus, *gen & pl* **leòis** *nm* 1 a light, a ray of light, *Cf more usu* **gath 3, solas**; 2 a torch, *Cf* **lampa, lanntair**; 3 a blister, *Cf* **balg 2**

leusair, leusair, leusairean *nm* a laser, **teicneolas** *m* **leusair** laser technology, **gath leusair** a laser beam

liagh, lèigh, liaghan *nf* 1 a ladle, a large spoon, *Cf* **ladar 1, spàin**; 2 a scoop, *Cf* **ladar 2**

liath *vti, pres part* **a' liathadh**, make or become grey, (*song*) **ged tha mo cheann air liathadh** though my head/hair has turned/gone/become grey

liath *adj* grey, **falt** *m* **liath** grey hair, **creag** *f* **liath** grey rock/crag, *Cf* **glas** *adj* 1

liathadh, *gen* **liathaidh** *nm* (*the act or process of*) greying, turning grey (*see* **liath** *v*)

liath-reothadh, *gen* **liath-reothaidh** *nm* hoar frost

lìbhrig *vt, pres part* **a' lìbhrigeadh**, deliver (*goods &c*)

lìbhrigeadh, lìbhrigidh, lìbhrigidhean *nm* 1 (*the act of*) delivering; 2 delivery, a delivery (*of goods &c*)

lide, lide, lidean *nm* a syllable

lighiche, lighiche, lighichean *nm* a (medical) doctor, *Cf less trad* **do(c)tair**

lili(dh), lili(dh), lilidhean *nf* a lily

lìnig *vt, pres part* **a' lìnigeadh**, (*curtains &c*) line

lìnigeadh, lìnigidh, lìnigidhean *nm* 1 (*the act of*) lining; 2 (*material*) lining, a lining

linn, linn, linntean *nmf* 1 an age, a time, **Na Linntean Dorcha** The Dark Ages, **Na Linntean Meadhanach** The Middle Ages, **ri linn ar sinnsirean** in our ancestors' time, *Cf* **rè** *n* 2; 2 a generation, **bho linn gu linn** from generation to generation, *Cf more usu* **ginealach 1**; 3 a century, **san fhicheadamh linn** in the twentieth century

linne, *gen* **linne,** *pl* **linneachan** *&* **linntean** *nf* 1 a pool, (*esp in placenames*) a pool below a waterfall, (*Sc*) a linn, *Cf* **glumag 1, lòn² 1**; 2 (*esp in placenames*) a waterfall, falls, *Cf* **eas, leum-uisge, spùt** *n* 2

liomaid, liomaide, liomaidean *nf* a lemon

lìomh *vt, pres part* **a' lìomhadh**, polish, shine (*shoes &c*)

lìomh, *gen* **lìomha** *nf* polish, a polish, a gloss, a shine (*on shoes &c*)

lìomharra *adj* polished, shiny, glossy

lìon *vti, pres part* **a' lìonadh**, fill (up), become full, **lìon botal-teth dhomh** fill me a hot water bottle, **lìon am muir/a' mhuir** the tide came in

lìon, lìn, lìontan *nm* **1** net, netting, a net, a web, **lìon-iasgaich** a fishing net, **lìon damhain-allaidh** a spider's web, a cobweb; **2** lint, flax

lìonadh, *gen* lìonaidh *nm* (*the act of*) filling &c (*see* lìon *v*)

lìonmhor *adj* numerous, copious, plentiful, abundant, (*trad*) **bu lìonmhor a luchd-leanmhainn** numerous were his followers, **na h-èildean lìonmhor** the numerous/abundant hinds, *Cf* **pailt 1**

lionn, lionna, lionntan *nm* liquid, a liquid, a fluid, **'s e lionn a th' ann am bùrn** water is a liquid, *also in expr* **eadar-dhà-lionn** undecided, *also* neither one thing nor the other

lionsa, lionsa, lionsaichean *nf* a lens, **lionsa-suathaidh** a contact lens

lìonta *adj* filled, full

liopard, liopaird, liopardan *nm* a leopard

lios, *gen* liosa & lise, *pl* liosan *nmf* **1** a garden, *Cf* **gàrradh 2**; **2** (*trad*) an enclosure, *Cf* **lann² 1**

Liosach, *gen* & *pl* Liosaich *nm* someone from Lismore (**Lios Mòr**), *also as adj,* **Liosach** from, of or pertaining to Lismore

liosda *adj* boring, tedious, *Cf* **fadalach 2, màirnealach 2**

liosta, liosta, liostaichean *nf* a list (*of items*)

liotach *adj* lisping

liotachas, *gen* liotachais *nm* a lisp, lisping

liotair, liotair, liotairean *nm* a litre

lip, lipe, lipean *nf* a lip, *Cf more usu* **bile** *nf* **1**

lite *nf invar* porridge, *Cf* **brochan**

litearra *adj* literate

litearras, *gen* litearrais *nm* literacy

litir, litreach, litrichean *nf* a letter, **litrichean na h-aibidile** the letters of the alphabet, **tapadh leat airson na litreach a chuir thu thugam** thank you for the letter you sent me

litireil *adj* literal

litreachadh, *gen* litreachaidh *nm* spelling, orthography, **tha i math air litreachadh** she's good at spelling

litreachail *adj* literary

litreachas, *gen* litreachais *nm* literature, **litreachas na Gàidhlig** Gaelic literature, **fèis** *f* **litreachais** a literature/literary festival

litrich *vti, pres part* **a' litreachadh**, spell

liùdhag, liùdhaig, liùdhagan *nf* a doll

liut, *gen* liuit *nf* a knack, a flair, **chan eil an liut agam air sin** I haven't got the knack of/for that

lobh *vi, pres part* **a' lobhadh**, rot, decay, decompose, go bad or rotten, putrefy, *Cf* **grod** *v*

lobhadh, *gen* **lobhaidh** *nm* **1** (*the act or process of*) rotting, decaying &c (*see senses of* **lobh** *v*); **2** rottenness, putrefaction, rot, decay; *Cf* **grodadh**

lobhar, *gen & pl* **lobhair** *nm* a leper, *Cf* **luibhre**

lobht(a), lobhta, lobhtaichean *nm* **1** (*in tenement &c*) a storey, a floor, a flat (*ie both storey & individual dwelling*); **2** a loft (*ie roofspace*), *Cf* **seòmar-mullaich** (*see* **seòmar**)

lobhte *adj* putrid, rotted, rotten, *Cf* **grod** *adj*

locair, locair, locairean *nf also* **locar**, *gen* **locair**, *pl* **locaran** & **locraichean** *nmf* (*carpentry*) a plane

lòcast, *gen & pl* **lòcaist** *nm* a locust

loch, locha, lochan *nm* a loch, a lake, **loch-mara** a sea loch, a fjord, **loch-tasgaidh** a reservoir

lochan, lochain, lochanan *nm* (*dimin of* **loch**) a lochan, a small loch; a pond

lochd, lochda, lochdan *nm* **1** fault, blame; **2** harm; *Cf more usu* **cron**

lochdach *adj* harmful, *Cf more usu* **cronail**

Lochlann, *gen* **Lochlainn** *nf* **1** (*trad*) Norway, *Cf now more usu* **Nirribhidh**; **2** Scandinavia

Lochlannach, *gen & pl* **Lochlannaich** *nm* **1** (*trad*) a Norwegian; **2** a Scandinavian; **3** (*hist*) a Norseman, a Viking; *also as adj* **Lochlannach** **1** (*trad*) Norwegian; **2** Scandinavian; **3** (*hist*) Norse, Viking

lòchran, *gen & pl* **lòchrain** *nm* a lamp, a lantern, *Cf more usu* **lampa**, **lanntair**

lof, lofa, lofaichean *nmf* a (*shop-bought*) loaf, a breadloaf, *Cf* **aran** & *less usu* **buileann**

loidhne, loidhne, loidhnichean *nf* a line, **tarraing** *v* **loidhne** draw a line, **cò a th' agam air an loidhne?** who have I got on the (*phone*) line?, (*IT*) **air loidhne** on line

loingeas & **luingeas**, *gen* **loingeis** *nm* **1** shipping; **2** a fleet, a navy, *Cf more usu* **cabhlach, nèibhi(dh)**

lòinidh *nmf invar, with art*, **an lòinidh** rheumatism, rheumatics

loisg *vti, pres part* **a' losgadh**, **1** burn, (*prov*) **fear sam bith a loisgeas a mhàs, 's e fhèin a dh'fheumas suidhe air** any man who burns his backside must sit on it himself, **cnàmh-loisg** smoulder, *Cf* **las** **1** & **2**; **2** fire, shoot (*a firearm*), *Cf* **tilg** **4**

loisgte *adj* burnt

lòistear & **loidsear**, *gen* **lòisteir**, *pl* **lòistearan** *nm* a lodger

lòistinn, lòistinn, lòistinnean *nm* lodging(s), digs, accommodation, *Cf less usu* **fàrdach 2**

lom *vt, pres part* **a' lomadh, 1** bare, lay bare, strip, *Cf* **rùisg 1; 2** shave (*Cf* **beàrr 1**); (*esp of sheep*) shear, clip (*Cf* **rùisg 2**); **3** (*lawn, grass*) mow, **feur air a lomadh** mown grass

lom *adj* **1** bare, naked, nude, *Cf more usu* **lomnochd, rùisgte; 2** bare, bleak, **sliabh** *m* **lom** a bare/bleak moor, (*prov*) **is lom an leac air nach buaineadh tu bàirneach** it's a bare rock from which you couldn't gather a limpet; **3** thin, threadbare, **còta lom** a worn/threadbare coat, **brochan lom** thin porridge/gruel; **4** (*weight, sum &c*) net

lomadair, lomadair, lomadairean *nm* a sheep-shearer

lomadh, *gen* **lomaidh** *nm* (*the act of*) baring, shearing &c (*see senses of* **lom** *v*)

loma-làn *adj* completely full, full up, full to the brim, packed, **bha an talla loma-làn** the hall was packed

lomnochd *adj* (*of person*) naked, unclothed, undressed, bare, *Cf* **lom** *adj* **1, rùisgte**

lòn¹, *gen* **lòin** *nm* **1** food, nourishment, sustenance, provisions, fare, (*song*) **cha bhi lòn oirnn a dhìth** we will not want for food, *Cf more usu* **biadh 1; 2** (*trad*) a meal, *Cf* **biadh 2, diathad 1**

lòn², **lòin, lòintean** *nm* **1** a pool, *Cf* **glumag 1, linne 1; 2** a puddle, *Cf* **glumag 2; 3** a meadow; a lawn, *Cf* **clua(i)n, dail 1, faiche**

lònaid, lònaide, lònaidean *nf* a lane, *Cf* **caol-shràid**

lon-dubh, loin-duibh, loin-dubha *nm* a blackbird

long & **lung**, *gen* **luinge**, *pl* **longan** *nf* a ship, a (sailing) vessel, **long-chogaidh** a warship, a battleship, **long-bhriseadh** *m* a shipwreck

lorg *vt, pres part* **a' lorg** & **a' lorgadh, 1** look for, be in search of *or* on the track of, *Cf* **sir** & *less usu* **siubhail 4; 2** find, track down, trace, **lorg mi a' chaora a bha a dhìth** I found the missing sheep, *Cf* **amais 2, faigh 2, lorg** *n* **3**

lorg, luirge, lorgan *nf* **1** (*the act of*) looking for, finding &c (*see senses of* **lorg** *v*); **2** (*left by person, animal, object*) a print, a footprint, a path, a trace, a track, a mark, a vestige, an imprint, **meur-lorg** a fingerprint, (*book title*) **Mo Lorgan Fhìn** My Own Tracks/traces, my own footsteps, **air lorg an fhèidh** on the track/path/trail of the deer, **chan eil lorg air** there's no trace/sign of him/it, *Cf* **comharra(dh) 3, làrach 1; 3** *in expr* **faigh** *v* **lorg air** find, locate, track down, **fhuair am poileas lorg air ann an Lunnainn** the police found/located him in London, *Cf* **faigh 2, lorg** *v* **2**

los *nm invar* **1** (*trad*) a purpose, an intention, **air mo los** (*trad*) for me/ my sake, on my account, because of me (*Cf more usu* **airson 3, sgàth 3**); **2** *also in expr* **los gu(n)** *conj* so that, in order that, to, *Cf more usu* **dòigh 5, gus** *conj*

lòsan, *gen & pl* **lòsain** *nm* a pane of glass

losgadh, losgaidh, losgaidhean *nm* **1** (*the act of*) burning &c (*see senses of* **loisg** *v*); **2** a burn, **losgadh-bràghad** heartburn, **losgadh-grèine** sunburn

losgann, losgainn, losgannan *nm* a frog

lot *vti, pres part* **a' lotadh**, wound, *Cf more usu* **leòn** *v*

lot, lota, lotan *nm* a wound, *Cf more usu* **leòn** *n*

lot, lota, lotaichean *nf* a piece *or* holding of land, (*in some districts*) a croft (*Cf more usu* **croit 1**)

lotadh, *gen* **lotaidh** *nm* (*the act of*) wounding

loth, lotha, lothan *nmf* **1** a filly; **2** (*occas*) a foal, a colt, *Cf more usu* **searrach**

luach *nm* **1** *invar* worth, value, **dè an luach a th' ann?** what's it worth? **gun luach** worthless, *Cf more usu* **fiù** *n* **1**; **2** (*fin*) a rate, **luach na h-iomlaide** the rate of exchange, **luach rèidh** an interest rate; **3** *in expr* **cuir** *v* **luach air** evaluate, value, *Cf* **luachaich**

luachachadh, luachachaidh, luachachaidhean *nm* (*the act of*) evaluating &c (*see senses of* **luachaich** *v*); **2** (*also* **luachadh, luachaidh, luachaidhean** *nm*) valuation, a valuation, an evaluation, *Cf* **meas**[1] **2**

luachaich *vt, pres part* **a' luachachadh**, evaluate, value, put a price or value on, *Cf* **luach 2, meas** *v* **3**

luachair, *gen* **luachrach** *nf* a rush (*ie the plant*), rushes

luachmhor *adj* valuable, precious, *Cf* **prìseil**

luadhadh, *gen* **luadhaidh** *nm* **1** (*trad*) (*the act of*) waulking *or* fulling cloth (*by hand or with the feet*); **2** (*also* **luadh**, *gen* **luaidh** *nm*) a waulking (*ie occasion when fulling was done*), **òrain** *mpl* **luadhaidh** (*also* **òrain luaidh**) waulking songs (*to accompany fulling of cloth*)

luaidh *vt, pres part* **a' luaidh**, **1** praise, *Cf* **mol** *v* **1**; **2** mention

luaidh *vti, pres part* **a' luadhadh**, waulk *or* full cloth, hold or be engaged in a waulking

luaidh *nm invar* **1** (*the act of*) praising, mentioning *Cf* **moladh 1**; **2** praise, **dèan luaidh (air)** praise (*Cf* **mol** *v* **1**); *Cf* **cliù 2, moladh 2**

luaidh, luaidhe, luaidhean *nmf* a beloved person, *often in voc*, **a luaidh!/ mo luaidh!** love!/my love! darling!/my darling! *Cf* **eudail 2, gaol 2, gràdh 2, laogh 2**

luaidhe *nmf invar* lead, **bha dath na luaidhe air a' mhuir** the sea was the colour of lead, **saighdear luaidhe** a lead soldier

luaisg *vi, pres part* **a' luasgadh**, rock, shake, oscillate, sway, swing, toss, wave, *Cf* **tulg 1**

luaithre *nf invar, also* **luath**, *gen* **luaith** & **luatha(inn)** *nf*, ash, ashes

luamhan, *gen* **luamhain**, *pl* **luamhain** & **luamhanan** *nm* a lever

luas & **luaths**, *gen* **luai(th)s** *nm* **1** speed, velocity, *Cf* **astar 2**; **2** agility, *Cf* **lùth 2**

luasgadh, *gen* **luasgaidh** *nm* (*the act of*) rocking &c (*see senses of* **luaisg** *v*)

luasgan, *gen* **luasgain** *nm* **1** a rocking, shaking &c movement (*see senses of* **luaisg** *v*), oscillation; **2** giddiness, dizziness, *Cf more usu* **tuainealaich**

luath *nf see* **luaithre**

luath *adj* **1** (*phys*) fast, swift, speedy, rapid, quick, **each** *m* **luath** a fast horse, **luath-thrèana** *f* a fast/an express train, *Cf* **astarach**; **2** (*mentally*) quick, sharp, agile, **tha e luath na inntinn** he's quick/sharp, he's mentally agile, *Cf* **grad 2**; **3** *in expr* **cho luath agus/is** as soon as, no sooner than, **thòisich iad ri trod cho luath 's a thàinig iad a-steach** they started squabbling as soon as/the moment they came in; **4** *also in expr* **luath no mall** sooner or later, eventually

luathachadh, *gen* **luathachaidh** *nm* **1** (*the act of*) accelerating, hurrying &c (*see senses of* **luathaich** *v*); **2** acceleration

luathaich *vti, pres part* **a' luathachadh**, **1** accelerate, speed up, **bha an càr/an dràibhear a' luathachadh** the car/the driver was accelerating, **luathaich sinn ar ceum** we quickened/increased our pace; **2** *as vt* hurry (on), **bha an tidsear gar luathachadh aig deireadh an leasain** the teacher was hurrying us on at the end of the lesson, *Cf* **greas 2**

luaths *see* **luas**

lùb *vti, pres part* **a' lùbadh**, **1** bend, curve, bow, **lùb a' ghlùin** bend/bow the knee (*esp for prayer*), *Cf* **crom** *v* **1** & **2**, **fiar** *v*; **2** (*river &c*) meander

lùb, **lùib**, **lùban** *nf* **1** a bend, a curve, **tha lùb mhòr air/anns a' bhata** the stick has a big bend in it, *Cf* **caime**; **2** a loop, a noose; **3** *in expr* **an lùib** (*with gen*) involved in *or* with, implicated in, under the influence of, *also* associated with, connected with, attached to, **tha dealbh an lùib gach facail** a picture accompanies/is associated with each word (*Cf* **cas** *n* **4**)

lùbach *adj* **1** bending, having bends; **2** pliant, flexible, bendy, **bata lùbach** a pliant stick, *Cf* **sùbailte**; **3** (*road, river, argument &c*) meandering, tortuous, winding

lùbadh, *gen* **lùbaidh** *nm* (*the act of*) bending, curving &c (*see senses of* **lùb** *v*)

lùbte *adj* bent, curved, bowed, *Cf* **cam**, **crom** *adj*, **fiar** *adj* **1**

luch, *gen* **lucha** & **luchainn**, *pl* **luchan** *nf* a mouse

lùchairt, lùchairte, lùchairtean *nf* a palace, *Cf less trad* **pàileis**

luchd¹, luchda, luchdan *nm* a cargo, a load, *Cf* **cargu, uallach**

luchd² *nm invar* people, *used only in gen exprs, as pl of* **fear**, **neach**, *eg* (*song*) **tha mi sgìth de luchd na Beurla** I'm weary of people of English speech, **luchd-casaid** accusers, prosecutors, **luchd-eòlais** acquaintances, **luchd-frithealaidh** attendants, **luchd-turais** tourists, *Cf* **duine 5, fear 2, neach 2**

luchdachadh, *gen* **luchdachaidh** *nm* (*the act or process of*) loading

luchdaich *vt, pres part* **a' luchdachadh**, load (*boat, vehicle &c*)

luchdmhor *adj* capacious, able to take a large cargo

luchraban, *gen* & *pl* **luchrabain** *nm* a dwarf, a midget, *Cf* **troich**

Lucsamburgach, *gen* & *pl* **Lucsamburgaich** *nm* someone from Luxembourg (**Lucsamburg**), *also as adj* **Lucsamburgach** of, from or pertaining to Luxembourg

lùdag, lùdaig, lùdagan *nf* **1** a little finger, (*Sc*) a pinkie (finger); **2** a hinge, *Cf* **banntach**

lugha (*in comp exprs* **(n)as** (*&c*) **lugha**) *see* **beag**

lùghdachadh, *gen* **lùghdachaidh** *nm* **1** (*the act of*) lessening &c (*see senses of* **lùghdaich** *v*); **2** shrinkage, diminution, a diminution, abatement, an abatement, reduction, a reduction, decrease, a decrease, **lùghdachadh màil** a rent reduction

lùghdaich *vti, pres part* **a' lùghdachadh**, lessen, decrease, diminish, reduce, shrink, make or become smaller, abate

luibh, luibhe, luibhean *nmf* a herb, a plant, a weed, **luibh-eòlas** *m* botany, *Cf* **lus 1** & **2**

luibheach *adj* botanical

luibhre *nf invar* leprosy, *Cf* **lobhar**

luideach *adj* shabby, scruffy, slovenly, untidy, ragged, *Cf* **cearbach 2**

luideag, luideig, luideagan *nf* a rag, *Cf* **cearb 1**

luidhear, luidheir, luidheirean *nm* a ship's funnel, a (*usu non-domestic*) chimney, *Cf* **similear**

luime *nf invar* (*abstr noun corres to* **lom**) nakedness, bleakness &c (*see senses of* **lom** *adj*)

Luinneach, *gen* & *pl* **Luinnich** *nm* someone from Luing (**Eilean Luinn**), *also as adj* **Luinneach** of, from or pertaining to Luing

luinneag, luinneig, luinneagan *nf* a ditty, a short song, (*song title*) **Luinneag MhicLeòid** MacLeod's Ditty, *Cf* **duan 2**

Lùnasdal, *gen* **Lùnasdail** *nm, with art,* **an Lùnasdal** August, **Là Lùnasdail** Lammas Day, August 1st

lurach *adj* (*trad*) pretty, nice; beloved, (*song*) **bò lurach thu, bò na h-àirigh** you nice/beloved cow you, shieling cow, *Cf more usu* **àlainn, laghach, snog 2**

lurgann, *gen* **lurgainn**, *pl* **lurgannan** & **luirgnean** *nf* a shin (*also* **faobhar na lurgainn**)

lus, *gen* **luis** & **lusa**, *pl* **lusan** *nm* 1 a herb, **lus MhicCuimein** cumin; 2 a plant, a weed, **lus a' chrom-chinn** the daffodil, *Cf* **luibh**

lùth, *gen* **lùtha** *nm, also* **lùths**, *gen* **lùiths** *nm,* 1 movement, the power or faculty of movement, **tha e gun lùth** he is unable to move/without the power of motion; 2 (*power of swift movement*) agility, nimbleness, *Cf* **cliseachd, luas 2**; 3 energy, vigour, bodily strength, *Cf* **brìgh 4, neart, spionnadh**

lùthmhor *adj* 1 strong, (*phys*) powerful, *Cf* **làidir 1, neartmhor**; 2 agile, nimble, athletic, *Cf* **clis**; 3 energetic, vigorous, *Cf* **brìghmhor 2**

lùths *see* **lùth**

M

ma *conj* if, *neg* **mur(a)** if … not, **leig d' anail ma tha thu sgìth** have a break if you're tired, **cha tig mi ma bhios Anndra ann** I won't come if Andrew will be there, **cha tèid mise mura bheil** (*fam* **mur eil**) **thusa air a shon** I won't go if you're not keen on it, **dùin an doras, mas e** (*for* **ma is e**) **do thoil e** close the door, please (*lit* if it is your will), *Cf* **nan** *conj*; **2** *in expr* **ma-thà** *or* **ma-tà** then, in that case, **tha an doras fosgailte, dùin e ma-tà!** the door's open, close it then! **ceart, ma-thà!** right, then!, *Cf* **a-rèist**

màb *vt, pres part* **a' màbadh**, abuse (*verbally*), revile, vilify

màbadh, *gen* **màbaidh** *nm* (*the act of*) abusing &c (*see senses of* **màb** *v*)

mac, *gen & pl* **mic** *nm* a son, **tha dithis mhac** (*gen pl*) **aca** they have two sons, **mac mo bhràthar** *&* **mac mo pheathar** my nephew, **am mac stròdhail/struidheil** the prodigal son; **2** *in various exprs & excls eg* **a mhic an donais!** damn it! (*lit* son (*voc*) of the evil one), **mac-na-bracha** (*a nickname for*) malt whisky (*lit* son of the malt), **mac-talla** an echo, **mac-an-aba** the ring finger (*lit* son of the abbot); **3** *in clan surnames* (*also surnames adapted to the Gaelic system*), a (*male*) descendant of the real or supposed progenitor of the clan, **MacAonghais** MacInnes, a descendant of Angus, **Mac an Tàilleir** Taylor, *Cf* **nic**

macanta *adj* meek, submissive, *Cf* **umha(i)l 2**

mach *see* **a-mach**

machair(e), **machrach**, **machraichean** *nmf, applied to grassy stretches of land adjoining the Atlantic seaboard affording excellent grazing, similar to links but usu more level*, machair-land, a machair; **2** a plain, low-lying level land, *esp in* **(air) a' Mhachair Ghallda** (in) the (Scottish) Lowlands (*Cf* **Galldachd**)

machlag, machlaig, machlagan *nf* a womb, a uterus, *Cf* **broinn 1, brù 1**

mac-meanmna, *gen* **mic-meanmna** *nm* imagination, an imagination

mac-meanmnach *adj* **1** imaginary; **2** imaginative

mac-samhail, *gen & pl* **mic-samhail** *nm* **1** a replica, a duplicate, a facsimile of something, *Cf* **lethbhreac 2**; **2** the equal, match, 'fellow' (*Cf Sc* marrow), 'image', like or likeness of someone or something, *Cf* **leithid, lethbhreac 1, samhail, seis(e)**

mac-talla *see* **mac 2**

madadh, madaidh, madaidhean *nm, an animal of the canine species*, **1** a dog, *Cf* **more usu** **cù**; **2** (*esp* **madadh-ruadh**) a fox, (*prov*) **cho carach ris a' mhadadh-ruadh** as wily as the fox, *Cf* **balgair 1, sionnach**; **3** (*esp* **madadh-allaidh**) a wolf, *Cf* **faol**

madainn, maidne, maidnean *nf* morning, (*news programme*) **aithris na maidne** morning report/bulletin, **bha uisge ann air a' mhadainn** it rained during/in the course of the morning, **rugadh i sa mhadainn an-diugh/an-dè** she was born this/yesterday morning, **trì uairean sa mhadainn** three in the morning, 3 am

ma dh'fhaodte *see* **faod 2**

mag *vi, pres part* **a' magadh**, mock, deride, jeer, scoff, make fun (**air** at, of), **clann (is iad) a' magadh air a' bhodach bhochd** children mocking/making fun of the poor old man, *Cf* **fanaid 1**

màg, màig, màgan *nf* a paw, **air a** (*&c*) **mhàgan** *also* **air mhàgaran**, on all fours, on (his *&c*) hands and knees, *Cf* **cròg 1, spòg 1**

magadh, *gen* **magaidh** *nm* **1** (*the act of*) mocking &c (*see senses of* **mag** *v*); **2** mockery; *Cf* **fanaid 1**

magail *adj* mocking, jeering, scoffing, making fun; apt to mock, jeer &c

magairle, magairle, magairlean *nmf* a testicle, *Cf* (*more fam*) **clach** *n* **3**

maghar, maghair, maghairean *nm* **1** a fly (*for fly-fishing*); **2** bait, *Cf* **baoit**

maide, maide, maidean *nm* **1** wood, timber, a piece of wood or timber *usu shaped or worked for a specific purpose*, *Cf* **fiodh** *which is rather wood in general or in its natural state*, **maide-droma** *&* **maide-mullaich** a ridge-pole, a roof-tree; **2** a stick, **maide poite** a spirtle, **am maide-crochaidh** the hanging stick (*formerly a stick hung around the neck of children caught speaking Gaelic at school*), *Cf* **bata 1**

maids(e), maidse, maidsichean *nm* **1** a match (*ie for lighting*), *Cf more trad* **lasadair**; **2** (*sport, esp football*) a match, *Cf* **geama 2**

màidsear, màidseir, màidsearan *nm* (*army &c*) a major

Màigh, *gen* **Màighe** *nf, with art* **a' Mhàigh** (the month of) May, *Cf more trad* **Cèitean**

maighdeann, *gen* **maighdinn,** *pl* **maighdeannan** *&* **maighdinnean** *nf* **1** (*trad*) a maiden, a maid, a young woman, **maighdeann mo rùin** my beloved maiden, **maighdeann-mhara** a mermaid, *common in songs eg* **maighdeannan na h-àirigh** the sheiling maidens, *Cf* **gruagach, nighean 2, nìghneag 2, rìbhinn**; **2** a virgin, *Cf* **ainnir**; **3** an unmarried woman, a spinster, **seana-mhaighdeann** an elderly spinster, an old maid; **4** *in formal address, corres,* Miss, **A Mhaighdeann(-uasal) Chaimbeul,** *abbrev* **A Mh(-uas) Chaimbeul,** (Dear) Miss Campbell

maighdeannas, *gen* **maighdeannais** *nm* (*phys & abstr*) virginity, maidenhood, maidenhead

maigheach, maighiche, maighichean *nf* a hare, *Cf* **geàrr** *n*

maigh(i)stir, maigh(i)stir, maigh(i)stirean *nm* **1** a master, **maighistir-sgoile** a schoolmaster, a schoolteacher (*usu primary*), *also* a head-teacher (*usu secondary*), **ban(a)-mhaighstir-sgoile** *f* a schoolmistress (*Cf* **fear-teagaisg** (*see* **teagasg**), **tìdsear**); **2** *in formal address, corres*, (*abbrev* **Mgr**) Mister, **A Mhaighstir Fhriseil** (*abbrev* **A Mhgr Fhriseil**) (Dear) Mr Fraser

màileid, màileide, màileidean *nf various kinds of leather &c bags*, a suitcase, a briefcase, a (*large*) bag, a satchel, **màileid-làimh** a handbag, **màileid-droma** a rucksack, a backpack (*Cf* **paca 1**), *Cf* **baga, ceus** *n*, **poca**

maille *nf invar* **1** (*abstr noun corres to* **mall**) slowness; **2** delay, a delay, **cuir** *v* **maille air** *or* **ann** delay, impede, hold back, retard, slow down (*a process &c*), **ma thèid maille orra** if they're held up/delayed, *Cf* **dàil 2**

mailleachadh, *gen* **mailleachaidh** *nm* (*the act of*) procrastinating &c (*see senses of* **maillich** *v*)

maille ri *prep* with, along with, **bidh sinn a' falbh maille ri càch** we'll be leaving along with the others, *Cf* **cuide ri, mar 5**, & *more usu* **còmhla 2, le 1**

maillich *vti, pres part* **a' mailleachadh**, procrastinate, delay, defer, retard

mair *vi, pres part* **a' mairsinn**, *also* **a' maireann** & **a' maireachdainn**, last, continue (in existence), **cha mhair e dà là** he/it won't last two days, **mair beò** live, survive, **ma mhaireas mi** if I live/survive, if I'm spared, (*prov*) **cha mhair a' ghrian mhaidne rè an latha** the morning sun won't last all day

maireann (*verbal noun of* **mair** *v*) **1** *in expr* **rim (&c) mhaireann** during my (&c) lifetime, as long as I (&c) live, *Cf* **beò 2, saoghal 2; 2** *in expr* **nach maireann** the late …, **Seonaidh Caimbeul nach maireann** the late Johnny Campbell

maireannach *adj* **1** eternal, everlasting, **beatha mhaireannach** everlasting life; **2** durable, lasting, **sìth mhaireannach** a lasting peace; **3** (*of individual*) long-lived; *Cf* **buan**

mairg *adj* (*trad*) pitiable, to be pitied, *esp in expr* **(is) mairg a** … woe to …, (*song*) **('s) mairg a dhèanadh mo bhualadh** woe to him who would strike me, **is mairg a thigeadh faisg air** woe to/pity anyone who would come near him

màirnealach *adj* **1** slow, dilatory, *Cf* **athaiseach** & *more usu* **mall, slaodach 1; 2** long drawn out, boring, tedious, *Cf* **fadalach 2, slaodach 2**

màirnealaich *vi, pres part* **a' màirnealachadh**, delay, procrastinate, drag one's heels (*fig*)

mairtfheoil, *gen* **mairtfheòla** *nf* beef

maise *nf invar* beauty, loveliness, gracefulness, **maise na nighinne** the girl's beauty, **ball-maise** *m* an ornament, *also* a beauty spot (*on face*), *Cf* **bòidhchead**

maiseach *adj* (*esp of woman*) beautiful, lovely, graceful, handsome, *Cf* **àlainn, bòidheach**

maiseachadh, maiseachaidh, maiseachaidhean *nm* 1 (*the act of*) decorating &c (*see senses of* **maisich** *v*); 2 decoration, a decoration, embellishment, an embellishment, *Cf* **sgeadachadh** 2

maisich *vt, pres part* **a' maiseachadh**, 1 decorate, beautify, embellish, *Cf* **brèaghaich, sgeadaich** 1; 2 make up, **mhaisich i a h-aodann** she made up her face

maith *see* **math** *v & n*

màithreil *adj* motherly, maternal

màl, *gen & pl* **màil** *nm* rent, **gabh** *v* **taigh air mhàl** rent a house (*as tenant*), **thoir** *v* **seachad taigh air mhàl** rent (out) a house (*as landlord*), **taigh air mhàl** a rented house

mala, mala, malaichean *nf* 1 an eyebrow; 2 a brow, *Cf* **bathais** 1, **clàr** 2, **maoil**

malairt, malairt, malairtean *nf* 1 trade, business, commerce, a business, **dèan** *v* **malairt** trade, do business (*Cf* **malairtich**), *Cf* **gnìomhachas** 2, **gnothach** 1; 2 barter, exchange, *Cf* **iomlaid** 1

malairteach *adj* commercial, **ealain mhalairteach** commercial art

malairtich *vi, pres part* **a' malairteachadh**, 1 trade, engage in trade or commerce, *Cf* **malairt** 1; 2 barter, exchange

màlda *adj* coy, bashful, modest, *Cf* **nàrach** 2

mall *adj* slow, tardy, *Cf* **athaiseach** *& more usu* **màirnealach** 1, **slaodach** 1

mallachadh, *gen* **mallachaidh** *nm* (*the act of*) cursing (*see* **mallaich** *v*)

mallachd & mollachd, *gen* **mallachd,** *pl* **mallachdan** *nf* a curse, malediction, a malediction, (*song*) **mallachd nan Gàidheal gu lèir air Rìgh Uilleam 's air a threud** the curse of every Gael on King William and on his gang

mallaich *vt, pres part* **a' mallachadh**, curse

mallaichte *adj* cursed, accursed, damned

mamaidh, mamaidh, mamaidhean *nf* (*child's lang*) mammy, mummy, *Cf* **màthair** 1

manach, *gen & pl* **manaich** *nm* a monk

manachainn, manachainne, manachainnean *nf* a monastery

manadh, manaidh, manaidhean *nm* an omen

manaidsear, manaidseir, manaidsearan *nm* a manager, **bana-mhanaidsear** *f* a manageress, *Cf* **fear-riaghlaidh** (*see* **riaghladh** 3), **fear-stiùiridh** (*see* **stiùireadh**)

Manainneach, *gen & pl* **Manainnich** *nm* a Manxman, *also as adj* **Manainneach** Manx, of, from or pertaining to the Isle of Man (**Eilean Mhanainn, an t-Eilean Manainneach**)

mànas, mànais, mànasan *nm* (*agric*) the mains or home farm of an estate

mang, mainge, mangan *nf* a fawn

maodal, maodail, maodalan *nf* a (large) stomach, a paunch, a belly, *Cf* **balg** 1, **brù** 2, **stamag**

maoidh *vi, pres part* **a' maoidheadh, 1** threaten, menace (*with prep* **air**), **bha e a' maoidheadh orm** he was threatening me, *Cf* **bagair** 1; **2** bully

maoidheadh, maoidhidh, maoidhidhean *nm* **1** (*the act of*) threatening, menacing, bullying; **2** a threat, a menace; **3** bullying

maoidhear, maoidheir, maoidhearan *nm* a bully

maoil, maoil, maoilean *nf* a forehead, a brow (*not eyebrow, Cf* **mala** 1), *Cf* **bathais** 1, **clàr** 2, **mala** 2

Maoil, *gen* **Maoile** *nf, with art,* **a' Mhaoil** the Minch

maoile *nf invar, also* **maoilead,** *gen* **maoileid,** baldness (*abstr nouns corres to* **maol** *adj*)

maoin, maoine, maoinean, *nf* **1** goods (*not usu at point of sale, Cf* **bathar**); **2** one's wordly goods, possessions, goods and chattels, (*Sc*) gear; **3** worldly wealth, riches, assets, *Cf more usu* **beartas, saidhbhreas**

maol, *gen & pl* **maoil** *nm* **1** a cape, a promontory (*usu rounded*), *Cf* **àrd** *n* 2, **rubha, sròn** 2; **2** (*topog*) a rounded bare hill

maol *adj* **1** (*knife &c*) blunt; **2** bald, *Cf* **sgallach; 3** hornless, **bò mhaol odhar agus bò odhar mhaol** six and half a dozen (*lit* a hornless dun cow and a dun hornless cow)

maor, *gen & pl* **maoir** *nm* **1** (*trad*) *referring to a number of subordinate & middle-ranking positions in the law, land-management &c, eg* a bailiff (*Cf* **bàillidh** 1), a land/township constable (*Cf* **con(a)stabal**), a factor (*Cf* **seumarlan** 1), a (land) steward (*Cf* **stiùbhard**); **2 maor-eaglais** a church officer, **maor(-obrach)** a foreman, a gaffer, **maor dùthcha/ pàirce** a countryside/park ranger, **maor-cladaich** a coastguard

maorach, *gen* **maoraich** *nm* shellfish, a shellfish

maoth *adj* **1** (*phys or emotionally*) soft, tender, delicate, *Cf* **bog** *adj* 1; **2** tender(-hearted), affectionate, loving, *Cf* **gaolach** 1, **gràdhach**

maothachadh, *gen* **maothachaidh** *nm* (*the act of*) softening (*see* **maothaich** *v*)

maothaich *vti, pres part* **a' maothachadh**, soften, make or become soft or softer

mapa, mapa, mapaichean *nm* a map, **mapa na Roinn-Eòrpa** the map of Europe, *Cf* **clàr 4**

mar 1 *prep,* in the manner of, like, *Note: a noun without the art after* **mar** *is in the dat, & aspirated/lenited, eg* **a' cluich mar chaileig** playing like a girl, *(but Cf)* **mar a' chaileag** like the girl; **thug e Canada air dìreach mar a bhràthair** he went off to Canada just like his brother, *(common saying)* **is ann mar sin a tha agus a bha agus a bhitheas** that's how/the way it is and always was and always will be; **2** *in expr* **mar sin so, chaill mi mo mhàileid-pòca 's mar sin chan eil sgillinn ruadh agam** I lost my wallet and so I haven't a brass farthing, *also in leave-taking* **mar sin leat/leibh!** 'bye then!, 'bye just now! *(Cf* **tìoraidh!** *& more formal* **beannachd 4**); **3** *in exprs* **mar sin** *&* **mar sin air adhart** and so on, **briogais, brògan 's mar sin** trousers, shoes and so on/that kind of thing, **thuirt i gun robh sinn leisg, mì-mhodhail, luideach . . . 's mar sin air adhart** she said we were lazy, rude, scruffy . . . and so on; **4** *in expr* **mar eisimpleir** for example *(abbrev* **me** *&* **m.e.**); **5** *(trad)* **mar ri** *prep* with, along with, **'s truagh nach eil thu mar rium** it's sad that you aren't with me, *Cf more usu* **còmhla 2**; **6** *in expr* **mar an ceudna** *adv* likewise, too, similarly, **bha athair an sàs ann am poileataics – mar an ceudna e fhèin** his father was involved in politics himself too/likewise, *Cf* **cuideachd** *adv*; **7** *as conj* **mar a** as, how, **bitheadh sin mar a bhitheas e** be that as it may, **mar a chanas iad** as they say, **thachair a h-uile càil mar a thogradh sinn** everything happened as we would wish, **tha sinn dòigheil mar a tha sinn** we're fine/contented as we are, **dh'innis i dha mar a chuala i** she told him what she had heard, **is truagh mar a thachair** it's sad the way things turned out, it's a shame what happened, *(prov)* **mar as** *(for* **mar a is**) **sine am boc 's ann as cruaidhe an adharc** the older the buck the harder the horn; **8** *as conj* **mar gun/nach** as if, as though, **lean e air mar nach robh e gu diofar** he carried on as if/though it didn't matter, **bha i, mar gum biodh, fad às** she was, as it were, withdrawn; **9** *in expr* **mar a tha** *also* **mar-thà** *adv* already, *see* **tràth** *adj & adv* **3**

marag, maraig, maragan *nf* **1** a pudding *(savoury not sweet – Cf* **mìlsean**), **marag dhubh/gheal** black/white pudding; **2** *(occas)* a haggis, *Cf* **taigeis**

maraiche, maraiche, maraichean *nm* a sailor, a seaman, a seafarer, a mariner, *(song)* **('s e) 'n fhìrinn a th' agam nach maraiche mi** I'm no sailor and that's the truth, *Cf* **seòladair**

marbh *vt, pres part* **a' marbhadh**, kill, slay, *(poem)* **creachadh, losgadh agus marbhadh** plundering, burning and killing, *Cf* **murt** *v*

marbh *adj* dead, **corp marbh** a dead body, a corpse, **a' mhìos mharbh** the dead month (February), (*calque*) **ann am marbh na h-oidhche** in the dead of night, **uisge marbh** stagnant water

marbhadh, *gen* **marbhaidh** *nm* (*the act of*) killing &c (*see senses of* **marbh** *v*)

marbhaiche, marbhaiche, marbhaichean *nm* a killer, a murderer, *Cf* **murtair**

marbhan, marbhain, marbhanan *nm* a corpse, a dead body, *Cf more usu* **corp 2**

marbhphaisg, marbhphaisge, marbhphaisgean *nf* a shroud, a winding-sheet, *trad, in curses*, (*song*) **mìle marbhphaisg air a' ghaol/air na fearaibh** (*obs dat pl*) a thousands shrouds on love/on men

marbhrann, marbhrainn, marbhrannan *nm* (*trad*) a poem in praise of a dead hero &c, an elegy, *Cf* **cumha** *nm*

marbhtach *adj* deadly, fatal, mortal, death-dealing, **buille mharbhtach** a deadly/mortal (&c) blow, *Cf* **bàsmhor 2**

marcachadh, *gen* **marcachaidh** *nm, also* **marcachd** *nf invar*, **1** (*the act of*) riding (*see senses of* **marcaich** *v*); **2** horsemanship, **sgoil mharcachd** a riding school

marcaich *vi, pres part* **a' marcachd** & **a' marcachadh**, ride (*esp horse*)

marcaiche, marcaiche, marcaichean *nm* a (*horse*) rider, a horseman

marcaid *see* **margadh**

margadh, margaidh, margaidhean *nmf, also* **marcaid, marcaide, marcaidean** *nf*, **1** a (*weekly &c*) market, **ionad-margaidh** *m* a market-place, **baile-margaidh** *m* a market town, *Cf* **fèill 3**; **2** (*economics*) a market, **am Margadh Coitcheann** the Common Market, **eaconomaidh saor-mhargaidh** a free market economy, **am bi margadh air?** will there be a market for it? (*Cf* **fèill 4**)

margarain *nm invar* margarine

màrmor, *gen* **màrmoir** *nm* marble

màrsail, *gen* **màrsaile** *nf* marching, a march, *sometimes used as pres part*, **a' màrsail** marching, *Cf* **caismeachd 2, mèarrsadh**

Màrt, *gen* **Màirt** *nm* **1** (*the planet*) Mars; **2** *with art* **am Màrt** March

mart, *gen & pl* **mairt** *nm* (*trad*) any bovine, (*now usu*) a beef animal, (*Sc*) a mart

màs, màis, màsan *nm* **1** a buttock; **2** (*fam*) an arse, a bottom, a bum, a backside, *Cf* **tòn 2**

masg, masg, masgan *nm* a mask, *Cf* **aghaidh-choimheach, aodannan**

ma sgaoil *see* **sgaoil** *n*

maslach *adj* disgraceful, shameful, *Cf* **nàr, tàmailteach 1**

maslachadh, *gen* **maslachaidh** *nm* (*the act of*) disgracing &c (*see* **maslaich** *v*)

masladh, maslaidh, maslaidhean *nm* disgrace, shame, **'s e cùis-mhaslaidh a th' ann!** it's a disgrace! *Cf* **nàire 1, tàmailt 1**

maslaich *vt, pres part* **a' maslachadh**, disgrace, shame, put to shame, **chaidh mo mhaslachadh** I was put to shame, *Cf* **nàraich**

matamataig(s) *nm invar* mathematics, maths

math & **maith** *vi, pres part* **a' mathadh**, forgive, **maith dhuinn, a Dhia/ a Chruitheir!** forgive us, O God!

math, *gen* **maith** *nm* good, **am math is an t-olc** good and evil, **dè am math a bhith a' bruidhinn?** what's the good/use of talking? (*Cf* **feum** *n* 3)

math *adj* (*comp* **(n)as** (&c) **fheàrr** better, best, *see* **feàrr**), **1** good (*quality*) **biadh math** good food, (*quantity*) **pìos math coiseachd** a good/ fair bit of walking, (*morally*) **duine math** a good man, (*attainment, ability*) **cluicheadair math** a good player, **math air òrain** good at singing, (*accuracy*) **mas math mo chuimhne** if I remember rightly/ correctly, (*wish, greeting*) **madainn/oidhche mhath!** good morning/ night! (*expr approval, pleasure*) **glè mhath!** very good/excellent! **'s math sin!** that's good/smashing!, **math dha-rìribh!** very good indeed!, splendid!, **math thu fhèin!** good for you!, well done!, **'s math d' fhaicinn!** it's good to see you, **'s math gu bheil thu a' cumail sùil air** it's good that you're keeping an eye on him; **2** *as adv* well, **nach math a rinn thu!** didn't you do well!, well done!; **3** *in expr* **cho math ri** as well as, in addition to, **dh'ith e marag cho math ri pìos math feòla** he ate a pudding as well as a good bit of meat; **4** *in expr* **gu math** *adv* well, quite, **tha mi gu math** I am well, **bha iad gu math aosta** they were quite/pretty old, (*calque*) **tha e gu math dheth** he's well off; **5** (**is**) **ma(th) dh'fhaodte** *see* **faod 2**

mathachadh, *gen* **mathachaidh** *nm* manure, fertilizer &c (*used to enrich land*), *also* the act of adding this to land, *Cf* **inneir, leasachadh 4, todhar**

mathadh, *gen* **mathaidh** *nm* (*the act of*) forgiving (*see* **math** *v*)

mathaich *vt, pres part* **a' mathachadh**, manure, enrich, fertilize land (*by adding manure &c*), *Cf* **leasaich 3**

màthair, màthar, màthraichean *nf* **1** a mother, **màthair-chèile** a mother-in law, **bràthair-màthar** an uncle (*on mother's side*); **2** (*occas, esp in compounds*) the origin or prime example of something *eg* **màthair-adhbhar** *m* a prime cause, **màthair-uisge** *m* a fountainhead

màthaireachd *nf invar* motherhood, maternity

mathan, mathain, mathanan *nm* a (brown) bear, **mathan bàn** a polar bear

mathanas, *gen* **mathanais** *nm* forgiveness, pardon, **thoir** *v* **mathanas do** forgive (*Cf* **math** *v*)

mathas, *gen* **mathais** *nm* goodness

me & **m.e.** (*abbrev*) *see* **mar 4**

meadhan, **meadhain**, **meadhanan** *nm* **1** a middle, a centre, **meadhan a' bhaile** the town centre/middle of the town, **ann an teis-meadhan** (*also* **ceart-mheadhan**) **an achaidh** in the dead centre of the field; **2** an average, a mean; **3** a medium, a mechanism, a means, **foghlam tro mheadhan na Gàidhlig** Gaelic medium education, (*press, TV &c*) **na meadhanan** the media; **4** a waist, **crios mum mheadhan** a belt around my middle/waist; **5** *adjectivally in compound exprs eg* **meadhan-aois** *f* middle age, **meadhan-aoiseil** *adj* medieval, **am meadhan-chearcall** *m* the equator, **meadhan-là/-oidhche** *m* noon/ midnight

meadhan-sheachnach *adj* centrifugal

meadhanach *adj* **1** middling, tolerable, average, so-so, **chan eil mi ach meadhanach an-diugh** I'm only middling (well)/so-so today, **cha do rinn thu ach meadhanach math** you only did tolerably/ middling well; **2** middle, **An Ear Mheadhanach** the Middle East

Meadhan-thìreach *adj* Mediterranean

meal *vt, pres part* **a' mealadh** & **a' mealtainn**, enjoy (*Cf* **còrd** *v* **2**), *esp in exprs* **meal do naidheachd!** congratulations! (*lit* enjoy your news) & **cuir** *v* **meal-a-naidheachd air cuideigin** congratulate someone

mealadh, *gen* **mealaidh** *nm, also* **mealtainn** *nm invar*, **1** (*the act of*) enjoying (*see* **meal** *v*); **2** enjoyment

meal-bhucan, **meal-bhucain**, **meal-bhucanan** *nm* a melon

meall *vt, pres part* **a' mealladh**, **1** deceive, trick, cheat, **carson, a ghaoil, a mheall thu mi?** why, my love, did you deceive me?; **2** beguile, entice, tempt, **mheall an nathair Eubha** the serpent beguiled Eve, *Cf* **tàlaidh 2**

meall, *gen* & *pl* **mill** *nm* **1** a lump of anything, **meall an sgòrnain** the adam's apple, *Cf* **cnap 1**; **2** (*topog*) a (*usu lumpy*) hill, a lump of a hill, *Cf* **cnap 3**; **3 meall uisge** *m* a shower of rain (*heavier than* **fras** *n* **1**)

meallach *adj* alluring, enticing, beguiling, bewitching, (*song*) **Teàrlach òg nan gorm-shùl meallach** young Charles (*Edward Stewart*) of the bewitching blue eyes

mealladh, *gen* **meallaidh** *nm* **1** (*the act of*) deceiving, beguiling &c (*see senses of* **meall** *v*); **2** deceit, deception, *Cf* **foill 1**; **3** enticement, allurement; **4** (*also* **mealladh-dùil**) disappointment, *Cf more usu* **bris(t)eadh-dùil**

meallta(ch) *adj* deceitful, cheating, false, deceptive, *Cf* **brèige** *adj* **1**, **fallsa**

meallta *adj* deceived, cheated, taken in

mealltair, mealltair, mealltairean *nm* a cheat, a deceiver, *Cf* **cealgair(e)**

mealtainn *see* **meal** *v & * **mealadh**

meamhair, meamhrachadh, meamhraich *see* **meomhair, meòmhrachadh, meòmhraich**

mean *adj* little, tiny, *often in expr* **mean air mhean** little by little, gradually, *Cf* **beag 1, meanbh, mion 1**

mèanan, mèananaich *see* **mèaran, mèaranaich**

meanbh *adj* (very) little, tiny, diminutive, minute, *usu in compounds eg* **meanbh-chuileag** *f* a midge (*lit* tiny fly), **meanbh-thonn** *nf & adj* (a) microwave, **meanbh-reic** *m* (*commerce*) retailing, *Cf* **crìon** *adj* **1, mion 1**

meang, *gen* **meanga** *&* **meing**, *pl* **meangan** *nf* **1** (*moral*) a fault, a defect, a flaw, a blemish, **an laoch gun mheang** the flawless hero, *Cf* **fàillinn 1, gaoid; 2** (*phys*) a defect, an abnormality

meang(l)an, *gen* **meang(l)ain**, *pl* **meang(l)ain** *&* **meang(l)anan** *nm* (*of tree*) a branch, a bough

meann, *gen & pl* **minn** *nm* a kid (*ie young goat*)

mearachd, mearachd, mearachdan *nf* a mistake, an error, a slip-up, **cha dèan mi mearachdan idir** I never make mistakes

mearachdach *adj* mistaken, wrong, incorrect, erroneous, **aithris mhearachdach** an incorrect report, **beachd mearachdach** a mistaken opinion, *Cf* **iomrallach**

mèaran *&* **mèanan**, *gen* **mèarain**, *pl* **mèaranan** *nm* a yawn

mèaranaich *&* **mèananaich**, *gen* **mèaranaiche** *nf* yawning, **'s ann ort a tha a' mhèaranaich an-diugh!** you're yawning a lot today!

mèarrsadh, *gen* **mèarrsaidh** *nm* marching, a march, *Cf* **caismeachd 2, màrsail**

meas *vti*, *pres part* **a' meas(adh)**, **1** think, reckon, consider, *Cf* **creid 2, saoil, smaoin(t)ich 3; 2** esteem, respect, value; **3** (*surveyors, valuers &c*) evaluate, assess, value, appraise, estimate, *Cf* **luachaich, luach 2**

meas[1] *nm invar* **1** respect, regard, esteem, **tha meas mòr agam oirre** I have a great deal of respect/regard for her, (*corres*) **is mise le meas** yours sincerely (*lit* I am, with respect …), *Cf* **urram 1; 2** (*surveyor &c*) valuation, a valuation, evaluation, an evaluation, assessment, an assessment, *Cf* **luachachadh 2**

meas[2], **measa, measan** *nm* fruit, a fruit, **meas-chraobh** *f* a fruit tree, **sùgh-measa** *m* fruit juice

measach *adj* fruity, full of *or* tasting of fruit

measadh, *gen* **measaidh** *nm* (*the act of*) considering, esteeming, valuing &c (*see senses of* **meas** *v*)

measail *adj* 1 respectable, respected, esteemed, valued, highly regarded; 2 fond (**air** of), (*poem*) **a chionn 's gu robh mi measail air** (Meg Bateman) because I was fond of him, *Cf* **dèidheil**

measarra *adj* moderate, sober, temperate, modest (*ie not excessive*), *Cf* **stuama 1**

measg *see* **am measg**

measgachadh, **measgachaidh**, **measgachaidhean** *nm* 1 (*the act of*) mixing &c (*see senses of* **measgaich** *v*); 2 mixture, a mixture

measgaich *vt, pres part* **a' measgachadh**, 1 mix, mingle, **air am measgachadh ri chèile** mixed/mingled together, (*calque*) **measgaich suas rudan eadar-dhealaichte** mix up/confuse different things; 2 combine, *Cf stronger* **co-mheasgaich**

measgaichear, **measgaicheir**, **measgaichearan** *nm* (*food, cement &c*) a mixer

meata *adj* faint-hearted, timid, feeble, lacking in spirit, *Cf* **gun smior** (*see* **smior 3**)

meatailt, **meatailte**, **meatailtean** *nf* metal, (*also as adj*) **dorsan meatailt** *or* **dorsan de mheatailt** metal doors

meatair, **meatair**, **meatairean** *nm* a metre

meatrach *adj* metric

meidh, **meidhe**, **meidhean** *nf* 1 (*weighing*) a balance, a scale, scales; 2 balance, equilibrium, *esp in exprs* **air mheidh** balanced & **cuir** *v* **air mheidh** balance, **chuir i an t-eallach air mheidh air a ceann** she balanced the load/burden on her head; *Cf* **cothrom** *n* 4

meil *vti, pres part* **a' meileadh**, (*corn &c*) mill, grind, *Cf* **bleith** *v* 1

meileabhaid, *gen* **meileabhaide** *nf* velvet

meileachadh, *gen* **meileachaidh** *nm* (*the act of*) chilling, numbing

meilich *vti, pres part* **a' meileachadh**, chill, make or become chilled, make or become numb (*esp with cold*), *Cf* **fuaraich**

mèilich *nf invar* a bleat (*esp sheep*), a baa, bleating, baaing, **dèan** *v* **mèilich** bleat, baa

mèinn, *gen* **mèinne** *nf* 1 character, disposition, temperament, nature, *Cf* **aigne 2**, **nàdar 2**; 2 (*occas, more temporary*) look, appearance, mien, expression, *Cf* **dreach 1**, **fiamh 3**, **tuar**

mèinn(e), **mèinne**, **mèinnean** *nf* 1 ore; 2 a mine, **mèinn(e)-ghuail** a coalmine

mèinneadair, **mèinneadair**, **mèinneadairean** *nm* a miner

mèinneach & **mèinneil** *adj* mineral

mèinnear, mèinneir, mèinnearan *nm, also* **mèinnearach,** *gen & pl* **mèinnearaich** *nm,* a mineral

mèinnearachd *nf invar* 1 mineralogy, *Cf* **mèinn-eòlas; 2** mining

mèinneil *see* **mèinneach**

mèinn-eòlas, *gen* **mèinn-eòlais** *nm* mineralogy

meirg *vti, pres part* **a' meirgeadh,** *also* **meirgich** *vti, pres part* **a' meirgeachadh,** rust, make or become rusty or rustier

meirg, *gen* **meirge** *nf* rust, **meirg-dhìonach** *adj* rust proof

meirgeach *adj* rusty, (*calque*) **tha mo chuid Gàidhlig** (&c) **gu math meirgeach** my Gaelic (&c) is pretty rusty

meirgich *see* **meirg** *v*

mèirle *&* **meirle** *nf invar* theft, thieving, stealing, **dèan** *v* **meirle** steal, thieve, (*prov*) **breac à linne, slat à coille is fiadh à fireach – meirle nach do ghabh duine a-riamh nàire aiste** a trout from the pool, a wand from the wood and a deer from the hill – theft no man was ever ashamed of, *Cf* **braid, goid** *n & v*

mèirleach *&* **meirleach,** *gen & pl* **meirlich** *nm* a thief, *Cf* **gadaiche**

meomhair *&* **meamhair,** *gen* **meomhair(e),** *pl* **meomhairean** *nf* (*the faculty of*) memory, **cùm** *v* **air mheomhair** memorise

meòmhrachadh *&* **meamhraich,** *gen* **meòmhrachaidh** *nm* (*the act of*) recalling, meditating &c (*see senses of* **meòmhraich** *v*)

meòmhraich *&* **meamhraich** *vi, pres part* **a' meòmhrachadh,** 1 recall, recollect, remember, think over the past; 2 meditate, ponder, muse, think, contemplate (**air** on, about), *Cf* **beachd-smaoin(t)ich, cnuas 2; 3** memorise, commit to memory

meud *nm invar* 1 size, extent, **meud an taighe/an achaidh** the size of the house/the field, **meud a h-iomagain** the extent of her anxiety, **rach** *v* **am meud** increase in size, grow bigger; 2 amount, quantity, number, (*trad*) **a mheud 's a bha an làthair** as many as were present, *Cf* **uimhir 1; 3** *esp in expr* **co** (*also* **cia**) **mheud** how many, how much, **co mheud a th' ann?** how many are there? *or* how much is there? **co mheud bliadhna a bha thu ann?** how many years were you there?

meudachadh, meudachaidh, meudachaidhean *nm* 1 (*the act of*) increasing &c (*see senses of* **meudaich** *v*); 2 increase, an increase, enlargement, an enlargement, addition, augmentation

meudachd *nf invar* bigness, magnitude, greatness, size, **meudachd nam fiachan aca** the greatness of their debts, **mu mheudachd muice** about the size of a pig

meudaich *vti, pres part* **a' meudachadh,** increase, enlarge, add to, augment, make or become bigger, *Cf* (*vi*) **fàs** *v* **2,** (*vti*) **leudaich**

meur, *gen & pl* **meòir** *nf* **1** a finger, **meur-lorg** *f* a fingerprint, *Cf* **corrag**; **2** (*of piano, computer &c*) a key, **meur-chlàr** *m* a keyboard; **3** (*of tree, family, river, organisation &c*) a branch

meuran, *gen* **meurain**, *pl* **meurain** & **meuranan** *nm* a thimble

mi, *emph form* **mise**, *pers pron* I, me

mì- *a common neg prefix corres to Eng* un-, in-, dis-, mis-, -less *&c* (*ie it negativises second part of compound*), *eg* **mì-bhlasta** *adj* tasteless, unsavoury, **mì-cheartas** *m* injustice, **mì-dhìleas** *adj* disloyal, **mì-earbsa** *m* mistrust, distrust, **gu mì-fhortanach** *adv* unfortunately, **mì-rùn** *m* malice, ill-will, malevolence, *Cf* **eas-, eu-, neo-**

mial, **miala**, **mialan** *nf* **1** a louse; **2** a tick (*ie the parasite*), **mial-chaorach** a sheep-tick

mialaich *nf invar*, *also* **miamhail** *nf invar*, mewing, miauling, **rinn an cat mialaich/miamhail** the cat mewed

miann, **miann**, **miannan** *nmf* **1** desire, a desire, longing, a longing, a wish, **tobar** *m* **miann** a wishing well, (*trad*) **is e mo mhiann a bhith còmhla riut** my desire/wish is to be with you, **is miann/bu mhiann leam** I wish, **bu mhiann leam gum faighinn duais sa chrannchur** I wish I could win a prize in the lottery, *Cf* **rùn 3**; **2** (sexual) desire, **dh'fhairich e lasair beag miann** he felt a small flame of desire, **ana-miann** lust, *Cf* **drùis**

miannachadh, *gen* **miannachaidh** *nm* (*the act of*) desiring &c (*see senses of* **miannaich** *v*)

miannaich *vt*, *pres part* **a' miannachadh**, **1** desire, long for, wish for, **na miannaich rudan nach faigh thu** do not desire/wish for things you won't get, *Cf* **togair 1**; **2** (*sexually*) desire, lust after

mias, *gen* **mias** & **mèise**, *pl* **miasan** *nf* **1** a basin, **mias-ionnlaid** a wash basin; **2** a (large) dish, a platter

miastachd *nf invar* hooliganism, loutish behaviour

mil, **meala(ch)**, **mealan** *nf* honey, **pògan air blas na meala** honeyed/honey-sweet kisses, **cìr-mheala** *f* a honeycomb

mìle[1], **mìle**, **mìltean** *nm* **1** a thousand, **dà mhìle saighdear** two thousand soldiers, **thàinig iad nam mìltean** they came in their thousands

mìle[2], **mìle**, **mìltean** *nmf* a mile

milis *adj*, *comp* **(n)as (&c) mìlse**, sweet, **rudan milis** sweet things (*to eat*), *also* sweet(ie)s, (*song*) **gur milis Mòrag** how sweet is Mòrag, (*song*) **'s mìlse leam do phògan gu mòr na na cìrean-meala** (Murchadh MacPhàrlain) your kisses are sweeter to me by far than the honeycombs

mill *vti*, *pres part* **a' milleadh**, **1** spoil, ruin, mar, damage, destroy, wreck, **mhill e an doras** he damaged the door, **mhill na gunnaichean an tùr** the guns destroyed the tower, *Cf stronger* **sgrios** *v*; **2** spoil (*ie over-indulge*) **tha an cuilean ud air a mhilleadh!** yon pup's spoilt!

milleadh, *gen* **millidh** *nm* **1** (*the act of*) spoiling, ruining &c (*see senses of* **mill** *v*); **2** destruction, (*trad*) **is esan a rinn ar milleadh** it is he who brought about/wrought our destruction, *Cf* **sgrios** *n*

millean, millean, milleanan *nm, also* **muillean, muillean, muilleanan** *nm*, a million

millte *adj* spoilt, marred, damaged

millteach *adj* destructive, ruinous, apt to spoil, damage or wreck, *Cf* **sgriosail 1**

milltear, millteir, milltearan *nm* a vandal

mìlseachd *nf invar* sweetness

mìlsean, *gen* **mìlsein**, *pl* **mìlsein** & **mìlseanan** *nm* a dessert, a pudding, a sweet (course), **spàin-mhìlsein** *f* a dessert spoon

mì-mhodhail *adj* rude, ill-mannered, impolite, ill-bred, discourteous

mìn *adj* smooth, soft, **aodach/falt mìn** soft/smooth material/hair

min, *gen* **mine** *nf* **1** meal, **min-choirce** oatmeal, **min-èisg** fish meal; **2** (*occas*) flour (*more often* **min-flùir**), *Cf* **flùr²**; **3** *other finely-ground or fragmented substances eg* **min-iarainn** iron filings, **min-sàibh** sawdust

mìneachadh¹, mìneachaidh, mìneachaidhean *nm* **1** (*the act of*) explaining, interpreting (*see* **mìnich** *vt*); **2** explanation, an explanation, interpretation, an interpretation

mìneachadh², *gen* **mìneachaidh** *nm* (*the act of*) smoothing, making smooth

mìneachail *adj* explanatory

mìnich *vt, pres part* **a' mìneachadh**, (*vt*) explain, interpret, **bha an tidsear a' mìneachadh brìgh an fhacail** the teacher was explaining the sense/meaning of the word, *Cf* **soilleirich 2**

mìnich *vt, pres part* **a' mìneachadh**, smoothe, make smooth

minig *adj* used *adverbially* frequent, (*trad*) **is minig a chì thu caora air leth-shùil** you'll often see/many's the time you'll see a one-eyed ewe, *now usu as adv* **gu minig** often, frequently, *Cf more usu* **tric 1**

minig *vt, pres part* **a' minigeadh**, (*fam*) mean, **dè a tha thu a' minigeadh?** what do you mean?, *Cf* **ciallaich**

ministear, ministeir, ministearan *nm* **1** a minister (of religion), *Cf* **clèireach** *n* **1, pears-eaglais, sagart**; **2** a (government) minister, **Ministear na Stàite** the Minister of State, **Ministear a' Chosnaidh** the Employment Minister

ministrealachd, ministrealachd, ministrealachdan *nf* (*church, government*) ministry, a ministry

miodal, *gen* **miodail** *nm* flattery, fawning, buttering up, **dèan** *v* **miodal do chuideigin** flatter, fawn on, butter up someone, *Cf* **brìodal 3, sodal**

mìog, mìoga, mìogan *nf* a smirk, a sly smile

miogadaich *nf invar* bleating, a bleat *esp of goats*

mìol-chù, *gen & pl* **mìol-choin** *nm* a greyhound

mion *adj, usu used as prefix* **1** small, minute, tiny, on a small scale, **mion-bhraide** *f* petty pilfering, **mion-gheàrr** *vt* cut up finely, **mion-fhacal** *m* (*gram*) a particle, *Cf* **crìon** *adj* **1**, **meanbh**; **2** detailed, exact, punctilious, **mion-cheasnaich** *v* question minutely/in detail, (*fam*) grill, **mion-eòlas** *m* detailed/thorough/intimate knowledge or acquaintance, **mion-phuing** *f* a detail, **mion-chùiseach** *adj* meticulous, punctilious, attentive to detail, *Cf* **mionaideach**, **pongail 1**; **3** minor, minority, lesser, **mion-chànan** *m* a minority/lesser used language, **mion-aoiseach** *adj* minor (*ie under age*), **mion-chuid** *f* a minority (*ie a lesser part, Cf* **mòr-chuid** a majority)

mionach, mionaich, mionaichean *nm* **1** entrails, guts, innards, **mionach èisg** fish guts, *Cf* **caolan, greallach, innidh**; **2** (*fam*) a stomach, a belly, a gut, *Cf* **broinn 1, brù 2, stamag**

mionaid, mionaide, mionaidean *nf* a minute, **fichead mionaid** twenty minutes, **fuirich mionaid!** wait a minute!

mionaideach *adj* thorough, meticulous, detailed, in detail, **sgrùdadh mionaideach** a detailed/thorough/meticulous enquiry *or* study, *Cf* **mion 2, pongail 1**

mionn, mionna, mionnan *nmf, also* **mionnan**, *gen* **mionnain**, *pl* **mionnain** *&* **mionnanan** *nm*, **1** an oath, **thoir** *v* **mionnan** make/swear an oath; **2** a curse, an oath, (*Sc*) a swear, *Cf* **droch cainnt** (*see* **cainnt 2**)

mionnachadh, *gen* **mionnachaidh** *nm* (*the act of*) swearing &c (*see senses of* **mionnaich** *v*)

mionnaich *vi, pres part* **a' mionnachadh**, **1** swear (*ie testify &c on oath*); **2** curse, swear, use bad or foul language

mionnan *see* **mionn**

mìorbhail, mìorbhaile, mìorbhailean *nf* **1** a marvel, a wonder, *Cf* **iongnadh 1**; **2** a miracle

mìorbhaileach *adj* **1** marvellous, wonderful, *Cf* **iongantach**; **2** miraculous

mìos, mìosa, mìosan *nmf* a month, **mìos nam pòg** a honeymoon (*lit* the month of the kisses)

miosa *see* **dona**

mìosach *adj* monthly

mìosachan, *gen & pl* **mìosachain** *nm* a calender

miotag, miotaig, miotagan *nf* **1** a glove, *Cf* **làmhainn**; **2** a mitten

mìr, mìre, mìrean *nm* a bit, a small piece, particle or scrap of anything, *Cf* **bìdeag, criomag**

mire *nf invar* merriment, mirth, light-heartedness, (*song*) **thèid sinn le mire a-null air an linne** merrily we will cross the channel/sound, *Cf* **aighearachd**, **cridhealas**

mìrean, *gen & pl* **mìrein** (*dimin of* **mìr**) *nm* **1** a particle of anything; **2** (*gram*) a particle

misde *see* **miste**

misg, *gen* **misge** *nf* drunkenness, intoxication, **air mhisg** drunk, **cuir** *v* **air mhisg** make drunk, inebriate, **air leth-mhisg** tipsy, merry, half drunk, (*trad*) **misg chatha** battle frenzy (*lit* battle drunkenness), *Cf* **daorach 1, pòitearachd, smùid** *n* **3**

misgeach *adj* intoxicated; drunken; heady

misgear, misgeir, misgearan *nm* a drunkard, a boozer, *Cf* **pòitear**

misionairidh, misionairidh, misionairidhean *nm* a missionary, *Cf trad* **teachdaire 2**

misneach, *gen* **misnich** *nf*, *also* **misneachd** *nf invar*, courage, bravery, fortitude (*esp moral*); confidence, morale, *Cf* **cridhe 2, smior 3**

misneachadh, *gen* **misneachaidh** *nm* **1** (*the act of*) inspiring with courage &c (*see senses of* **misnich** *v*); **2** encouragement, **cha d'fhuair i misneachadh bhuapa** she got no encouragement from them, *Cf* **brosnachadh 2**

misneachail *adj* **1** courageous, brave (*esp morally*), *Cf* **smiorail**; **2** spirited, of good cheer, in good heart; **3** encouraging, *Cf* **brosnachail**

misneachd *see* **misneach**

misnich *vt, pres part* **a' misneachadh, 1** inspire or fill someone with courage, awaken someone's courage or confidence; **2** encourage; *Cf* **brosnaich**

miste *&* **misde** *adj* worse, the worse, *esp in expr* **is miste mi** (&c) ... I am (&c) the worse for ..., **cha mhiste sibh e** you are none the worse for it, **cha bu mhiste mi pinnt** I'd be none the worse for a pint, a pint wouldn't do me any harm, *Cf opposite* **feàirrde**

mithich *adj* timeous, timely, opportune

mithich *nf invar* the proper or appointed time for something, *esp in expr* **ron mhithich** premature, prematurely

mnà, mnaoi, mnathan *see* **bean** *nf*

mo *poss adj* my, **mo dhachaigh** my home, **m' athair** my father, *Cf* **aig 2**

mò *see* **mòr**

moch *adj, now usu as adv*, early, (*trad*) **anns a' mhoch-mhadainn** in the early morning, **moch sa mhadainn** early in the morning, *also as noun in expr* **bho mhoch gu dubh** from morning till night/dawn to dusk (*lit* from early till darkness), *Cf* **tràth** *adj* **1** *& opposite* **anmoch**

mòd, mòid, mòdan *nm* **1** (*trad*) a (*legal*) court, *Cf more usu* **cùirt 2; 2** (*now usu*) a Gaelic mod, (*a session of literary and musical events and competitions*), **mòd ionadail** a local mod, **am Mòd Nàiseanta** the National Mod, *Cf* **fèis 1**

modh, modha, modh(ann)an *nmf* **1** a way, a manner, a mode (of doing something), **feumaidh tu a dhèanamh air mhodh àraidh** you must do it in a particular way/manner, **modh riaghlaidh** a mode/way/ system of governing, *Cf* **dòigh 1** *& less usu* **nòs 2; 2** *in expr* **air mhodh eile** otherwise, alternatively, or, on the other hand, *Cf* **air neo; 3** manners, (good) behaviour, (good) breeding, civility, *Cf* **beus 2, giùlan 3; 4** (*gram*) a mood, **a' mhodh àithneach** the imperative mood

modhail *adj* polite, well-mannered, well-bred, *Cf* **cùirteil 1** *& opposite* **mì-mhodhail**

modhalachd *nf invar* politeness, courtesy

Mohamadanach, *gen & pl* **Mohamadanaich,** a Mohammedan, a Muslim, *also as adj* **Mohamadanach** Mohammedan, Muslim, Islamic, *Cf* **Ioslamach**

mòine, *gen* **mòna, mònadh** *& ** **mònach,** *nf* peat, **poll** *m* **mòna(ch)** a peat bank/bog/hag, **fàd/fòid** *m* **mònach** a (single) peat, **bha iad ris a' mhòine** they were (working) at the peats, **dèan/buain** *v* **mòine** win/cut/gather peat

mòinteach, mòintich, mòintichean *nf* moorland, a moor (*rough hill land at low to medium altitude*), *Cf* **monadh 1, sliabh 1**

moit, *gen* **moite** *nf* pride, *often legitimate, Cf* **àrdan, pròis**

moiteil *adj* proud, *often legitimately,* **tha sinn moiteil asad** we're proud of/pleased with you, *Cf* **àrdanach, pròiseil**

mol *vt, pres part* **a' moladh, 1** praise, *Cf* **luaidh** *vt;* **2** suggest, propose, recommend, **mholainn dha an t-airgead a thoirt seachad** I'd advise/recommend him to give the money away, **tha a' chomhairle a' moladh meadhan a' bhaile a leasachadh** the council is proposing to develop/improve the town centre

mol, *gen* **moil** *&* **mola,** *pl* **molan** *nm* **1** shingle; **2** a shingly or pebbly beach

molach *adj* **1** hairy, rough, shaggy, 'wild and woolly', (*song*) **bonaid bhiorach, mholach, ghorm** a blue, hairy/rough, pointed bonnet, *Cf* **robach 1, ròmach 1; 2** furry

moladh, molaidh, molaidhean *nm* **1** (*the act of*) praising, proposing &c (*see senses of* **mol** *v*); **2** praise, (*song*) **Moladh Mòraig** (in) Praise of Mòrag, *Cf* **cliù 2, luaidh** *nm* **2; 3** a proposal, a recommendation, a suggestion, **molaidhean Oifis na h-Alba airson drochaid ùire** Scottish Office proposals/recommendations for a new bridge

moll, *gen* **muill** *nm* chaff, *Cf* **càth**

mollachd *see* **mallachd**

molldair, molldair, molldairean *nm* a mould (*ie for forming, shaping*)

molt *see* **mult**

mòmaid, mòmaide, mòmaidean *nf* a moment, an instant, (*loosely*) a second, *Cf more usu* **tiota(n) 2, tiotag**

monadail *adj* hilly, mountainous, *Cf* **cnocach**

monadh, monaidh, monaidhean *nm* 1 moorland, a moor, rough hill land, *Cf* **aonach, mòinteach, sliabh 1;** 2 (*crofting*) **am monadh** the hill (*the common hill grazing land associated with a crofting township*), **tha caoraich agam air a' mhonadh** I've sheep on the hill

mòr *adj, comp* **(n)as** (&c) **mò/motha**, 1 big, large, great in size or quantity, **eilean mòr** a big island, **Aonghas Mòr** Big Angus, **sluagh mòr** a big/numerous/great crowd (*Cf* **lìonmhor**), **airgead mòr** 'big' money, a lot/great deal of money, (*trad*) **bu mhòr mo mhulad** great was my sadness; 2 important, great, **bàrd/fear-ciùil mòr** a great poet/musician, (*ironic*) **na daoine mòra** the big shots/bigwigs, **tha sinn mòr aig a chèile** we are great friends/get on famously; 3 *in compounds, eg* **a' mhòr-chuid** the majority, **mòr-iongnadh** *m* astonishment, **mòr-roinn** *f* a continent; 4 *in expr* **cha mhòr** *conj* barely, hardly, scarcely, **cha mhòr gun do leig e às dà fhacal** he barely/scarcely uttered two words (*Cf* **gann 2**), *also* almost, nearly, (*note double neg*) **cha mhòr nach do chaill mi an sporan agam** I almost/nearly lost my purse (*Cf* **theab 2**); 5 **cha mhòr** *adv* nearly, almost, just about, **bidh sinn ga faicinn a h-uile là, cha mhòr** we see her every day, almost, *Cf* **ìre 4;** 6 *in expr* **nas motha** *adv* either, neither, **cha tèid mi dhachaigh! cha tèid mise nas motha!** I won't go home! neither will I!, I won't either!; 7 **cha mhotha (a)** *conj* neither, nor, **cha mhotha (a) chunnaic duine eile mi** nor/neither did anyone else see me

mòrachd *nf invar* greatness, grandeur, majesty

morair, morair, morairean *nm* a lord, **Taigh nam Morairean** the House of Lords, *Cf* **tighearna 1**

mòran, *gen* **mòrain** *nm* 1 many, a lot, a large number, *with gen pl noun*, **mòran dhaoine** a lot of/many people, **mòran dhiubh/aca** many of them, *Cf* **iomadach, iomadh 1** *& opposite* **beagan** *n*; 2 much, a lot, a great deal, a large quantity, *with gen sing n*, **mòran bìdh** much/a lot of food, **mòran taing!** many thanks!, thanks a lot!, **a bheil airgead agad? chan eil mòran** have you any money? not much, (*fam*) **dè tha dol? chan eil mòran** what's doing? not a lot, *Cf opposite* **beagan** *n*; 3 *as adv* much, a great deal, **tha an t-sìde mòran nas fheàrr an-diugh** the weather's a great deal better today, *Cf* **fada 3**

mòr-chòrdte *adj* popular, well-liked

mòr-chuid *see* **cuid 1**

mòrchuis, *gen* **mòrchuise** *nf* pride, conceit, *Cf* **leòm**

mòrchuiseach *adj* proud, conceited; pompous

morgaidse, morgaidse, morgaidsean *nm* a mortgage

morghan, *gen* **morghain** *nm* **1** gravel, *Cf* **grinneal 1**; **2** shingle, *Cf* **mol** *n* **1**

mort, mortadh, mortair *see* **murt, murtadh, murtair**

mòr-thìr, mòr-thìre, mòr-thirean *nf* a continent, a mainland, *Cf* **tìr-mòr** (*see* **tìr 1**)

mosach *adj* **1** nasty, dirty, scruffy, *Cf* **dràbhail, grodach, rapach**; **2** niggardly, *Cf* **spìocach**

mosg, mosga, mosgan *nm* a mosque

mosgail *vti, pres part* **a' mosgladh**, awake, wake, waken, rouse from sleep, *Cf more usu* **dùisg 1**

mosgladh, *gen* **mosglaidh** *nm* (*the act of*) awakening &c (*see senses of* **mosgail** *v*), an awakening, *Cf* **dùsgadh 1**

motair, motair, motairean *nm* a motor, **motair-rothar** a motor-bike

motha *see* **mòr**

mothachadh, *gen* **mothachaidh** *nm* **1** (*the act of*) noticing, feeling &c (*see senses of* **mothaich** *v*); **2** (*the sense or faculty of*) feeling, sensibility, sensitivity, sensation; **3** consciousness, awareness

mothachail *adj* **1** aware, observant, perceptive, *Cf* **beachdail 1, lèirsinneach 2**; **2** sensitive, feeling, sympathetic (*also* **co-mhothachail**), *Cf* **tuigseach 2**; **3** conscious

mothaich *vt, pres part* **a' mothachadh**, **1** notice, observe, perceive, **mhothaich mi e san dol seachad** I noticed it in passing (*also* **mhothaich mi dha** I noticed it/him), *Cf* **aire 2, fa-near 3**; **2** feel, experience, be conscious of, **mhothaich sinn gluasad a' bhàta** we felt the movement of the boat, *Cf* **fairich 1**

mu *prep, takes the dat, Note: the pers prons* **mi, thu, e** *&c combine with* **mu** *to form the prep prons* **umam(sa), umad(sa), uime(san), uimpe(se), umainn(e), umaibh(se), umpa(san)** around me, you &c; **1** around, about, **bann mu cheann** a bandage around his head (*Cf* **timcheall air**), **chuir i uimpe** she got dressed, **cuir umad do chòta** put your coat on/about you, *Cf* **air 1**; **2** about, concerning, **sgeulachd mu iasgair/mun chogadh** a story about a fisherman/about the war, *Cf* **air 4**; **3** *in expr* **mu dheidhinn** *prep, takes gen*, about, concerning, **a' bruidhinn mum dheidhinn** talking about me, **prògram mu dheidhinn foghlaim** a programme about education, (*calque*) **dè mu dheidhinn?** what about it?; **4** (*with* **deas** *n* & **tuath** *n*) in, to,

chaidh e mu dheas he went to the south, **na h-eileanan mu thuath** the islands in the north, the northern/northerly islands, **anns a' chùil mu dheas de bhàgh farsainn** in the southern corner of a broad bay; *Note: for other prep expressions with* **mu** *see under second word of expression*

muc, muice, mucan *nf* a pig, a sow, **muicfheoil** *f* pork, *Cf* **cràin, cullach, torc**

mùch *vt, pres part* **a' mùchadh, 1** (*fire*) extinguish, quench, smother, *Cf* **smà(i)l, tùch 2; 2** (*person*) choke, strangle, suffocate, smother, throttle, *Cf* **tachd; 3** (*spirit, rebellion &c*) quell, repress, put down, *Cf* **ceannsaich 2**

mùchadh, *gen* **mùchaidh** *nm* **1** (*the act of*) extinguishing, choking &c (*see senses of* **mùch** *v*); **2** suffocation; **3** (*pol &c*) repression, *Cf* **ceannsachadh 2**

mu choinneimh *see* **coinneamh 2**

mu chuairt *see* **cuairt 4**

muc-mhara, muic-mhara, mucan-mara *nf* a whale

mu dheas *see* **mu 4**

mu dheidhinn *see* **mu 3**

mu dheireadh *see* **deireadh 4**

muga, *gen* **muga,** *pl* **mugannan** & **mugaichean** *nf* a (*drinking*) mug

mùgach *adj* **1** morose, gloomy, *Cf* **gruamach 1; 2** surly, sullen, *Cf* **gnù, iargalt(a)**

muicfheoil *see* **muc**

muidhe, *gen* **muidhe,** *pl* **muidhean** & **muidheachan** *nm* a churn, *Cf* **crannag 2**

mùig, mùig, mùigean *nm* a frown, a scowl, a sulk, **chuir e mùig air** he frowned/scowled/sulked, *Cf* **gruaim 2** & **3, sgraing**

Muileach, *gen* & *pl* **Muilich** *nm* someone from Mull (**Muile**), *also as adj* **Muileach** of, from or pertaining to Mull, **An t-Eilean Muileach** The Isle of Mull

muileann, *gen* **muilinn,** *pl* **muilnean** & **muileannan** *nmf, also* **muilinn, muilne, muilnean** *nf*, a mill, **muileann-uisge** a water-mill, **muileann-gaoithe** a windmill, **muileann-pàipeir** a paper-mill

muile-mhàg, muile-mhàg, muileacha-màg *nf* a toad

muil(i)cheann *see* **muin(i)chill**

muilinn *see* **muileann**

muillean *see* **millean**

muillear, muilleir, muillearan *nm* a miller

muiltfheoil *see* **mult**

muime, muime, muimeachan *nf* a step-mother, *Cf* **oide**

muin *nf invar* **1** a back (*esp of an animal*), **air muin eich** on horse back, on the back of a horse, **leum e air muin na h-asail** he leapt on the donkey's back, *Cf* **druim 1**; **2** the top of something, **muin a' chnuic** the top of the hill (*Cf more usu* **mullach 1**), **chuir i blobhs oirre agus air muin sin seacaid** she put on a blouse and on top of that a jacket; **3** *with sexual meaning* **rach** *v* **air muin** (*with gen*) have intercourse with, fuck; (*animals*) mount, serve, **chaidh e air a muin** he had intercourse with her, **chaidh an tarbh air muin na bà** the bull mounted/served the cow; **4** *also in expr* **faigh** *v* **muin** have sex, have sexual intercourse, copulate, *Cf* **co-ghin, cuplaich**

mùin *vi, pres part* **a' mùn**, urinate, pass water, piss, *Cf* **dèan** *v* **mùn** (*see* **mùn**)

muinchill & **muinichill**, *gen* **muin(i)chill**, *pl* **muin(i)chillean** *nm*, *also* **muil(i)cheann, muil(i)chinn, muil(i)chinnean** *nm*, a sleeve (*of garment*), **thruis e a mhuilchinnean** he rolled up his sleeves

muineal, muineil, muinealan *nm* a neck, *Cf* **amha(i)ch 1**

muing, muinge, muingean *nf* (*of horse &c*) a mane, **muing an leòmhainn** the lion's mane

muinntir, *gen* **muinntire** *nf* **1** (*in the sense of one's associates, relatives, household &c*) people, folk(s) **dh'fhàg e an dùthaich ach cha deachaidh a mhuinntir còmhla ris** he left the country but his people/folks/followers didn't go with him; **2** (*now more usu in gen exprs*) the people, folk, inhabitants *of a particular place or locality*, **muinntir a' bhaile seo** the people of this town(ship), **muinntir Uibhist** the people of Uist, Uist folk, (*prov*) **ged as e an taigh, chan e a' mhuinntir** though it's the (same) house, these are not its people; *Cf* **duine 6, sluagh 2**

muir, mara, marannan *nmf* sea, a sea, **am muir** & **a' mhuir** the sea, **air muir 's air tìr** on land and sea, **rach gu muir** go to sea, **tha e aig muir** he's at sea, he's a sailor/seaman, **ceòl na mara** the song/ sound of the sea, **seòl-mara** *m* tide, *Cf* **cuan** & *less usu* **fairge**

muir-làn, *gen* & *pl* **muir-làin** *nm* a (high) tide, *Cf* **làn** *n* 2, **seòl-mara** (*see* **muir**), **tràigh** *n* 2

muir-thìreach *adj* amphibious, *Cf* **dà-bheathach** (*see* **dà 2**)

mulad, *gen* **mulaid** *nf* grief, sadness, **tha mi fo mhulad** or (*less trad*) **tha mulad orm** I'm sad, *Cf* **bròn 1**

muladach *adj* sad, (*song*) **gur muladach sgìth mi** I am sad and weary, *Cf* **brònach, tùrsach**

mullach, mullaich, mullaichean *nm* **1** the top of something, **clach mhòr is eun air a mullach** a great stone with a bird on top (of it), **mullach beinne** the top/summit of a mountain, *Cf less usu* **muin 2**; **2** a roof,

mullach taighe a house roof, **bha an t-uisge a' sileadh tron mhullach** the rain was pouring through the roof

mult & **molt**, *gen* & *pl* **muilt**, a wether, a wedder (*castrated sheep*), **muilt-fheòil** *gen* **muiltfheòla** *nf* mutton

mùn, *gen* **mùin** *nm* urine, piss, **dèan** *v* **mùn** urinate, **theab mi mo mhùn a chall leis cho èibhinn 's a bha e** I almost wet myself, it was so funny, *Cf* **fual**

mun *conj see* **mus**

mùnadh, *gen* **mùnaidh** *nm* (*the act of*) urinating; urination

muncaidh, muncaidh, muncaidhean *nm* a monkey

mun cuairt *see* **cuairt 4** & **5**

mur, mura *conj see* **ma**

mùr, mùir, mùirean *nm* (*trad*) a wall (*esp defensive or fortified*), a bulwark, a rampart, *Cf* **bàbhan**

murt *vt*, *pres part* **a' murt** (**adh**), murder, assassinate, *Cf* **marbh** *v*

murt, *gen* & *pl* **muirt**, *nm* murder, manslaughter, assassination, (*hist*) **Murt Ghlinne Comhainn** the Massacre of Glencoe

murtadh, *gen* **murtaidh** *nm*, (*the act of*) murdering, assassinating (*see* **murt** *vt*)

murtair, murtair, murtairean *nm*, a murderer, an assassin

mus & **mun** *conj* **1** before, **mus/mun tig an geamhradh** before the winter comes, **cha do phàigh e mus do dh'fhalbh e** he didn't pay before he left, **an oidhche mus do chaochail i** the night before she died; **2** lest, in case, for fear, **chùm e grèim math air an fhàradh mus tuiteadh i** he kept a good grip on the ladder lest/for fear she should fall, *Cf* **eagal 2**, **fios 5**

mu seach *see* **seach 3**

mu sgaoil *see* **sgaoil** *n*

mùth *vti*, *pres part* **a' mùthadh**, **1** change, alter; (*often*) change for the worse, deteriorate, *Cf more usu* **atharraich**; **2** mutate

mùthadh, mùthaidh, mùthaidhean *nm* **1** (*the act of*) changing, mutating &c (*see senses of* **mùth** *v*); **2** change, a change, alteration, an alteration (*often for the worse*), *Cf more usu* **atharrachadh 2, caochladh 2**; **3** mutation, a mutation; **4** (*phys*) corruption, decay

mu t(h)imcheall *see* **timcheall 4**

mu thràth *see* **tràth** *adj* **3**

N

na *neg imperative particle* don't, do not, **na fàg air an làr e!** don't leave it on the floor! **na bi gòrach!** don't be silly/stupid!

na *inter particle equivalent to* **an do** *before v in the past*, **na chùm e air ais sibh?** did he keep you back?

na *conj* than, **tha iad nas sine na mise** they are older than me

na *rel pron* **1** that, what, (all) that which, (all) those which, **thug mi dha na bha agam de bhiadh** I gave him what food/all the food I had (*lit* that which I had of food), **chuir i iongnadh air mòran de na bha ann** she surprised many of those that were there; **2** *in comp constrs* **tha am fear seo nas** (*for* **na is**) **mò** this one's bigger, **bha an trèana na b' fhaide** the train was longer

na *form of the art, see table p 401*

na *prep pron see* **an** *prep 3*

na b' (*in comp constrs*) *see* **na** *rel pron 2*

nàbaidh, nàbaidh, nàbaidhean *nm* a neighbour, *Cf less usu* **coimhearsnach**

nàbaidheachd *nf invar* a neighbourhood, *Cf* **coimhearsnachd**

nàbaidheil *adj* neighbourly

nach *neg particle* **1** *in inter clauses,* **nach do rinn thu e?** didn't you do it? **tha i fuar, nach eil?** it's cold, isn't it? **nach bi iad ann?** won't they be there? **nach truagh sin?** isn't that a shame/pity? **nach math a rinn thu!** didn't you do well!, well done! **2** *in rel clauses,* **an tè nach tàinig 's nach tig** the woman who didn't come and won't come, (*prov*) **cha chaoidh duine an rud nach fhaic e** a man doesn't grieve over what he doesn't see; **3** *forming neg with conjs,* **a chionn 's nach eil stailc ann** because there isn't a strike, **ged nach robh e tinn** though he wasn't ill, **air dhòigh 's nach bithinn mì-mhodhail** so that I wouldn't be impolite

nad *prep pron see* **an** *prep 3*

nàdar, *gen* **nàdair** *nm,* **1** nature (*ie the natural world*), **glèidhteachas** *m* **nàdair** nature conservancy, conservation; **2** nature, temperament, character, disposition, *Cf* **aigne 2, mèinn 1**

nàdarra(ch) *adj* natural

naidheachd, naidheachd, naidheachdan *nf* **1** news, a piece of news, **meal do naidheachd!** congratulations! (*lit* enjoy your news), **bha Iain a' gabhail do naidheachd** Iain was asking after you, (*TV, Radio &c*) **na naidheachdan** the news, **fear-naidheachd** a journalist (*Cf* **naidheachdair**); **2** (*at ceilidh &c*) an anecdote, a short (*usu humorous*) story

naidheachdair, naidheachdair, naidheachdairean *nm* a journalist

nàidhlean, *gen* **nàidhlein** *nm* nylon

nàimhdeas, *gen* **nàimhdeis** *nm* (*abstr noun corres to* **nàmhaid**) enmity, hostility

nàimhdeil *adj* hostile, inimical

nàire *nf invar* 1 shame, ignominy, **a bhoireannaich** (*voc*) **gun nàire!** shameless woman! **gabh** *v* **nàire** be/feel ashamed, **fo nàire** ashamed, **mo nàire!** for shame! **mo nàire oirbh!** shame on you! *Cf* **masladh; 2** bashfulness, *Cf* **diùide**

nàireach *see* **nàrach**

nàisean, nàisein, nàiseanan *nm* a nation (*people & territory*)

nàiseanta *adj* national, **Am Mòd Nàiseanta** The National Mod

nàiseantach, *gen & pl* **nàiseantaich** *nm* a nationalist, *also as adj* **nàiseantach** nationalist

nàiseantachd *nf invar* 1 nationalism; 2 nationhood

naisgear, naisgeir, naisgearan *nm* (*gram*) a conjunction

nam *prep pron see* **an** *prep* 3

nàmhaid, nàmhad, nàimhdean *nm* an enemy, a foe, an adversary

nan *conj* (**nam** *before b,f,m,p*) if (*in hypothetical contexts in past & conditional tenses*), (*song*) **nam biodh agams' an sin cupan, dh'òlainn dith mo shàth** if I had had a cup there, I would have drunk my fill of it, **nan robh mi beartach, thogainn caisteal dhut** if I was/were rich, I'd build you a castle, *Cf* **ma** 1

nan (**nam** *before b,f,m,p*) *form of the article see table p 401*

nan *prep pron see* **an** *prep* 3

naoi & naodh *num* nine, **naoi-deug & naodh-deug** nineteen

naoidhean, naoidhein, naoidheanan *nm* an infant, a baby, a young child, *Cf* **leanaban, leanabh, pàiste**

naoinear *nmf* people numbering nine, **cha tàinig ach naoinear** only nine (people) came, **naoinear mhac/chaileag** (*gen pl*) nine sons/ girls

naomh, *gen & pl* **naoimh** *nm* a saint

naomh *adj* holy, sacred, saintly

naomhachd *nf invar* 1 saintliness; 2 holiness, sanctity

nàr *adj* shameful, disgraceful, **is nàr sin!** that's disgraceful!, *Cf* **maslach, tàmailteach** 1

nar *prep pron see* **an** *prep* 3

nàrach & nàireach *adj* 1 shame-faced, sheepish, ashamed; 2 bashful, modest, diffident, *Cf* **diùid, màlda**

nàrachadh, *gen* **nàrachaidh** *nm* (*the act of*) shaming &c (*see senses of* **nàraich** *v*)

nàraich *vt, pres part* **a' nàrachadh**, shame, put to shame, abash, disgrace, *Cf* **maslaich**

nas (*in comp exprs*) *see* **na** *rel pron* **2**

nathair, **nathrach**, **nathraichean** *nf* **1** an adder; **2** a snake, a serpent, *also in Bibl context* **mheall an nathair Eubha** the serpent beguiled Eve

neach *nm invar* **1** a person, one, someone, an individual, (*in neg constr*) no-one, **an neach ris an do bhruidhinn mi** the person/individual I spoke to, **chan fhaca mi neach sam bith** I saw no-one/didn't see anyone at all, **gaol nach cuireadh neach an cèill** a love no-one could/one couldn't express, *Cf* **duine 2**, **urra 1**; **2** *in numerous compounds as politically correct alternative to* **fear-**, *eg* **neach-ciùil** a musician, *pl* **luchd-ciùil**, **neach-cathrach** a chairperson, **neach-labhairt** a spokesperson, **neach-obrach** a worker, a workperson, *Cf* **bana-**, **fear 2**, **luchd**[2]

neach-ionaid, *pl* **luchd-ionaid** *nm* a replacement, (*sport &c*) a substitute, (*theatre &c*) a stand-in, (*med*) a locum, *also* an agent

neactar, *gen* **neactair** *nm* nectar

nead, *gen & pl* **nid** *nm* a nest, (*song*) **thig gach eun a dh'ionnsaigh nid** each bird will make for its nest

nèamh, **nèimh**, **nèamhan** *nm* **1** heaven, a heaven, *Cf* **flaitheas**, **pàrras**; **2** (*occas*) the heavens, *Cf* **iarmailt**, **speur 2**

nèamhaidh *adj* heavenly, celestial

neapaigear, **neapaigeir**, **neapaigearan** *nm* a handkerchief

neapaigin, **neapaigine**, **neapaiginean** *nf* a napkin

nearbhach *adj* nervy, nervous

neart, *gen* **neirt** *nm* (*usu phys*) strength, force, might, vigour, (*prov*) **thèid neart thar ceart** might before right, **an trèine a neirt** at the height of his strength/powers, in his prime, *Cf* **lùth 3**, **spionnadh**

neartachadh, *gen* **neartachaidh** *nm* (*the act of*) strengthening &c (*see senses of* **neartaich** *v*)

neartaich *vti, pres part* **a' neartachadh**, strengthen, make or become strong or stronger, invigorate

neartmhor *adj* (*phys*) strong, mighty, powerful, *Cf* **làidir 1**, **lùthmhor 1**

neas, **neasa**, **neasan** *nm* **1** a weasel; **2** a stoat (*also* **neas mhòr**); **3** a ferret

neasgaid, **neasgaide**, **neasgaidean** *nf* a boil, an ulcer, a carbuncle

nèibhi(dh), **nèibhi(dh)**, **nèibhidhean** *nmf* a navy, (*song*) **saoilidh balaich … nach eil ceàrd as fheàrr na 'n Nèibhi gus an tèid iad**

innte (Murchadh MacLeòid, Siabost) young fellows think there's no trade better than the Navy, until they join it, *Cf* **cabhlach 2**, **loingeas 2**

neimh *see* **nimh**

Neiptiùn, *gen* **Neiptiùin** *nm* Neptune

neo *see* **no**

neo- *prefix corres to Eng* un-, in-, -less *&c* (*ie negativises second element of compound*), *eg* **neo-àbhaisteach** *adj* unusual, **neo-chiontach** *adj* guiltless, innocent, **neo-chomasach** *adj* incapable, incompetent, **neo-chùramach** *adj* irresponsible, **neo-iomlan** *adj* incomplete **neo-thruacanta** *adj* pitiless, **neo-eisimeileachd** *f* independence, *Cf* **eas-, eu-, mì-**

neodrach *adj* (*gram &c*) neuter

neòinean, *gen* **neòinein**, *pl* **neòinein** & **neòineanan** *nm* a daisy, **neòinean-grèine** a sunflower

neònach *adj* odd, strange, curious, (*trad*) **nach neònach sin?** isn't that strange?, *Cf stronger* **iongantach**

neoni *nf invar* nothing, nought, zero, (*scores*) nil, (*tennis*) love, **rach** *v* **gu neoni** come to nought/nothing

neo-phàirteach *adj* unbiased, impartial, objective

neul, *gen & pl* **neòil** *nm* **1** a cloud, (*song*) **a' fuadach neul na h-oidhche** banishing the clouds of night, *Cf* **sgòth**; **2** (*of face*) a complexion, a hue, *Cf* **dreach 2, tuar**; **3** a faint, a fainting fit, **rach** *v* **an neul** faint, *Cf* **laigse 2**

neulach *adj* cloudy, *Cf* **sgòthach**

neulaich *vti*, *pres part* **a' neulachadh**, cloud, cloud over, obscure

nì *pt of irreg v* **dèan** *see tables p 407*

nì, nì, nithean *nm* **1** a thing, **a h-uile nì** everything, **nì sam bith** anything at all, **nitheigin** something, *Cf* **càil** *nm* **1, dad 1, rud 1, sian 3**; **2** a circumstance, a matter, an affair, a business, **'s e droch nì a bh' ann** it was a bad business/affair, (*song*) **bidh i daonnan air mo chùram anns gach nì** she's always on my mind in every circumstance, (*prov*) **deiseil air gach nì** sunwise in every circumstance, *Cf* **gnothach 2**; **3** *in expr* **(an) Nì Math** God

nic *a prefix found in clan surnames & surnames adapted to Gaelic form*, female descendant of (*lit* grand-daughter of), **Mòrag Nic-Dhòmhnaill** Mòrag MacDonald, **Seònaid NicBhàtair** Janet Watson, *Cf* **mac 3**

nigh *vt*, *pres part* **a' nighe**, wash, *Cf* **failc, ionnlaid**

nighe *nm invar* (*the act of*) washing

nigheadair, nigheadair, nigheadairean *nm* a washer, a washing machine (*Cf* **inneal-nighe** – *see* **inneal** 1), **nigheadair-shoithichean** a dishwasher

nigheadaireachd *nf invar* washing (*ie a batch of washing*)

nighean, *gen* **nighinne** & **ìghne**, *pl* **nigheanan** & **ìghnean** *nf* 1 a (*young*) girl, **clann-nighean** *f* girls, girl children; 2 a young woman up to the late teens or early twenties; *Cf* **caileag** 2, **nìghneag**; 3 a daughter, **nighean bràthar/peathar** a niece

nìghneag & **nìonag**, *gen* **nìghneig**, *pl* **nìghneagan** *nf* (*affectionate dimin of* **nighean**) 1 a (*young*) girl; 2 (*freq in songs*) a young woman up to the late teens or early twenties, (*song*) **nìghneag a' chùil duinn, nach fhan thu?** brown haired girl/lass, won't you wait?; *Cf* **caileag** 2, **gruagach**, **nighean** 1 & 2, **maighdeann** 1, **rìbhinn**

nimh & **neimh**, *gen* **n(e)imhe** *nm* 1 poison, venom, *Cf* **puinnsean**; 2 (*abstr*) venom, bitterness, malice, *Cf* **mì-rùn** (*see* **mì-**)

nimheil *adj* 1 poisonous, (*phys*) venomous, *Cf* **puinnseanach**; 2 (*abstr*) venomous, malicious

nìonag *see* **nìghneag**

Nirribhidh *nf* Norway, *Cf* **Lochlann** 1

nis(e) *see* **a-nis(e)**

nitheil *adj* concrete, actual, real, *Cf* **fìor** 2, **rudail**, & *opposite* **beachdail** 2

niuclasach *adj* nuclear, **sgudal** *m* **niuclasach** nuclear waste

no (*older sp* **neo**) *conj* or, **cogadh no sìth** war or peace

nobhail, nobhaile, nobhailean *nf* a novel

nochd *vti, pres part* **a' nochdadh**, 1 (*vt*) show, reveal, **nochd dhomh e** show me it, *Cf* **seall** 2; 2 (*vi*) appear, come into view or sight, **an uair a nochd e a-staigh** when he turned up/rolled in, **cò às a nochd thusa?** where did you (*emph*) appear/spring from? (*song*) **a' nochdadh ri beanntan na Hearadh** coming in sight of the mountains of Harris, (*book &c*) **nochd an clò** appear in print, come out, be published

Nollaig, Nollaige, Nollaigean *nf* Christmas, **Nollaig Chridheil!** Merry Christmas! **Là/Oidhche Nollaig** Christmas Day/Eve, **aig àm na Nollaige** at Christmas time

norradaich, *gen* **norradaiche** *nf* a nap (*ie short sleep*)

norrag, norraig, norragan *nf* a doze, a nap, a snooze, **cha d'fhuair mi norrag chadail** I didn't get a wink of sleep, *Cf* **cadal** 2, **dùsal**, **suain** *n*

nòs, nòis, nòsan *nm* **1** a custom, a habit, a usage, *Cf more usu* **àbhaist 1**, **cleachdadh 2**; **2** a way *or* manner of doing something, *esp* (*under influence of Irish*) **an seann nòs** the traditional style/manner (*esp of singing*), *Cf more usu* **dòigh 1**, **modh 1**

nota, nota, notaichean *nf* **1** (*money*) *earlier* a bank-note, *now usu* a pound, **tha ceithir notaichean agam oirbh** you owe me four pounds, *Cf trad* **punnd 2**; **2** a (written) note, an aide-mémoire, **bha na h-oileanaich a' gabhail notaichean** the students were taking notes; **3** a short letter or written message, a note

nuadh *adj* new, novel (*can stress difference from what has gone before rather than a pristine state*), **an Tiomnadh Nuadh** the New Testament, **nuadh-fhacal** *m* a neologism, *Cf more usu* **ùr 1**, *& opposite* **sean**

nuadhachadh, *gen* **nuadhachaidh** *nm*, **1** (*the act of*) making new &c (*see senses of* **nuadhaich** *v*); **2** (*of house &c*) a renovation

nuadhaich *vt, pres part* **a' nuadhachadh**, make new, renovate, do up, *Cf* **ùraich 1** *& stronger* **ath-nuadhaich 2**

nuair a *see* **an uair a**

nuallaich *vi, pres part* **a' nuallaich**, (*usu of animals*) howl, roar, bellow, *Cf* **beuc** *v*, **geum** *v*, **langanaich**

nur *prep pron see* **an** *prep* **3**

nurs, nurs, nursaichean *nf* a nurse, *Cf more trad* **banaltram, bean-eiridinn**

O

o & **bho** *prep* from, *takes dat & aspirates/lenites following noun, Note: the pers prons* **mi**, **thu** &c *combine with* **o/bho** *to form the prep prons* **(bh)uam(sa)**, **(bh)uat(sa)**, **(bh)uaithe(san)**, **(bh)uaipe(se)**, **(bh)uainn(e)**, **(bh)uaibh(se)**, **(bh)uapa(san)** from me, you &c; **1** (*time*) **o mhoch gu dubh** from morn till night, **bhon àm sin air adhart** from that time forward/on, **bho Dhiluain gu Dihaoine** from Monday to Friday; **2** (*movement, direction*) **chaidh i suas bhon chladach** she went up from the beach, **litir o Mhurchadh** a letter from Murdo, (*story collection*) **Oiteagan on Iar** Breezes from the West, (*trad story collection*) **Ugam agus Bhuam** To Me and from Me, *also fig in exprs* **thig** *v* **bhuaithe** recover (*from illness*), get better, & **rach** *v* **bhuaithe** go off, get worse, deteriorate; **3** *as conj*, since (*esp of time, but see also* **on a**), (*song*) **'s cian nan cian bhon dh'fhàg mi Leòdhas** it's a very long time since I left Lewis, **bho dh'fhàg mi an sgoil** since I left school, **'s fhada o nach fhaca mi thu!** I haven't seen you for a long time!, long time no see!, *Cf* **on a**

òb, **òba** & **oìb**, **òban** *nm* a bay, *Cf* **bàgh**, **camas 1**

obair, *gen* **obrach** & **oibre**, *pl* **obraichean** *nf* **1** work, labour, **tha obair agam ri dhèanamh** I've (got) work to do, **obair chruaidh** hard work, **obair-taighe** housework, (*prov*) **'s e obair latha tòiseachadh** it's a day's work getting started, *Cf* **cosnadh 3**, **saothair 1**; **2** *freq as pres part* **ag obair** working, **ag obair gu trang** working busily, **bha sinn ag obair fad an latha an-dè** we were working all day yesterday; **3** work (*ie the product of labour*), **obair-ghrèis** needlework, **obair-làimhe** handiwork, (*poetry collection*) **Sàr-obair nam Bàrd Gàidhealach** The Masterwork of the Gaelic Poets; **4** a job, an occupation, employment, **a bheil obair agad?** have you got a job?, are you working? **gun obair** unemployed, (*calque*) **a-mach à obair** out of work, **luchd-obrach** *m* workers, employees, a workforce (*Cf* **obraiche**), *Cf* **cosnadh 2**, **dreuchd**

obann *adj* sudden, *Cf* **grad 1**

obh *excl*, *usu as* **obh! obh!** dear oh dear!, my goodness me!, good heavens! &c, *expressing sympathy, concern, surprise* &c

obraich *occas* **oibrich** *vti*, *pres part* **ag obrachadh**, **1** (*vi*) work, (*usu in sense of*) function properly, succeed, **chan eil an t-inneal-nighe ag obrachadh** the washer isn't working, **dh'fheuch sinn ri car a thoirt aiste ach cha do dh'obraich e** we tried to play a trick on her but it didn't work; **2** (*vt*) work, operate, work at *or* on, **obraich inneal** operate/work a machine, **obraich fearann/croit** work land/a croft (*Cf* **àitich 1**)

obraiche (*also* **oibriche**), **obraiche**, **obraichean** *nm* a worker, a workman, a labourer, *Cf* **neach-obrach** (*see* **neach 2**)

och *excl usu expr sadness, common in songs eg* **och nan och, tha mi fo mhulad** alas/woe is me, (for) sadness is upon me

ochd *num & adj* eight, **ochd-deug** eighteen, **ochdamh** eighth

ochdad *nm* eighty (*in alt numbering system*)

ochdnar *nmf* people numbering eight, an 'eightsome', **ruidhle-ochdnar** *m* an eightsome reel

o chionn *also* **bho chionn** *prep, with gen* **1** *corres to* ago, **bho chionn ghoirid** a short time ago, recently, **o chionn mìos(a)** a month ago; **2** since, for (*of time*), **tha mi ag obair aige bho chionn bliadhna** I've been working for him for a year/since a year ago

ocsaidean, *gen* **ocsaidein** *nm* oxygen

odhar *adj* **1** dun(-coloured), **bò odhar** a dun cow, *can occur in placenames as* our, **Beinn Odhar** Ben Our, dun mountain, *Cf* **ciar 3**, **lachdann 1**; **2** sallow, **Coinneach Odhar Fiosaiche** Sallow Kenneth the Seer (*the Brahan Seer*)

òg *adj* **1** young, **caileag òg** a young girl; **2** (*usu poet*) fresh, new, early, **san òg-mhadainn** in the early morning, **an t-Ogmhios** June, *Cf* **ùr 1**

ògan, ògain, òganan *nm* (*plants &c*) a shoot, a tendril, *Cf* **bachlag 2**, **gas**

òganach, *gen & pl* **òganaich** *nm* **1** a young man, (*folk group*) **Na h-Oganaich** The Young Ones; **2** a youth, a stripling, an adolescent (male), (*Sc*) a halflin, *Cf* **òigear**

ogha, *gen* **ogha**, *pl* **oghachan** & **oghaichean** *nm* a grandchild, a grandson, a grand-daughter, **iar-ogha** a great-grandchild

Ogmhios *see* **òg 2**

oibrich, oibriche *see* **obraich, obraiche**

oide, oide, oidean *nm* a step-father, *Cf* **muime**

oideachas, *gen* **oideachais** *nm* **1** learning, education, instruction, *Cf more usu* **foghlam 2**, **ionnsachadh 2**; **2** *esp in expr* **beul-oideachas** traditional learning, knowledge and lore orally transmitted, *Cf* **beul-aithris**

oidhche, oidhche, oidhcheannan *nf* **1** night, a night, **air feadh na h-oidhche** during/all through the night, **Oidhche Mhàirt** Tuesday night, **oidhche mhath (leat/leibh)!** goodnight!; **2** the eve (*of specific days*), **Oidhche Challainn** New Year's Eve, Hogmanay, **Oidhche Shamhna** Halloween

oidhirp, oidhirpe, oidhirpean *nf* **1** an attempt, a try, (*Sc*) a shot, **dèan/ thoir** *v* **oidhirp** make an attempt, try (**air** at/to), **thug e oidhirp eile air** he had another try/shot at it, *Cf* **ionnsaigh 2**; **2** an effort (*ie* *the concrete result of an attempt at something*), **cha bu toigh leis an fhear-deasachaidh na h-oidhirpean agam** the editor didn't like my efforts

oifigeach, *gen & pl* **oifigich** *nm, also* **oifigear, oifigeir, oifigearan** *nm* **1** (*forces &c*) an officer; **2** an official, **tha e na oifigeach aig a' chomhairle** he's a council official/an official with the council

oifigeil *adj* official, **cuir fios thuca gu h-oifigeil** let them know officially

oifig, oifige, oifigean *nf, also* **oifis, oifise, oifisean** *nf*, **1** an office (*ie the phys place*) **tha an oifis na bùrach** the office is untidy/in a mess, **cheannaich mi stampaichean an oifis a' phuist** I bought some stamps at the post office; **2** (*abstr*) an office, a position, a function, *Cf* **dreuchd, obair 4**; **3** an office (*ie the institution*) **Oifis na h-Alba** the Scottish Office

òige *nf invar* youth, **làithean m' òige** the days of my youth, my young days, **gaol** *m* **na h-òige** young love

òigeachd *nf invar* adolescence

òigear, òigeir, òigearan *nm* a youngster, an adolescent, a teenager (*of either sex*), a youth, *Cf* **deugaire, òganach 2**

òigh, òighe, òighean *nf* **1** a virgin, *Cf* **ainnir**; **2** a maiden, a young (*single*) woman, *Cf* **caileag 2, gruagach, maighdeann 1, nighean 2, nìghneag 2, rìbhinn**

òigheil *adj* virginal

oighre, oighre, oighreachan *nm* an heir, an inheritor

oighreachd, oighreachd, oighreachdan *nf* **1** an inheritance, an estate (*ie property left as an inheritance*), **cìs** *f* **oighreachd** inheritance tax, *Cf* **dìleab**; **2** an estate (*ie large land unit*), **tha e na gheamair air an oighreachd** he's a gamekeeper on the estate

òigridh *nf coll invar*, young people, youngsters, young folk, (*song*) **le òigridh ghuanach tha nis air fuadach** (Màiri Mhòr) with carefree young folk who are now in exile, **buidheann** *mf* **òigridh** a youth club/group

oilbheum, oilbheim, oilbheuman *nm* offence, **dèan** *v* **oilbheum do chuideigin** offend/give offence to someone, *Cf stronger* **tàmailt 2**

oilbheumach *adj* offensive, *Cf stronger* **tàmailteach 2**

oileanach, *gen & pl* **oileanaich** *nm* (*university, college &c*) a student

oileanachadh, *gen* **oileanachaidh** *nm* **1** (*the act of*) training, instructing, teaching; **2** instruction, training; *Cf* **teagasg**

oileanaich *vt, pres part* **ag oileanachadh**, train, instruct, teach, *Cf* **teagaisg 2**

oillt, oillte, oilltean *nf* terror, horror, dread, **cuir** *v* **oillt air** terrify, horrify, **thàinig oillt orm** dread/horror came over me, *Cf* **eagal 1, uabhas 1, uamhann**

oillteil *adj* horrible, dreadful, frightful, *Cf* **uabhasach 1**

oilltich *vt, pres part* **ag oillteachadh**, terrify, *Cf* **cuir oillt air** (*see* **oillt**)

oilthigh, oilthigh, oilthighean *nm* a university, **Oilthigh Ghlaschu** Glasgow University, *with art*, **tha i aig an oilthigh/a' dol don oilthigh** she's at university/going to university, **an t-Oilthigh Fosgailte** the Open University

òinseach, òinsiche, òinsichean *nf* an idiot, a fool, *trad a female but also used of males*, *Cf* **amadan**

oir, oire, oirean *nf* **1** an edge, a margin, a fringe, (*of road*) a verge, **oir na coille** the edge/margin/fringe of the wood, **oir a' chabhsair** the kerb, **air oir na creige** on the cliff-edge; **2** (*of jug &c*) a rim, a lip; *Cf* **bile** *nf* **2, iomall 2**

oir *conj* (*rather formal*) for, **dh'fhalbh e, oir bha an oidhche a' fàs dorcha** he left, for the night was growing dark

oirbh(se) *prep pron see* **air**

òirdheirc *adj* **1** glorious, magnificent, *Cf more usu* **glòrmhor**; **2** distinguished, illustrious, *Cf more usu* **ainmeil, cliùiteach, iomraiteach**

òirleach, *gen & pl* **òirlich** *nmf* an inch (*ie measurement*), (*prov*) **is duine gach òirleach dheth** he's every inch a man

oirnn(e), oirre(se) *prep prons see* **air**

oirthir, oirthire, oirthirean *nf* a coast, a littoral, a seaboard, *Cf* **costa**

oisean, oisein, oiseanan *nm, also* **oisinn, oisne, oisnean** *nf*, a corner, (*external*) **aig oisean an taighe** at the corner of the house, (*internal*) **anns an oisean** in the corner (*Cf* **cùil 1** & *less trad* **còrnair**)

oiteag, oiteig, oiteagan *nf* a breeze, (*story collection*) **Oiteagan on Iar** Breezes from the West, *Cf* **gaoth 1, osnadh 2**

òl *vti, pres part* **ag òl, 1** (*vt*) drink, **òl cupan teatha** drink a cup of tea, *Cf* **gabh 1; 2** (*vi*) drink (*alcoholic drinks*), **cha bhi mi ag òl idir** I don't drink at all

ola, ola, olaichean *nf* oil, **ola-luis** vegetable oil, **ola-thalmhainn** mineral oil

olann, *gen* **olainn** *nf* wool, *Cf* **clòimh**

olc, *gen* **uilc** *nm* evil, badness, wickedness, *Cf less strong* **donas 1**

olc, *comp* **(n)as (&c) miosa,** *adj* evil, wicked, bad, **tha an t-athair olc ach tha am mac nas miosa** the father is wicked but the son is more wicked/worse, *Cf less strong* **dona 1**

ollamh, ollaimh, ollamhan *nm* **1** (*trad*) a learned man; **2** (*now*) a (*non-medical*) doctor, someone holding a doctorate, **An t-Ollamh Caimbeul** Doctor Campbell

òmar, *gen* **òmair** *nm* amber

on a & **bhon a** *conj* since, as (*often causal, though Cf eg* **'s fhada on a bha mi san sgoil** it's a long time since I was at school; *see also* **o 3**), **chuir iad an sprèidh dhan mhonadh on a bha an t-ionaltradh math shuas an sin** they put the stock on the hill as/since the grazing was good up there, *Cf* **a chionn 2, oir** *conj*

onair, onaire, onairean *nf* **1** (personal) honour, (*trad*) **air m' onair!** (up)on my honour!; **2** honour, esteem, respect, *Cf* **urram 1** & **2**; **3** honesty, *Cf* **ionracas 1**

onarach *adj* **1** honourable; **2** honorary, **ball onarach den chomann** an honorary member of the society; **3** honest, *Cf* **ionraic 1**

onarachadh, *gen* **onarachaidh** *nm* (*the act of*) honouring

onaraich *vt, pres part* **ag onarachadh, 1** honour (*ie bestow an honour on*), *Cf* **urram 2; 2** honour (*ie respect, revere*)

opairèisean, opairèisein, opairèiseanan *nmf* an operation (*ie medical*), **tha i a' faighinn seachad air opairèisean** she's recovering from an operation

òr, *gen* **òir** *nm* **1** gold, (*song*) **bidh airgead nad phòcaidean is òr nach cuir thu feum air** you'll have silver in your pockets and more gold than you'll be able to use; **2** *gen used adjectivally*, gold, golden, of gold, **bonn** *m* **òir** a gold coin/medal

òraid, òraide, òraidean *nf* a speech, a talk, a lecture, an address, **thoir seachad/dèan** *v* **òraid** give a talk, **thug i seachad òraid don chomann eachdraidh ionadail** she gave a talk to/addressed the local history society

òraidiche, òraidiche, òraidichean *nm* a speaker, someone who gives talks or lectures, a lecturer

orain(d)s *adj* orange, **dè an dath a th' air? (tha) orains** what colour is it? orange

orain(d)sear, orain(d)seir, orain(d)searan *nm* an orange

òran (*in some areas* **amhran**), *gen* & *pl* **òrain** *nm* a song, (*19th century poetess*) **Màiri Mhòr nan Oran** Big Mary of the Songs, **òrain luadhaidh** waulking songs (*see* **luadhadh**), **na h-òrain mhòra** the big songs (*the classic songs of Gaelic tradition*), (*at ceilidh &c*) **gabh òran!** give us/sing a song!, *Cf* **duan 2, luinneag**

orc, *gen* **oirc** *nm*, *with art*, **an t-orc** (*muscular*) cramp

òrd, *gen* **ùird,** *pl* **ùird** & **òrdan** *nm* a hammer

òrdachadh, *gen* **òrdachaidh** *nm* (*the act of*) ordering, organising &c (*see senses of* **òrdaich** *v*)

òrdag, òrdaig, òrdagan *nf* **1** a thumb; **2** (*also* **òrdag-coise**) a toe, **an òrdag mhòr** the big toe

òrdaich *vti, pres part* **ag òrdachadh**, **1** (*vi*) order, command, tell, **dh'òrdaich iad dhomh na geataichean a dhùnadh** they ordered me to shut the gates; **2** (*vti*) (*in café &c*) order, *Cf* **iarr 3**; **3** put in order, organise, tidy, *Cf* **òrdugh 3**; **4** (*med &c*) prescribe

òrdaighean *see* **òrdugh 4**

òrdail *adj* **1** ordered, orderly, regular, methodical, *Cf* **riaghailteach, rianail**; **2** (*arith*) ordinal, **cunntair òrdail** an ordinal number

òrdugh, òrduigh, òrduighean *nm* **1** an order, a command; **2** (*café &c*) an order, (*med*) **òrdugh cungaidh** a prescription; **3** orderliness, a proper order, state or sequence, **cuir** *v* **an òrdugh** put in order, organise, tidy up, *Cf* **òrdaich 3**; **4** (*Presbyterianism*) *in pl, usu as* **na h-òrdaighean**, Communion (*also the sequence of services leading up to the sacrament of Communion*), *Cf* **comanachadh**

òrgan, òrgain, òrganan *nm* (*mus*) an organ

orm(sa), orra(san), ort(sa) *prep prons see* **air**

òrraiseach *adj* **1** squeamish; **2** fastidious

ortha, ortha, orthannan *nf* a spell, a charm, an incantation, *Cf* **geas 1, seun 1**

os (*trad*) *prep* **1** above, *now usu in compound prep* **os cionn** above, over, *with gen*, **neòil os cionn a' chuain** clouds over the ocean, (*song*) **os mo chionn sheinn an uiseag ghreannmhor** (Màiri Mhòr) above me/overhead sang the joyful skylark; **2** *occas as prefix corres to Eng* super- &c, *eg* **os-nàdarrach** *adj* supernatural, **os-rathad** *m* a fly-over

osan, *gen* **osain**, *pl* **osain** & **osanan** *nm* a stocking, hose, *Cf* **stocainn**

osann *see* **osna**

os cionn *see* **os 1**

os ìosal *see* **ìosal 3**

os làimh *see* **làmh 1**

osna (*nf*) & **osnadh** (*nm*), *gen* **osnaidh**, *pl* **osnaidhean** *nm, also* **osann**, *gen* & *pl* **osainn** *nm*, **1** a sigh, **leig/dèan** *v* **osna** sigh, heave a sigh (*Cf* **osnaich**), *Cf less usu* **ospag 1**; **2** (*occas*) a breeze, a breath of wind, *Cf more usu* **oiteag, ospag 2**

osnachadh *see* **osnaich** *n*

osnaich *vi, pres part* **ag osnaich** & **ag osnachadh**, sigh, *Cf* **osna 1**

osnaich, *gen* **osnaiche** *nf, also* **osnachadh**, *gen* **osnachaidh** *nm*, (*the act of*) sighing

ospadal, ospadail, ospadalan *nm* a hospital, *usu with art*, **anns an ospadal** in hospital, *Cf more trad* **taigh-eiridinn** (*see* **eiridinn**)

ospag, ospaig, ospagan *nf* 1 a sigh, *Cf more usu* **osna 1**; **2** a breath or gentle gust of wind, *Cf* **oiteag**, *&* (*occas*) **osna 2**

òstair *&* **òsdair**, *gen* **òstair**, *pl* **òstairean** *nm* a hotelier, an innkeeper, (*pub &c*) a landlord, a licensee, *Cf* **fear-taighe** (*see* **fear 2**)

Ostair, *gen* **Ostaire** *nf, with art* **an Ostair** Austria

Ostaireach, *gen & pl* **Ostairich** *nm* an Austrian, *also as adj* **Ostaireach** Austrian, of, from or pertaining to Austria

othail, othaile, othailean *nf* a hubbub, an uproar, a tumult, a din, *Cf* **gleadhar, iorghail, ùpraid 1**

othaisg, *gen* **othaisge**, *pl* **othaisgean** *occas* **òisgean** *nf* a hog(g) (*ie a ewe lamb between 1 & 2 years old*)

òtrach, òtraich, òtraichean *nm* a dunghill, a midden, a manure heap, *Cf* **dùnan 2, siteag**

P

paca, paca, pacannan *nm* **1** a pack (*ie as carried on back*); **2** a pack (*ie a bundle or collection of something*), **paca clòimhe** a pack of wool, **paca chairtean** a pack of cards

pacaid, pacaide, pacaidean *nf* a packet

pàganach, *gen & pl* **pàganaich** *nm* a pagan, *also as adj* **pàganach** pagan

paidhir, *gen* **paidhir** (*m*) *&* **paidhreach** (*f*), *pl* **paidhirichean** *nmf* a pair, **paidhir thrìlleachan/mhiotagan** a pair of oystercatchers/gloves

paidir, paidire, paidrichean *nf, with art,* **a' phaidir** the Lord's Prayer, the Paternoster, *Cf* **Urnaigh an Tighearna** (*see* **ùrnaigh**)

paidirean, paidirin, paidirinean *nm* (*relig*) **1** a rosary (*ie the beads*); **2** a rosary (*ie the prayers*); *Cf* **conaire**

pàigh *vt, pres part* **a' pàigheadh, 1** pay, pay for, **pàigh bileag** pay a bill, **pàigh fear-obrach** pay a worker, **cha do phàigh e am pinnt/airson a' phinnt a ghabh e** he didn't pay for the pint he had, **dh'fhalbh e gun phàigheadh** he left without paying, *Cf less usu* **ìoc** *v*; **2** pay, make amends, suffer or atone for, **pàighidh tu (airson) do pheacaidhean** you'll pay (*&c*) for your sins

pàigh *nm invar,* pay, remuneration, **àrdachadh** *m* **pàigh/pàighidh** a pay rise, *Cf* **cosnadh 4, pàigheadh 2, tuarasdal**

pàigheadh, *gen* **pàighidh** *nm* **1** (*the act of*) paying &c (*see senses of* **pàigh** *v*), payment; **2** *as* **pàigh** *n*

pàileis, pàileis, pàileiscan *nf* a palace, *Cf more trad* **lùchairt**

pàillean, pàillein, pàilleanan *nm* **1** a pavilion; **2** a (*sizeable*) tent, *Cf* **puball, teanta**

pailt *adj* **1** plentiful, ample, abundant, copious, **biadh pailt** copious food, **sitheann phailt** abundant game, *Cf* **lìonmhor**; **2** *expr good measure,* **trì troighean pailt de dh'fhad** a good/full three feet in length, **punnd pailt de fhlùr** a good/generous pound of flour

pailteas, *gen* **pailteis** *nm* plenty, abundance, an abundance, an ample sufficiency, *Cf* **leòr 2**

pàipear, pàipeir, pàipearan *nm* **1** paper, **pàipear-balla** wallpaper; **2** (*for* **pàipear-naidheachd**), a newspaper, (*fam*) **Am Pàipear Beag** (*lit* the wee paper) The West Highland Free Press

pàirc(e), pàirce, pàircean *nf* **1** a field, (*Sc*) a park, *Cf* **achadh**; **2** a (public) park

paireafain *nm invar* paraffin

pàirt, **pàirt**, **pàirtean** *nmf* 1 a part, **bha an t-ugh math, pàirt dheth co-dhiù** the egg was good, part of it at any rate, **ghabh iad pàirt san ar-a-mach** they took part/participated in the rising (*Cf* **com-pàirtich** 2), *Cf* **cuid** 1, **earrann**, **roinn** *n* 2; 2 (*cars &c*) a part, **pàirtean-càraidh** spare parts, spares

pàirteacheadh, *gen* **pàirteachaidh** *nm* (*the act of*) sharing, dividing &c (*see senses of* **pàirtich** *v*); division, partition

pàirtich *vt, pres part* **a' pàirteachadh**, share, divide into shares or parts, *Cf* **roinn** *v* 2

pàirtiche, **pàirtiche**, **pàirtichean** *nm* 1 an associate, a partner, *Cf* **companach** 2, **co-obraiche** 2; 2 an accomplice, an abettor

pàisde *see* **pàiste**

paisg *vt, pres part* **a' pasgadh**, wrap (up), roll (up), fold (up), pack (up) (*objects, material, parcels &c*), *Cf* **fill** 1 & 2

pàiste (*also* **pàisde**), *gen* **pàiste**, *pl* **pàistean** *nm* an infant, a baby, a small child, **bha pàiste aice** she had a baby/child, *Cf* **leanaban**, **leanabh**, **naoidhean**

pàiteach *adj* thirsty, *Cf* **ìotmhor**, **tartmhor**

pana, **pana**, **panaichean** *nm* (*kitchen &c*) a pan, *Cf more trad* **aghann**

pannal, **pannail**, **pannalan** *nm* 1 (*building &c*) a panel, **pannal fiodha** a wooden panel; 2 (*official body*) a panel, **Pannal na Cloinne** the Children's Panel, *Cf* **bòrd** 1, **comataidh**

Pàp(a), *gen* **Pàpa**, *pl* **Pàpan** & **Pàpachan** *nm, with art*, **am Pàp(a)** the Pope

pàpanach, *gen* & *pl* **pàpanaich** *nm* (*derog*) a papist, a Roman Catholic, *also as adj* **pàpanach** (*derog*) papist, popish, Catholic

pàrant, **pàrant**, **pàrantan** *nm* a parent

pàrlamaid, **pàrlamaide**, **pàrlamaidean** *nf* a parliament

pàrlamaideach *adj* parliamentary

pàrras, *gen* **pàrrais** *nm* paradise, a paradise, heaven, a heavenly or idyllic place, *Cf* **flaitheas**, **nèamh** 1

parsail, **parsail**, **parsailean** *nm* a parcel, a package, *Cf* **pasgan** 2

pàrtaidh, **pàrtaidh**, **pàrtaidhean** *nm* 1 (*body, group &c*) a party, **pàrtaidh poileataigeach** a political party, **Am Pàrtaidh Làborach/Liberalach Democratach/Tòraidheach** the Labour/Liberal Democrat/Tory Party, **Pàrtaidh Nàiseanta na h-Alba** the Scottish National Party; 2 (*social gathering*) a party, *Cf* **hò-ro-gheallaidh** 1

partan, **partain**, **partanan** *nm* a crab (*usu edible*), (*Sc*) a partan, *Cf larger* **crùbag**

pasgadh, *gen* **pasgaidh** *nm* packing, a package, *Cf* **parsail**, **pasgan** 1 & 2

pasgan, *gen & pl* **pasgain** *nm* **1** a bundle, a package, *Cf* **pasgadh**; **2** a parcel, *Cf more usu* **parsail**; **3** (*stationery &c*) a folder

pastra *nf invar* pastry

pathadh, *gen* **pathaidh** *nm* thirst, **bha/thàinig am pathadh oirre** she was/she grew thirsty, *Cf stronger* **tart**

pàtran, **pàtrain**, **pàtranan** *nm* **1** a pattern (*ie a design, arrangement &c*) **pàtran brèagha air a' phàipear-balla** an attractive pattern on the wallpaper; **2** (*as model to be copied*) a pattern, **tha am pàtran seo ro dhoirbh, chan urrainn dhomh a leantainn** this pattern's too difficult, I can't follow it

peacach, *gen & pl* **peacaich** *nm* a sinner

peacach *adj* sinful

peacadh, **peacaidh**, **peacaidhean** *nm* sin, a sin, **peacadh-bàis** a mortal sin, **peacadh-gin(e)** original sin, *Cf* **ciont(a) 2**

peacaich *vi, pres part* **a' peacachadh**, (*usu in relig sense*) sin, transgress, *Cf* **ciontaich**

peanas, **peanais**, **peanasan** *nm*, punishment, a punishment, a penalty, **peanas corporra** corporal punishment

peanasachadh, *gen* **peanasachaidh** *nm*, (*the act of*) punishing, chastising; punishment

peanasaich *vt, pres part* **a' peanasachadh**, punish, chastise

peann, *gen & pl* **pinn** *nm* a pen

peansail, **peansail**, **peansailean** *nm* a pencil

peant *vti, pres part* **a' peantadh**, paint

peanta, *gen* **peanta**, *pl* **peantan** & **peantaichean** *nm* paint

peantadh, *gen* **peantaidh** *nm* (*the act of*) painting

peantair, **peantair**, **peantairean** *nm* a painter (*artist or tradesman*)

pearraid, **pearraide**, **pearraidean** *nf* a parrot

pearsa, **pearsa**, **pearsachan** *nm* **1** a person, *Cf* **duine 2**, **neach 1**; **2** (*in novel &c*) a character, *Cf more usu* **caractar**

pearsanta *adj* personal, **beachd pearsanta** a personal opinion, **coimpiutair pearsanta** a personal computer

pearsantachd *nf invar* personality

pears-eaglais, *gen* **pears-eaglais**, *pl* **pearsan-eaglais** & **pearsachan-eaglais** *nm* a clergyman, *Cf* **clèireach** *n* **1**, **ministear 1**, **sagart**

peasair, **peasrach**, **peasraichean** *nf* a pea (*ie the vegetable*)

peata, *gen* **peata**, *pl* **peatan** & **peatachan** *nm* a pet

peathrachas, **peathrachais**, **peathrachasan** *nm* sisterhood, a sisterhood, sisterliness

peatra(i)l, *gen* **peatrail** *nm, also* **peatro(i)l**, *gen* **peatroil** *nm* petrol

peighinn, peighinne, peighinnean *nf* 1 (*trad*) a penny, *orig* a penny Scots, (*prov*) **cha dlighe do pheighinn fois** a penny has no right to be idle, *Cf usu* **sgillinn 1**; 2 (*hist & in placenames*) a pennyland, **Peighinn a' Chaisteil** Pennycastle, the pennyland of the castle

peile, peile, peilichean *nm* a pail, **peile-frasaidh** a watering can, *Cf* **bucaid 1**, *& more trad* **cuinneag, cuman**

pèileag, pèileig, pèileagan *nf* a porpoise

peilear *&* **peileir**, *gen* **peileir**, *pl* **peilearan** *&* **peileirean** *nm sing coll* a bullet, a pellet (*ie as projectile*)

pein(n)sean, peinnsein, peinnseanan *nm* a pension, **luchd** *m* **peinnsein** pensioners

peirceall, *gen* **peircle** *&* **peircill**, *pl* **peirclean** *&* **peirceallan** *nm* 1 a jaw, *Cf* **giall**; 2 a jawbone

pèist, pèiste, pèistean *nf* a reptile

peitean, peitein, peiteanan *nm* 1 a vest; 2 a waistcoat

peitseag, peitseig, peitseagan *nf* a peach

peur, peura, peuran *nf* a pear

pian *vt, pres part*, **a' pianadh**, 1 pain, distress, **tha an dol-a-mach (a th')
aice gam phianadh** her behaviour pains/distresses me; 2 (*stronger*) torment, torture, *Cf* **cràidh**

pian, pèin, piantan *nf* pain, a pain

piàna *also* **piàno**, *gen* **piàna**, *pl* **piànathan** *nm* a piano

pianadh, *gen* **pianaidh** *nm* 1 (*the act of*) paining, tormenting &c (*see senses of* **pian** *v*); 2 torture

pianail *adj* painful (*phys or mentally*), *Cf* **crài(dh)teach, goirt 1**

pic, pice, picean *nm* (*tool*) a pick, a pickaxe

picil, *gen* **picile** *nf* pickle, a pickle

pile, *gen* **pile**, *pl* **pilichean** *&* **pileachan** *nf* (*med*) a pill

pìleat, pìleat, pìleatan *nm, also* **poidhleat, poidhleit, poidhleatan** *nm*,
1 (*seafaring*) a pilot, **thàinig pìleat air bòrd a nuair a ràinig sinn
beul na h-aibhne** a pilot came on board when we reached the river mouth; 2 (*aviation &c*) a pilot

pill, pilleadh *see* **till, tilleadh**

pillean, pillein, pilleanan *nm* 1 a cushion; 2 a pillion seat or saddle

pinc *adj* pink

pinnt, pinnt, pinntean *nm* 1 (*measure*) an imperial pint; 2 a pint, *esp of
beer*, **tha mi airson pinnt** I fancy a pint

pìob, pìoba, pìoban *nf* **1** a pipe, a tube, **pìoban-uisge** water pipes, *Cf* **feadan 2**; **2** (*also* **pìob-thombaca**) a pipe (*for smoking*); **3** (*music*) a pipe, (*esp*) the great Highland bagpipe, a set *or* stand of pipes (*also* **pìob mhòr**), **gabh** *v* **port air a' phìob** play a tune on the pipes, **ceòl na pìoba** pipe music, **pìob-uilne** uileann pipes

pìobaire, pìobaire, pìobairean *nm* a piper, **pìobair an aona phuirt** the piper with only one tune

pìobaireachd *nf invar* **1** piping, the act and art of playing on the great Highland bagpipe; **2** *used at competitions &c, & often Anglicised as* pibroch, *a* pibroch, *to refer to the classical music of the pipes, which is strictly speaking* **ceòl mòr**

piobar, *gen* **piobair** *nm* pepper

piobraich *vt, pres part* **a' piobrachadh, 1** add pepper to; **2** (*lit & fig*) pep up, spice up

pioc *vti, pres part* **a' piocadh, 1** (*birds feeding*) peck; **2** (*persons &c*) pick (*at food*), nibble, *Cf* **creim 1**

pìos, pìos, pìosan *nm* **1** a bit or a piece of something, **pìos arain** a piece/bit of bread, **pìos math coiseachd** a fair bit of walking, **pìos air falbh** a bit away, some distance away; **2** a snack, a sandwich &c (*esp eaten away from one's house*), a (*worker's, pupil's &c*) packed lunch, (*Sc*) a piece

piseach, *gen* **pisich** *nm* **1** progress, improvement (*in skill, activity &c*), **tha (am) piseach a' tighinn oirnn** we're improving/making progress/getting better, *Cf* **adhartas, leasachadh 2**; **2** *occas* (*trad*) luck, good fortune

piseag, piseig, piseagan *nf* a kitten

pit, pite, pitean *nf* **1** female genitals, a vulva, *Cf* **faighean, ròmag; 2** (*vulg*) *us* **a phit!** *occas used as an oath or swear*

piuthar, peathar, peathraichean *nf* a sister, **piuthar-chèile** a sister-in-law, **piuthar mo mhàthar** my aunt (*on mother's side*)

plaide, plaide, plaidean *nf* a blanket, *Cf* **plangaid**

plàigh, plàighe, plàighean *nf* **1** a plague, a pestilence, **plàigh de luch-ainn** a plague/an infestation of mice; **2** a pest, a nuisance

plàigheil *adj* pestiferous, pestilential

plana, plana, planaichean *nm* **1** a plan (*ie intention*), **planaichean na comhairle airson a' bhaile** the council's plans for the village/town, *Cf* **moladh 3; 2** a plan (*ie map, diagram &c*)

planaid, planaide, planaidean *nf* a planet

planaig *vti, pres part* **a' planaigeadh,** plan, make a plan or plans, *Cf* **dealbh** *v* **3**

planaigeadh, *gen* **planaigidh** *nm* (*the act of*) planning, *Cf* **dealbhadh**

plangaid, **plangaide**, **plangaidean** *nf* a blanket, *Cf* **plaide**

plaoisg *vt*, *pres part* **a' plaosgadh**, (*fruit, vegetables, nuts &c*) shell, pod, peel, skin, husk, *Cf* **rùisg 3**

plaosg, **plaoisg**, **plaosgan** *nm* (*nuts, eggs, peas & beans*) shell, a shell, a pod (*Cf* **cochall 1**), (*fruit, vegetables*) skin, peel, husk, *Cf* **rùsg 1**

plap *vi*, *pres part* **a' plapail**, (*esp wings, heart*) flutter, *Cf more severe* **plosg** *v* **2**

plap *nm invar* fluttering (*esp of heart, wings*), *Cf more severe* **plosg** *n* **2**

plàsd & **plàst**, *gen* **plàsda**, *pl* **plàsd(aidhe)an** *nm* a (sticking) plaster

plastaig, **plastaige**, **plastaigean** *nf* plastic, a plastic, *also as adj* **plastaig** plastic

plathadh, **plathaidh**, **plathaidhean** *nm* **1** a glance, a glimpse, *Cf* **aiteal**; **2** an instant, a flash, **chaidh e seachad orra ann am plathadh** he went past them in a flash, *Cf* **priobadh 2**

pleadhag, **pleadhaig**, **pleadhagan** *nf* a paddle (*of canoe &c*)

pleadhagaich *vti*, *pres part* **a' pleadhagaich**, **1** paddle (*canoe &c*); **2** paddle (*one's feet*)

plèana, **plèana**, **plèanaichean** *nmf* a plane, an aeroplane, an aircraft, *Cf more trad* **itealan**

ploc, **pluic**, **plocan** *nm* **1** (*earth*) a clod, a turf, a divot, *Cf* **fòid 1**; **2** a block of wood, (*song*) **chuir iad a cheann air ploc daraich** they placed his head on a block/stump of oak, *Cf* **sgonn**; **3** a rounded piece or lump of something, **ploc-prìne** a pinhead, *Cf* **ceap 1**, **cnap 1**

plosg *vi*, *pres part* **a' plosgadh** *also* **a' plosgail** & **a' plosgartaich**, **1** gasp (*for breath*), pant, (*Sc*) pech; **2** (*esp heart*) palpitate, throb, **tha mo chridhe a' plosgadh** my heart is palpitating/beating very fast, *Cf less severe* **plap** *v*

plosg, **ploisg**, **plosgan** *nm* **1** gasping (*for breath*), a gasp, panting, a pant; **2** (*esp of heart*) palpitation, a palpitation, throbbing, a throb, *Cf less severe* **plap** *n*

plosgadh, *gen* **plosgaidh** *nm*, *also* **plosgail** *nf invar* & **plosgartaich** *nf invar*, (*the act of*) gasping, palpitating &c (*see senses of* **plosg** *v*); palpitation

plub *vi see* **plubraich**

plub, **pluba**, **pluban** *nm* **1** (*sound*) a splash, a plop; **2** a sloshing or sploshing or glugging sound

plubraich *vi*, *pres part* **a' plubraich**, *also* **plub** *vi*, *pres part* **a' plubadaich** & **a' plubarsaich**, **1** (*sound of impact on water*) splash, plop; **2** (*sound of motion of liquids*) slosh, splosh, glug, splash

plubraich, *gen* plubraiche *nf (the act & sound of)* splashing, sloshing &c (*see senses of* plubraich *v*)

plucan, plucain, plucanan *nm* 1 a pimple, *(Sc)* a plouk; 2 a plug *(for sink, container, powerpoint &c)*, *Cf* cnag *n* 4

pluic, pluice, pluicean *nf* a cheek *(esp plump, rosy)*, *(prov)* cha dèan a' phluic a' phìobaireachd there's more to piping than distended cheeks, *Cf* lethcheann 1 *& more usu* gruaidh

plumair, plumair, plumairean *nm* a plumber

Pluta *nm invar* the planet Pluto

poball, pobaill, poballan *nm* a people, poball na h-Eireann the Irish people, the people of Ireland, *Cf more usu* muinntir 2, sluagh 2

poblach *&* poballach *adj* public, companaidh phoballach a public company, leabharlann poblach a public library, an roinn phoballach the public sector, *Cf* coitcheann 1, *& opposite* prìobhaideach

poblachd, poblachd, poblachdan *nf* a republic

poca, poca, pocannan *nm* 1 a bag *(usu for small purchases &c – Cf Sc* poke)*; 2 a larger bag, a sack, poca-cadail a sleeping-bag, *Cf* sac

pòcaid, pòcaide, pòcaidean *nf, also more trad* pòca, pòca, pòcan(nan) *nm* a pocket, airgead pòca(id) pocket money

pòg *vti, pres part* a' pògadh, kiss, *(humorous car sticker)* na pòg mo thòn don't kiss my arse (keep your distance)

pòg, pòige, pògan *nf* a kiss, *(trad dance)* ruidhle nam pòg the kissing reel, *(pibroch)* thug mi pòg do làimh an Rìgh I got a kiss of the King's hand

poidhleat *see* pìleat

poidsear, poidseir, poidsearan *nm* a poacher

puileas, *gen* poilis *nm*, 1 police, càr-poilis a police car; 2 a policeman, *Cf* poileasman

poileasaidh, poileasaidh, poileasaidhean *nm (government &c)* a policy, poileasaidh-urrais an insurance policy

poileasman, *gen & pl* poileasmain *nm* a policeman, chaidh e na phoileasman ann an Glaschu he became a policeman/joined the police in Glasgow, *Cf* poileas 2

poileataiceach *&* poileataigeach *adj* political, pàrtaidhean poileataigeach political parties

poileataics *nf invar* politics, ann an saoghal na poileataics in the world of politics, luchd-poileataics *m* politicians

poit, poite, poitean *nf* a pot *(as container, cooking utensil &c)*, poit-fhlùran a flowerpot, poit na lite the porridge pot, poit teatha a teapot, *also* a pot of tea, poit-dhubh a *(whisky)* still, *Cf* prais

poitean, *gen* **poitein** *nm* poteen, illicitly distilled whisky

pòitear, pòiteir, pòitearan *nm* a drinker, a tippler, a boozer, a drunkard, **co-phòitear** a drinking companion, a fellow boozer, *Cf* **misgear**

pòitearachd *nf invar* drinking, tippling, boozing, (*Sc*) bevvying, *Cf* **daorach 1, misg**

pòla, pòla, pòlaichean *nm* **1** a (magnetic) pole, **am Pòla a Deas** the South Pole; **2** a (*wooden &c*) pole, *Cf* **cabar 2**

Pòlach, *gen & pl* **Pòlaich** *nm* a Pole, *also as adj* **Pòlach** Polish

Pòlainn *nf invar, with art*, **a' Phòlainn** Poland, (*POW poem*) **Deargadan na Pòlainn** The Fleas of Poland

polas, polasman, *same as* **poileas, poileasman**

poll, *gen & pl* **puill** *nm* **1** mud, mire, silt, *Cf* **eabar**; **2** a bog, a mire, *Cf* **boglach, fèith(e), sùil-chritheach**; **3** *esp* **poll-mòna(ch)** a peat(y) bog, a peat hag, a peat bank

pònaidh, pònaidh, pònaidhean *nm* a pony

pònair, *gen* **pònarach** *nf* a bean, (*more often as coll*) beans, **pònair leathann/Fhrangach** broad/French beans

pong, puing, pongan *nm* (*music*) a note

pongail *adj* **1** (*person, work &c*) punctilious, meticulous, exact, painstaking, thorough, *Cf* **mion 2, mionaideach**; **2** (*speech &c*) concise, pointed, to the point; **3** punctual

pòr, pòir, pòran *nm* **1** (*trad*) seed, *Cf* **fras** *n* **2**, *& more usu* **sìol 1**; **2** crops, *Cf* **bàrr 2**; **3** growth (*of plants*), *Cf* **fàs** *n*

port[1], *gen & pl* **puirt** *nm* a tune, **gabh** *v* **port air an fhidhill** play a tune on the fiddle, **port-à-beul** mouth music (*lit* a tune from a mouth) *singing to dance tunes, using vocables, or nonsensical or humorous words*, *Cf* **fonn 1**

port[2], *gen & pl* **puirt** *nm* a port, a harbour, **'s e port a th' ann an Glaschu** Glasgow is a port, **port-adhair** an airport, *Cf* **acarsaid, cala**

Portagail *nf, with art*, **a' Phortagail** Portugal

Portagaileach, *gen & pl* **Portagailich** *nm* a Portuguese, *also as adj* **Portagaileach** Portuguese

portair, portair, portairean *nm* **1** a porter, a bearer, *Cf more trad* **fear-giùlain** (*see* **giùlan 1**); **2** a porter, a doorman, *Cf more trad* **dorsair**

pòs *vti, pres part* **a' pòsadh**, marry, get married, **phòs iad an-uiridh** they (got) married last year, **am pòs thu mi? cha phòs!** will you marry me? no!

pòsadh, pòsaidh, pòsaidhean *nm* **1** (*the act of*) marrying, getting married; **2** marriage, a marriage, **gealladh-pòsaidh** *m* an engagement (*lit* a promise of marriage - *see* **gealladh**), **sgaradh-pòsaidh** *m* divorce, a divorce, separation, *Cf* **banais**

pòsda & **pòsta** *adj* married, wed, **pòsda aig Anndra** married to Andrew, **nuadh-phòsda** *adj* newly married, **càraid** *f* **phòsda** a married couple, (*song*) **ged nach eil sinn fhathast pòsd', tha mi 'n dòchas gum bi** though we are not yet married, I hope we will be

post[1], *gen* **puist** *nm* post, mail, **am Post Rìoghail** the Royal Mail, **oifis a' phuist** *f* the post office (*ie the institution & a branch*), *also* **post-oifis** *m* a post-office, **post-adhair** air mail, **post a-mach/a-steach** outgoing/incoming mail, **post-dealain** electronic mail, e-mail

post[2], *gen* **puist** *nm* a (wooden) post, a stake, a stob, **post-seòlaidh** a signpost, *Cf* **stob 1**

post(a), **posta**, **postaichean** *nm* a postman, (*Sc*) a postie, (*Highland Eng*) a post, **Ailig Post** Alec the Post(ie)

pòsta *see* **pòsda**

prab-shùileach *adj* having bleary, rheumy or runny eyes

prabar, **prabair**, **prabairean** *nm* a rabble, a mob, a crowd (*derog*), *Cf* **gràisg**

prais, **praise**, **praisean** *nf* a (cooking) pot, *Cf* **poit**

pràis, *gen* **pràise** *nf* brass

pràiseach *adj* brass, made of brass

preantas, **preantais**, **preantasan** *nm* an apprentice

preas *vt*, *pres part* **a' preasadh**, 1 fold, crease, *Cf* **fill 1** & **2**; 2 furrow, wrinkle, corrugate; 3 crush, squeeze, *Cf* **fàisg**

preas[1], *gen* **pris**, *pl* **pris** & **preasan** *nm* a bush, a shrub, *Cf less usu* **dos 1**

preas[2], **preasa**, **preasan** *nm*, *also* **preasadh**, **preasaidh**, **preasaidhean** *nm*, a wrinkle

preas(a), *gen* **pris**, *pl* **pris** & **preasan** *nm* a cupboard, (*Sc*) a press, **preas-aodaich** a wardrobe, a clothes cupboard, **preas-leabhraichean** a bookcase

preasach *adj* 1 wrinkly, wrinkled; 2 corrugated, **iarann/pàipear preasach** corrugated iron/paper

preasadh *see* **preas**[2]

preasag, **preasaig**, **preasagan** *nf* a crease, a wrinkle, *Cf* **preas**[2]

prìbheideach, **prìbheiteach** *see* **prìobhaideach**

prìne, **prìne**, **prìnichean** *nm* a pin (*Cf Sc* preen), **prìne-banaltraim** a safety pin, *Cf* **dealg 4**

priob *vti*, *pres part* **a' priobadh**, wink, blink, *Cf* **caog**

priobadh, **priobaidh**, **priobaidhean** *nm* 1 (*the act of*) winking, blinking; 2 a wink, a blink, **ann am priobadh na sùla** in an instant, in the twinkling of an eye, *Cf* **plathadh 2**

prìobhaideach, *also* **prìbheideach** & **prìbheiteach**, *adj* private, (*industry &c*) **an roinn phrìobhaideach** the private sector, *Cf opposites* **coitcheann 1, poblach**

prìomh *adj* (*precedes the noun*) main, foremost, principal, chief, head, prime, premier, **prìomh-chlèireach** *m* a chief/head clerk, **prìomh-àireamh** *f* a prime number, **a' phrìomh-oifis** the head ofice, **prìomh adhbhar a ghiùlain** the main/principal reason for his conduct, (*ed*) **prìomh chuspair** a core subject, *Cf* **àrd** *adj* **3**

prìomhaire, prìomhaire, prìomhairean *nm* a prime minister, a premier

prionnsa, prionnsa, prionnsan *nm* a prince, **Bliadhna a' Phrionnsa** the year of the Prince (1745–6), **bana-phrionnsa** *f* a princess

prionnsabal, prionnsabail, prionnsabalan *nm* a principle, **ann am prionnsabal** in principle

prìosan, prìosain, prìosanan *nm* a prison

prìosanach, *gen* & *pl* **prìosanaich** *nm* a prisoner, *Cf more trad* **bràigh** *n*, **ciomach**

prìs, prìse, prìsean *nf* a price, the cost of something, **dè a' phrìs a th' air?** how much does it cost?, **prìsean àrda** high prices, *Cf* **cosg** *n* **2**, **cosgais 1**

prìseil *adj* precious, valuable, *Cf* **luachmhor**

pròbhaist, pròbhaiste, pròbhaistean *nm* (*civic admin*) a provost

prògram, prògraim, prògraman *nm* a programme, (*IT*) a program(me), **a' craobh-sgaoileadh phrògraman air an rèidio** broadcasting programmes on the radio, (*IT*) **prògram chleachdaidhean** an applications programme

proifeasair, proifeasair, proifeasairean *nm* a professor, (*children's book*) **Clann a' Phroifeasair** (Maoilios M. Caimbeul) The Professor's Children, *Cf more trad* **àrd-ollamh**

proifeiseanta *adj* professional, *Cf* **dreuchdail 2**

pròis, *gen* **pròise** *nf* pride (*often legitimate*), *Cf* **moit**, & *usu more excessive* **àrdan, uabhar, uaibhreas**

pròiseict & **pròiseact,** *gen* **pròiseict,** *pl* **pròiseictean** *nmf* a project, *Cf* **plana 1**

pròiseil *adj* (*often legitimately*) proud, **bha sinn pròiseil asad** we were proud of you, **pròiseil aiste fhèin** proud of herself, *Cf* **moiteil**, & *often more excessive* **àrdanach, uaibhreach**

pronn *vt, pres part* **a' pronnadh, 1** mash, pound, grind, pulverise, break up small, (*saying*) **chaidh a phronnadh na shùgh fhèin** he was mashed in his own juice; **2** (*fam, in fight &c*) bash, maul, beat up; **3** *in expr* (*fam*) **bha mi air mo phronnadh** I was drunk/smashed/steaming

pronn *adj* mashed, pounded, ground, pulverised, broken up small, **buntàta pronn** mashed potato, **airgead pronn** small change

pronnadh, *gen* **pronnaidh** *nm* (*the act of*) mashing, bashing &c (*see senses of* **pronn** *v*)

pronnasg, *gen* **pronnaisg** *nm* sulphur, brimstone

prosbaig, prosbaig, prosbaigean *nf* **1** binoculars, field glasses; **2** a telescope

Pròstanach, *gen & pl* **Pròstanaich** *nm* a Protestant, *also as adj* **Pròstanach** Protestant

prothaid, prothaide, prothaidean *nf* (*usu fin*) profit, a profit, gain, a gain, benefit, a benefit, **dèan** *v* **prothaid** make a profit

puball *&* **pùball**, *gen* **pubaill**, *pl* **puballan** *nm* a (vcry) large tent, a marquee, *Cf* **pàillean 1**, **teanta**

pùdar *&* **fùdar**, *gen* **pùdair**, *pl* **pùdaran** *nm* powder, a powder

pùdaraich *&* **fùdaraich** *vt, pres part* **a' pùdarachadh**, **1** powder, put powder on something; **2** reduce to powder

puing, puinge, puingean *nf* **1** a point in a scale, series &c, (*heat, angles*) a degree; **2** a point (*made in an argument &c*); **3** (*typog*) a stop, a mark, **stad-phuing** a full stop, **clisg-phuing** an exclamation mark, **dà-phuing** a colon

puinnsean, puinnsein, puinnseanan *nm* poison, a poison, *Cf more trad* **nimh 1**

puinnseanach *also* **puinnseanta**, *adj* poisonous, *Cf more trad* **nimheil 1**

puinnseanaich *vt, pres part* **a' puinnseanachadh**, poison

pumpa, pumpa, pumpaichean *nm* a pump

punnd, *gen & pl* **puinnd** *nm* **1** (*weight*) a pound; **2** (*money*) a pound, **punnd Eireannach** an Irish pound, a punt, (*trad*) **punnd Sasannach** a pound Sterling, *Cf* **nota 1**

purgadair, *gen* **purgadaire** *nm* purgatory

purpaidh *adj* purple, *Cf* **còrcair**

purpar *&* **purpur**, *gen* **purpair** *nm* the colour purple

put *vti, pres part* **a' putadh**, **1** push, shove, *Cf* **brùth 2**, **sàth** *v* **2**; **2** jostle, *Cf* **uillnich**; **3** (*IT & c*) **put ann** key in (*data &c*)

put, puta, putan *nm* a buoy

putadh, *gen* **putaidh** *nm* (*the act of*) pushing, shoving, jostling

putan, putain, putanan *nm* **1** a button, **dùin/fuasgail** *v* **putanan** fasten/ undo buttons; **2** (*calculator &c*) a key, a button

R

rabaid, rabaide, rabaidean *nf* a rabbit, *Cf* **coineanach**

rabhadh, rabhaidh, rabhaidhean *nm* warning, a warning, an alarm, a caution, **clag-rabhaidh** *m* a warning bell, an alarm bell, **thug iad rabhadh dhomh** they warned/alerted/cautioned me, *Cf* **earalachadh 3, earalaich 3**

rabhd, *gen* **rabhda** *nm, also* **ràbhart,** *gen* **ràbhairt** *nm,* **1** idle, boastful or far-fetched talk, tales or chatter, a 'spiel'; **2** obscene talk, *Cf* **drabastachd, draostachd**

ràc *vti, pres part* **a' ràcadh,** (*gardening &c*) rake

ràc, ràic, ràcan *nm* a drake, *Cf* **dràc**

racaid, racaide, racaidean *nf* (*sport*) a racket

ràcan, ràcain, ràcanan *nm* (*tool*) a rake

rach *vi irreg* (*for forms see tables p 410*), *pres part* **a' dol, 1** go, **thèid mi don bhaile** I'll go to the town, **a bheil an trèana seo a' dol do Ghlaschu?** is this train going to Glasgow?, **rach a chadal** go to bed, **chaidh i bhuaithe** she went downhill/off, she deteriorated, *Cf* **falbh 1, gabh 2, triall; 2** happen, go on, take place, **a bheil/am bi na cèilidhean a' dol fhathast?** are the ceilidhs still going (strong)? (*fam*) **dè tha dol?** what's doing/happening/going on?, how's things?, **bha mi sa chùirt an-dè! ciamar a chaidh dhut? cha deach ach gu dubh dona!** I was in court yesterday! how did you get on/ how did it go? just terrible!, *Cf* **èirich 2; 3** become, grow, get, *with abstract nouns* **tha e a' dol am meud/feabhas** (*&c*) it's getting bigger/better (*&c*), *Cf* **fàs** *v* **3; 4** become, take a job (*&c*) as, **chaidh e na phoileas** he became a policeman; **5** *in expr* **rach agam** (*&c*) **air** manage to, succeed in, **an tèid agad air obair fhaighinn?** will you manage to find/get a job? **rinn i e cho math 's a rachadh aice** she did it as well as she could (manage); **6** *used to expr passive,* **chaidh talla a' bhaile a pheantadh** the town hall was painted, **cha tèid sin a dhèanamh** that won't be done; **7** *misc exprs,* **rach thar a chèile** fall out, quarrel (with each other), **rach an sàs anns an obair** (*&c*) get involved in the work (*&c*), get stuck into the work (*&c*), **rach an urras gu** ... guarantee that ..., **chaidh e às mo chuimhne** I forgot it, **rach ri taobh cuideigin** take after (*ie* resemble) someone

rachadh, rachaibh, rachainn, racham, rachamaid *pts of irreg v* **rach** *see tables p 410*

radan, *gen & pl* **radain** *nm* a rat

ràdh *nm invar* **1** a saying, a proverb, an adage, *Cf more usu* **facal 2**, **seanfhacal**; **2 ag ràdh** *prep part see* **abair**

radharc *see* **fradharc**

rag *adj* **1** (*phys*) stiff, rigid, inflexible; **2** (*character &c*) stubborn, obstinate, inflexible, (*Sc*) thrawn, *Cf* **dùr 1**, **rag-mhuinealach**

ragaich *vti, pres part* **a' ragachadh**, stiffen, make or become stiff or rigid

rag-bharaileach *adj* dogmatic, stubborn or overbearing in one's opinions or beliefs

rag-mhuinealach *adj* very stubborn or obstinate, pig-headed, *Cf* **dùr 1**, **rag 2**

raidhfil, raidhfil, raidhfilean *nf* a rifle

raige *nf invar* (*abstr noun corres to* **rag**) **1** stiffness, rigidity; **2** obstinacy

raineach, *gen* **rainich** *nf* bracken, fern(s)

ràinig *pt of irreg v* **ruig** *see tables p 411*

ràith, ràithe, ràithean *nf* **1** a season, a quarter (*of year*); **2** a period, a while, a time, *Cf* **greis, ùine 2**

ràitheachan, *gen & pl* **ràitheachain** *nm* (*publishing*) a quarterly (magazine), a periodical, *Cf* **iris**

ràmh, *gen & pl* **ràimh** *nm* an oar

ràn *vi, pres part* **a' rànail** *&* **a' rànaich**, **1** roar, yell, bellow, *Cf* **beuc** *v*, **geum** *v*; **2** cry, weep (*usu vigorously*), *Cf* **caoin 2, guil**

ràn, *gen & pl* **ràin** *nm* a roar, a yell, a bellow, *Cf* **beuc** *n*, **geum** *n*

rànail *nm invar* **1** roaring, yelling, bellowing; **2** (*usu vigorous*) crying, weeping

rann, *gen* **rainn**, *pl* **rannan** *&* **ranntaichean** *nf* **1** verse, poetry, **rosg is rann** prose and verse, *Cf* **bàrdachd, dànachd**; **2** a (*single*) verse, a stanza

rannaigheachd *nf invar* (*poet*) versification, metre, metrics, **saor-rannaigheachd** free verse

rannsachadh, *gen* **rannsachaidh** *nm* **1** (*the act of*) searching, rummaging &c (*see senses of* **rannsaich** *v*); **2** research

rannsaich *vti, pres part* **a' rannsachadh**, **1** search; **2** rummage (*esp in search of something*), *Cf* **ruamhair 2, rùraich 1**; **3** research, study, investigate, **tha i a' rannsachadh eachdraidh na dùthcha** she's researching the history of the country; **4** explore; **5** (*trad*) ransack

raon, *gen* **raoin**, *pl* **raontan** *&* **raointean** *nm* **1** a field, a piece of (*usu*) level ground (*often for a specific purpose*), **raon-cluiche** a playing field, a pitch, **raon goilf** a golf course, **raon-adhair** an airfield, **raon gnìomhachais** an industrial estate, a business park, **raon-ola** an oil field; **2** (*fig*) a field, an area, an aspect (*of activity, knowledge, experience &c*), **raon eile anns an robh e fìor eòlach** another field/area he was highly knowledgeable about; **3** (*IT*) a field

rapach *adj* slovenly, scruffy, dirty, *Cf* **dràbhail, grodach, luideach, mosach 1**

rath, *gen* **ratha** *nm* (*trad*) luck, good fortune, prosperity, *now usu in proverbs, eg* **is duilich rath a chur air duine dona** it's hard to put luck on a worthless (*or* unlucky) man

rathad, *gen* **rathaid** & **rothaid**, *pl* **rathaidean** & **ròidean** *nm* **1** a road, **rathad beag** a minor road, **rathad mòr** a main road, **rathad singilte/dùbailte** a single/double track road; **2** a way, a route, **air an rathad dhachaigh** on the way home, **chaidh iad an rathad sin** they went that way, (*calque*) **an rathad teaghlaich** in the family way, *Cf* **slighe**

Ratharsach, *gen* & *pl* **Ratharsaich** *nm* someone from Raasay (**Ratharsair** & **Ratharsaigh**), *also as adj* **Ratharsach** of, from or pertaining to Raasay

rè *nf invar* **1** a time, a period, *Cf more usu* **ùine 2**; **2** one's time, day or lifetime, **an rè mo sheanar** in my grandfather's time/day, *Cf more usu* **linn 2**

rè *prep, with gen*, during, through(out), in the course of, **rè nam bliadhnachan dh'fhàs i nas sèimhe** through/over the years she became calmer, *Cf* **air feadh**

reachd *nm invar* **1** rule, command, authority, **a' Ghrèig fo reachd nan seanailearan** Greece under the generals' rule, (*prov*) **ge cruaidh reachd a' bhàillidh, chan fheàrr reachd a' mhinisteir** though the factor's rule is harsh, the minister's is no better, *Cf* **smachd**; **2** a rule, a command, a statute, an ordinance, a law, *Cf more usu* **lagh, riaghailt 1**

reamhar *adj* fat, *Cf* **sultmhor 1**

reamhraich *vti, pres part* **a' reamhrachadh**, fatten, make or become fat

reic *vt, pres part* **a' reic**, sell, **chan eil càil agam ri reic** I've nothing to sell, **reic air deagh phrìs** sell at a good price

reic *nm invar* selling, a sale, **chan eil e airson a reic** it's not for sale, **fear-reic** *or* **neach-reic** a salesman/salesperson

reiceadair, reiceadair, reiceadairean *nm* **1** a seller, a vendor; **2** a salesman, *Cf more usu* **fear-reic** (*see* **reic** *n*); **3** an auctioneer

rèidh *adj* **1** level, even, *Cf* **còmhnard** *adj*; **2** smooth, *Cf* **mìn**; **3** (*area of ground &c*) clear, cleared, (*wool &c*) disentangled, straightened out; **4** *in expr* **bi rèidh ri cuideigin** get on well/smoothly with someone, be on good terms with someone

rèidhlean, rèidhlein, rèidhleanan *nm* a meadow, (*village &c*) a green

rèidio, rèidio, rèidiothan *nm* radio, a radio, **dè a th' air an rèidio?** what's on the radio?

rèile, rèile, rèilichean *nf* 1 a rail; 2 *pl* rèilichean railings

rèilig, rèilige, rèiligean *nf* a kirkyard, a churchyard, a graveyard, *Cf* cill 2, clachan 3, cladh

rèir *see* a-rèir

rèis, rèise, rèisean *nf* (*sports &c*) a race

rèisde, rèist *see* a-rèist

rèiseamaid, rèiseamaide, rèiseamaidean *nf* a regiment

rèite, rèite, rèitean *nf* 1 agreement, an agreement; 2 reconciliation, a reconciliation; 3 atonement, expiation; 4 *also used for* rèiteach

rèiteach, rèitich, rèitichean *nm* (*trad*) a betrothal, *involving family discussion, agreement and associated celebrations*

rèiteachadh, *gen* rèiteachaidh *nm* 1 (*the act of*) conciliating, settling &c (*see senses of* rèitich *v*); 2 *also used for* rèiteach

rèitear, rèiteir, rèitearan *nm* (*sport*) a referee

reithe, reithe, reitheachan *nm* a tup, a ram, *Cf* rùda

rèitich *vti, pres part* **a' rèiteachadh,** 1 (*opposing parties &c*) conciliate, reconcile, appease, arbitrate; 2 (*situations, relationships &c*) settle, sort out, put right/in order, put/set on an even keel, adjust, clear up, **rèitich an gnothach** settle/sort out the matter; 3 disentangle, **rèitich a' chlòimh seo dhomh** disentangle this wool for me, *Cf* fuasgail 2; 4 (*objects, spaces*) clear (away), clear up, **rèitich an rùm agad!** clear up/sort your room! (*Cf* sgioblaich), **rèitich an rathad** clear the road/way

reòdh *&* reòth *vti, pres part* **a' reodhadh** *&* **a' reothadh,** freeze

reòdhta *see* reòta

reòiteag, reòiteig, reòiteagan *nf* ice cream, an ice cream

reòta, *also* reòdhta *&* reòthte *adj*, frozen, **biadh** *m* **reòta** frozen food, **tha mo chasan reòthte!** my feet are frozen!

reòth *see* reòdh

reothadair, reothadair, reothadairean *nm* a freezer, a deep freeze

reothadh, *gen* reothaidh *nm* frost, a frost, **bha reothadh ann sa mhadainn (an-diugh)** there was (a) frost this morning

reotha(i)rt, reothairt, reothartan *nmf* a spring-tide, (*poetry collection*) **Reothairt is Contraigh** (Somhairle MacGill-Eain) Spring tide and Neap tide, (*saying*) **reothart an-diugh is contraigh a-màireach** too much today and too little tomorrow

reòthte *see* reòta

reub *vti, pres part* **a' reubadh**, *(materials, flesh &c)* tear, rend, rip, lacerate, mangle, *(song)* **an dèidh a reubadh le claidheamh** after ripping/ mangling him with a sword, *Cf* **srac**

reubadh, reubaidh, reubaidhean *nm* **1** *(the act of)* tearing, rending &c *(see senses of* **reub** *v)*; **2** a rip, a rent

reubalach, *gen & pl* **reubalaich** *nm* a rebel

reudan, reudain, reudanan *nm* a wood-louse, *(Sc)* a slater

reul, rèil, reultan *nf* a star, *(story)* **Iain am measg nan Reultan** (Iain Mac a' Ghobhainn) Iain among the Stars, **reul-bhad** *m* a constellation, **an reul-iùil** the pole star, **reul-eòlas** *m* astronomy, *Cf* **rionnag**

reuladair, reuladair, reuladairean *nm* an astronomer

reultag, reultaig, reultagan *nf* *(typog)* an asterisk

reusan, *gen* **reusain** *nm* reason *(ie the faculty)*, sanity, *Cf* **ciall 2, rian 3**

reusanta *adj* **1** reasonable, sensible, *Cf* **ciallach**; **2** reasonable, fair, *Cf* **cothromach**

ri, *before art* **ris**, *prep, takes dat, Note: the pers prons* **mi, thu**, *&c combine with* **ri** *to form the prep prons* **rium(sa), riut(sa), ris(-san), rithe(se), rinn(e), ribh(se), riutha(san)**; **1** *often expresses opposition, some degree of struggle or effort,* **chaidh i ris an t-sruth** she went upstream/ against the current, **ris a' ghaoith** against the wind, **bha iad a' trod ri chèile** they were squabbling (with each other); **2** *expr proximity* **taobh ri taobh** side by side, **bha mo dhruim ris a' bhalla** my back was against/to the wall, **an tacsa ri craoibh** leaning/propped up against a tree, **còmhla rium/cuide rium/mar rium** with me, in my company, **dhealaich sinn riutha** we parted from them/took our leave of them; **3** *in exprs of comparison* **coltach ri chèile** like each other, **cho seang ri seangan** as slim as an ant; **4** *expr that something is or needs to be done* **tha mòran agam ri dhèanamh** I've lots to do, **tha an taigh sin ri reic** that house is to be sold/is for sale, **tha iad rim moladh** they are/deserve to be praised; **5** during, in *(of time)*, **ri linn mo sheanar** in my grandfather's time/day, **gheibh sinn ri tìde e** we'll get it in time/in due course/eventually; **6** *expr exposure, visibility,* *(song)* **(a') nochdadh ri beanntan na Hearadh** appearing/ coming in sight of the mountains of Harris, **bha a h-uileann ris** her elbow was showing/visible, **ris a' ghrèin** exposed to the sun; **7** engaged in an activity, **tha iad ris an iasgach** they are at the fishing *(either just now, or as an occupation)*, **dè a tha sibh ris?** what are you up to?, **a bheil thu ri bàrdachd fhathast?** are you still writing poetry?, *Note:* **ri** *in this sense is used by some speakers in the place of* **ag** *or* **a'** *to form the pres part*

riabhach *adj* (*trad*) **1** brindled, marked with spots or stripes, *freq in placenames as* -reoch, **Dail Riabhach** Dalreoch, brindled haugh or meadow, *Cf* **ballach, breac** *adj*; **2** *of a range of dull colourings*, grizzled, drab, dun, yellowish-brown, *Cf* **lachdann 1, odhar 1**

riadh, *gen* **rèidh** *nm* (*fin*) interest

riaghail *vti*, *pres part* **a' riaghladh**, *also* **riaghlaich** *vti*, *pres part* **a' riaghlachadh**, **1** rule, rule over, govern (a country &c); **2** regulate, administer, manage (*a body, firm* &c), *Cf* **stiùir** *v* 2

riaghailt, riaghailte, riaghailtean *nf* **1** a rule, a regulation, an ordinance, *Cf* **lagh, reachd 2**; **2** system, order, *Cf* **òrdugh 3, rian 1**

riaghailteach *adj* **1** regular, systematical, orderly, conforming to the rules or norms, *Cf* **òrdail 1**

riaghailteachd *nf invar* orderliness, regularity

riaghailtich *vt*, *pres part* **a' riaghailteachadh**, regularise, make regular, regulate, put or keep in order

riaghaltas, riaghaltais, riaghaltasan *nm* government, a government, **riaghaltas nàiseanta/ionadail** national/local government

riaghladair, riaghladair, riaghladairean *nm* **1** a ruler (*ie head of state* &c), a governor; **2** a regulator

riaghladh, *gen* **riaghlaidh** *nm* **1** (*the act of*) ruling, regulating &c (*see senses of* **riaghail** *v*); **2** (*of country* &c) (*abstr*) government; **3** (*of business, body* &c) (*abstr*) administration, management, **neach-riaghlaidh** *m* a manager, an administrator (*Cf less trad* **manaidsear**), **an luchd-riaghlaidh** the administrators, (*con*) the administration

riamh *see* **a-riamh**

rian, rian, rianan *nm* **1** method, methodicalness, orderliness, system, **cuir rian air rudeigin** impose order, system, method &c on something, *Cf* **òrdugh 3**; **2** (*trad*) a mode or manner (*of doing something*), *Cf more usu* **dòigh 1**; **3** reason, senses, sanity, **cha mhòr nach deach mi às mo rian** I nearly went out of my mind/lost my reason, **tha thu às do rian!** you're out of your mind! *Cf* **ciall 2, reusan**; **4** (*music*) an arrangement

rianachd *nf invar* administration

rianadair, rianadair, rianadairean *nm* **1** (*music*) an arranger; **2** a computer, *Cf usu* **coimpiuta(i)r**

rianail *adj* methodical, *Cf* **òrdail**

rianaire, rianaire, rianairean *nm* an administrator

riarachadh, *gen* **riarachaidh** *nm* (*the act of*) pleasing, dividing &c (*see senses of* **riaraich** *v*)

riaraich *vt, pres part* **a' riarachadh**, 1 please, content, satisfy, *Cf* **còrd** *v*, **sàsaich 1**, **toilich**; 2 divide, share (out), distribute, (*playing cards*) deal, *Cf* **pàirtich**, **roinn** *v* 2

riaraichte *adj* pleased, satisfied, *Cf* **sàsaichte 1**, **toilichte**

riatanach *adj* essential, necessary, indispensable, *Cf* **deatamach**

rib *vt, pres part* **a' ribeadh**, trap, ensnare

ribe, **ribe**, **ribeachan** *nmf* a snare, a trap

ribh *prep pron see* **ri**

ribheid, **ribheide**, **ribheidean** *nf* 1 (*music*) a reed; 2 *in expr* (*fam*) **fliuch do ribheid!** wet your whistle!

rìbhinn, **rìbhinne**, **rìbhinnean** *nf* (*trad, freq in songs*) a maiden, a young woman, a girl (*as object of affections*), (*song*) **a rìbhinn òg, bheil cuimhn' agad?** young lass, do you remember?, *Cf* **caileag 2**, **gruagach**, **nighean 2**, **nìghneag 2**, **maighdeann 1**

ridhil *see* **ruidhle**

ridire, **ridire**, **ridirean** *nm* a knight

rìgh, **rìgh**, **rìghrean** *nm* 1 a king, (*prov*) **'Tiugainn,' ars an rìgh, 'Fuirich,' ars a' ghaoth** 'Come,' said the king, 'Stay,' said the wind; 2 (*occas*) God, Lord (God), **a Rìgh, glèidh sinn!** Lord save us! **Rìgh nan dùl** the Lord of the elements/universe, *Cf* **Dia 1**

righinn *adj* (*materials &c*) tough, (*prov*) **bidh an iall righinn gu leòr gus am brist i** the thong is tough enough until it breaks

rinn, **rinne**, **rinnean** *nm* 1 a point (*of pencil, pin &c*), *Cf* **bior 1**; 2 a point of land, a promontory, *Cf more usu* **àird 2**, **rubha**

rinn, *pt of irreg v* **dèan** (*see tables p 407*)

rinn *prep pron see* **ri**

rioban, **riobain**, **riobanan** *nm* ribbon, a ribbon, **rioban-tomhais** a tape measure

riochd, **riochda**, **riochdan** *nm* form, likeness, appearance, **nochd an taibhse an riochd cait** the ghost appeared in the likeness of a cat, **breug-riochd** *m* a disguise (*lit* a false appearance)

riochdachadh, **riochdachaidh**, **riochdachaidhean** *nm* 1 (*the act of*) representing, portraying &c (*see senses of* **riochdaich** *v*); 2 (*by lawyer, spokesperson &c*) representation; 3 (*actor, artist &c*) representation, a representation, portrayal, a portrayal

riochdaich *vt, pres part* **a' riochdachadh**, 1 (*lawyer, spokesman &c*) represent; 2 (*actor, artist &c*) represent, portray, impersonate

riochdair, **riochdair**, **riochdairean** *nm* (*gram*) a pronoun

riochdaire, **riochdaire**, **riochdairean** *nm* 1 a representative, **riochdaire aonaidh** a union representative, a shop steward; 2 (*film &c*) a producer

rìoghachadh, rìoghachaidh, rìoghachaidhean *nm* reigning, a reign

rìoghachd, rìoghachd, rìoghachdan *nf* a kingdom

rìoghaich *vi, pres part* **a' rìoghachadh**, reign

rìoghail *adj* royal, kingly, regal, **is rìoghail mo dhream** royal is my race (*motto of Clan Gregor*)

rìomhach *adj* beautiful, fine, splendid, (*song*) **air luing rìomhaich nam ball airgid** on a splendid/beautiful ship with silver rigging, *Cf* **àlainn, eireachdail**

rionnach, *gen & pl* **rionnaich** *nm* mackerel, a mackerel

rionnag, rionnaig, rionnagan *nf* a star, (*fam*) **chan eil fhios a'm o na rionnagan ruadha** I haven't the faintest idea, *Cf* **reul**

ris *prep pron see* **ri**

ri taobh *see* **taobh 2**

ro *adv, aspirates/lenites following adj &c,* **1** too, excessively, **tha e ro anmoch airson cuairt a ghabhail** it's too late to go for a walk; **2** *also occurs as prefix* **ro-** over-, **ro-throm** *adj* over-weight, **ro-nochd** *v* over-expose; **3** (*trad*) *as intensifying element* very, extremely, (*before noun*) great, extreme, **ro-gheal** *adj* extremely white, **ro-chùram** *m* extreme anxiety/care

ro, roi- *&* **roimh**, *before art* **ron**, *prep, takes dat, Note: the pers prons* **mi, thu,** *&c combine with* **ro** *to form the prep prons* **romham(sa), romhad(sa), roimhe(san), roimhpe(se), romhainn(e), romhaibh(se), romhpa(san)** before me, you &c; **1** before (*in time*), **dh'fhalbh sinn ron àm** we left early (*lit* before the time), **ron mhithich** *adv* before the appointed time, prematurely, **ro-làimh** *adv* beforehand, (*trad tales*) **fada fada ron a seo** long long ago (*lit* before this), once upon a time; **2** in front of, before (*in space*), **choisich sinn romhainn** we walked along/on (*lit* before ourselves), **bha càr ron doras** a car was in front of the door, *Cf* **air beulaibh**; **3** *expr reaction to or in the presence of someone,* **bha eagal air roimhpe** he was afraid of her; **4** *prep pron* **roimhe** *used adverbially*, before (*in time*), **duine nach fhaca sinn a-riamh roimhe** a man we never saw before, (**chaidh mi ann** *&c*) **an là roimhe** (I went there *&c*) the other day; **5** *in expr* **cuir** *v* **romham** (*&c*) decide, determine, resolve, propose, intend, make up my (*&c*) mind, **chuir iad romhpa taigh ùr a thogail** they resolved to build a new house; **6 ro-,** *also* **roi(mh)-,** *prefix corres to Eng* pre-, fore-, **ro-ràdh** *m* a foreword, a preamble, a prologue, (*relig*) **ro-òrdachadh** *m* predestination, **ro-chraiceann** *m* a foreskin, (*gram*) **ro-leasachan** *m* a prefix, **ro-phàigheadh** *m* pre-payment, **ro-thaghadh** *m* pre-selection, *also* predestination, (*esp weather*) **ro-aithris** *f* a forecast

robach *adj* **1** shaggy, hairy, *Cf* **molach, ròmach 1; 2** slovenly, untidy, *Cf* **luideach**

robh *pt of irreg v* **bi** (*see tables p 414*)

roc, *gen & pl* **ruic** *nf* a wrinkle, *Cf more usu* **preas²**

rocaid, rocaide, rocaidean *nf* a rocket

ròcail, *gen* **ròcaile** *nf* croaking, a croak, (*crows &c*) cawing, a caw

ròca(i)s, ròcais, ròcaisean *nf*, a rook, **bodach-ròcais** *m* a scarecrow

roghainn, roghainn, roghainnean *nmf* choice, choosing, a choice, an option, a preference, **chan eil roghainn againn** we've no choice, **mo roghainn fhìn de cheòl** my own choice of/preference in music, *Cf* **taghadh 2**

roghnachadh, *gen* **roghnachaidh** *nm* (*the act of*) choosing &c (*see senses of* **roghnaich** *v*)

roghnaich *vti, pres part* **a' roghnachadh**, choose, select, pick, *Cf* **tagh 1**

roi-, roimh, roimhe *see* **ro** *prep*

roilig *vti, pres part* **a' roiligeadh**, roll

roimh- *prefix see* **ro 6**

roimhe 1 *prep pron see* **ro** *prep;* **2** *adv* (*of time*) before, **cha do rinn mi sin a-riamh roimhe** I never did that before, *see* **ro** *prep* **4**

roimhear, roimheir, roimhearan *nm* (*gram*) a preposition

roimhpe *prep pron see* **ro** *prep*

ròineag, ròineig, ròineagan *nf* a (single) hair, *Cf* **fuiltean**

roinn *vt, pres part* **a' roinneadh**, **1** divide (up), split (up), separate (*into smaller quantities, shares &c*); **2** divide, distribute, share (out), apportion, (*cards*) deal, **roinn i an t-airgead oirnn** she divided/shared (*&c*) the money between us, *Cf* **pàirtich, riaraich 2; 3** (*arith*) divide, **72 air a roinneadh le 3** 72 divided by 3

roinn, roinne, roinnean *nf* **1** a division (*incl football*), (*arith &c*) division, a sector, (*pol*) **roinn taghaidh** a constituency, (industry &c) **an roinn phoballach/phrìobhaideach** the public/private sector; **2** a share, a portion, a part, a section, *Cf* **cuibhreann 1, cuid 1, earrann; 3** (*in organisation &c*) a department, **roinn na rùnaireachd** the secretarial department, (*ed*) **Roinn na Fraingis** the French Department; **4** (*local government, formerly*) a region, **Roinn na Gàidhealtachd** Highland Region; **5** a continent, *esp* **an Roinn-Eòrpa** Europe, the continent of Europe

ròist *&* **ròsd** *vt, pres part* **a' ròstadh** *&* **a' ròsdadh**, **1** roast (*meat &c*); **2** fry, *Cf* **frighig**

ròlaist, ròlaist, ròlaistean *nm* (*Lit*) a romance, a romantic novel

ròm *nmf invar* pubes, pubic hair, *Cf* **gaoisid 2**

ròmach *adj* **1** woolly, hairy, shaggy, *Cf* **molach, robach 1**; **2** bearded, hirsute

ròmag, ròmaig, ròmagan *nf* female genitals, the female pubic area, *Cf* **faighean, pit**

Romàinianach, *gen & pl* **Romàinianaich** *nm* a Romanian, *also as adj* **Romàinianach** of, from or pertaining to Romania (**Romàinia** *f*)

romhad, romhaibh, romhainn, romham, romhpa *prep prons see* **ro** *prep*

ròn, *gen & pl* **ròin** *nm* a seal (*ie the sea creature*)

ron *see* **ro**

rong, *gen* **roinge** *&* **ronga**, *pl* **rongan** *nf, also* **rongas**, *gen & pl* **rongais** *nm*, **1** a rung; **2** a spar, a (wooden) crosspiece, a dwang; **3** a (wooden) hoop

rong, *gen & pl* **roing** *nm* a spark, *esp* a spark of life, a vital spark, **chan eil rong innte** there's not a spark of life in her, *Cf* **deò**

ronn, roinn, ronnan *nm* **1** mucus, phlegm; **2** slaver, *Cf* **seile**

ròp(a), *gen* **ròpa**, *pl* **ròpaichean** *&* **ròpannan** *nm* a rope, **ròp-aodaich** a clothes-line, *Cf* **ball**[2] **4, còrd** *n*

ròsda *&* **ròsta** *adj* **1** roast, roasted; **2** fried, **buntàta ròsda** *m* fried potatoes, chips

ròs, ròis, ròsan *nm* a rose

rosg[1]**, ruisg, rosgan** *nm* prose, **rosg-rann** *f* (*gram*) a sentence (*Cf less trad* **seantans**), *Cf* **rann 1**

rosg[2]**, ruisg, rosgan** *nm* an eyelash, *Cf* **fabhra 1**

roth, rotha, rothan *nmf* a wheel, *Cf less trad* **cuibhle**

rothach *adj* wheeled, having wheels

rothar, rothair, rotharan *nm* a bicycle, *Cf less trad* **baidhsagal**

ruadh *adj* **1** (*of hair, animal's coat &c*) red, ginger, **falt** *m* **ruadh** red/ginger hair, **fear** *m* **ruadh** a red-haired man, **madadh** *m* **ruadh** a fox (*lit a red dog/canine*); **2** red (*a less true red than* **dearg**), **sgillinn** *f* **ruadh** a (*brass or copper*) penny, *esp in expr* **chan eil sgillinn ruadh agam** I don't have a brass farthing, I'm completely broke, *Cf* **dearg 1**

ruagadh, *gen* **ruagaidh** *nm* (*the act of*) chasing, routing &c (*see senses of* **rua(i)g** *v*)

rua(i)g *vt, pres part* **a' ruagadh, 1** chase, chase away, put to flight, pursue, drive out *or* away; **2** (*military*) rout

ruaig, ruaige, ruaigean *nf* **1** chasing, a chase, pursuing, a pursuit, *Cf* **tòir 1**; **2** (*military &c*) a flight, a rout; **3** (*hunting*) a chase, a hunt

ruamhair *vi, pres part* **a' ruamhar, 1** dig, *Cf* **cladhaich 1**; **2** rummage (*esp in search of something*), *Cf* **rannsaich 2, rùraich 1**

rubair, rubair, rubairean *nm* rubber, a rubber

rubha, rubha, rubhaichean *nm* (*topog, usu coastal*) a point, a promontory, *Cf* **àird** *n* 2

rùchd *vi, pres part* **a' rùchdail**, **1** (*esp pig*) grunt; **2** belch, *Cf* **brùchd** *v* 1; **3** retch, *Cf* **dìobhair, sgeith**

rùchd, rùchda, rùchdan *nm* **1** (*esp pig*) a grunt; **2** a belch, *Cf* **brùchd** *n*; **3** retching, (*vulg*) **chuir mi a-mach rùchd mo chaolanan** I spewed my guts up

rud, rud, rudan *nm* **1** a thing, **rud sam bith** anything at all (*after neg verb*) nothing at all (*Cf* **rudeigin**), (*fam*) **dè an rud?** what?, what did you say? (*Cf more polite* **àill** 2), *Cf* **càil** *nm* 1, **dad** 1, **nì** *n* 1, **sian** 3; **2** a fact, **mas e an rud e 's gu bheil stoirm a' tighinn oirnn &c**) if it is true/a fact/the case that we are in for a storm, **nam b' e rud e 's gun caochladh iad** if they were to die; **3 rud beag** *adv see* **beag** 4

rùda, rùda, rùdan *nm* a ram, a tup, *Cf* **reithe**

rudail *adj* concrete, real, actual, *Cf* **nitheil**, & *opposite* **beachdail** 2

rùdan, *gen* **rùdain**, *pl* **rùdain** & **rùdanan** *nm* a knuckle, a finger-joint, **tha altas nad rùdain** you've got arthritis in your knuckles

rudeigin 1 *pron* something, anything, **a bheil rudeigin ceàrr? tha rudeigin nam shùil** is anything/something wrong? there's something in my eye, *Cf less usu* **nitheigin** (*see* **nì** *n* 1); **2** *as adv* a little, a bit, somewhat, rather, **bha mi rudeigin sgìth** I was a bit/ rather tired, *Cf* **beag** 4, **beagan** *adv*, **car** *n* 7, **caran**

rudhadh, *gen* **rudhaidh** *nm* **1** (*the act of*) blushing, flushing (*of face*); **2** (*also* **rudhadh-gruaidhe**) a blush, a flush (*on face*)

rug, rugadh *pts of irreg v* **beir** *see tables p 405*

ruidhle, ruidhle, ruidhlea(cha)n *nm, also* **ridhil, ridhle, ridhlea(cha)n** *nm,* (*dance*) a reel, **ruidhle-ochdnar** an eightsome reel, **Ruidhle Thulachain** the Reel o Tulloch, (*prov*) **tha car eile air ruidhle a' bhodaich** there's another turn left in the old man's reel

ruig *vti irreg* (*see tables p 411*), *pres part* **a' ruigsinn**, **1** (*vi*) arrive, (*vt*) arrive at, reach (*a place*), **an dèidh dhuinn an cladach a ruigsinn** after we reached/arrived at the shore; **2** *in expr* **ruig air** reach, reach for, take, seize (*object &c, esp with hand*), **an ruig thu air an sgeilp as àirde?** can you reach the top shelf? **ruig air mo làimh** reach for/ take my hand; **3** attain (*an aim &c*); **4** *for expr* **cha ruig mi** (&c) **a leas** *see* **leas** 2

ruige *see* **gu ruige**

ruighe, ruighe, ruighean *nmf* **1** a forearm; **2** (*topog*) a hillslope, *Cf* **aodann** 2, **bruthach** 1, **leathad, leitir**

rùilear, rùileir, rùilearan *nm* a ruler, a rule (*ie for measuring*), *Cf more trad* **slat-thomhais** (*see* **slat 3**)

Ruis (an) *see* **Ruisia**

ruisean, *gen* **ruisein** *nm, with art* **an ruisean** the midday meal, lunch

Ruiseanach, *gen & pl* **Ruiseanaich** *nm* a Russian, *also as adj* **Ruiseanach** Russian

Ruiseanais *nf invar* (*lang*) Russian

rùisg *vt, pres part* **a' rùsgadh, 1** (*body &c*) bare, uncover, undress, strip, **rùisg e a ruighe** he bared his forearm, *Cf* **lom** *v* **1; 2** (*sheep*) shear, clip, fleece; **3** (*vegetables &c*) peel, skin; **4** (*sword &c*) unsheathe, bare, draw, (*trad*) **an àm rùsgadh nan lann** in the time of baring of blades; **5** (*peatbank*) strip, open up (*by removing turf*); **6** chafe, graze, scrape (*skin of hand &c*)

rùisgte *adj* bare, bared, naked, stripped, peeled &c (*see senses of* **rùisg** *v*), **buntàta rùisgte** peeled potatoes, **casruisgte** *adj* barefoot, **ceannruisgte** *adj* bare-headed

Ruisia *nf, also* **an Ruis** *nf,* Russia

ruiteach *adj* **1** (*of colour*) ruddy, *Cf* **dearg 1; 2** (*face*) blushing, flushed

ruith *vti, pres part* **a' ruith, 1** run, **ruith i dà mhìle an-dè** she ran two miles yesterday, **chan eil an trèana/an t-uisge a' ruith** the train's/the water's not running, (*calque*) **ruith an gual a-mach** the coal ran out; **2** (*liquids*) run, flow, stream, *Cf* **sil 2, sruth** *v*; **3** chase, run after, *Cf* **rua(i)g** *v* **1**

ruith, ruithe, ruithean *nf* **1** running, a run, **dh'fhalbh iad nan ruith** they went away at a run, **nan dian-ruith** at full tilt, hell for leather; **2** (*military &c*) a pursuit, a flight, a rout, *Cf more usu* **ruaig** *n* **2; 3** a rate (*of speed, progress &c*), **air an ruith seo cha bhi e seachad ron oidhche** at this rate it won't be finished/over before night, **cùm ruith ri cuideigin** keep up/keep pace with someone; **4** a sequence

rùm, rùim, rumannan *nm* **1** room, space, **cha robh rùm sa bhàta** there was no room in the boat; **2** a room, (*Sc*) an apartment, **rùm is cidsin** a room and kitchen, **rùm-bìdh** a dining-room, **thalla don rùm agad!** go to your room!, *Cf* **seòmar**

Rùmach, *gen & pl* **Rùmaich** *nm* someone from Rum (**Eilean Ruma &** **Eilean Rùim**), *also as adj* **Rùmach** of, from or pertaining to Rum

rùn, rùin, rùintean *nm* **1** love, affection, **tìr mo rùin(-sa)** the land I love, **mì-rùn** ill-will, malice, *Cf* **dèidh 2, gaol 1, gràdh 1; 2** an object of love or affection, a thing, place or person loved, (*song*) **Mo Rùn Geal Dìleas** My Faithful Fair Loved One; **3** ambition, an ambition, a desire, an intention, a purpose, a motive; a wish, a hope, *Cf* **miann**

1; 4 *also in expr* **a dh'aon rùn (gu)** deliberately/on purpose (to), with the sole/express intention (of) (*Cf similarly used* **gnothach 5**); 5 a secret

rùnachadh, *gen* **rùnachaidh** *nm* (*the act of*) wishing, intending &c (*see senses of* **rùnaich** *v*)

rùnaich *vi*, *pres part*, **a' rùnachadh**, wish, desire, propose, resolve, intend (*to do something*), *Cf* **cuir** *v* **romham** (*see* **ro** *prep* **5**)

rùnaire, rùnaire, rùnairean *nm* a secretary, **Rùnaire na Stàite** the Secretary of State

rùrachadh, *gen* **rùrachaidh** *nm* (*the act of*) rummaging, exploring &c (*see senses of* **rùraich** *v*)

rùraich *vi*, *pres part* **a' rùrachadh**, 1 rummage, grope (*esp in search of something*), *Cf* **rannsaich 2, ruamhair 2**; 2 *vti* explore

rus, *gen* **ruis** *nm* rice

rùsg, rùisg, rùsgan *nm*, *refers to covering of many objects*, 1 (*fruit &c*) peel, skin, husk, (*sheep*) fleece, (*wood*) bark, *Cf* **cochall 1, plaosg**; 2 *in expr* **rùsg na Talmhainn** the Earth's crust

rùsgadh, *gen* **rùsgaidh** *nm* (*the act of*) baring, shearing &c (*see senses of* **rùisg** *v*)

S

's *see* **agus** *conj* & **is** *v*

sa (*for* **anns a'**) *see* **anns an**

sa[1] *corres to* **seo**, this, **air an t-seachdain sa** this week

-sa[2] *a suffix used to emphasise poss adj*, (*song*) **Cailin Mo Rùin-sa** the lass (who is) my very own love, **air do shon-sa** for you (*emph*), for your (*emph*) part,

Sàbaid, Sàbaid, Sàbaidean *nf, also* **Sàboint, Sàboint, Sàbointean** *nf*, a sabbath, (*esp in Protestant usage*) **Là na Sàbaid** the Sabbath (Day), Sunday, *Cf* **Didòmhnaich**

sabaid *vi, pres part* **a' sabaid**, *also* **sabaidich** *vi, pres part* **a' sabaidich**, fight, scrap, brawl, (**ri** with, against)

sabaid, sabaide, sabaidean *nf* fighting, brawling, a fight, a brawl, a scrap, **dèan** *v* **sabaid** fight, have a fight, *Cf* **còmhrag, tuasaid 2**

sàbh *vti, pres part* **a' sàbhadh**, saw

sàbh, *gen* **sàibh**, *pl* **sàbhan** & **sàibh** *nm* a saw

sàbhail *vt, pres part* **a' sàbhaladh**, **1** save, rescue (*from accident, danger*), **chaidh an sàbhaladh le bàta-teasairginn** they were saved by a lifeboat, *Cf* **teasairg**; **2** (*spiritually*) save, **sàbhail na pàganaich** save the heathens, *Cf* **saor** *v* **2**; **3** (*money*) save, economise, put aside, *Cf* **caomhain, glèidh 2**

sàbhailte *adj* safe, *Cf* **tèarainte 1**

sabhal, *gen* **sabhail**, *pl* **sabhalan** & **saibhlean** *nm* a barn

sàbhaladh, *gen* **sàbhalaidh** *nm* **1** (*the act of*) saving, rescuing &c (*see senses of* **sàbhail**); **2** (*relig*) salvation, *Cf* **saorsa 2**; **3** (*fin*) savings

sabhs, saibhse, sabhsan *nm* (*cookery*) sauce, a sauce, *Cf* **leannra**

Sàboint *see* **Sàbaid**

sac, *gen* **saic**, *pl* **sacan** & **saic** *nm* **1** a sack, *Cf* **poca 2**; **2** *with art*, **an sac** asthma, *Cf* **cuing**[2]

sad *vt, pres part* **a' sadail** & **a' sadadh**, throw (*carelessly*), toss, chuck, fling, **sad an cùl na làraidh e** throw it in the back of the lorry, *Cf* **tilg 1**

sagart, sagairt, sagartan *nm* a priest, *Cf* **clèireach** *n* **1, ministear 1, pears-eaglais**

saibhear & **sàibhear**, *gen* **saibheir**, *pl* **saibhearan** *nm* **1** a culvert, a conduit; **2** a sewer

saideal, saideil, saidealan *nm* a satellite

saidhbhir *adj* wealthy, rich, affluent, opulent, *Cf* **beartach**

saidhbhreas, *gen* **saidhbhreis** *nm* wealth, riches, affluence, opulence, *Cf* **beartas, ionmhas, stòras 2**

saidheans, saidheans, saidheansan *nm* science, a science, **'s e saidheans an cuspair as fheàrr leam** science is my favourite subject

saighdear, saighdeir, saighdearan *nm* a soldier, **bha e na shaighdear** he was a soldier, (*hist*) **na saighdearan dearga** the red soldiers, the redcoats (*government troops, esp in Jacobite period*), (*prov*) **ceannard ar fhichead air fichead saighdear** twenty-one captains leading twenty soldiers

saighead, saighde, saighdean *nf* an arrow, (*trad song*) **Saighdean Ghlinn Lìobhann** The Arrows of Glen Lyon

sail, saile, sail(th)ean *nf* (*building*) a beam, a joist, *Cf* **spàrr** *n* **1**

sàil, sàile, sàil(t)ean *nf* a heel (*of foot & shoe*)

sailead, saileid, saileadan *nm* salad, a salad

saill *vt, pres part* **a' sailleadh**, **1** (*fish, meat &c*) salt, preserve, pickle &c (*with salt*); **2** season with salt

saill, *gen* **saille** *nf* fat (*not bodily, Cf* **sult**), grease, *Cf* **crèis, geir 2**

saillear, sailleir, saillearan *nf* a salt-cellar

saillte *adj* salty, salted, salt, **sgadan saillte** salt herring

saimeant *nm invar* cement, concrete

sal, *gen* **sail** *nm* **1** filth, *Cf more usu* **salchar**; **2** dross, *Cf* **smùr**; **3** a stain, *Cf* **smal**

sàl, *gen* **sàil(e)** *nm* **1** salt water, brine; **2** (*esp in songs*) **an sàl** the sea, the ocean, the 'briny', **thar an t-sàile** over/beyond the salt sea, *Cf* **fairge**, *& more usu* **cuan, muir**

salach *adj* dirty, filthy, foul

salachadh, *gen* **salachaidh** *nm* (*the act of*) dirtying, defiling &c (*see senses of* **salaich** *v*)

salaich *vt, pres part* **a' salachadh**, **1** dirty, make dirty, soil; **2** defile, sully, *Cf* **truaill 1 & 2**

salann, *gen* **salainn** *nm* salt

salchar, *gen* **salchair** *nm* dirt, filth, *Cf less usu* **sal 1**

salm, *gen & pl* **sailm** *nmf* a psalm, (*Bibl*) **Leabhar nan Salm** the Book of Psalms

salmadair, salmadair, salmadairean *nm* a psalm book, a psalter

saltair *vt, pres part* **a' saltairt**, tread, trample, **saltair fìon-dearcan** tread grapes

sam bith *see* **bith** *n* **2**

sàmhach *adj* **1** quiet, silent, **bi sàmhach!** be quiet! (*Cf* **ist!**), *Cf* **tosdach**; **2** (*weather, person &c*) peaceful, still, quiet, tranquil, **feasgar sàmhach** a peaceful/quiet evening, (*prov*) **far an sàmhaiche** (*superlative*) **an t-uisge, is ann as doimhne e** the water's deepest where it's stillest, *Cf* **ciùin**

samhail, samhla, samhailean *nm* an equivalent, a match, a likeness, the (spitting) image of someone, the like(s) of something or someone, **cha robh a samhail ann a-riamh** the like(s) of her never existed before, *Cf* **leithid, mac-samhail 2, seis(e)**

Samhain, *gen* **Samhna** *nf* **1** Hallowtide, All Souls' *or* All Saints' Day (1st November), **Oidhche Shamhna** Halloween; **2** *with art*, **an t-Samhain** November

sàmhchair, *gen* **sàmhchaire** *nf* **1** quiet, quietness, silence, *Cf* **tosd**; **2** peacefulness, stillness, tranquility, *Cf* **ciùineas**

samhla(dh), samhlaidh, samhlaidhean *nm* **1** a resemblance, a likeness; **2** a symbol, a sign, **is e '-an' samhla an iolra** '-an' is a sign of the plural, *Cf* **comharra(dh) 2**; **3** (*Lit &c*) a simile, a comparison; **4** an allegory, a parable, *Cf* **cosamhlachd**

samhlaich *vti, pres part* **a' samhlachadh, 1** (*vt*) compare, liken (**ri** to); **2** (*vi*) *in expr* **samhlaich ri cuideigin** resemble someone

samhradh, samhraidh, samhraidhean *nm* summer, a summer, **as t-samhradh** in (the) summer, **sgoil** *f* **shamhraidh** a summer school

san *see* **anns an**

sanas, sanais, sanasan *nm* **1** a (written) announcement, notice or message (*publicly displayed*), an advertisement, a placard, **sanas-reic** an advertisement; **2** a hint, a sign, **thug e sanas dhomh le priobadh a shùla** he gave me a hint/sign with a wink of his eye

sanasaich *vti, pres part* **a' sanasachadh**, advertise

sannt, *gen* **sannta** *nm* avarice, greed (*esp for wealth*), covetousness

sanntach *adj* greedy (*esp for wealth*), avaricious, covetous, *Cf* **gionach 1**

sanntaich *vt, pres part* **a' sanntachadh**, covet (*wealth &c of others*)

saobh *adj* foolish, misguided, wrong-headed (*applied to what is false or foolish or goes against the established norm*), *now esp in compounds, eg* **saobh-smuain** *m* a whim, **saobh-shruth** *m* an eddy *or* counter-current, **saobh-chràbhadh** *m* superstition

saobhaidh, saobhaidh, saobhaidhean *nf* (*of animal*) a den, a lair

saoghal, saoghail, saoghalan *nm* **1** a world, **an saoghal** the world (*Cf* **talamh 1**), **mo chuid-sa den t-saoghal** my worldly possessions (*lit* my share of the world), **càit air an t-saoghal a bheil iad?** where on earth/in the world are they? **ann an saoghal a' ghnìomhachais** in the business world/the world of business; **2** (*trad*) a life, a lifetime,

rim shaoghal in/during my life(time) (*Cf* **beò 2, maireann 1**), **saoghal fada dhuibh!** long life to you!, *Cf* **beatha 1**

saoghalta *adj* **1** wordly, pertaining to the world, *Cf* **talmhaidh; 2** materialistic

saoil *vi, pres part* **a' saoilsinn**, think, consider, suppose, believe, **saoilidh mi gu bheil thu ceart** I think/consider that you're right, **saoil(ibh) am bi stoirm ann?** do you think there'll be a storm?, *also* I wonder if there'll be a storm, *Cf* **creid 2, smaointich 3**

saor *vt, pres part* **a' saoradh, 1** free, set free, liberate, rescue (*from captivity, oppression &c*), *Cf* **sgaoil** *n*; **2** save, redeem, deliver (*esp from sin*), *Cf* **sàbhail 2**

saor, *gen & pl* **saoir** *nm* a joiner, a carpenter, **saor-àirneis** a cabinetmaker

saor *adj* (*opposite of* **daor**) **1** free, at liberty, **tha na prìosanaich saor a-nis** the prisoners are free now, **saor-làithean** *mpl &* **làithean-saora** *mpl* holidays; **2** *in expr* **saor o** free from, untroubled by, without, (*song*) **gheibh thu do roghainn saor o dhearbhadh** you'll get what you want without dispute/argument, *also* **saor is** free/shut/quit of (*Cf* **cuidhteas 2**); **3** free (of charge), *esp in expr* **saor 's an asgaidh** free of charge, absolutely free; **4** cheap, **biadh saor** cheap food

saoradh, *gen* **saoraidh** *nm* **1** (*the act of*) freeing, saving &c (*see senses of* **saor** *v*); **2** liberation, deliverance

saorsa *nf invar, also* **saorsainn**, *gen* **saorsainne** *nf*, **1** freedom, liberty; **2** salvation, redemption, deliverance (*esp from sin*), *Cf* **sàbhaladh 2**

saothair, saothrach, saothraichean *nf* **1** labour, toil, hard work, **chan fhiach dhut do shaothair** it's not worth your while/effort; **2** (*childbirth*) labour; **3** (*industry &c*) labour, **cosgaisean saothrach** labour costs

saothrachadh, *gen* **saothrachaidh** *nm* **1** (*the act of*) labouring, manufacturing &c (*see senses of* **saothraich** *v*); **2** manufacture

saothraich *vti, pres part* **a' saothrachadh, 1** labour, toil, work very hard, (*as vt*) **shaothraich iad am fearann** they laboured at the land; **2** manufacture

saothraichte *adj* manufactured

sàr *adv, adj & prefix* (*precedes noun &c, & aspirates/lenites where possible*), (*trad*) very, extremely, true &c (*according to context*), **sàr-Ghàidheal** *m* a Gael through and through, a true Gael, **sàr-obair** *f* a master work, a masterpiece, **sàr-mhath** *adj* excellent

sàrachadh, *gen* **sàrachaidh** *nm* **1** (*the act of*) oppressing, vexing &c (*see senses of* **sàraich** *v*); **2** oppression

sàraich *vt, pres part* **a' sàrachadh, 1** (*phys*) oppress, do violence to; **2** (*emotionally &c*) vex, harass, trouble, bother, weary, fatigue, distress, **air mo shàrachadh le fiachan** harassed/troubled by debts, *Cf* **claoidh** *v* **2, cuir dragh air** (*see* **dragh 1**), **leamhaich**

sàraichte *adj* boring, tedious, *cf* **fadalach 2**

sàs, *gen* **sàis** *nm* **1** the state of being caught, trapped or captured, *esp in expr* **an sàs** caught *&c*, **chaidh i an sàs sna drisean** she got caught in the brambles, **tha iad an sàs** they are in captivity, **radan an sàs ann an ribe** a rat caught in a trap, **cuir** *v* **an sàs** capture, arrest, *Cf* **làmh 2**; **2** the state of being busy at, engaged or involved in, something, **bha mi an sàs ann am poileataics aig an àm sin** I was involved in politics at that time; **3** *in expr* **bi** *v* **an sàs ann an cuideigin** nag, natter, pester, be on at, someone, **bha i an sàs annam fad na h-ùine airson an taigh a pheantadh** she was on at me all the time to paint the house

sàsachadh, *gen* **sàsachaidh** *nm* **1** (*the act of*) pleasing, satisfying &c (*see senses of* **sàsaich** *v*); **2** satisfaction

sàsaich *vt, pres part* **a' sàsachadh**, **1** please, content, satisfy, *Cf* **riaraich 1**; **2** satisfy, fill, sate, satiate

sàsaichte *adj* **1** contented, pleased, satisfied, *Cf* **riaraichte, toilichte**; **2** full, sated, satiated, glutted

Sasainn *nf* (*invar*) England

Sasannach, *gen & pl* **Sasannaich** *nm* an Englishman, *also as adj* **Sasannach** English

sàsar, sàsair, sàsaran *nm* a saucer, *Cf* **flat**

sàth *vti, pres part* **a' sàthadh**, **1** stab; **2** thrust, push, shove, **sàth a-steach sa phreas e** shove/push it into the cupboard, *Cf* **brùth 2, put 1, spàrr** *v*

sàth, *gen* **sàith** *nm* one's fill, **fhuair sinn ar sàth dheth** we got our fill/ more than enough of it, (*song*) **nam biodh agams' an sin cupan, dh'òlainn dhith mo shàth** if I had had a cup there, I would have drunk my fill of it, *Cf* **làn** *n* **1, leòr 1**

sàthadh, sàthaidh, sàthaidhean *nm* **1** (*the act of*) stabbing, thrusting &c (*see senses of* **sàth** *v*); **2** a stab; **3** a thrust, a push, a shove

seabhag, seabhaig, seabhagan *nmf* a hawk, a falcon, (*prov*) **cha dèanar seabhag den chlamhan** you can't make a hawk out of a buzzard

seac *&* **seachd**, *reinforcing adverbial element, eg* **seac àraidh** (*adv*) especially, particularly (*Cf* **àraidh 3, sònraichte 3**), **tha mi seac searbh sgìth dheth!** I'm sick and tired/heartily sick of it/him

seacaid, seacaide, seacaidean *nf* (*clothing, book &c*) a jacket

seach *prep* **1** instead of, rather than, **gabhaidh sinn iasg seach feòil** we'll take fish rather than/instead of meat; **2** compared to, in comparison to, **tha gròiseidean searbh seach mil** gooseberries are bitter compared to honey, *Cf* **coimeas** *n* **3**; **3** (*esp of a sequence*) after, **fear seach fear, chaidh iad tron doras** one (man) after another/

one by one/each one in turn, they went through the door, *also in expr* **mu seach** *adv* in turn, alternately, turn and turn about, *also* one by one, one after the other, **thug iad greis mu seach air an spaid** they each spent a while in turn/each took a turn for a while at the spade, **thog i na piseagan tè mu seach** she picked up the kittens one after the other; **4** (*trad*) *adv & prep* past, by, **chaidh i seach** she passed/went by (*Cf more usu* **seachad**), **chaidh i seach an taigh** she passed/went past the house (*Cf more usu* **seachad air**)

seachad *adv* **1** (*movement*) past, by, **chaidh bus làn seachad** a full bus went past/by, **bhuail e a-steach san dol seachad** he dropped in in passing/(*Sc*) in the by-gaun; **2** (*time*) past, **cuir** *v* **seachad ùine** pass/spend time, (*Sc*) put by time, **tha an oidhche a' dol seachad gu luath** the night is passing quickly; **3** past, over, finished, **tha na làithean ud seachad** yon days are over, (*of task &c*) **is math seachad e!** it's good that it's finished!; *Cf more trad* **seach 4**; **4** *in expr* **thoir** *v* **seachad** give, give away, **thoir seachad òraid** *f* give a talk, **thoir seachad airgead** *m* give away money

seachad air *prep* (*esp movement*) past, by, **ruith a' chlann seachad oirnn** the children ran past us, *Cf more trad* **seach 4**

seachain(n) *vt, pres part* **a' seachnadh**, avoid, shun, abstain from, keep away from, **seachain meadhan a' bhaile, tha cus trafaig ann** avoid the town centre, there's too much traffic, **seachain boireannaich gun nàire** shun/keep away from shameless women

seachanta *adj* avoidable, **neo-sheachanta** unavoidable, inevitable

seachd *adj & num* seven

seachd *adv see* **seac**

seachdad, seachdaid, seachdadan *nm* seventy (*in alt numbering system*)

seachdain, seachdaine, seachdainean *nf* a week, **seachdain an-diugh** a week today, **air an t-seachdain sa** (during) this week

seachdamh *adj* seventh

seachdnar *nmf invar* seven (*used of people*)

seachnadh, *gen* **seachnaidh** *nm* (*the act of*) avoiding, shunning &c (*see senses of* **seachain** *v*), (*poem*) **An Seachnadh** (Aonghas MacNeacail) The Avoiding, (*on single track road*) **àite** *m* **seachnaidh** passing place

seachran, *gen* **seachrain** *nm* **1** wandering, **rach** *v* **air seachran** go wandering (*see also* **2**), *Cf* **allaban, fuadan 1**; **2** (*the act of*) getting lost or going astray (*phys or morally*), **rach** *v* **air seachran** go astray, err, *Cf* **iomrall 2 & 3**

seada, seada, seadaichean *nmf* a shed

seadag, seadaig, seadagan *nf* a grapefruit

seadh (*v* is *plus obs neuter* **eadh**) *adv expressing non-affirmative* yes, *ie not in answer to a question*, **Aonghais! seadh?** Angus! yes? **bha mi sa bhaile an-dè ... seadh(?) ... agus chunna mi Ailean, Ailean às a' bhùth ... A, seadh! seadh!** I was in town yesterday ... yes/uh-huh/so?/and? ... and I saw Alan, Alan from the shop ... Ah yes, of course!, **seadh dìreach!** absolutely!, definitely!

seadh *nm see* **seagh**

seagal, *gen* **seagail** *nm* rye, **aran seagail** rye bread

seagh *occas* **seadh**, *gen* **seagha**, *pl* **seaghan** *nm* sense, meaning, *esp of words & exprs*, **cha chleachdar am facal san t-seagh sin** the word isn't used in that sense, **tha thu ceart, ann an seagh** you're right, in a sense/way, *Cf* **brìgh 1**

seàla, seàla, seàlaichean *nf* a shawl

sealbh, *gen* **seilbh** *nm* **1** luck, fortune (*usu good*), **sealbh ort!** good luck!, *Cf* **fortan; 2** providence, heaven, **gun glèidh an Sealbh mi!** Heaven help/protect me! (*see also* **seall 3**), **aig sealbh tha brath (carson &c)!** heaven knows (why &c)!, *Cf* **freasdal 3; 3** *same senses as* **seilbh**

sealbhach *adj* **1** lucky, fortunate, **mì-shealbhach** unlucky, unfortunate, *Cf* **fortanach; 2** *same sense as* **seilbheach**

sealbhadair *see* **seilbheadair**

sealbhaich *same senses as* **seilbhich**

sealg *vti*, *pres part* **a' sealg**, hunt, hunt for, chase, **sealg na daimh** hunt the stags

sealg, seilg, sealgan *nf* hunting, a hunt, a chase, (*poem*) **Oran Seachran Seilg** song on a hunt that went wrong

sealgair, sealgair, sealgairean *nm* a hunter, a huntsman, **an Sealgair Mòr** (the constellation) Orion

seall *vti*, *pres part* **a' sealltainn**, **1** see, look (**air** at), behold, **seall orm** look at me, **seall seo!** look at/see this! *Cf* **coimhead 2; 2** (*vt*) show, **seall dhomh na dealbhan a ghabh thu** show me the photos you took, *Cf* **nochd 1; 3** watch over, preserve &c, *usu in excls, to express surprise, indignation &c*, **gu sealladh (Dia/Sealbh) orm!** My Goodness!, For Pete's/Heaven's sake! &c, (*lit* God/Providence/Heaven preserve me!)

sealladh, seallaidh, seallaidhean *nm* **1** sight, eyesight, vision, (*trad*) **is lag mo shealladh** weak is my sight, **an dà shealladh** second sight (*Cf* **taibhsearachd**), *Cf more usu* **fradharc 1, lèirsinn 1; 2** a look, **thug e sealladh neònach orm** he gave me a strange look/looked at me strangely, **sealladh-taoibh** a sideways glance/look, *Cf* **sùil 2; 3** sight (*ie what one can see at a given time*), **a-mach às mo shealladh!** out of my sight!, **thig** *v* **an sealladh/san t-sealladh** come in(to) sight, **rach** *v* **à sealladh/às an t-sealladh** go out of sight, (*song*) **fad mo sheallaidh mun cuairt** as far as I could see all around me, **chaill sinn sealladh air** we lost sight of him, *Cf* **fradharc 2**; **4** a sight, a view, a spectacle, a prospect, (*song*) **seallaidhean bu bhrèagha riamh chan fhaca sùil** (Màiri Mhòr) eye never saw more beautiful views/sights/prospects; **5** a point of view, **tha sin math bhon t-sealladh is gum bi i nas fhaisge a-nise** that's good from the point of view that she'll be nearer now

Sealtainn *nm* Shetland

Sealtainneach, *gen & pl* **Sealtainnich** *nm* a Shetlander, *also as adj* **Sealtainneach** of, from or pertaining to Shetland

seamrag, seamraig, seamragan *nf* **1** shamrock; **2** clover, *Cf* **clòbhar**

sean, *before d, s, t, l, n or r* **seann**, *lenites/aspirates exc for d, s, & t, comp* **(n)as sine**, (*past*) **(n)a bu shine**, *adj* **1** *of people*, old, aged, **tha i a' fàs sean** she's getting old, **dachaigh nan seann daoine** the old folk's/people's home, *Cf* **aosta**; **2** *of objects &c*, old, **seann chaisteal** *m* an old castle, *Cf* **àrsaidh**; **3** old, former, **sna seann làithean** in the old days, **is e seann phoileasman a th' ann dheth** he's a former policeman; **4** *as noun in expr* **o shean** of old, **bha mo dhaoine san sgìre o shean** my people/folks/family were in the district of old/from way back/since long ago; **5** *as prefix,* **sean(n)-** old-, **sean(n)-fhasanta** old-fashioned; **6** (*family relationships*) grand-, great-, **seann-phàrant** *m* a grandparent, *Cf* **sinn-**

seana- *adj prefix* old, (*esp*) **seana-ghille** an old bachelor, **seana-mhaighdeann** an old maid, a spinster

seanailear, seanaileir, seanailearan *nm* a general

seanair, seanar, seanairean *nm* **1** a grandfather; **2** an ancestor, a forebear, **an àm ar seanairean** in our ancestors' time, *Cf* **sinnsear**

seanchaidh, seanchaidh, seanchaidhean *nm* **1** a (traditional) storyteller (*Cf* **sgeulaiche**), a tradition-bearer; **2** (*trad*) a shenachie, *one of the 'office-bearers' of Gaelic society, keeper of the history, tradition. genealogy &c of the clan or race*

seanchas, seanchais, seanchasan *nm* **1** (*trad*) traditional knowledge and lore, culture and tradition, the knowledge in the keeping of a **seanchaidh**, *Cf* **beul-aithris, beul-oideachas**; **2** talk, chat, gossip, news, **tha iad ri seanchas aig ceann a' bhaile** they're busy talking/gossiping at the end of the township, **seanchasan bhon taigh** news/gossip from home, **tha mi air a dhol seachad air mo sheanchas** I've strayed/wandered from the/my point

seanfhacal, seanfhacail, seanfhaclan *nm* a proverb, a saying, an adage, *Cf* **facal 2, ràdh 1**

seang *adj* slim, slender, skinny, lanky, thin, *Cf* **caol** *adj* 2, **tana** 1

seangan, *gen* **seangain**, *pl* **seanganan** & **seangain** *nm* an ant

seanmhair, seanmhar, seanmhairean *nf* a grandmother, *Cf* **seanair** 1

seann *see* **sean**

seantans, seantans, seantansan *nm* (*gram*) a sentence, *Cf more trad* **rosg-rann** (*see* **rosg**¹)

Seapan, *gen* **Seapain** *nf, with art*, **an t-Seapan** Japan

Seapanach, *gen* & *pl* **Seapanaich** *nm* someone from Japan, a Japanese, *also as adj* **Seapanach** Japanese

sear *adj* & *adv, corres to* **an ear** (*see* **ear**), east, eastern, **an taobh sear** & **an taobh an ear** the east(ern side of the country), **sear air Eden** east of Eden, *Cf* **deas** 1, **ear, iar, siar, tuath**¹

searbh *adj* 1 (*esp tastes*) bitter, sour, tart, acrid, harsh, pungent, sharp, unpleasant, *Cf* **geur** 3; 2 (*situation &c*) disagreeable, hard to swallow, **searbh is gun robh sin leatha** disagreeable though that was to her, (*prov*) **ge milis am fìon, tha e searbh ri dhìol** though the wine is sweet, it is bitter to pay for; 3 sarcastic, sardonic, *Cf* **geur** 4; 4 acid

searbhadair, searbhadair, searbhadairean *nm* a towel, *Cf* **tubhailte**

searbhag, searbhaig, searbhagan *nf* acid, an acid

searbhanta, searbhanta, searbhantan *nmf* a servant, a maid-servant, *Cf* **seirbheiseach, sgalag** 2

searg *vti, pres part* **a' seargadh**, (*vti*) dry up, fade, shrivel, wither, decay, (*vi*) fade, waste or pine away, (*vt*) blight, **shearg a' ghaoth an duilleach ùr** the wind blighted/withered the new foliage, **a' seargadh le aois** drying up/fading away/shriveling with age, *Cf* **crìon** *v*

seargach *adj* 1 apt to dry up, fade &c, (*see senses of* **searg** *v*); 2 (*trees*) deciduous

seargadh, *gen* **seargaidh** *nm* (*the act of*) drying up, blighting &c (*see senses of* **searg** *v*); 2 decay; 3 blight

searmon, searmoin, searmonan *nm* a sermon

searmonaich *vi, pres part* **a' searmonachadh**, preach, give or deliver a sermon

searrach, *gen* & *pl* **searraich** *nm* a colt, a foal

searrag, searraig, searragan *nf* 1 a bottle, *Cf more usu* **botal**; 2 a flask

seas *vti, pres part* **a' seasamh**, 1 (*vi*) stand, get on one's feet, **sheas an luchd-èisteachd** the audience stood up, **seas suas/an-àird!** stand up!; 2 (*vt*) stand up for, stand by, support, **seas an còir** stand up for their rights, **cò a sheasas thu?** who will support you/take your part?; 3 (*vi*) endure, last, **aoibhneas a sheasas** joy that will endure, *Cf* **mair**

seasamh, *gen* **seasaimh** *nm* **1** a standing position, *esp in expr* **nam (&c) sheasamh** standing, **bha i na seasamh** she was standing (up); **2** one's footing (*also* **seasamh-chas** *m*), **ghlèidh e a sheasamh(-chas)** he kept his footing; **3** *in expr* **an seasamh nam bonn** on the spot, on the spur of the moment

seasg *adj* **1** (*livestock &c*) barren, sterile; **2** (*dairy or suckling animals*) dry, giving no milk

seasgad, seasgaid, seasgadan *nm* sixty (*in alt numbering system*), **anns na seasgadan** in the sixties

seasgair *adj* **1** cosy, comfortable, snug, **cùil sheasgair** a cosy nook/ corner, *Cf* **cofhurtail**; **2** (*fin*) comfortable, comfortably off, *Cf* **airgeadach**

seasmhach *adj* (*phys & morally*) **1** firm, stable, steady, reliable, dependable, consistent, **gun àite-còmhnaidh seasmhach** of no fixed abode; **2** constant, enduring, durable, lasting, *Cf* **buan, maireannach**

seatlair, seatlair, seatlairean *nm* a settler, *esp in expr* (*pej*) **seatlair geal** a white settler, *applied esp to well-to-do incomers perceived as making little attempt to integrate into or identify with the local community and way of life, Cf* **srainnsear 2**

seic, seice, seicichean *nf* a cheque, **seic-leabhar** *m* a chequebook

Seic, *gen* **Seice** *nf, with art* **an t-Seic** the Czech Republic

Seiceach, *gen & pl* **Seicich** *nm* a Czech, *also as adj* **Seiceach** Czech

seiche, seiche, seicheannan *nf* a skin, a pelt, a hide, **seiche bhàrr laoigh a bhàsaich** a hide from a calf that died, **chaidh a fhliuchadh chun na seiche** he got soaked to the skin, *Cf* **bian 2**

sèid *vti, pres part* **a' sèideadh, 1** (*vi*) blow, **shèid a' ghaoth an ear** the east wind blew, **a' sèideadh air mo chorragan** blowing on my fingers; **2** (*vi*) swell, puff up, *Cf* **at** *v*, **bòc; 3** (*vt*) (*trad*) **sèid a' phìob** blow/play the pipes, (*calque*) **sèid do shròn!** blow your nose!, (*calque*) **sèid suas (ball-coise &c)** blow up, inflate (a football &c)

seilbh (*also* **sealbh**), *gen* **seilbhe**, *pl* **seilbhean** *nf* property, possession, a possession, **gabh** *v* **seilbh air** take possession of

seilbheach (*also* **sealbhach**) *adj* possessive, (*gram*) **buadhair seilbheach** a possessive adjective

seilbheadair (*also* **sealbhadair**), *gen* **seilbheadair**, *pl* **seilbheadairean** *nm* an owner, a proprietor

seilbhich *vt, pres part* **a' seilbheachadh,** own, possess

seilcheag, seilcheig, seilchagan *nf* **1** a snail; **2** a slug

seile *nm invar* saliva, spittle, slaver, *Cf* **ronn 2**

seileach, seilich, seileachan *nm* willow, a willow

seillean, *gen* **seillein**, *pl* **seilleanan** & **seillein** *nm* a bee, **seillean-mòr** a bumble-bee, *Cf* **beach 1**

sèimh *adj* (*person, weather &c*) calm, mild, gentle, **maighdeann shèimh** a gentle maiden, **feasgar sèimh** a calm evening, *Cf* **ciùin; 2** pacific, **an Cuan Sèimh** the Pacific Ocean

sèimhe *nf invar* (*person, weather &c*) calm(ness), mildness, gentleness, *Cf* **ciùineas**

sèimheachadh, *gen* **sèimheachaidh** *nm* (*gram*) aspiration, lenition, *Cf* **analachadh**

seinn *vti, pres part* **a' seinn, 1** sing; **2** (*trad*) play, sound (*a musical instrument*), **sheinn e a' phìob** he played the pipes, *Cf more usu* **cluich** *v*

seinn, *gen* **seinne** *nf* singing, (*instrument, trad*) playing

seinneadair, seinneadair, seinneadairean *nm* a singer

seirbheis, seirbheise, seirbheisean *nf* **1** serving, service, *ie the role or work of a servant, waiter &c*; **2** a service, a favour, **an dèan thu seirbheis bheag dhomh?** will you do me a small service/favour? *Cf* **bàidh 2, fàbhar; 3** (*church*) a service; **4** (*misc contexts, tennis, garage &c*) a service

seirbheiseach, *gen* & *pl* **seirbheisich** *nm* a servant, *Cf* **searbhanta, sgalag 2**

seirc, *gen* **seirce** *nf* **1** (*non-sexual*) love, affection, *Cf more usu* **gràdh 1; 2** (*in Bibl sense*) charity, *Cf* **carthannachd 1**

seirm *vti, pres part* **a' seirm**, ring, ring out, sound, **seirm na cluig** ring the bells, **sheirm a' phìob** the pipe(s) sounded/rang out

seis(e), seise, seisean *nm* **1** the like(s) of something or someone, *Cf* **leithid, samhail; 2** an equal, a match (*ie a worthy or superior opponent*), **fhuair i a seis an là sin!** she met her match that day!

seisean, seisein, seiseanan *nm* **1** a kirk session; **2** (*of meetings, college &c*) a session

sèist, sèist, sèistean *nmf* a siege, **fo shèist** under siege, **dèan/cuir** *v* **sèist air caisteal** &c besiege/lay siege to a castle &c

sèist, sèist, sèistean *nmf* (*song, poetry*) a refrain, a chorus

sèithear, sèithir, sèithrichean *nm* a chair, *Cf* **cathair 1, suidhe 3**

seo & (*trad*) **so** *adj* this, **am fear seo** this man/one, **aig an àm seo** at this time, **an t-seachdain seo chaidh** last week (*lit* this week that went), **an t-seachdain seo tighinn** next week, *Cf* **sa¹, sin** *adj* **1, ud**

seo & (*trad*) **so 1** *pron* this, **cò/dè a tha seo?** who's/what's this? **seo an càr agam** this is my car; **2** *pron* & *adv* here, **seo agad tiodhlac** here's a present for you, **cà'il do bhràthair? seo e** where's your brother? here he is, (*to dog &c*) **a-mach à seo (leat)!** get out of here!; **3** *in exprs*

an seo & (*sometimes more emph*) **ann an s(h)eo**, *advs*, here, **dè a tha thu a' dèanamh an seo?** what are you doing here? (*song*) **chan eil mo leannan ann an seo** my sweetheart isn't here, **tha Seumas an seo! càite? ... ann an sheo?** James is here! where? ... right here?; **4** *corres to* now, *in exprs* **gu ruige seo** & **chun a seo** *advs* up until now, up to now, **cha chuala sinn sgeul air gu ruige seo** we haven't heard anything of him up to now (*lit* up to this), **bho seo a-mach** from now on; *Cf* **sin** *pron*, **siud**

seòbhrach & **sòbhrach**, *gen* **s(e)òbhraich**, *pl* **s(e)òbhraichean** *nf* also **sòbhrag, sòbhraig, sòbhragan** *nf*, a primrose

seòclaid *see* **teòclaid**

seòd, *gen* & *pl* **seòid** *nm* a hero, (*song*) **eilean beag Leòdhais, dachaigh nan seòid** little isle of Lewis, home of heroes, *Cf* **curaidh, gaisgeach, laoch**

seòl *vti, pres part* **a' seòladh**, **1** (*vi*) sail, **a' seòladh dhachaigh** sailing homewards; **2** (*vt*) sail, navigate, steer, **bha Iain ga seòladh** Iain was sailing/steering her; **3** (*vt*) guide, steer, direct, manage (*persons, organisation &c*), govern (*country &c*); **4** (*vt*) direct, show (someone) the way; *Cf* **stiùir** *v*

seòl[1], *gen* & *pl* **siùil** *nm* a sail, **seòl-toisich** a foresail

seòl[2], *gen* & *pl* **siùil** *nm* **1** a way, a method, a means, an expedient, **air an t-seòl seo** in this way, **chan eil seòl air** there's no way/means of doing it, **faigh seòl air rudeigin a dhèanamh** find a way/contrive/manage to do something, **seòl-beatha** a way of life, *Cf* **dòigh 1**; **2** a course or direction of travel, *Cf more usu* **cùrsa 2, iùl 1**

seòladair, seòladair, seòladairean *nm* a sailor, a mariner, a seaman, *Cf* **maraiche**

seòladh, seòlaidh, seòlaidhean *nm* **1** (*the act of*) sailing, navigating, directing &c (*see senses of* **seòl** *v*); **2** an address (*ie postal*); **3** *usu in pl* **seòlaidhean** guide-lines, instructions, directions

seòl-mara *see* **muir**

seòlta *adj* **1** cunning, artful, crafty, wily, *Cf* **carach 1, fiar** *adj* **4**; **2** *occas in more favourable sense*, ingenious, resourceful, full of expedients, shrewd

seòmar, seòmair, seòmraichean *nm* a room, (*Sc*) an apartment (& *Cf Sc* chaumer), **seòmar-cadail** & **seòmar-leapa** a bedroom, **seòmar-ionnlaid** a bathroom, **seòmar-mullaich** an attic, a garret, (*Cf* **lobht(a) 2**), *Cf* **rùm 2**

seòrsa, *gen* **seòrsa**, *pl* **seòrsaichean** & **seòrsachan** *nm* **1** a sort, a kind, a type, a category, **dè an seòrsa là a th' ann?** what sort of a day is it? **rudan de gach seòrsa** things of every kind, all sorts/kinds of things, **cha do leugh mi leabhar den t-seòrsa** I haven't read such a book/

a book of that kind (*Cf* **leithid**), *Cf* **gnè** 1; 2 (*natural hist*) a genus, a species, *Cf* **cineal** 2, **gnè** 2; 3 a (social) class, **chan ionann do sheòrsa 's mo sheòrsa-sa** your class and mine are not alike

seòrsachadh, *gen* **seòrsachaidh** *nm* 1 (*the act of*) classifying &c (*see senses of* **seòrsaich** *v*); 2 classification

seòrsaich *vt, pres part* **a' seòrsachadh**, classify, sort, arrange (*according to type &c*), *Cf* **òrdaich** 3

seud, *gen* **seòid**, *pl* **seudan** & **seòid** *nm* a jewel, a gem, a precious stone, *Cf* **àilleag** 1, **leug**

seumarlan, *gen* & *pl* **seumarlain** *nm* 1 (*estates &c*) a factor, a land-agent, *Cf* **maor** 1; 2 a chamberlain

Seumasach, *gen* & *pl* **Seumasaich** *nm* (*hist*) a Jacobite, *also as adj* **Seumasach** Jacobite

seun, **seuna**, **seun(t)an** *nm* 1 a spell, a charm, *Cf* **geas** 1, **ortha**; 2 (*magic &c*) an amulet (*or other object to protect against spells &c*), a charm

seunta *adj* enchanted, bewitched, spellbound, charmed (*by magic*), *Cf* **geas** 2

sgadan, *gen* & *pl* **sgadain** *nm* herring, a herring, (*trad, hist*) **clann-nighean an sgadain** the herring lasses/girls (*itinerant fish gutters*)

sgàil *vt, pres part* **a' sgàileadh**, shade, darken, veil, mask, cloak in darkness or shade, eclipse, *Cf* **duibhrich**

sgàil *nf see* **sgàil(e)**

sgailc *vt, pres part* **a' sgail(eadh)**, slap, smack

sgailc, **sgailce**, **sgailcean** *nf* 1 a sharp blow, a slap, a smack, (*Sc*) a skelp, **sgailc mun chluais** a crack/slap around the ear, *Cf* **sgealp** 1, **sgleog**; 2 a sharp sound, a crack, *Cf* **brag**; 3 a swig, a good swallow or drink of liquid, **ghabh e sgailc mhath uisge-bheatha** he took a good swig of whisky, *Cf* **balgam** 2, **steallag**; 4 baldness, *Cf* **sgall** 2

sgàil(e), **sgàile**, **sgàilean** *nf* 1 shade, shadow, a shade, a veil, a mask, a film, a covering, **sgàil-sùla** an eyelid, **sgàil-lampa** a lampshade, **fo sgàil na h-oidhche** under the shadow/veil/covering of night, **fo sgàil craoibhe** in/beneath the shade of a tree, *Cf* **dubhar**; 2 a ghost, a spectre, a (*ghostly*) shade, *Cf* **tannasg** & *more usu* **taibhse**

sgàileadh, *gen* **sgàilidh** *nm* (*the act of*) shading, masking &c (*see senses of* **sgàil** *v*)

sgàilean, **sgàilein**, **sgàileanan** *nm* 1 *dimin of* **sgàil(e)**; 2 an umbrella (*also* **sgàilean-uisge**), **sgàilean-grèine** a parasol, a sun-shade; 3 (*TV &c*) a screen

sgàin *vti, pres part* **a' sgàineadh**, burst, crack, split, **bha am baraille air sgàineadh** the barrel was/had split, (*prov*) **cha sgàin màthair leanaibh** a mother with a child to raise doesn't burst (*with over-eating*), *Cf* **sgoilt**

sgàineadh, sgàinidh, sgàinidhean *nm* **1** (*the act of*) bursting, cracking, splitting; **2** a split, a crack, **sgàineadh sa chreig** a split in the rock; *Cf* **sgoltadh**

sgàird, *gen* **sgàirde** *nf, with art*, **an sgàird** diarrhoea, *Cf* **buinneach**

sgairt[1], **sgairte, sgairtean** *nf* a diaphragm

sgairt[2], **sgairte, sgairtean** *nf* **1** a yell, **dèan** *v* **sgairt** yell, *Cf* **glaodh** *n*; **2** energy, activity, bustle, enthusiasm, gusto, vigour, *Cf more usu* **brìgh 4, lùth 3, spionnadh**

sgairteil *adj*, **1** (*persons*) brisk, energetic, active, bustling, enthusiastic, vigorous, *Cf* **brìghmhor 2, lùthmhor 3**; **2** (*weather*) blowy, blustery, gusty (*ie windy but not stormy*)

sgait, sgaite, sgaitean *nf* a skate (*ie the fish*)

sgal *vi, pres part* **a' sgaladh**, yell, squeal, cry out (*esp shrilly and suddenly*)

sgal, sgala, sgalan *nm* **1** an onset or outburst of something, *esp* a squall, a blast of wind; **2** a yell, a squeal, a cry (*esp shrill & sudden*)

sgàl, *gen & pl* **sgàil** *nm* a tray

sgàla, sgàla, sgàlaichean *nf* (*music*) a scale

sgaladh, *gen* **sgalaidh** *nm* (*the act of*) yelling &c (*see senses of* **sgal** *v*)

sgalag, sgalaig, sgalagan *nf* **1** (*trad*) a farm servant; **2** a skivvy, a menial, a flunkey

sgalanta *adj* (*sound, voice*) shrill

sgall, *gen* **sgaill** *nm* **1** a bald patch (*on head*); **2** baldness, *Cf* **sgailc 4**

sgallach *adj* bald(-headed), *Cf* **maol 2**

Sgalpach, *gen & pl* **Sgalpaich** *nm* someone from Scalpay (**Sgalpaigh na Hearadh**), *also as adj*, **Sgalpach** of, from or pertaining to Scalpay

sgamhan, sgamhain, sgamhanan *nm* a lung

sgaoil *vti, pres part* **a' sgaoileadh**, **1** spread, spread out, scatter, disperse, **sgaoil i a gàirdeanan** she stretched/spread out her arms, **sgaoil na fògarraich air feadh an t-saoghail** the cleared people scattered throughout the world, **sgaoil an sgoil** the school dispersed/(*Sc*) skailed, **seallaidhean brèagha air an sgaoileadh fodhpa** beautiful views spread out beneath them, *Cf* **sgap**; **2** (*vt*) release, free, loosen, untie, disentangle, *Cf more usu* **fuasgail 1 & 2**

sgaoil *nm invar* liberty, freedom, *esp in exprs* **fa/ma/mu sgaoil** *adv* free, at liberty, **cuir/leig** *v* **mu sgaoil** set free, liberate, release (*Cf* **fuasgail 1, saor** *v* **1**), *Cf more usu* **saorsa 1**

sgaoileadh, *gen* **sgaoilidh** *nm* **1** (*the act of*) spreading, scattering, releasing &c (*see senses of* **sgaoil** *v*); **2** dispersal, (*Sc*) skailin, (*Sc*) lowsin

sgaoth, sgaotha, sgaothan *nm* **1** a great mass or multitude; **2** *esp* a swarm of insects

sgaothaich *vi, pres part* **a' sgaothachadh**, **1** flock, mass, assemble in great numbers; **2** *esp (of insects &c)* swarm

sgap *vti, pres part* **a' sgapadh**, scatter, *Cf less brusque* **sgaoil** *v* **1**

sgar *vti, pres part* **a' sgaradh**, separate, break up *or* apart, split up *or* apart, sever

sgaradh, sgaraidh, sgaraidhean *nm* **1** (*the act of*) separating &c (*see senses of* **sgar** *v*); **2** separation, a separation, severance &c, (*see senses of* **sgar** *v*); **3** (*esp of marriage*) separation, **sgaradh-pòsaidh** divorce, a divorce, *Cf* **dealachadh 2**

sgarbh, *gen & pl* **sgairbh** *nm* a cormorant, **sgarbh an sgumain** a shag (*lit* tufted cormorant)

sgarfa, sgarfa, sgarfaichean *nmf* a scarf, *Cf more trad* **stoc**²

sgàrlaid *adj* scarlet

sgath *vt, pres part* **a' sgath(adh)**, cut off, lop off, prune

sgàth, sgàtha, sgàthan *nm* **1** (*trad*) shadow, shade, protection; **2** (*trad*) fear; **3** *now usu in expr* **air sgàth** *prep, with gen,* on account of, because of, **air sgàth na h-aimsire** because of the weather, **'s ann air mo sgàth-sa a rinn e e** it was because of me/on my account/ for my sake that he did it, **ealain air sgàth ealain** art for art's sake, *Cf* **a chionn, airson 3, brìgh 5**

sgàthan, sgàthain, sgàthanan *nm* a mirror, a looking-glass, (*saying*) **is math an sgàthan sùil caraid** a friend's eye makes a good mirror

sgeadachadh, *gen* **sgeadachaidh** *nm* **1** (*the act of*) adorning, clothing &c (*see senses of* **sgeadaich** *v*) *Cf* **sgèimheachadh**; **2** embellishment, *Cf* **maiseachadh 2**

sgeadaich *vt, pres part* **a' sgeadachadh**, **1** adorn, decorate, ornament, embellish, beautify, prettify, *Cf* **maisich, sgèimhich**; **2** dress (up), clothe (*esp attractively*); **3** attend to (*various objects to tidy them or make them function better*), *eg* **sgeadaich an teine/an lampa** make up the fire, trim the lamp

sgealb *vti*, **1** split, splinter, shatter, dash/break into pieces, (*esp wood or stone*) chip, *Cf* **sgoilt, smùid** *v* **2**, **spealg** *v*; **2** carve, *Cf* **snaigh**

sgealb, sgeilb, sgealban *nf* **1** a chip, a splinter, a fragment *esp one broken or cut from wood or stone*; **2** (*IT*) a chip

sgealbag, sgealbaig, sgealbagan *nf* an index finger

sgealp, sgealpa, sgealpan *nf* **1** a sharp blow, a slap, a smack, (*Sc*) a skelp, *Cf* **sgailc** *n* **1, sgleog**; **2** a sharp sound, a crack, *Cf* **brag, sgailc** *n* **2**

sgeap, sgip, sgeap(aiche)an *nf* a beehive, (*Sc*) a skep

sgeilb, sgeilbe, sgeilbean *nf* a chisel, *Cf* **gilb**

sgeileid, sgeileide, sgeileidean *nf* a skillet

sgeilp, sgeilp, sgeilpichean *nf* a shelf

sgèimheach & **sgeumhach** *adj* beautiful, elegant, graceful, *Cf* **bòidheach, eireachdail, maiseach**

sgèimheachadh, *gen* **sgèimheachaidh** *nm* **1** (*the act of*) adorning, ornamenting &c (*see senses of* **sgèimhich** *v*), *Cf* **sgeadachadh 1**; **2** adornment, ornamentation

sgèimhich, *also* **sgeumhaich** & **sgiamhaich,** *vt, pres part* **a' sgèimheachadh,** adorn, ornament, beautify, deck (**le** with), *Cf* **maisich 1, sgeadaich 1**

sgeir, sgeire, sgeirean *nf* a skerry, a rock (*in the sea near the shore, usu covered & uncovered by the tide*)

sgeith *vti, pres part* **a' sgeith(eadh),** vomit, spew, throw *or* bring up, be sick, *Cf* **dìobhair, tilg 3**

sgeul, *gen & pl* **sgeòil** *nm* **1** a story, a tale (*often trad in content*), **sgeul air na daoine-sìth** a tale about the fairy folk, (*poem*) **gun bhristeadh cridhe an sgeòil** (Somhairle MacGill-Eain) without the heartbreak of the tale, *Cf* **sgeulachd**; **2** news, information, tidings, a piece of news, a report, (*song*) **bochd an sgeul a chuala mi** sad is the report/ news I have heard, *Cf* **fios 3, naidheachd 1**; **3** (*fam*) a sign (*of something or someone*), **a bheil sgeul air Ruairidh?** is there any sign of Rory?

sgeulach *adj* **1** like a tale; **2** fond of tales; **3** *esp in adv expr* **gu h-aon-sgeulach** unanimously

sgeulachd, sgeulachd, sgeulachdan *nf* a story (*usu less trad in content than* **sgeul**), **sgeulachdan goirid** short stories, **innis sgeulachd dhuinn!** tell us a story! *Cf* **naidheachd 2, sgeul 1, stòiridh**

sgeulaiche, sgeulaiche, sgeulaichean *nm* a storyteller

sgeunach *adj* (*esp of animals*) **1** timid, apt to take fright or bolt or shy; **2** skittish, mettlesome

sgiamh *vi, pres part* **a' sgiamhadh, a' sgiamhail** & **a' sgiamhaich,** squeal, shriek, yell, *Cf* **sgreuch** *v*

sgiamh, sgiamha, sgiamhan *nm* a squeal, a shriek, a yell, *Cf* **sgairt**² **1, sgreuch** *n*

sgian, *gen* **sgine** & **sgeine,** *dat* **sgithinn,** *pl* **sgeinan** & **sgineachan** *nf* a knife

sgiath, sgèithe, sgiathan *nf* **1** a wing, (*song*) **an uiseag air a sgiath** (Màiri Mhòr) the lark on the (*lit* its) wing; **2** (*armour &c*) a shield; **3** (*occas*) shelter, protection, *Cf more usu* **dìon** *n*

sgiathaich *vi, pres part* **a' sgiathadh,** fly, *Cf* **itealaich**

Sgiathanach *same as* **Sgitheanach**

sgil, sgil, sgilean *nm* skill, a skill

sgileil *adj* skilful, skilled

sgillinn, sgillinne, sgillinnean *nf* **1** a penny, **deich sgilinn** 10p, *also in expr* **gun sgillinn ruadh (no geal)** without a penny/cent/brass farthing, stony broke, penniless, skint; **2** (*trad*) a shilling Scots; **3** (*hist*) *in land valuation* a shilling-land, (*placename*) **Fichead Sgillinn** Twenty Shilling Land

sgioba, sgioba, sgioban *nmf* **1** a crew (*of boat &c*); **2** a team, **sgioba ball-coise** a football team

sgiobair, sgiobair, sgiobairean *nm* a skipper, a captain (*of boat, team &c*), *Cf* **caiptean 1**

sgiobalta *adj* **1** (*of room, space &c*) neat, tidy, tidied up; **2** (*of person, object*) neat, tidy, trim, *Cf* **cuimir 2, grinn 3, snasail; 3** (*esp of persons*) active, quick, handy, *Cf* **deas 4, èasgaidh, tapaidh 1**

sgioblachadh, *gen* **sgioblachaidh** *nm* (*the act of*) tidying &c (*see senses of* **sgioblaich** *v*)

sgioblaich *vti, pres part* **a' sgioblachadh**, tidy (up), put right or straight, **sgioblaich an rùm agad!** tidy your room!

sgiorradh, sgiorraidh, sgiorraidhean *nm* **1** an accident, *Cf more usu* **tubaist; 2** slipping, a slip, stumbling, a stumble, *Cf* **tuisleadh 1 & 2**

sgiort, sgiorta, sgiortan *nf* a skirt

sgìos & **sgìths** *nmf invar* tiredness, weariness, fatigue, **bha coltas na sgìths oirre** she looked tired/weary

sgìre, sgìre, sgìrean *nf* **1** a district, an area, a locality, **muinntir na sgìre** the people of the district, the local people, (*formerly*) **comhairle na sgìre** the district council, *Cf* **ceàrn; 2** a parish, *Cf* **sgìreachd**

sgìreachd, sgìreachd, sgìreachdan *nf* a parish, *Cf* **sgìre 2**

sgi, sgi(the), sgithean *nf* a ski

sgìth *adj* tired, weary (*phys or emotionally*), *see also* **seac**

sgitheach, *gen* & *pl* **sgith(e)ich** *nm* whitethorn; hawthorn

sgìtheachadh, *gen* **sgìtheachaidh** *nm* (*the act of*) tiring, wearying (*see senses of* **sgìthich** *v*)

Sgitheanach, *gen* & *pl* **Sgitheanaich** *nm* a Skyeman, someone from Skye (**an t-Eilean Sgitheanach**), *also as adj*, **Sgitheanach** of, from or pertaining to Skye

sgìtheil *adj* tiring, wearying, wearisome

sgìthich *vti, pres part* **a' sgìtheachadh**, tire, weary, make or become tired or weary

sgithich *vi, pres part* **a' sgitheadh**, ski

sgìths *see* **sgìos**

sgiùrs *vt, pres part* **a' sgiùrsadh**, scourge, whip, *Cf more usu* **cuip** *v*

sgiùrsair, sgiùrsair, sgiùrsairean *nm* a scourge, a whip, *Cf more usu* **cuip** *n*

sglàib *nf invar (building)* plaster

sglàibeadair, sglàibeadair, sglàibeadairean *nm (building)* a plasterer

sglèat, sglèata, sglèatan *nm* slate, a slate, **mullach sglèata** a slate roof

sglèatair, sglèatair, sglèatairean *nm (building)* a slater

sgleog, sgleoig, sgleogan *nf* a slap, a sharp blow, *Cf* **sgailc** *n* **1**, **sgealp 1**

sgob *vti, pres part* **a' sgobadh**, **1** snatch; **2** sting, bite; **3** peck

sgoch *vt, pres part* **a' sgochadh**, sprain, strain *(ankle &c)*, *Cf* **siach**

sgoil, sgoile, sgoiltean *nf* **1** a school, **sgoil-àraich** a nursery school, **bun-sgoil** a primary school, **àrd-sgoil** a high/secondary school, **tha i anns an sgoil** she's at school; **2** schooling, education, **fhuair sinn ar sgoil san Oban** we were educated/got our schooling in Oban, *Cf* **foghlam**

sgoilear, sgoileir, sgoilearan *nm* **1** a (school) pupil; **2** a scholar

sgoilearachd, sgoilearachd, sgoilearachdan *nf* **1** scholarship, learning, erudition; **2** a scholarship, a bursary

sgoilt & **sgolt** *vti, pres part* **a' sgoltadh**, split, cleave, crack, slit, *Cf* **sgàin**

sgoinneil *adj (fam)* great, super, smashing, **duine** *m* **sgoinneil** a great/super guy, **là** *m* **sgoinneil** a smashing day, **bha sin dìreach sgoinneil!** that was just great/grand!, *Cf* **gasta 2, glan** *adj* **2**

sgol *vt, pres part* **a' sgoladh**, rinse

sgolt *see* **sgoilt**

sgoltadh, sgoltaidh, sgoltaidhean *nm* **1** *(the act of)* splitting, cleaving &c *(see senses of* **sgoilt** *v)*; **2** a split, a cleft, a crack, a slit, a chink; *Cf* **sgàineadh**

sgona, sgona, sgonaichean *nmf* a scone, *Cf more trad* **bonnach 3**

sgonn, *gen* **sgoinn** & **sguinn,** *pl* **sgonnan** & **sguinn** *nm* a block, a lump, a hunk of anything, **sgonn cloiche** a block/lump of stone, **sgonn arain** a thick slice/a hunk of bread, *Cf* **ceap 1, cnap 1, ploc 2** & **3**

sgòr, sgòir, sgòraichean *nm (games &c)* a score, *Cf* **cunntas 5**

sgòrnan, sgòrnain, sgòrnanan *nm* a gullet, a throat, a windpipe, **meall an sgòrnain** *m* the adam's apple

sgoth, sgotha, sgothan *nf* a skiff, a sailing boat, **sgoth-long** a yacht sgòth, sgòtha, sgòthan *nf* cloud, a cloud, *Cf* neul 1

sgòthach *adj* cloudy, *Cf* neulach

sgraing, sgrainge, sgraingean *nf* a frown, an angry or sullen look, a scowl, *Cf* gruaim 2, mùig

sgreab, sgreaba, sgreaban *nf* a scab

sgread *vi, pres part* a' sgreadadh & a' sgreadail, scream, screech, shriek, *Cf* sgreuch *v*

sgread, sgreada, sgreadan *nm* a scream, a screech, a shriek, *Cf* sgreuch *n*

sgreadhail, sgreadhaile, sgreadhailean *nf* a trowel

sgreamh, *gen* sgreamha & sgreimhe *nm* loathing, disgust, *Cf* gràin 2

sgreamhail *adj* disgusting, loathsome, nauseating, (*Sc*) scunnersome, *Cf* gràineil 1 & 2, sgreataidh

sgreataidh *adj same senses as* sgreamhail

sgreuch *vi, pres part* a' sgreuchail, scream, screech, *Cf* sgread *v*

sgreuch, sgreucha, sgreuchan *nm* a scream, a screech, *Cf* sgread *n*

sgrìob *vti, pres part* a' sgrìobadh, 1 scratch or scrape the surface of something, sgrìob e am bòrd ùr he scratched the new table; 2 scrape or rub the surface of something (*to clean it*), sgrìob am buntàta scrape the potatoes; 3 scratch (*with fingernails*), *Cf* sgròb, tachais; 4 furrow (*esp the ground*)

sgrìob, sgrìoba, sgrìoban *nf* 1 a scratch, a scrape on surface of something; 2 (*farming*) a furrow, *Cf* clais 3; 3 a trip, an excursion, a jaunt, (*song*) bheir mi sgrìob do dh'Uibhist leat I'll take a trip to Uist with you, *Cf* cuairt 3, turas 1 & 2

sgrìobadh, *gen* sgrìobaidh *nm* (*the act of*) scratching, scraping &c (*see senses of* sgrìob *v*)

sgrìoban, sgrìobain, sgrìobanan *nm* a hoe, *Cf* todha

sgrìobh *vti, pres part* a' sgrìobhadh, 1 write, sgrìobh iad thugam they wrote to me, bidh e a' sgrìobhadh bàrdachd he writes poetry

sgrìobhadair, sgrìobhadair, sgrìobhadairean *nm* a writer, *Cf* sgrìobhaiche

sgrìobhadh, sgrìobhaidh, sgrìobhaidhean *nm* 1 (*the act of*) writing; 2 writing, a piece of writing, tha am balach beag math air sgrìobhadh the wee boy's good at writing, sgrìobhaidhean Aristotle the writings of Aristotle; 2 (*also* làmh-sgrìobhadh) handwriting, script

sgrìobhaiche, sgrìobhaiche, sgrìobhaichean *nm* a writer, *Cf* sgrìobhadair

sgriobtar, sgriobtair, sgriobtairean *nm* Scripture

sgrios *vti, pres part* **a' sgrios** & **a' sgriosadh**, destroy, ruin, wreck, *Cf* **creach** *v* 2, **mill** 1

sgrios, sgriosa, sgriosan *nm* destruction, ruin, (*excl*) **mo sgrios!** my ruin is upon me!, woe is me!, *Cf* **creach** *n* 2

sgriosadh, *gen* **sgriosaidh** *nm* (*the act of*) destroying &c (*see senses of* **sgrios** *v*)

sgriosail *adj* 1 destructive, apt to ruin or wreck, *Cf* **millteach**; 2 pernicious; 3 (*more fam*) terrible, dreadful, awful, **chaill mi m' obair! tha sin sgriosail!** I lost my job! that's awful!

sgriubha, sgriubha, sgriubhaichean *nmf* (*joinery*) a screw, *Cf* **bithis**

sgriubhaire, sgriubhaire, sgriubhairean *nm* a screwdriver

sgròb *vti, pres part* **a' sgròbadh**, scratch (*with fingernails*), *Cf* **sgrìob** *v* 3, **tachais** 1

sgrùd *vt, pres part* **a' sgrùdadh**, 1 scrutinize, examine, look into, investigate, study, **tha sinn a' sgrùdadh dhòighean ùra air cosgaisean a lùghdachadh** we're looking at/into new ways of decreasing costs, *Cf* **rannsaich** 3; 2 (*accounts*) audit

sgrùdadh, sgrùdaidh, sgrùdaidhean *nm* 1 (*the act of*) scrutinizing, studying &c (*see senses of* **sgrùd** *v*); 2 scrutiny, investigation, an investigation, an examination (*not school &c*), **sgrùdadh air beatha na speacha** a study of/investigation into the life of the wasp; 3 (*accounts*) an audit

sguab *vti, pres part* **a' sguabadh**, sweep, brush

sguab, sguaibe, sguaban *nf* 1 a brush, a broom, **sguab fhliuch** a mop, *Cf less trad* (& *often smaller*) **bruis**; 2 a sheaf of corn

sguabadair, sguabadair, sguabadairean *nm* a hoover, a vacuum-cleaner

sgud *vti, pres part* **a' sgudadh**, chop, **a' sgudadh fiodha** chopping wood

sgudal, *gen* **sgudail** *nm* 1 rubbish, refuse, garbage, **tha làraidh na comhairle a' togail sgudail** the council lorry's collecting/uplifting rubbish, *Cf less usu* **fuighleach**; 2 (*calque, fam*) rubbish, nonsense, **'s e tòrr sgudail a th' ann!** it's a load of rubbish!

sguir *vi, pres part* **a' sgur**, stop, cease, give up, leave off, desist (**de** from), **sguir sinn aig meadhan-làtha** we stopped at noon, **sguir dheth!** stop it!, *Cf* **stad** *v* 2

sgur, *gen* **sguir** *nm* 1 (*the act of*) stopping, ceasing &c (*see senses of* **sguir** *v*); 2 *esp in expr* **gun sgur** *adv* unceasingly, continually, constantly, endlessly, **ag obair/a' bruidhinn gun sgur** working/talking nonstop, **tha iad an sàs annam gun sgur** they're constantly/always on at me

sgùrr, sgurra, sgurran *nm* a peak, a pinnacle, a steep, sharp mountain-top, **Sgùrr Alasdair** Alasdair's Pinnacle

shìos *adv* down (*expr position*), **shìos bhuaithe** down below him, **am baile ud shìos** the township down yonder, *Cf* **sìos, shuas, suas**

shuas *adj* up (*expr position*), **tha uiseag a' seinn shuas an sin** a lark's singing up there, *Cf* **shìos, sìos, suas**

sia *adj & num* six

siab *vti, pres part* **a' siabadh, 1** wipe, rub (*esp to clean*), **siab am bòrd** wipe the table, *Cf* **suath 1; 2** *vi* (*snow &c*) drift, blow away

siabann, *gen & pl* **siabainn** *nm* soap

siach *vt, pres part* **a' siachadh**, (*ankle &c*) sprain, strain. *Cf* **sgoch**

sia-deug *adj & num* sixteen

sia-deugach *adj* (*IT &c*) hexadecimal

sian, sìne, siantan *nf*, *also* **sìon, sìon, sìontan** *nm*, **1** a storm, a blast (*of wind, rain &c*), *Cf* **doineann, gailleann, stoirm 1; 2** *in pl*, the elements, the climate, (*face &c*) **air dath nan sian** weather-beaten, *esp in expr* **sìde nan seachd sian** appalling weather, the worst weather imaginable; **3** a thing, something, anything, (*in neg expr*) nothing, **a h-uile sian** everything, **cha robh sian againn** we had nothing, *Cf* **càil** *nm* **1 & 2, dad 1, nì** *n* **1, rud 1**

sianar *nmf invar* six (*used of people*)

siar *adj & adv*, *corres to* **an iar** (*see* **iar**), west, western, **na h-Eileanan Siar** the Western Isles, **an Cuan Siar** the Atlantic Ocean, **an taobh siar** *or* **an taobh an iar** the west(ern side of the country), **siar air a' bhaile** west of the township/village, *Cf* **deas 1, ear, iar, sear, tuath**[1]

sibh *emph* **sibhse**, *pron pl*, *also expr formal sing*, you, **ciamar a tha sibh? tha gu math, ciamar a tha sibh fhèin?** how are you? well, how are you yourself/yourselves? **am bi sibhse ann?** will you (*emph*) be there? *Note: There are two systems governing the use of* **sibh** *&* **thu** *in the sing, based on status and familiarity respectively. In some areas one's parent or a close friend who was, eg, a minister or an elderly neighbour, would be addressed as* **sibh** *out of respect for their status. Where the familiarity criterion prevails they might be addressed as* **thu**; **sibh** *is best when in any doubt!; Cf* **thu**

sìde *nf invar* weather, **deagh/droch shìde** good/bad weather, **tuairmse sìde** a weather forecast, *see also* **sian 2**, *Cf* **aimsir 3, tìde 2**

sil *vi, pres part* **a' sileadh**, (*of liquids*) **1** drip, drop, **uisge a' sileadh tron tughadh** rain/water dripping through the thatch, *Cf* **snigh; 2** flow, (*song*) **mo chùl rid chùl 's na deòir a' sileadh** my back to your back and the tears flowing, *Cf* **ruith** *v* **2; 3** rain (*often heavily*) **tha e a' sileadh** it's raining/pouring, *Cf* **uisge 2**

sileadh, *gen* **silidh 1** *nm* (*the act of*) dripping, flowing &c (*see senses of* **sil** *v*); **2** rainfall, precipitation

silidh *nm invar* **1** jam, (*Sc*) jeelie; **2** jelly, a jelly

silteach *adj* fluid, dripping, dropping, flowing, apt to drip &c, (*of eye*) tearful, (*song*) **dh'fhàg thu silteach mo shùil** you caused my eye to shed tears (*Cf* **deurach**)

similear, simileir, similearan *nm* a chimney, *Cf* **luidhear**

sìmpleachadh, *gen* **sìmpleachaidh**, *nm* **1** (*the act of*) simplifying (*see* **sìmplich** *v*); **2** simplification

sìmplich *vt*, *pres part* **a' sìmpleachadh**, simplify

simplidh *adj* **1** simple, easy, uncomplicated, elementary, *Cf* **furasta**, **soirbh**; **2** simple, plain, unpretentious, *Cf* **aon-fhillte**; **3** simple, simple-minded, *Cf* **baoth**

sin *adj* **1** that, those, **na coin sin** those dogs, **aig an àm sin** at that time, **thoir dhomh am fear sin** give me that one; **2** *as emphasising element* **chan eil mi cho math sin!** I'm not that (*emph*) good, **b' iad sin an fheadhainn a chunnaic mi** those ones/they (*emph*) were the ones that I saw, **chùm e grèim air an laogh ach thuit e sin air a mhuin** he kept hold of the calf but it fell on top of him; *Cf* **seo** *adj*, **ud**

sin 1 *pron* that, **cò/dè a tha sin?** who's/what's that? **sin an càr agam** that is my car, **sin e** that's it, **'s e sin** … that is …, i.e. …, namely …, **is e sin ri ràdh** … that is to say …, **'s e sin a' chùis!** that's the point/problem!; **2** *pron & adv* there, **sin agad leabhar** there's a book (for you), **cà'il do bhràthair? sin e** where's your brother? there he is, (*to dog &c*) **a-mach à sin (leat)!** get out of there!; **3** *in exprs* **an sin** & (*sometimes more emph*) **ann an s(h)in**, *adv*, there, **rugadh mi an sin** I was born there, **dè a tha thu a' dèanamh an sin?** what are you doing there? **tha an cat ann an sin** the cat's there; **4** *in expr* **an sin** *adv* then, thereupon, **an sin dh'fhàg e an dùthaich** then/at that he left the country; **5** *in expr* **sin thu (fhèin)!** well done!; **6** *as emphasising element* **a bheil thu sgìth? tha mi sin!** are you tired? I am that!, I sure am!; *Cf* **seo, siud** *prons*

sìn *vti*, *pres part* **a' sìneadh**, **1** stretch, make or become longer by stretching, **tha an ròpa air a shìneadh** the rope has been stretched; **2** stretch, stretch out, extend (*one's body*), **shìn i a-mach a cas chlì** she stretched out her left foot/leg; **3** pass, reach, hand, **shìn i thugam am pàipear-naidheachd** she passed/handed me the newspaper

sinc *nm invar* zinc

sinc(e), since, sincean *nmf* a sink

sine, sine, sinean *nf* a nipple, a teat, **a' deoghal air sine** sucking at/on a teat

sineach, *gen & pl* **sinich** *nm* a mammal; *also as adj*, **sineach** mammalian

sìneadh, *gen* **sìnidh** *nm* **1** (*the act of*) stretching, stretching out, extending &c (*see senses of* **sìn** *v*); **2** an outstretched position or posture, *esp in expr* **nam** (&c) **shìneadh** stretched out, **bha i na sìneadh air a' bheinge** she was stretched out on the bench, *Cf* **laighe 2**

singilte *adj* **1** single, **leabaidh shingilte** a single bed, **rathad singilte** a single-track road; **2** single, unmarried, (*song*) **nuair a bha mi singilte, 's a bha mo phòca gliongadaich** when I was single and my pocket did jingle; **3** (*gram*) singular, **ainmear singilte** a singular noun

sinn *emph* **sinne**, *pron*, we, **is truagh nach robh sinn còmhla** it's a shame we weren't together, **sinn fhìn** ourselves

sinn- *prefix used in family relationships*, great-, **sinn-seanair** *m* a great-grandfather, **sinn-sinn-seanmhair** *f* a great-great-grandmother, *Cf* **sean 6**

sinnsear, **sinnsir**, **sinnsirean** *nm* an ancestor, a forefather, a forebear, **ri linn ar sinnsirean** in the time of our ancestors, *Cf* **seanair 2**

sìnteag, **sìnteig**, **sìnteagan** *nf* **1** a hop, a (long) stride; **2** a stepping-stone

siobhag, **siobhaig**, **siobhagan** *nf* a wick, *Cf* **buaic**

sìobhalta *adj* **1** civil, polite, courteous, (*song*) **labhair mi rithe gu sìobhalta blàth** I addressed her politely and warmly, *Cf* **cùirteil 1**, **modhail**; **2** (*legal &c*) civil, pertaining to the citizens of a state, **lagh sìobhalta** civil law, **cogadh sìobhalta** (a) civil war

sìobhaltair, **sìobhaltair**, **sìobhaltairean** *nm* a civilian

sìochail *see* **sìtheil**

sìoda, **sìoda**, **sìodachan** *nm* silk, (*song*) **sìoda reamhar ruadh na Spàinne** the full/sleek red silk of Spain

sìol, *gen* **sìl** *nm coll* **1** seed, **sìol eòrna** barley seed, **sìol-cuir** seed-corn, *Cf less usu* **fras** *n* **2**; **2** (*also* **sìol-ginidh**) semen; **3** a race, a clan, progeny of the same real or supposed ancestor, **sìol Diarmaid** the race/descendants/children of Dermid, the Campbells, *Cf* **clann 2**, **gineal**, **sliochd**; **4** (*livestock &c*) a breed

sìolachadh, *gen* **sìolachaidh** *nm* **1** (*the act of*) engendering, seeding &c (*see senses of* **sìolaich** *v*); **2** (*med &c*) insemination, **sìolachadh fuadain** artificial insemination

sìol(t)achan, *gen & pl* **sìol(t)achain** *nm* (*for coffee &c*) a strainer, a filter

sìoladh, *gen* **sìolaidh** *nm* (*the act of*) subsiding, filtering &c (*see senses of* **sìolaidh** *v*)

sìolaich *vti, pres part* **a' sìolachadh**, **1** (*trad*) engender, beget, propagate; **2** (*vi*) seed; **3** (*vt*) inseminate

sìolaidh *vti, pres part* **a' sìoladh**, 1 subside, lower, settle, sink, cause to subside or lower, **shìolaidh na h-uisgeachan** the waters subsided/settled, *Cf* **tràigh** *v* 2; 2 filter, strain (*liquids*), **tha an cofaidh a' sìoladh** the coffee's filtering

siolp *vi, pres part* **a' siolpadh**, (*of surreptitious movement*) slip, steal, **siolp a-steach/air falbh** slip in(side)/away, *Cf* **èalaidh** 2

sìoman, sìomain, sìomanan *nm* straw rope, a straw rope

sìon *see* **sian**

Sìonach, *gen & pl* **Sìonaich** someone from China (**Sìona** *f*), *also as adj* **Sìonach** Chinese

sionnach, *gen & pl* **sionnaich** *nm* a fox, *Cf* **balgair** 1, **madadh** 2

sionnsar, sionnsair, sionnsaran a bagpipe chanter, *Cf* **feadan** 1

sìor- *a prefix corres to Eng* ever-, eternally, constantly, (*song*) **a' sìor-ionndrainn tìr a bhruadair** ever yearning for the land he dreams of, **sìor-mhaireannach** *adj* eternal, everlasting, immortal, **sìor-uaine** *adj* evergreen, *Cf* **bith-**

siorrachd, siorrachd, siorrachdan *nf also* **siorramachd** *nf invar* 1 (*hist*) a sheriffdom; 2 (*now*) a county, a shire, **Siorrachd Rois** Ross-shire

siorraidh, siorraidh, siorraidhean *nm &* **siorram, siorraim, siorraman** *nm* a sheriff, **cùirt** *f* **an t-siorraim** the sheriff court

sìorraidh *adj* 1 everlasting, eternal, *Cf* **bith-bhuan** (*see* **bith-**); 2 *usu as adv* ever, for ever, (*with neg verb*) never, (*song*) **cha till iad gu sìorraidh** they will never return, **gu sìorraidh bràth** for ever and ever, *Cf* **a-chaoidh, a-riamh, bràth** 2 & 3; 3 *in excls, eg* **a shìorraidh!** Heavens!, Goodness!, for Pete's sake!, *Cf* **sealbh** 2

sìorraidheachd *nf invar* eternity

siorram *see* **siorraidh**

siorramachd *see* **siorrachd**

sìos *adv* down (*expr movement, NB from point of view of the person moving, Cf* **a-nìos, a-nuas**), **thuit e sìos an staidhre** he fell down the stair (*Cf* **tha e shìos an staidhre** he's downstairs/down the stair), **chaidh iad sìos** they went down, *also* (*trad, of army*) they charged, *Cf* **a-bhàn, a-nìos, a-nuas, shìos, shuas, suas**

siosar, siosair, siosaran *nmf* scissors, a pair of scissors

siosarnaich *nf invar* 1 (*the act or sound of*) hissing, a hiss, *also used as pres part* **tha e a' siosarnaich** he is hissing; 2 whispering, a whisper, *Cf* **cagar** 2; 3 a rustling noise

sìothchail *see* **sìtheil**

sir *vt, pres part* **a' sireadh**, seek, search for, look for, **tha e a' sireadh mnà/obrach** he's looking for a wife/work, **tha a' chompanaidh a' sireadh luchd-obrach** the company is looking for/requires workers, *Cf* **lorg** *v* 1

sireadh, *gen* **siridh** *nm* (*the act of*) seeking &c (*see senses of* **sir** *v*)

siris(t), siris(t), siris(t)ean *nf* a cherry

siteag, siteig, siteagan *nf &* **sitig, sitig, sitigean** *nf* a dunghill, a manure heap, a midden, *also in expr* **thoir an t-siteag ort!** get out(side)!, *Cf* **dùnan 2, òtrach**

sìth, *gen* **sìthe** *nf* **1** peace (*ie opposite of war*), **cogadh no sìth** war or peace; **2** peace, tranquillity, quiet, *Cf* **fois 1**

sìth *adj* fairy, of or pertaining to fairies, **daoine sìth** fairy folk, **a' Bhratach Shìth** the Fairy Flag (*at Dunvegan*)

sìtheachadh, *gen* **sìtheachaidh** *nm* **1** (*the act of*) pacifying &c (*see senses of* **sìthich** *v*); **2** pacification

sìthean, *gen & pl* **sìthein** *nm* a small rounded hill (*often one thought to be a fairy hill*)

sitheann, *gen* **sìthne &** **sithinn** *nf* **1** venison; **2** game in general

sìtheil & **sìo(th)chail** *adj* **1** peaceful, tranquil; **2** peaceable

sìthich *vti, pres part* **a' sìtheachadh, 1** (*vt*) pacify; **2** (*vti*) make or become peaceful or tranquil; *Cf* **ciùinich, socraich 1**

sìthiche, sìthiche, sìthichean *nm* a fairy, *Cf* **daoine sìth** (*see* **sìth** *adj*)

sitig *see* **siteag**

sitir, *gen* **sitire** *nf* braying, neighing, whinnying

siubhail *vti, pres part* **a' siubhal, 1** (*vi*) travel, **'s toigh leam a bhith a' siubhal** I like travelling; **2** (*vt*) travel, cross, **a' siubhal na mòintich** travelling/crossing the moor; **3** (*vi*) die, pass away, *Cf more usu* **bàsaich, caochail 2; 4** (*vt*) seek, look for, *Cf more usu* **lorg** *v* **1, sir**

siubhal, siubhail, siùbhlaichean *nm* **1** travel, travelling, **luchd-siubhail** *m* travellers, **cosgaisean** *fpl* **siubhail** travel(ling) costs/expenses; **2** time, *esp in expr* **fad an t-siubhail** all the time, *Cf more usu* **tìde 1, ùine 1**

siùbhlach *adj* **1** speedy, swift, fleet, moving easily, *Cf* **clis, luath** *adj* **1; 2** (*speech*) fluent, fluid; **3** transient, fleeting, *Cf* **diombuan**

siùcar, siùcair, siùcairean *nm* **1** sugar; **2** *in pl* sweets, sweeties, *Cf* **suiteas**

siud & *more trad* **sud** *pron* **1** that (*more distant or remote than* **sin**), (*Sc*) yon, **dè a bha siud?** what was that/yon? (*song*) **siud mar chuir mi 'n geamhradh tharam** that's how I spent the winter; **2** *in expr* **an siud &** (*sometimes more emph*) **ann an s(h)iud** *adv* there (*more distant or remote than* **an sin**), (*Sc*) yonder, **thall an siud** over yonder, **an siud 's an seo** here and there, *also* hither and thither, ... **is siud is seo** ... and so on and so on, ... blah, blah, blah, (*can be more pej than* **sin**) **tha am biadh sgriosail ann an siud!** the food's terrible in yon place!; *Cf* **seo, sin, ud**

siuga, siuga, siugannan *nmf* a jug

siùrsach, siùrsaich, siùrsaichean *nf* a prostitute, *Cf* **strìopach**

siùrsachd *nf invar* prostitution

siuthad, *pl* **siuthadaibh** *imperatives of def verb, excl giving encouragement*, on you go! go to it! get on with it! (*song*) **siuthadaibh, 'illean, gabhaibh am port** on you go, lads, strike up the tune

slabhraidh, slabhraidh, slabhraidhean *nf* a chain, *Cf* **cuibhreach**

slac *vt*, *pres part* **a' slacadh**, (*esp with heavy object*) thrash, drub, beat, thump, bruise, maul

slacadh, slacaidh, slacaidhean *nm*, *also* **slacadaich** *nf invar*, **1** (*the act of*) thrashing &c (*see senses of* **slac** *v*); **2** (**slacadh** *only*) a thrashing

slàinte *nf invar* **1** (*public*) health, **Seirbheis na Slàinte** the Health Service, **ministear na slàinte** the health minister, **foghlam na slàinte** health education, **slàinte inntinn** mental health; **2** health (*of individual*), **ma cheadaicheas mo shlàinte dhomh** if my health allows/permits me; **3** *freq in toasts, wishes &c*, **deoch-slàinte** *f* a toast, **slàinte!** good health!, cheers!, **slàinte mhath/mhòr!** the best of health!, **air do dheagh shlàinte!** (to) your very good health!

slaman, *gen* **slamain** *nm* (*dairying*) curds, crowdie, *Cf* **gruth**

slàn *adj* **1** healthy, well, in good health, **pàiste slàn** a healthy child, *Cf* **fallain 1**; **2** healthy (*ie healthgiving*), **biadh slàn** healthy food, *Cf* **fallain 2**; **3** *in expr* **slàn leat!** goodbye!, farewell!; **4** complete, whole, entire, in one piece, intact, **facal slàn** a whole word, **àireamh shlàn** a whole number **tursa Cruithneach slàn** a complete/intact Pictish standing stone, *Cf* **iomlan** *adj* **2**

slànachadh, *gen* **slànachaidh** *nm* (*the act of*) healing, curing (*see senses of* **slànaich** *v*)

slànaich *vti*, *pres part* **a' slànachadh**, heal, cure, (*of ill person*) make or get better, *Cf* **leighis**

slànaighear, *gen & pl* **slànaigheir** *nm* a saviour (*esp relig*), *with art*, **an Slànaighear** the Saviour

slaod *vti*, *pres part* **a' slaodadh**, *usu of heavy objects* drag, haul, pull, **shlaod e a' chaora a-mach às a' bhoglaich** he dragged/hauled the ewe out of the bog, *Cf* **tarraing** *v* **1**

slaod, slaoid, slaodan *nm* a sledge, **slaod-uisge** a raft

slaodach *adj* **1** slow (*in a trailing, dragging way*), **chaidh an tìde seachad cho slaodach** the time dragged so, *Cf* **mall**; **2** boring, tedious, **obair shlaodach** a tedious/long-drawn-out job, *Cf* **fadalach 2**, **màirnealach 2**; **3** (*person*) slow, dilatory

slaodadh, *gen* **slaodaidh** *nm* (*the act of*) dragging &c (*see senses of* **slaod** *v*)

slaodair, slaodair, slaodairean *nm* (*transport*) a trailer

slaoightear, slaoighteir, slaoightearan *nm* a knave, a rascal, a rogue, a villain, *Cf* **balgair 2**

slapag, slapaig, slapagan *nf* a slipper

slat, slait, slatan *nf* **1** (*measure*) a yard; **2** a twig; **3** a rod, a switch, a wand, **slat-iasgaich** a fishing rod, **slat-thomhais** a rule, a measure, a yardstick, (*also, abstr*, a criterion), **slat-rìoghail** a sceptre; **4** (*fam, vulg*) a penis, a prick, a cock, *Cf* **bod**

sleagh, sleagha, sleaghan *nf* a spear, a lance, a javelin, *Cf* **gath 2**

sleamhainn *adj* slippy, slippery, **cabhsair sleamhainn** a slippery pavement

sleamhnachadh, *gen* **sleamhnachaidh** *nm* (*the act of*) sliding, slipping (*see* **sleamhnaich** *v*)

sleamhnag, sleamhnaig, sleamhnagan *nf* **1** (*also* **sleamhnan, sleamhnain, sleamhnanan** *nm*) a slide (*made on ice*); **2** (*in playpark &c*) a (*children's*) slide, (*Sc*) a chute

sleamhnaich *vi, pres part* **a' sleamhnachadh**, slide, slip (*on ice &c*)

sleuchd *vi, pres part* **a' sleuchdadh**, **1** kneel, kneel down, *Cf* **lùb** *v* **1**; **2** bow down, prostrate oneself

sleuchdadh, sleuchdaidh, sleuchdaidhean *nm* **1** (*the act of*) kneeling, bowing down &c (*see senses of* **sleuchd** *v*); **2** prostration; a bow

sliabh, slèibh, slèibhtean *nm* **1** a moor, an expanse of moorland, a muir, (*placename*) **Sliabh an t-Siorraim** Sheriffmuir, *Cf* **aonach, mòinteach, monadh 1**; **2** a hill or mountain, *Cf* **beinn 2, cnoc**

sliasaid, sliasaide, sliasaidean *nf* a thigh, *Cf less usu* **leis**

slige, slige, slige(ach)an *nf* **1** a shell (*of egg, nut, shellfish*), *Cf* **cochall 1, plaosg**; **2** (*artillery*) a shell

slighe, slighe, slighean *nf* (*with rather abstract connotation*) a path, a road, a track, a way, a route, **gabh an t-slighe sin** take that road/route, **thachair sinn riutha air an t-slighe** we met them on the way/en route, (*at road junction &c*) **gèill** *v* **slighe** give way, **còir-slighe** *f* right of way, **fàsach** *m* **gun slighe** a trackless wilderness, **slighe na fìreantachd** the path of righteousness, *Cf* **rathad 2**

slinnean, slinnein, slinneinean *nm* a shoulder, **cnàimh-slinnein** *m* a shoulder-blade, *Cf more usu* **gualann 1**

slìob *vt, pres part* **a' slìobadh**, *also* **slìog** *vt, pres part* **a' slìogadh**, (*dog &c*) stroke

sliochd, sliochda, sliochdan *nm coll* descendants, offspring, progeny, lineage (*of real or supposed ancestor*), *Cf* **clann 2, gineal, sìol 3**

slìog *see* **slìob**

slios, sliosa, sliosan *nm* (*of object, living thing &c*) a side, a flank, *Cf more usu* **cliathaich, taobh 1**

slis, slise, slisean *nf, & dimin* **sliseag, sliseig, sliseagan** *nf,* **1** a slice cut from something, (**sliseag** *only*) a (bacon) rasher; **2** (*kitchen tool*) **sliseag-èisg** a fish-slice

slisnich *vt, pres part* **a' slisneadh,** slice

sloc, *gen* **sluic,** *pl* **slocan** *nm* **1** (*topog*) a hollow, a low-lying area surrounded by higher ground, *freq in placenames, Cf* **lag** *n*; **2** a pit, **sloc-buntàta** a potato pit

sloinn *vi, pres part* **a' sloinneadh,** trace or research one's family tree

sloinneadh, sloinnidh, sloinnidhean *nm* **1** (*the act of*) tracing one's family tree (*see* **sloinn** *v*); **2** a surname, a second name, a family name, **dè an sloinneadh a th' agad/a th' ort?** what's your second name?; **3** a patronymic

sluagh, *gen* **sluaigh,** *pl* **slòigh,** *gen pl* **slògh** *nm* **1** (trad) an army, a host; **2** people, population, populace (*of a country, locality &c*), **aimhreit am measg an t-sluaigh** unrest among the people/population, **an sluagh dom buineadh e** the people he belonged to, *Cf* **muinntir 2, poball**; **3** a crowd, **bha sluagh mòr ann** there was a big crowd (there), **mòr-shluagh** a multitude, a huge crowd

sluagh-ghairm, sluagh-ghairme, sluagh-ghairmean *nf* **1** (*trad, clan hist*) a war-cry, a gathering cry, **'s e 'Cruachan' sluagh-ghairm nan Caimbeulach** 'Cruachan' is the war-cry of the Campells; **2** (*now, pol, advertising &c*) a slogan

sluaghmhor *adj* populous, well populated

sluasaid, sluasaide, sluasaidean *nf* a shovel

slug *see* **sluig**

slugadh, slugaidh, slugaidhean *nm* **1** (*the act of*) swallowing, gulping &c (*see senses of* **sluig** *v*); **2** a swallow, a gulp

sluig & slug *vti, pres part* **a' slugadh,** swallow, gulp (down), devour

smachd *nm invar* authority, control, command, discipline, rule, subjection, **fo smachd nan Ròmanach** under the authority/control/rule of the Romans, **cùm** *v* **smachd air sgoilearan** keep control of/maintain discipline over pupils, **sluagh** *m* **fo smachd** a subject people, *Cf* **cumhachd 1, reachd 1, ùghdarras 1**

smachdaich *vt, pres part* **a' smachdachadh, 1** discipline, punish, keep in order; **2** impose (one's) authority or power upon (*people, country &c*)

smachdail *adj* authoritative, commanding

smà(i)l *vt, pres part* **a' smàladh,** (*esp fire*) put out, extinguish, snuff (out), quench, **smàil às an teine** put the fire out, **smàil na coinnlean** snuff the candles, *Cf* **mùch 1, tùch 2**

smal, smail, smalan *nm* a stain, a spot (*on clothing &c*), *Cf* **sal 3**, **spot 1**

smàladair, smàladair, smàladairean *nm* candle-snuffers

smàladh, *gen* **smàlaidh** *nm* (*the act of*) extinguishing &c (*see senses of* **smà(i)l** *v*), **inneal-smàlaidh** *m* a fire-extinguisher, **einnsean-smàlaidh** *m* a fire engine, **luchd-smàlaidh** *m coll* firefighters

smalan, *gen* **smalain** *nm* gloom, melancholy, **fo smalan** (*also* **smalanach** *adj*) gloomy, melancholy, *Cf* **bròn 1**, **gruaim 1**

smaoin, smaoine, smaointean *nf* & **smuain, smuaine, smuaintean** *nf* a thought, a notion, a reflection, an idea, **smaointean dubhach** melancholy thoughts, **cha do chòrd an dàn rium ach chòrd an smuain** I didn't enjoy the poem but I liked the idea/theme

smaoin(t)eachadh, *gen* **smaoin(t)eachaidh** *nm* (*the act of*) thinking, supposing, considering &c (*see senses of* **smaoin(t)ich** *v*)

smaoin(t)ich *vi, pres part* **a' smaointinn** & **a' smaoin(t)eachadh**, *also* **smuain(t)ich** *vi, pres part* **a' smuain(t)eachadh**, **1** think, reflect, **is tric a bhios mi a' smaoineachadh mu dheidhinn** I often think about it/him; **2** think, imagine, suppose, **bidh an t-acras ort, tha mi a' smaoineachadh** you'll be hungry, I imagine/I'm thinking, *Cf* **saoil**; **3** think, consider, believe, be of the opinion, **tha mi a' smaointeachadh gun robh thu ceàrr** I think you were wrong (*some speakers would say that* **smaoin(t)ich** *should not be used in this sense*), *Cf* **saoil**

smàrag, smàraig, smàragan *nf* an emerald

smèid *vi, pres part* **a' smèideadh**, **1** beckon, **smèid air cuideigin** beckon to someone; **2** wave, **smèid ri cuideigin** wave to someone, *Cf* **crath 1**

smèideadh, *gen* **smèididh** *nm* (*the act of*) beckoning, waving (*see* **smèid** *v*)

smeòrach, smeòraich, smeòraichean *nf* a thrush, (*prov*) **cha dèan aon smeòrach samhradh** one thrush doesn't make it summer

smeur *v see* **smiùr**

smeur, smeura, smeuran *nf* a bramble, a blackberry (*ie the berry*, *Cf* **dris**), (*poetry collection*) **Smeur an Dòchais** (Ruaraidh MacThòmais) Bramble of Hope

smeuradh, *gen* **smeuraidh** *nm* (*the act of*) smearing &c (*see senses of* **smiùr/smeur** *v*)

smid, smide, smidean *nf* a word, a syllable, *esp in expr* (*fam*) **cha tubhairt e smid** he didn't say a word/utter a syllable, *Cf* **bìd 2**

smig, smig, smigean *nm* & *more usu* **smiogaid, smiogaid, smiogaidean** *nm* a chin

smiogaid *see* **smig**

smior, *gen* **smior** & **smir** *nm* **1** marrow, (*prov*) **briseadh a' chnàimh agamsa, an smior aig càch** I get to break the bone, the others get the marrow; **2** the best part of something, the best example of something, **smior an t-sìl** the best/pick of the seed, **dhèanadh e smior a' mhaighstir-sgoile** he'd make a great schoolmaster, *Cf* **brod** *n* **2**, & *opposite* **diù**; **3** (*esp inner or moral*) courage, spirit, strength, pluck, 'guts', **duine gun smior** a spineless/'wet' individual, *Cf* **misneach**; **4** manliness, vigour, *Cf* **duinealas 1**

smiorach *adj* pithy, *Cf* **brìghmhor 1**

smiorail *adj* **1** (*esp in character*) strong, spirited, plucky, *Cf* **misneachail**; **2** manly, vigorous, *Cf* **duineil 1**

smiùr *vt, pres part* **a' smiùradh**, & **smeur** *vt, pres part* **a' smeuradh**, smear, daub, grease

smoc *vti, pres part* **a' smocadh**, smoke (*tobacco &c*), **am bi thu a' smocadh?** do you smoke?

smocadh, *gen* **smocaidh** *nm* smoking, the act of smoking, (*notice*) **chan fhaodar smocadh** no smoking, smoking not allowed

smuain, smuain(t)ich *see* **smaoin, smaoin(t)ich**

smuais *vt, pres part* **a' smuaiseadh**, smash, splinter, break into pieces, *Cf* **smùid** *v* **2**, **spealg** *v*

smùch *vi, pres part* **a' smùchadh**, snivel

smugaid, smugaide, smugaidean *nf* spit, spittle, *esp in expr* **tilg** *v* **smugaid** spit

smùid *vti, pres part* **a' smùideadh**, **1** (*of chimney &c*) smoke; **2** smash into pieces, *Cf* **smuais, spealg** *v*

smùid, smùide, smùidean *nf* **1** steam, vapour, (*song*) **fàgaidh sinn Malaig air bàta na smùide** we'll leave Mallaig on the steamer/ steam boat; **2** smoke, *esp in expr* **cuir** *v* **smùid** smoke, **tha an teine a' cur smùide** the fire's smoking; **3** fumes, *Cf* **deatach**; **4** (*fam*) a state of drunkenness, **ghabh e smùid mhath a-raoir** he got well and truly drunk last night, **tha smùid orra** they're drunk/ steaming/smashed, *Cf* **daorach 1, misg**

smùr, *gen* **smùir** *nm* dust, dross, **smùr mòna** peat dross, *Cf* **sal 2**

sna *see* **anns an**

snàgadh, *gen* **snàgaidh** *nm*, & **snàgail**, *gen* **snàgaile** *nf*, (*the act of*) stealing, creeping &c (*see senses of* **snàig** *v*)

snagan-daraich, snagain-daraich, snaganan-daraich *nm* a woodpecker

snaidhm, snaidhm, snaidhmean(nan) *nm* a knot (*in rope &c*), *fig* (*song*) **'s mi ri cromadh leis a' ghleann, thàinig snaidhm air mo chridh'** as I came down the glen my heart knotted/a pang came upon my heart

snàig *vi, pres part* **a' snàgail** & **a' snàgadh**, **1** crawl, **shnàig mi a' dh'ionnsaigh an taighe** I crawled towards the house, *Cf* **crùb 4**; **2** (*walk stealthily*) creep, steal, **shnàig sinn sìos an staidhre** we crept/ stole down the stair, *Cf* **èalaidh 1**

snaigh *vt, pres part* **a' snaigheadh**, (*wood, stone &c*) hew, chip, carve

snàith *n see* **snàth**

snàmh *vi, pres part* **a' snàmh**, swim, float

snàmh, *gen* **snàimh** *nm* **1** (*the act or activity of*) swimming *or* floating, **math air snàmh** good at swimming, **an dèan thu snàmh?** can/do you swim?; **2** *in expr* **air snàmh** deluged, inundated, flooded, **cuir** *v* **an seòmar air snàmh** flood the room with water, **bha an taigh air snàmh** the house was swimming in water/awash

snasail & **snasmhor** *adj* neat, trim, **eathar beag snasmhor** a trim wee boat, *Cf* **cuimir 2, sgiobalta 2**

snàth & **snàith**, *gen* **snàith** & **snàtha**, *pl* **snàithean** *nm coll* (*needlework &c*) thread, *Cf* **snàthainn**

snàthad, **snàthaid**, **snàthadan** *nf* a (*sewing*) needle, **crò snàthaid** the eye of a needle

snàthainn, *gen* **snàithne** & **snàthainne**, *pl* **snàithnean** & **snàthainnean** *nm* (*needlework &c*) a single thread, *Cf coll* **snàth**

sneachd(a), *gen* **sneachda** *nm* snow, **tha e a' cur an t-sneachda** it's snowing, **bodach-sneachda** a snowman

snèap, **snèip**, **snèapan** *nf* a turnip, a swede, (*Sc*) a neep

snigh *vi, pres part* **a' snighe**, (*of liquids*) drip, seep, **uisge a' snighe tron tughadh** rain seeping through the thatch, *Cf* **sil 1**

snighe *nm invar* (*the act of*) dripping, seeping (*see* **snigh** *v*)

snìomh *vti, pres part* **a' snìomhadh** & **a' snìomh**, **1** spin (*yarn &c*); **2** twist, wring, **shnìomh e an ròpa** he twisted the rope, **tha thu a' snìomhadh mo chridhe** you're wringing my heart(-strings), **na snìomh d' adhbrann!** don't twist/sprain your ankle!

snìomhadh, *gen* **snìomhaidh** *nm* (*the act of*) spinning, twisting &c (*see senses of* **snìomh** *v*)

snìomhair(e), **snìomhaire**, **snìomhairean** *nm* (*tools*) a drill, an auger, *Cf less trad* **drile**

snodha-gàire, **snodha-gàire**, **snodhan-gàire** *nm* a smile, *Cf* **faite**

snog *adj* (*slightly fam*) **1** (*esp of people, places*) pretty, bonny, **tha i uabhasach snog** she's ever so pretty, *Cf* **brèagha**; **2** (*people, objects, situations*) nice, **duine snog** a nice man, **chuir sinn seachad feasgar còmhla, bha e snog** we spent an evening together, it was nice, **àite snog** a nice (*also* pretty) place, *Cf* **laghach**, & *stronger* **sgoinneil**

snuadh, *gen* **snuaidh** *nm* (*esp of people*) **1** appearance, aspect, (*song*) **dh'fhàg thu tana-ghlas mo shnuadh** you left me looking/made me look thin and wan, *Cf* **coltas 1**, **dreach 1**; **2** hue, colour, complexion, *Cf* **dreach 2**, **fiamh 1**, **tuar**

so *see* **seo** *adj & pron*

so- *prefix corres to Eng* -able, -ible, *eg* **so-ruighinn** *adj* attainable, reachable, accessible, **so-thuigsinn** *adj* intelligible, understandable, comprehensible, **so-dhèanta** *adj* possible, feasible, able to be done, **so-lùbadh** *adj* flexible, pliable, **so-leughte** legible *Cf* **ion-**, **neo-**, **mì-**

sòbair, *also* **sòbarr(a)**, *adj* sober, *esp* not drunk, **cha tric a tha e sòbair** it's not often he's sober, *Cf* **stuama 2**

sòbhrach & **sòbhrag** *see* **seòbhrach**

socair, *gen* **socrach** & **socaire** *nf* comfort, ease, leisure, **gabh** *v* **socair** take one's ease, **gabh** *v* **air do** (&c) **shocair** take things easily/comfortably, *excl* **socair!** *or* **air do shocair!** steady on!, take it easy!, go easy!

socair *adj* **1** (*weather &c*) mild, tranquil, calm, *Cf more usu* **ciùin**, **sèimh**; **2** (*esp people*) at ease, at peace, relaxed

socais, **socais**, **socaisean** *nf* a sock (*ie footwear*)

sochar, *gen* **sochair** *nf* **1** bashfulness, shyness, *Cf more usu* **diùide**; **2** (*of character*) softness, weakness, (excessive) compliance or indulgence

socharach *adj* **1** bashful, shy, *Cf more usu* **diùid**; **2** (*of character*) soft, weak, tame, (too) compliant or indulgent, *Cf more usu* **bog** *adj* **2**, **lag**, **maoth 1**

socrach *adj* **1** at ease, sedate, comfortable, leisurely, **ceum socrach** a leisurely/comfortable pace

socrachadh, *gen* **socrachaidh** *nm* (*the act of*) settling, solving, establishing &c (*see senses of* **socraich** *v*)

socraich *vti*, *pres part* **a' socrachadh**, **1** settle, make or become calm or tranquil, **shocraich a' ghaoth** the wind settled/abated, **cha tèid am fearg a shocrachadh** their anger cannot/will not be calmed/assuaged, *Cf* **ciùinich**, **sìthich 1** & **2**; **2** (*vt*) (*dispute &c*) settle, solve, arrange, sort out, **shocraich a' chomataidh na duilgheadasan air fad** the committee solved/settled all the problems, *Cf* **fuasgail 3**; **3** (*vt*) set, settle, fix, establish, **socraich an ìomhaigh air a' cholbh** set the statue on the column, **shocraich i a cridhe air** she set her heart on it, **chan urrainn dhomh m' inntinn a shocrachadh air a' chùis** I can't fix/concentrate my mind on the matter, *Cf* **suidhich 1**

sodal, *gen* **sodail** *nm* adulation, fawning, flattery, *also in expr* **dèan** *v* **sodal ri cuideigin** fawn on/butter up/suck up to someone

sòfa, **sòfa**, **sòfathan** *nf* a sofa, *Cf more trad* **langasaid**

sògh, *gen* **sòigh** *nm* luxury

sòghail *adj* luxurious

soilire, *gen* **soilire** *nm* celery

soilleir *adj* **1** (*light &c*) bright, clear, **là soilleir** a bright/clear day, **deàlraich** *v* **gu soilleir** shine brightly; **2** (*facts &c*) clear, apparent, evident, obvious, manifest, **tha a chionta soilleir** his guilt is clear/obvious, *Cf* **follaiseach 1**; **3** (*argument &c*) clear, easy to follow, **mìneachadh soilleir** a clear explanation

soilleirich *vti, pres part* **a' soilleireachadh, 1** (*vi*) (*light &c*) become bright(er), become clear(er), **shoilleirich an là** the day brightened up; **2** (*vt*) (*problems &c*) clear up, clarify, elucidate, explain, enlighten, **shoilleirich an tidsear an cuspair dhuinn** the teacher clarified/elucidated the subject for us, *Cf* **mìnich**

soillse *nm invar* light (*esp natural*), *Cf more usu* **solas**

soillseachadh, *gen* **soillseachaidh** *nm* **1** (*the act of*) becoming bright, clarifying, shining (*see senses of* **soilleirich** *&* **soillsich** *v*); **2** explanation, an explanation, clarification, enlightenment, (*hist, philo*) **an Soillseachadh** the Enlightenment

soillsich *vti, pres part* **a' soillseachadh, 1** *same senses as* **soilleirich; 2** (*vi*) (*of lights*) shine, gleam, *Cf* **deàlraich 1**

soineannta *adj* naive

soirbh *adj, opposite of* **doirbh,** easy, **rud soirbh** an easy thing, **chan eil e soirbh a ràdh** it's not easy to say, *Cf* **furasta, sìmplidh 1**

soirbheachail *adj* (*business &c*) successful, thriving, prosperous

soirbheachas, *gen* **soirbheachais,** *nm* prosperity, success (*esp material*)

soirbhich *vi, pres part* **a' soirbheachadh,** succeed, turn out well, thrive, prosper, (*with prep* **le**) **an soirbhich an gnìomhachas leotha?** will the business succeed/turn out well for them?, (*as impersonal verb*) **shoirbhich leis** he succeeded *or* he throve/prospered

sòisealach, *gen & pl* **sòisealaich** *nm & adj* (*pol*) a socialist, *also as adj* **sòisealach** socialist, **pàrtaidh sòisealach** a socialist party

sòisealta *adj* social, **tèarainteachd shòisealta/seirbheisean sòisealta** social security/services

soisgeul, *gen* **soisgeil** *nm* a gospel, **an Soisgeul a rèir Mhata** the Gospel according to Matthew

soisgeulach *adj* evangelical

soisgeulaiche, soisgeulaiche, soisgeulaichean *nm* an evangelist; an evangelical preacher

soitheach, soithich, soithichean *nmf* **1** a vessel, a container, *now usu food or kitchen-related*, a dish, **nigh** *v* **na soithichean** wash the dishes, do the washing-up; **2** a ship, a (*sailing*) vessel, *Cf* **bàta, long**

soitheamh *adj* gentle, tractable, good-natured, *Cf more usu* **ciùin**, **sèimh**

sòlaimte *adj* solemn, dignified, ceremonious

solair *vt, pres part* **a' solar(adh)**, *(of trader &c)* purvey, supply, provide, procure, **buidheann a' solaradh àirneis-oifis** a firm supplying office furniture, **solair fasgadh don luchd-turais** provide shelter for the tourists

solas, *gen & pl* **solais** *nm (natural & artificial)* light, a light, **solas an latha** daylight, **solas dealain** electric light, **cuir** *v* **air an solas** put/switch the light on, *Cf less usu* **soillse**

sòlas, *gen* **sòlais** *nm* solace, consolation, *(esp spiritual, emotional)* comfort, *Cf* **furtachd**; **2** joy, gladness, delight, *(song)* **seòlaidh sinn thairis le sòlas** we'll sail across joyfully, *Cf more usu* **gàirdeachas**

sòlasach *adj* **1** *(esp spiritually, emotionally)* comforting, consoling; **2** joyful, glad, well contented, *Cf more usu* **aoibhneach 2 & 3**

solt(a) *adj* **1** meek, harmless, gentle, quiet, *Cf* **macanta** *& more usu* **ciùin**, **sèimh**

son *(in exprs* **air a son**, **air mo shon** *&c) see* **airson 1**

sona *adj (opposite of* **dona**) **1** happy, content, **phòs iad 's tha mi an dòchas gun robh iad sona** they married and I hope they were happy, *Cf stronger* **toilichte**; **2** *occas (trad)* lucky, fortunate

sònrachadh, *gen* **sònrachaidh** *nm (the act of)* distinguishing, specifying, pointing out &c *(see senses of* **sònraich** *v)*

sònraich *vt, pres part* **a' sònrachadh**, **1** distinguish (**bho** from); **2** specify, choose, single out, **shònraich an seanailear e airson na teachdaireachd** the general singled him out/chose him to deliver the message; **3** point out; **4** *(admin)* allocate *(resources &c)*

sònraichte *adj* **1** particular, **tha mi a' sireadh seòrsa sònraichte** I'm looking for a particular sort/kind/variety, *Cf* **àraidh 1**; **2** special, **'s e àite sònraichte a th' ann dhomh** it's a special place to me, *Cf* **leth 2**; **3 gu sònraichte** *adv* particularly, especially, **chòrd na h-òrain rium, gu sònraichte am fear mu dheireadh** I enjoyed the songs, particularly/especially the last one, *Cf* **àraidh 3**, *& see* **seac**

sop, *gen* **suip**, *pl* **sopan** *&* **suip** *nm* a wisp *(esp of straw, hay)*

soraidh *nf invar & excl* **1** *(trad)* a farewell, **soraidh leibh!** farewell, fare ye well! *Cf* **beannachd 4**; **2** *(trad)* a greeting, **thoir mo shoraidh thar a' chuain** carry my greeting beyond the ocean, *Cf* **dùrachd 2**

spaid, **spaide**, **spaidean** *nf* a spade, *Cf less usu* **caibe 1**

spaideil *adj (dress &c)* smart *(perhaps in a slightly showy way)*

spai(s)dirich *vi, pres part* **a' spai(s)dearachd**, walk *or* march in a proud or showy way, strut, parade

spàin, spàine, spàin(t)ean *nf* a spoon, làn-spàine *m* a spoonful

Spàinn, *gen* Spàinne *nf, with art,* an Spàinn Spain

Spàinnis *nf invar,* Spanish (*ie the lang*)

Spàinn(t)each, *gen & pl* Spàinn(t)ich *nm* a Spaniard, *also as adj* Spàinn(t)each Spanish

spàirn, *gen* spàirne *nf* exertion, hard physical effort, an effort, struggling, a struggle, leis gach spàirn a rinn e with every effort he made

spanair, spanair, spanairean *nm* a spanner

spàrr *vt, pres part* a' sparradh, drive or thrust one object into another, spàrr tarrag ann an dèile drive a nail into a plank, spàrr do làmh sa phoca thrust/shove your hand into the sack, *Cf* brùth 2, put *v* 1, sàth 2

spàrr, sparra, sparran *nm* 1 (*building*) a joist, a beam, *Cf* sail; 2 *in expr* cuir *v* air an spàrr put aside, save, store/stow away, *Cf* glèidh 2 & 3, stò(i)r; 3 (*for hen &c*) a roost, *Cf* spiris

sparradh, *gen* sparraidh *nm* (*the act of*) driving, thrusting (*see senses of* spàrr *v*)

speach, speacha, speachan *nf* a wasp

speal, speala, spealan *nf* a scythe

spealg *vti, pres part* a' spealgadh, splinter, smash to pieces, *Cf* smuais, smùid *v* 2

spealg, speilg, spealgan *nf* a splinter, a fragment, bhris e am bòrd na spealgan he smashed the table into splinters/to bits, *Cf* sgealb *n*

spealgadh, *gen* spealgaidh *nm* (*the act of*) splintering &c (*see* spealg *v*)

spèil *vi, pres part* a' spèileadh, skate (*on ice*)

spèil, spèile, spèilean *nf* a skate, an ice-skate

spèis, *gen* spèise *nf* 1 (*esp in songs*) love, affection, gur òg thug mi mo spèis dhut when young I gave you my love/affection, *Cf* dèidh 2, & *more usu* gaol 1; 2 (*of friends &c*) liking, fondness, affection, regard, esteem, fèin-spèis conceit, self-regard, (*in letter*) le mòran spèis ... sincerely yours ..., *Cf* bàidh 1

speuclairean *nm pl* spectacles, glasses, speuclairean-grèine sunglasses, *Cf* glainne 2

speur, speura, speuran *nm* 1 sky, shuas san speur up in the sky, *Cf* adhar; 2 *esp in pl* na speuran the heavens, the firmament, reultan nan speuran the stars of the heavens, *Cf* iarmailt; 3 space, speur-sheòladh *m* space travel, *Cf* fànas 1

speuradair, speuradair, speuradairean *nm* an astrologer

speuradaireachd *nf invar* astrology

speurair, speurair, speurairean *nm* a spaceman, an astronaut spìc, spìce, spìcean *nf* a spike

spideag, spideig, spideagan *nf* a nightingale

spìocach *adj* mean, miserly, niggardly, stingy, *Cf* mosach 2

spìocaire, spìocaire, spìocairean *nm* a miser, a mean, stingy person

spìon *vt, pres part* **a' spìonadh**, 1 snatch, grab, tug, tear or wrench away; 2 (*less strong*) pluck (*flower, harpstring &c*)

spìonadh, *gen* spìonaidh *nm* (*the act of*) snatching, plucking &c (*see senses of* spìon *v*)

spionnadh, *gen* spionnaidh *nm* energy, strength, vigour, **leis na bha de spionnadh air fhàgail aige** with his remaining strength/energy, *Cf* lùth 3, neart

spiorad, spioraid, spioradan *nm* 1 (*relig*) a spirit, **an Spiorad Naomh** the Holy Spirit/Ghost; 2 a spirit, a ghost, *Cf* taibhse, tannasg

spioradail *adj* (*relig*) spiritual, pertaining to the spirit, **dàin spioradail** spiritual songs, hymns

spìosradh, spìosraidh, spìosraidhean *nm* (*culinary*) spice, a spice

spìosraich *vt, pres part* **a' spìosrachadh**, 1 spice, add spices to food; 2 (*body*) embalm

spiris, spirise, spirisean *nf* a perch, a roosting or perching place, *Cf* spàrr *n* 3

spleuchd *vi, pres part* **a' spleuchdadh**, 1 stare, gaze, gape, 'gawp', (**air** at); 2 squint

spleuchd, spleuchda, spleuchdan *nm* 1 a stare, a gaze, a 'gawping' expression; 2 a squint, *Cf* claonadh 4, fiaradh 2

spleuchdadh, *gen* spleuchdaidh *nm* (*the act of*) staring, squinting &c (*see senses of* spleuchd *v*)

spliùchan, spliùchain, spliùchanan *nm* a pouch (*esp for tobacco*)

spòg, spòig, spògan *nf* 1 a paw, *Cf* cròg 1, màg; 2 a hand of a clock or watch, **spòg mhòr/bheag** a minute/an hour hand; 3 a spoke

spong, spuing, spongan *nm* sponge, a sponge

sporan, *gen & pl* sporain *nm* 1 a purse; 2 (*highland dress*) a sporran, (*song*) **gheibh mi fèileadh is sporan garbh** I will get a kilt and a rough sporran

spòrs, *gen* spòrsa *nf* 1 sport, a sport, **'s e ball-coise an spòrs as fheàrr leam** football's my favourite sport; 2 fun, **bha spòrs againn a-raoir** we had fun/had a good time/enjoyed ourselves last night, **faigh** *v* **spòrs air cuideigin** have fun at someone's expense, *Cf* dibhearsan

spot, spot, spotan *nm* 1 a spot, a stain, *Cf* smal; 2 a spot, a place, (*calque*) **air an spot** on the spot, *Cf* bad 1

spoth *vt, pres part* **a' spoth** *&* **a' spothadh**, castrate, geld, spay, *Cf* **geàrr** *v* 2

spothadh, *gen* **spothaidh** *nm* 1 (*the act of*) castrating (*see* **spoth** *v*); 2 castration

spreadh *vti, pres part* **a' spreadhadh**, 1 (*vi*) burst; 2 (*vti*) explode, blow up

spreadhadh, spreadhaidh, spreadhaidhean *nm* 1 (*the act of*) bursting, exploding, blowing up; 2 an explosion

sprèidh, *gen* **sprèidhe** *nf* livestock, stock, (*esp*) cattle, (*song*) **chan iarrainn sprèidh no fearann leat** I wouldn't ask for cattle or land with you (*ie as a dowry*), *Cf* **bò, crodh, stoc¹** 3

spreig *vt, pres part* **a' spreigeadh**, incite, prompt, urge (*someone to do something*), *Cf* **brod** *v* 1 *&* 2, **brosnaich, stuig**

spreigeadh, *gen* **spreigidh** *nm* (*the act of*) inciting &c (*see senses of* **spreig** *v*)

sprùilleach, *gen* **sprùillich** *nm coll* 1 crumbs, *Cf* **criomag, sprùilleag;** 2 debris

sprùilleag, sprùilleig, sprùilleagan *nf* a crumb, *Cf* **criomag**, *& coll* **sprùilleach** 1

spùill *vt, pres part* **a' spùilleadh**, *also* **spùinn** *vt, pres part* **a' spùinneadh**, plunder, rob, despoil, *Cf* **creach** *v* 1

spùinneadair, spùinneadair, spùinneadairean *nm* a robber, a plunderer, a despoiler, a brigand, **spùinneadair-mara** a pirate, a buccaneer

spu(i)r, spuir, spuirean *nm* a claw (*esp of bird*), a talon, *Cf* **ìne** 2

spùt *vti, pres part* **a' spùtadh**, (*of liquids*) spout, spurt, squirt, *Cf* **steall** *v*, **srùb** *v* 1

spùt, spùta, spùtan *nm* 1 a spout (*ie jet of liquid*), a gush, a spurt, *Cf* **steall** *n* 1; 2 a (*large*) waterfall, *freq in placenames as* spout, **Spùt Roilidh** Spout Rollo, *Cf* **eas, leum-uisge, linne** 2; 3 *with the art*, **an spùt** diarrhoea, *Cf* **buinneach, sgàird**

spùtadh, *gen* **spùtaidh** *nm* (*the act of*) spouting, spurting &c (*see senses of* **spùt** *v*)

sràbh, sràibh, sràbhan *nm* a (drinking) straw

srac *vt, pres part* **a' sracadh**, tear, rip, rend, *Cf* **reub**

sracadh, *gen* **sracaidh** *nm* (*the act of*) tearing, ripping, rending (*see* **srac** *v*)

sradag, sradaig, sradagan *nf* a spark

sràid, sràide, sràidean *nf* a street

sràidearaich *vi, pres part* **a' sràidearachd**, stroll, saunter, walk about, (*song*) **air madainn dhomh 's mi (a') sràidearachd** one morning as I strolled about

srainnsear, srainnseir, srainnsearan *nm* **1** a stranger, **na bi nad shrainnsear!** don't be a stranger! (*ie* keep in touch!), *Cf* **coigreach 2**; **2** an incomer, **tha am baile làn shrainnsearan a-nis** the township's full of incomers now, *Cf* **seatlair**

srann *vi, pres part* **a' srannail**, snore

srann, srainn, srannan *nmf, also* **srannail** *nf invar, &* **srannartaich**, *gen* **srannartaiche** *nf,* snoring, a snore

sreang, sreinge, sreangan *nf* string (*not of instrument, Cf* **teud**)

sreath, sreatha, sreathan *nmf* **1** (*of people, objects*) a row, a line, (*of platoon &c*) a rank, (*of hills, mountains*) a range, (*on roadway*) a lane, *also in expr* (**an treas bliadhna** *&c*) **an sreath a chèile** (the third year *&c*) in a row, running, in succession (*Cf* **an ceann a chèile** – *see* **ceann 3**); **2** a layer, a stratum; **3** a series, **am prògram mu dheireadh san t-sreath** the last programme in the series

sreothart, sreothairt, sreothartan *nm* a sneeze, **dèan** *v* **sreothart** sneeze

sreothartaich, *gen* **sreothartaiche** *nf* sneezing, a bout or fit of sneezing, **dè an sreothartaich a th' ort!** what a lot of sneezing you're doing!

srian, *gen* **srèine**, *pl* **srèinean** *&* **sriantan** *nf* **1** a bridle, a rein, reins; **2** a streak, a stripe, *Cf* **stiall** *n* **1**

sròn, *gen* **sròine**, *pl* **srònan** *&* **sròintean** *nf* **1** a nose, **tha mo shròn a' leum** my nose is bleeding, **gabh rudeigin anns an t-sròin** take offence at something, **sròn bròige** a toe of a shoe; **2** (*topog*) a ridge, point or promontory, *often in placenames as* stron(e), **Sròn Iasgair** Stronesker, fisher's point or promontory, *Cf* **àrd** *n* **2**

sròn-adharcach, *gen & pl* **sròn-adharcaich** *nm* a rhinoceros

srùb *vti, pres part* **a' srùbadh**, **1** spout, spurt, *Cf* **spùt** *v*, **steall** *v*; **2** suck or slurp in (*a drink &c*)

srùb, srùib, srùban *nm* a spout (*of container, teapot &c*)

srùbadh, *gen* **srùbaidh** *nm* (*the act of*) spouting, sucking &c (*see senses of* **srùb** *v*)

srùbag, srùbaig, srùbagan *nf* **1** a sip, a small drink (*Cf* **srùb** *v* **2**); **2** (*esp*) a snack, a cup of tea (*plus biscuits, sandwich &c*), (*Highland Eng*) a stroupach, **an tig thu a-steach airson srùbaig?** will you come in for a cup of tea/a stroupach?

srùban, *gen & pl* **srùbain** *nm* a cockle, *Cf* **coilleag**

sruth *vi, pres part* **a' sruthadh**, (*esp of liquids*) flow, stream, run, *Cf* **ruith** *v* **2**, **sil 2**

sruth, *gen* **sruith** *&* **srutha**, *pl* **sruthan** *nm* **1** a stream, a burn, *occurs in placenames as* stru(ie), strow(ie) *&c*, *Cf* **allt**; **2** a flow, a rush (*of running water*); **3** a current, **ris/leis an t-sruth** against/with the current

sruthach *adj* **1** (*of liquids*) streaming, running, flowing; **2** liquid

sruthadh, *gen* **sruthaidh** *nm* (*the act of*) flowing &c (*see senses of* **sruth** *v*)

sruthan, *gen & pl* **sruthain** *nm, dimin of* **sruth** *n*, a small stream or burn, *can occur in placenames as* struan

stàball, stàbaill, stàballan *nm* a stable

stad *vti, pres part* **a' stad(adh)**, **1** stop, halt, pause, come or bring to a halt or stop, **stad iad aig bun na beinne** they halted at the foot of the mountain, **stad e an làraidh** he stopped the lorry; **2** stop, cease, desist from doing something, *Cf more usu* **leig 5**, **sguir**

stad, stada, stadan *nm* **1** a stop, a halt, a pause (*in motion, activity &c*), **nì sinn stad an seo** we'll stop/wait here (*usu briefly*), **thàinig i gu stad** she came to a halt/stop, *Cf* **stad** *v* **1**; **2** the state or condition of being stationary, **bha am bus na stad** the bus was stationary, **tha a' chùis na stad** the affair/matter/business is at a standstill; **3** an end, a cessation, a stop, *esp in expr* **cuir** *v* **stad air** stop, put a stop or end to, **cuiridh mi stad air do shràidearachd!** I'll put a stop to your stravaigin! **thoir** *v* **rudeigin gu stad** bring something to an end, *Cf* **crìoch 1**

stad-phuing, stad-phuinge, stad-phuingean *nf* a full stop

staid, staide, staidean *nf* a state, a condition, **ann an droch staid** in a bad state/condition, (*of person*) in a bad way, *Cf* **cor 1**, **dòigh 3**

staidhir, staidhreach, staidhrichean *nf, &* **staidhre, staidhre, staidhrichean** *nf,* **1** a (*single*) stair, a step (*in staircase*); **2** a staircase, a flight of stairs, (*Sc*) a stair; *Cf* **ceum 3**

stailc, stailc, stailcean *nf* (*industry &c*) a strike, **air stailc** on strike

stàilinn, *gen* **stàilinne** *nf* steel, *Cf* **cruaidh** *n*

staing, stainge, staingean *nf* a difficulty, a tight corner, a fix, **ann an droch staing** in a very difficult situation/a bad fix, *Cf* **cruaidh-chàs 2**

stàirn, *gen* **stàirne** *nf* **1** a crashing or clattering noise; **2** a loud rumbling noise

stairs(n)each, stairs(n)ich, stairs(n)ichean *nf* a threshold

stais, staise, staisean *nf* a moustache

stàit, stàite, stàitean *nf* (*pol &c*) a state, **Na Stàitean Aonaichte** the United States, **an stàit Bhreatannach** the British state, **Rùnaire na Stàite** the Secretary of State

stàiteil *adj* stately, **ceum stàiteil** a stately pace/gait

stalc, *gen* **stailc** *nm* starch

stalcair(e), stalcaire, stalcairean *nm* a fool, a blockhead, *Cf* **amadan, bumailear, ùmaidh**

stalcaireachd *nf invar* **1** stupidity; **2** a stupid action

stamag, stamaig, stamagan *nf* a stomach, *Cf* **balg 1, broinn 1, brù 2, maodal**

stamh, *gen* **staimh,** *pl* **staimh & stamhan** *nm* (*seaweed*) tangle

stamp *vti, pres part* **a' stampadh,** stamp (*with foot*), **bha i a' stampadh a casan ris** she was stamping her feet at him, *Cf* **breab** *v* 2

stamp(a), stampa, stampaichean *nf* a (postage) stamp

staoig, staoige, staoigean *nf* steak, a steak

staoin, *gen* **staoine** *nf* tin

steall *vti, pres part* **a' stealladh,** (*of liquids*) spout, squirt, spurt, gush, *Cf* **spùt** *v*, **srùb** *v* 1

steall, still, steallan *nf* 1 an outpouring of liquid, a spout, a spurt, a gush, a squirt, *Cf* **spùt** *n* 1; 2 a large drink, a swig, a slug, *Cf* **balgam 2, sgailc 3, steallag**

stealladh, *gen* **steallaidh** *nm* (*the act of*) spouting &c (*see senses of* **steall** *v*)

steallag, steallaig, steallagan *nf, dimin of* **steall** *n*, a copious drink, a swig, **ghabh e steallag mhath às a' bhotal** he took a good swig from the bottle, *Cf* **balgam 2, sgailc 3, steall** *n* 2

steallair(e), steallaire, steallairean *nm* a syringe

stèidh, stèidhe, stèidhean *nf* 1 (*phys*) a base, a foundation, (*Bibl*) **stèidh na talmhainn** the foundation of the earth, *Cf more usu* **bonn 1;** 2 (*philo, relig &c*) a basis, a foundation, a fundamental or founding principle, *Cf* **bunait**

stèidheachadh, *gen* **stèidheachaidh** *nm* 1 (*the act of*) founding &c (*see senses of* **stèidhich** *v*); 2 (*abstr*) foundation, establishment

stèidhich *vt, pres part* **a' stèidheachadh,** found, establish, set up, *Cf* **bonn 5, cas** *n* 6

stèidhichte *adj* founded, established, set up, **stèidhichte ann an 1923** founded in 1923, **an Eaglais Stèidhichte** the Established Church

stèisean, stèisein, stèiseanan *nm* (*transport, radio &c*) a station

stiall *vt, pres part* **a' stialladh,** stripe, streak, mark with streaks or stripes

stiall, stèill, stiallan *nf* 1 a streak, a stripe (*on material, skin &c*); 2 tape, a tape, a strip (*of material &c*), *Cf less trad* **teip 1;** 3 a scrap or stitch of clothing, **chuir e dheth a h-uile stiall ach a bhriogais** he took off every scrap/stitch of clothing except his trousers

stialladh, *gen* **stiallaidh** *nm* (*the act of*) striping &c (*see senses of* **stiall** *v*)

stìopall, *gen & pl* **stìopaill** *nm* a steeple, (*song*) **Glaschu mòr nan stìopall** great Glasgow of the steeples

stiùbhard, stiùbhaird, stiùbhardan *nm* a steward

stiùir *vt, pres part* **a' stiùireadh**, **1** (*boat, vehicle &c*) steer; **2** (*firm &c*) direct, run, manage, *Cf* **riaghail 2**; **3** direct, lead, conduct, show the way (*to someone in street &c*); *Cf* **seòl** *v*

stiùir, stiùire(ach), *also* **stiùrach, stiùir(ich)ean** *nf* **1** (*of boat*) a rudder; **2** a helm, *Cf* **failm, falmadair**; **3** *in expr* **uisge na stiùrach** (*lit*) the wake (*of boat &c*), (*fig*) **cha tig iad** (*&c*) **an uisge na stiùrach dhut** (*&c*) they (&c) can't hold a candle to/aren't in the same league as/ can't compete with you (&c)

stiùireadair, stiùireadair, stiùireadairean *nm* a steersman, a helmsman

stiùireadh, *gen* **stiùiridh** *nm* (*the act of*) steering, directing &c (*see senses of* **stiùir** *v*), **fear-stiùiridh** *m* a director, a manager (*of firm, organisation &c*), **an luchd-stiùiridh** the managers, the directors, (*coll*) the management, *Cf* **manaidsear, riaghladh 3**

stiùiriche, stiùiriche, stiùirichean *nm* (*esp admin*) a director, **Stiùiriche Foghlaim/Ionmhais** Director of Education/Finance, **stiùiriche riaghlaidh** a managing director

stob, stuib, stoban *nm* **1** a fence post, a stake, a stob, *Cf* **post**^{2}; **2** a stump

stòbh(a), stòbha, stòbhaichean *nf* a stove

stoc^1, *gen & pl* **stuic** *nm* **1** a trunk, *also* a stump (*of tree*), *Cf* **stob 2**; **2** a root(-stock), *Cf* **freumh**; **3** stock, livestock, *Cf* **sprèidh**

stoc^2, *gen & pl* **stuic** *nm* a scarf, a cravat, *Cf less trad* **sgarfa**

stocainn, stocainne, stocainnean *nf* a stocking, *Cf* **osan, socais**

stoidhle, stoidhle, stoidhlichean *nf* style, a style, **tha stoidhle throm air a chuid sgrìobhaidh** there's a ponderous style about his writing

stò(i)r *vt, pres part* **a' stòradh**, store, put in store, *Cf* **spàrr** *n* **2, gleidh 3**

stòiridh (*&* **stòraidh**), *gen* **stòiridh**, *pl* **stòiridhean** *nm* a story (*often a joke, a humorous story or anecdote*), *Cf* **naidheachd 2, sgeul 1, sgeulachd**

stoirm, stoirme, stoirmean *nmf* **1** a storm, *Cf* **doineann, gailleann, sian 1**; **2** *occas for* **toirm**

stòl, *gen* **stòil** *&* **stòla**, *pl* **stòlan** *nm* (*furniture*) a stool, *Cf* **furm 2** *& trad* **creapan**

stòlda *adj* (*of temperament, behaviour*) **1** sedate, serious, slow and steady, staid, sober; **2** serious (*ie opposite of* in jest), *Cf* **da-rìribh 1**

stòr *v see* **stò(i)r**

stòr, stòir, stòran *nm* **1** a store (*ie repository, shop &c, also stock, hoard &c*), (*IT*) **stòr-dàta** a database; **2** *same senses as* **stòras**

stòradh, *gen* **stòraidh** *nm* (*the act of*) storing (*see* **stò(i)r** *v*)

stòras, *gen* **stòrais** *nm* (*trad*) riches, wealth, possessions, (*song*) **ged a bhiodh mo phòcaid falamh, chì mi stòras air gach bealach** though my pocket may be empty, I see riches on every side, *Cf* **beartas, ionmhas 2, saidhbhreas**

stràc, stràic, stràcan *nm* **1** a stroke (*of scythe, strap, pen &c*), a blow, *Cf* **buille 1**; **2** an accent (*ie diacritic mark*), **tha stràc air 'a' san fhacal 'stràc'** there's an accent on 'a' in the word 'stràc', *Note: in Gaelic the 'accents' are really length marks*

stràic, stràice, stràicean *nm* (*formerly, in school*) a belt, a strap, a tawse, a lochgelly

streap *vti, pres part* **a' streap(adh)**, climb, *Cf* **dìrich**²

streap(adh), *gen* **streapaidh** *nm* (*the act of*) climbing, **streap mhonaidhean** hill/mountain climbing, hillwalking

strì *vi, pres part* **a' strì**, struggle, strive, battle, contend, compete (**ri** with, against), **a' strì ri chèile** struggling against each other

strì *nf invar* **1** (*the act of*) struggling, striving &c (*see senses of* **strì** *v*); **2** strife, contention, a struggle, a contest, **bhris an claidheamh anns an strì** the sword broke in the struggle, **buidheann strì** a pressure group, (*trad*) **strì nam bàrd** the contest of the poets, *Cf* **gleac** *n* **1**

strìoch, strìocha, strìochan *nf* (*typog*) a hyphen, *Cf* **tàthan**

strìochag, strìochaig, strìochagan *nf* (*typog*) a tick

strìochd *vi, pres part* **a' strìochdadh**, **1** submit, surrender, yield, *Cf* **gèill 1**; **2** cringe, *Cf* **crùb 3**

strìochdadh, *gen* **strìochdaidh** *nm* **1** (*the act of*) submitting, cringing &c (*see senses of* **strìochd** *v*); **2** surrender

strìopach, strìopaiche, strìopaichean *nf* a prostitute, *Cf* **siùrsach**

strìopachas, *gen* **strìopachais** *nm* prostitution

stròdhail *see* **struidheil**

structair, structair, structairean *nm* structure, a structure

struidh *vt, pres part* **a' struidh** waste, spend lavishly, squander, dissipate, *Cf* **caith 3**

struidhear, struidheir, struidhearan *nm* a waster, a wastrel, a spend-thrift

struidheil & **stròdhail** *adj* extravagant, prodigal, *esp in expr* (*Bibl, humorous &c*) **am mac struidheil/stròdhail** the prodigal son

struth, strutha, struthan *nmf* an ostrich

stuadh & **stuagh**, *gen* **stuaidh**, *pl* **stuadhan(nan)** *nf* **1** (*sea &c*) a wave, *Cf* **tonn 1**; **2** a gable (*of building*)

stuaim, *gen* **stuaime** *nf, also* **stuamachd** *nf invar*, abstemiousness, moderation, restraint, temperance, sobriety

stuama *adj* **1** (*in general behaviour, temperament*) abstemious, moderate, temperate, restrained, *Cf* **measarra, stòlda 1**; **2** (*as regards drink*) sober, abstemious, **'s e duine stuama a th' ann, cha bhi e ag òl idir** he's a sober/abstemious man, he doesn't drink at all, *Cf* **sòbair**

stùiceach & **stùirceach** *adj* surly, morose, *Cf* **gnù, mùgach 2**

stuig *vt, pres part* **a' stuigeadh**, incite, prompt, urge (*someone to do something*), *Cf* **brod** *v* 1 & 2, **brosnaich, spreig**

stuigeadh, *gen* **stuigidh** *nm* **1** (*the act of*) inciting &c (*see senses of* **stuig** *v*); **2** incitement; *Cf* **brosnachadh 1** & **3**

stùr, *gen* **stùir** *nm* dust, (*Sc*) stour, *Cf* **duslach, dust**

stuth, stutha, stuthan *nm* **1** (*textiles &c*) material(s); **2** (*sing*) material (*for making something*), **stuth bhròg** shoe-making material(s), *Cf* **adhbhar 3**; **3** stuff, matter, material, **stuth leughaidh** reading matter, **stuth math a tha sin!** that's good stuff! **chuir an naidheachdair stuth air falbh chun an fhir-deasachaidh** the journalist sent some stuff/material off to the editor

suaicheantas, *gen* & *pl* **suaicheantais** *nm* **1** (*clan, regiment, organisation &c*) a badge, an emblem, insignia, **is e an t-aiteann suaicheantas MhicLeòid** the badge/emblem of MacLeod of MacLeod is the juniper; **2** (*occas*) a novelty, a rarity, a phenomenon, (*prov*) **cha shuaicheantas còrr air cladach** a heron on a beach is no marvel

suaimhneach *adj* calm, composed, quiet, *Cf more usu* **ciùin, socair 1** & **2**

suain *vt, pres part* **a' suaineadh**, wrap, entwine (*in flexible object such as rope, foliage*), envelop

suain, *gen* **suaine** *nf* sleep (*usu deep*), slumber, *Cf more usu* **cadal 2**

Suaineach, *gen* & *pl* **Suainich** *nm* a Swede, *also as adj* **Suaineach** Swedish, of, from or pertaining to Sweden (**an t-Suain**)

suaineadh, *gen* **suainidh** *nm* (*the act of*) wrapping, entwining (*see* **suain** *v*)

suairc(e) *adj* **1** affable, approachable; **2** kind, gentle; **3** courteous, mannerly, *Cf* **beusach 2, cùirteil 1, modhail, sìobhalta 1**

suarach *adj* **1** insignificant, petty, mean, trifling, paltry, *Cf* **crìon** *adj* 2; **2** (*stronger*) contemptible, despicable, *Cf* **tàireil**

suarachas, *gen* **suarachais** *nm* **1** insignificance, pettiness, paltriness, *esp in expr* **cuir** *v* **rudeigin/cuideigin an suarachas** belittle *or* slight something/someone; **2** contemptible or despicable nature of something

suas *adv* up (*expr movement, NB from point of view of the person moving, Cf* **a-nìos, a-nuas**), **cuiridh mi suas sanas** I'll put up a notice (*Cf* **àrd** *n* 4), **chaidh e suas an staidhre** he went up the stair (*Cf* **tha e shuas an staidhre** he's upstairs), (*fam*) **cha do chuir e suas no sìos mi** it didn't affect me in the least/one way or the other, *Cf* **a-nìos, a-nuas, shìos, shuas, sìos**

suath *vti, pres part* **a' suathadh**, 1 rub, wipe (*esp for cleaning*), *Cf* **siab** 1; 2 rub or brush (**ri** against), (*autobiography title*) **Suathadh ri Iomadh Rubha** (Aonghas Caimbeul) Rubbing/Brushing against Many a Point/headland, (*fig*) **shuath mi ri iomadh carraig** I (have) knocked about a good deal (*lit* I (have) brushed against many a rock); 3 massage

suathadh, *gen* **suathaidh** *nm* 1 (*the act of*) rubbing, brushing &c (*see senses of* **suath** *v*); 2 friction; 3 massage

sùbailte *adj* supple, flexible (*material, mind &c*), *Cf* **lùbach** 2

sùbh, sùibh, sùbhan *nm* a berry, **sùbh-làir** a strawberry, *Cf more usu* **dearc**

sud *see* **siud**

sùgan, sùgain, sùganan *nm* (*trad*) rope made of twisted straw

sùgh & **sùigh** *vti, pres part* **a' sùghadh**, (*liquids*) absorb, suck (up), soak (up), **shùigh mo chòta an t-uisge** my coat absorbed/soaked up the rain, **pàipear-sùghaidh** blotting paper

sùgh, *gen* **sùgha** & **sùigh**, *pl* **sùghan** *nm* 1 (*fruits &c*) juice; 2 (*trees, plants &c*) sap

sùghach *adj* absorbent

sùghadh, *gen* **sùghaidh** *nm* 1 (*the act of*) absorbing &c (*see senses of* **sùgh** *v*); 2 suction

sùghmhor *adj* juicy, sappy

sùgradh, *gen* **sùgraidh** *nm* 1 (*trad*) mirth, merry-making, **dèan** *v* **sùgradh** make merry, revel, (*song*) **dhèanainn sùgradh ris an nigh'n duibh** I would make merry/would sport with the black-haired girl; 2 (*occas*) lovemaking

suidh *vi, pres part* **a' suidhe**, sit (down), **suidh an sin** sit there, **suidh sìos/a-bhàn!** sit down! **shuidh e sa bhus** he sat in the bus, *Cf* **suidhe** *n* 1 & 2

suidhe, suidhe, suidhe(ach)an *nm* 1 the act of sitting down, **dèan** *v* **suidhe** sit down, take a seat, be seated; 2 the state of being seated, **tha mi nam shuidhe** I am seated/sitting down, **cuir** *v* **cuideigin na shuidhe** seat someone, sit someone down, **àite-suidhe** *m* a seat, a sitting place, **cha robh àite-suidhe ann** there was nowhere to sit; 3 (*occas*) a seat

suidheachadh, suidheachaidh, suidheachaidhean *nm* 1 (*the act of*) settling, arranging, placing, etc (*see senses of* **suidhich** *v*); 2 a setting, a physical situation, a site, **b' e sin suidheachadh air leth math airson taigh-dhealbh** that was an exceptionally good site/situation for a cinema; 3 (*freq*) an abstract situation, a state of affairs, **tha an teaghlach ann an suidheachadh gu math cugallach** the family's in a pretty dodgy/dicy/uncertain situation

suidheachan, *gen & pl* **suidheachain** *nm* a seat (*Cf* **suidhe** *n* 3), a stool (*Cf* **stòl**), (*church*) a pew

suidhich *vt, pres part* **a' suidheachadh**, 1 place, seat, plant, settle or install (*an object in its location*), **suidhich stèidh** lay down a foundation, **suidhich gàrradh** plant/establish a garden, **suidhich ìomhaigh air colbh** place/install a statue on a column, *Cf* **socraich** 3; 2 set, settle, arrange, agree upon (*details, plans &c*), **suidhich là na coinneimh** arrange/settle the date of the meeting; 3 appoint, set up, establish, **suidhich comataidh** appoint a committee, **modh-riaghlaidh a shuidhich na Lochlannaich** a way/mode of governing that the Vikings established/set up

suidhichte *adj* 1 settled, arranged, placed, etc (*see senses of* **suidhich**); 2 determined, resolute, **suidhichte nach fairtlicheadh e orm** determined it wouldn't get the better of me; 3 (*of persons, status &c*) settled, established, steady; 4 (*persons*) sedate, grave, respectable, *Cf* **stòlda** 1

suidse, suidse, suidsichean *nmf* (*elec*) a switch

suigeart, *gen* **suigeirt** *nm* cheerfulness, *Cf more usu* **sunnd** 1

sùigh *see* **sùgh** *v*

sùil, sùla, sùilean *nf* 1 an eye, **dùin** *v* **do shùilean** close your eyes, **sùil gheur** a sharp eye, **ann am priobadh na sùla** in the twinkling of an eye, in a flash, (*song*) **Tearlach òg nan gorm-shùl meallach** young Charlie of the bewitching blue eyes, **cùm** *v* **sùil air** keep an eye on him/it; 2 a look, a glance, **sùil aithghearr air a' chleoc** a quick look/glance at the clock, **an toir thu sùil air a' chàr agam?** will you take/have a look at my car?; 3 *in expr* **tha sùil aig ... ri ...** expect, **tha sùil aige rithe** he's expecting her, **cha robh sùil aca ri ar faicinn** they didn't expect to see us, *Cf* **dùil**[1] 2, **sùilich**

sùil-chritheach, *gen & pl* **sùil-chrithich** *nf* a quagmire

suilbhir *adj* cheerful, *Cf* **aoibhneach** 2, **sunndach**

sùilich *vi, pres part* **a' sùileachadh**, expect (*with prep* **ri**), **chan eil mi ga shùileachadh** I don't expect it, *Cf more usu* **dùil**[1] 2, **sùil** 3

sùim, sùime, suimeannan *nf* 1 regard, respect; 2 attention, concern, interest, care, **chan eil sùim agam de na thuirt iad** I'm not paying any attention to what they said, **gabh** *v* **sùim** care, **cuir** *v* **sùim ann an rudeigin** be interested/take an interest in something, *Cf* **aire** 2, **ùidh** 2; 3 an amount, a sum, **sùim airgid** a sum of money; 4 a sum (*ie arithmetical problem*)

suipear *& suipeir, gen **suipeire(ach)**, *also* **suipearach** *pl* **suiperan** *nf* a supper

suirghe & **suiridhe** *nf invar* courting, courtship, *also as pres part* **a'**/**ri suirghe** courting, **fear-suirghe** a suitor, **dèan** *v* **suirghe ri nighean** court a lass, *Cf* **brìodal 4**, **leannanachd**

suiridhe *see* **suirghe**

suiteas, *gen* & *pl* **suiteis** *nm* a sweet, *(Sc)* a sweetie, **poca** *m* **shuiteas** a bag of sweet(ie)s, *Cf* **siùcar 2**

sùith(e), *gen* **sùithe** *nmf* soot

sùlaire, **sùlaire**, **sùlairean** *nmf* a gannet, a solan goose, *Cf* **guga**

sult, *gen* **suilt** *nm (bodily)* fat, fatness, plumpness, *(fig)* **cha robh a bheag de shult na talmhainn ann** there was none of the earth's fatness/ abundance there

Sultain, *gen* **Sultaine** *nf* & **Sultuine** *nf invar*, *with art*, **an t-Sultain**/**an t-Sultuine** September

sultmhor *adj* **1** fat, plump, corpulent, *Cf* **reamhar**; **2** in rude health, lusty, sleek; **3** wealthy, prosperous, opulent

sumainn, **sumainne**, **sumainnean** *nf* billowing *(of sea)*, a billow, surge, swell *(of sea)*, *Cf* **ataireachd**

sunnd *nm invar* **1** cheerfulness, alacrity, good humour, good cheer; **2** frame of mind, mood, humour, **dè do shunnd?** how are you? *(Aberdeenshire)* fit like?, **ann an deagh**/**droch shunnd** in a good/ bad humour/mood, in good/bad spirits, **tha deagh shunnd oirre** she's in good spirits, *Cf* **cor 1**, **dòigh 3**, **fonn 2**, **gean**, **gleus 2**

sunndach *adj* lively, cheerful, merry, in good spirits, hearty, *Cf* **aoibhneach 2**, **beòthail**, **cridheil**, **suilbhir**

Suòmach, *gen* & *pl* **Suòmaich** *nm* a Finn, someone from Finland (**Suòmaidh** *f*), *also as adj* **Suòmach** Finnish

sùrd, *gen* **sùird** *nm* **1** cheerfulness; **2** alacrity, eagerness, willingness, **chuir e ris le sùrd** he set to with a will

sùrdag, **sùrdaig**, **sùrdagan** *nf* a jump, a skip, a bounce, a caper, **dèan** *v* **sùrdag** jump, skip &c, *Cf* **leum** *n* **2**

sùrdagaich *vi, pres part* **a' sùrdagaich**, jump, skip, bounce, caper, *Cf* **leum** *v* **1**, **dèan sùrdag** *(see* **sùrdag**)

suth, **sutha**, **suthan** *nm (biol, med)* an embryo

sutha, **sutha**, **suth(ach)an** *nmf* a zoo

T

t' *see* **do** *poss adj*

tàbhachdach *adj* sound, solid, substantial, **gnìomhachas tàbhachdach** a sound/solid business, **cho tàbhachdach 's a bha a h-inntinn** how substantial her intellect was

tabhainn *see* **tabhannaich** *v*

tabhair, tabhairt *pts of irreg v* **thoir** (*see tables p 413*)

tabhairteach, *gen & pl* **tabhairtich** *nm, also* **tabhairtiche, tabhairtiche, tabhairtichean** *nm*, a giver, a donor, a benefactor

tabhann *see* **tabhannaich** *n*

tabhannaich *vi, pres part* **a' tabhannaich**, *also* **tabhainn** *vi, pres part* **a' tabhann**, bark, *Cf* **comhartaich**

tabhannaich, *gen* **tabhannaiche** *nf also* **tabhann**, *gen* **tabhainn** *nm* (*the act & sound of*) barking, *Cf* **comhart**

tabhartach *adj* **1** giving, liberal, apt to give; **2** *esp* (*gram*) dative, **an tuiseal tabhartach** the dative case

tabhartas, tabhartais, tabhartasan *nm* a donation, an offering, a presentation, a grant, a gift, *Cf* **tiodhlac**

taca *nf invar* **1** proximity, *Cf* **taic(e)** 2; **2** *now usu in expr* **an taca ri** compared to, alongside, **tha i glic an taca ri a bràthair** she's clever compared to/alongside her brother, *Cf* **coimeas** *n* 3 , **seach** 2

tacaid, tacaide, tacaidean *nf* **1** (*esp for footwear*) a tack, (*Sc*) a tacket, a hobnail; **2** (*also* **tacaid-balla**) a drawing pin

tacan, tacain, tacanan *nm* a (short) time, a (little) while, (*song*) **an sin suidhidh i tacan a' tachas a cinn** then she'll sit for a while scratching her head, *Cf more usu* **greis, tamall, treis**

tachair *vi, pres part* **a' tachairt**, **1** happen (**do** to), occur, take place, **dè a tha a' tachairt? chan eil càil** what's happening? nothing, **thachair sin an-uiridh** that happened last year, **dè a thachair do Sheumas?** what happened to James? (*Cf* **èirich** 3); **2** *can occur without subject eg* **'s ann mar sin a thachair** that's how it happened/turned out, **mar a thachair, bha trì dhiubh ann** as it happened/turned out, there were three of them; **3** *in expr* **tachair air** happen upon, chance upon, come across, **thachair mi air an-dè** I came across/happened to meet him yesterday, *Cf* **amais** 2; **4** *in expr* **tachair ri**, meet (*more intentionally*), **thachair mi rithe sa bhaile** I met her in town, *Cf* **coinnich** 2; **5** meet, make the acquaintance of, **an do thachair thu ris a-riamh?** did you ever meet him?, *Cf* **coinnich** 2

tachais *vti, pres part* **a' tachas**, **1** (*vt*) scratch (*for an example, see* **tacan**), *Cf* **sgrìob** *v* 3, **sgròb**; **2** (*vi*) itch, tickle, *Cf vti* **diogail**

tachartas, tachartais, tachartasan *nm* a happening, an event, an incident, an occurrence, *Cf* **tuiteamas 1**

tachas, *gen* **tachais** *nm* 1 (*the act of*) scratching (*esp an itch*); itching (*see* **tachais** *v*); 2 an itch, a tickling sensation

tachd *vt, pres part* **a' tachdadh**, smother, choke, throttle, strangle; (*aperture &c*) stop up, *Cf* **mùch 2**

tachdadh, *gen* **tachdaidh** *nm* 1 (*the act of*) smothering, choking &c (*see senses of* **tachd** *v*); 2 suffocation

tadhail *vti, pres part* **a' tadhal**, 1 visit, go to see, call (**air** on), **tha sinn a' dol a thadhal orra** we're going to visit/see/call on them, *Cf* **cèilidh 1, tathaich**

tadhal, tadhail, tadhalaichean *nm* 1 (*the act of*) visiting &c (*see senses of* **tadhail** *v*); 2 a visit, a call, *Cf* **cèilidh 1**; 3 (*sport*) a goal

tagair *vt, pres part* **a' tagairt** & **a' tagradh**, 1 claim (*rights, possessions, in insurance &c*), **a' tagairt a dhuais** claiming his prize/reward; 2 (*a cause, & esp a legal case*) plead, argue, prosecute or conduct

tagairt, tagairte, tagairtean *nf* 1 (*the act of*) claiming, pleading &c (*see senses of* **tagair** *v*); 2 a claim; a petition

tagh *vt, pres part* **a' taghadh**, 1 choose, select, **thagh e an sgioba** he chose/selected the team, *Cf* **roghnaich**; 2 (*pol*) elect, vote for, vote into office, **cha deachaidh an taghadh** they weren't elected, *Cf* **bhòt**

taghadh, taghaidh, taghaidhean *nm* 1 (*the act of*) choosing, electing &c (*see senses of* **tagh** *v*); 2 choice, a choice, selection, a selection, *Cf* **roghainn**; 3 (*pol*) an election

taghta *adj* 1 chosen, selected, elected; 2 choice, (*fam*) great! fine! perfect! smashing!, *as excl* **an dèan mi na soithichean dhut? taghta!** will I do the dishes for you? great!

tagradh, tagraidh, tagraidhean *nm* 1 & 2 *same as* **tagairt 1** & **2**; 3 (*law courts &c*) a plea

tagsaidh, *gen* **tagsaidh**, *pl* **tagsaidhean** *nmf* a taxi, a cab

taibhse, taibhse, taibhsean *nmf* a ghost, *Cf less usu* **tannasg**

taibhsearachd *nf invar* second sight, (*the ability and activity of*) seeing visions (*freq announcing death*), *Cf* **an dà shealladh** (*see* **sealladh 1**)

taic(e), *gen* **taice** *nf* 1 (*lit or fig*) support, a support, a buttress, a prop; patronage, **fear-taice** *m* a supporter, a patron, a backer, **cùm** *v* **taic ri cuideigin** support someone, **taic airgid** financial support/ backing/help, **taic-beatha** life support, **cuir** *v* **do thaic orm/rium** lean on me, *also* depend on me; 2 contact, proximity, *now usu in expr* **an taic ri** leaning on/against, propped up against, *Cf* **taca 1**

taiceil *adj* supporting, supportive

taidhr, taidhre, taidhrichean *nf* a tyre

taifeid, taifeid, taifeidean *nm* a bowstring

taigeis, taigeise, taigeisean *nf* haggis, a haggis

taigh, taighe, taighean *nm* & **tigh, tighe, tighean** *nm* **1** a (dwelling) house, **fear an taighe** the man of the house/head of the family, *also* the landlord (*of hotel, pub &c*) & the MC (*at ceilidh &c*), **bean an taighe** the lady/woman of the house, the housewife, *also* the landlady (*of hotel, pub, boarding house &c*), **taigh dubh** a black house, *a trad type of low-walled, thatched, round-ended Highland dwelling now virtually disappeared, also* an illicit distillery, a shebeen (*Cf* **bothan 3**), *Cf* **fàrdach 1**; **2** home *in exprs* **aig an taigh** at home, **on taigh** away from home, not at home, out, *Cf* **baile 5, dachaigh 1**; **3** *other kinds of building, or part of a building, usu for a specific use, eg* **Taigh nan Cumantan/nam Morairean** the House of Commons/of Lords, **taigh-beag** a toilet (*public or private*), **taigh-bìdh** a café, a restaurant, **taigh-chon** a kennel, **taigh-cluiche** a theatre, **taigh-dhealbh** a cinema, **taigh-nighe** a wash-house, a laundry, **taigh-òsta** a hotel, an inn, (*loosely*) a public house/pub, **taigh-tasgaidh** a museum, **taigh-staile** a distillery, *Cf* **ionad 2**

taigheadas, *gen* **taigheadais** *nm* housing, **Comataidh** *f* **an Taigheadais** the Housing Committee

tailceas, tailceasach *see* **tarcais, tarcaiseach**

tàileasg, *gen* **tàileisg** *nm* **1** chess; **2** backgammon

tàillear, tàilleir, tàillearan *nm* a tailor

taing, *gen* **tainge** *nf* **1** thanks, gratitude, **gus mo thaing a nochdadh** to show my thanks/gratitude, *Cf* **buidheachas**; **2** *usu in exprs* **mòran taing!** many thanks! thank you very much! thanks a lot!, (*less usu*) **taing dhut/dhuibh!** thank you!, **ceud taing!** thanks very much (indeed)!, *Cf* **tapadh 2**

taingeil *adj* thankful, grateful, *Cf* **buidheach**

tàinig *pt of irreg v* **thig** (*see tables p 412*)

tàir *v see* **tàrr**

tàir, tàire, tàirean *nf* contempt, disparagement, **dèan** *v* **tàir air cuideigin** despise, disparage someone, *Cf* **tarcais 1**

tairbhe *nf invar* advantage, gain, profit, benefit, *Cf* **leas 1** & *more usu* **buannachd 1**

tairbheach & **tarbhach** *adj* advantageous, beneficial, profitable

tairbhich *vi, pres part* **a' tairbheachadh**, *also* **tarbhaich** *vi, pres part* **a' tarbhachadh**, profit, gain, benefit

tàireil *adj* contemptible, *Cf* **suarach 2**

tairg *vti, pres part* **a' tairgse**, **1** offer, propose, **thairg e a chuideachadh** he offered his help, **thairg e a dhèanamh** he offered/proposed to do it; **2** offer, bid (*at sale &c*), *Cf* **tairgse 2**

tairgse, tairgse, tairgseachan *nf* **1** (*the act of*) offering &c (*see senses of* **tairg** *v*); **2** an offer, **thoir** *v* **tairgse (air)** make an offer/a bid (for), **cuir** *v* **an tairgse muinntir eile** offer/make available to other people

tàirneanach, *gen* **tàirneanaich** *nm* thunder

tairsgeir, tairsgeir, tairsgeirean *nf* a peat iron, a peat spade

tais *adj* damp, moist, humid, *Cf* **bog** *adj* 5

taisbean & **taisbein** *vt, pres part* **a' taisbeanadh**, display, show, present, reveal, exhibit, demonstrate, *Cf* **nochd 1, seall 2**

taisbeanach *adj* **1** (*esp sounds, sights*) clear, distinct, **chunnaic/chuala e gu taisbeanach iad** he saw/heard them clearly; **2** (*gram*) indicative, **a' mhodh thaisbeanach** the indicative mood

taisbeanadh, taisbeanaidh, taisbeanaidhean *nm* **1** (*the act of*) displaying, showing &c (*see senses of* **taisbean** *v*); **2** (*of art, goods, techniques &c*) an exhibition, a display, a show, a demonstration, a presentation

taisbeanlann, taisbeanlainn, taisbeanlannan *nf* an exhibition hall, an art gallery

taise *nf invar* & **taiseachd** *nf invar* moistness, moisture, dampness, humidity

taiseachadh, *gen* **taiseachaidh** *nm* (*the act of*) dampening &c (*see senses of* **taisich** *v*)

taisg *vt, pres part* **a' tasgadh**, **1** (*esp in museums &c*) store, put in store, deposit, *Cf* **stò(i)r**; **2** hoard; **3** (*fin*) invest, deposit

taisich *vt, pres part* **a' taiseachadh**, dampen, moisten, make damp, moist or humid

taitinn *vi, pres part* **a' taitinn** & **a' taitneadh**, (*with prep* **ri**), please, be pleasant, *Cf* **còrd** *v* 2

taitneach *adj* (*persons, also things, situations*) agreeable, pleasant, pleasing (**ri** to), *Cf* **ciatach 1, tlachdmhor 1**

taitneadh, *gen* **taitnidh** *nm* (*the act of*) pleasing &c (*see senses of* **taitinn** *v*)

taitneas, taitneis, taitneasan *nm* **1** pleasure, the state of being pleased, *Cf* **tlachd 1**; **2** pleasantness, agreeableness

talachadh, *gen* **talachaidh** *nm* (*the act of*) complaining &c (*see* **talaich** *v*)

tàladh, tàlaidh, tàlaidhean *nm* **1** (*the act of*) attracting, enticing, soothing &c (*see senses of* **tàlaidh** *v*); **2** attraction; **3** enticement, allurement; **4** (*also* **òran** *m* **tàlaidh**) a lullaby

talaich *vi, pres part* **a' talachadh**, complain, grumble, be dissatisfied, *Cf more usu* **gearain**

tàlaidh *vt, pres part* **a' tàladh**, **1** attract, *Cf* **tarraing 5**; **2** entice, allure, tempt, **tàlaidh an luchd-ceannachd air ais** attract/tempt the customers back, *Cf* **meall** *v* **2**; **3** hush, soothe, calm, *Cf* **ciùinich**; **4** sing and/or rock to sleep

tàlaidheach *adj* attractive, *Cf* **tarraingeach**

talamh, talmhainn, talamhan *nm* (*f in gen sing*) **1 an Talamh** the Earth, **air aghaidh na talmhainn** on the face of the earth, *Cf* **cruinne-cè**, **saoghal 1**; **2** earth, soil, **chuir iad san talamh e** they put him into the earth, *Cf* **ùir**; **3** land, ground, **talamh àitich** arable/cultivated land, **talamh bàn** fallow ground, *Cf* **fearann**, **tìr 4**

tàlann, tàlainn, tàlann(t)an *nm* a talent, a (natural) gift, *Cf less strong* **comas**

tàlantach *adj* talented, gifted, *Cf less strong* **comasach**

talla, talla, tallachan *nm* a hall (*trad, hist*) **talla MhicLeòid** MacLeod's (*ancestral or chiefly*) hall, *now usu public*, **talla a' bhaile** the village hall, the town hall; **2** *in expr* **mac-talla** *m* an echo (*lit* son of (the) hall)

talmhaidh *adj* **1** earthly, **creutair talmhaidh** an earthly creature; **2** (*opposite of spiritual*) worldly, *Cf* **saoghalta**

tàmailt, tàmailte, tàmailtean *nf* **1** disgrace, shame, *Cf* **masladh**, **nàire 1**; **2** an insult, an indignity

tàmailteach *adj* **1** scandalous, shameful, disgraceful, *Cf* **maslach**, **nàr**; **2** insulting

tàmailtich *vt, pres part* **a' tàmailteachadh**, insult, make ashamed

tamall, tamaill, tamallan *nm* a time, a while, **an ceann tamaill** in/after a while, (*song*) **ma dh'fhanas tu tamall** if you'll tarry a while, *Cf more usu* **greis**, **tacan**, **treis**

tàmh *vi, pres part* **a' tàmh**, **1** rest, *Cf more usu* **gabh fois** (*see* **fois 2**); **2** dwell, live, stay, (*song*) **gruagach an taobh shuas dhìom a' tàmh** a girl living up the way from me, *Cf* **còmhnaich** *& more usu* **fuirich 2**

tàmh, *gen* **tàimh** *nm* **1** (*the act of*) resting, dwelling &c (*see senses of* **tàmh** *v*); **2** rest, peace, **tha iad nan tàmh** they are at rest, (*esp of dead*) they are at peace, *Cf* **fois 1**, **sìth**; **3** (*not necessarily pej*) idleness, inactivity, freedom from work, **a bheil thu nad thàmh?** are you at leisure/free?, **tha an luchd-obrach nan tàmh air sgàth na stailc** the workers are idle because of the strike, (*prov*) **am fear a bhios na thàmh, cuiridh e an cat san teine** the man with nothing to do will put the cat in the fire

tàmhadair, tàmhadair, tàmhadairean *nm* a tranquilizer

tana *adj* **1** (*of build, dimensions*) thin, *Cf* **caol** *adj* **2**; **2** (*of liquids*) thin, runny, **brochan tana** thin gruel/porridge; **3** (*opposite of dense*) thin, sparse, **falt tana** thin(ning) hair, *Cf* **gann 1**, *& opposite* **dlùth 2**; **4** (*of water*) shallow; **5** (*material &c*) flimsy

tanaich *vti, pres part* **a' tanachadh**, thin, make or become thin &c (*see senses of* **tana**)

tancair, tancair, tancairean *nm* a tanker, **tancair-ola** an oil tanker

tannasg, *gen & pl* **tannaisg** *nm* a ghost, *Cf more usu* **taibhse**

taobh, taoibh, taobhan *nm* **1** a side, **tha pian nam thaobh** there's a pain in my side (*Cf* **cliathaich**), **bhuail an làraidh taobh an taighe** the lorry struck the side of the house, **taobh-duilleige** a page (*of book &c*), (*abbrev*) **td a seachd** p7, **rim thaobh** at my side, beside me, **ri taobh a' chidhe** beside/alongside the quay, **taobh ri taobh** side by side, **an taobh a-muigh/a-staigh** the outside/inside, **an taobh siar** & **an taobh an iar** the west (side of the country); **2** a way, a direction, **tha iad a' tighinn an taobh seo** they're coming this way, *Cf* **rathad 2**; **3** (*in dispute &c*) a side, a part, **ghabh sinn a taobh** we took her part/side, we sided with/supported her, **cùm** *v* **taobh ri** side with, favour, *Cf* **leth 1**; **4** *in expr* (*in family &c*) **rach ri taobh cuideigin** take after someone; **5** *in expr* **(a-)thaobh** (*with gen*) concerning, regarding, touching on, in connection with, **tha duilgheadasan aige a-thaobh airgid** he has problems concerning money, **thaobh an taghaidh** ... as for the election ..., as far as the election is concerned ...; **6** *also in expr* **a-thaobh (is gun)** *prep* (*& conj*) because of, on account of, **a-thaobh sin** because of that, **a-thaobh is gun chaochail e** because he died, *Cf more usu* **a chionn 1 & 2**

taois, taoise, taoisean *nf* dough

taom *vti, pres part* **a' taomadh**, (*esp liquids from container &c*) pour, pour or flow out, empty; (*cookery &c*) drain, **taom na currain** drain the carrots, *Cf* **dòirt** (*vti*), **ruith** (*vi*), **sil** (*vi*)

taomadh, *gen* **taomaidh** *nm* (*the act of*) pouring &c (*see* **taom** *v*)

tap, tapa, tapaichean *nmf* a (water) tap, *Cf* **goc**

tapachd *nf invar, abstr noun corres to* **tapaidh**, cleverness, sturdiness &c (*see senses of* **tapaidh**)

tapadh, *gen* **tapaidh** *nm* **1** (*trad*) the state of being handy, willing, smart &c; a smart (&c) action (*see senses of* **tapaidh**); **2** *now usu in expr* **tapadh leat/leibh!** thank you!, *Cf* **taing 2**

tapag, tapaig, tapagan *nf* a slip of the tongue, an exclamation

tapaidh *adj* **1** (*of persons*) willing, handy; clever, quick, smart, *Cf* **deas 4**; **2** sturdy, manly, active, *Cf* **calma, duineil 1, fearail**

tarbh, *gen & pl* **tairbh** *nm* a bull

tarbhach *adj see* **tairbheach**

tarbhaich *see* **tairbhich**

tarbh-nathrach, *gen & pl* **tairbh-nathrach** *nm* a dragonfly

tarcais, *gen* **tarcaise** *nf, &* **tailceas**, *gen* **tailceis** *nm*, **1** contempt, reproach, disdain, scorn, **dèan** *v* **tarcais air** despise, *Cf* **tàir** *n*; **2** spite

tarcaiseach *adj &* **tailceasach** *adj* **1** contemptuous, reproachful, scornful, disdainful; **2** spiteful

targaid, **targaide**, **targaidean** *nf* **1** a target; **2** (*trad*) a targe, a shield, *Cf* **sgiath 2**

tàrmachadh, *gen* **tàrmachaidh** *nm* (*the act of*) begetting, breeding &c (*see senses of* **tàrmaich** *v*)

tàrmaich *vt, pres part* **a' tàrmachadh**, **1** (*trad*) beget, *Cf more usu* **gin** *v* **1**; **2** (*plants, animals*) breed, propagate; **3** produce, originate

tàrr *vi, pres part* **a' tàrradh**, *also* **tàir** *vi, pres part* **a' tàireadh**, *usu in expr* **tàrr/tàir às** escape, flee, make off, run away, *Cf* **teich**

tàrradh, *gen* **tàrraidh** *nm* (*the act of*) escaping, making off &c (*see senses of* **tàrr** *v*)

tarrag *see* **tarrang**

tarraing *vti, pres part* **a' tarraing**, **1** draw, drag, pull, haul, heave, tug (**air** at, on), *Cf* **slaod** *v*, **spìon 1**; **2** draw (*liquids &c*), **tarraing pinnt** draw/pull a pint, **tarraing anail/fuil** draw breath/blood; **3** (*lit & fig*) approach, draw near (**gu** to), **tarraing gu crìch** draw to an end, **bha iad a' tarraing gu h-aois** they were getting on (in years), **bha an oidhche a' tarraing faisg air a' mhadainn** the night was drawing close to morning, *Cf* **teann** *v* **3**; **4** (*artist &c*) draw, **tarraing dealbh** draw a picture; **5** (*person, magnet &c*) attract, *Cf* **tàlaidh 1**; **6** *in expr* **tarraing à cuideigin** tease, kid someone, pull someone's leg, *Cf* **farranaich 1**; **7** (*spirits*) distil

tarraing, *gen* **tarrainge** *&* **tàirgne**, *pl* **tarraingean** *&* **tàirgnean** *nf* **1** (*the act of*) drawing, pulling, attracting &c (*see senses of* **tarraing** *v*); **2** a pull, a tug; **3** (*liquids*) a draught; **4** (*spirits*) distillation

tarraingeach *adj* attractive, *Cf* **tàlaidheach**

tarrang, **tàirnge**, **tàirngean** *nf, also* **tarrag**, **tarraig**, **tarragan** *nf &* **tarran**, **tarrain**, **tàirnean** *nm*, (*joinery*) a nail

tarsainn 1 *adv* (*expr position or movement*) across, over; **2** *usu as prep* **tarsainn air** (*with dat*) across, over, **bha craobh mhòr tarsainn air an rathad** a great tree was across the road, **chaidh iad tarsainn air an drochaid/na beanntan** they crossed/went over the bridge/ mountains; *Cf* **thairis 1** *&* **2**, **thar 1**

tart, *gen* **tairt** *nm* thirst, dryness, *stronger than* **pathadh**

tartmhor *adj* thirsty, dry, *Cf* **ìotmhor**, **pàiteach**

tasgadh, *gen* **tasgaidh** *nm* **1** storing, depositing &c (*see senses of* **taisg** *v*), **taigh-tasgaidh** *m* a storehouse, a museum, **ionad-tasgaidh** *m* a repository; **2** investment, **airgead-tasgaidh** *m* an investment (*ie the funds invested*), **neach-tasgaidh** *m* an investor

tasgaidh, tasgaidhe, tasgaidhean *nf* a store, a treasure, a hoard, *Cf* **stòr, stòras**

tastan, tastain, tastanan *nm* (*former currency*) a shilling, *Cf* **sgillinn 2**

tàth *vt, pres part* **a' tàthadh,** join or fix together (*by various means & substances*), glue (together), cement, solder, weld

tathaich *vi, pres part* **a' tathaich,** (*with prep* **air**) frequent, visit (*usu frequently*); haunt, (*song*) **a fhleasgaich** (*voc*) **tha tathaich air srathan is glinn, a' mealladh nan caileag** young fellow who haunts/hangs about in straths and glens, enticing the lassies, **tathaich air càirdean** visit/call on friends, *Cf* **tadhail**

tàthan, tàthain, tàthanan *nm* (*typog*) a hyphen, *Cf* **strìoch**

tè *nf invar* **1** one (*denoting object or living thing having female gram or phys gender*), **tha a' phiseag/a' chroit seo nas lugha na an tè sin** this kitten/croft is smaller than that one, *Cf* **fear 3; 2** a woman, a female, **tè-mhalairt** a business woman, **thàinig tè gam fhaicinn an-dè** a woman came to see me yesterday, *Cf* **boireannach, fear 1**

teachd *&* **tiochd** *vi defective* **1** (*trad*) come, *virtually obs in this sense exc in set expr* **an t-àm ri teachd** the time to come, the future, *Cf usu* **thig 1; 2** fit, **an teachd e an cùl do chàir?** will it fit in the back of your car?

teachd *nm invar* an arrival, a coming, **teachd an earraich** the coming of spring, *also in exprs* **teachd-an-tìr** a living, a livelihood, **teachd-a-steach** an income (*also* an entry/entrance)

teachdail *adj* future, (*gram*) **an tràth teachdail** the future tense

teachdaire, teachdaire, teachdairean *nm* **1** a messenger, a courier; **2** a missionary, *Cf less trad* **misionairidh**

teachdaireachd *nf invar* **1** a mission, a message, a commission, an errand, **a' dol air theachdaireachd** going on an errand/a mission (*Cf* **gnothach 3**); **2** news, information &c carried (*by messenger &c*), *Cf* **fios 3, naidheachd 1**

teadhair, teadhrach, teadhraichean *nf* a tether, (*calque*) **aig ceann mo theadhrach** at the end of my tether

teagaisg *vt, pres part* **a' teagasg, 1** teach, **theagaisg mo sheanair dhomh na th' agam de ghliocas** my grandfather taught me what wisdom I have; **2** (*formally*) teach, instruct, educate, **teagaisg matamataig** teach maths, **teagaisg an ginealach ùr** teach/educate the new generation (*Cf* **foghlaim**)

teagamh, teagaimh, teagamhan *nm* **1** a doubt, an uncertainty, **gun teagamh** without (a) doubt, doubtless, **an tig i a-màireach? thig gun teagamh!** will she come tomorrow? without a doubt! definitely! *in expr* **cuir** *v* **(an) teagamh** doubt, cast doubt on, **cha do chuir iad**

teagamh nach fhaca sinn e (*note double neg*) they didn't doubt that we saw/had seen it, **cuir** *v* **teagamh ann an rudeigin** doubt (*the existence, truth &c of*) something, *Cf* **amharas; 2** *as conj* **theagamh** perhaps, maybe, **theagamh nach tig i** perhaps she won't come, *Cf more usu* **dòcha 3, faod 2**

teagasg, *gen* **teagaisg** *nm* (*ed, Bibl &c*) teaching, **fear-/neach-teagaisg** *m* a teacher (*Cf* **tidsear**)

teaghlach, teaghlaich, teaghlaichean *nm* a family, *Cf* **caraid 2, duine 6**

teagmhach *adj* doubtful, doubting, dubious, sceptical, *Cf* **amharasach**

teallach, teallaich, teallaichean *nm* a hearth, a fireside, a fireplace, **leac** *f* **an teallaich** a hearthstone, **teallach ceàrdaich** a forge (*in smithy*), *Cf* **cagailt, teinntean**

teampall, *gen & pl* **teampaill** *nm* a temple

teanchair, teanchair, teanchairean *nm, also* **teannachair, teannachair, teannachairean** *nm,* **1** a vice, a clamp; **2** a pair of pincers; **3** a pair of tongs

teanga, teangaidh, teangan *nf* **1** a tongue, **air bàrr mo theangaidh** on the tip of my tongue; **2** (*occas*) a tongue, a language, *Cf more usu* **cainnt 2, cànain**

teann *vi, pres part* **a' teannadh, 1** (*trad*) move, go, come, proceed, (*song*) **teann a-nall 's thoir dhomh do làmh** come over here and give me your hand, *Cf* **gabh 2, imich 2, rach 1, thig 1; 2** (*lit & fig*) **teann air** approach, near, draw near to, **bha e a' teannadh air meadhan-oidhche** it was nearing midnight, *Cf* **tarraing** *v* **3; 3** begin, start, set about, set to, **theann e ri streap** he began/set to/set about climbing, *Cf* **tòisich**

teann *adj* **1** tight, tense, **ròpa teann** a tight rope; **2** firm, fixed, solid, **ceangail** *v* **gu teann** join firmly, *Cf* **daingeann; 3** (*person, discipline &c*) severe, strict, *Cf* **cruaidh 2; 4** close, near (**air** to), **teann air mìos air ais** close on/nearly a month ago, **bha an t-arm teann orra** the army was hard on their heels/close by them, *Cf more usu* **dlùth 1, faisg**

teannachadh, *gen* **teannachaidh** *nm* **1** (*the act of*) tightening, constricting &c (*see senses of* **teannaich** *v*); **2** constriction

teannaich *vti, pres part* **a' teannachadh, 1** tighten, tense, tension; **2** constrict, squeeze

teanntachd-cuim *nf invar* constipation

teanta, teanta, teantaichean *nf* a tent, *Cf more trad* **pàillean 2, puball**

Tearach *see* **Hearach**

tèarainte *adj* **1** safe, secure (*from danger &c*), **àite-falaich tèarainte** a safe/secure hide-out, *Cf* **sàbhailte; 2** secure (*ie guaranteed*), **gabhaltas tèarainte** secure tenure (*of land &c*), **inbhe thèarainte airson na Gàidhlig** secure (*legal &c*) status for Gaelic

tèarainteachd *nf invar* 1 security, safety, **an tèarainteachd** in safety; 2 security (*of tenure &c*); 3 (*IT*) **tèarainteachd dàta** data protection/ security

tearc *adj* scant, scarce, few, rare, *Cf* **ainneamh** *& more usu* **gann**

tèarmann, *gen* **tèarmainn** *nm* (*abstr*) protection, safeguard, refuge, sanctuary, asylum, (*con*) a refuge, a sanctuary, **fo thèarmann na cùirte** in/under the court's protection, **tèarmann poileataigeach** political asylum, **tèarmann nàdair** a nature reserve, *Cf* **comraich**, **dìon** *n*

teàrn *&* **teàrnadh** *see* **teirinn**

teàrr, *gen* **tearra** *nf* tar, pitch, *Cf* **bìth** 1

teas *nm invar* heat, *Cf* **blàths**

teasach, teasaich, teasaichean *nf* fever, a fever, *Cf* **fiabhras**

teasachadh, *gen* **teasachaidh** *nm* 1 (*the act of*) heating (*see* **teasaich** *v*); 2 (*domestic &c*) heating, **uidheam** *f* **teasachaidh** a heater, a heating appliance

teasaich *vti, pres part* **a' teasachadh**, heat, heat up, *Cf* **blàthaich**, **teòthaich**

teasairg *&* **teasraig** *vt, pres part* **a' teasairginn** *&* **a' teasraiginn**, save, rescue, **is e an luchd-tadhail a theasairg an t-eilean** it was the visitors who saved the island, **bata-teasairginn** *m* a lifeboat, a rescue boat, *Cf* **sàbhail** 1

teas-mheidh, teas-mheidh, teas-mheidhean *nf* a thermometer

teatha *nf invar* & **tì** *nf invar* tea (*ie the drink*), **cupa tì** a cup of tea

teich *vi, pres part* **a' teicheadh**, flee, escape, run away, **theich na saighdearan** the soldiers fled *or* the soldiers deserted, *Cf* **tàrr**

teicheadh, *gen* **teichidh** *nm* 1 (*the act of*) running away &c (*see senses of* **teich** *v*); 2 flight, escape; 3 desertion (*from army &c*)

teicneolach *adj* technical, technological, *Cf* **teignigeach**

teicneolaiche, teicneolaiche, teicneolaichean *nm* a technician, a technologist

teicneolas, *gen* **teicneolais** *nm* technology, (*IT*) **teicneolas fiosrachaidh** information technology

tèid *pt of irreg v* **rach** (*see tables p 410*)

teignigeach *adj* technical, *Cf* **teicneolach**

teine, teine, teintean *nm* fire, a fire, **taobh** *m* **an teine** the fireside, (*Cf* **cagailt, teallach, teinntean**), **teine-dealain** an electric fire, **cuir** *v* **air/cuir** *v* **às an teine** light/put out the fire, **rach** *v* **na theine** go on fire, **chaidh talla a' bhaile na theine** the village hall went on fire, **cuir** *v* **teine ri togalach** set fire to a building

teinntean, *gen & pl* **teinntein** *nm* a hearth, a fireplace, *Cf* **cagailt, teallach**

teip, teip, teipichean *nf* 1 tape, a tape, **tcip-thomhais** a measuring tape, **dùin** *v* **am parsail le teip** seal the parcel with tape, **teip-clàraidh** recording tape; 2 a tape, a cassette, a recording on tape, **an cuala tu an teip ùr aca?** have you heard their new tape?

teirce *nf invar, abstr noun corres to* **tearc**, scarceness, scarcity &c (*see senses of* **tearc**)

teirinn & **teàrn** *vti, pres part* **a' teàrnadh, 1** come or go down, descend (*from hill &c*), **theirinn e às a' chùbaid** he came down from the pulpit, (*as vt*) **a' teàrnadh a' bhruthaich** coming down/descending the hillside; **2** alight, dismount, climb/get down (*from horse, vehicle &c*), **theirinn i bhàrr a' ghàrraidh** she climbed down from the wall; *Cf* **crom** *v* 4

teis-meadhan *see* **meadhan 1**

teisteanas, teisteanais, teisteanasan *nm* **1** testimony, a testimony, evidence, a piece of evidence (*in court &c*), *Cf* **dearbhadh 2, fianais 2; 2** (*proof of something, usu written*) attestation, an attestation, a certificate, a diploma, **teisteanas-breith** a birth certificate; **3** (*of character, qualifications &c*) a reference, a testimonial

telebhisean, telebhisein, telebhiseanan *nm* television, a television set, *used with & without art,* **chunnaic mi prògram math air (an) telebhisean** I saw a good programme on (the) television, **cead** *m* **telebhisein** a television licence

teòclaid & **seòclaid**, *gen* **teòclaid**, *pl* **teòclaidean** *nmf* chocolate, a chocolate, *also as adj* **teòclaid** chocolate

teòdh *see* **teòthaich**

teodhachd & **teothachd** *nf invar* temperature, a temperature

teòthaich *also* **teothaich** *vti, pres part* **a' teòthachadh**, *also* **teòdh** *vt, pres part* **a' teòthadh**, warm, warm up, **teòthaich am brot** warm up the soup, (*as vi*) **teòdh ri cuideigin** warm/take to someone, *Cf* **blàthaich, teasaich**

teòma *adj* **1** expert, skilful, *Cf* **ealanta 2, sgileil; 2** ingenious, *Cf* **innleachdach 1, tionnsgalach**

teth *comp* **(n)as (&c) teotha** *adj* hot, **botal** *m* **teth** a hot water bottle, *Cf weaker* **blàth** *adj* 1

teud, *gen* **tèid** & **teuda**, *pl* **teudan** *nm* a string (*of instrument*), **sheinneadh teudan na fìdhle** the fiddle strings would/used to sing

tha *pt of irreg v* **bi** (*see tables p 414*)

thabhair *pt of irreg v* **thoir** (*see tables p 413*)

thàinig *pt of irreg v* **thig** (*see tables p 412*)

thairis *adv* 1 (*usu expr movement*) across, over, beyond, **chaidh iad thairis** they went over/across, (*trad*) they went abroad, (*now usu*) **chaidh iad a-null thairis** they went abroad, (*expr position*) **tha iad thall thairis** they are abroad, **cuir** *v* **thairis** overflow, run over, (*of boat*) capsize, turn over, overturn, **chuir an t-uisge thairis** the water overflowed, (*fig*) **tìr a' cur thairis le creutairean de gach seòrsa** a land overflowing with creatures of every kind, **chuir iad thairis i** they capsized her; 2 *as prep* **thairis air** across, over, **chaidh am plèana thairis air na beanntan** the plane passed over the mountains, *Cf* **tarsainn 2**; 3 beyond, (*fig*) **chaidh thu thairis air na bha mi ag iarraidh** you went beyond what I required, *Cf* **thar 2**

thairis, thairte, *prep prons see* **thar**

thall *adv* over there, (over) yonder (*usu expr position*), (*song*) **a bhean** (*voc*) **ud thall a rinn an gàire** woman over there who laughed, **thall 's a-bhos** here and there, (*expr motion*) hither and thither, **ann an Ameireagaidh thall** over (yonder)/far away in America, *Cf* **a-bhos, a-nall, a-null**; 2 (*in exprs of time*) *expr idea* furthest, latter, **mu dheireadh thall** at long last, **aig a' cheann thall** in the end, ultimately, at the latter end; 3 *for* **thall thairis** *see* **thairis 1**

thalla *pl* **thallaibh** *imper* go, be off, get, **thalla(ibh) dhachaigh!** off you go home!, (get) away home!, *Cf* **falbh 1, tiugainn, trobhad**

thar *prep* (*with gen*), *Note: the pers prons* **mi**, **thu**, **e** *&c combine with* **thar** *to form the prep prons* **tharam(sa), tharad(sa), thairis(-san), thairte(se), tharainn(e), tharaibh(se), tharta(san)**; 1 across, over (*expr position*), **bha raidhfil aige thar a ghuailne** he had a rifle over/across his shoulder, *Cf more usu* **tarsainn 2**; 2 over, beyond (*expr motion*) **thoir mo shoraidh thar a' chuain** carry my greeting over/beyond the ocean, (*fig*) **tha sin uile thar mo chomasan** all that's beyond my capabilities, (*with numbers*) upon, **mìltean thar mhìltean** thousands upon thousands; 3 *in expr* **thar a chèile** in a state of confusion, *also* at loggerheads, **sgioblaich an rùm agad, tha a h-uile càil thar a chèile** tidy your room, everything's in a complete jumble/mess (*Cf* **bun-os-cionn**), **chuir mi thar a chèile iad** I set them at each other's throats, **chaidh iad thar a chèile** they fell out, *Cf* **tro 2**

tharad, tharaibh, tharainn, tharam, tharta, *prep prons see* **thar**

theab *v def*, 1 (*trad*) miss; 2 *now normally used only in preterite tense, expressing the idea* almost, nearly, **theab mi tuiteam** I almost fell, **theab iad mo sgriosadh** they almost/nearly ruined me

theagamh *see* **teagamh 2**

thèid *pt of irreg v* **rach** (*see tables p 410*)

their, theireadh, theirinn *pts of irreg v* **abair** (*see tables p 403*)

thig *vi irreg* (*see tables p 412*), *pres part* **a' tighinn, 1** come, approach, **thig gam fhaicinn!** come to/and see me! **cha tàinig i còmhla rium** she didn't come with me, **a' tighinn an taobh seo** coming this way; **2** arrive, come, get here, **cuin a thig iad?** when will they come/get here? (*Cf* **ruig**), **mus tig an geamhradh** before winter comes, (*fig*) **thàinig e a-steach orm nach robh iad ag èisteachd** I realised/it occurred to me that they weren't listening; **3** *in expr* **thig air** *expr the onset of an emotion, state &c*, **thàinig eagal/mulad/acras orm** I grew afraid/sorrowful/hungry; **4** *in expr* **thig do** suit, please, fit, be appropriate for, **ciamar a tha an dreuchd ùr a' tighinn dhut?** how's the new job suiting you?, how do you like the new job? (*trad song*) **is tu as fheàrr don tig deise** it is you whom a suit of clothes best becomes/fits, *also* **thig ri** suit, **cha tàinig an t-àite ri a shlàinte** the place didn't suit his health, *Cf* **còrd** *v*, **freagair 2; 5** *misc exprs* **thig beò** live, **ciamar a thig sinn beò san àite seo?** how will we live in this place?, **thig suas/beò air** live on, survive on, **cha tig mi suas/ beò air sin!** I can't live/manage/survive on that!, **thàinig e (&c) bhuaithe** he (&c) recovered/got over it/got better, **thàinig orm sin a dhèanamh** I had to do that

thogras *see* **togair 2**

thoir & **tabhair,** *occas* **thabhair** *vt irreg* (*see tables p 413*), *pres part* **a' toirt** *occas* **a' tabhairt, 1** give (**do** to), **thug i tiodhlac dhuinn** she gave us a present, **thoir comhairle** give advice, **thoir dhomh do làmh** give me your hand, **thoir an aire** pay (*lit* give) attention, *also* take care, **thoir oidhirp** make an attempt (**air** at), **thoir tarraing air rudeigin** mention, touch on, allude or refer to something (*Cf* **iomradh 1**); **2** **thoir seachad** give, give away, present, deliver, hand over **bha iad a' toirt seachad airgid air an t-sràid an-diugh** they were giving away money in the street today, **bheir i seachad òraid** she'll give/ deliver a speech/talk (*Cf* **gabh 3**), **thoir seachad an gunna** hand over the gun; **3** take, bring, (*song*) **thoir am fios seo thun a' bhàird** take this news/message to the poet, (*song*) **thoir a-nall Ailean thugam** bring Alan over to me, **bheir mi sgrìob do Ghlaschu** I'll take a trip to Glasgow, **a' toirt sùil air a' phàipear-naidheachd** taking/having a look at the paper, **thoir gu buil** bring to a conclusion, achieve, **thoir am bith** bring into being/existence, **thoir do chasan leat!** take yourself off!, clear off! **thug iad na buinn asta** they took to their heels, **thoir an t-siteag ort!** get out! **thug i Ameireagaidh oirre** she took herself off/off she went to America; **4** *in expr* **thoir air** make, force, **thug i orm falbh** she made me leave, **bheir e orm a dhèanamh aig a' cheann thall** he'll force me to do it eventually, *Cf* **co-èignich**

thu, *emph* **thusa**, *pers pron* you (*sing & fam - for note on use of* **thu** *&* **sibh** *see* **sibh**); *Note:* **tu** *tends to be used after all parts of the verb* is (**is tu, cha tu, nach tu?, an tu?, bu tu** *&c*) *& when it is the subject of a verb in the conditional* (*eg* **bhiodh tu** you would be) *or the relative future* (*eg* **'s ann an sin a bhitheas tu** it's there that you'll be); *contrast* **is esan a bhuaileadh/bhuaileas thu** it's he who would/will strike you, *where* **thu** *is the object of the verb*

thubhairt *pt of irreg v* **abair** (*see tables p 403*)

thuca, thugad, thugaibh, thugainn, thugam, thuice, thuige, *prep prons see* **gu**[1]

thug, thugadh, *pts of irreg v* **thoir** (*see tables p 413*)

thuirt *pt of irreg v* **abair** (*see tables p 403*)

thun *see* **gu**[1]

tì *see* **teatha**

tiamhaidh *adj* melancholy, plaintive, poignant, pulling at the heartstrings, (*song*) **'s tiamhaidh buan dha thar nan stuaghan seinn nam maighdeannan san àirigh** melancholy and enduring for him beyond the waves is the singing of the maidens in the sheiling

tibhre, tibhre, tibhrean *nm* a dimple

ticead, ticeid, ticeadan *nf, also* **ticeard, ticeaird, ticeardan** *nf &* **tiocaid, tiocaid, tiocaidean** *nf*, a ticket, *Cf* **bileag 4**

tìde, tìde, tìdean *nf* 1 time, **tha an tìde a' dol seachad** the time's going by/passing, **sgrìobh Murchadh thugainn, agus bha a thìde aige** Murdo wrote to us, and about time too! **bidh uisge ann fad na tìde** it rains all the time, **ri tìde** in time, in due course, eventually, **an ceann uair a** (*for* **de**) **thìde** after an hour, in an hour's time, *Cf* **ùine 1**; 2 weather (*for more usu* **sìde**), *Cf* **aimsir**; 3 *usu with art* **an tìde** (*also* **an tìde-mhara**) the tide, **tha an tìde(-mhara) nar n-aghaidh** the tide's against us, *Cf* **seòl-mara** (*see* **muir**)

tidsear, tidseir, tidsearan *nm* a teacher, *Cf* **fear-teagaisg** (*see* **teagasg**)

tig, tigeadh, tiginn, *pts of irreg v* **thig** (*see tables p 412*)

tigh *see* **taigh**

tighead *see* **tiughad**

tighearna, tighearna, tighearnan *nm* 1 (*hist*) a lord (*ie ruler*), **Tighearna nan Eilean** Lord of the Isles; 2 a landowner, a laird, *Cf* **uachdaran 2**; 3 (*relig*) **an Tighearna** the Lord; 4 *excl* **a Thighearna!** (Oh) Lord!

tighinn *pt of irreg v* **thig** (*see tables p 412*)

Tìleach, *gen & pl* **Tìlich** *nm* an Icelander, someone from Iceland (**Innis** *m* **Tìle**), *also as adj* **Tìleach** Icelandic

tilg *vt, pres part* **a' tilgeadh** & **a' tilgeil, 1** throw, fling, toss, cast (**air** at), **na tilg clachan!** don't throw stones! **tilg air falbh** throw away, **thilg i searrach** she cast a foal, *Cf* **caith 4, sad; 2** accuse of, reproach with, **thilg iad orm nach robh mi dìcheallach** they accused me of/reproached me with not being conscientious; **3** throw up, vomit, sick up, **thilg am balach a dhìnnear** the boy threw up his dinner, *Cf* **dìobhair, sgeith; 4** fire, shoot (*a firearm*), *Cf* **loisg 2**

tilgeadh, tilgidh, tilgidhean *nm* **1** (*the act of*) throwing, accusing &c (*see senses of* **tilg** *v*); **2** a throw

till, *formerly also* **pill**, *vi, pres part* **a' tilleadh** & **a' pilleadh**, return, come or go back, (*trad song*) **cha till MacCruimein** MacCrimmon will never return, **a' tilleadh dhachaigh** going back/returning home

tilleadh, *gen* **tillidh** *nm* returning, a return, **turas-tillidh** *m* a return journey

tìm, tìme, tìmean *nf* (*the abstr phenomenon*) time, (*poem*) **Tha tìm, am fiadh, an coille Hallaig** (Somhairle MacGill-Eain) Time, the deer, is in the wood of Hallaig, *Cf more usu* (*for time as it is lived*) **àm, tìde 1**

timcheall 1 *adv* round, around, **bha dealbh na teilidh a' dol timcheall, timcheall** the picture on the telly was going round and round, **cuir** *v* **timcheall na briosgaidean** pass/send round the biscuits, *Cf* **cuairt 4; 2** *as prep* **timcheall** (*with gen*) round, around, **thèid sinn timcheall an locha** we'll go round the loch, **tha luchd-reic a' dol timcheall a' bhaile** there are salesmen going round the town, *Cf* **cuairt 5; 3** *as prep* **timcheall air** round, around, about, **bha craobhan timcheall orm** there were trees around me, **a bheil bùithtean timcheall air an seo?** are there any shops around/about here? **thog iad taighean timcheall air a' ghàrradh aige** they built houses around his garden, **bidh timcheall air deichnear ann** there'll be around/about ten people there, *Cf* **cuairt 5; 4** *as prep* **mu thimcheall** about, concerning (*with gen*), **tha iad ag ràdh rudan oillteil mum thimcheall/mu timcheall** they're saying dreadful/shocking things about me/her, *Cf more usu* **mu 3**

timcheallan, *gen* & *pl* **timcheallain** *nm* (*at road junction,* & *in playpark* &c) a roundabout

tinn *adj* ill, sick, unwell, ailing, *Cf* **bochd 3, euslainteach** *adj*

tinne, *gen* **tinne**, *pl* **tinnean** & **tinneachan** *nm* a link (*in chain*)

tinneas, tinneis, tinneasan *nm* illness, an illness, disease, a disease, sickness, **tinneas-mara** seasickness, **tinneas cridhe** heart disease, **tinneas an t-siùcair** diabetes, *Cf* **euslaint(e), galar, gearan 3**

tiocaid *see* **ticead**

tiodhlac, tiodhlaic, tiodhlacan *nm* a gift, a present, a donation, *Cf* **tabhartas**

tiodhlacadh, tiodhlacaidh, tiodhlacadhan *nm* 1 (*the act of*) burying, giving &c (*see senses of* **tiodhlaic** *v*); 2 burial, a burial, a funeral, *Cf* **adhlacadh 2, tòrradh**

tiodhlaic *vt, pres part* **a' tiodhlacadh,** 1 (*of people*) bury, inter, *Cf* **adhlaic;** 2 give as a present, donate, gift, *Cf more usu* **thoir 1 & 2**

tiomnadh, tiomnaidh, tiomnaidhean *nm* 1 a will, a testament; 2 the act of bequeathing, a bequest, *Cf* **dìleab;** 3 (*Bibl*) **an Seann Tiomnadh** the Old Testament, **an Tiomnadh Nuadh** the New Testament

tiomnaich *vt, pres part* **a' tiomnachadh,** bequeathe, leave in one's will

tiompan, *gen* **tiompain,** *pl* **tiompain** & **tiompanan** *nm* a cymbal

tionail *vti, pres part* **a' tional,** 1 (*vi*) (*esp of people*) assemble, come together, gather, congregate, collect, meet, *Cf* **cruinnich 1, thig còmhla** (*see* **còmhla** *adv* 1); 2 (*vt*) (*esp of livestock*) gather, *Cf* **cruinnich 3, tru(i)s 3**

tional, tionail, tionalan *nm* 1 (*the act of*) assembling, gathering, collecting &c (*see senses of* **tionail** *v*); 2 assembly, an assembly, collection, a collection, a gathering, a rally, *Cf* **cruinneachadh 2**

tionndadh, tionndaidh, tionndaidhean *nm* 1 (*the act of*) turning (*see senses of* **tionndaidh** *v*); 2 a turn (*ie a deviation or revolution*)

tionndaidh *vti, pres part* **a' tionndadh,** 1 (*vi*) turn (*phys & fig*), **thionndaidh e chun an taoibh a thàinig e** he turned towards the way/direction he had come, **cò ris a thionndaidheadh e?** who(m) could he turn to? **tha an tìde-mhara a' tionndadh** the tide's turning; 2 (*vt*) turn, cause to revolve or change orientation, **cha do thionndaidh i a ceann** she didn't turn her head, **tionndaidh a' chuibhle(-stiùiridh)** turn the steering wheel, **tionndaidh an sgàthan chun a' bhalla** turn the mirror to the wall; 3 (*vti*) turn (**gu** to) (*ie convert or become*), **thionndaidh an luaidhe gu òr** the lead turned to gold

tionnsgail & **tionnsgain** *vt, pres part* **a' tionnsgal** & **a' tionnsgain** & **a' tionnsgnadh,** contrive, devise, invent, *Cf more usu* **innlich**

tionnsgal, tionnsgail, tionnsgalan *nm* 1 (*the act of*) contriving &c (*see senses of* **tionnsgail** *v*); 2 ingenuity, inventiveness, invention, an invention, a contraption, *Cf more usu* **innleachd 1**

tionnsgalach *adj* 1 inventive, *Cf* **innleachdach 1;** 2 industrial, *Cf* **gnìomhachail**

tionnsgalair, tionnsgalair, tionnsgalairean *nm* an inventor

tìoraidh! (*fam*) *excl on parting*, cheerio!, *Cf more formal* **beannachd 4, soraidh 1**

tioram *adj* **1** dry, **seo agad tubhailte thioram** here's a dry towel, **bha an loch tioram** the loch was dry; **2** dry, thirsty, *Cf* **ìotmhor, tartmhor; 3** (*climate, landscape*) dry, arid

tiormachadh, *gen* **tiormachaidh** *nm* (*the act of*) drying, drying up

tiormachd *nf invar* **1** dryness; **2** drought, a drought, *Cf less extreme* **turadh**

tiormadair, tiormadair, tiormadairean *nm* a dryer

tiormaich *vti, pres part* **a' tiormachadh,** dry, dry up, **chan eil na soithichean air an tiormachadh** the dishes haven't been dried

tiota, tiota, tiotaidhean *nm, also* **tiotan,** *gen & pl* **tiotain** *nm,* **1** (*clock time*) a second, *Cf* **diog; 2** an instant, a moment, a short while, a tick, a 'jiffy', *Cf* **mòmaid, priobadh 2,** *& longer* **greis(eag), tacan, treis**

tiotag, tiotaig, tiotagan *nf, dimin of* **tiota**

tiotal, tiotail, tiotalan *nm* **1** a title (*of book &c*); **2** (*TV &c*) **fo-thiotalan** subtitles; **3** (*rank &c*) a title

tìr, tìre, tìrean *nmf* **1** land (*as opposed to sea*), terra firma, **muir is tìr** sea and land, **tha iad a' tighinn gu tìr** they're coming ashore, (*song*) **'s truagh nach do dh'fhuirich mi tioram air tìr** it's a pity I didn't stay dry on terra firma, **tìr-mòr** a mainland, (*not usu with art*) **air tìr-mòr** on the mainland; **2** a land, a country, **tìrean cèin** distant/ foreign lands, **tha mi sona san tìr seo** I'm happy/content in this country, **tìr-eòlas** geography (*Cf* **cruinn-eòlas**), *Cf* **dùthaich 1; 3** an area, a region, a district, **ciamar a thig sinn beò san tìr seo?** how will we live/make a living in this area/part of the world (*also here* . . . in this landscape/terrain), *Cf more usu* **ceàrn, dùthaich 2, sgìre 1; 4** land, ground, *Cf more usu* **fearann, talamh 3**

Tirt, Tirteach *see* **Hiort, Hiortach**

tiugainn *imper* come along, come on ('with me' *understood*), let us go, *Cf* **thalla, trobhad**

tiugh *comp* **(n)as** (*&c*) **tighe** *adj* **1** (*phys*) thick, dense, *Cf* **dlùth 2, dòmhail 2; 2** (*fam*) (*mentally*) thick, dense, slow-witted

tiughad, *gen* **tiughaid** *nm &* **tighead,** *gen* **tigheid** *nm* density, denseness, thickness

tlachd *nf invar* **1** pleasure, enjoyment, *Cf* **toileachadh 2; 2** affection, attachment, liking, (*trad*) **is beag mo thlachd dheth** I have little affection/liking for him, *Cf* **bàidh 1, dèidh 2, spèis**

tlachdmhor *adj* **1** pleasant, pleasing, *Cf* **taitneach; 2** enjoyable, pleasurable; **3** (*of people*) attractive, likeable

tnù(th), *gen* **tnùtha** *nm* envy, jealousy; malice, *Cf more usu* **eud 1, farmad**

tobar, *gen* **tobair** (*m*) *&* **tobrach** (*f*), *pl* **tobraichean** *nmf* **1** a spring, a (natural) well, **tobar fìor-uisge** a spring of pure water, *Cf* **fuaran; 2** a (*dug*) well (*unlike* **fuaran**)

tobhta, tobhta, tobhtaichean *nmf* a ruin (*of building*), (*song*) **an tobht' aig Anndra 's e làn de dh'fheanntaig** (Màiri Mhòr) the ruins of Andrew's house, overrun with nettles, *Cf* **làrach 1**

tobhta, *gen* **tobhta,** *pl* **tobhtan** & **tobhtachan** *nmf* (*of boat*) a thwart

tocasaid & **togsaid,** *gen* **tocasaid,** *pl* **tocasaidean** *nf* a large barrel; (*orig*) a hogshead, *Cf* **baraille**

tòchd *nm invar* a stink, a bad or foul smell

tochradh, tochraidh, tochraidhean *nm* a dowry, (*Sc*) a tocher

todha, todha, todhaichean *nm* (*tool*) a hoe, **bha obair-thodha ri dèanamh** there was hoeing to be done, *Cf* **sgrìoban**

todhaig *vti, pres part* **a' todhaigeadh,** hoe

todhair *vt, pres part* **a' todhar, 1** manure (*land*), *Cf* **leasaich 3, mathaich; 2** bleach, *Cf* **gealaich 2**

todhar, *gen* **todhair** *nm* manure, dung (*to put on fields &c*), *Cf* **inneir, mathachadh**

tog *vt, pres part* **a' togail, 1** raise, lift, pick up, hoist, **tog do cheann** lift/raise your head, **togaibh na siùil** hoist the sails, **thog sin mo chridhe** that raised my spirits (*lit* heart), (*song*) **hì-ri-o-rì togaidh sinn fonn** we will sing/strike up (*lit* raise) a song; **2** build, **thog e taigh dha fhèin** he built a house for himself, **taigh air a dheagh thogail** a well built house; **3** (*of people*) raise, bring up, rear, **thogadh mi ann an Cola** I was brought up/I grew up in Coll, (*of livestock &c*) raise, rear, breed, *Cf* **àraich; 4** stir, rouse, *in expr* **tog ort!** rouse yourself!, stir your stumps!, get a move on!, *also* be off with you!; **5** pick up, acquire, **'s ann san Eilean Sgitheanach a thog mi mo chuid Gàidhlig** I picked up/acquired/learned my Gaelic in Skye, *Cf* **ionnsaich 1**

togail, *gen* **togalach** *nf* (*the act of*) raising, building, rousing &c (*see senses of* **tog** *v*)

togair *vti, pres part* **a' togradh, 1** wish for, desire, covet, *Cf more usu* **miannaich 1; 2** *now usu in rel fut tense,* **thèid sinn air làithean-saora, ma thogras tu** we'll go on holiday, if you like/want, **dìreach mar a thogras sibh** just as you like, *Cf* **iarr 1**

togalach, togalaich, togalaichean *nm* a building

togradh, tograidh, tograidhean *nm* **1** (*the act of*) wishing for &c (*see senses of* **togair** *v*); **2** a wish, a desire, an inclination

togsaid *see* **toc(a)said**

toibheum, toibheim, toibheuman *nm* blasphemy, a blasphemous utterance

toigh *adj* **1** (*trad*) pleasing, agreeable, dear, *Cf more usu* **taitneach; 2** *now in expr* **is toigh leam** (&c) I (&c) like, find pleasing, **an toigh leat càise? cha toil** (*for* **cha toigh leam**)! do you like cheese? no! **nach toigh leat a bhith a' snàmh?** is toil don't you like to swim? yes, *Cf* **còrd**

toil, toile, toilean *nf* **1** will, **toil Dhè** God's will, **deagh-thoil** goodwill, (*prov*) **far am bi toil, bidh gnìomh** where there's a will there's a way, *Cf* **miann 1, rùn 3; 2** *also in expr* **mas e do thoil/ur toil e!** please! (*lit* if it is your will)

toileach *adj* **1** willing, **tha mi toileach sin a dhèanamh dhut** I'm willing/ happy/glad to do that for you, *Cf* **deònach; 2** (*also* **saor-thoileach**) voluntary; **3** content, contented, glad, *Cf* **riaraichte, sona,** & *stronger* **toilichte**

toileachadh, *gen* **toileachaidh** *nm* **1** (*the act of*) pleasing &c (*see senses of* **toilich** *v*); **2** satisfaction, gratification

toileachas, *gen* **toileachais** *nm* content, contentment, gladness

toileachas-inntinn *see* **toil-inntinn**

toilich *vt*, *pres part* **a' toileachadh**, please, content, satisfy, *Cf* **riaraich 1**

toilichte *adj* happy, well pleased or satisfied, *Cf usu weaker* **sona**

toil-inntinn, toil-inntinne, toil-inntinnean *nf* **1** (*also, in this sense,* **toileachas-inntinn**, *gen* **toileachas-inntinne** *nm*) (mental) pleasure, contentment, or gladness; **2** something that causes the foregoing, a source of contentment &c; **3** peace of mind

toill *vt*, *pres part* **a' toilltinn**, deserve, merit

toillteanach *adj* worthy, deserving (**air** of), (*poem*) **toillteanach air pòg** deserving (of) a kiss, *Cf more usu* **airidh**

tòimhseachan, *gen* & *pl* **tòimhseachain** *nm* **1** a puzzle, a riddle, a brainteaser, a conundrum, **tòimhseachan-tarsainn** a crossword puzzle

toinisg, *gen* **toinisge** *nf* sense, common sense, 'gumption', *Cf* **ciall 1, tuigse 1**

toinisgeil *adj* **1** sensible, having common sense and/or sound judgement or understanding, *Cf* **ciallach, tuigseach 1; 2** mentally bright or smart, intelligent, *Cf* **geur-chùiseach**

toinn *vti*, *pres part* **a' toinneadh**, twist, wind, twine, wreathe, *Cf* **snìomh 2**

tòir, *gen* **tòrach** & **tòire**, *pl* **tòirichean** & **tòirean** *nf* **1** a pursuit, a chase, *Cf* **ruaig 1; 2** *now usu in expr* **an tòir air** in pursuit of, in search of, after, (*song*) **Dòmhnall dubh an Dòmhnallaich a-nochd an tòir air Mòraig** MacDonald's black-haired Donald tonight in pursuit of/after Morag, **chaidh e dhan bhaile an tòir air càr ùr** he went to the town after/looking for a new car, *Cf* **lorg** *v* **1, sir**

toireadh, toirinn *pts of irreg v* **thoir** *see tables p 413*

toirm, toirme, toirmean *nf* noise, a noise, a din, a hubbub, (*song*) **is toirm mum chluais** and a din about my ear(s), *Cf* **faram, othail**

toirmeasg, *gen* **toirmisg** *nm* **1** (*the act of*) forbidding, prohibiting (*see* **toirmisg** *v*); **2** prohibition, a prohibition

toirmeasgach *adj* prohibitive, apt to prohibit or forbid

toirmisg *vt, pres part* **a' toirmeasg**, forbid, prohibit

toirt *nf invar* (*the act of*) giving, taking, bringing &c (*see senses of* **thoir** *v*)

toiseach, toisich, toisichean *nm* **1** (*in time*) a start, a beginning, **toiseach an t-samhraidh** the start/beginning of summer, *esp in expr* **an toiseach** *adv* first, at first, **thàinig Flòraidh an toiseach** Flora came first/was first to arrive, **cha bu toigh leam e an toiseach** I didn't like him at first, (*emph*) **an toiseach tòiseachaidh** in the very beginning, originally; **2** (*in space*) the front part of anything, a prow or bow (*of boat*), **an comhair a thoisich** frontwards, front end first, *also* head on, **ann an toiseach na làraidh** in the front (*ie cab*) of the lorry, **cas-toisich** a foreleg/front leg, **toiseach an airm** the van(guard) of the army; **3** *also in expr* **air thoiseach air** *prep* ahead of, **bha e a' coiseachd roimhe, fada air thoiseach oirnn** he was walking along, far ahead/a long way in front of us, **air thoiseach air na dùthchannan eile** ahead of the other countries

tòiseachadh, *gen* **tòiseachaidh** *nm* **1** (*the act of*) beginning, starting &c (*see senses of* **tòisich** *v*), (*saying*) **is e obair latha tòiseachadh** getting started is a day's work; **2** a beginning, a start, **tòiseachadh ùr** a fresh start, *Cf* **toiseach 1**

tòisich *vti, pres part* **a' tòiseachadh**, start, commence, begin, **tòisich as ùr** start afresh, make a fresh start, **tòisichidh sinn air an treabhadh a-màireach** we'll make a start at the ploughing tomorrow, **tòisich a' seinn** start singing, (*more trad*) **tòisich air/ri seinn** start to sing, *Cf* **teann** *v* **3**

toit, toite, toitean *nf* **1** steam, (*prov*) **cha tig às a' phoit ach an toit a bhios innte** you can't get out of the pot more steam than is in it; **2** smoke; *Cf* **smùid** *n* **1** *&* **2**

toitean, toitein, toiteanan *nm* a cigarette

toll *vti, pres part* **a' tolladh**, bore, hole, dig or make a hole, drill, perforate, pierce, puncture, **chaidh am bàta a tholladh** the boat was holed

toll, *gen & pl* **tuill** *nm* **1** a hole, a bore; **2** a pit, a hollow; **3** (*vulg*) an anus, an arsehole, **'s e an t-àite seo toll an t-saoghail** this place is the arsehole of the world

tolladh, *gen* **tollaidh** *nm* (*the act of*) boring, perforating &c (*see senses of* **toll** *v*), **clàr-tollaidh** *m* a drilling platform

tolltach *adj* full of holes

tolman, tolmain, tolmanan *nm* (*topog*) a small knowe, knoll or mound

tom, tuim, tomannan *nm* **1** (*topog*) a small hill or hillock (*usu rounded*); **2** *now mainly in placenames*, a thicket, a bush; **Tom Beithe** birch thicket (*or* birch hillock)

tomadach & **tomaltach** *adj* **1** large, sizeable, bulky, ample; **2** (*of person*) big, brawny, burly

tombaca, tombaca, tombacan *nm* tobacco

tomhais *vt, pres part* **a' tomhas, 1** measure (*esp dimensions, also speed, weight*); **2** (*land &c*) survey; **3** calculate, compute (*distance, speed &c*); **4** guess, **tomhais cia mheud a th' ann** guess how many there are

tomhas, *gen* **tomhais,** *pl* **tòimhsean** & **tomhasan** *nm* **1** (*the act of*) measuring, surveying, guessing &c (*see senses of* **tomhais** *v*), **teip-thomhais** *f* a measuring tape, **fear-tomhais** *m* a surveyor; **2** measurement, a measurement, a dimension, a size, **gabh** *v* **tomhasan** take measurements; **3** a measure (*ie device*), **tomhas-teas** a thermometer; **4** (*land &c*) a survey; **5** calculation, a calculation, computation, a computation, **aig astar gun tomhas** at an incalculable/immeasurable speed; **6** a guess, *Cf* **tuaiream**

tòn, tòine, tònan *nf* **1** an anus (*also* **toll-tòine** *m*), a rectum, *Cf* (*vulg*) **toll** *n* 3; **2** (*fam*) an arse, a bum, a bottom, a backside, (*humorous car sticker*) **na pòg mo thòn** don't kiss my bum (*ie keep your distance*), *Cf* **màs** 2; **3** the back part or section of something, **tòn an taighe/an talla** the back of the house/the hall, *Cf more usu* **cùl** 2

tonn, *gen* **tuinn(e),** *pl* **tuinn** & **tonnan** *nmf* **1** (*in sea*) a wave, **cumhachd** *m* **tuinne** wave power, *Cf* **stuadh** 1; **2** (*physics &c*) a wave, **fuaim-thonn** a sound wave, **tonn-teasa** (*also* **teas-tonn** *m*) a heat wave

tonna & **tunna,** *gen* **tonna/tunna,** *pl* **tonnachan/tunnachan** *nm* a ton, a tonne

topag, topaig, topagan *nf* a (sky)lark, *Cf more usu* **uiseag**

torach *adj* **1** (*land, plants &c*) fruitful, productive, high-yielding, fertile, (*lit & fig*) bearing fruit; **2** (*also, in this sense,* **torrach**) pregnant, with young (*Cf* **trom** 4), fecund, fertilised, **ugh torrach** a fertilised egg, (*prov*) **ge b' e bhios saor, cha dèan gaoth torrach** whoever may be innocent/blameless, it's not the wind that causes pregnancy

torachadh, *gen* **torachaidh** *nm* **1** (*the act of*) fertilising &c (*see senses of* **toraich** *v*); **2** fertilisation

torachas, *gen* **torachais** *nm* fertility

toradh, toraidh, toraidhean *nm* **1** (*of land, plants &c*) produce, fruit(s), (*fin &c*) yield, **toradh na talmhainn** the produce/fruit(s) of the earth; **2** (*of action &c*) a result, a consequence, an effect, **toradh do dhol-a-mach** the consequence(s) of your behaviour, **toradh deuchainn** an exam result, **mar thoradh air sin** as a result of that, *Cf* **buaidh 4, buil 1, èifeachd; 3** (*industry &c*) output

toraich *vt, pres part* **a' torachadh**, (*gynaecology &c*) fertilise, make fertile, cause to conceive

torc, *gen & pl* **tuirc** *nm* a boar, **torc allaidh/fiadhaich** a wild boar, *Cf* **cràin, cullach, muc**

torman, tormain, tormanan *nm* a continuous (*usu low*) sound, murmuring, a murmur, droning, humming, a hum, **torman an uillt** the murmur(ing) of the stream, *Cf* **crònan 1; 2** (*occas louder*) rumbling, a rumble

tòrr, torra, torran *nm* **1** a heap, a mound, **tòrr airgid** a heap of money/silver, **tòrr gainneimh** a heap/mound of sand, *Cf* **cruach** *n* **1, dùn 1; 2** (*fam*) lots, heaps, loads, many, much, (*with gen*) **tha tòrr dhaoine den bheachd sin** lots of people are of that opinion, *Cf* **grunn 2, mòran 1; 3** (*topog*) a hill (*esp conical or mound-shaped*)

torrach *see* **torach 2**

tòrradh, tòrraidh, tòrraidhean *nm* a funeral, a burial, *Cf* **adhlacadh 2, tiodhlacadh 2**

tosd *nm invar* **1** silence, the state of being silent or quiet, (*esp of persons*) **bha a' chlann nan tosd** the children were silent, *also as command* **tosd!** silence!; **2** (*music*) a rest

tosdach *adj* silent, quiet, **dh'fhalbh iad gu tosdach** they left quietly/silently, *Cf* **sàmhach 1**

tosgaid *same as* **tocasaid**

tosgaire, tosgaire, tosgairean *nm* an ambassador, an envoy

tosgaireachd, toisgaireachd, tosgaireachdan *nf* an embassy

tràchdas, *gen & pl* **tràchdais** *nm* a thesis, a dissertation

tractar, tractair, tractaran *nm* a tractor

tràghadh, *gen* **tràghaidh** *nm* **1** (*the act of*) draining, emptying, subsiding, ebbing &c (*see senses of* **tràigh** *v*); **2** (*of engine*) exhaust, **pìob** *f* **thràghaidh** an exhaust pipe

trafaig, *gen* **trafaige** *nf* (*road &c*) traffic

tràigh *vti, pres part* **a' tràghadh**, *also* **traogh** *vti, pres part* **a' traoghadh**, *esp of liquids*, **1** drain, empty, exhaust (*container &c*); **2** (*vi*) subside, settle, sink, **thraogh na tuiltean** the floods subsided, *Cf* **sìolaidh 2; 3** (*vi*) (*of sea, tide*) ebb, subside

tràigh, *gen* **tràgha(d)** & **tràighe**, *pl* **tràighean** *nf* **1** a shore, a beach (*esp tidal*), a strand, *Cf* **cladach**; **2** a tide (*insofar as it covers & uncovers a beach*), **tha tràigh mhòr ann an-diugh** there's a very low tide today, *Cf* **seòl-mara** (*see* **muir**)

tràill, **tràill(e)**, **tràillean** *nmf* **1** a slave; **2** a drudge; **3** an addict, **tha e na thràill do cheàrrachas/dhrogaichean** he's addicted to gambling/drugs, *Cf* **urra 3**

tràilleachadh, *gen* **tràilleachaidh** *nm* (*the act of*) enslaving

tràilleachd *nf invar* & **tràillealachd** *nf invar* **1** slavery, enslavement; **2** drudgery; **3** addiction

tràillich *vt*, *pres part* **a' tràilleachadh**, enslave

traisg *vi*, *pres part* **a' trasg(adh)**, fast

tràlair, **tràlair**, **tràlairean** *nm* a (fishing) trawler

trang *adj* busy, (*Sc*) thrang, **trang ris an iasgach** busy at/with the fishing, *Cf* **dripeil**, **sàs 2**

trannsa, **trannsa**, **trannsaichean** *nf* a corridor, a passage (*in building*)

traogh *see* **tràigh** *v*

trasg, **traisg**, **trasgan** *nf* & **trasgadh**, **trasgaidh**, **trasgaidhean** *nm* fasting, a fast, **là-traisg** *m* a fast day, **tha iad nan trasg** they are fasting (*Cf* **traisg** *v*)

trastanach *adj* diagonal

tràth *adj* & (*esp*) *adv* **1** early (*ie at an early stage*), **tràth feasgar** early in the afternoon, **tràth sa mhadainn** early in the morning, *Cf* **moch**; **2** early, in good time, soon (*ie before time, premature*), **tràth airson na coinneimh** early for the meeting, **ro thràth airson ùbhlan abaich** too early/soon for ripe apples; **3** *in expr* **mu thràth** (*also found as* **mar a tha** & **mar-thà**) *adv* already, **leugh mi e mu thràth** I've read it already, **mar a thubhairt mi mu thràth** as I have said already, *Cf* **a cheana**

tràth, *gen* **tràith** & **tràtha**, *pl* **tràthan** *nm* **1** a time, a season, a period (*incl school*), (*trad*) **tràth air tàileasg** a time/while spent at backgammon, *esp an appointed, right or habitual time*, **tràth-bìdh** a mealtime, **tràth-ùrnaigh** prayer time, **facal na thràth** a word in season/at the right time, *Cf more usu* **àm**, **greis**, **ràith 2**; **2** (*gram*) a tense, **an tràth caithte** the past tense

tràthach, *gen* **tràthaich** *nm* hay, *Cf more usu* **feur 2**

treabh *vt*, *pres part* **a' treabhadh**, plough

treal(l)aich, **treal(l)aich**, **treal(l)aichean** *nf* **1** jumble, lumber, assorted rubbish, trash or junk, *Cf* **truileis** & (*more worthless*) **sgudal 1**; **2** (*assorted possessions &c*) odds and ends, bits and pieces, gear, stuff,

sgioblaich do threallaich tidy your stuff; **3** *in pl* **treal(l)aichean** one's luggage, baggage, belongings

trèan *vti, pres part* **a' trèanadh, 1** (*vt*) (*ed &c*) train, *Cf* **ionnsaich 3, oileanaich; 2** (*vti*) (*sport*) train

trèan(a), trèana, trèanaichean *nf* a (railway, tube &c) train, **chaill mi an trèana** I missed the train, **luath-thrèana** an express

treas *num adj* third, **an treas là den mhìos** the third of the month, **treas deug** thirteenth

trèig *vt, pres part* **a' trèigsinn**, abandon, desert, forsake, leave, quit, relinquish, **thrèig e a theaghlach** he deserted/abandoned his family, **thrèig i a dreuchd** she quit/relinquished her post, **trèigibh creideamh ur sinnsirean** forsake the faith of your forefathers, **thrèig na daoine an t-eilean** the people deserted/abandoned the island, *Cf* **dìobair, fàg**

trèigsinn *nm invar* **1** (*the act of*) abandoning, deserting &c (*see senses of* **trèig** *v*); **2** desertion

treis, treise, treisean *nf* a while, a time, *Cf* **greis**

treiseag, treiseig, treiseagan *nf* (*dimin of* **treis**), a short while *or* time, (*Sc*) a whilie, *Cf* **greiseag**

treòrachadh, *gen* **treòrachaidh** *nm* **1** (*the act of*) guiding, directing, conducting, leading (*see senses of* **treòraich** *v*), **neach-treòrachaidh** *m* a (*tourist &c*) guide; **2** (*ed &c*) guidance, **tidsear-treòrachaidh** *m* a guidance teacher

treòraich *vt, pres part* **a' treòrachadh, 1** guide, direct, conduct, **treòraich luchd-turais** *m* guide/conduct tourists, *Cf* **seòl** *v* **3; 2** lead, **threòraich e a choitheanal gu Canada** he led his congregation to Canada, *Cf* **stiùir** *v* **3**

treubh, *gen* **trèibh** *&* **treubha**, *pl* **treubhan** *nf* a tribe

treud, *gen* **trèid** *&* **treuda**, *pl* **treudan** *nm* **1** (*animals*) a flock, a herd, *Cf* **buar, greigh; 2** (*people*) a group, a band, *Cf more usu* **buidheann 1, còmhlan; 3** (*derog*) a gang, a crowd, (*song*) **mallachd ... air Rìgh Uilleam 's air a threud** a curse ... on King William and on his gang, *Cf* **gràisg, prabar**

treun, *comp* (**n)as** (*&c*) **treine, treise** *&* **treasa**, *adj* strong (*with overtones of bravery, endurance*), stout, **gaisgich threuna** stout heroes, (*poem*) **còmhdach an spioraid bu trèine** (Somhairle MacGill-Eain) garment of the bravest spirit, *Cf* **calma, làidir 1**

treun *nf invar* **1** (*trad*) strength, the height of one's strength, *now usu in expr* **ann an treun a neirt** at the height of his/her powers/strength, in his/her prime

trì *num adj* three, **trì fichead** sixty, three score

triall *vi, pres part* **a' triall**, travel, make one's way, move about, journey, (*trad song*) **bha seo ort a' triall** this is what you had when on the move, (*song*) **nach fhaod mi triall do chladaichean** that I cannot travel/go along your shores, *Cf* **imich 2, rach 1, siubhail 1**

trian *nm invar* a third, **chaill mi dà thrian de na shàbhail mi** I lost two thirds of my savings

triath, triaith, triathan *nm* (*trad*) a lord, *Cf now usu* **tighearna 1**

tric *adj, usu as adv* **1** often, frequent(ly), **cha tig i cho tric agus a chleachd (i)** she doesn't come as often as she used to, **is tric a rachadh sinn ann** we often used to go there, *Cf* **minig**; **2** *in adv expr* **mar as trice** usually

tricead, *gen* **triceid** *nm* (*abstr*) frequency, (*elec*) a frequency

trì-cheàrnag, trì-cheàrnaig, trì-cheàrnagan *nf* a triangle

trìd 1 *prep* (*trad*) through (*Cf* **tro**); **2** *now as prefix corres to Eng* trans-, *eg* **trìd-shoilleir** transparent

trì-deug *n & adj* thirteen

trioblaid, trioblaide, trioblaidean *nf* trouble (*ie misfortune, difficulties &c*), **thàinig trioblaid oirnn** trouble came upon us, **b' e call m' obrach toiseach ar trioblaidean** the loss of my job was the start of our troubles, *Cf* **duilgheadas**

trìthead, trìtheid, trìtheadan *nm & num* thirty (*in alt numbering system*)

triubhas, triubhais, triubhasan *nm* a pair of trews or trousers, *Cf* **briogais**

triùir *nmf invar* (*of people*) three, a threesome, (*with gen pl*) **triùir bhràithrean** three brothers, (*prov*) **bheir aon duine triùir bhàrr an rathaid** one man will lead three off the road

triuthach, *gen* **triuthaich** *nf*, *with art*, **an triuthach** whooping cough

tro & troimh *prep* (*takes dat, & aspirates/lenites following cons*), *Note: the pers prons* **mi, thu** *&c combine with* **tro** *to form the prep prons* **tromham(sa), tromhad(sa), troimhe(san), troimhpe(se), tromhainn(e), tromhaibh(se), tromhpa(san)** through me, you *&c*; **1** through, (*story collection*) **Dorcha tro Ghlainne** Through a Glass Darkly, **thàinig iad tron choille** they came through the wood, (*occas as prefix*) **tro-shlighe** *f* a thoroughfare; **2** *in expr* **troimh-chèile** (*of people*) at loggerheads, having fallen out (*Cf* **thar 3**), *also* upset, (*of things, situations, places*) in confusion, in a mess, very untidy (*Cf* **bun 2, bùrach**)

trobhad, *pl* **trobhadaibh** *imper of def verb* **1** come, come here, come to me (*common in calling hens, pets &c*); **2** come along, come (along) with me, *Cf* **tiugainn**

tròcair, tròcaire, tròcairean *nf* mercy, an act of mercy, **tròcairean Dhè** God's mercies, *Cf* **iochd, truacantas, truas**

tròcaireach *adj* merciful, *Cf* **iochdmhor, truacanta**

trod, *gen & pl* **troid** *nm* **1** (*the act of*) quarreling, squabbling &c (*see senses of* **troid** *v*), **chan urrainn dhomh cadal air sgàth an troid** I can't sleep on account of their quarreling; **2** a quarrel, a squabble, a row, **dh'èirich trod eatarra** a quarrel arose between them, *Cf* **argamaid 3, tuasaid**

troich, troiche, troichean *nmf* a dwarf, *Cf* **luchraban**

troid *vi, pres part* **a' trod,** quarrel, row, squabble, fight (*now usu verbally*), *Cf* **sabaid** *v*

troigh, troighe, troighean *nf* **1** a foot, *Cf more usu* **cas** *n*; **2** (*measure*) a foot, **dà throigh a dh'fhad** two feet long

troighean, troighein, troigheanan *nm* a pedal

troimh *prep,* **troimhe, troimhpe** *prep prons see* **tro**

trom *adj* **1** heavy, **parsailean troma** heavy parcels, **ceum trom** a heavy/ ponderous step, (*fam*) **trom air an deoch** heavy on the booze; **2** weighty, serious, important, **cuspairean aotroma is troma** light/ unimportant and serious/important matters, *Cf* **cudthromach 2; 3** heavy (*in spirit*), depressed, dejected, melancholy, **le cridhe trom** with a heavy heart, *Cf* **brònach; 4** pregnant, *Cf* **torach 2; 5** (*typog*) bold

tromalach, *gen* **tromalaich** *nf* a preponderance, a majority, the greater part of something

trombaid, trombaide, trombaidean *nf* a trumpet

tromhad, tromhaibh, tromhainn, tromham, tromhpa *prep prons see* **tro**

trom-laighe, trom-laighe, trom-laighean *nmf* a nightmare, **mar neach a bhiodh fo throm-laighe** like a person in the grip of/having a nightmare

trosg, *gen & pl* **truisg** *nm* cod, a cod

trotan, *gen* **trotain** *nm* trotting, a trot, **dèan** *v* **trotan** trot

truacanta *adj* compassionate, pitying, humane, *Cf* **iochdmhor, tròcaireach**

truacantas, *gen* **truacantais** *nm* compassion, pity, humaneness, *Cf* **iochd, truas**

truagh *adj* **1** poor (*ie unfortunate*), wretched, pitiable, piteous, pitiful, abject, **bochdainn thruagh** wretched/abject poverty, (*trad*) **is truagh mo chor** wretched/piteous is my state/condition, *Cf* **bochd 2; 2** sad, miserable, *Cf* **brònach, muladach; 3** *with v* is, sad, a pity, a shame, **is truagh sin!** that's a pity/shame!, (*song*) **is truagh nach**

robh mis' ann an gleannan mo ghaoil it is sad/a pity that I were not in my beloved little glen, *Cf* bochd 2, duilich 4

truaghan, truaghain, truaghanan *nm* 1 a poor or wretched person, a (poor) wretch, chaochail e aig a' cheann thall, an truaghan a bh' ann dheth he died in the end, poor man that he was; 2 *often as excl, expr pity &c*, a thruaghain! poor man/fellow/craitur!

truaighe, truaighe, truaighean *nf* misery, woe, wretchedness, *esp in excls* mo thruaighe! woe is me!, (*trad*) mo thruaighe sibh! woe unto you!

truaill *vt, pres part* a' truailleadh, 1 (*environment &c*) pollute, contaminate, *Cf* salaich 1 & 2; 2 (*relig, morals &c*) defile, profane; 3 (*persons*) corrupt, abuse, pervert, debauch, *Cf* claon 3, coirb

truailleadh, *gen* truaillidh *nm* 1 (*the act of*) polluting, defiling, corrupting &c (*see senses of* truaill *v*); 2 pollution, corruption, defilement, contamination

truas, *gen* truais *nm* pity, compassion, nach gabh thu truas dhìom? won't you take pity on me?, tha truas agam rium fhìn I'm sorry for myself, *Cf* iochd, tròcair, truacantas

truileis *nf invar* rubbish, junk, trash, mess, *Cf stronger* sgudal

truimead, *gen* truimeid *nm* heaviness, the state of being heavy (*esp emotionally*), truimead mo chridhe the heaviness of my heart

truinnsear, truinnseir, truinnsearan *nm* a (dinner &c) plate

tru(i)s *vt, pres part* a' trusadh & a' truiseadh, 1 truss, bundle up or together; 2 (*of clothing*) tuck up, gather, roll up, bha a còtaichean-bàna air an trusadh her petticoats were tucked up/kilted, thruis e a mhuilchinnean he rolled up his sleeves; 3 gather, collect (*livestock*), a' trusadh chaorach gathering sheep, *Cf* cruinnich 3, tionail 2

trusadh, *gen* trusaidh *nm* (*the act of*) bundling up, gathering &c (*see senses of* tru(i)s *v*)

trusgan, trusgain, trusganan *nm* 1 clothes, clothing, *Cf more usu* aodach 2; 2 a suit (*of clothes*), *Cf* culaidh 2, deise

tu *see* thu

tuagh, tuaigh(e), tuaghan *nf* an axe, (*hist*) tuagh-chatha a battle-axe, a Lochaber axe

tuainealach *adj* dizzy, giddy

tuainealaich, *gen* tuainealaiche *nf* dizziness, giddiness, vertigo, *Cf* luasgan 2

tuaiream, tuaireim, tuaireaman *nf*, & tuairmeas, tuairmeis, tuairmeasan *nm*, guessing, a guess, conjecture, a conjecture, an estimate, speculation, thoir *v* tuaiream air take a guess at it, air thuaiream at random, *Cf* tomhas 6

tuaireamach *adj* **1** random, arbitrary; **2** conjectural, speculative

tuairisgeul, tuairisgeil, tuairisgeulan *nm* a description (*of person or thing*), **tha tuairisgeul a' mhèirlich aig a' phoileas mu thràth** the police already have the thief's description

tuairmeas *see* **tuaiream**

tuar, tuair, tuaran *nm* (*at a given moment, not nec permanent*) complexion, hue or colour (*of features*), appearance, look, *Cf* **dreach 1, fiamh 3, snuadh 2**

tuarasdal & **tuarastal,** *gen* **tuarasdail,** *pl* **tuarasdalan** *nm* a salary, a wage, wages, earnings; a stipend; a fee, *Cf* **cosnadh 4, duais 1, pàigh** *n*

tuasaid, tuasaide, tuasaidean *nf* **1** (*verbal*) a quarrel, a squabble, a row, *Cf* **argamaid 3, connsachadh 2, trod; 2** (*more phys*) a scrap, a tussle, *Cf usu more serious* **sabaid** *n*

tuath¹ *nf invar* & *adj* north, northern, **an àird(e) tuath** north (*ie the compass point*), **Uibhist a Tuath** North Uist, **a' fuireach/a' dol mu thuath** living in/going to the north, **oiteag on tuath** a breeze from the north, **an taobh tuath** the north, the north country, **tha Peairt tuath air Ceann Rois** Perth is north of Kinross

tuath², *gen* **tuatha** *nf* (*trad*) peasantry, tenantry, indigenous people of a district, (*song*) **sliochd na tuath bha gun uaill, gun ghò** (Màiri Mhòr) the native peasant stock who were without vanity, without guile

tuathal *adj* **1** anti-clockwise, *Cf* **deiseil 4; 2** contrary to the movement of the sun, (*Sc*) widdershins, *Cf* **deiseil 5; 3** awry, wrong, in a somewhat untidy or confused state, (*Sc*) agley

tuathanach, *gen* & *pl* **tuathanaich** *nm* a farmer

tuathanachas, *gen* **tuathanachais** *nm* farming, agriculture, *Cf* **àiteachd**

tuathanas, tuathanais, tuathanasan *nm* a farm

tubaist, tubaiste, tubaistean *nf* an accident, a mishap, a mischance, **tubaist-rathaid** a road accident, *Cf less usu* **sgiorradh 1**

tubhailte, tubhailte, tubhailtean *nf* a towel, **tubhailte-shoithichean** a tea-towel, *Cf* **searbhadair**

tubhairt, tuirt *pts of irreg v* **abair** *see tables p 403*

tùch *vi, pres part* **a' tùchadh, 1** make hoarse, **chaidh mo thùchadh** I have become (*lit* been made) hoarse; **2** (*flame* &c) smother, extinguish, *Cf* **mùch 1, smà(i)l**

tùchadh, *gen* **tùchaidh** *nm* hoarseness, the state of being hoarse; **thàinig an tùchadh oirre** she became hoarse

tùchanach *adj* hoarse

tudan & **tùdan,** *gen* **tudain,** *pl* **tudanan** *nm* **1** a stack (*of corn* &c), *Cf* **cruach** *n* **1; 2** a turd

tug *pt of irreg v* **thoir** (*see tables p 413*)

tugh *vt, pres part* **a' tughadh,** thatch

tughadh, *gen* **tughaidh** *nm* **1** (*the act of*) thatching; **2** thatch

tuig *vti, pres part* **a' tuigsinn,** understand, comprehend, 'twig'

tuigse *nf invar* **1** understanding (*ie the mental faculty or capacity*), intelligence, judgement, sense, insight, perception, *Cf* **ciall 1, toinisg; 2** (*sympathetic*) understanding

tuigseach *adj* **1** (*mentally*) understanding, sensible, intelligent, perceptive, *Cf* **ciallach, toinisgeil 1; 2** (*sympathetically*) understanding, **caraid tuigseach** an understanding friend

tuigsinn *nf invar* (*the act of*) understanding &c (*see senses of* **tuig** *v*)

tuil, tuile, tuiltean *nf* a flood, a deluge, *Cf* **dìle 2**

tuilleadh *nm invar* **1** more, an additional amount or number, **tuilleadh fiosrachaidh** more/additional information, **a bheil thu ag iarraidh tuilleadh?** do you want any more/some more?, **carson nach eil an tuilleadh chlàran gan dèanamh?** why aren't more records being made?, *Cf* **barrachd 2; 2** *as adv* again, any more, **na dèan sin tuilleadh** don't do that again/any more, **cha till e gu bràth tuilleadh** he won't ever come back; **3** *in expr* **a thuilleadh air** *prep* in addition to, as well as, **a thuilleadh air sin** ... moreover ..., **tha dà lobhta againn a thuilleadh air an taigh** we have two flats in addition to the house; **4** *in expr* **tuilleadh 's a' chòir** more than enough, too much, **pìos eile? tha tuilleadh 's a' chòir agam mu thràth, tapadh leat** another piece? I've more than enough already, thanks, *Cf* **cus**

tuineachadh, *gen* **tuineachaidh** *nm* **1** (*the act of*) settling, dwelling (*see* **tuinich** *v*); **2** (*habitational*) settlement, **tuineachadh sgaoilte/cruinn** dispersed/nucleated settlement

tuinich *vi, pres part* **a' tuineachadh,** dwell, settle, **a' chiad chinneadh a thuinich ann an Ameireagaidh** the first race that settled in America

Tuirc *nf, with art,* **an Tuirc** Turkey

tuireadh, tuiridh, tuiridhean *nm* mourning, lamentation, a lament, **dèan** *v* **tuireadh** mourn, lament, *Cf* **bròn 2, caoin** *v* **1**

tùirse & **tùrsa** *nf invar* sorrow, *Cf more usu* **bròn 1, mulad**

tuirt *pt of irreg v* **abair** *see tables p 403*

tuiseal, tuiseil, tuisealan *nm* (*gram*) a case, **an tuiseal ginideach** the genitive case

tuisleadh, tuislidh, tuislidhean *nm* **1** (*the act of*) stumbling, tripping, slipping; **2** a stumble, a trip, a slip; *Cf* **sgiorradh 2**

tuislich *vi, pres part* **a' tuisleachadh** & **a' tuisleadh**, stumble, trip, slip

tuit *vi, pres part* **a' tuiteam, 1** fall, drop, tumble, **a' tuisleadh 's a' tuiteam** stumbling and falling, **thuit sèaraichean an-diugh** shares fell today; **2** happen (**do** to), befall, chance, **thuit dhomh fhaicinn air an t-sràid** I happened/chanced to see him on the street, (*more permanently*) **thuit dha a bhith na shaighdear** it was his lot/it fell to him to be a soldier, *Cf* **èirich 3, tachair 1**

tuiteam, tuiteim, tuiteaman *nm* **1** (*the act of*) falling, befalling &c (*see senses of* **tuit** *v*); **2** a fall

tuiteamach *adj* accidental, fortuitous, chance, contingent, **tachartasan tuiteamach** chance occurrences

tuiteamas, tuiteamais, tuiteamasan *nm* **1** an event, a happening, an occurrence, an incident, *Cf* **tachartas; 2** an accident (*not necessarily unpleasant, Cf* **tubaist**), something happening by chance, **le tuiteamas** by chance/accident, **co-thuiteamas** a coincidence; **3** (*med*) epilepsy

tulach, *gen* **tulaich**, *pl* **tulaichean** & **tulachan** *nm* a hillock, a mound (*usu small to medium*), a knoll, (*Sc*) a knowe, *in placenames as* tulloch, tilloch, tullo &c

tulg *vti, pres part* **a' tulgadh, 1** (*seas, ship, trees &c*) rock, roll, pitch, lurch, swing, toss, *Cf* **luaisg; 2** (*also more gently*) **tulg a' chreathail** rock the cradle

tulgach *adj* **1** rocking, liable to rock, roll &c (*see senses of* **tulg** *v*); **2** (*seat &c*) unsteady, rocky, (*Sc*) shooglie, *Cf* **cugallach**

tulgadh, *gen* **tulgaidh** *nm* (*the act of*) rocking, rolling &c (*see senses of* **tulg** *v*), **tulgadh a' chuain** the tossing of the ocean, **sèithear-tulgaidh** *m* a rocking-chair

tum *vt, pres part* **a' tumadh**, dip, duck, immerse, steep, plunge (*in liquid*), *Cf* **bog** *v* **1**

tumadh, tumaidh, tumaidhean *nm* **1** (*the act of*) dipping, immersing &c (*see senses of* **tum** *v*); **2** immersion; **3** a dip, a plunge, a ducking

tunna *see* **tonna**

tunnag, tunnaig, tunnagan *nf* a duck, *Cf* **lach**

tùr[1], *gen* **tùir** *nm* sense, understanding, *Cf more usu* **ciall 1, toinisg, tuigse 1**

tùr[2], *gen* & *pl* **tùir** *nm* a tower, *Cf* **turaid**

tur *adj* **1** (*trad*) whole, complete, *Cf more usu* **iomlan** *adj* **2; 2** *now in expr* **gu tur** *adv* completely, entirely, altogether, totally, quite, **tha an dà rud gu tur eadar-dhealaichte** the two things are quite different, *Cf* **iomlan** *adj* **3, gu lèir, uile 4**

turadh, *gen* **turaidh** *nm* dry, fine or fair weather, a dry spell, **is math an turadh!** it's a good dry spell!, *or* it's good to see it dry!, *Cf* **tiormachd 2**

turaid, turaide, turaidean *nf* a tower, a turret, *Cf* **tùr**²

tùrail *adj* sensible, *Cf more usu* **ciallach, toinisgeil 1**

turas, turais, tursan *nm* **1** a journey, an expedition, a trip, **turas-mara** a (sea-)voyage, **turas-adhair** a flight, *Cf* **cuairt 3, sgrìob** *n* **3**; **2** (*now esp holidays &c*) touring, a tour, **luchd-turais** *m coll* tourists; **3** a time, **aon turas** once, one time, **'s e seo an turas mu dheireadh** this is the last time, *Cf* **uair 3**

turasachd *nf invar* tourism, **oifis turasachd** a tourist office, **Bòrd Turasachd na h-Alba** the Scottish Tourist Board

Turcach, *gen & pl* **Turcaich** *nm* a Turk, *also as adj* **Turcach** Turkish

tursa, tursa, tursachan *nm* a standing stone, a monolith, *in pl* **tursachan** a stone circle, **Tursachan Chalanais** the Callanish (*standing*) Stones, *Cf* **carragh 2, gallan**

tùrsach *adj* sorrowful, (*song*) **dh'fhàg thu tùrsach mo chridh'** you left me with a sorrowful heart/made my heart sorrowful, *Cf* **brònach, muladach**

tùs, *gen* **tùis** *nm* **1** the beginning, start or origin of something, **tùs an t-samhraidh** the start/beginning of summer, (*prov*) **'s e tùs a' ghliocais eagal Dhè** the fear of God is the beginning/origin of wisdom, *Cf* **bun 3, toiseach 1**; **2** *also in expr* **o/bho thùs** from, since *or* in the beginning, originally, **tha e air a bhith ag obair an seo o thùs** he's been working here from/since the (very) beginning, **bhon a bha clann Adhaimh san àite o thùs** since the children of Adam were first/originally in the place

tùsanach, *gen & pl* **tùsanaich** *nm* an aborigine

tuthag, tuthaig, tuthagan *nf* a patch (*of material &c*), *Cf* **brèid 2**

U

uabhann *see* **uamhann**

uabhar, *gen* **uabhair** *nm* pride (*usu excessive*), haughtiness, *Cf* **àrdan**, **pròis**, **uaibhreas 1** & **2**

uabhas, *gen* **uabhais**, *pl* **uabhasan** *nm* **1** dread, horror, terror, *Cf* **oillt**, **uamhann**; **2** a dreadful or horrible thing or action, an atrocity, a horror, **uabhasan an àm cogaidh** horrors/atrocities in time of war

uabhasach *adj* **1** dreadful, awful, terrible, atrocious (*Cf* **oillteil**), (*now often with attenuated colloquial force*), **chaill thu ceud not? tha sin uabhasach!** you lost a hundred pounds? that's dreadful/awful/ terrible!, *Cf* **eagalach 2, sgriosail 3**; **2** *as adv* terribly, awfully, dreadfully, **bha am biadh uabhasach math** the food was terribly good/very very good, **rinn thu uabhasach fhèin math** you did amazingly well/very well indeed, *Cf* **cianail 3, eagalach 3**

uachdar, uachdair, uachdaran *nm, opposite of* **ìochdar**, **1** a surface, **air uachdar na talmhainn/nan tonn** on the surface of the earth/the waves, **thig** *v* **an uachdar** surface; manifest itself, *Cf* **bàrr 1**; **2** the top or upper surface of anything, *Cf more usu* **bàrr 1, mullach 1**; **3** (*of milk*) cream, top of the milk, *Cf* **bàrr 1**; **4** (*topog*) an upland, *can occur in placenames as* **auchter** & **ochter**, *Cf* **bràigh** *nm* **2**; **5** *in expr* **làmh-an-uachdair** the upper hand, **gheibh sinn làmh-an-uachdair orra** we'll get the upper hand over them, *Cf* **cùis 5, gnothach 6**

uachdarach *adj, opposite of* **ìochdarach**, **1** (*phys*) upper; **2** (*in status &c*) superior; **3** superficial; **4** creamy, *Cf* **barragach**

uachdaran, uachdarain, uachdaranan *nm, opposite of* **ìochdaran**, **1** (*status &c*) a superior; **2** a landowner, a laird, *Cf* **tighearna 2**

uachdar-fhiaclan, uachdair-fhiaclan, uachdaran-fhiaclan *nm* toothpaste

uaibh *prep pron see* **o**

uaibhreach *adj* **1** proud; **2** (*excessively*) proud, haughty, arrogant; *Cf* **àrdanach, dàna 4**

uaibhreas, *gen* **uaibhreis** *nm* **1** pride; **2** (*excessive or insolent*) pride, haughtiness, arrogance; *Cf* **àrdan, pròis, uabhar**

uaigh, *gen* **uaighe** & **uaghach**, *pl* **uaighean** *nf* a grave, (*song*) **nach robh mi san uaigh!** if only I were dead and buried!

uaigneach *adj* **1** (*person*) lonely, lonesome, *Cf* **aonaranach**; **2** (*place &c*) solitary, lonely, deserted, secluded; **3** (*esp place*) private, secret, *Cf* **dìomhair 1**

uaim, *gen* **uaime** *nf* (*poetry &c*) alliteration

uaimh & **uamh**, *gen* **uaimhe** & **uamha**, *pl* **uamhan** & **uaimhean** *nf* a cave, (*trad song*) **uaimh an òir** the cave of gold

uaine *adj* green, *Cf* **glas** 2, **gorm** 2

uainfheòil, *gen* **uainfheòla** *nf* lamb (*ie the meat*)

uainn, uaipe *prep prons see* **o**

uaipear, uaipeir, uaipearan *nm* a botcher, a bungler, *Cf* **cearbair(e)**

uair, uarach, uairean *nf* 1 (*clock time*) an hour, *esp* **uair a** (*for de*) **thìde** & **uair an uaireadair** an hour, **cairteal na h-uarach** a quarter of an hour, **dè an uair a tha e?** what time is it? (*lit* what hour is it?), **tha e trì uairean** it's three o'clock, **tha e leth-uair an dèidh a ceithir** it's half past four, **cha dèan mi sin aig an uair seo!** I won't do that at this hour/time! (*Cf* **àm**); 2 (*as adv*) a time, an occasion, once, **bha mi ann uair** I was there once/one time/on one occasion, **aon uair 's gun tòisicheadh e** once he got started, **thig gam fhaicinn uair sam bith** come and see me any time, **chì mi (uair no) uaireigin thu** I'll see you some time or other, **air uairean** (*trad* **air uairibh**) at times, sometimes, occasionally (*Cf* **uaireannan**), *see also* **an uair a** *conj*; 3 a time (*ie a repetition*), **uair is uair** time and time again, again and again, over and over again, **rinn sinn dà uair e** we did it twice, **a' chiad uair a chunna mi i** the first time I saw her, *Cf* **turas** 3

uaireadair, uaireadair, uaireadairean *nm* 1 *trad used for timepieces of various kinds, eg* **uaireadair-grèine** a sundial, **uaireadair-glainne** an hour-glass; 2 a clock, **uair an uaireadair** an hour's (clock) time, an hour by the clock, *Cf more usu* **gleoc**; 3 (*now esp*) a watch

uaireannan *adv* at times, sometimes, occasionally, *Cf* **air uairean** (*see* **uair** 2)

uaireigin *adv* (at) some time or other

uaisle *nf invar* (*abstr, of birth, character &c*) nobility, gentility, aristocracy

uaislean *see* **uasal** *n* 2

uaithe *prep pron see* **o**

uallach, *gen* & *pl* **uallaich** *nm* 1 (*mostly fig*) a burden, a load, **is trom an t-uallach an aois** age is a heavy burden, (*prov*) **chan fhuirich muir air uallach** the sea won't wait on a cargo, *Cf* **eallach**; 2 a charge, a responsibility, an onus, **chuir iad orm uallach an turais** they charged me with the responsibility for the journey, **bha uallach na dachaigh oirre** hers was the responsibility for the home, **'s ann oirbhse a tha an t-uallach** the onus is on you, *Cf* **cùram** 1, **eallach**, **urra** 2; 3 (*psych*) stress, pressure, **tha an duine agam fo uallach an-dràsta air sgàth dhuilgheadasan san fhactaraidh** my husband's under pressure/stress just now because of difficulties in the factory; **4** worry, **bha uallach oirre air sgàth a màthar** she was worried about/on account of her mother, **gabh** *v* **uallach** become worried, *Cf* **dragh 3**

uam *prep pron see* **o**

uamh *see* **uaimh**

uamhann & **uabhann,** *gen* **uamhainn** *nm* dread, horror, terror, *Cf* **oillt, uabhas 1**

uan, *gen* & *pl* **uain** *nm* a lamb

uapa *prep pron see* **o**

uasal *adj* **1** noble, aristocratic, *(trad)* **duine uasal** a nobleman, a gentleman, *(Sc, hist)* a duniwassal, *(trad, formal address, in corres &c)* **a bhean-uasail** Madam; **2** *(in manners &c)* genteel; **3** precious, *esp in expr* **clach** *f* **uasal** a precious stone

uasal, uasail, uaislean *nm* **1** *(trad)* a gentleman, **mòr-uasal** a nobleman, an aristocrat; **2** *in pl, esp with art (coll)* **na h-uaislean** the nobility, the aristocracy

uat *prep pron see* **o**

ubhal, ubhail, ùbhlan *nm* an apple

ubhalghort, ubhalghoirt, ubhalghoirtean *nm* an orchard

uchd, uchda, uchdan *nm* **1** a breast *(ie general breast area)*, a bosom, **theannaich i am balach ri a h-uchd** she clasped the boy to her bosom, *Cf* **broilleach 1, com 1; 2** a lap, **bha am balach na shuidhe na h-uchd** the boy was sitting on her lap, *Cf* **glùn; 3** *in expr* **ri uchd** at the point of, on the verge of, *esp in expr* **ri uchd bàis** at the point of death, at death's door; **4** *as prefix* **uchd-** adoptive, pertaining to adoption, *eg* **uchd-leanabh** *m* an adopted child, **uchd-mhacaich** *vt* adopt

ud *adj* that *(usu more distant or remote than* **sin)**, yon, yonder, **am faic thu an taigh ud, aig ceann a' bhaile?** do you see that/yon house, at the end of the village?, *(can be slightly pej)* **cha toigh leam an duineachan ud** I don't like that/yon mannie, *Cf* **seo, sin, siud**

ud, ud! *excl expr disapproval, reservations &c,* tut, tut!, now, now!, no, no!, come on now! **ud, ud, a bhalaich, chan eil mi airson sin idir!** now now/wait a minute, boy, I don't approve of that at all!

uèir, uèir, uèirichean *nf* wire, **uèir-bhiorach** barbed wire

ugan, ugain, ugannan *nm* the upper part of the chest area, *esp in expr* **cnàimh** *m* **an ugain** the collar bone

ugh, uigh, uighean *nm* an egg, **ughlann** *nf* an ovary

ughach *adj* oval, egg-shaped

ughach, *gen & pl* **ughaich** *nm* an oval

ughagan, *gen & pl* **ughagain** *nm* custard, a custard

ùghdarraichte *adj* authorised; licensed

ùghdar, ùghdair, ùghdaran *nm* an author

ùghdarras, ùghdarrais, ùghdarrasan *nm* 1 (*abstr*) authority, *Cf* **smachd**; 2 (*con*) an authority, **ùghdarrasan ionadail** local authorities, *Cf* **comhairle 2**

Uibhisteach, *gen & pl* **Uibhistich** *nm* someone from Uist (**Uibhist**), *also as adj* **Uibhisteach** of, from or pertaining to Uist

ùidh, ùidhe, ùidhean *nf* 1 (*trad*) hope; intention; fondness; 2 *now usu* interest, **chan eil ùidh agam ann** I'm not interested in it, **gabh** *v* **ùidh ann** take an interest/be interested in, *Cf* **suim 2**

uidh, *gen* **uidhe** *nf* 1 (*trad*) a step, a degree, a gradation; *also* a journey; 2 *now in expr* **uidh air n-uidh** step by step, bit by bit, gradually; 3 *in expr* **ceann-uidhe** *m* a destination, a terminus, a journey's end, **togalach uidhe** a terminal building

uidheam, uidheim, uidheaman *nf coll* 1 (*tools, machinery &c*) equipment, gear, apparatus, tackle; 2 furnishings, accoutrements, trappings, fittings; 3 (*of horse &c*) harness; 4 (*of boat*) rigging; *Cf* **acainn**

uidheamachadh, *gen* **uidheamachaidh** 1 (*the act of*) equipping &c (*see senses of* **uidheamaich** *v*); 2 preparation, *Cf* **ullachadh 2**

uidheamaich *vt, pres part* **ag uidheamachadh**, equip, gear up, furnish, fit out, get ready, prepare

uidheamaichte *adj* 1 equipped, geared up, fitted out, *Cf* **acainneach**; 2 (*person*) qualified

uile *adj & adv* 1 all, **dh'fhalbh na saighdearan uile** the soldiers all left, **tha sin uile seachad** all that's over; 2 *often occurs as* **a h-uile** every, (*precedes the noun*), **a h-uile càil/duine** everything/everybody, **a h-uile là** every day, **a h-uile fear aca** every one of them, *Cf* **gach 1**; 3 *as noun & pron* **na h-uile** everyone, everybody, **chaill na h-uile an cuid airgid** everyone/they all lost their money; 4 *as adv* (*trad*) **tha mi uile-thoileach** I am fully willing, *now esp in expr* **uile-gu-lèir** *adv* completely, totally, altogether, fully, absolutely, **shoirbhich leinn uile-gu-lèir** we succeeded totally, **gun fheum uile-gu-lèir** absolutely useless, *Cf* **buileach, tur 2**; 5 *as prefix corres to Eng* all-, omni-, *eg* **uile-chumhachdach** *adj* all-powerful, omnipotent, **uile-fhiosrach** *adj* all-knowing, omniscient

uileann & uilinn, *gen* **uilinn & uilne**, *pl* **uilnean & uileannan** *nf* 1 an angle, **ceart-uilinn** a right angle; 2 a corner (*usu external*), *Cf* **còrnair, cùil 1, oisean**; 3 an elbow

uilebheist, uilebheist, uilebheistean *nmf* a monster, **Uilebheist Loch Nis** the Loch Ness Monster

uilinn *see* **uileann**

ùilleach *adj* oily

uilleagan, *gen & pl* **uilleagain** *nm* a spoilt brat

uillnich *vti, pres part* **ag uillneachadh,** jostle, elbow, *Cf* **put** *v* 2, **ùpag**

uime *prep pron see* **mu**

uimhir *nf invar* 1 a number, an amount, a quantity, **a' cheart uimhir** the same amount/quantity, **dè uimhir 's a th' ann?** how much is there?, how many are there?, *Cf* **meud** 2; 2 a certain amount, a measure, a modicum of something, **bha na h-uimhir de thèarainteachd againn** we had a measure/a certain amount of security; 3 the same number, quantity &c, **thoir dhomh uimhir eile** give me as much again/the same again, **na toir dhomh uimhir ri Seumas!** don't give me as much as James!; 4 (*also* **na h-uimhir**) a great number or quantity, so much, so many, **bha (na h-)uimhir de dhaoine ann** there were so many/such a lot of people there, **bha (na h-)uimhir de dh'airgead agam** I had so much/such a lot of money; *Cf* **uiread**

uimpe *prep pron see* **mu**

ùine *nf invar* 1 time, **cuir** *v* **seachad ùine** spend/pass time, **fad na h-ùine** all the time, **tha ùine gu leòr againn** we've plenty of time, *Cf* **tìde** 1; 2 a period of time, **ùine ghoirid roimhe sin** a short time before that; 3 (*fam*) *non-trad pl* **ùineachan** ages, **ùineachan is ùineachan air ais** ages and ages ago

uinneag, uinneige, uinneagan *nf* a window, **coimhead** *v* **a-mach air an uinneig** (*dat*) look out (of) the window

uinnean, uinnein, uinneanan *nm* an onion

uinnseann, *gen* **uinnsinn** *nm* (*tree & wood*) ash

ùir, *gen* **ùire** *&* **ùrach** *nf* 1 soil, earth, **sìol air a chur san ùir** seed sown in the earth; 2 (*trad*) *euphemism for* a grave, **chuireadh e san ùir** he was lain in the earth, he was buried, *Cf* **fòid** 1, **uaigh**

uircean, uircein, uirceanan *nm* a piglet

uiread *nm invar* 1 a certain amount, a measure, a modicum of something, **bha na h-uiread de thèarainteachd againn** we had a certain amount/a modicum of security, *Cf* **uimhir** 2; 2 the same number, quantity or amount, **uiread eile** as much again, the same again, **leth uiread** half as much, **thoir dhomh uiread 's a tha aig Iain** give me as much as Ian has, *Cf* **uimhir** 3; 3 *in neg exprs*, **uiread is/agus** even, so much as, **gun uiread agus leth-cheud sgillinn** without even/so much as fifty pence, *Cf* **eadhon, fiù** *n* 2; 4 (*also* **na**

h-uiread) a great number or quantity, so much, so many, **chaill mi (na h-)uiread de thìde** I lost so much/such a lot of time, **uiread de dhaoine** so many people, *Cf* **uimhir 4**; **5** (*arith &c*) times, multiplied by, **a dhà uiread a dhà** two times two, twice two

uireasbhach *adj* **1** (*persons*) needy, indigent, *Cf* **ainniseach**; **2** needful, much needed, lacking, *Cf* **dìth 2, gann 1**

uireasbhach, *gen & pl* **uireasbhaich** *nm* a needy or indigent person

uireasbhaidh, uireasbhaidhe, uireasbhaidhean *nf* **1** want, need, indigence; **2** a lack, a deficiency, a shortage, *Cf* **cion 1**

uirsgeul & ùirsgeul, *gen* **uirsgeil**, *pl* **uirsgeulan** *nm* **1** a fable, a legend, a myth, *Cf* **fionnsgeul**; **2** (*Lit &c*) fiction, a piece of fiction, **dh'fhaighnich iad am b' e uirsgeul a bh' agam** they asked if I was making it up

uirsgeulach *adj* **1** legendary, relating to legend; **2** (*Lit &c*) fictional, fictitious, made up

uiseag, uiseig, uiseagan *nf* a lark, a skylark, *Cf* **topag**

uisge, uisge, uisgeachan *nm* **1** water, **deoch uisge** a drink of water, **tobar fìor-uisge** a well of pure water, *Cf* **bùrn**; **2** (*usu with art*) rain, **tha an t-uisge ann fhathast** it's still raining, **sguir an t-uisge mu dheireadh thall** the rain stopped at long last, **uisge-searbhaig** acid rain

uisge-beatha, *gen* **uisge-bheatha** *nm* whisky

uisgeachadh, *gen* **uisgeachaidh** *nm* **1** (*the act of*) watering, irrigating; **2** irrigation

uisgich *vt, pres part* **ag uisgeachadh**, **1** water; **2** irrigate

ulaidh, ulaidhe, ulaidhean *nf* **1** treasure, a treasure, a precious object; **2** (*expr affection*) **m' ulaidh!** my darling!, precious!; *Cf* **eudail**

ulbhag, ulbhaig, ulbhagan *nf* a large stone or boulder

ulfhart, *gen & pl* **ulfhairt** *nm* (*esp dog*) howling, a howl, **dèan** *v* **ulfhart** howl

ullachadh, *gen* **ullachaidh** *nm* **1** (*the act of*) preparing, providing *&c* (*see senses of* **ullaich** *v*); **2** preparation, **gun ullachadh** unprepared, impromptu, *Cf* **deasachadh 2**; **3** provision, **ullachadh ionmhais** provision of finance

ullaich *vt, pres part* **ag ullachadh**, **1** prepare, get ready, *Cf* **deasaich 1 & 2**; **2** (*esp admin &c*) provide, **ullaich ionmhas airson ospadail ùir** provide finance for a new hospital

ullamh *adj* **1** ready, prepared, **a bheil thu ullamh?** are you ready, *Cf* **deiseil 1** & *less usu* **deas 3**; **2** finished, **bha iad ullamh de cheasnachadh** they had finished/they were through asking questions, *Cf* **deiseil 2** & *less usu* **deas 3**; **3** handy, ready to hand, **airgead** *m* **ullamh** ready money, cash, *Cf* **deiseil 3**, **goireasach**

ultach, ultaich, ultaichean *nm* **1** a load (*ie as much as can be carried at one time*), an armful (*Cf* **achlasan**), **ultach-droma** as much as can be carried on the back; **2** a bundle

umad, umaibh *prep prons see* **mu**

ùmaidh, ùmaidh, ùmaidhean *nm* a blockhead, a dolt, a dunce, a fool, *Cf* **bumailear**, **stalcaire**

umainn, umam *prep prons see* **mu**

umha *nm invar* bronze, (*hist*) **Linn an Umha** the Bronze Age

umha(i)l *adj* **1** humble, meek, lowly, *Cf* **iriosal 2**; **2** obedient, submissive, compliant, deferential, **umhail do mhàthair** obedient to his mother, *Cf* **macanta**; **3** obsequious

ùmhlachadh, *gen* **ùmhlachaidh** *nm* **1** (*the act of*) becoming humble, humiliating &c (*see senses of* **ùmhlaich** *v*); **2** humiliation, a humiliation, mortification

ùmhlachd *nf invar* **1** humbleness, lowliness, meekness, *Cf* **irioslachd**; **2** obedience, submissiveness, deference; **3** obsequiousness; **4** (*before royalty &c*) homage, obeisance, a bow

ùmhlaich *vti, pres part* **ag ùmhlachadh**, **1** become or make humble; **2** (*vt*) humiliate, mortify, humble, chasten, *Cf* **irioslaich**

umpa *prep pron see* **mu**

Ungair *nf, with art*, **an Ungair** Hungary

Ungaireach, *gen* & *pl* **Ungairich** *nm* a Hungarian, *also as adj* **Ungaireach** Hungarian

ùnnlagh, ùnnlagha, ùnnlaghan *nm* a fine

ùnnsa, ùnnsa, ùnnsachan *nm* an ounce

ùpag, ùpaig, ùpagan *nf* (*in crowd, squabble &c*) a jostle, a jab (*with elbow &c*), *Cf* **uillnich**

ùpraid, ùpraide, ùpraidean *nf* **1** (*noise*) uproar, an uproar, *Cf* **gleadhar**, **othail**; **2** (*in crowds, disturbance &c*) confusion, a commotion, a dispute, **am measg na h-ùpraide shiolp e air falbh** amidst the confusion/commotion he slipped away, *Cf* **aimhreit 1**

ùpraideach *adj* uproarious, rowdy, unruly, full of confusion or commotion

ùr *adj* **1** new, fresh, recent, **càr** *m* **ùr** a new car, **càirdean ùra** new friends, **leabhar** *m* **ùr** a new/recent book, **sgadan/ìm ùr** fresh herring/butter, *Cf* **nuadh**; **2** modern, **na h-amannan ùra seo** these modern times, *Cf* **nuadh**, **ùr-nodha**; **3** *in expr* **às ùr** *adv* afresh, anew, (for) a second time, **tòisich** *v* **às ùr** start afresh/all over again, make a fresh start; **4** *occas as prefix* new, newly, fresh, freshly, *eg* **air ùr-thighinn à Glaschu** newly arrived from Glasgow, **ùr-fhàs** *m* new / fresh growth

ur, *also less usu* **bhur**, *poss adj*, **(bh)ur n-** *before a vowel, pl & formal* your (*corres to pron* **sibh**), **ur pàrantan** your parents, **leigibh ur n-anail** take a breather, **is math ur faicinn** it's good to see you, **'s e ur beatha!** you're welcome!, *Cf sing/fam* **do** *poss adj*

ùrachadh, *gen* **ùrachaidh** *nm* **1** (*the act of*) renewing &c (*see senses of* **ùraich** *v*); **2** renewal; **3** modernisation; **4** a change, **bidh sin na ùrachadh dhut** that will be/make a change for you

ùraich *vti, pres part* **ag ùrachadh**, **1** become or make new or fresh, renew, refresh; **2** modernise, bring up to date

urchair, **urchrach**, **urchraichean** *nf* **1** (*from firearm*) a shot, **chuala mi urchair** I heard a shot, (*distance*) **urchair gunna air falbh** a gun-shot away; **2** a missile

urchasg, **urchaisg**, **urchasgan** *nm* an antidote

ùrlar, **ùrlair**, **ùrlaran** *nm* **1** a floor, **ùrlar taighe** a house floor, **ùrlar cloiche** a stone floor, **a' dannsadh air an ùrlar** dancing on the (dance) floor, **àrd-ùrlar** a stage, a platform, *Cf* **làr** 2; **2** a floor (*ie storey*), *Cf* **lobht(a)** 1; **3** (*music*) a theme, *esp in pibroch* a ground

ùrnaigh, **ùrnaigh**, **ùrnaighean** *nf* praying, a prayer, **dèan** *v* **ùrnaigh** pray (**ri** to), **Urnaigh an Tighearna** the Lord's Prayer, **coinneamh** *f* **ùrnaigh** a prayer meeting, *Cf* **guidhe** *n* 4

ùr-nodha *adj* **1** brand new, modern, up-to-date, (*Sc*) split new

urra, **urra**, **urraidhean** *nf* **1** (*trad*) a person, an individual, *occas in expr* **an urra** *adv* each, per capita, **mìle nota an urra** a thousand pounds each, *Cf more usu* **duine** 2, **neach** 1; **2** authority, responsibility (*mainly moral*), *now usu in expr* **an urra** responsible, **bha mi an urra ri Oifis a' Phuist** I was responsible for/in charge of the Post Office, *Cf* **cùram** 1, **uallach** 2; **3** *in expr* **an urra ri** *prep* dependent on, **an urra ri drogaichean** dependent on/addicted to drugs, *Cf* **tràill** 3

urrainn *nf invar* **1** (*trad*) power, ability, *Cf trad* **feudar** 1; **2** *now in verbal expr* **is urrainn do** can, is able, **chan urrainn dhomh slugadh** I can't swallow, **nach urrainn dhut a dhèanamh? chan urrainn** can't you do it? no, **cha b' urrainn dhomh gun a bhith brònach** I couldn't help being sad, I couldn't but be sad

urram, *gen* **urraim** *nm* **1** respect, deference, **àrd-urram** reverence, **thoir urram don fheadhainn a tha airidh air** respect those who are worthy of it, *Cf* **meas**[1] 1; **2** honour, an honour, **cuir** *v* **urram air cuideigin** honour/confer an honour on someone (*Cf* **onaraich** 1 & 2)

urramach *adj* **1** honourable, reverend, venerable, worthy of respect or honour; **2** honorary, **ball** *m* **urramach** an honorary member; **3** *(of minister)* Reverend, *with art*, **an t-Urramach Uilleam Caimbeul** the Reverend William Campbell

urras, urrais, urrasan *nm* **1** *(esp in fin matters)* a guarantee, a bond, surety, **rach** *v* **an urras air** stand as surety/guarantee for, vouch for, *Cf* **bar(r)antas 2**; **2** *(legal)* bail, **fuasgail** *v* **air urras** release on bail; **3** insurance, assurance, **poileasaidh-urrais** an insurance policy; **4** *(legal, fin, business)* a trust, **ciste-urrais** *f* a trust fund

urrasach *adj* (*person, business &c*) trustworthy, sound, secure, dependable, *Cf* **earbsach 2**

ursainn, ursainn, ursainnean *nf* **1** *(trad)* a prop, a support, *(fig, trad)* **ursainn chatha** a champion, a staunch support in battle; **2** *(now usu)* a jamb, a doorpost

usgar, usgair, usgaran *nm* a jewel *(esp one worn as an ornament)*, an item of jewellery, *Cf* **seud**

uspag, uspaig, uspagan *nf* a start, *(horse &c)* a shying movement, **thoir** *v* **uspag** start, shy, *Cf* **clisgeadh 2**

ùth, ùtha, ùthan(nan) *nm* an udder

The Forms of the Article

	Singular		Plural
	Masculine	**Feminine**	**Both Genders**
Nom & Acc	**an** (*before consonants, exc b, f, m, p*) **am** (*before b, f, m, p*) **an t-** (*before a vowel*)	**an** (*before a vowel or fh*) **a'** (*before bh, ch, gh, mh, ph*) **an t-** (*before s followed by l, n, r, or by a vowel*)	**na** **na h-** (*before a vowel*)
e.g.	an taigh, an sìol, an sruth am bodach, **am** fraoch an t-eilean	an ite, an fhras a' chraobh, a' ghaoth an t-sìde, an t-sròn	na caileagan na h-òrain
Gen	**an** **a'** } *Same as Nom Feminine* **an t-**	**na** **na h-** (*before a vowel*)	**nan** **nam** (*before b, f, m, p*)
e.g.	an eilein, an taighe, an fhraoich a' bhodaich an t-sil, an t-sruith	na gaoithe, na craoibhe, na sròine na h-ite	nan taighean, **nan** òran **nam** bodach
Dat	**an** **a'** } *Same as Nom Feminine* **an t-**	**an** **a'** } *Same as Nom Feminine* **an t-**	**na** **na h-** } *Same as Nom Plural*
e.g.	an eilean, an taigh, an fhraoch a' bhodach an t-sìol, an t-sruth	an tràigh a' ghaoith, a' chraoibh an t-sùil, an t-slait, an t-sròin	na caileagan na h-òrain

Note: In the Dative Singular, for both genders, after a preposition ending in a vowel the article is shortened to **'n** or **'n t-**, and combined with the preposition. E.g. **don** bhùth, **on** taigh, **bhon** t-sìol, **tron** choille, **fon** t-sruth, **mun** bhòrd.

401

The Most Commonly Used Forms of the Gaelic Irregular and DefectiveVerbs

ABAIR

abair say (*pres part* **ag ràdh** saying, *infinitive* **a ràdh** to say)

Important Note: It is very common for the forms of this verb, except for the Past (Preterite), to be supplied by the defective verb **can**. See next page.

IMPERATIVE

abram let me say

abair (*sing*) say

abradh e/i let him/her say

abramaid let us say

abraibh (*pl*) say

abradh iad let them say

na h-abram let me not say

na h-abair (*sing*) don't say

na h-abradh e/i let him/her not say

na h-abramaid let us not say

na h-abraibh (*pl*) don't say

na h-abradh iad let them not say

FUTURE (AND HABITUAL PRESENT)

their mi I will say, I say

an abair mi? will I say? do I say?

chan abair mi I won't say, I don't say

nach abair mi? won't I say? don't I say?

RELATIVE FUTURE

dè a their mi? what will I say?

PAST (PRETERITE)

thuirt mi I said

an tuirt mi did I say?

cha tuirt mi I didn't say

nach tuirt mi? didn't I say?

Note: **thuirt** also occurs as **thubhairt; tuirt** occurs as **tubhairt, dubhairt** and **duirt**

PERFECT AND PLUPERFECT

tha mi air a ràdh I have said

tha mi air a ràdh I have said it

bha mi air a ràdh I had said

bha mi air a ràdh I had said it

Note: In the Future, Relative Future, Past, Perfect and Pluperfect, the same forms of the verb are used for all persons.

CONDITIONAL

theirinn I would say

theireadh* tu you would say

theireamaid we would say

an abrainn? would I say?

an abradh* tu? would you say?

an abramaid? would we say?

chan abrainn I wouldn't say

chan abradh* tu you wouldn't say

chan abramaid we wouldn't say

nach abrainn? wouldn't I say?

nach abradh* tu? wouldn't you say?

nach abramaid? wouldn't we say?

The forms marked * are used for all persons except the first singular, I. The forms in -**maid** are alternative forms for the second person singular, we.

CAN

can say (*pres part* **a' cantainn** saying, *infinitive* **a chantainn** to say)

Note: The following forms of this defective verb are very commonly used instead of the corresponding forms of **abair** (see previous page).

IMPERATIVE

canam let me say   **na canam** let me not say
can (*sing*) say   **na can** (*sing*) don't say
canadh e/i let him/her say   **na canadh e/i** let him/her not say
canamaid let us say   **na canamaid** let us not say
canaibh (*pl*) say   **na canaibh** (*pl*) don't say
canadh iad let them say   **na canadh iad** let them not say

FUTURE AND HABITUAL PRESENT

canaidh mi I will say, I say   **cha chan mi** I won't say, I don't say
an can mi? will I say? do I say?   **nach can mi?** won't I say? don't I say?

RELATIVE FUTURE

dè a chanas mi? what will I say?

PERFECT AND PLUPERFECT

tha mi air cantainn I have said   **bha mi air cantainn** I had said
tha mi air a chantainn I have said it   **bha mi air a chantainn** I had said it

Note: In the Future, Relative Future, Perfect and Pluperfect, the same forms of the verb are used for all persons.

CONDITIONAL

chanainn I would say   **cha chanainn** I wouldn't say
chanadh* tu you would say   **cha chanadh* tu** you wouldn't say
chanamaid we would say   **cha chanamaid** we wouldn't say
an canainn? would I say?   **nach canainn?** wouldn't I say?
an canadh* tu? would you say?   **nach canadh* tu?** wouldn't you say?
an canamaid? would we say?   **nach canamaid?** wouldn't we say?

The forms marked * are used for all persons except the first singular, I. The forms in -**maid** are alternative forms for the second person singular, we.

BEIR

beir bear, catch (*pres part* **a' breith** bearing/catching, *infinitive* **a bhreith** to bear/catch)

IMPERATIVE

beiream let me bear	**na beiream** let me not bear
beir (*sing*) bear	**na beir** (*sing*) don't bear
beireadh e/i let him/her bear	**na beireadh e/i** let him/her not bear
beireamaid let us bear	**na beireamaid** let us not bear
beiribh (*pl*) bear	**na beiribh** (*pl*) don't bear
beireadh iad let them bear	**na beireadh iad** let them not bear

FUTURE (AND HABITUAL PRESENT)

beiridh mi I will bear, I bear	**cha bheir mi** I won't bear, I don't bear
am beir mi? will I bear? do I bear?	**nach beir mi?** won't I bear? don't I bear?

RELATIVE FUTURE

dè a bheireas mi? what will I bear?

PAST (PRETERITE)

rug mi I bore	**cha do rug mi** I didn't bear
an do rug mi did I bear?	**nach do rug mi?** didn't I bear?

PERFECT AND PLUPERFECT

tha mi air breith I have borne	**bha mi air breith** I had borne
tha mi air a bhreith I have borne it	**bha mi air a bhreith** I had borne it

CONDITIONAL

bheirinn I would bear	**cha bheirinn** I wouldn't bear
bheireadh* tu you would bear	**cha bheireadh* tu** you wouldn't bear
bheireamaid we would bear	**cha bheireamaid** we wouldn't bear
am beirinn? would I bear?	**nach beirinn?** wouldn't I bear?
am beireadh* tu? would you bear?	**nach beireadh* tu?** wouldn't you bear?
am beireamaid? would we hear?	**nach beireamaid?** wouldn't we hear?

The forms marked * are used for all persons except the first singular, I. The forms in -**maid** are alternative forms for the second person singular, we.

PAST PASSIVE

rugadh e he was born	**cha do rugadh e** he wasn't born
an do rugadh e? was he born?	**nach do rugadh e?** wasn't he born?

Note: In the Future, Relative Future, Past, Perfect, Pluperfect and Past Passive, the same forms of the verb are used for all persons.

CLUINN

cluinn hear (*pres part* **a' cluinntinn** hearing, *infinitive* **a chluinntinn** to hear)

IMPERATIVE

cluinneam let me hear	**na cluinneam** let me not hear
cluinn (*sing*) hear	**na cluinn** (*sing*) don't hear
cluinneadh e/i let him/her hear	**na cluinneadh e/i** let him/her not hear
cluinneamaid let us hear	**na cluinneamaid** let us not hear
cluinnibh (*pl*) hear	**na cluinnibh** (*pl*) don't hear
cluinneadh iad let them hear	**na cluinneadh iad** let them not hear

FUTURE AND HABITUAL PRESENT

cluinnidh mi I will hear, I hear	**cha chluinn mi** I won't hear, I don't hear
an cluinn mi? will I hear? do I hear?	**nach cluinn mi?** won't I hear? don't I hear?

RELATIVE FUTURE

dè a chluinneas mi? what will I hear?

PAST (PRETERITE)

chuala mi I heard	**cha chuala mi** I didn't hear
an cuala mi? did I hear?	**nach cuala mi?** didn't I hear?

PERFECT AND PLUPERFECT

tha mi air cluinntinn I have heard	**bha mi air cluinntinn** I had heard
tha mi air a chluinntinn I have heard it	**bha mi air a chluinntinn** I had heard it

Note: In the Future, Relative Future, Past, Perfect and Pluperfect, the same forms of the verb are used for all persons.

CONDITIONAL

chluinninn I would hear	**cha chluinninn** I wouldn't hear
chluinneadh* tu you would hear	**cha chluinneadh* tu** you wouldn't hear
chluinneamaid we would hear	**cha chluinneamaid** we wouldn't hear
an cluinninn? would I hear?	**nach cluinninn?** wouldn't I hear?
an cluinneadh* tu? would you hear?	**nach cluinneadh* tu?** wouldn't you hear?
an cluinneamaid? would we hear?	**nach cluinneamaid?** wouldn't we hear?

The forms marked * are used for all persons except the first singular, I. The forms in -**maid** are alternative forms for the second person singular, we.

DEAN

dèan do/make (*pres part* **a' dèanamh** doing/making, *infinitive* **a dhèanamh** to do/make)

IMPERATIVE

dèanam let me do	**na dèanam** let me not do
dèan (*sing*) do	**na dèan** (*sing*) don't do
dèanadh e/i let him/her do	**na dèanadh e/i** let him/her not do
dèanamaid let us do	**na dèanamaid** let us not do
dèanaibh (*pl*) do	**na dèanaibh** (*pl*) don't do
dèanadh iad let them do	**na dèanadh iad** let them not do

FUTURE AND HABITUAL PRESENT

nì mi I will do, I do	**cha dèan mi** I won't do, I don't do
an dèan mi? will I do? do I do?	**nach dèan mi?** won't I do? don't I do?

RELATIVE FUTURE

dè a nì mi? what will I do?

PAST (PRETERITE)

rinn mi I did	**cha do rinn mi** I didn't do
an do rinn mi? did I do?	**nach do rinn mi?** didn't I do?

PERFECT AND PLUPERFECT

tha mi air dèanamh I have done	**bha mi air dèanamh** I had done
tha mi air a dhèanamh I have done it	**bha mi air a dhèanamh** I had done it

Note: In the Future, Relative Future, Past, Perfect and Pluperfect, the same forms of the verb are used for all persons.

CONDITIONAL

dhèanainn I would do	**cha dèanainn** I wouldn't do
dhèanadh* tu you would do	**cha dèanadh* tu** you wouldn't do
dhèanamaid we would do	**cha dèanamaid** we wouldn't do
an dèanainn? would I do?	**nach dèanainn?** wouldn't I do?
an dèanadh* tu? would you do?	**nach dèanadh* tu?** wouldn't you do?
an dèanamaid? would we do?	**nach dèanamaid?** wouldn't we do?

The forms marked * are used for all persons except the first singular, I. The forms in -**maid** are alternative forms for the second person singular, we.

FAIC

faic see (*pres part* **a' faicinn** seeing, *infinitive* **a dh'fhaicinn** to see)

IMPERATIVE

faiceam let me see

faic (*sing*) see

faiceadh e/i let him/her see

faiceamaid let us see

faicibh (*pl*) see

faiceadh iad let them see

na faiceam let me not see

na faic (*sing*) don't see

na faiceadh e/i let him/her not see

na faiceamaid let us not see

na faicibh (*pl*) don't see

na faiceadh iad let them not see

FUTURE AND HABITUAL PRESENT

chì mi I will see, I see

am faic mi? will I see? do I see?

chan fhaic mi I won't see, I don't see

nach f(h)aic mi? won't I see? don't I see?

RELATIVE FUTURE

dè a chì mi? what will I see?

PAST (PRETERITE)

chunnaic/chunna mi I saw

am faca mi? did I see?

chan fhaca mi I didn't see

nach f(h)aca mi? didn't I see?

PERFECT AND PLUPERFECT

tha mi air faicinn I have seen

tha mi air fhaicinn I have seen it

bha mi air faicinn I had seen

bha mi air fhaicinn I had seen it

Note: In the Future, Relative Future, Past, Perfect and Pluperfect, the same forms of the verb are used for all persons.

CONDITIONAL

chithinn I would see

chitheadh* tu you would see

chitheamaid we would see

am faicinn? would I see?

am faiceadh* tu? would you see?

am faiceamaid? would we see?

chan fhaicinn I wouldn't see

chan fhaiceadh* tu you wouldn't see

chan fhaiceamaid we wouldn't see

nach f(h)aicinn? wouldn't I see?

nach f(h)aiceadh* tu? wouldn't you see?

nach f(h)aiceamaid? wouldn't we see?

The forms marked * are used for all persons except the first singular, I. The forms in -**maid** are alternative forms for the second person singular, we.

FAIGH

faigh get (*pres part* **a' faighinn** getting, *infinitive* **a dh'fhaighinn** to get)

IMPERATIVE

faigheam let me get

na faigheam let me not get

faigh (*sing*) get

na faigh (*sing*) don't get

faigheadh e/i let him/her get

na faigheadh e/i let him/her not get

faigheamaid let us get

na faigheamaid let us not get

faighibh (*pl*) get

na faighibh (*pl*) don't get

faigheadh iad let them get

na faigheadh iad let them not get

FUTURE AND HABITUAL PRESENT

gheibh mi I will get, I get

chan fhaigh mi I won't get, I don't get

am faigh mi? will I get? do I get?

nach f(h)aigh mi? won't I get? don't I get?

RELATIVE FUTURE

dè a gheibh mi? what will I get?

PAST (PRETERITE)

fhuair mi I got

cha d'fhuair mi I didn't get

an d'fhuair mi? did I get?

nach d'fhuair mi? didn't I get?

PERFECT AND PLUPERFECT

tha mi air faighinn I have got

bha mi air faighinn I had got

tha mi air fhaighinn I have got it

bha mi air fhaighinn I had got it

Note: In the Future, Relative Future, Past, Perfect and Pluperfect, the same forms of the verb are used for all persons.

CONDITIONAL

gheibhinn I would get

chan fhaighinn I wouldn't get

gheibheadh* tu you would get

chan fhaigheadh* tu you wouldn't get

gheibheamaid we would get

chan fhaigheamaid we wouldn't get

am faighinn? would I get?

nach f(h)aighinn? wouldn't I get?

am faigheadh* tu? would you get?

nach f(h)aigheadh* tu? wouldn't you get?

am faigheamaid? would we get?

nach f(h)aigheamaid? wouldn't we get?

The forms marked * are used for all persons except the first singular, I. The forms in -**maid** are alternative forms for the second person singular, we.

RACH

rach go (*pres part* **a' dol** going, *infinitive* **a dhol** to go)

IMPERATIVE

racham let me go

rach (*sing*) go

rachadh e/i let him/her go

rachamaid let us go

rachaibh (*pl*) go

rachadh iad let them go

na racham let me not go

na rach (*sing*) don't go

na rachadh e/i let him/her not go

na rachamaid let us not go

na rachaibh (*pl*) don't go

na rachadh iad let them not go

FUTURE AND HABITUAL PRESENT

thèid mi I will go, I go

an tèid mi? will I go? do I go?

cha tèid mi I won't go, I don't go

nach tèid mi? won't I go? don't I go?

RELATIVE FUTURE

cuin a thèid mi? when will I go?

PAST (PRETERITE)

chaidh mi I went

an deach(aidh) mi? did I go?

cha deach(aidh) mi I didn't go

nach deach(aidh) mi? didn't I go?

PERFECT AND PLUPERFECT

tha mi air dol/air a dhol
   I have gone

bha mi air dol/air a dhol
   I had gone

Note: In the Future, Relative Future, Past, Perfect and Pluperfect, the same forms of the verb are used for all persons.

CONDITIONAL

rachainn I would go

rachadh* tu you would go

rachamaid we would go

an rachainn? would I go?

an rachadh* tu? would you go?

an rachamaid? would we go?

cha rachainn I wouldn't go

cha rachadh* tu you wouldn't go

cha rachamaid we wouldn't go

nach rachainn? wouldn't I go?

nach rachadh* tu? wouldn't you go?

nach rachamaid? wouldn't we go?

The forms marked * are used for all persons except the first singular, I. The forms in -**maid** are alternative forms for the second person singular, we.

RUIG

ruig *as vi* arrive, *as vt* reach (*pres part* **a' ruigsinn** arriving *&c, infinitive* **a ruigsinn** to arrive *&c*)

IMPERATIVE

ruigeam let me arrive	**na ruigeam** let me not arrive
ruig (*sing*) arrive	**na ruig** (*sing*) don't arrive
ruigeadh e/i let him/her arrive	**na ruigeadh e/i** let him/her not arrive
ruigeamaid let us arrive	**na ruigeamaid** let us not arrive
ruigibh (*pl*) arrive	**na ruigibh** (*pl*) don't arrive
ruigeadh iad let them arrive	**na ruigeadh iad** let them not arrive

FUTURE AND HABITUAL PRESENT

ruigidh mi I will arrive, I arrive	**cha ruig mi** I won't arrive, I don't arrive
an ruig mi? will I arrive? do I arrive?	**nach ruig mi?** won't I arrive? don't I arrive?

RELATIVE FUTURE

cuin a ruigeas mi? when will I arrive?

PAST (PRETERITE)

ràinig mi I arrived	**cha do ràinig mi** I didn't arrive
an do ràinig mi? did I arrive?	**nach do ràinig mi?** didn't I arrive?

PERFECT AND PLUPERFECT

tha mi air ruigsinn I have arrived	**bha mi air ruigsinn** I had arrived
tha mi air a ruigsinn I have reached it	**bha mi air a ruigsinn** I had reached it

Note: In the Future, Relative Future, Past, Perfect and Pluperfect, the same forms of the verb are used for all persons.

CONDITIONAL

ruiginn I would arrive	**cha ruiginn** I wouldn't arrive
ruigeadh* tu you would arrive	**cha ruigeadh* tu** you wouldn't arrive
ruigeamaid we wouldn't arrive	**cha ruigeamaid** we wouldn't arrive
an ruiginn? would I arrive?	**nach ruiginn?** wouldn't I arrive?
an ruigeadh* tu? would you arrive?	**nach ruigeadh* tu?** wouldn't you arrive?
an ruigeamaid? would we arrive?	**nach ruigeamaid?** wouldn't we arrive?

The forms marked * are used for all persons except the first singular, I. The forms in -**maid** are alternative forms for the second person singular, we.

411

THIG

thig come (*pres part* **a' tighinn** coming, *infinitive* **a thighinn** to come)

IMPERATIVE

thigeam let me come	**na tigeam** let me not come
thig (*sing*) come	**na tig** (*sing*) don't come
thigeadh e/i let him/her come	**na tigeadh e/i** let him/her not come
thigeamaid let us come	**na tigeamaid** let us not come
thigibh (*pl*) come	**na tigibh** (*pl*) don't come
thigeadh iad let them come	**na tigeadh iad** let them not come

FUTURE AND HABITUAL PRESENT

thig mi I will come, I come	**cha tig mi** I won't come, I don't come
an tig mi? will I come? do I come?	**nach tig mi?** won't I come? don't I come?

RELATIVE FUTURE

cuin a thig mi? when will I come?

PAST (PRETERITE)

thàinig mi I came	**cha tàinig mi** I didn't come
an tàinig mi? did I come?	**nach tàinig mi?** didn't I come?

PERFECT AND PLUPERFECT

tha mi air tighinn/a thighinn I have come	**bha mi air tighinn/a thighinn** I had come

Note: In the Future, Relative Future, Past, Perfect and Pluperfect, the same forms are of the verb used for all persons.

CONDITIONAL

thiginn I would come	**cha tiginn** I wouldn't come
thigeadh* tu you would come	**cha tigeadh* tu** you wouldn't come
thigeamaid we would come	**cha tigeamaid** we wouldn't come
an tiginn? would I come?	**nach tiginn?** wouldn't I come?
an tigeadh* tu? would you come?	**nach tigeadh* tu?** wouldn't you come?
an tigeamaid? would we come?	**nach tigeamaid?** wouldn't we come?

The forms marked * are used for all persons except the first singular, I. The forms in -**maid** are alternative forms for the second person singular, we.

THOIR

thoir give/take/bring (*pres part* **a' toirt** giving *&c, infinitive* **a thoirt** to give *&c*)

IMPERATIVE

thoiream let me give	**na toiream** let me not give
thoir (*sing*) give	**na toir** (*sing*) don't give
thoireadh e/i let him/her give	**na toireadh e/i** let him/her not give
thoireamaid let us give	**na toireamaid** let us not give
thoiribh (*pl*) give	**na toiribh** (*pl*) don't give
thoireadh iad let them give	**na toireadh iad** let them not give

Note: In the first person sing and pl imperative **t(h)ugam** and **t(h)ugamaid** are also found, and in the third person sing and pl **t(h)ugadh**

FUTURE AND HABITUAL PRESENT

bheir mi I will give, I give	**cha toir mi** I won't give, I don't give
an toir mi? will I give? do I give?	**nach toir mi?** won't I give? don't I give?

RELATIVE FUTURE

dè a bheir mi? what will I give?

PAST (PRETERITE)

thug mi I gave	**cha tug mi** I didn't give
an tug mi? did I give?	**nach tug mi?** didn't I give?

PERFECT AND PLUPERFECT

tha mi air toirt I have given	**bha mi air toirt** I had given
tha mi air a thoirt I have given it	**bha mi air a thoirt** I had given it

Note: In the Future, Relative Future, Past, Perfect and Pluperfect, the same forms of the verb are used for all persons.

CONDITIONAL

bheirinn I would give	**cha toirinn** I wouldn't give
bheireadh* tu you would give	**cha toireadh* tu** you wouldn't give
bheireamaid we would give	**cha toireamaid** we wouldn't give
an toirinn? would I give?	**nach toirinn?** wouldn't I give?
an toireadh* tu? would you give?	**nach toireadh* tu?** wouldn't you give?
an toireamaid? would we give?	**nach toireamaid?** wouldn't we give?

The forms marked * are used for all persons except the first singular, I. The forms in **-maid** are alternative forms for the second person singular, we.

Note: **toir, thoir** and **toirt** are occasionally found as **tabhair, thabhair** and **tabhairt**

BI

bi be (*infinitive* a bhith to be)

IMPERATIVE

bitheam let me be	**na bitheam** let me not be
bi (*sing*) be	**na bi** (*sing*) don't be
bitheadh e/i let him/her be	**na bitheadh e/i** let him/her not be
bitheamaid/biomaid let us be	**na bitheamaid/biomaid** let us not be
bithibh (*pl*) be	**na bithibh** (*pl*) don't be
bitheadh iad let them be	**na bitheadh iad** let them not be

PRESENT

tha mi I am	**chan eil mi** I am not
a bheil mi? am I?	**nach eil mi** am I not?

FUTURE AND HABITUAL PRESENT

bithidh/bidh mi I will be, I am	**cha bhi mi** I won't be, I'm not
am bi mi? will I be? am I?	**nach bi mi?** won't I be? am I not?

RELATIVE FUTURE

ma bhitheas (*or* **ma bhios**) **mi** if I will be, if I am

PAST (PRETERITE)

bha mi I was	**cha robh mi** I wasn't
an robh mi? was I?	**nach robh mi?** wasn't I?

PERFECT AND PLUPERFECT

tha mi air a bhith I have been	**bha mi air a bhith** I had been

Note: In the Future, Relative Future, Past, Perfect, and Pluperfect, the same forms of the verb are used for all persons.

CONDITIONAL

bhithinn I would be	**cha bhithinn** I wouldn't be
bhitheadh/bhiodh* tu you would be	**cha bhitheadh/bhiodh* tu** you wouldn't be
bhitheamaid/bhiomaid we would be	**cha bhitheamaid/bhiomaid** we wouldn't be
am bithinn? would I be?	**nach bithinn?** wouldn't I be?
am bitheadh/biodh* tu? would you be?	**nach bitheadh biodh* tu?** wouldn't you be?
am bitheamaid/biomaid? would we be?	**nach bitheamaid/biomaid?** wouldn't we be?

The forms marked * are used for all persons except the first singular, I. The forms in -**maid** are alternative forms for the second person singular, we.

See also following page.

CONSTRUCTIONS USING BI AS AN AUXILIARY VERB

PRESENT AND PAST CONTINUOUS (ACTIVE, REFLEXIVE AND PASSIVE)

tha/bha e a' bualadh he is/was striking
tha/bha e gam bualadh he is/was striking them
tha/bha e ga bhualadh fhèin he is/was striking himself
tha/bha e ga bhualadh he is/was being struck (*also* he is/was striking him)

PERFECT TENSES (PRESENT, PLUPERFECT, FUTURE AND CONDITIONAL), ACTIVE AND PASSIVE

tha/bha e air bualadh he has/had struck
tha/bha e air am bualadh he has/had struck them
tha/bha e air a bhualadh he has/had been struck (*also* he has/had struck him)
bidh e air bualadh he will have struck
bidh e air am bualadh he will have struck them
bidh e air a bhualadh he will have been struck (*also* he will have struck him)
bhiodh e air bualadh he would have struck
bhiodh e air am bualadh he would have struck them
bhiodh e air a bhualadh he would have been struck (*also* he would have struck him)

IMPERSONAL PASSIVE

thathar ag ràdh it is said, it is being said
bhathar ag ràdh it was said, it was being said
bithear ag ràdh it will be said
bhite/bhithist ag ràdh it would be said, it used to be said